The Great Chicago Fire and the Myth of Mrs. O'Leary's Cow

by Richard F. Bales

FOREWORD BY THOMAS F. SCHWARTZ

McFarland & Company, Inc., Publishers
Jefferson, North Carolina, and London

Library of Congress Cataloguing-in-Publication Data

Bales, Richard F., 1951–
The Great Chicago Fire and the myth of Mrs. O'Leary's cow /
by Richard F. Bales ; foreword by Thomas F. Schwartz.
p.   cm.
Includes bibliographical references and index.

ISBN 0-7864-1424-3 (illustrated case binding : 50# alkaline paper)

1. Great Fire, Chicago, Ill., 1871.   2. Chicago (Ill.)—History—
To 1875.   I. Title.
F548.42.B23   2002   977.3'11041—dc21   2002010361

British Library cataloguing data are available

Cover image: "The Cause of the Great Chicago Fire Oct. 9 1871,"
Kellogg & Bulkeley Company (*author's collection*)

Manufactured in the United States of America

McFarland & Company, Inc., Publishers
Box 611, Jefferson, North Carolina 28640
www.mcfarlandpub.com

*The Great Chicago Fire and
the Myth of Mrs. O'Leary's Cow*

To
Joanne;
Mike & Tom;
Phyllis, my mother;
and to Jack, naturally.

In Memoriam

Catherine O'Leary
Catherine O'Leary Ledwell
Eileen Knight

Acknowledgments

I could not have written this book without the enthusiastic assistance of Kenneth Grenier, retired survey officer of Chicago Title Insurance Company. Ken's career at Chicago Title spanned fifty-three years, and almost all of it was spent in its land records department. Ken and Chicago Title employees Jack Moore and Welton Pryor, Jr., plumbed the company's ante-fire tract books and other resources to ferret out information that has never before been utilized by fire historians. Simply put, this book exists because of their efforts.

But if Ken, Jack, and Welton made this book possible, then my brother Jack Bales made it as good as possible. Jack is reference librarian of Mary Washington College, Fredericksburg, Virginia. He was always willing to help and patiently answered my countless reference and editing questions and routinely mailed me (usually at his expense) research materials. Both he and my mother Phyllis Bales read and critiqued every chapter of this book and offered innumerable words of advice and encouragement.

I had always envisioned this book to be primarily an exposition of the printed word. It was not until I saw the work of artist Marshall Philyaw that I realized the importance of art and pictures in conveying the drama of the Chicago Fire. His wonderful drawings brought to life the many individuals who sought their fifteen minutes of post-fire fame by lying their way into the O'Leary limelight.

My initial findings concerning the fire's origin were published by the Illinois Historic Preservation Agency in the Spring 1997 issue of the *Illinois Historical Journal*.[1] This article included a diagram by an extraordinary graphic artist, Douglas A. Swanson. This drawing, as well as several additional diagrams, proves that a picture is indeed worth a thousand words in illustrating the thoughts, theories, and conclusions presented in this book.

I owe a tremendous debt of gratitude to four individuals who believed in this project from the very beginning and supported me throughout this endeavor: Professor James E. Davis, Illinois College, Jacksonville, Illinois; Christi Parsons of the *Chicago Tribune*; Evelyn R. Taylor of the Illinois Historic Preservation Agency; and Thomas F. Schwartz, Illinois State Historian. Tom kindly agreed to write the foreword to this book.

In 1958 Robert Cromie wrote in his popular history *The Great Chicago Fire* of the tremendous help he received from the staff at the Chicago Historical Society. More than forty years later, only the names have changed. Archie Motley and Russell Lewis were unflagging in their assistance and enthusiasm for this project. Keshia Whitehead generously allowed me to publish annotated portions of the transcript of the investigation into the cause of the fire. These are reproduced in Appendix D. Jessica Meyer patiently (and repeatedly) searched the Society's files of prints and photographs, looking for the illustrations that appear in this book. John Alderson, Tiffany Charles, Jay Crawford, Rob Kent, and Julie Thomas helped me obtain new photographs that have never before appeared in a book about the fire.

For more than six years I prowled the Research Center of the Chicago Historical Society, transcribing the minutes of the inquiry investigation, reading microfilmed newspapers, and poring over numerous reference works. During this time countless staff members helped bring this book to fruition. They include John Anderson, Patrick Ashley, Olivia Chen, Linda Evans, Melissa Gasparotto, Jennifer Hartz, Michael Glass, Justin Huyck, Heather Keepes, Debbie Meiko King, Jessica Koscielniak, Darmon Lewis, Jan McNeill, Lesley Martin, Paula Murphy, Ramon Nunez, Steve Peters, Ralph Pugh, Leith Rohr, and Tim Samuelson. If I have missed any others, I am sorry.

The historical society is not the only venerable research institution in Chicago. The Newberry Library is without peer when it comes to genealogical material, and I thank its staff for helping me secure 1870 and 1880 United States census information.

The following people also contributed their knowledge, expertise, assistance, and support, and their contributions are gratefully acknowledged: Max Armstrong, Jon Austin, Carla Bailey, Robert Bales, Mary Basich, Anne Beatty, Fredda Berman, Pam Belluck, Edward M. Burke, Edward Byers, William Clark, the late Robert Collins, Lisa Compton, Nancy Knight Connolly, Denise Crosby, Anthony DeBartolo, John D. DeHaan, John Doe, Sally Dolphin, Brian Downes, Burton S. Ehrlich, John Franch, Andrea E. Friedman, Chris Froemke, Carol Gats, Brian Gray, Greg Hannon, the late Clyde Hewitt, John T. Huntington, Robert James, William Jerousek, Janet M. Johnson, Thomas J. Joyce, Jeff Karrow, Rob Karsa, Boyd Kidwell, Jean Loe, Melvin Loe, Walter S. Mitchell III, Bill Mitchinson, Manly W. Mumford, John Musial, Phyllis Newquist, Charles O'Connor, Steve Olson, Ron Otto, Riva Pollard, JoAnne Prichard, Michael Raimondi, Nicholas Raimondi, Ralph Ruebner, Herman Schell, Allison Slomovitz, Melissa Smart, Carl Smith, Kelli M. Smith, Robert Steinkamp, Rebecca Swartz, Guy Trayling, Laura Tumminello, Ingolf Vogeler, Win Wehrli, and Eric Zorn.

William Tubbs of the Illinois Historic Preservation Agency provided invaluable research assistance. Mary Michals of the Illinois State Historical Library helped me obtain copies of photographs from the library's collections.

Thanks to Dale Cohen and Sandy Spikes of the *Chicago Tribune* and Rick Hibbert of *Oak Leaves* (Oak Park, Illinois) for graciously allowing Marshall Philyaw to reproduce illustrations that originally appeared in their respective newspapers.

I thank Ken Little, co-author of *History of Chicago Fire Houses of the 19th Century*, whose encyclopedic knowledge of Chicago Fire Department history is matched only by his kindness in sharing it. Thanks also to David Lewis, curator of the Aurora

Regional Fire Museum, Aurora, Illinois, for both his boundless enthusiasm for this project and his aid in helping me complete it.

I must acknowledge the old world craftsmanship of Donald I. Stephens and his wife Althea "Sue" Stephens of Assell Photo Shop, Aurora, Illinois, who were somehow able to transform worn photos, faded pictures, and even grainy microfilm copies into quality photographs.

I thank Bill Radke and my co-workers at the Wheaton, Illinois, office of Chicago Title Insurance Company for their many kindnesses. They may not have always understood this obsession, but at least they tolerated it.

And finally, a special thank you to my wife, Joanne, and my two sons, Mike and Tom. I thank them for their reluctant blessing for the hundreds of hours I was away, either in our basement, surrounded by books, index cards, photocopies, and a computer, or in Chicago on countless research trips. I owe them much.

Richard F. Bales
Aurora, Illinois
July 2002

Notes

1. Richard F. Bales, "Did the Cow Do It? A New Look at the Cause of the Great Chicago Fire," *Illinois Historical Journal* 90 (Spring 1997), pp. 2–24.

Table of Contents

Foreword

Catastrophes invite investigation. The sheer magnitude of destruction and loss of life raise the obvious question of causality: "How did it happen?" When evidence is not conclusive—and, at times, even when it is determinative—folk traditions arise, offering explanations that become embedded in popular culture. Such is the case with the 1871 Great Chicago Fire, Mrs. O'Leary, and her cow.

Chicago has always had a fondness for bovines. Whether it be Elsie, the trademarked logo for the Borden Dairy Company, sports announcer Harry Carey's "Holy Cow" restaurant, or the summer when world renowned artists painted cows for public display throughout the city streets, Chicagoans display a continued fascination toward this four-legged creature with four stomachs. The one exception, until recently, has been Mrs. O'Leary's cow, which is credited with kicking over the lamp and beginning the Chicago Fire. Scholarly studies have examined the issues analyzing larger questions of the impact and significance of the disaster. But the question of what caused the fire is hardly addressed. That the fire occurred is evidence enough for most academics.

When Richard Bales began his search for the origin of the fire, he brought with it a talent that most historians do not possess. Bales' many years at Chicago Title Insurance Company honed his skill at reading plat maps and legal descriptions. Bringing this knowledge to bear on evaluating the official recorded testimony of witnesses collected by the Chicago Board of Police and Fire Commissioners, Bales concluded that long-accepted explanations for the origin of the fire did not make sense. And of one thing he was certain: Mrs. O'Leary's cow was not the culprit.

This one finding resonated throughout Illinois, the United States and, indeed, the world. The Chicago City Council passed a resolution officially exonerating Mrs. O'Leary's cow from wrongdoing. Bales' detective work was a front page story for the *Chicago Tribune* and a feature story for the Sunday edition of *The New York Times*. His research was noted in popular publications such as *People* magazine. Word soon spread overseas, resulting in interviews with foreign correspondents and a lengthy piece on the BBC.[1]

History comes in many forms. What the reader will find in the following pages

1

is an intricate unraveling of evidence collected to explain one of the great disasters of nineteenth-century America. It is an engaging and entertaining piece of detective work that lays certain explanations aside and allows for a fresh look at an old question. Readers will discover why Bales' research findings resonated so widely among the general public in the aftermath of the one hundred and twenty-fifth anniversary of the Great Chicago Fire.

—Thomas F. Schwartz, Ph.D.
Illinois State Historian

Notes

1. Steve Mills, "Uncowed Aldermen Clear Mrs. O'Leary in 1871 Fire," *Chicago Tribune*, 7 October 1997, sec. 2, p. 8; Christi Parsons, "Historian Finds a New Suspect for Chicago Fire," *Chicago Tribune*, 7 January 1997, sec. 1, pp. 1, 14; Pam Belluck, "Barn Door Reopened on Fire After Legend Has Escaped," *New York Times*, 17 August 1997, p. 10; "A Dairy Tale," *People* 48 (22 September 1997), p. 155.

Preface

When Paul Angle, former director of the Chicago Historical Society, wrote the introduction to Robert Cromie's superb book, *The Great Chicago Fire* (1958), he commented that "one could collect a sizable shelf of books which already have been written."[1] More than forty years later, what was then a shelf is now a small bookcase, with several fine works added in just the last few years. Why then, another book on the fire?

Because despite these new additions to Angle's collection, there is still a sizable void in fire-related scholarship—two matters have never before been studied by fire historians. One is the cause of the fire, and the other is the inquiry investigation by Chicago's Board of Police and Fire Commissioners into both the origin of the fire and the conduct of the city's firemen during the blaze.

Almost from the time Mrs. O'Leary's barn erupted into flames on the evening of October 8, 1871, she has been blamed for starting the fire. The legend dates back to October 9, only hours after the fire started, when the staff of the *Chicago Evening Journal* managed to cobble together a small edition even as the city continued to burn

around them. One sentence gave this working class Irishwoman immortality: "The fire broke out on the corner of DeKoven and Twelfth streets, at about 9 o'clock on Sunday evening, being caused by a cow kicking over a lamp in a stable in which a woman was milking."[2] Although the story of her cow and the lantern has survived to this day, many other theories have been suggested, even in the first few days and weeks after the fire. In this book, I discuss and debunk the more prominent theories and in the process attempt to salvage Mrs. O'Leary's reputation.

O'Leary was never able to rid herself of her unwanted and unwarranted notoriety. In the years after the fire, as each October 8 drew near, newspaper reporters would track her down and attempt to interview her for a "fire anniversary" article. After her death in 1895, people like Jacob John Schaller and Louis M. Cohn—people who were probably in all other respects upstanding members of their respective communities—began to come forward to tell their stories. They either claimed to have fabricated the "cow and lantern" explanation for the fire's cause, to have been in the barn when the fire started, or (what was

3

surely the ultimate insult to the O'Leary family) to have heard Mrs. O'Leary confess to milking the cow, causing it to kick over the lantern. Although their stories were different, it appears that the people who told them all craved the same thing—each wanted Andy Warhol's "fifteen minutes of fame." It seems clear that they all wanted to hitch a ride on the legend of Mrs. O'Leary, who by this time (conveniently) was not alive to protest their lies and innuendoes. Drawings of most of these charlatans appear in this book. The pictures are based on photos and sketches that I have culled primarily from old newspaper accounts of their "confessions." These pictures have never before been published in a fire history, probably because until now their stories have never before been discredited in a book about the fire.[3]

But as I debunk the tall tales of Jacob Schaller and Louis Cohn, I must acknowledge the ante-fire records of Chicago Title Insurance Company. Although this book is not the first Chicago history to use these documents, it appears that it is the first history of the Chicago Fire to rely on them.[4] And it is both ironic and appropriate that I utilize these materials. The fire destroyed the Cook County Courthouse and with it the official real estate records. The public quickly realized the enormity of the problem. The *Chicago Times* did not publish its first post-fire issue until October 18, but on the very next day it wrote:

> The matter of the most vital importance to the people of Chicago as a community is the ability to fix the titles to the real estate.... [It is] a necessity of the future, upon which, more than all else, the credit of the city and the facilities for rapid reconstruction must depend.[5]

Fortunately, three small abstract companies managed to rescue their holdings from the blaze, and soon they were housed together in the untouched western outskirts of the city. In April of 1872, the Illinois legislature passed the Burnt Records Act, and the documents of these three companies were made admissible as evidence in Illinois courts. More than 130 years later, these same records are a foundation for many of the conclusions presented in this book.[6]

The Board of Police and Fire Commissioners conducted an investigation after the fire in an attempt to determine the fire's cause. The Board interviewed fifty people in nine days of testimony over the course of twelve days—November 23 to December 4, 1871. A shorthand reporter took down the witnesses' testimony, which was later transcribed into longhand. The minutes of this investigation consist of four volumes of over 1100 pages that are still preserved at the Chicago Historical Society. The handwriting of these minutes ranges from glorious script to crabbed scratchings. I spent two years at the historical society methodically transcribing the testimony of every witness. Using Chicago Title's records and other source materials, I was able to reconstruct a scale drawing of the O'Leary property and the surrounding neighborhood. I then attempted to verify the accuracy of key statements made during the inquiry by comparing them to this drawing. When I did so, numerous inconsistencies became apparent, inconsistencies that have led me to the person I believe really *did* cause the Great Chicago Fire.

The investigation by the Board of Police and Fire Commissioners has never before been fully researched and reported by fire historians. The Board's final report, published in the Chicago newspapers on December 12, 1871, indicated that the commissioners were unable to determine the fire's cause. By poring over hundreds of pages of microfilmed newspapers, I was able to reconstruct the events that led up to these hearings. But furthermore, by scrutinizing the testimony of the fifty witnesses, I concluded that the Board *could* have determined the cause of the fire had it really wanted to. But it apparently did not care to do so, possibly because it was more concerned with repairing the fire department's tattered reputation, a reputation that was ravaged by post-fire stories of incompetence, drunkenness, and bribery.

This book is *not* merely a chronological account of the fire, which for the most part raged unchecked until it burned itself out in the early morning hours of Tuesday, October 10. Robert Cromie has already written that story, and *The Great Chicago Fire* is marvelous in its detail. The original 1958 book is readily available through one of the many Internet book services, and a new "illustrated edition" is now in print. H. A. Musham's 1941 monograph, *The Great Chicago Fire, October 8–10, 1871,* is also good, and although out of print, it too is available online.[7] Having said that, I do include a fairly complete chronology of the fire in the first chapter, which brings a sense of continuity and cohesiveness to the succeeding chapters. In relating the story of the fire, I have used the inquiry transcript and unpublished letters to describe incidents that have not always appeared in previous fire histories in an effort to bring a human touch to a catastrophe that affected thousands of nineteenth-century Chicagoans.[8]

Furthermore, the book is not a study of the sociological implications of the transmutation of Mrs. O'Leary into a lightning rod for anti–Irish/foreign born/working class sentiment. This is ground already covered by fire historians Karen Sawislak and Carl Smith in their respective works, *Smoldering City: Chicagoans and the Great*

Fire, 1871–1874 and *Urban Disorder and the Shape of Belief: The Great Chicago Fire, the Haymarket Bomb, and the Model Town of Pullman.*[9]

Nor is it a pictorial history of the fire. This book has 90 photographs, diagrams, and drawings, half of which have never before appeared in a book about the fire. Nonetheless, it should not be compared to Herman Kogan and Robert Cromie's illustrated chronology, *The Great Fire: Chicago 1871,* which contains more than 200 photographs and drawings.[10]

And finally, it is not a study of the rebuilding of Chicago. There is no need to compete with Ross Miller's *American Apocalypse: The Great Fire and the Myth of Chicago,* recently reissued as *The Great Chicago Fire.*[11]

As mentioned above, I have augmented the book's text with a number of illustrations. Strangely, although there are many photos of fire ruins and later reconstruction, there is not one extant photograph of the city burning or of anything else that occurred during those terrifying hours on October 8, 9, and 10, such as the frenzied fleeing to Chicago's lake shore. The closest the most stubborn researcher will ever find of the city on fire might be a photo of coal piles smoldering along the Chicago River. Historians Herman Kogan and Robert Cromie have suggested several reasons for this: perhaps the primitive photographic equipment of the time would not work satisfactorily in the intense heat. Perhaps photographers were too frightened to take the time to set up their cameras for even one picture. Or perhaps any photographs that were taken were later destroyed in the flames or lost among the crowds rushing to escape a conflagration.[12]

A researcher will search the holdings of the Chicago Historical Society in vain for a single photograph of the infamous

Mrs. O'Leary. As explained in the epilogue, Catherine O'Leary was shocked at how history satirized her and her alleged connection to the fire. She vowed that if history was going to ridicule her, it would have to do so without the aid of a photograph of her features. Her doctor apparently spoke the truth when he commented in 1894, "She has not a likeness in the world and will never have one."[13]

The cause of the fire is probably Chicago's ultimate historical whodunit. But there are lesser known but still equally fascinating mysteries associated with the fire. At what time did the fire start? Did a neighbor hear Mrs. O'Leary scream as her barn began to blaze? Did another neighbor attempt to turn in an alarm at a nearby drug store, only to be rebuffed by the store owner? These and other questions are discussed in one of several appendices. Another appendix includes the complete and annotated inquiry testimony of twelve of the fifty witnesses—including, of course, Mrs. O'Leary.

Catherine O'Leary was the fifth person to testify in the investigation. If she and her cow did not cause the fire, am I certain I know who did? More than a century has passed since Chicago burned down. At this late date it is impossible to prove guilt beyond a reasonable doubt. All the witnesses are dead. The city has been rebuilt. The trail has long been cold, covered over by skyscrapers and expressways. It is somehow appropriate that where the O'Leary barn once harbored cows (and the perpetrator), a fire academy now stands. But have I dug through its concrete floors and unearthed a fingerprint-covered lantern or other evidence sufficient to convict the guilty party in a criminal court? No, I have not. I have no smoking gun; there is no longer even a smoking city that might give testimony to what happened on that Sunday evening. But the evidence that I do

have is substantial, and I am convinced that I have solved the mystery of who started the Great Chicago Fire.

Historian H. A. Musham remarked that after the fire, every person in Chicago who lived through it had a story to tell and that these people never tired of telling it. Many of them wrote and even published their own personal histories in the months and years after October 8, 1871, and I have relied on some of them in writing this book. After reading these works, it is clear that the story of the Great Chicago Fire is a compendium of hundreds of incidents and accounts. I am confident that there is still memorable fire history in untold stories that has yet to be uncovered. It might be someone's unpublished reminiscences found in a library, minutes of a proceeding or meeting unearthed in an archive, or even a letter purchased on the Internet. Perhaps these materials will one day provide historians with even more information about the men and women I only allude to in this book—heroes like Thomas Ockerby and John Tolland or hucksters like Robert Critchell and Mary Callahan. Because in every sense of the word, Mrs. O'Leary and her cow are only the beginning of the history of the Great Chicago Fire.[14]

Notes

1. Robert Cromie, *The Great Chicago Fire* (New York: McGraw-Hill Book Co., 1958), p. x.

2. "The Great Calamity of the Age!," *Chicago Evening Journal-Extra*, 9 October 1871, p. 1.

3. As author Gerald Posner remarked in one of the hundreds of books about the Kennedy assassination: "As in every famous case, people have come out of the woodwork for their fifteen minutes of fame." See Gerald Posner, *Case Closed: Lee Harvey Oswald and the Assassination of JFK* (New York: Random House, 1993), p. xi. Jim Fisher made a similar observation in his book about the Lindbergh kidnapping. See Jim Fisher, *The Ghosts*

of Hopewell: Setting the Record Straight in the Lindbergh Case (Carbondale: Southern Illinois University Press, 1999), pp. 72–73, 169.

4. For example, see Robin L. Einhorn, *Property Rules: Political Economy in Chicago, 1833–1872* (Chicago: University of Chicago Press, 1991).

5. "Titles to Property," *Chicago Times*, 19 October 1871, p. [2].

6. *Chicago Title and Trust Co.: The First 150 Years* (privately printed, [1997]), p. [2]; "A Marvellous Achievement," *Chicago Tribune*, 23 October 1871, p. 1; A[lfred] T[heodore] Andreas, *History of Chicago: From the Earliest Period to the Present Time*, vol. 2, *From 1857 Until the Fire of 1871* (Chicago: A. T. Andreas Co., 1885), pp. 586–89; A[lfred] T[heodore] Andreas, *History of Chicago: From the Earliest Period to the Present Time*, vol. 3, *From the Fire of 1871 Until 1885* (Chicago: A. T. Andreas Co., 1886), pp. 248–49; E[dgar] J[ohnson] Goodspeed, *History of the Great Fires in Chicago and the West* (New York: H. S. Goodspeed & Co., 1871), pp. 257–61; James W. Sheahan and George P. Upton, *The Great Conflagration....* (Chicago: Union Publishing Co., 1871), pp. 228–32; Joseph Kirkland, *The Story of Chicago* (Chicago: Dibble Publishing Co., 1892), vol. 1, pp. 307–17; Loretto Dennis Szucs, *Chicago and Cook County: A Guide to Research* (Salt Lake City: Ancestry, 1996), pp. 374–80; "Helped to Save Records of Real Estate from Fire Half a Century Ago," *Chicago Daily Journal*, 8 October 1921, p. [2]; "Aged Employe Tells of Saving Title Records," *Chicago Evening Post*, 8 October 1921, sec. 1, p. [13].

7. H[arry] A[lbert] Musham, "The Great Chicago Fire, October 8–10, 1871," *Papers in Illinois History and Transactions for the Year 1940* (Springfield: Illinois State Historical Society, 1941), hereafter cited in preface as Musham; Robert Cromie, *The Great Chicago Fire*, illustrated ed. (Nashville: Rutledge Hill Press, 1994).

8. For ease of reading, I have very lightly edited these letters and unpublished personal accounts. For example, I have changed "dont" to "don't" and "+" to "and" and corrected the occasional misspelled word.

9. Karen Sawislak, *Smoldering City: Chicagoans and the Great Fire, 1871–1874* (Chicago: University of Chicago Press, 1995); Carl Smith, *Urban Disorder and the Shape of Belief: The Great Chicago Fire, the Haymarket Bomb, and the Model Town of Pullman* (Chicago: University of Chicago Press, 1995).

10. Herman Kogan and Robert Cromie, *The Great Fire: Chicago 1871* (New York: G. P. Putnam's Sons, 1971), hereafter cited in preface as Kogan and Cromie.

11. Ross Miller, *American Apocalypse: The Great Fire and the Myth of Chicago* (Chicago: University of Chicago Press, 1990); Ross Miller, *The Great Chicago Fire*, paperback ed. (Urbana: University of Illinois Press, 2000).

12. Kogan and Cromie, p. [5]; Harold M. Mayer and Richard C. Wade, *Chicago: Growth of a Metropolis* (Chicago: University of Chicago Press, 1969), p. 107.

13. "Fire Alley Is Paved," *Chicago Daily Tribune*, 25 May 1894, p. 1.

14. Musham, p. 69.

ok:

• *Chapter One* •

A City on Fire

In a city where time was everything, and durability was not a matter much considered, street after street was lined with wooden buildings, not with oaken beams and floorings, but an aggregation of flimsily constructed and inflammable pine.

—*Chicago Daily Tribune*, October 9, 1872

Chicago Before the Fire

In 1871 Chicago was on the cusp of greatness. First organized in 1833, it had quickly grown from a town of less than a square mile in size, inhabited by about two hundred people, to a city of more than 334,000. Half of this population were native-born Americans; the other half were emigrants, practically all from northern Europe. Both halves now lived in an area about thirty-six square miles in size. Chicago had become the fourth largest city in the country, and in the process had become the industrial, commercial, and cultural mecca of the Midwest as well, even rivaling its older big-city brethren to the east.[1]

"Location, location, and location" is the mantra consistently intoned as the three most important factors to consider in choosing a place to live. This was especially appropriate to Chicago, for it was the city's unique geography, more than any-

thing else, that determined its destiny. Nestled along Lake Michigan and the Chicago River these two bodies of water from the very beginning helped to make Chicago one of the largest ports of entry in the United States. By 1870 more vessels docked at Chicago than at the ports of New York, Philadelphia, Baltimore, San Francisco, Charleston, and Mobile combined. The excavation of the Illinois and Michigan Canal, which connected Lake Michigan to the Illinois River and eventually to the Mississippi River, made Chicago's location even more lucrative. Chicago was now more than just a lake port; it had an inland water route as well. After the canal opened up in 1848, anyone with access to a river and goods to sell or money in his pocket could ship to or buy from Chicago. Because of the advent of the railroad in the 1850s, the canal never did become a significant trade artery. But that did not matter, because by 1871, virtually all railroads led to Chicago anyway.[2]

It was the city's geography that served to internally define the city as well. The Chicago River divided the city into three parts or divisions, appropriately called the South Side, the North Side, and the West Side (Figure 1). Extending west from Lake Michigan, the trunk of the river forked about half a mile from the lake, so that its two branches ran north and south, looking somewhat like the letter "T" but tipped over to the left and lying on its side. Between the trunk and southern arm of the "T" was the city's South Side, which contained the main business section of the city as well as the worst of its slums. North, across the trunk of the "T," was the North Side, which contained Chicago's finest residential district. West of the two branches of the river was the West Side, which included both an industrial section of factories, grain elevators, and warehouses located near the river as well as the crowded frame homes of the working class. Industry, commerce, and trade—facts and figures indicated that statistically Chicago was clearly a city on its way to the top[3] (Figures 2–4).

Or was it? A careful examination of Chicago in 1871 by someone other than the casual observer revealed that there were cracks in its seemingly impenetrable façade.

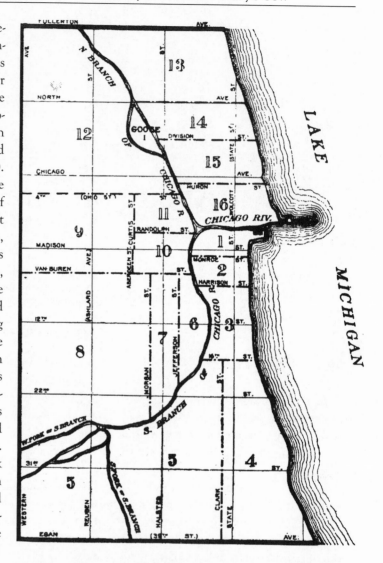

FIGURE 1—MAP OF CHICAGO SHOWING THE THREE DIVISIONS. This map of Chicago (circa 1863) shows how the Chicago River divides the city into three divisions. The map originally appeared in Hugo S. Grosser's *Chicago: A Review of Its Governmental History from 1837 to 1906.*

Certainly there was the red-light and saloon district just blocks from the business section. There was also Conley's Patch, a slum of crime and vice once colorfully called a collection of hundreds of the "dirtiest, vilest, most rickety, one-sided, leaning forward, propped up, tumbled-down, sinking fast, low-roofed and most miserable shanties"[4] (Figure 5).

FIGURE 2—WOOD'S MUSEUM, PRE-FIRE. This pre-fire photograph of Chicago's business district was taken in 1868 or 1869 from the courthouse roof looking east and northeast. Colonel J. H. Wood's famous museum can be seen to the left. The museum was on the north side of Randolph Street between Clark and Dearborn streets, on Chicago's South Side. It was founded in 1863 and contained such oddities as a pair of mummies reportedly once owned by the Mormon prophet Joseph Smith. The main attraction was the "Zeuglodon," a ninety-six-foot-long skeleton of a prehistoric whale. The museum was an immediate success, with ten thousand people passing through its doors during its first six weeks of operation. The building also contained a theater with a seating capacity of about 1,500. (Chicago Historical Society ICHi-33546)

But there was more than just these obvious imperfections. In the thirty-eight years since Chicago was first organized as a town, the city had grown quickly, perhaps too quickly. Buildings were slapped together with little or no regard for fire-resistant materials or construction methods. Even though stone and brick were used in many of the South Side businesses and the more elegant North Side homes, wood was still the construction material of choice for the rank and file Chicagoan, as wood was readily available and much lighter and easier to work with than brick, stone, iron, or steel. Although an advantage of wood was its abundance, one disadvantage was its impermanence. That is, as Chicagoans would soon discover, it had an unfortunate propensity to burn.[5]

But the fire department already knew this. Since 1865 the department had been managed by a Board of Police and Fire Commissioners. During the next few years, the Board lobbied unsuccessfully for more

FIGURE 3—CORNER OF LAKE STREET AND WABASH AVENUE, PRE-FIRE. This lithograph (circa 1866) by artists Otto Jevne and Peter M. Almini illustrates the pre-fire hustle and bustle of the corner of Lake Street and Wabash Avenue. The lettering on the cart in the foreground indicates that its driver works for the Merchants Union Express Company. Express companies delivered baggage and parcels throughout Chicago. Fire Marshal Robert A. Williams commented after the fire that "the barn of the 'Merchants Union' was burning north side of Monroe Street. The cornice got afire, and we couldn't reach it." Looking west down Lake Street, the cupola of what appears to be the Tremont House looms above the other buildings. Like the express company barn, this hotel would not survive the fire. (Chicago Historical Society ICHi-06852)

fire hydrants, a limitation on the use of wood as a building material, and the elimination of the use of tar as a roofing material. As the Board so succinctly observed in its annual report of 1868: "The style of constructing buildings throughout the city, is generally too unsubstantial. In many cases, ornament is substituted for strength, and safety is sacrificed for cheapness." Although the city had fire limits, which were areas in which no frame buildings were allowed, the ordinances governing these areas were enforced as haphazardly as the buildings were erected. Furthermore, these fire limits were just that, of *limited* extent. The Chicago Fire Department's pleas to expand the boundaries of these areas apparently fell on the deaf and uncaring ears of the citizenry of Chicago, who opposed all laws that would regulate the use of their property.[6]

If the fire department received little support from the general public, it apparently received even less from the city

FIGURE 4—LAKE STREET, PRE-FIRE. In 1871, Lake Street was one of Chicago's primary commercial thoroughfares. This view of Lake Street looking east from Clark Street reveals a myriad of merchandise that Chicagoans could purchase: watches and jewelry; hats, caps, and furs; dry goods and carpets; and far down on the left hand side, rare books. Services were also available, as the signs for book binding and printing indicate. (Chicago Historical Society ICHi-04316)

government. Although the Board of Police and Fire Commissioners managed the fire department, it was the city's Common Council that controlled the department's purse strings, and it appeared that it did so with alacrity. Robert A. Williams became fire marshal in 1868 (Figure 6). In his annual report for 1868–69, Williams recommended that the city obtain one or more floating steam fire engines that could be used on the Chicago River. In 1870 Williams suggested that larger water mains be installed throughout the city. The Common Council failed to fund these proposals. Williams requested 15,000 feet of new hose for 1871, but he received only 10,000 feet.[7]

Assuming that the Common Council was tight with a dollar, did its frugality pose a danger to the city of Chicago? At first one

FIGURE 5—CONLEY'S PATCH, PRE-FIRE. Shortly after midnight on October 9, the fire reached Conley's Patch, a block of tenements on Chicago's South Side. Historians James W. Sheahan and George P. Upton describe Conley's Patch as an area "densely covered with saloons, tumble-down hovels and sheds, and peopled by the lowest class in the city. For years this spot had been the terror of the neighborhood beyond it, and had been stained with every conceivable crime." Artist Marshall Philyaw brings these words to life with this imaginative illustration that is consistent with other descriptions of this infamous area and similar to a drawing of a Chicago alley scene that appeared in the *Chicago Tribune* a few years after the fire.

FIGURE 6—FIRE MARSHAL ROBERT A. Born in Canada in 1828, Williams came to Chicago in 1848. A year later he joined the Volunteer Fire Department, becoming a member of Engine Company No. 6. Williams served as first assistant to the popular fire chief Uriah P. Harris until Harris resigned in 1868. Williams was then appointed Chief Fire Marshal and served in this capacity until 1873. (Chicago Historical Society ICHi-12924)

payroll for the month ending October 31, 1871, indicates that all this equipment was manned by 193 firemen and that twenty-three additional men worked at the department headquarters. There was an average of only two fires a day during the year preceding the Great Chicago Fire. Fireman Leo Meyers observed shortly after the blaze that "it has been the remark that we had better facilities for the last three or four years for the extinguishment of a fire than we ever had before in Chicago." Can one blame the Common Council for declining to spend $12,000 for Williams' floating folly—a hybrid boat and fire engine capable of throwing up to twelve streams of water and having a dockside fire alarm telegraph connection?[8]

Possibly yes. The Chicago Fire Department was very good, but its force was spread too thin. The department did not have enough resources to protect a wooden city of thirty-six square miles. Although the city had sixteen steam engines, on average each engine had to cover more than two square miles of combustible territory. It appears that Williams knew this, but unfortunately, the Common Council apparently did not.[9]

As the summer of 1871 unfolded in

might argue that it is doubtful that parsimonious politicians ever truly imperiled the city. In 1871 the fire department had sixteen steam engine companies (with one additional engine in reserve), six hose carts, four hook-and-ladder companies, and one hose elevator (Figures 7–9). The engines were the most modern ones of the day. All but two of them were less than six years old, and four engines were less than two years old. The Chicago Fire Department

FIGURE 7—STEAMER *LITTLE GIANT* NO. 6. The steam engine *Little Giant* was built in 1860 by the Amoskeag Manufacturing Company of Manchester, New Hampshire. This engine was designed to throw four streams of water. It was drawn by four horses and weighed 8,100 pounds. A steam boiler mounted on the back of the engine provided power to the pump, which was located at the center. The manufacturer claimed that at an average working speed, it could pump 600 gallons of water per minute. During a test in 1865, a Chicago steam engine threw a stream of water from a one-and-one-fourth inch nozzle to a height of 175 feet and a horizontal stream from the same size nozzle a distance of 230 feet. (Drawing by Marshall Philyaw)

sweltering drought, perhaps the city fathers wished they had listened to their fire marshal. That summer was exceptionally hot and dry in Chicago. In the twenty-two days from September 17 to October 8, only 0.11 inch of rain fell. Indeed, there had been very little rainfall since July 4. Prevailing southwest winds brought to the already seared and withered city the scorching heat of the great plains. The wind sucked what little moisture there was out of Chicago's wooden buildings, leaving them as dry as the leaves that had already fallen from the trees and now lay scattered over the parched grass. By the first week of October, Chicago was a desiccated husk of a city, and as its residents either broiled in the sun or merely simmered in the shade, all were aware of the danger that fire could bring to their city.[10]

Even in 1871 children undoubtedly learned in school that in order for fire to ignite there must be three elements: heat, fuel, and oxygen. Unfortunately, all three were in abundance by October. The overpowering presence of stifling heat was, of course, continually apparent to all of the city's beleaguered residents. A ready supply

FIGURE 8—TEMPEST HOSE CART NO. 1. The machinery needed to power a steam engine and operate its pump left little room for other fire fighting equipment, such as hose. Instead, a two-wheeled hose cart drawn by one horse was assigned to each engine company. Other hose carts, such as this one, the *Tempest*, were not part of any engine company. The company called *Tempest* Hose Cart No. 1 was composed of a foreman, two hosemen, and a driver. This cart was built by George W. Hannis of Chicago. It carried 500 feet of two-and-one-half inch hose. With driver and hose, the cart weighed about 1,800 pounds. Its foreman, Leo Meyers, was one of the 27 firemen who testified at the investigation into the cause of the fire. (Drawing by Marshall Philyaw)

of the second element was wood—besides wooden homes and businesses, there were grain elevators, furniture factories and lumber mills, which, if not made of wood, contained wooden materials. And if that were not enough, many of these industries had stockpiles of coal for their steam-powered boilers. As Chicago Fire historian Robert Cromie observed: "It might be said, with considerable justice, that Chicago specialized in the production, handling, and storage of combustible goods."[11]

The third and final element was oxygen. Besides the obvious aboveground supply, the 561 miles of wooden sidewalks provided a subterranean resource as well. In an attempt to alleviate Chicago's swampy conditions, some of the city's streets, particularly in the business section, were raised above ground level. Many of Chicago's sidewalks were raised as well, some apparently as much as five to seven feet. There were few partitions underneath, and so these underground passages were lengthy and high enough so that a person could walk from one end of the street to the other—or even, as fireman Leo Meyers recalled, large enough to drive a good-sized cart through. As a result, they were like gigantic horizontal pine chimneys; if set ablaze, they would draw thousands of cubic feet of oxygen and encircle the city in a stranglehold of fire.[12]

All three ingredients combined to

GEORGE W. HANNIS,

No. 76 Michigan Street, Chicago, Illinois,

MANUFACTURER OF

HOSE CARTS.

Fire Ladders, Hook and Ladder Pike Poles, Trucks, Hooks and Chains,

AND ALL KINDS OF FIRE APPARATUS.

REFERENCES { R. A. WILLIAMS, Chief Marshal, Fire Dept. Chicago.   E. G. MEGRUE, Esq., Chief Engineer Fire Dept., Cincinnati { H. B. HINSDALE, Chief Engineer, Fire Dept. Kenosha, Wis.

FIGURE 9—PIONEER HOOK AND LADDER NO. 1. This advertisement for George W. Hannis, manufacturer of fire company equipment, appeared in the "Fire Edition" of *Edwards' Chicago Directory*. The ad depicts a hook and ladder truck. This piece of equipment derives its name from the hooks and ladders it carried. The hooks were attached to chains and used to pull down frame sheds, barns, and small houses in order to create a fire break. The ladders provided firemen access to the roofs of buildings, allowed them to bring hose lines to the upper floors of buildings, and were used to evacuate people from burning buildings. This piece of equipment was officially called a "hook and ladder," but as the advertisement indicates, the term "truck" was also used. When fully equipped, it weighed 4,500 pounds. It was pulled by two horses.

At first glance, the advertisement does not appear to indicate that this is a picture of any particular hook and ladder truck. But barely discernible are the words "Pioneer No. 1" and "Pioneer," emblazoned on the rear and fronts seats respectively of the truck. Also, this same picture appeared in the 1869 *Report of the Board of Police* next to a description of the "*Pioneer* Hook and Ladder Truck No. 1." Francis T. Swenie was the foreman of this hook and ladder company. He was the thirty-fifth person to testify at the fire department investigation.

The list of references in this advertisement includes Marshal Robert A. Williams. This ad is almost identical to one that appeared in the 1870 city directory. In this earlier ad, however, the references included the late Uriah P. Harris, Williams' predecessor.

produce twenty-eight significant fires during that first week of October, the most serious of which broke out on the evening of Saturday, October 7, in the Lull & Holmes planing mill on Chicago's West Side[13] (Figure 10). The fire started at about eleven o'clock that evening, and firemen fought the fire all night and through Sunday afternoon. On Sunday the *Chicago Tribune*

gave extensive coverage to this fire. The lead paragraph seemed especially foreboding: "For days past, alarm has followed alarm, but the comparatively trifling losses have familiarized us to the pealing of the Court House bell, and we had forgotten that the absence of rain for three weeks had left everything in so dry and inflammable a condition that a spark might start a fire

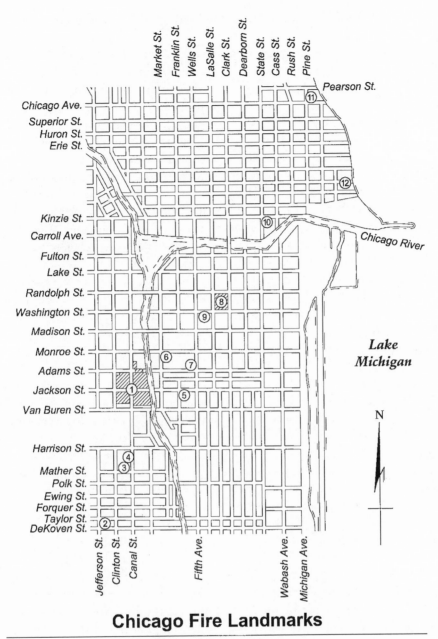

Chicago Fire Landmarks

October 8, 1871

1. Lull & Holmes planing mill (October 7 fire)
2. O'Leary barn
3. St. Paul's Catholic Church
4. Bateham's mills
5. Parmelee Omnibus and Stage Company
6. Gas Works

7. Conley's Patch
8. Courthouse
9. Union National Bank
10. Wright Brothers Stables
11. Water Works
12. The Sands

FIGURE 10—CHICAGO FIRE LANDMARKS. Chapter One, which is a history of the Chicago Fire, refers to various buildings and locations throughout this city. These places, numbered and in chronological order, are shown on this street map of Chicago in 1871. (Diagram by Douglas A. Swanson)

which would sweep from end to end of the city"[14] (Figure 11).

A City Ablaze

Only a few hours later, the words of the *Tribune* proved to be devastatingly prescient. Shortly after nine o'clock on the evening of Sunday, October 8, 1871, fire broke out in the barn of Patrick and Catherine O'Leary, who lived on the city's West Side (Figure 12). The blaze spread quickly through the shanties, sheds, and other buildings that adjoined the O'Learys' DeKoven Street cottage, traveling, generally speaking, in a northeasterly direction. Directly north of and parallel to DeKoven Street was Taylor Street; in less than an hour the fire crossed Taylor and a weary fire department, exhausted from fighting the Lull & Holmes blaze, tried in vain to contain the ever-growing maelstrom. The heat was already so strong that fireman Charles Anderson was able to hold the fire hose to the flames only when shielded by a door that a friend had scavenged. Within half a minute, however, the door caught fire, and as his friend dropped it, Anderson's clothes began to smoke, and his hat began to twist on his head from the intense heat. It appeared to many that the fire was quickly getting out of control. When First Assistant Fire Marshal John Schank told Third Assistant Mathias Benner to send all spare engines to the fire, Benner asked, "John, where has this fire gone to?" Schank aptly summarized the situation when he replied, "She has gone to hell and gone."[15]

In the coming days and weeks, when Chicagoans wrote letters to loved ones about the fire, and years later, when they penned their reminiscences of what they lived through that October, many of them wrote in awe of the gale-like wind that whipped the flames into walls of fire more than one hundred feet high. Mrs. Anna E. Higginson, burned out of her home and living for the moment in Elmhurst, Illinois, wrote in November of 1871 that "the wind, blowing a hurricane, howling like myriads of evil spirits, drove the flames before it with a force and fierceness which could never be described or imagined...." Actually, the wind at this time was never greater than thirty miles an hour. What Mrs. Higginson and other soon-to-be homeless Chicagoans thought was a tornado of fire were in fact "convection whirls," masses of superheated air that rose from the flames and developed a whirling motion on contact with the cooler surrounding air. At the time, the average citizen, fleeing for his life, probably would not have wanted or even cared to stop and debate the finer points of thermodynamics and meteorology. Nonetheless, it was these convection whirls, sometimes called "fire devils," that were the death knell of Chicago. They carried burning masses of fire forward for distances of up to a half mile or more, starting new fires far from where they originated, creating new centers of destruction from which fire flowed in all directions.[16]

Chicago firemen quickly got a lesson in the power of these convection whirls. As the fire poured onto Taylor Street and onward to the north, the fire marshal and his men raced ahead of the fire, as Williams still thought that he could get the blaze under control. But at about ten P.M., while the fire was still just a few hours old, a mass of burning material about two feet long and one foot thick spun off of the fire north of Taylor Street. Whirling northward, it struck the steeple of St. Paul's Catholic Church four blocks away (and at least two blocks north of the firemen), engulfing the church in flames almost instantaneously. Williams immediately assigned

THE FIRE FIEND.

A Terribly Destructive Conflagration Last Night.

Twenty Acres of Buildings in the West Division in Ruins.

Lumber, Wood, and Coal Yards, Planing Mills, Stores, and Dwellings Burned.

The Adams Street Viaduct Destroyed---Narrow Escape of the Bridge.

Thousands of Citizens Witness the Grand but Awful Illumination.

The Loss Supposed to be in the Neighborhood of $1,000,000.

Scenes, Incidents, and Accidents Occasioned by the Fire.

DISCOVERED.

THE SOUNDING OF THE FIRE ALARM from Box No. 248, at about 11 o'clock last night, was the solemn prelude to one of the most disastrous and imposing conflagrations which has ever visited a city which has already enrolled in her anuals numbers of such visitations, many of them so terrible that they can serve as eras in her history. For days past, alarm has followed alarm, but the comparatively trifling losses have familiarized us to the pealing of the Court House bell, and we had forgotten that the absence of rain for three weeks had left everything in so dry and inflammable a condition that a spark might start a fire which would sweep from end to end of the city.

additional manpower to fight this new fire. His men might even have succeeded had it not been for one of the many ironies that seem to be entwined with the history of the Great Chicago Fire—the church just happened to be within several feet of the shingle mill, box factory, and furniture factory of William B. Bateham. Even worse, the Frank Mayer Furniture Company and the Roelle Furniture Finishing Company were located on the Bateham property. In a combination as deadly as Chicago baseball's "Tinker to Evers to Chance" of a few decades later, the church set fire to the Roelle factory, which in turn touched off the Mayer Furniture Company, which quickly spread through the Bateham mills. Williams later described what he saw as he entered the Bateham property: "I went in there, but the fire was coming down thicker than any snowstorm you ever saw, and the yard between the two mills was all filled with shavings, and chunks of fire came in of all sizes, from the length of your arm down to three inches." By ten-thirty the firemen were driven away by the intense heat, and as Mr. Bateham turned from the incineration of his property, he prophetically remarked, "The materials from this mill will fire the South Side, and nothing can prevent it now."[17]

FIGURE 11—OCTOBER 8, 1871, *TRIBUNE* ARTICLE ABOUT THE LULL & HOLMES PLANING MILL FIRE. On Sunday, October 8, the *Tribune* covered the Lull & Holmes planing mill fire of the previous evening. Surely the lead paragraph would later haunt Chicagoans: "For days past, alarm has followed alarm, but the comparatively trifling losses have familiarized us to the pealing of the Court House bell, and we had forgotten that the absence of rain for three weeks had left everything in so dry and inflammable a condition that a spark might start a fire which would sweep from end to end of the city."

FIGURE 12—O'LEARY BARN ON FIRE. The O'Leary barn burst into flames on Sunday evening, October 8, 1871. In this drawing, artist Marshall Philyaw depicts the first few minutes of the fire and how the scene might have appeared to someone watching from the opposite side of DeKoven Street. A close examination reveals some of the people who have been memorialized in Chicago Fire lore: Mrs. O'Leary's tenant, Mr. McLaughlin, holding his fiddle, and two neighbors, Daniel "Peg Leg" Sullivan and Dennis Regan, using buckets of water to help extinguish the flames. Also shown are some of the incidents linked with the fire's history: the rain of sparks and embers on adjoining buildings, which helped to spread the flames, and firemen ripping up the sidewalks so that they can be used as fuel for the steam engines.

The Fire Strikes the South Side

It took only an hour for the fire to prove Bateham correct. At eleven-thirty more burning debris was blown across the Chicago River and ignited a horse stable, but not just any stable. This was the new building of the Parmelee Omnibus and Stage Company, which had just been completed at a cost of $80,000. Said to be the finest of its kind in the country, it would have been occupied for the first time on Wednesday, October 11. About half an hour later, a burning shingle was carried across the river and dropped into the tar tank of Barrett & Arnold, a manufacturer of roofing material. "A sheet of fire and smoke rushed right up," and within seconds the flames spread to an adjoining coal shed of the Chicago Gas Light and Coke Company, commonly called the gas works. At the time there was about 200,000 cubic feet of gas in the gas holders. The possibility of an explosion must have seemed imminent, for when Fire Marshal Williams arrived, someone yelled at him to leave, screaming,

"You'll be blown to pieces!" Police Captain Michael C. Hickey later described the scene: "There was such confusion! Men, women, and children hollering and yelling and drawing out their things—the streets were just perfectly thronged with these human beings trying to get out of these patches, and they were all hollering and running in every direction. It was nothing but excitement." And in the midst of this hell stood Mr. Thomas Ockerby.[18]

The legend and lore of the Great Chicago Fire is replete with a myriad of characters. There were foolish men like David Green, night superintendent of mail for the post office. With the fire looming only a block away, a postal clerk named Alonzo Hannis asked Green for permission to begin packing letters for removal. As the city burned around them, Green, a government lackey to the end, responded: "If you touch any letters without orders from headquarters, you will get your discharge!" There were also scoundrels, like the possibly apocryphal lout who threw a glass of liquor on the burning blond hair of a girl running past him. The fire "flared up and covered her with a blue flame." And there were heroes. On Saturday, December 2, Thomas Ockerby testified at the Board of Police and Fire Commissioners' investigation of the fire. If one can believe his testimony, then Thomas Ockerby was a hero. Ockerby was night superintendent of the gas works. Afraid that the facility would burn, Ockerby asked a fireman to go into the works with a "lead," or fire hose, to cool down a gas holder. The fireman refused, and so Ockerby went in with the hose instead—until firemen inexplicably shut the hose off and took it away. As Ockerby explained to the Board:

A. [Ockerby] One of our men came and told me there was a fire engine out on the corner, and I went out there and saw a man that appeared to be in charge. I do not know whether he was captain of the machine or who he was, and I asked him to take a lead into the works to play on the gas holder, and he said that he would not go there nor he would not send his men there.

Q. [Board] Give any reason?

A. I told him, said I, "It is perfectly safe, and I will go down there with you." Said he, "I do not take any man's soul in my hands. You can take the lead in there if you want to." Said I, "You request your men to surrender the lead to me, and I will." He did so, and I took the lead in there and I led on the gas holder until they shut it off and reeled up the hose and took it away.[19]

And it probably was safe. There apparently was little danger of an explosion, because even before the fire had crossed the river, the gas had already been transferred to the gas holders on the city's North Side. But the firemen did not know this at the time. Even Fire Marshal Williams had declared that "in case of explosion, I won't put my men down in there." But Ockerby did remain in there; after his hose was taken away, he checked to be sure some horses were safe. He then went to the gas works retort house to make sure that no gas was escaping. And what was Ockerby's reward for his diligence? No good deed goes unpunished. In a letter to the editor published in the *Chicago Tribune* on November 17, 1871, Williams claimed that the gas was deliberately let out of the works into the surrounding neighborhood, causing the entire area to burn even more fiercely than otherwise. Peter T. Burtis, another gas works superintendent, bitterly protested this allegation in a subsequent *Tribune* letter, arguing that "the gas holders were in the position we wanted them before the fire reached the works, and not one foot of gas was allowed to escape at the works...." Williams eventually softened his position, contending in his 1893 reminiscences only that "when the fire reached the gas works and destroyed them there must have been some outlet for the gas that was there."[20]

Shortly after midnight on October 9, at approximately the same time the gas works caught fire, another burning brand was carried across the river, where it landed on the roof of a three-story tenement house. The fire quickly spread to the shacks and shanties of the infamous "Conley's Patch," a block of South Side wooden buildings near the gas works. The men of this not-so-upscale address were all out on the city's West Side at the time, enjoying the free entertainment of watching someone else's property being destroyed. Accordingly, it was only the women and children who were home when the flames swooped upon them. Although most of the residents escaped the fiery onslaught, Chicago Fire historians James Sheahan and George Upton later suggested that "undoubtedly some were overtaken by the fire and miserably perished." Fellow historian Joseph Kirkland concurred, commenting starkly that "the death harvest probably began at about this time." Indeed, death filled the air with burning brands swirling above the city and engulfing the sky. In one of the simplest but most hauntingly evocative post-fire descriptions, fireman Thomas Byrne later told of what he saw: "You couldn't see anything over you but fire. No clouds, no stars. Nothing else but fire."[21]

In a sense the courthouse was similar to Conley's Patch. Located in the heart of the city, a contemporary guidebook called the building "one of the homeliest of its kind in the country" (Figure 13). As the county jail was in the courthouse basement, it housed, like Conley's Patch, the worst of Chicago's ne'er-do-wells (some who, when they signed the jail's guest book upon checking in, undoubtedly listed "The Patch" as their previous address). But the courthouse was more than just a repository for thieves and murderers. Shared by both the county and the city, it contained numerous administrative offices and warehoused a multitude of records. Rogues *vs.* Records—it made no difference, the fire was prepared for equal opportunity destruction.[22]

Almost from the beginning the courthouse was in danger of being ignited by the rain of fire that was blown over it. Twice that Sunday night Mathias Schaefer, fire department watchman in the courthouse cupola, had to leave his post to go out onto the roof and stamp out errant fires. Unfortunately, one of the cupola's windows was broken, and some sparks blew into this tower and set the woodwork ablaze. Schaefer tried to put out the flames but was driven away by the smoke. As the stairs leading down from the cupola were on fire, he was forced to slide down the bannisters, scorching his whiskers and burning his hands and face. In order to warn Chicagoans of Armageddon, Schaefer had been ringing the courthouse bell throughout the night. Now, at about 1:30 Monday morning, as he and another watchmen, Denis Deneen, fled the cupola, one of them set the bell on "automatic," to ring continually as long as it could. "Continually" lasted only thirty-five minutes, for at 2:05 A.M. the bell went booming downward through the courthouse and was silenced. (After the fire, part of the bell was melted down into tiny souvenir bells. Years later, one former fire relic dealer, reminiscing about the large number of bell mementos that were sold

FIGURE 13—COURTHOUSE, PRE-FIRE. Although this building housed both the Cook County Courthouse and Chicago City Hall, Chicagoans invariably called it "the courthouse." The center portion was constructed in 1853. The two-story tower held the courthouse bell, and around the tower was the walkway manned by fire department watchman Mathias Schaefer on the night of October 8. The west and east additions were built in 1870, and this photograph was taken just after these improvements were completed. The west wing housed City Hall and contained the offices of the mayor, Board of Police, fire marshal, fire department telegraph, and other municipal departments. In the east or county wing were courtrooms and county records. The jail was in the basement of the east wing. (Chicago Historical Society ICHi-32031)

and perhaps commenting on their questionable pedigree, wrote: "If all that were sold came from that bell, it sure was a wonderful big one")[23] (Figures 14–16).

As the jail filled with smoke, the prisoners began to scream, fearful of being burned alive. Outside, Captain Hickey went to the jail door and implored Edward Longley, deputy sheriff and jail keeper, to release the prisoners, telling him that "the courthouse is on fire. It won't be five minutes before this roof will go in." Longley, speaking like a true bureaucrat, allegedly replied, "I hate to take the responsibility."

Hickey retorted, "I will take the responsibility." Those prisoners charged with murder were taken away in handcuffs and under guard to the North Side. The rest were released into the streets. According to one rather improbable anecdote, as the men rushed out of the jail, a clothing truck happened to be passing by, and in an instant the now ex-prisoners swarmed over it and quickly emptied the vehicle. The men then ran off to disguise themselves and, some claimed, to plunder the city. Minutes later, at 2:20 A.M., Hickey's words proved true. The roof of the courthouse crashed

AUCTION SALES.

BY WM. A. BUTTERS & CO.

PUBLIC AUCTION.

THE REMAINING PORTION

OF THE

Court-House Bell

Will be sold at PUBLIC AUCTION,

TO-DAY, SATURDAY, DEC. 16.

At the Northwestern M'fg Co.'s Warehouse, on Jefferson street, between Randolph and Lake. Sale to commence at 2 o'clock sharp, and to be sold for cash on day of sale. There will be about 7.200 pounds of the metal.
J. McARTHUR, W. H. CARTER, R. PRINDIVILLE, Board of Public Works.

WM. A. BUTTERS & CO,
Auctioneers.

del6dlt

FIGURE 14—AUCTION ADVERTISEMENT OF THE COURTHOUSE BELL. The *Chicago Tribune* of December 17, 1871, reported that the courthouse bell "was among the last to leave the tower, the watchman having deserted his post some minutes before. It took an air line route to the ground, and when the ruins were cleared away was found in a half-melted state." The Chicago Board of Public Works placed the remains of the bell in storage with the Northwestern Manufacturing Company. This ad from the December 16, 1871, *Chicago Times* publicizes the auction sale of the melted bell. It was sold to Thomas B. Bryan of the Fidelity Safe Depository, who kept a portion of it but sold most of what he purchased to H. S. Everhart & Company. This company made miniature bells, one-half inch high, out of the metal and sold them to the public as souvenirs of the fire.

earthward, taking with it the legal history of Chicago but sparing the city's miscreants[24] (Figures 17–19).

Pillage and Plunder

As newspapers across the country vied with each other in attempting to write the story of the century, their reporters became

Left: FIGURE 15—ADVERTISEMENT FOR THE MINIATURE COURTHOUSE BELLS. This advertisement for the miniature courthouse bells appeared in the February 1872 issue of *The Land Owner: A Journal of Real Estate Building & Improvement.* H. S. Everhart & Co., mindful of "bogus, spurious, and inferior" imitation bells, admonished Chicagoans to "procure with EACH BELL our certificate from the Chicago Board of Public Works, and Thomas B. Bryan, as proof of the veracity of our statements relative to Bells, made by us, of the metal of the Chicago Court House Bell." *Above:* FIGURE 16—MINIATURE COURTHOUSE BELL. Smaller than a Lincoln penny, this is one of the miniature courthouse bells made by H. S. Everhart & Company. (Chicago Historical Society DIA-506)

less and less objective and more and more lurid as they wrote of the fire and its aftermath. The release of the prisoners from the courthouse was just one of several incidents that captured the attention of many newspaper editors who believed that although truth may be stranger than fiction, it doesn't sell as many papers at the corner newsstand. The following description of this event, for example, is typical of many of these post-fire newspaper accounts: "Like devils incarnate they rushed pell-mell into the street, yelling and cursing with the utmost fiendishness. Hastening to the district threatened by the conflagration, they commenced a series of outrages almost unparalleled in the history of crime"[25] (Figures 20–21).

FIGURE 17—COURTHOUSE ON FIRE. In this picture that originally appeared in the October 28, 1871, issue of *Frank Leslie's Illustrated Newspaper*, smoke swirls around the courthouse cupola where Mathias Schaefer stood only a few hours earlier. Frank Leslie was "editor and proprietor" of this New York City weekly newspaper. The *Chicago Press* complained bitterly of the sensationalism of its eastern brethren. With graphic tales of exotic punishments meted out to alleged incendiaries, Leslie's paper must have been one of the most lurid of these eastern newspapers. One of the tamer passages from the article "The Tornado of Fire" appropriately describes the melee outside the burning courthouse: "The streets were thronged with people flying for their lives. Children were carried, screaming with terror; women were shrieking, men shouting, and all running. Some of the old and sick and helpless were carried on stretchers— some apparently demented or stupefied were dragged along. Close to their heels, in hot pursuit, came the belching, roaring and crackling flames. In some places they actually advanced as fast as a man ran."

Actually, the charges of looting and robbery were greatly exaggerated. As the fire swept over the city, the prisoners, like most other Chicagoans, were primarily concerned with running for their lives, not running to snatch what they could from the nearest store. It would make little sense for anyone to race the fire into the business district to pillage and plunder, knowing that at any time the flames could cut off an escape route. Granted, there was some looting of stores during the fire. Police captain Michael Hickey told of trying "to stop a quarrel on Canal Street. They were gutting a saloon there—trying to take everything out of it." He also commented that "there was a lot of thieves who were stealing this property on Wabash Avenue through the wholesale stores there. They were fetching it along in loads." There were

FIGURE 18—WOOD'S MUSEUM ON FIRE. As noted in Figure 2, Colonal Wood's museum was near the courthouse, and as shown in this drawing by artist Marshall Philyaw, the museum suffered the same fate as this city and county government building. The *Chicago Evening Journal* of November 18, 1871, included a chronology of when certain buildings were overtaken by the flames. This newspaper indicates that the museum was ablaze at three o'clock Monday morning, October 9.

FIGURE 19—COURTHOUSE RUINS; VIEW ALONG RANDOLPH STREET. Looking east along Randolph Street, this stark view of what remains of the courthouse bears testimony to the complete and utter desolation created by the fire. Historians Robert Cromie and Herman Kogan plausibly suggest that this photograph may have been taken from the roof of the Lind Block, which was at the northwest corner of Market (now Wacker Drive) and Randolph streets. The Lind Block was one of the few buildings in the South Side burnt district that escaped the flames. As measured along Randolph Street, it was almost directly west of the courthouse. The only other surviving structure of note in the South Side business section was the unfinished Nixon Building, but this was at the northeast corner of Monroe and LaSalle streets, almost due south from the courthouse and nowhere near Randolph Street. (Courtesy of the Illinois State Historical Library)

Opposite: FIGURE 20—"THE HORRORS OF CHICAGO." Many post-fire newspapers and periodicals sensationalized the events of October 8–10, 1871, with lurid tales of roving marauders and incendiaries. This drawing is from the appropriately named booklet *The Horrors of Chicago.* It depicts a woman holding a baby and leaping to her death from a burning building, an arsonist at work, an apparent looter, and a lynching that suggests the attempted hanging allegedly witnessed by Police Captain Michael C. Hickey: "One other thing that I remember in regard to lynching was a man on the corner of Harrison and Clark streets, a peaceable man, a man I knew and a good citizen. About five hundred people got around him. That was two nights after the fire, I think it was. They licked him on the start and got together to lynch him on a lamppost."

"THE RUINED CITY."

THE
Horrors of Chicago

THE AMERICAN NEWS CO., 119, 121 Nassau St., N. Y:

similar crimes of opportunity in the private sector as well. In her *Memories of the Chicago Fire*, Mrs. Mary Emily Blatchford wrote of her wedding dress that was stolen by a group of men but later recovered. In an article printed in the *New York Tribune* on October 14, William Bross of the *Chicago Tribune* recounted the following story: "I met a man at my door looking decidedly corpulent. 'My friend,' said I, 'you have on a considerable invoice of my clothes, with the hunting suit outside. Well, go along, you might as well have them as to let them burn.'" There was undoubtedly even some thievery in the days after the fire, as homeless and hungry throngs wandered about the city. But there certainly was not the crime wave like that reported in many of the nation's newspapers. Accordingly, Chicagoans like Joel Bigelow accepted these graphic tales of marauders, incendiaries, and lynchings with some skepticism:

> There are so many reports, one don't know what to believe—there are some who assert that it is a preconcerted plan by a lot of villains to meet here and burn the city for plunder—I saw one party who says that two parties were caught in the act of setting fire to sidewalks in the West Division—and that they were both hung to lampposts—the party asserted that he saw the bodies hanging—an acquaintance of mine says that he is reliably informed—that in the South Division two men has [sic] been hung and one shot—I have just returned from the police headquarters and was informed that such reports are confirmed from reports brought in by police officers—*though I am inclined to accept these statements with some degree of allowance* [emphasis added].[26]

Probably closer to the truth were the stories of wagon and cart drivers who charged exorbitant fees to haul away the household belongings of the hapless victims fleeing the fire. In some instances the price demanded would be paid, but the dri-

ver would carry the goods and owner only a few blocks before unceremoniously emptying both onto the street, so that he could go back and again ply his extortion. Such practices outraged the press, with the *Chicago Evening Journal* proclaiming: "We are glad to learn that our police authorities are making efforts to find out all such cases, and in the event of proof being presented of the guilt of any licensed hackman or expressman, his license will be promptly revoked and his name published broadcast, to his eternal disgrace."[27]

Occasionally, though, the victims would refuse to be victimized. More than once a driver would attempt to liberate himself of his load, only to have the occupant "persuade" him at the point of a gun to move on. On October 17, for example, Thomas Foster wrote his parents a long letter recounting in vivid prose his experiences during the fire. At one point, after colorfully describing the fire as "a white melting heat" and the constant shower of sparks as "a fall of golden snow," he matter-of-factly added another comment, surely to the horror of his mother back home:

> One expressman that we employed was going to drop our things out on the street after he got a few yards when one of my newly made acquaintances drew his revolver, and told him he would blow his brains out if he did. He drove quietly on after that.[28]

Just like the story of the fish that got away, some tales of bravado got bigger and better with the retelling. In 1896 attorney James B. Bradwell reminisced of his struggle to save both his life and his law books from his burning home. He managed to do so only by throwing the books out the window and then running down the fiery stairs. Lying outside on the sidewalk, exhausted from his efforts, he offered an express man fifty dollars to take his books to

FIGURE 21—CHICAGO FIRE SENSATIONALISM. In this imaginative drawing, artist Marshall Philyaw captures the vivid, if inaccurate, prose of *The Horrors of Chicago*: "The great crowd of flying citizens, distracted women, of women carrying distracted children, of men bearing fainting wives or mothers, of children totally helpless, are forced to pause terrified by a sight more dreadful than the wild, flaring ruin behind them. An incendiary.... The phrenzied populace seize the wretch, and in another minute his body hangs dangling from a lamp-post. Even now we seem to hear his yells, entreaties and fierce imprecations, and see his eye-balls starting from their sockets, struggling in vain to save his justly forfeited life."

safety, but the driver only laughed at him. Bradwell added that "had it been ten minutes later I would have gagged the expressman, thrown him in the wagon, loaded in the books and saved them." Thirty years later, his daughter Bessie Bradwell Helmer recalled the same story. Now, though, the express man agrees to move not only a trunk (but not of law books) but also her parents for the same fifty dollars. In this new and improved version, the driver does not laugh at her father. Instead, the express man places the trunk on his wagon, but then, seeing the looming clouds of smoke, he reneges and pulls the trunk off. But after resting thirty years her father has his strength back, because this time he roars at the hapless driver: "Take your choice of three things: take us as you agreed to do, and we may go through in safety; or we may die in the attempt; or you may stay right here and die now." In Mrs. Helmer's revisionist account of her father's exploits, the express man wisely chose option number one.[29]

Blowing Up the City

On the night of October 8, James H. Hildreth, war veteran and former alderman, was also concerned about safety. He was in bed when the fire broke out, but upon hearing the fire alarm and engines and seeing the ominous glare of the flames through his window, he got up, dressed, and went to DeKoven Street. As he watched the firemen work, he realized that the wind, which he described as "blowing a pretty good gale," was quickly driving the fire northward, beyond the control of the firemen. He suggested to Joseph Locke, assistant city engineer, that some buildings should be either torn down or blown up. This would create a firebreak that would

halt the advancing flames. Hildreth and Locke tracked down Marshal Williams, and the three men discussed the matter further. At first Williams was reluctant to authorize the demolition work, explaining that he did not have the authority to destroy the buildings. But when he finally told Hildreth to "get your powder, then," the ex-alderman was off and running.[30]

He almost didn't get the powder. Luckily for him, Roswell H. Mason, the son of Mayor Roswell B. Mason (Figure 22), was more enthusiastic about this project than Williams, and the younger Mason made arrangements for obtaining a powder wagon for Hildreth and Captain Hickey. The mayor issued an order to Hildreth that authorized him to use the powder. But before Hildreth and Hickey could take delivery of the powder wagon, some frightened Chicagoans discovered it. Hickey later claimed that these men were so enraged that gunpowder had been brought into their midst, they set out to lynch the driver from a telegraph post. As Hickey ran over to stop the hanging, he heard the men ask the driver, "Where are you going with that powder?" When the driver replied, "Captain Hickey and the mayor sent it there," the men replied, "Damn Captain Hickey and the mayor!" Hickey disbursed the crowd, telling them, "If you will go about your business, we will try and do some good."[31]

Hildreth's initial attempts at urban renewal were less than satisfactory. First of all, he had no fuse (he later pointed out the obvious, observing that "the places where fuse was sold are all burned up"), so he had to make do by substituting "wicking" or by sprinkling gunpowder onto paper. Second, he knew little about the proper placement of powder for maximum effect. His first effort, an attempt to blow up the Union National Bank, resulted in

FIGURE 22—MAYOR ROSWELL B. MASON. This picture of Mayor Roswell B. Mason was published in Frank Luzerne's *The Lost City!* In his *History of Chicago*, A. T. Andreas lauded Mason, proclaiming that at the time of the fire, "it was well, truly, that a man of such rugged common sense and brave character had control of the city government." But the *Times* had a different opinion of Mason. Shortly after the fire, the newspaper attacked him in a scathing editorial, calling him "an old granny" who was "completely dazed by the calamity." The fire struck Chicago less than a month before its citizens were due to elect a new mayor, and Mason was a self-avowed lame duck. Apparently noting Mason's desire to leave public office, the *Times* sneered: "One mason who will never help to rebuild the city—Mayor Mason."

could not get them to stop.... I grabbed hold of them, took right hold of them with more force than I would if I'd been sheriff, for that matter, and made them, but they would leave me just as quick as I would take my hand off them and cut. The word 'powder' was a terror to them. They could not stand the word 'powder.'"[33]

But circumstances changed. Possibly bolstered by words of encouragement from Board of Police Commissioner Mark Sheridan, who told him that "buildings were coming down very nicely, and we could not ask to have them fall better than they did," Hildreth's skills improved remarkably. Eventually he formed a small cadre of volunteers who took to their work with enthusiasm—almost too much enthusiasm. The men would sit on the powder kegs and smoke. As the men took the kegs into a building, the barrels would be uncovered and unprotected, so that burning coals would fall on them. Going into one building, Hildreth recounted, "We had to shut the back door to keep the fire out of the room where the powder was." He added, almost as an afterthought, an obvious observation: "We had no time to lose."[34]

little damage, possibly no more than just the breaking of the bank's windows.[32]

Hildreth also had trouble recruiting members for his demolition team: "I tried with a great many, maybe twenty or thirty men, to get them to stop and assist in blowing up the buildings, to stop the fire on a line that was feasible to me at that time, but

As Lieutenant General Philip H. Sheridan watched the flames advance, the famous Civil War hero must have thought the same thing (Figure 23). In 1871 Sheridan was commanding officer of the Military Division of the Missouri with headquarters at Chicago, and he also wanted to practice his demolition skills, but in an area that in Hildreth's judgment was already safe from burning. Unfortunately for Sheridan, Hildreth had placed Cornelius Mahoney, the foreman of Munn and Scott's grain elevator, in charge of the gunpowder. Hildreth described him as "a very trusty man, a man who would be like the boy that stood on the burning deck. You could not drive him from his post...." When Sheridan went to Mahoney and requested powder, Mahoney refused to give it to him. Sheridan came back again, this time with an accomplice. Mahoney was unimpressed. Sheridan left and came back a third time, now accompanied by a policeman, and again demanded powder, whereupon "Mahoney very quietly took his revolver out of his pocket and told them that if they took any powder, it would be after he emptied that revolver, and he was the man that would do it." Hildreth had just sent for five more kegs of powder, and Mahoney told Sheridan that if he wanted to help, he could carry the powder. Sheridan declined to do so and asked Mahoney if he knew who he was. Mahoney replied that "he did not care a damn. He could not have the powder."[35]

Hildreth and his wrecking crew eventually blew up "thirty or forty" buildings (Figure 24). Hildreth claimed that this demolition helped halt the progress of the fire. Although some historians have agreed with this conclusion, others have

FIGURE 23—GENERAL PHILIP H. SHERIDAN. Lieutenant General Philip H. Sheridan was a Civil War hero who had lived in Chicago since 1867. On October 11, Mayor Roswell B. Mason, concerned about an outbreak of lawlessness, issued the following proclamation that transferred all police authority to the general: "PROCLAMATION! The preservation of the good order and peace of the city is hereby entrusted to Lieut. General P. H. Sheridan, U.S. Army. The Police will act in conjunction with the Lieut. General in the preservation of the peace and quiet of the city, and the Superintendent of Police will consult with him to that end. The intent hereof being to preserve the peace of the city, without interfering with the functions of the City Government. Given under my hand this 11th day of October, 1871. R. B. MASON, Mayor." (Chicago Historical Society ICHi-12451)

questioned whether or not Hildreth's work had any real effect as a firebreak. (See

FIGURE 24—DEMOLISHED BUILDING. In an attempt to halt the spread of the fire, former alderman James H. Hildreth spearheaded the blowing up of buildings with gunpowder. Historians Herman Kogan and Robert Cromie comment in their book *The Great Fire: Chicago 1871* that this demolished building near Wabash Avenue and Congress Street marks the end of the fire's southward march. (Chicago Historical Society ICHi-02745)

Appendix A.) Regardless of the impact of Hildreth's efforts, his sense of civic pride must have been dampened by post-fire threats of lawsuits against the city. Fortunately for the former alderman, these rumblings apparently never crystallized into litigation.[36]

The Fire Spreads to the North Side

At 2:30 A.M., just minutes after the courthouse roof fell in, a train of railroad cars containing oil caught fire, possibly from a barrage of sparks and brands hurled across the river by convection whirls. These cars were on the North Side, about three-eighths of a mile from the courthouse.

They quickly touched off nearby Wright Brothers Stables, and as the fire began to spread out and engulf surrounding homes and buildings, it commenced an inexorable trek northward. By then the city water works remained the only hope for Chicago, and so, as historian Joseph Kirkland remarked, the flames crept stealthily towards it, "like a wild beast intent on destroying its worst enemy, the enemy which it must either kill or be killed by."[37]

The water works and the adjoining water tower were essentially a pumping facility. The water works drew water from Lake Michigan through a two-mile tunnel under the lake bed and pumped it to the top of the 130-foot-high water tower. The water in the tower would then flow by its own weight to the various water mains throughout the city. The water works was made of stone and its massive timber roof was covered with slate (Figure 25). With open area all around it, the building must have seemed invulnerable to Chicagoans. To them, possibly, but not to the fire that roared upon it at one-half mile an hour. At 3:20 Monday morning, a burning brand about twelve feet in length struck one of the water work's corners, and in seconds its roof was ablaze. Despite the efforts of the

FIGURE 25—WATER TOWER AND WATER WORKS, PRE-FIRE. The city's water tower and water works were built in 1867. The water works drew water from Lake Michigan via a tunnel and then pumped it to the top of the adjoining tower, which was 130 feet high. The water was then forced by its own pressure through Chicago's 275 miles of water mains. (Chicago Historical Society ICHi-33548)

employees stationed there, the interior of the building soon turned into a raging furnace, and by four o'clock the men were forced to abandon it. Once the pumps stopped working, the only water available was the so-called "dead" water left in the mains and in the only slightly damaged water tower. When that was exhausted, the streams from the firemen's hoses dwindled and died. With hydrants now useless, the fire engines were ineffective except along the river and the lake shore. If Chicago was not doomed, it was certainly now helpless.[38]

From the water works the fire spread across the North Side. Although the scenes of commotion and confusion on the South Side were horrible, the terror in this north division was perhaps even more so. Many North Side residents went to bed Sunday evening, content that the fire on the South Side would never cross the river. They then awoke in the early morning to find themselves surrounded by walls of flame and fire that traveled "faster than a man could run." Unlike their South Side compatriots, they had little time to pack their belongings

FIGURE 26—FLEEING FROM THE BURNING CITY. In 1858, Alfred R. Waud came to America from England and became a leading artist for *Harper's Weekly*. In 1870, he was hired by the illustrated journal *Every Saturday*. A year later, Waud teamed up with roving correspondent Ralph Keeler to do a series of articles on the lower Mississippi River and its cities. They were in St. Louis when they heard about the fire, and they immediately rushed to Chicago by train to cover the story, arriving while the city still burned. This picture is captioned "Fleeing from the Burning City." Herman Kogan and Robert Cromie describe it as a "study in light and darkness, which suggests most wonderfully the tension of this frozen moment." Details include the woman running without shoes, the man carrying a baby, and the child clinging to a coattail with his right hand as the glare of the fire dapples his left arm. (Chicago Historical Society ICHi-02991)

FIGURE 27—FLEEING THE NORTH SIDE; NEAR THE WATER TOWER. **The Chicago River divides the city into three (north, south, and west) divisions. Many North Side residents went to bed on the evening of October 8, certain that the fire, then raging on the city's South Side, would never cross the river. But the flames, propelled by masses of superheated air called convection whirls, proved them wrong, and many North Siders awoke in the early morning to find themselves surrounded by walls of fire. With Chicago's famous water tower in the background, these two Chicagoans, with a few hastily packed belongings, make a frenzied dash to safety. (Drawing by Marshall Philyaw)**

before being forced to flee for safety. Depending on where they lived, they could either go to the prairies on the West Side, north to Lincoln Park and the outskirts of the city, or east to the Sands[39] (Figures 26–28).

The Sands was a strip of lakeshore north of the Chicago River. In years past it was home to numerous gambling parlors and brothels. These dens of inequity flourished in such flagrant violation of the law that in 1857, bowing to enraged public opinion, Mayor "Long John" Wentworth revoked the Sands's favored nation status and moved in with steel hooks and chains and demolished its "rows of wretched wooden shanties." By 1871 it was primarily vacant sandy beach.[40]

But it was anything but vacant on that early morning of Monday, October 9. As fire consumed the North Side, "thousands of men, women, and children, and hundreds of horses and dogs" took refuge on the shores of Lake Michigan. Groups huddled around their bits of furniture and other possessions, all that they had managed to save before being driven east by the fire, a fire which soon encircled the refugees, "until the whole city in every direction, looking north, west and south, was a mass of smoke and flames." The sparks and cinders fell "as fast and thick as hailstones in a storm," and soon the piles of household belongings began to burn, driving people closer and closer to the water's edge.[41]

And then the lumberyards to the south took fire. Dense clouds of smoke and cinders that poured from thousands of board feet of burning timber rolled over and enveloped the fugitives, forcing them into the lake. Some people drove their horses and wagons into the water as far as the animals could go and then clamored aboard for safety. Others stood in the lake for hours, scorching heat above the water line, chilling cold below it, all with their backs to the firestorm that raged behind them, a storm that sent down a deadly shower of thousands of burning brands that fell hissing into the water. One man buried his wife and children under a foot of sand, leaving only small air holes for them to breathe through. A woman implored her husband that "if I took fire to put me in the lake and drown me, not let me burn to death." Eventually, when the lumberyards were destroyed and the heat

and smoke had subsided somewhat, the wet and weary Chicagoans began a slow exodus out of the water to what was left of their homes, which was nothing at all.[42]

At about eleven o'clock Monday evening, rain began to fall. Although by then the fire had just about run its course, until the rain came there was still the chance that the wind might change and the fire return again to the now waterless West Side. Surely Mary Fales, one of many homeless North Siders, echoed the beliefs of all Chicagoans in a letter to her mother written the next day: "I never felt so grateful in my life as to hear the rain pour down...."[43]

Mary Fales was only one of 100,000 made homeless by the fire. By the time it died out completely in the early morning of Tuesday, October 10, the flames had cauterized the heart of Chicago, ravaging a swath approximately three-and-one-third square miles in size. Property valued at $192,000,000 was destroyed and about 300 people lost their lives (Figures 29–30). In a strange twist of fate, a fact not overlooked by the rabid post–October 8 press, the fire ironically spared Mr. and Mrs. O'Leary's home (Figure 31). And although they were probably grateful for that, their troubles were only just beginning.[44]

Notes

1. A[lfred] T[heodore] Andreas, *History of Chicago: From the Earliest Period to the Present Time,* vol. 1, *Ending with the Year 1857* (Chicago: A. T. Andreas, 1884), p. 128, hereafter cited in text as Andreas, vol. 1; A[lfred] T[heodore] Andreas, *History of Chicago: From the Earliest Period to the Present Time,* vol. 2, *From 1857 Until the Fire of 1871* (Chicago: A. T. Andreas Co., 1885), p. 702, hereafter cited in text as Andreas, vol. 2; *Report of the Chicago Relief and Aid Society of Disbursement of Contributions for the Sufferers by the Chicago Fire* (Cambridge, [Mass.]: Riverside Press, 1874), pp. 2–5, hereafter cited in text as *Report of the Chicago Relief and Aid Society;* Robert Cromie, *The Great*

Chicago Fire (New York: McGraw-Hill Book Co., 1958), p. 2, hereafter cited in text as Cromie; H[arry] A[lbert] Musham, "The Great Chicago Fire, October 8–10, 1871," *Papers in Illinois History and Transactions for the Year 1940* (Springfield: Illinois State Historical Society, 1941), pp. 71, 74, hereafter cited in text as Musham; Elias Colbert and Everett Chamberlin, *Chicago and the Great Conflagration* (Cincinnati: C. F. Vent, 1871), pp. 34–35, 125, 167, 175, hereafter cited in text as Colbert and Chamberlin; Ulrich Danckers and Jane Meredith, *A Compendium of the Early History of Chicago to the Year 1835 When the Indians Left* (River Forest, Ill.: Early Chicago, 1999), pp. 37–38.

2. Andreas, vol. 1, pp. 165–73; Andreas, vol. 2, p. 73; Bessie Louise Pierce, *A History of Chicago*, vol. 2, *From Town to City, 1848–1871* (New York: Alfred A. Knopf, 1940), pp. 37–40, hereafter cited in text as Pierce, vol. 2; Musham, pp. 71–72; Robert P. Howard, *Illinois: A History of the Prairie State* (Grand Rapids, Mich.: William B. Eerdmans Publishing Co., 1972), pp. 238–42; Colbert and Chamberlin, pp. 131, 169–74; Rufus Blanchard,

Discovery and Conquests of the North-West, with the History of Chicago (Wheaton, [Ill.]: R. Blanchard & Co., 1879), pp. 445–51.

3. Cromie, p. 3; Colbert and Chamberlin, pp. 174–76, 202–3; Andreas, vol. 2, p. 701.

4. Emmett Dedmon, *Fabulous Chicago* (New York: Random House, 1953), p. 32, hereafter cited in text as Dedmon; Stephen Longstreet, *Chicago: 1860–1919* (New York: David McKay Co., 1973), pp. 61–66, hereafter cited in text as Longstreet; Cromie, p. 7; Alfred L. Sewell, *The Great Calamity! ...* (Chicago: privately printed, 1871), p. 59, hereafter cited in text as Sewell.

5. Cromie, pp. 5–6.

6. Andreas, vol. 2, pp. 91, 703–4, 710; "Our Next Public Improvement," *Chicago Tribune*, 10 September 1871, p. [2]; "Anniversary of the Great Fire," *Chicago Daily Tribune*, 9 October 1872, p. [5], hereafter cited in text as "Anniversary of the Great Fire"; Donald L. Miller, *City of the Century: The Epic of Chicago and the Making of America* (New York: Simon & Schuster, 1996), pp. 143–44, hereafter cited in text as Miller; Musham, pp. 75–81;

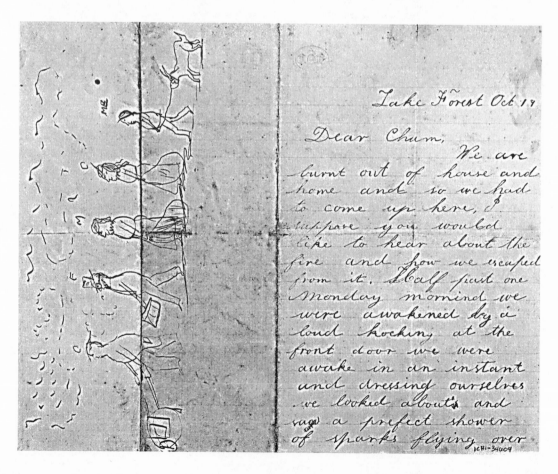

Ken Little and John McNalis, *History of Chicago Fire Houses of the 19th Century* (privately printed, 1996), pp. 37, 99, hereafter cited in text as Little and McNalis; "Preparing for the Next Fire," *Chicago Tribune*, 15 October 1871, p. [2]; "The Great Fire," *Chicago Evening Journal*, 12 December 1871, p. [4]; *Report of the Board of Police in the Fire Department, to the Common Council of the City of Chicago: For the Year Ending March 31st, 1869* (Chicago: Illinois Staats-Zeitung, 1869), pp. 16–17, hereafter cited in text as *1869 Report of the Board of Police*; Cromie, p. 15; Karen Sawislak, *Smoldering City: Chicagoans and the Great Fire, 1871–1874* (Chicago:

University of Chicago Press, 1995), p. 125, hereafter cited in text as Sawislak; Robin L. Einhorn, *Property Rules: Political Economy in Chicago, 1833–1872* (Chicago: University of Chicago Press, 1991), pp. 128–133.

7. Musham, pp. 81, 84; *1869 Report of the Board of Police*, p. 21; *Report of the Board of Police, in the Fire Department, to the Common Council of the City of Chicago: For the Year Ending March 31st, 1872* (Chicago: Hazlitt & Reed, 1872), p. 20, hereafter cited in text as *1872 Report of the Board of Police*; Little and McNalis, pp. 99, 119; "On the Defensive," *Chicago Tribune*, 17 November 1871, p. 4, hereafter

Opposite: FIGURE 28—LETTER AND ILLUSTRATION BY JUSTIN [BUTTERFIELD]. Alfred Waud was not the only person in October of 1871 drawing pictures of the fire. "Justin" wrote this letter to a friend, Philip Prescott, shortly after the fire. It is one of the few letters or reminiscences in the collections of the Chicago Historical Society that was written by a child. The fact that the letter is also illustrated makes it even more notable, perhaps even unique.

In his letter Justin tells how he and his family escaped the fire in the early morning of Monday, October 9. His picture depicts them fleeing to safety as a "perfect shower of sparks" rain down upon them. Justin wrote the letter from "up here" in Lake Forest, Illinois, a city north of Chicago. The complete text of the letter (edited only for punctuation and spelling) reads as follows:

> Lake Forest Oct. 19
> Dear Chum,
>
> We are burnt out of house and home, and so we had to come up here. I suppose you would like to hear about the fire and how we escaped from it. Half past one Monday morning we were awakened by a loud knocking at the front door. We were awake in an instant, and dressing ourselves, we looked about and saw a perfect shower of sparks flying over our house. I got some water and went out in the yard while my brother went up on the roof. We worked for one or two hours. At the end of that time we had to give up. We tried to get a wagon but could not, so we put two trunks on a wheelbarrow, and each of us shouldered a bundle, and we marched for the old skating park, I leading my goat. We got along very well until the Peshtigo lumberyard caught on fire. Then it was all we could do to breathe. Mother caught on fire once, but we put it out. At last we heard that there was a little shanty that hadn't burnt down, so we marched there but had to leave our trunks and everything else, but Charlie and father went back and got one but could not get the other as the sand was blowing in their faces and cut like glass. At last a wagon drove up, and we all piled in and escaped. So good-by.
>
> Yours, Justin
>
> Address Lake Forest
> Lake County
> Care of Mr. Rossiter

It appears that Justin's last name was Butterfield. In his reminiscences of the fire, Judge Lambert Tree wrote that "my wife, son, father, sister, the mother of Mrs. Bliss, the French girl, and myself, and also Mr. and Mrs. Butterfield, their daughter Clara, and their son Justin, with his pet goat, which he had been carefully trying to shelter and protect through the day, all packed ourselves into the wagon and started for the West Side."

Justin has labeled all the people in his picture. He is obviously the last figure in the procession. No doubt the people lettered from left to right as "C," "F," "M," and "C" are respectively Charlie (probably his brother), his father, mother and Clara. (Chicago Historical Society ICHi-34604)

FIGURE 29—PEOPLE GATHERED AROUND THE WATER TOWER, POST-FIRE. This post-fire photograph shows Chicagoans gathered near the city's water tower. Historians Herman Kogan and Lloyd Wendt claim that this picture was taken a day after the fire burned itself out. But there appears to be scaffolding and piles of building materials near the tower. If so, this would indicate that the picture was taken later, after reconstruction began on the North Side.

The water tower has always been Chicago's cherished symbol of not only the fire but also the city's amazing recovery from disaster. When Oscar Wilde visited Chicago in the 1880s, he aroused the ire of its citizens by referring to the water tower as "a castellated monstrosity with pepperboxes stuck all over it."

Most of the people seem to be posing for the camera. What appears to be a young girl, sitting down, staring at the devastation and alone in her thoughts, is a particularly haunting exception. (Courtesy of the Illinois State Historical Library)

cited in text as "On the Defensive"; "Story of the Great Chicago Fire as Told by the Men Who Fought It," *Chicago Daily Tribune*, 9 October 1893, sec. 3, p. 20, hereafter cited in text as "Story of the Great Chicago Fire"; E[dgar] J[ohnson] Goodspeed, *History of the Great Fires in Chicago and the West....* (New York: H. S. Goodspeed & Co., 1871), p. 351, hereafter cited in text as Goodspeed; "The Great Fire," *Chicago Evening Journal*, 12 December 1871, p. [4]; Cromie, p. 15; Robert A. Williams,

"Transcript of Inquiry into Cause of Chicago Fire and Actions of Fire Department Therein" [1871], Chicago Fire of 1871 Collection, Chicago Historical Society, vol. [4], pp. 283–85. The transcript of the investigation consists of four unnumbered bound volumes. This proceeding is hereafter cited in text as *Inquiry* followed by the volume number in brackets.

8. Musham, pp. 79, 83, 86, 181–87; Andreas, vol. 2, pp. 91–92; Little and McNalis, p. 99; Robert

FIGURE 30—CHICAGO FIRE RUINS; VIEW OF PINE STREET (NOW MICHIGAN AVE.) FROM THE TOP OF
THE WATER TOWER. Looking south from the top of the water tower, Pine Street runs diagonally to the upper right corner of this picture. The large building near the top of
the photograph and right of center is the grain elevator known as Central Elevator
B. Built in 1857 and later enlarged, this elevator had a capacity of 1,600,000 bushels
in 1871. It was the only elevator in the burnt district unharmed by the fire. (Chicago
Historical Society ICHi-02805)

A. Williams, *Inquiry*, vol. [4], pp. 284–85; Leo Meyers, *Inquiry*, vol. [2], p. 99; *1872 Report of the Board
of Police*, pp. 28–84; Pay Roll for the Month Ending October 31, 1871, Chicago Fire Department
Collection, Chicago Historical Society, hereafter
cited in text as 1871 Pay Roll.

9. Cromie, p. 15; Little and McNalis, p. 99;
1872 Report of the Board of Police, p. 22.

10. Henry J. Cox and John H. Armington,
The Weather and Climate of Chicago (Chicago: University of Chicago Press, 1914), p. 197, hereafter
cited in text as Cox and Armington; Statement of

FIGURE 31—SOUTHEASTERN VIEW OF THE O'LEARY AND MCLAUGHLIN HOMES. The October 21, 1871, issue of the *Chicago Evening Journal* offers the perfect description of this southeastern view of the O'Leary property: "In the center of the block stands a small one-story tenement. On every side are ashes and cinders. Not a house or shed remains west, south or north of it, and half a dozen ash piles tell the passer-by where stood houses on the east of the solitary shanty (for it is that and nothing more). It is past explanation that all the rest went and that remained." (Chicago Historical Society ICHi-32462)

Lambert Tree, "The Experience of Lambert Tree and the Several Members of His Family During the Great Chicago Fire of Sunday and Monday Oct. 8th and 9th 1871," n.d., Chicago Fire of 1871 Personal Narratives Collection, Chicago Historical Society; "Anniversary of the Great Fire," p. [5]; Musham, pp. 87–89; Andreas, vol. 2, pp. 703–4; "Common Council," *Chicago Republican*, 6 December 1871, p. [3]; "The Fire Fiend," *Chicago Tribune*, 8 October 1871, p. [3], hereafter cited in text as "The Fire Fiend."

11. Cromie, pp. 9–12.

12. Musham, p. 74; Cromie, p. 5; Leo Meyers, *Inquiry*, vol. [2], pp. 102–3; Frank J. Loesch, *Personal Experiences During the Chicago Fire, 1871* (Chi-

cago: privately printed, 1925), p. 6, hereafter cited in text as Loesch; Robert A. Williams, *Inquiry*, vol. [4], pp. 288–89; Andreas, vol. 2, pp. 57–58; "On the Defensive," p. 4.

13. The location of the Lull & Holmes planing mill and all other landmarks mentioned in this chapter are shown in Figure 10. The mill is identified by the number 1. The accompanying shading delineates the area burned by the Saturday night fire.

14. "The Fire Fiend," p. [3]; Andreas, vol. 2, pp. 704–7, 713; Musham, pp. 89–94; William Musham, *Inquiry*, vol. [1], p. 29; Christian Schimmals, *Inquiry*, vol. [1], pp. 131–33; Michael Sullivan, *Inquiry*, vol. [1], pp. 98–99; Lewis Fiene, *Inquiry*,

vol. [1], pp. 216–18; *Edwards' Thirteenth Annual Directory of the Inhabitants, Institutions, Incorporated Companies, and Manufacturing Establishments of the City of Chicago, Embracing a Complete Business Directory for 1870* (Chicago: Richard Edwards, 1870), vol. 13, p. 1083; hereafter cited in text as *1870 City Directory*.

15. Andreas, vol. 2, pp. 707–16; Charles Anderson, *Inquiry*, vol. [3], p. 101; Mathias Benner, *Inquiry*, vol. [4], pp. 130–31. Although Andreas persuasively argues that the fire began as early as 8:45 P.M., it is quite possible that the fire started much later, at about 9:20 P.M. See Andreas, vol. 2, pp. 701, 711–16; see also Appendix A, "When Did the Fire Start?"

16. Paul M. Angle, ed., *The Great Chicago Fire* (Chicago: Chicago Historical Society, 1946), p. 48, hereafter cited in text as Angle; Musham, pp. 163–67; Frank Luzerne, *The Lost City! Drama of the Fire-Fiend!....* (New York: Wells & Co., 1872), pp. 69–70, hereafter cited in text as Luzerne; John D. DeHaan, *Kirk's Fire Investigation*, 4th ed. (Upper Saddle River, N. J.: Prentice-Hall, 1997), p. 28, hereafter cited in text as *Kirk's Fire Investigation*; Stephen J. Pyne, *Fire in America: A Cultural History of Wildland and Rural Fire*, paperback ed. (Seattle: University of Washington Press, 1997), pp. 22–26, hereafter cited in text as Pyne, Cox and Armington, pp. 367–69; "Erroneous Impressions," *Chicago Tribune*, 20 October 1871, p. [2], hereafter cited in text as "Erroneous Impressions." In his study of the Mann Gulch forest fire in Montana, Norman Maclean points out that convection whirls can also be created by winds shearing off large obstacles, such as cliffs. Historian Donald L. Miller suggests that this is what happened in Chicago's business district, with the "cliffs" being the city's four-and-five-story brick buildings. See Norman Maclean, *Young Men & Fire* (Chicago: University of Chicago Press, 1992), pp. 36, 136, 287; Miller, p. 152. At the time of the fire, John Tolland was stationed on the city's water crib, which was in Lake Michigan, almost two miles from shore. He later told of fiery pieces of boards, between three and six inches in size, raining down on him. See John Tolland, *Inquiry*, vol. [2], pp. 184–86.

17. Robert A. Williams, *Inquiry*, vol. [4], pp. 241–48; Andreas, vol. 2, p. 717; Musham, pp. 105–7; Erroneous Impressions," p. [2].

18. Peter T. Burtis, *Inquiry*, vol. [3], p. 50; Thomas Ockerby, *Inquiry*, vol. [4], pp. 1–8, 33–34; Robert A. Williams, *Inquiry*, vol. [4], p. 254; Michael C. Hickey, *Inquiry*, vol. [2], pp. 150, 156; *1870 City Directory*, p. 66; Andreas, vol. 2, p. 719; Musham, pp. 109–12; "The Gas Works," *Chicago Tribune*, 20 November 1871, p. 2, hereafter cited in

text as "The Gas Works." Musham claims that a burning brand blew across the river and fell onto the tar house of the gas works and then spread to the adjoining roofing plant of Powell, Getchell & Co. This is contrary, however, to the inquiry testimony of Thomas Ockerby, who told the Board that he saw fiery debris fall into the Barrett & Arnold tar tank, starting the fire that quickly spread to the gas works. (Both Ockerby and the 1870 city directory refer to the manufacturer as "Barrett & Arnold," but the 1871 directory lists the firm as "Barrett, Arnold & Kimball.") See Musham, p. 111; Thomas Ockerby, *Inquiry*, vol. [4], pp. 1–2; *1870 City Directory*, p. 1097; *Edwards' Fourteenth Annual Directory of the Inhabitants, Institutions, Incorporated Companies and Manufacturing Establishments of the City of Chicago, Embracing a Complete Business Directory for 1871* (Chicago: Richard Edwards, 1871), vol. 14, pp. 99, 726, 1078, [1079], hereafter cited in text as *1871 City Directory*. Andreas discusses the "embarrassment of conflicting statements" as to when and where the fire struck the South Side at Andreas, vol. 2, pp. 719–20.

19. Cromie, pp. 103–4; Bessie Louise Pierce, ed., *As Others See Chicago: Impressions of Visitors, 1673-1933* (Chicago: University of Chicago Press, 1933), p. 202, hereafter cited in text as *As Others See Chicago*; Thomas Ockerby, *Inquiry*, vol. [4], pp. 7–11; Andreas, vol. 2, p. 723; Luzerne, p. 126.

20. Peter T. Burtis, *Inquiry*, vol. [3], pp. 50–52; Thomas Ockerby, *Inquiry*, vol. [4], pp. 12–14, 46, 48–49; Robert A. Williams, *Inquiry*, vol. [4], pp. 254–55; Thomas B. Burtis, *Inquiry*, vol. [3], p. 77; "On the Defensive," p. 4; "The Gas Works," p. 2; "Story of the Great Chicago Fire," sec. 3, p. 20; Luzerne, p. 174; Goodspeed, p. 350.

21. James W. Sheahan and George P. Upton, *The Great Conflagration....* (Chicago: Union Publishing Co., 1871), p. 74, hereafter cited in text as Sheahan and Upton; Musham, p. 112; Andreas, vol. 2, pp. 719–20; Joseph Kirkland, "The Chicago Fire," *The New England Magazine*, n.s., 6 (August 1892), p. 731, hereafter cited in text as Kirkland; "The Great Conflagration," *Chicago Tribune*, 11 October 1871, p. 1; Thomas Byrne, *Inquiry*, vol. [2], p. 136.

22. Herman Kogan and Robert Cromie, *The Great Fire: Chicago 1871* (New York: G. P. Putnam's Sons, 1971), p. 10, hereafter cited in text as Kogan and Cromie; Andreas, vol. 1, pp. 180–81; Andreas, vol. 2, p. 66; *1870 City Directory*, pp. [913]–18.

23. Andreas, vol. 2, pp. 719, 724–25; Luzerne, p. 94; Goodspeed, pp. 118–19; "The Great Fire," *Chicago Tribune*, 24 November 1871, p. 6;

"Boring for Facts," *Chicago Tribune*, 19 November 1871, p. 6; "Bell Relics," *Chicago Tribune*, 22 December 1871, p. 2; "Jottings About Town," *Chicago Times*, 7 December 1871, p. [4]; "Chicago Condensed," *Chicago Republican*, 23 December 1871, p. [4]; "Common Council," *Chicago Republican*, 10 November 1871, p. [2]; "The Co[urt] House Bell," *Chicago Tribune*, 17 December 1871, p. 7; Mathias Schaefer, *Inquiry*, vol. [1], pp. 5–9; Kirkland, p. 732; Liliana Gomez Roche, "From Ruins to Relics and Revitalization: The Debris from the Great Chicago Fire" (unpublished manuscript, Loyola University of Chicago, 4 November 1996); Charles R. Lott to the Chicago Historical Society, 7 October 1926, Chicago Fire of 1871 Personal Narratives Collection, Chicago Historical Society; *The City That a Cow Kicked Over* (Chicago: A. H. Andrews & Co., n.d.), p. [26], hereafter cited in text as *The City That a Cow Kicked Over*. On November 19 the *Chicago Times* voiced the same skepticism as this relic dealer: "It is safe to say that enough pieces of the court-house bell have been distributed throughout the world to make up a whole chime that should out ring the Bow Bells of London." See Untitled article, *Chicago Times*, 19 November 1871, p. [2].

24. Michael C. Hickey, *Inquiry*, vol. [2], pp. 153–55, 172–73; Andreas, vol. 2, pp. 724–25; Luzerne, p. 94; *1870 City Directory*, p. 504; Kirkland, p. 733; Michael Ahern, "1871 Reporter Writes Story of Great Fire," *Chicago Sunday Tribune*, 9 October 1921, sec. 1, p. 3, hereafter cited in text as "1871 Reporter"; "The Debtors," *Chicago Tribune*, 4 December 1871, p. 3, hereafter cited in text as "The Debtors"; "The Jail and Criminals," *Chicago Tribune*, 20 October 1871, p. [2]; "A City Laid Waste," *(Chicago) Daily Inter Ocean*," 9 October 1893, sec. 1, p. 1; Carl Smith, *Urban Disorder and the Shape of Belief: The Great Chicago Fire, the Haymarket Bomb, and the Model Town of Pullman* (Chicago: University of Chicago Press, 1995), pp. 57–58, hereafter cited in text as Smith.

25. *Full Account of the Great Fire in Chicago* (Racine, [Wis.]: Wm. L. Utley & Son, 1871), p. 5; "Incendiaries Killed," *Chicago Tribune*, 11 October 1871, p. 1, hereafter cited in text as "Incendiaries Killed"; "The Fire," *Chicago Times*, 18 October 1871, p. [4]. The *Chicago Evening Post* of October 18, 1871, was even more descriptive of the inhabitants of a slum neighborhood in the fire's path: "Villainous, haggard with debauch and pinched with misery, flitted through the crowd collarless, ragged, dirty, unkempt, these negroes with stolid faces and white men who fatten on the wages of shame, glided through the masses like vultures in search of prey. They smashed windows reckless of the severe wounds inflicted on their naked hands, and with bloody fingers rifled impartially till, shelf and cellar, fighting viciously for the spoils of their forays. Women, hollow-eyed and brazen-faced, with foul drapery tied over their heads, their dresses half torn from their skinny bosoms, and their feet thrust into trodden down slippers, moved here and there, stealing, scolding shrilly, and laughing with one another at some particularly 'splendid' gush of flame or 'beautiful' falling-in of a roof." See Smith, pp. 51–52, 302.

26. Joel Bigelow to S. and O. Bigelow, 10 October 1871, Chicago Fire of 1871 Personal Narratives Collection, Chicago Historical Society; Sewell, pp. 58–59; Smith, pp. 53–61; Sheahan and Upton, p, 193; "Working Up the Details," *Chicago Tribune*, 2 November 1871, p. 1; Miller, pp. 149–50; Michael C. Hickey, *Inquiry*, vol. [2], pp. 145, 162–63; Angle, p. 28; Goodspeed, pp. 125–29; "Jottings About Town," *Chicago Times*, 21 December 1871, p. 7; "Atrocious Fabrications," *Chicago Tribune*, 19 October 1871, p. [2], hereafter cited in text as "Atrocious Fabrications"; "Absurd Misstatements," *Chicago Tribune*, 19 October 1871, p. [2], hereafter cited in text as "Absurd Misstatements"; "Correcting False Impressions," *Chicago Tribune*, 3 November 1871, p. [4]; Mabel McIlvaine, ed., *Reminiscences of Chicago During the Great Fire* (Chicago: Lakeside Press, 1915), p. 84, hereafter cited in text as *Reminiscences of Chicago During the Great Fire*; M[ary] E[mily] and E[liphalet] W[ickes] Blatchford, *Memories of the Chicago Fire* (privately printed, 1921), p. 14.

27. *Reminiscences of Chicago During the Great Fire*, p. 69; "Sharks Among Us," *Chicago Evening Journal*, 16 October 1871, p. [2]; William Gallagher to his sister [Isabel], 17 October 1871, Chicago Fire of 1871 Personal Narratives Collection, Chicago Historical Society, hereafter cited in text as William Gallagher letter; Colbert and Chamberlin, pp. 219–20; Andreas, vol. 2, p. 757; "Scenes on Wabash Avenue," *Chicago Tribune*, 11 October 1871, p. 1.

28. Thomas D. Foster, *A Letter from the Fire* (Cedar Rapids, Iowa: privately printed, 1949), pp. 15, 30, hereafter cited in text as Foster; Colbert and Chamberlin, p. 220; "Story of the Great Chicago Fire," sec. 3, p. 20; William Gallagher letter. The *Tribune* related a similar story of a man on the lake shore who asked a tug boat captain to take him and his family to safety: "I brought one trunk on board, and found the other in the possession of the Captain, who brought it aboard while I was there, and claimed it as belonging to him. Seeing that kind words would not give me possession of my goods, I was obliged to present my revolver to the Captain's head and demand my trunk, which

I did." See "Miscellaneous Items," *Chicago Tribune*, 12 October 1871, p. [3].

29. "Stories of the Big Fire," *Chicago Daily News*, 9 October 1896, p. 13, hereafter cited in text as "Stories of the Big Fire"; Bessie Bradwell Helmer to Caroline M. McIlvaine, 7 October 1926, Chicago Fire of 1871 Personal Narratives Collection, Chicago Historical Society.

30. Musham, p. 117; James H. Hildreth, *Inquiry*, vol. [3], pp. 123–27; Cromie, pp. 47–48; *1871 City Directory*, p. 557. For a lengthy account detailing Hildreth's demolition efforts, see "The Gun-powder Plot," *Chicago Times*, 20 October 1871, p. [3], hereafter cited in text as "The Gunpowder Plot."

31. Andreas, vol. 2, p. 725; James H. Hildreth, *Inquiry*, vol. [3], pp. 132–37, 141; Michael C. Hickey, *Inquiry*, vol. [2], pp. 163–66; Musham, p. 117.

32. James H. Hildreth, *Inquiry*, vol. [3], pp. 137–39, 156, 160–62; Michael C. Hickey, *Inquiry*, vol. [2], p. 165; Musham, pp. 117–18.

33. James H. Hildreth, *Inquiry*, vol. [3], pp. 152–53.

34. James H. Hildreth, *Inquiry*, vol. [3], pp. 144, 154–55, 165. Hildreth's understatement concerning gunpowder is similar to the restrained observation of Third Assistant Fire Marshal Mathias Benner, who made the following comment after the fire: "About that time a man came to me and said, 'Matt, I have got some powder. What do you want to do with it?' That was on the corner of Wabash Avenue and Congress. Said I, 'I have been waiting for it. You go one block south and wait.' He started, and in three minutes after, I started to look for my powder. I went to the corner of Harrison and Michigan Avenue. I didn't see the wagon and went another block and couldn't find them there. Then I came back to Wabash Avenue up to the corner of Harrison and Wabash but still saw no powder wagon. I had inquired of several policemen if they had seen a mule team with two men in it that had powder. They told me they hadn't. I went back to Michigan Avenue again and went two blocks south. I crossed over to Wabash Avenue again and came up very near to the corner of Wabash and Harrison when I heard an explosion. Thinks I, 'They have got my powder now.'" See Mathias Benner, *Inquiry*, vol. [4], pp. 154–55.

35. Andreas, vol. 2, pp. 383–84, 774; Sawislak, p. 49; Musham, p. 134; James H. Hildreth, *Inquiry*, vol. [3], pp. 143–44, 148, 171–72; Cromie, p. 218; *1870 City Directory*, pp. 543, 919; *1871 City Directory*, pp. 39, 600, 818.

36. James H. Hildreth, *Inquiry*, vol. [3], pp.

156–57, 162, 164–65; "The Gun-powder Plot," p. [3]. At times, Hildreth's well-intentioned efforts to save the city must have been a mixed blessing for Chicago's fleeing citizens. William Bross of the *Chicago Tribune* commented a few days after the fire that "every now and then explosions, which seemed almost to shake the solid earth, would reverberate through the air and add to the terrors of the poor people." See *Reminiscences of Chicago During the Great Fire*, p. 80.

37. Musham, pp. 118–19, 122; Andreas, vol. 2, pp. 724, 740; Joseph Kirkland, *The Story of Chicago* (Chicago: Dibble Publishing Co., 1892), vol. 1, p. 293; David Lowe, ed., *The Great Chicago Fire: In Eyewitness Accounts and 70 Contemporary Photographs and Illustrations* (New York: Dover Publications, 1979), p. 42, hereafter cited in text as Lowe.

38. Musham, pp. 122–23; Andreas, vol. 2, pp. 66–70, 741, 752; Sheahan and Upton, pp. 32–34; Colbert and Chamberlin, pp. 154–55; John Schank, *Inquiry*, vol. [4], pp. 215–16. Andreas writes that the distance from the O'Leary barn to the water works was two miles and 1,252 feet, and that the flames traversed it in six hours and thirty-five minutes. See Andreas, vol. [2], p. 719.

39. Andreas, vol. 2, pp. 748, 750, 754–56; Cromie, pp. 146–47, 154–55; Sewell, pp. 30–31; Colbert and Chamberlin, pp. 211, 219–25; Angle, pp. 25, 39. H. R. Hamilton, the great nephew of Chicago pioneer Gurdon Hubbard, managed to humorously describe in his memoirs not only the fire leaping across the river to the North Side but also the premise (as set forth in Karen Sawislak's book *Smoldering City*) that the flames burned away (at least temporarily) the barriers between social classes: "When I got back to our house, the fire had jumped the river and was perceptibly nearer. Mrs. Barclay, our next door neighbor, a charming young woman, the mother of my friend Alex Barclay, had come out to the sidewalk and Mr. Kelly, who owned a large mansion next door to her, had also come out. Mr. Kelly was an Irishman who became rich in the whiskey business and was hardly in the same social set as Mrs. Barclay. She had never spoken to him before, but moved by a common peril she said, 'Oh! Mr. Kelly, do you think that the fire will come here?' He replied, 'H—l yes, Madam, we'll all burn up.' He was right, albeit somewhat inelegant." See H. R. Hamilton, *Footprints* (Chicago: Lakeside Press, 1927), pp. 22–24.

40. Andreas, vol. 2, p. 755; Colbert and Chamberlin, pp. 223–24; Pierce, vol. 2, pp. 433–34. For a descriptive account of Wentworth's raid on the Sands, see John J. Flinn, *History of the Chicago Police* (Chicago: Police Book Fund, 1887;

reprint, Montclair, N.J.: Patterson Smith Publishing Corp., 1973), pp. 82–83, hereafter cited in text as Flinn.

41. Andreas, vol. 2, p. 744; Goodspeed, pp. 153–54; Cromie, pp. 154–55.

42. Andreas, vol. 2, pp. 744–45; Cromie, p. 155; Sewell, pp. 50–51; Goodspeed, pp. 154–55; Colbert and Chamberlin, p. 224; Del Moore to [her father and mother], 14 October 1871, Chicago Fire of 1871 Personal Narratives Collection, Chicago Historical Society.

43. Musham, p. 138; Andreas, vol. 2, pp. 747, 750, 757; Cromie, p. 242; Angle, pp. 25, 31. In one sentence, stunning in its imagery, Joseph Kirkland describes the dawning of that Tuesday morning: "The fire is out, save only the scattered coal-piles, which will go on for weeks, filling the days with smoke and the nights with pitiful, ghostly gleamings; and save also the grain-piles marking the places of departed elevating warehouses, the smell whereof—an odor of roasted wheat and corn—is to remain, through all the long, hard winter, a pervading memento of the huge waste and loss." See Kirkland, p. 741.

44. Musham, p. 138; Catherine O'Leary, Inquiry, vol. [1], p. 64; Patrick O'Leary, Inquiry, vol. [1], p. 244; "Origin of the Fire," Chicago Evening Journal, 21 October 1871, supplement, p. [2], hereafter cited in text as "Origin of the Fire"; "A Lowly Monument of the Fire," Chicago Evening Journal, 13 October 1871, p. [2]; "City Wrapped in Angry Flames," Chicago Daily Tribune, 9 October 1893, sec. 3, p. [18]; "What Remains of the City," Chicago Tribune, 20 October 1871, p. 1; "How Many Perished," Chicago Times, 30 December 1871, p. 3; Report of the Chicago Relief and Aid Society, pp. 10–15. Andreas comments at vol. 2, p. 760, that the statistics of the Chicago Relief and Aid Society are possibly more accurate than those of other compilers, as the Society's data were the result of later and more careful estimates.

Chapter Two

The Exoneration of Mrs. O'Leary

One dark night, when people were in bed,
Old Mrs. 'Leary lit a lantern in her shed.
The cow kicked it over, and winked his eye,
   And said,
"There'll be a hot time in the old town tonight."
   —*Chicago Evening Post*, October 8, 1921

The O'Learys—Life Before the Fire

In 1871 Mr. and Mrs. Patrick and Catherine O'Leary lived in a tiny cottage at 137 DeKoven Street on Chicago's West Side. The O'Learys were Irish immigrants, as were many of the people in this working class West Side neighborhood. Patrick O'Leary, though only a laborer, had managed to buy his property in 1864 for $500. It was a spit of land stuck about halfway between Jefferson and Clinton streets, on the north side of DeKoven. Although this half-lot was only twenty-five feet wide, it was almost 101 feet deep, running north from the street to a fifteen-foot alley that cut the block in two. It certainly wasn't grandiose, even by 1871 standards, but the O'Learys called it home. Actually, only part of it was home, as there were two separate houses on the land, one directly behind the other.

The O'Learys rented the larger cottage that fronted DeKoven Street to Catharine and Patrick McLaughlin, who lived there with their five-year-old child. The O'Learys and their own five children lived in the smaller home in back. At the rear of their property, next to the alley, stood a barn. A narrower alleyway ran from the wooden sidewalk in front of the O'Leary house to their backyard. This path was perhaps five feet wide and ran along the east line of their land. On the other side of this alleyway was the home of James Dalton. Mrs. O'Leary sold milk throughout the neighborhood, and she kept her cows in her barn. Cottages, children, and cows, all tucked away in the middle of an Irish and Bohemian working class neighborhood in Chicago.[1]

Mrs. O'Leary led a rather inconspicuous existence on DeKoven Street, which simply means that little is known of her life prior to October 8, 1871. What reminiscences there are of her were written years after the fire, after she became a legend. At best, they are contradictory; at worst, they are complete fabrications. One person, for example, called her "shiftless and worthless" and "a drunken old hag with dirty hands." Another, though, allegedly remembered Mrs. O'Leary as "motherly, kind, a very good neighbor." Bouquets and brickbats aside, most likely she lived quietly in her West Side neighborhood, selling milk and collecting rent money. She prob-

ably would have continued to do so well into 1872 and beyond (or at least until her family outgrew its undoubtedly cramped living quarters), except for one thing, the Great Chicago Fire just happened to originate in the O'Leary barn. Although this fire irrevocably altered the landscape of nineteenth-century Chicago, it had a profound effect on Mrs. O'Leary as well. Forever branded as the owner of the cow that started it all, she became, against her will, part of the mythology of Chicago[2] (Figures 32–34).

FIGURE 32—A SYMPHATHETIC INTERPRETATION OF MRS. O'LEARY IN THE BARN; DRAWING BY THE KELLOGG & BULKELEY COMPANY. The *Chicago Evening Journal* of October 9, 1871, claimed that the fire was caused by "a cow kicking over a lamp in a stable in which a woman was milking." Although this newspaper contained no illustrations, this contemporary drawing printed by the Kellogg & Bulkeley Company could very well have accompanied the *Journal* account of the fire. The original drawing was entitled somewhat erroneously "The Cause of the Great Chicago Fire Oct. 9th 1871" and included the ominous sub-title: "A Warning to All Who Use Kerosene Lamps: Never forget that more lives have been lost, and more comfortable homes burned up by a Careless Use of this light than any other ever introduced into common use." Note that the lamp that the cow is kicking over is virtually identical to the lamp that appears in A. T. Andreas' *History of Chicago* and which is shown as Figure 55. (Chicago Historical Society ICHi-02949)

FIGURE 33—A NOT-SO KINDLY MRS. O'LEARY WITH RATS, A CHICKEN, AND A CAT; DRAWING BY L. V. H. CROSBY. In this highly imaginative painting by L. V. H. Crosby, both the cow and Mrs. O'Leary appear a lot more evil and a lot less benign than in Kellogg & Bulkeley's drawing. Crosby has added rats, a chicken, and a ghostly-looking cat to the scene. This sketch later appeared in a magazine, together with a poem allegedly quoting Mrs. O'Leary, who blames Crosby for starting the fire:

> How else could ye know,
>   I'd a cat and a sow,
> An' illegant chickens—
>   high perchin',
>
> If yerself had not been,
>   jist afore I coom in,
> Through my barn for rich
>   plunder a searchin'?

(Chicago Historical Society ICHi-02945)

Her fame was assured almost from the very beginning, because even before the fire died out on Chicago's northern outskirts, Mrs. O'Leary, her cow, and her lantern were being blamed for starting the fire that destroyed a city. This story first appeared in print in the October 9, 1871, issue of the *Chicago Evening Journal*, which reported that "the fire broke out on the corner of DeKoven and Twelfth streets, at about 9 o'clock on Sunday evening, being caused by a cow kicking over a lamp in a stable in which a woman was milking"[3] (Figure 35).

But in 1871 the press was not averse to occasionally mixing liberal doses of fiction with small amounts of fact. Although the fire did start in Mrs. O'Leary's barn, is it possible that she and her cow were not to blame? Assuming for the moment that the *Journal*'s account was either generously and intentionally laced with more than a touch of fantasy and fabrication or that a reporter failed to verify all facts before writing his story, what is the origin of the newspaper's tale of bovine terrorism? Existing historical records suggest at least two theories, one more probable than the other.[4]

FIGURE 34—MRS. O'LEARY AND MENAGERIE IN THE BARN; DRAWING BY W. O. MULL. In this exaggerated drawing by W. O. Mull, the artist has surrounded Mrs. O'Leary with an impressive menagerie of cats, rats, birds and a pig, dog, and second cow. But there is still the errant hoof, the falling lamp, and the sealing of Chicago's fate. (Chicago Historical Society ICHi-02826)

Theory Number One

Years after the fire Michael Ahern, a *Chicago Tribune* reporter who had worked for the *Chicago Republican* in 1871, asserted that Jim Haynie, a reporter for the *Chicago Times*, concocted the cow and lantern story.

This claim is doubtful, as the *Times* (and also the *Tribune* and *Republican*) issued their first "post-fire" editions subsequent to the famous October 9 issue of the *Evening Journal*. It is unlikely that a reporter for the acerbic *Times*, a newspaper the *Journal* once called "A Snarling Dog" because of its

Opposite: FIGURE 35—OCTOBER 9, 1871, CHICAGO EVENING JOURNAL. Even while Chicago burned, the staff of the *Chicago Evening Journal* managed to publish a small "Extra" on Monday, October 9. The sentence beginning at the end of the first column changed Mrs. O'Leary's life forever: "The fire broke out on the corner of DeKoven and Twelfth streets, at about 9 o'clock on Sunday evening, being caused by a cow kicking over a lamp in a stable in which a woman was milking." (Chicago Historical Society ICHi-06206)

EVENING JOURNAL-EXTRA.

CHICAGO, MONDAY, OCTOBER 9, 1871.

THE GREAT CALAMITY OF THE AGE!

Chicago in Ashes!!

Hundreds Of Millions of Dollars' Worth of Property Destroyed.

The South, the North and a Portion of the West Divisions of the City in Ruins.

All the Hotels, Banks, Public Buildings, Newspaper Offices and Great Business Blocks Swept Away.

The Conflagration Still in Progress.

Fury of the Flames.

Details, Etc., Etc.

Chicago is burning! Up to this hour of writing (1 o'clock p. m.) the best part of the city is already in ashes! An area of between six and seven miles in length and nearly a mile in width, embracing the great business part of the city, has been burned over and now lies a mass of smouldering ruins.

All the principal hotels, all the public buildings, all the banks, all the newspaper offices, all the places of amusement, nearly all the great business edifices, nearly all the railroad depots, the water works, the gas works, several churches, and thousands of private residences and stores have been consumed. The proud, noble, magnificent Chicago of yesterday, is to-day a mere shadow of what it was; and, helpless before the still sweeping flames, the fear is that the entire city will be consumed before we shall see the end.

The entire South Division, from Harrison street north to the river, almost the entire North Division, from the river to Lincoln Park, and several blocks in the West Division are burned.

It is utterly impossible to estimate the losses. They must in the aggregate amount to hundreds of millions of dollars. Amid the confusion and general bewilderment, we can only give a few details. The fire broke out on the corner of DeKoven and Twelfth streets, at about 9 o'clock on Sunday evening, being caused by a cow kicking over a lamp in a stable in which a woman was milking. An alarm was immediately given, but, owing to the high southwest wind, the building was speedily consumed, and thence the fire spread rapidly. The firemen could not, with all their efforts, get the mastery of he flames. Building after building was fired by the flying cinders, which, landing on the roofs, which were as dry as tinder, owing to the protracted dry weather, instantly took fire. Northwardly and northeastwardly the flames took their course, lapping up house after house, block after block, street after street, all night long.

The scene of ruin and devastation is beyond the power of words to describe. Never, in the history of the world, has such a scene of extended, terrible and complete destruction, by conflagration, been recorded; and never has a more frightful scene of panic, distress and horror been witnessed among a helpless, sorrowing, suffering population.

It is utterly impossible, in the fire hought, for the mind to take in any conception of the fearful ravages of the fire-fiend, although the astounding facts stated above is enough to appal the most heroic. The awful rush of the ul sa ion will be more fully comprehended by a glance a he following very imperfect list of he ci y's loss. It is, however, proper to state that, in his writing, the confusion in the police and fire departments is so complete as to render it impossible to give anything like a detailed account of he terrible conflagra ion.

PARTIAL DETAILS OF THE LOSSES.

The first to be mentioned, and possibly the most startling feature of the carnival of flame, is the total destruction of the City Water Works, by which calamity the firemen are rendered helpless to make the least endeavor to arrest the onward march of the devouring element. Should any other fires occur in parts of the city not burning, they must certainly have their sway. At about 12 o'clock last night the sheet of flame crossed the river in the neighborhood of Jackson street, first igniting a small wooden building, which communicated the fire to the Armory, and soon to the South Side Gas Works, the immense gasometer exploding with a fearful detonation, heard all over the city. Then commenced the fearful ravages, which in a few hours laid the entire South side in ashes, north of Harrison. The Post Office and Custom House, the Chamber of Commerce, the Court House and the rest soon went down in the ocean of fire and smoke. In brief, the following prominent buildings have perished with, in almost every case, their entire contents: the New Jerusalem Church, on Adams street, and the Catholic Church, on Desplaines stree .

The JOURNAL office, the Tribune, the Times, the Republican, the Post, the Mail, the Staats Zeitung, the Union, and many other publications.

Crosby's Opera-House, McVicker's Theater, Hooley's Opera-House, Dearborn Theater, and Wood's Museum.

First, Second, Third, Fourth, Fifth, Union, Northwestern, Manufacturers' Cook County, and Illinois National Banks.

The Second Presbyterian Church, St. Paul's Universalist Church, Trinity (Episcopal) Church.

The magnificent depot of the Chicago, Rock Island and Pacific and Lake Shore and Michigan Southern Railroads, on Van Buren street, at the head of La Salle street. The great Central Union depot, and the Wells street depots of the Chicago and Northwestern Railroad.

The National Elevator, corner of Adams and the river, Armour, Dole & Co's Elevator, corner Market and the river, Hiram Wheeler's Elevator, on same corner as the above, the Galena Elevator, corner Rush street bridge and river, and "A" of the Illinois Central, near the Illinois Depot, at the basin.

Tremont House, Sherman House, Briggs House, Metropolitan, Palmer, Adams, Bigelow, European, (Burke), Garden City, and the new Pacific, in process of erection, on Clark and La Salle streets.

The following prominent business houses are in ashes: Field, Leiter and Co. J. V. Farwell's block, and all the magnificent blocks in that locality. The Lake Side Publishing Company's new building, on Clark street, Terrace Row, on Michigan Av, and adjacent residences.

Farwell Hall burned at about four o'clock this morning.

The great breweries, on the North Side, are gone.

In fact, as stated above, the entire South and North sides, from Harrison street, northwardly, with a few isolated buildings left standing in some remarkable manner, are in hopeless ruins.

HELP COMING.

During the night, telegrams were sent to St. Louis, Cleveland, Milwaukee and nearer cities for aid, and at the time of going to press several trains are on the way to the city, bringing fire engines and men to assist us in this dire calamity.

BOARD OF TRADE.

The Board of Trade has leased for present use the northwest cor. of Washington and Canal streets.

We call attention to the card announcing a meeting of the Directors of the Chicago Board of Trade, to-morrow morning, at 10 o'clock, at 51 and 53 Canal street.

COUNCIL MEETING—A PROCLAMATION.

The Common Council and a number of prominent citizens are holding a meeting this afternoon in the First Congregational Church, to make such arrangements as may be possible for the safety of the city.

The Mayor has issued a proclamation that all fires in stoves in the city shall be extinguished.

THE EVENING JOURNAL.

We are under great obligations to the Interior Printing Company, 15 and 18 Canal street, for accommodations by which we are enabled to issue this *Extra*. We hope before many days, to be able to announce permanent arrangements for issuing THE EVENING JOURNAL regularly. We have saved a portion of our subscription books, and hope to be able to resume publication without great delay.

"reckless and mischievous blackguardism," would fabricate an explanation for Chicago's worst disaster and then hand it over to a rival paper, allowing that newspaper to publish it first.[5]

So is it possible that after *Times* reporter Haynie made up the story, the *Evening Journal* simply heard about it and ran it on page one? Yes, it is. But even assuming this possibility, or the possibility that Haynie would graciously turn his account concerning the origin of the fire over to the *Journal*, there are other irregularities in Ahern's tale. These irregularities prove Ahern to be less than credible and are sufficient to completely discredit his explanation for the legend of Mrs. O'Leary's cow (Figure 36).

As Chicagoans entered the twentieth century and as October 8, 1871, receded more and more into distant memory, Ahern, by then the ink-stained and venerable warhorse of Chicago journalism, was often trotted out on fire anniversaries to pen his recollections for the *Tribune*. But Ahern's chronicle of the cause of the fire kept changing, and with every version his role grew more and more prominent. He originally wrote in 1911 that he believed the fire was started by two women who had entered the barn to get milk for some punch. Nowhere in this lengthy newspaper article did he admit to knowing anything about the origin of the cow and lantern legend. But in 1915 he maintained that the fire was caused by the spontaneous combustion of hay and that Jim Haynie made up the tale of Mrs. O'Leary. And by 1921 Ahern had completely omitted Haynie's name from the credits. Instead, Ahern now claimed that *he* had a role in fashioning the now famous story: "I wish to state that the fire was not started by Mrs. O'Leary's cow kicking over a lamp. Nothing of the kind occurred. That version of the origin of the

FIGURE 36—MICHAEL AHERN. In 1871 Michael Ahern was a newspaper reporter for the *Chicago Republican*. While writing for the *Chicago Tribune* in 1921, he claimed that he helped concoct the story of the cow kicking over the lantern. Although later histories have repeated this assertion as fact, Ahern's statement appears instead to be fanciful. (Drawing by Marshall Philyaw)

fire was a concoction which the writer of these reminiscences confesses to a guilty part."[6]

Michael Ahern may not have been the only newspaperman who tried to bootstrap fame and possibly even fortune from the Chicago Fire. The day after the 1911 article was published, John Kelley, another reporter, charged that *he* authored the article, not Ahern, because "the booze got him [Ahern] many years ago, and he has not been able to do any newspaper work." Ahern died in 1927. A few days after his death, Kelley wrote the O'Learys' grandson, Patrick O'Leary, claiming that Ahern had always maintained that he (Ahern) and fellow newspapermen Jim Haynie and the appropriately named Johnny English made up the story of the cow kicking over the lamp. Not surprisingly, English's reminiscences of the fire, published in the *Tribune* in 1891, include no mention of his purported role in taking Mrs. O'Leary and her cow from obscurity to immortality. Although Ahern alleged in the 1911 article that the two women surreptitiously milking the cow were "the true cause of the fire," Kelley claimed in this letter that Ahern "was always of the opinion that someone emptied the ashes from his pipe in the alley in the rear of the cow shed, and this was what started the fire."[7]

Despite the many inconsistencies in Ahern's post–1871 newspaper articles, historians have continued to promulgate the "confession of Michael Ahern" as the basis for the O'Leary legend. And other penitents have joined Ahern in the confessional. In 1938 Dr. Frederick C. Hanmore wrote a letter to the Chicago Historical Society, offering to give it "a small item of great historical interest." Hanmore went on to profess that it was his father, a writer for the *New York Herald*, who conjured up the O'Leary cow story and that his father "often told me it was his idea...." But the elder Hanmore was obviously pulling his son's leg, as the story of the cow and the lantern did not appear in the *Herald* until October 11, 1871, two days after the *Journal* printed it.[8]

Theory Number Two

A more probable explanation also has its roots in Chicago's newspapers. On the fiftieth anniversary of the fire, the *Chicago Daily Journal* (formerly the *Evening Journal*) recalled that shortly after the city caught fire, an employee went to the West Side, to the area of "DeKoven and Twelfth streets,"

to investigate the blaze. He returned with the "common report" that the fire began after a cow kicked over a lamp. The *Daily Journal* added that "the editors of the *Journal* apparently found credence in the report, for they incorporated it in the 'Extra' which they printed."[9]

John J. McKenna, an author of one of the many post-fire personal histories that leaped into print in the months and years after the fire, appears to imply in his reminiscences that this "common report" originated with the children who lived in the O'Leary neighborhood. He alleged that "the story of the cow and the lamp is as old as the fire, for within that hour, the kids around Clinton and DeKoven streets were relating about the cow kicking over the lamp and causing the fire." Admittedly, recollections such as these can be unreliable. Many, like this one, were published years after the fire; still others appear to be colored with the tint of the author's interpretation of the facts, rather than the facts themselves. Nonetheless, this account remains a very plausible explanation for the origin of the legend of the lantern. There is a commonality that binds many post–Chicago Fire personalities. This tie is the "Andy Warhol factor"—the "fifteen minutes of fame" that so many of these figures apparently sought as they tried in varying ways to wrap themselves in the mantle of Mrs. O'Leary's infamy. Ahern claimed that he was responsible for the story of Mrs. O'Leary and her cow, and Hanmore maintained that his father came up with the idea. But McKenna sought no notoriety, no credit. McKenna's recollections of the fire are modest, ordinary, even mundane, not self-aggrandizing like Ahern's and Hanmore's statements, and it is these characteristics that make McKenna's reminiscences all the more believable[10] (Figure 37).

FIGURE 37—O'LEARY HOME; FROM JOHN J. MCKENNA'S BOOK. John J. McKenna published this photo in his 1918 book *Stories by the Original "Jawn" McKenna from "Archy Road" of the Sun Worshipers Club of McKinley Park in Their Political Tales and Reminiscences.* Unlike many other photographs of the O'Leary property, this view of the McLaughlin (front) and O'Leary (rear) homes clearly discloses a dark area on the right side of the east wall of the O'Leary cottage. This is surely their doorway, as photographs of the north and west sides reveal no entrance. Also, in an investigation held after the fire, Mrs. McLaughlin remarked that Mrs. O'Leary's door "reached out upon the side of Mr. Dalton's fence...." James Dalton owned the home immediately east of the O'Leary property.

Mrs. O'Leary Denies Starting the Fire

Regardless of who started the story, Mrs. O'Leary steadfastly denied starting the fire. From November 23 through De-

cember 4 (nine days of questioning over a twelve day period) the Board of Police and Fire Commissioners held an inquiry to determine, among other things, the cause of the fire. Mrs. O'Leary was the fifth witness to testify during the inquiry proceedings.

The first question the Board asked her was "What do you know about this fire?" (Figure 38). She replied, "I was in bed myself and my husband and five children when this fire commenced." But despite her claims of innocence and an alibi that was confirmed by others who testified, the story of her cow and lantern spread with the fervor of the fire itself. The embers had barely cooled before authors began battling with each other, vying to be the first off the publishers' starting blocks in order to satisfy an insatiable audience intent on reading anything about the fire. They eventually churned out a storm of books and pamphlets, and these works helped secure Mrs. O'Leary's niche in Chicago history.[11]

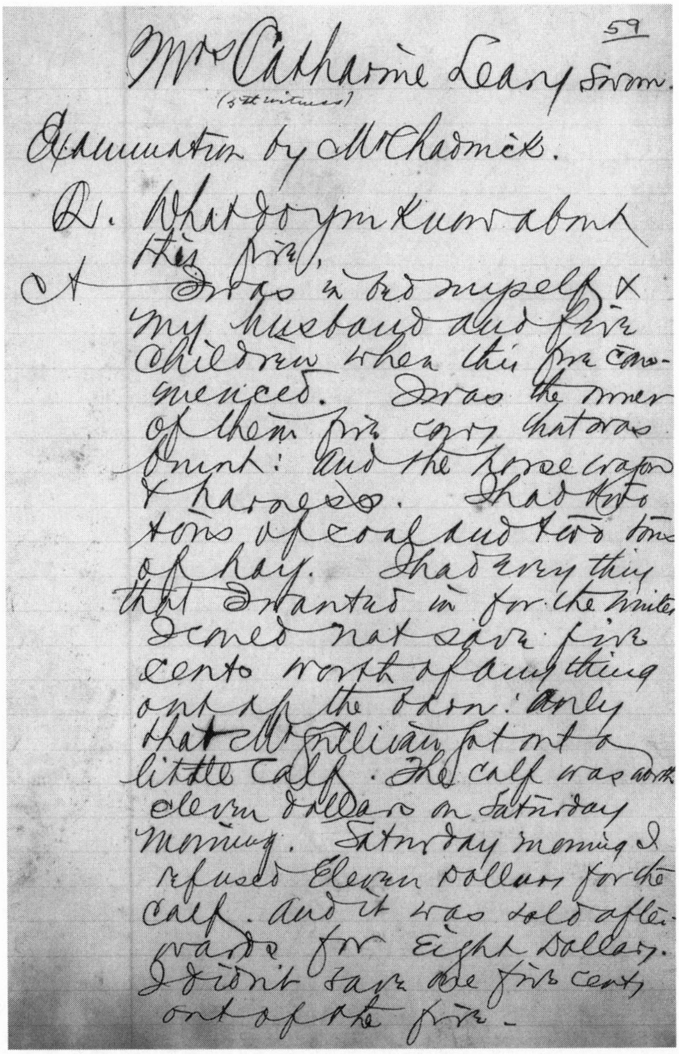

59

Mrs Catharine Leary Sworn.
(5th witness)
Examination by Mr Chadwick.
Q. What do you know about this fire.
A I was in bed myself & my husband and five children when this fire commenced. I was the owner of them five cows that was burnt: And the horse wagon & harness. I had two tons of coal and two tons of hay. I had every thing that I wanted in for the winter. I could not save five cents worth of any thing out of the barn: Only that Mr Sullivan got out a little calf. The calf was worth eleven dollars on Saturday morning. Saturday morning I refused Eleven dollars for the calf. and it was sold afterwards for Eight Dollars. I didn't save one five cents out of the fire.

FIGURE 38—FIRST PAGE OF MRS. O'LEARY'S INQUIRY TESTIMONY. **The transcript of the inquiry investigation is in four bound volumes that total 1,168 pages. Mrs. O'Leary was the fifth person to appear before the Board of Police and Fire Commissioners and fire marshals. She testified on November 24, 1871, and it appears that she was initially questioned by Commissioner James E. Chadwick. This is the first page of her testimony; it is page 59 of volume 1 of the transcript. (Chicago Historical Society ICHi-32210)**

Local writer Alfred L. Sewell drew first blood by cranking out *The Great Calamity!* before the end of 1871. The *Evening Journal* described him as a "conscientious gentleman," and if Mrs. O'Leary had known him, even she might have agreed, since Sewell merely matter-of-factly repeated the story of the cow:

> At about 9 o'clock on Sunday evening, October 8th, the fire-alarm was sounded for De Koven-street, in the West Division, near the scene of the previous night's fire, filled with shanties. There, as is alleged, an Irish woman had been milking a cow in a small stable, having a kerosene lamp standing on the straw at her side. The cow kicked over the lamp, which exploded and set fire to the straw, and speedily the stable was on fire....[12]

Other authors, though, were not so honorable. Taking indecent liberties with the story of Mrs. O'Leary and her cow, they greatly embellished the original *Evening Journal* account. For example, newspapermen Elias Colbert and Everett Chamberlin solemnly affirmed in their book *Chicago and the Great Conflagration* that "the great fire of the 9th October is attributed by the Fire Department of the city to the upsetting of a kerosene-lamp in a barn."[13]

The Official Investigation Into the Cause of the Fire

But in reality the Fire Department made no such determination. Despite interviewing fifty people during the course of its inquiry investigation, the Board of Police and Fire Commissioners failed to ascertain the fire's cause, stating merely in its report, which was issued in December of 1871 (and reprinted in Appendix E), that "whether it originated from a spark blown from a chimney on that windy night, or was set on fire by human agency, we are unable to determine." Curiously, a few months later Fire Marshal Robert A. Williams veered sharply away from this official position. In his annual report to the Board of Police, dated March 31, 1872, he wrote that "the origin of the fire could not be definitely arrived at, but from all the circumstances connected with the case, it is currently believed to have been set through the careless action of some person, or persons, at present unknown." In 1893, while reminiscing about the fire, he not only reaffirmed his opinion that the fire was accidentally set, he also suggested that someone subsequently helped spread the flames: "It may not have been of incendiary origin, but the incendiary had a hand in it before it was over." What was the basis for the fire marshal's dramatic departure from policy in his 1872 annual report? Williams cites no evidence to support his conclusion that

someone unintentionally caused the blaze, so perhaps this was merely his own opinion. But by 1893 did Williams have his own suspicions as to who started the fire? In 1872 he indicated that this "careless person" was "at present unknown," but twenty-one years later he voiced no such observation![14]

In 1893 did Williams believe that Mrs. O'Leary was this person? No one knows. But could she have been? Not likely, for an analysis of the original transcript of this inquiry, 1871 Chicago real estate records, and other period source materials provides powerful evidence that she, her cow, and her lantern were all unjustly accused of causing the Great Chicago Fire.

Attempting to Prove the Guilt of Mrs. O'Leary

Of all the fire historians, Harry A. Musham, author of the monograph *The Great Chicago Fire, October 8–10, 1871* (1941), is probably the most zealous in maintaining that Mrs. O'Leary was the guilty party. Musham, a naval architect and research engineer, was the son of William H. Musham, who was foreman of the fire company *Little Giant* No. 6 at the time of the fire. Harry Musham's work was the first scholarly treatment of the fire. Although an admirable effort, it is flawed by two biases. The first is Musham's tendency to embellish his father's firefighting acumen and the role his company had in fighting the fire. Swollen with filial pride, the author does so for an understandable reason. But what is not so understandable is his other bias—the bulldog tenacity that he exhibits in his single-minded quest to find Mrs. O'Leary guilty:

When all the evidence in the case is fairly considered, there can be but one conclusion and that is: that the Great Chicago Fire of October 8–10, 1871 was started in the barn of Mr. and Mrs. Patrick O'Leary, 137 De Koven Street, by one of their cows kicking over a lighted kerosene lamp between 8:30 and 9:00 P.M. on Sunday, October 8; that it was brought about by an accident; and that Mrs. O'Leary was in the barn at the time.[15]

Musham supports this statement by claiming that on the morning of October 9, Mrs. O'Leary admitted that the fire started when her cow kicked over a lamp or lantern. This alleged confession, supposedly made while Chicago still burned, is in direct contradiction to her later testimony at the inquiry hearings, where she indicated she did not know how the fire began. Musham blithely brushes off her denials, maintaining that Mr. and Mrs. O'Leary, fearing retribution for having caused the fire, "closed up like clams when questioned about it." Using Musham's own reasoning (that fearing punishment, she later stated at the hearings that she was not responsible) the story of her confession seems apocryphal. Even by October 9 she would have realized the enormity of the fire. Musham himself graphically writes that "with the coming of daylight on Monday, she could see the vast clouds of smoke that marked the destruction of the business district and the North Side." If she were predisposed to lie about causing the fire, she would have done so, even at this time. She would not have waited until November 24, the day she testified at the inquiry.[16]

Robert Critchell's Lie

There are other, more serious flaws in Musham's reasoning. He bases his conclusion in part on the words of one Robert S. Critchell (Figure 39), who wrote in his book, *Recollections of a Fire Insurance Man*

FIGURE 39—ROBERT S. CRITCHELL. Robert S. Critchell is the author of the 1909 book *Recollections of a Fire Insurance Man*. At the time of the fire, he was in charge of the Chicago agency of the Phenix Insurance Company. Critchell claimed that he interviewed Mrs. O'Leary and that "the old lady" told him the story of the cow kicking over the lantern was true. But as Mrs. O'Leary was only about forty-four years old at the time of the fire, his story appears to have little merit. (Drawing by Marshall Philyaw)

(1909), "I never saw the cow, but I did interview the old lady and was informed by her in rather an ungracious way that the story was true." Musham also refers to a 1915 book, *Reminiscences of Chicago During the Great Fire*, which quotes the *Chicago Times* of October 18, 1871. This newspaper contains an alleged "confession" by Mrs. O'Leary, who is referred to as "an old Irish woman ... about 70 years of age...."[17]

These three works—Critchell's book, the 1915 *Reminiscences*, and the October 18 *Times*—have one thing in common: they all describe Mrs. O'Leary as an *old* woman. The accuracy of these three sources, which are materials that Musham either relied on in making his arguments or at least noted in his monograph, is accordingly questionable because Mrs. O'Leary was *not* old in 1871!

Any historian attempting to determine the age of Mrs. O'Leary at the time of the fire will find the inconsistencies of history to be especially confounding. After her husband died, the *Chicago Tribune* of September 17, 1894, printed a lengthy obituary which included the statement that she was then seventy-six years old. This would mean that she was about fifty-three at the time of the fire. On the other hand, the 1870 federal census states that she was then forty years old, meaning she was only forty-one in 1871. Ten years later, the 1880 census indicated her age to be forty-five, and not, as one might think, fifty. But there is one seemingly irreproachable historical reference—Mrs. O'Leary's death certificate, filed with the Cook County Clerk, Division of Vital Statistics (Figure 40). Mrs. O'Leary died in 1895. This certificate indicates that she was sixty-eight years old when she died, meaning that she was only about forty-four at the time of the fire and nowhere near age seventy, as the *Times* indicates.[18]

It seems almost certain that Robert Critchell and the *Times* reporter never met Mrs. O'Leary, for if they had, they would not have misstated her age. Although the *Times* was the most widely read English-language daily newspaper in the city, it was also well-known for its general disregard for the facts of a story. Because of the *Times*'s reputation, it appears likely that this reporter completely fabricated the interview

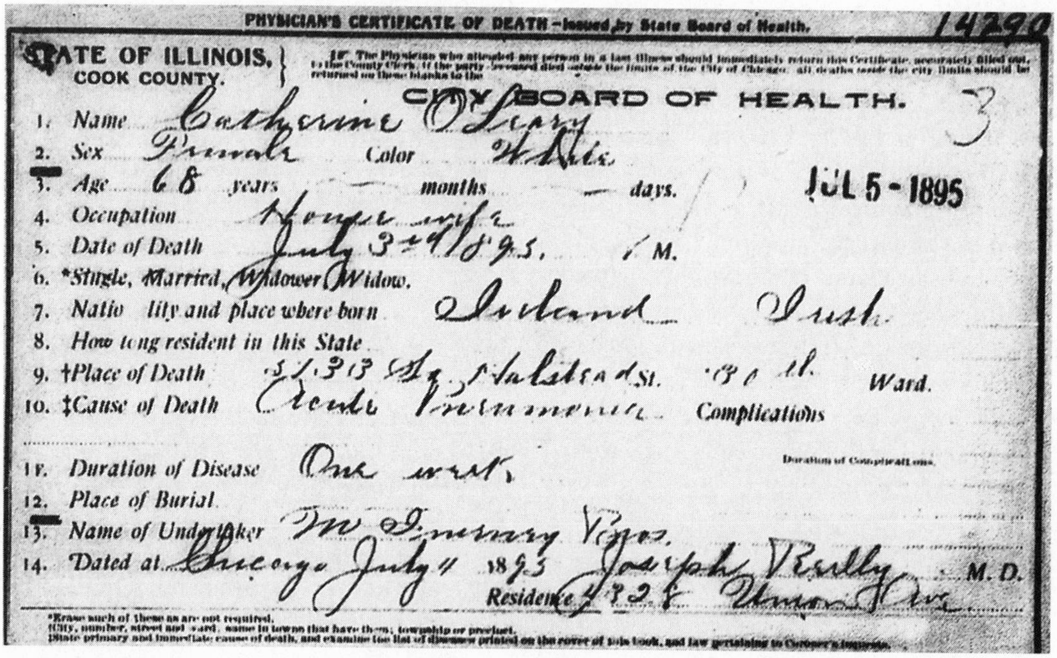
PHYSICIAN'S CERTIFICATE OF DEATH—Issued by State Board of Health. 14290

STATE OF ILLINOIS, COOK COUNTY.

CITY BOARD OF HEALTH. 3

1. Name Catherine O'Leary
2. Sex Female Color White
3. Age 68 years — months — days. JUL 5 - 1895
4. Occupation Housewife
5. Date of Death July 3rd 1895, M.
6. *Single, Married, Widower, Widow.
7. Nativity and place where born Ireland Irish
8. How long resident in this State
9. †Place of Death 313 S. Halsted St. 30th Ward.
10. ‡Cause of Death Acute Pneumonia Complications
11. Duration of Disease One week.
12. Place of Burial
13. Name of Undertaker McInerney Bros.
14. Dated at Chicago July 4 1895 Joseph Reilly M.D.

Residence 428 Union Ave.

FIGURE 40—CATHERINE O'LEARY'S DEATH CERTIFICATE. **The October 18, 1871, issue of the *Chicago Times* referred to Mrs. O'Leary as "an old Irish woman" and an "old hag" and described her as "about 70 years of age." But her death certificate indicates that she was only sixty-eight years old when she died in 1895, twenty-four years after the fire. (For privacy purposes, the place of burial has been removed from the certificate.)**

with Mrs. O'Leary. Thirty-eight years later, it seems equally likely that Robert Critchell, seeking a spot in the O'Leary limelight, followed the trend set by a newspaper dedicated to sensationalism and spun a similar tale of all fluff and no substance[19] (Figure 41).

But when it came to writing about Mrs. O'Leary and the Chicago Fire, the *Times* may not have been the only purveyor of tabloid-style journalism. An interview with Mrs. O'Leary that appeared in the October 21, 1871, issue of the *Evening Journal* appears at first to buttress this conclusion that Mrs. O'Leary was not old at the time of the fire. In the article she is described as "a stout Irish woman, some thirty-five years of age." But this interview also seems to be a complete fabrication. Mrs. O'Leary is quoted in the article as stating that the barn "must have been set afire." She then refers to the proverbial "mysterious stranger":

Two neighbors at the far end of the alley saw a strange man come up about half-past 9 in the evening. He asked them was the alley straight through. They told him it was, and he went through. It wasn't five minutes till they saw the barn on fire.[20]

But a month later, when she testified at the inquiry, she mentioned no such man. Mrs. O'Leary already had been pilloried in print for causing the fire; had she known of a "strange man" walking through the alley that night, surely she would have

FIGURE 41—NEWSPAPER ADVERTISEMENT OF THE PHENIX INSURANCE COMPANY AND ROBERT S. CRITCHELL. It appears that Robert S. Critchell was lying when he claimed that Mrs. O'Leary told him that the story of the cow kicking over the lantern was true. But he was telling the truth when he wrote in his book *Recollections of a Fire Insurance Man* that he was an agent of the Phenix Insurance Company. This ad is from the October 13, 1871, *Chicago Tribune*.

INSURANCE.

THE

PHENIX INS. CO.,

OF BROOKLYN,

Cash Assets, - - $1.850.000

Losses in the

GREAT FIRE

LESS THAN

$500,000

And has Opened an Office at

62 SOUTH CANAL-ST.

Property insured and Losses paid as usual. We have commenced paying. Policy-holders call and present their claims.

R. S. CRITCHELL, AGENT.

told the Board when she was questioned during the investigation.

Furthermore, when the *Evening Journal* reporter allegedly asked her, "Have you lived here long?" she supposedly replied, "Going on five years." But Chicago Title Insurance Company records indicate that Patrick O'Leary purchased this property in March of 1864, and the 1864 Chicago city directory lists Mr. O'Leary as living at this location. From March of 1864 to October of 1871 is seven-and-one-half years, not five years. This is a margin of error of 50 percent and another strong indication that this "interview" was a fraud.[21]

A third such indication can be gleaned from two apparently legitimate published statements made by Mrs. O'Leary in the early days after the fire. These appeared in the *Chicago Tribune* of October 19 and 20, 1871. In the October 19 *Tribune* article she stated that she did not milk her cows at night—a fact that the October 21 *Evening Journal* interview repeated. Her second statement consisted of her October 20 *Tribune* affidavit given before Michael McDermott, notary public and city surveyor, in which she attested that she owned five cows and a horse. These were the exact animals mentioned a day later in the *Evening Journal*. It seems possible that a *Journal* reporter saw the *Tribune* articles of October 19 and 20, collected a few facts from these two stories, and then fabricated from whole cloth a tale worthy of the Robert Critchell school of journalism that the *Journal* immediately published on October 21.[22]

Jacob Schaller's Hoax

But Robert Critchell barely rates an honorable mention when compared to some of the other charlatans of the nineteenth and twentieth centuries. For example, two years before the fire, cigar maker George Hull pulled off one of the greatest frauds of the 1800s by convincing much of New York State that a ten-foot tall, three-thousand-pound figure carved out of gypsum was actually an ancient petrified man eventually dubbed the "Cardiff Giant." Seventy years later, Jacob John Schaller perpetrated a similar scheme by convincing Harry A. (H. A.) Musham that Mrs. O'Leary told him that she and her cow started the Great Chicago Fire.[23]

The stage was set in October of 1939 when the Oak Park, Illinois, weekly newspaper *Oak Leaves* published a lengthy feature story entitled "Mrs. O'Leary's Delivery Boy Tells True Story of Great Fire." The article detailed the experiences of Jacob Schaller during the fire and explained why Schaller, by then an Oak Park resident, claimed that Mrs. O'Leary's cow kicked off the occasion. Just as George Hull set his plan in motion in the summer of 1868 by sending a block of stone to Chicago to have it carved, Jacob Schaller initiated his scheme by sending a letter dated October 15 to Chicago, to the home of H. A. Musham. Schaller invited Musham to meet with him to "hear what I know to be true about the great Chicago fire." Under separate cover, he sent a copy of *Oak Leaves*.[24]

But the fish was on the hook even before Schaller had cast his line. Musham had read about Schaller in the *Chicago Herald-American*. Musham's monograph was almost ready to go to press. It already included Critchell's story of Mrs. O'Leary admitting that the cow and lantern story was true. Eager for corroborating evidence, Musham wrote Schaller on October 14, asking for an interview. They met three days later at Schaller's home. A reporter from *Oak Leaves* was there, and a photograph of the two men was taken to memorialize the event. Schaller talked while Musham listened and wrote down Schaller's account in longhand. Later a final copy was typed, and both men signed it.[25]

Schaller claimed that, at the time of the fire, he lived on the first floor of a two-story frame house on the north side of DeKoven Street, about one block east of the O'Leary home, next to an alley. A map scrawled on Musham's notes, evidently drawn in Schaller's presence and with his approval, confirms this location. Schaller said that the house was owned by the father of "Bathhouse" John Coughlin, the infamous Chicago alderman. Schaller, then nine years old, delivered milk for Mrs. O'Leary who, he said, had but one cow. He delivered about fifteen pints a day to her customers. On the morning of October 9, 1871, he went to the O'Leary home and asked her, "How did the fire start?" She replied that she had company the night before and wanted to make some "Tom and Jerry" for her friends. She took the lantern and went to the barn and began to milk the cow, but the animal, upset at being disturbed twice in one day, kicked the lantern and knocked it over.[26]

But there are numerous discrepancies in Schaller's story. A search of Chicago Title Insurance Company's pre-fire land records discloses that no "Schaller" or "Coughlin" owned any of the lots on the north side of DeKoven Street in the two blocks east of the O'Leary block. (The railroad tracks of the Pittsburgh, Fort Wayne and Chicago Railway and non-residential property, possibly a lumberyard, were east of these two blocks.) No "Schaller" or "Coughlin" owned any lots on the south side of the street, either. This documentation also indicates that there was no alley in any of these blocks. A search of the 1870 and 1871 Chicago city directories fails to disclose a "Schaller," "Coughlin," or even a "Shaller" at any DeKoven Street address.[27]

Schaller's account contradicts the O'Learys' inquiry testimony as well. Schaller told Musham that he thought Mrs. O'Leary owned only one cow, but she indicated during the investigation that she owned six cows and a calf. As Schaller delivered the milk, surely he would have known how many cows she owned. Was Mrs. O'Leary lying about her animals? Not likely. She testified that five cows were burnt in the fire. This would have been common knowledge, a fact that the Board could have verified easily. There would have been no reason for her to lie about this inconsequential fact.[28]

Mrs. O'Leary testified that she was in bed when the fire began; her husband clarified the time, telling the commissioners that she retired sometime between eight o'clock and eight-thirty. Neither O'Leary said anything to the Board about having company on the night of the fire. Although two neighbors testified that they were in Mr. and Mrs. O'Leary's home that evening, the testimony of these two men indicates that both of them had left the house before the fire began. Therefore, Mrs. O'Leary would not have been in the barn getting milk for thirsty guests at the time the fire broke out.[29]

In the early 1800s the average dairy cow produced less than 1,500 liters of milk a year. This was less than nine pints a day. It is doubtful that in 1871 a single cow could produce fifteen pints a day for Schaller's alleged customers.[30]

But post-fire Chicago Title Insurance Company records reveal not only the most damning piece of evidence but also a possible explanation for Schaller's tale. John Coughlin's father was named Michael Coughlin. In 1868 a man by the name of "Anton Kohn" acquired a small property known as 79 DeKoven Street. This was a parcel of land about two blocks east of the

O'Leary home on the same, or north, side of the street. In October of 1872, a year *after* the fire, Kohn conveyed this parcel to a "Michael Coughlin." Is it possible that either Coughlin or the Schallers were renting this land from Kohn at the time of the fire, with the Schaller family being either a tenant of Kohn or a sub-tenant of Coughlin? Again, not likely. The 1870 Chicago City Directory indicates that it was Anton Kohn, not Schaller or Coughlin, who resided at 79 DeKoven Street. Although Anton Kohn is not shown as living at this address in the 1871 directory, Albert and Michael Kohn are; they also appear in Chicago's *1871 Census Report* as living at 79 DeKoven Street.[31]

Because immediate pre-fire and post-fire Chicago city directories do not indicate that the Schallers or Coughlin lived on DeKoven Street in 1871, Jacob Schaller's story might be a complete fabrication. But city directories are not infallible. Because Michael Coughlin did acquire 79 DeKoven Street in 1872, and because it was only a block east of the site indicated on Musham's map, it is possible that Schaller's tale does, after all, contain a grain or two of truth. Perhaps the Schallers *did* rent this house from Coughlin, but only *after* the fire, and only for a short time, not long enough for the family to be listed in a directory. Although Chicago Title Insurance Company records do not disclose the existence of any formally created alley, perhaps it was merely a dirt path, similar to the alleyway that ran between the O'Leary-McLaughlin and Dalton homes. If young Schaller did spend part of his childhood at 79 DeKoven Street, surely he grew up listening to stories of the Great Chicago Fire and the legendary Mrs. O'Leary. He might even have known her. As the years passed, and as the story of the fire, the cow, and the lantern took on mythic proportions, he

might also have grown to envy her, or at least her place in history. So much so that when he read about H. A. Musham and the book he was writing, he began to scheme.[32]

Musham should have wondered why Schaller waited sixty-eight years before coming forward. *Oak Leaves* gamely offered up his unconvincing but melodramatic explanation:

> He feels strongly that the truth should go down in history. It is only in the last year or so that the famous legend about Mrs. O'Leary's cow kicking over the lantern to start the fire has been doubted. Some have dared to say that there was no cow and no lantern at all. Such reports began to awaken Mr. Schaller to the fact that he was a living eye witness to the fire; that he was a personal friend of Mrs. O'Leary and knew her cow well and that from her own lips he had heard why she went back to the cow shed on that historic night for just one more quart of milk.[33]

But the more likely reason is disclosed in his letter to the editor that was published in the October 26 issue of *Oak Leaves*. It seems clear that Schaller made up the story simply because he wanted fame and glory. He knew that Musham was writing about the fire and he wanted to be a part of its history. Schaller had spent his childhood listening to stories about the cow and the lantern, and so he had already memorized the story he would tell Musham. But the text of his prepared speech was faulty. As he had only heard the story of her *cow* and the lantern, he indicated to Musham that Mrs. O'Leary owned only one cow. It never occurred to him that in 1871, one cow would probably not be able to provide fifteen pints of milk a day for his phantom customers. And recorded property records indicate that he did not live on DeKoven Street when the fire broke out in the barn.

But those details did not matter. All he had to do was rewind the videotape of history a few years, splice in a few fabricated statements, and then send his colorized version to H.A. Musham. As he explained in his letter to *Oak Leaves*:

> I have sent Mr. Musham, the Chicago historian who is writing a book about "The Great Chicago Fire," a copy of *Oak Leaves* which contains your story about me. I know when he sees what a fine paper *Oak Leaves* is and that you respected my word enough to print a big story about me the way you did, he will want an interview with me.[34]

And Musham got his interview. But in his rush to drive a stake through Mrs. O'Leary's reputation, he failed to verify Schaller's story. Instead, Musham accepted his lies without question, proclaiming in the October 19 *Oak Leaves* that "I consider Mr. Schaller's story of the Chicago fire of the utmost value"[35] (Figure 42).

But Schaller wasn't through with Mrs. O'Leary. On the day after his meeting with Musham, Schaller phoned him at eight o'clock in the morning. The message is still preserved with the rest of Musham's research materials at the Chicago Historical Society (Figure 43). It contained just a few sentences, and although all were ridiculous, the last one was patently absurd: "I can't say at any time she was intoxicated nor was there any signs of it." It is not clear if Musham asked Schaller if Mrs. O'Leary were inebriated or if Schaller volunteered this information. But it really doesn't matter. Before his interview Schaller claimed that "I want to tell Mr. Musham all I know about my friend Mrs. O'Leary and the cow whose milk I delivered daily." With "friends" like Jacob John Schaller, Mrs. O'Leary needed no enemies.[36]

From Barn Fire to Conflagration

In concluding that Mrs. O'Leary started the fire, Musham fails to consider the fact that under ordinary circumstances the fire would have been easily extinguished at its inception. A harried Chicago Fire Department had to fight 28 significant fires in Chicago during that first week of October. This large number was no doubt due, at least in part, to an unusual summer that was above average in temperature and below average in precipitation. But had it not been for an unlikely series of events, history books would have memorialized the fire of October 8, 1871, as nothing more than number 29. The seven factors that transformed an ordinary barn fire into what Fire Marshal Robert A. Williams called a "hurricane of fire and cinders" were:[37]

No. 1: Firemen Exhaustion

The firemen were exhausted from fighting the Saturday night Lull & Holmes planing mill fire. This was no small blaze; rather, it burned about sixteen acres. In fact, one contemporary author wrote that this fire of October 7 would have been memorialized in history as the "great Chicago fire" had it not been for the encore performance the following day. After fighting the fire through Sunday afternoon, many of the firemen had not eaten and had virtually no sleep before being called out to the O'Leary barn.[38]

The problem of firemen exhaustion was compounded by the "one platoon system" that was in effect in 1871. Under this form of personnel structure, there was only one working shift, which meant that all of the city's firemen were on duty all the time. In theory this may have been cost effective, as one shift of firefighters working full-time

FIGURE 42—HARRY A. MUSHAM AND JACOB JOHN SCHALLER. Harry A. Musham (left) and Jacob John Schaller met on October 17, 1939, at Schaller's home in Oak Park, Illinois. Schaller claimed that on the morning of October 9, 1871, Mrs. O'Leary told him that she had gone to the barn the night before to milk her cow. The animal, upset at this late night interruption, kicked the lantern and knocked it over. Musham failed to verify Schaller's story, which appears to be a complete fabrication. Instead, he sent his monograph *The Great Chicago Fire, October 8–10, 1871* to press, concluding in his otherwise scholarly work that Mrs. O'Leary and her cow caused the fire. (Drawing by Marshall Philyaw. Reproduced with permission of *Oak Leaves*, Oak Park, Illinois)

should cost less in salaries than two shifts working half as many hours. The cost of training only one shift of firemen should also be less than the cost of training two or more shifts. But on the evening of October 8, this personnel system resulted in all of the firemen being tired and worn out at the same time, with no fresh men ready to respond to and fight the O'Leary barn fire.[39]

NO. 2: EQUIPMENT DISREPAIR AND HOSE SHORTAGE

Because of this Saturday night fire, the firemen's equipment, including fire hose,

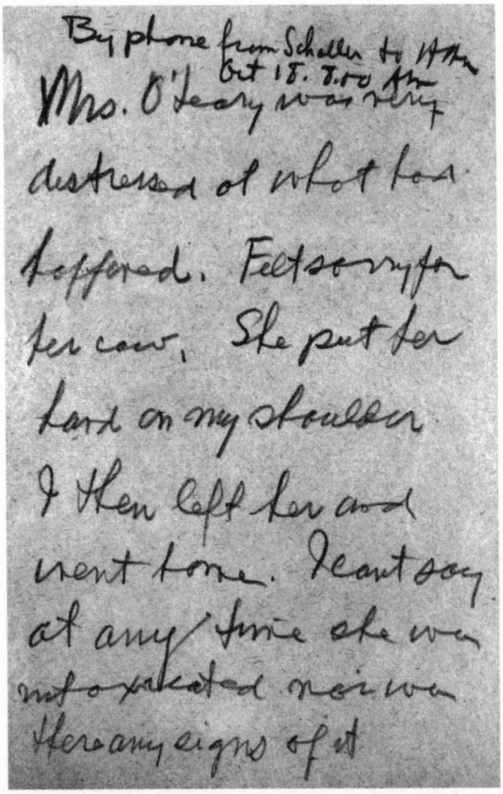

FIGURE 43—JACOB JOHN SCHALLER/HARRY A. MUSHAM TELEPHONE MESSAGE. **On what appears to be the day after Jacob Schaller and Harry Musham met, Schaller telephoned Musham at eight o'clock in the morning. Musham took notes of the conversation, and the message, along with the rest of his research materials, is still preserved at the Chicago Historical Society. The phone message reads as follows ("HAM" is an acronym for Harry A. Musham):**

By phone from Schaller to HAM
October 18, 8:00 A.M.
Mrs. O'Leary was very distressed at what had happened. Felt sorry for her cow. She put her hand on my shoulder. I then left her and went home. I can't say at any time she was intoxicated nor was there any signs of it.

(Chicago Historical Society ICHi-32029)

was not in the best condition. The hose that was available was in short supply.[40]

NO. 3: AN ERROR IN JUDGMENT?

The fire alarm telegraph system consisted of 172 alarm boxes that were connected to a central office located on the third floor of the courthouse. The boxes—numbered to indicate location—were placed outside firehouses and at various locations throughout the city. To prevent false alarms, the boxes were locked and keys were given to the occupants of nearby homes. The boxes were also placed at stores and the keys given to the storekeepers. A signal from any alarm box was automatically relayed to the central office, whereupon a telegraph operator would send a corresponding numbered alarm to the fire companies and at the same time ring the courthouse bell and other smaller bells scattered throughout the city. Any Chicagoan could listen to a bell and determine the location of the fire. For example, if a bell rang two times, then seven times, and then five times, a citizen could quickly look up "275" in a telegraph reference book and instantly determine that the fire was in the area of Randolph and Halsted streets.[41]

A watchman was also stationed in the cupola of the courthouse at all hours. His job was to scan the city for any unreported fires. Upon sighting one, he would estimate its location and then, via a voice tube, give the location of the fire to the telegraph operator in the central office, who would signal the fire houses and ring the city's bells.[42]

On the night of October 8, watchman Mathias Schaefer (Figure 44) was stationed in the courthouse cupola. When he noticed a light in the Southwest, he called down to William J. Brown, the night operator on duty, and told him to strike Box 342, located on the corner of Canalport Avenue and Halsted Street, in the same general direction as the O'Leary barn but about one mile farther southwest.[43]

As Schaefer examined the growing blaze from his location in the courthouse tower, he realized that he had made a mistake. It is possible that the autumn haze and smoke from the smoldering Saturday night fire obscured his vision, blurring the outlines of the landmarks that he would normally use to determine the location of fires. Also, the night was dark, with no moon yet in the sky. He called back down to Brown and asked him to strike Box 319, which was at the corner of Johnson and Twelfth streets. Although this box was closer to the fire, it was still seven-and-one-half blocks away. But Brown refused to ring the different alarm, stating that "he could not alter it now."[44]

And why not? Why didn't Brown direct the firemen to the correct location of the fire? The inquiry transcript reveals no clear answer. These four bound volumes contain the testimony of forty-nine people. With two exceptions these records consist of the verbatim account of what was said during the questioning. Unfortunately, the two exceptions are the statements of Schaefer and Brown. The *Chicago Tribune* of November 24, 1871, commented that on the first day of the inquiry "it was the intention to have a short-hand writer to take the evidence in full, but as one could not be procured, Mr. Brown [Thomas B. Brown, commissioner] wrote the testimony in long-hand. There were but two witnesses examined." Thomas Brown was a lawyer, not a stenographer; apparently unskilled in court reporting, he made only a summary of William Brown's testimony—a summary that does not com-

FIGURE 44—MATHIAS SCHAEFER. Mathias Schaefer was the fire department watchman. On the night of October 8, 1871, he was stationed in the courthouse cupola and so was one of the first people to see the O'Leary barn ablaze. But when he called down the fire's location to William J. Brown, the telegraph operator stationed on the third floor of the courthouse, he mistakenly told Brown that the fire was about one mile farther southwest than it actually was. In 1911, newspaper reporter Michael Ahern claimed that William Musham, foreman of the *Little Giant* steam engine, told him that had it not been for the Saturday night Lull & Holmes planing mill fire, which crippled the department, and Schaefer's misjudging the location of the burning O'Leary barn, "the 'big' fire, as it is called, would not have occurred." (Drawing by Marshall Philyaw)

pletely explain Brown's rationale in refusing to strike the closer Box 319. Perhaps the best explanation for Brown's behavior is set forth in this *Tribune* article: "In a short time the watchman called him [William Brown] again, and said he had been mistaken—that the fire was not so far off as he had thought when he gave him Box No. 342, which is located on the corner of Halsted street and Canalport avenue. As the box was on the line of the fire, Brown thought the firemen would not be misled, so he did not strike a nearer box. If he did so, confusion might ensue."[45]

But perhaps the firemen *were* misled. Robert Cromie contends that because of Brown's decision, fire companies that would otherwise have immediately answered the alarm failed to do so. Several firemen later maintained that had Schaefer given a closer location, they would have arrived at the fire sooner and the blaze could have been extinguished relatively quickly. But would these firemen have been at DeKoven Street any earlier if Brown had acceded to Schaefer's second request and struck Box 319, or would they have been delayed anyway because of the two different alarms? Was Brown's refusal to strike Box 319 the correct decision or was it a horrible error in judgment? Cromie also claims that Brown's reason for not changing the alarm was "arbitrary and foolish, since he must have known that Schafer's second estimate of the location was almost certain to be closer." Donald L. Miller succinctly states that "William Brown's stupid blunder helped doom Chicago." Even H. A. Musham, whose monograph clearly has a pro-firemen bent to it, refers to the fireman's refusal to strike Box 319 as "monumental stupidity."[46]

But historians Ken Little and John McNalis, authors of *History of Chicago Fire Houses of the 19th Century* (1996), convincingly argue otherwise. They point out that Brown knew that four steam engines, two hose units, and two trucks would respond to the Box 342 alarm. This equipment was capable of supplying six streams of water and producing at least fifteen hundred gallons of water per minute. Also, Brown thought that the firemen, together with this armament, would see the O'Leary fire on their way to Box 342. Therefore, Brown

did not strike another alarm because that would establish two locations for one fire, thus causing confusion and delay. Finally, today's Monday morning historians do not know what the fire department's official policy was in 1871 concerning alarm changes. Brown may have been following department procedure in not striking the second alarm for a fire that Brown could not have known at the time would eventually burn down Chicago.[47]

Nonetheless, it is possible that the firemen *were* delayed because of Brown's refusal to ring the closer alarm. Perhaps historians will agree that Brown cannot be criticized for making what he thought at the time was the proper decision, even though subsequent events indicate that this may have been an error in judgment.[48] This seems to have been the attitude of post-fire Chicagoans, who did not blame Brown personally, but chose instead to heap scorn and abuse on the shoulders of the fire department as a whole. Reminiscing years later about the events of October 8, 1871, several firemen did their share of finger pointing, but they blamed *Schaefer* for causing the delay! Brown should have said a silent prayer after the fire and nothing else, congratulating himself on his good fortune in escaping criticism. Instead, in what is probably one of the more interesting examples of *chutzpah* in Chicago history, he wrote his sister a few weeks after the fire and told her he was "still standing the *watch* that *burned Chicago* [emphasis in original]."[49]

NO. 4: BROWN'S DELAY

Brown saw the fire a few minutes after nine o'clock, almost one-half hour before Schaefer called down to him. But Brown (like other firemen) initially thought that the light in the southwest was a rekindling of the coal piles in the ruins of the previous night's fire. Accordingly, he did not sound the alarm, but chose instead to wait for Schaefer's signal. This also caused a delay in the fire department's arrival at the O'Leary barn.[50]

No. 5:
AN UNCOOPERATIVE DRUGGIST?

William Lee lived two houses east of the O'Leary home at 133 DeKoven Street, in a home owned by Walter Forbes. Upon seeing the fire, he ran southeast approximately three-and-one-half blocks to the drugstore of Bruno Goll, intending to turn in a fire alarm. Box 296 was located on an outside wall of this store, but Goll kept the key to the box inside (Figure 45). Lee later claimed that not only did Goll refuse to turn over the key, he also refused to turn in an alarm. Goll, on the other hand, argued differently, alleging in an affidavit that upon the request of two men, he turned in not one but two alarms. Although this may or may not have been true, neither alarm registered at the central office in the courthouse. As a result, the firemen were delayed in arriving at the fire.[51]

No. 6: INATTENTIVE NEIGHBORS

Alarm Box 295 was located only about two-and-one-half blocks northwest of the O'Leary barn, at the corner of Desplaines and Taylor streets (Figure 46). Although this box was even closer to the fire than the alarm at Goll's drug store, the O'Learys and their neighbors apparently did not attempt to turn in an alarm at this location until ten minutes after Schaefer had spotted the blaze from the courthouse cupola and called in the Box 342 alarm to William Brown. Firemen would have undoubtedly been at the O'Leary barn sooner

if a Box 295 alarm had been turned in promptly.[52]

No. 7: LACK OF ENGINE SUPPORT

Although the steam engine *Chicago* responded to Schaefer's call for Box 342, it was not delayed by his erroneous alarm. Rather, it was one of the first engines to appear at the scene of the fire. But Third Assistant Fire Marshal Mathias Benner later claimed that the *Chicago* was unprepared to fight the blaze when it arrived, apparently because of the Saturday night fire. As a result, the steamer's hoses were useless when it first took its position northwest of the O'Leary barn:

> If the *Chicago*, now No. 5, which I placed at the corner of Jefferson and Taylor streets, had done her duty the flames would have been checked at Taylor street. The engine had no steam on when she left her quarters on Jefferson street near Van Buren, and could do nothing when she reached the fire.... Their engine was uncleaned after her rough experience [on Saturday night]; there was no fire in the box, and everything was as it should not be. When No. 5 got to the corner of Taylor and Jefferson streets, they had no fire, and could do nothing. A picket fence was torn down and broken up to make the necessary blaze for heating the engine.[53]

The *Chicago's* troubles did not end there. Less than five minutes after it began pouring water on the flames, a spring in the steamer's pump broke. When foreman Christian Schimmals testified at the inquiry, he gave a colorful assessment of the problem and how his engineer was able to fix it, albeit somewhat artlessly:

> There was something cracked in her. I suppose [the engineer] knew what was the matter and shut her right down. I started back and said, "What does this mean?" Said he, "There is a spring broke in her pump." Said

FIGURE 45—BRUNO GOLL'S DRUGSTORE; FIRE ALARM BOX 296. An arrow drawn on this photograph of Bruno Goll's drugstore points to fire alarm Box 296. William Lee, a neighbor of the O'Learys, claimed that when he ran to the drugstore to turn in an alarm, Goll refused to give him the key to the box and would not turn in the alarm himself. Although Goll maintained that he turned in two alarms, neither one sounded at the central fire office in the courthouse. (Chicago Historical Society ICHi-02854)

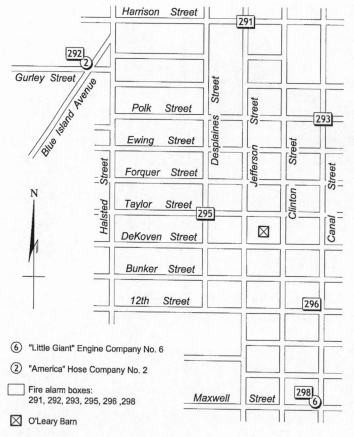

⑥ "Little Giant" Engine Company No. 6

② "America" Hose Company No. 2

☐ Fire alarm boxes:
    291, 292, 293, 295, 296 ,298

⊠ O'Leary Barn

Note:

Fire alarm box 296 was on the outside wall of Bruno Goll's store.

Fire alarm boxes 291, 293, and 295 were at the depicted street intersections, but their exact location at these intersections is unknown.

Location of Fire Companies and Fire Alarm Boxes in the O'Leary Neighborhood

October 8, 1871

FIGURE 46—LOCATION OF FIRE COMPANIES AND FIRE ALARM BOXES IN THE O'LEARY NEIGHBORHOOD. Although Patrick and Catherine O'Leary lived in a nondescript working class neighborhood on Chicago's West Side, they were not without fire department protection. Fire companies and fire alarm boxes were scattered throughout the area. This map indicates that Box 296, which was on the outside of Bruno Goll's drugstore, was about three-and-one-half blocks away from the O'Leary home. Box 295 was even closer, only about two-and-one-half blocks away. (Diagram by Douglas A. Swanson.)

I, "Is it going to do her any hurt to run her?" Said he, "I do not know. It is running a big risk. I might smash that pump all to pieces." Said I, "This is going to be a big fire. Smash her! We have got to run her and run the risk of its breaking her." Said I, "Break her completely and then it is broke!" He started her up and she run first rate. He struck her with a hammer and claimed it was all right again, but we could not depend on her.[54]

Schimmals later testified that the engine was shut down only about three minutes, but by then the damage was done. In that short interim blazing wood shavings, sparks, and shingles whirled across Taylor Street, and as the flames crept northeasterly, many felt that the fire was already out of control. Echoing the words of Fire Marshal Robert Williams and the belief of numerous firemen, historian A. T. Andreas wrote: "After the fire had crossed Taylor Street, and had found lodgment among the wooden buildings which filled that block, the destroying element became the master, and nothing could hold it back."[55]

Although Musham concludes otherwise, maintaining that even

after the blaze spread north past Taylor Street, the firemen still had a chance to subdue it, both he and Andreas agreed that another steam engine, the *Waubansia*, also failed to pull its weight after it drove up to the burning O'Leary neighborhood. In fact, Musham maintains that the failure of this engine to start working immediately after reaching the fire was a determining factor in the blaze spreading out of control. (Musham claims that the *Waubansia* went first to Box 342, but then apparently lost steam during its run to the fireplug at the corner of Clinton and Taylor streets, possibly due to a lack of fuel.) Understandably, Michael Sullivan, foreman of this engine company, failed to mention the *Waubansia*'s alleged inefficacy when interviewed during the inquiry hearings. Instead, he told the Board that when the alarm came in from Box 342, "We came on to the fire as quick as possible and took a plug on the corner of Taylor Street.... I put two streams on then. We worked there quite awhile, half an hour or so, and the fire got pretty warm at that time on Taylor Street."[56]

A Case for Exoneration

One fireman stated that at first the blaze "was a nasty fire, but not a particularly bad one, and with the help of two more engines we could have knocked it cold." But as another fireman noted, "From the beginning of that fatal fire everything went wrong," and all those things that went wrong combined to form a seven-act tragic comedy of errors. It is the inevitable conclusion that is drawn from these seven factors and from other circumstances that exonerates Mrs. O'Leary. That is, when the fire first broke out in her barn, there would have been no reason for her to think that the blaze would be of any more conse-

quence than any of the previous twenty-eight fires of that first week of October. Therefore, if she had been in the barn when the fire broke out, she would not have run back into her home and later feigned surprise, fearful of being blamed for starting the fire that would eventually destroy Chicago. Rather, she would have stayed outside, cried for help, and attempted to save the barn and its contents and extinguish what was then just one more October fire.[57]

And the contents of her barn were substantial. At the time of the fire, it appears that the barn contained five cows, a calf, a horse, and at least two tons of hay. Winter would soon inflict itself on the denizens of Chicago, therefore there were also two tons of coal in a small adjoining shed south of the barn. A sixth cow and a new wagon stood nearby in the alley. As none of this property was insured, it seems highly unlikely that she would turn her back on her burning barn and let her home, her comfort, and her livelihood both literally and figuratively go up in smoke.[58]

Unlikely, it seems, to everyone except for historian H. A. Musham. Instead of evaluating Mrs. O'Leary's behavior from an October 8, 1871, perspective, he comments on her reaction to the fire with post-fire hindsight, acquired years after her barn burned its way into Chicago history. In his zeal to bring Mrs. O'Leary to justice, he either ignores or fails to reach what would appear to be an inescapable conclusion—that the story of her cow kicking over a lantern was merely the combined product of the overly imaginative minds of neighborhood children and the overly gullible mind of an unknown and long-forgotten *Chicago Evening Journal* reporter. Furthermore, his obsession blinds him to the real (and only) significance of the O'Leary legend, that it was a harbinger of the sensational-ism that would immediately characterize many of the newspaper accounts and much of the literature of the fire.[59]

Much of this sensationalism was di-rected towards the unfortunate Mrs. O'Leary. Although it seems obvious that she and her cow were not responsible for the fire, she remained, nonetheless, a hapless target of the vitriolic press of the day. The October 18, 1871, issue of the *Chicago Times*, for ex-ample, described her as being "an old Irish woman" who was "bent almost double with the weight of many years of toil, and trou-ble, and privation." The article implied that she deliberately set her barn afire be-cause she was taken off of the welfare rolls: "The old hag swore she would be revenged on a city that would deny her a bit of wood or a pound of bacon." On the other hand, the December 3, 1871, issue of this same newspaper inconsistently described her ap-pearance at the inquiry hearings as being "a tall, stout Irish woman, with no intelli-gence...." Far from indicating she was old, the article stated that she appeared before the Board, carrying a baby, and that "dur-ing her testimony the infant kicked its bare legs around and drew nourishment from immense reservoirs."[60]

So why such invective, if Mrs. O'Leary did not cause the fire? Historians Carl Smith and Karen Sawislak suggest that she suffered the vituperative pen of the fourth estate, not so much because of any culpa-bility as to the fire, but rather because of the prejudices and stereotypes of the na-tive-born. On one level, the tale of the cow kicking over the lantern is merely the quin-tessential urban legend. But the story of the unfortunate Mrs. O'Leary also repre-sents a means by which middle- and upper-class Chicagoans could blame conflagra-tion, chaos, and calamity on not only an immigrant constituent of the urban work-

ing poor, but on a card-carrying member of the "dangerous classes" of their city as well. Although most assuredly innocent, Mrs. O'Leary and the people she represented be-came a focal point of all the fears of many of the elite Yankee Chicagoans of the day. Consequently, in the weeks after the fire, as citizens began to rebuild their city, the shadow of that broken lantern continued to cast a pall on the occupants of an un-burned cottage at 137 DeKoven Street[61] (Figures 47–48).

Notes

1. *1870 City Directory*, p. 486; Catherine O'Leary, *Inquiry*, vol. [1], pp. 59, 65–66, 77–78; Catharine McLaughlin, *Inquiry*, vol. [1], pp. 223, 237–39; Daniel Sullivan, *Inquiry*, vol. [1], pp. 259–61, 271–72; George Rau, *Inquiry*, vol. [1], p. 179; William Musham, *Inquiry*, vol. [1], p. 19; Kogan and Cromie, pp. 50–51; Sawislak, p. 11; *1872 Report of the Board of Police*, p. 12; John Drury, "Chicago's 'Forgotten House,'" *Chicago Daily News*, 14 April 1939, sec. 1, p. 18, hereafter cited in text as "Chicago's Forgotten House"; "Anniversary of the Great Fire," p. [5]; "How It Originated," *Chicago Tribune*, 20 October 1871, p. [2], hereafter cited in text as "How It Originated"; Musham, pp. 94–95; Andreas, vol. 2, p. 708; Chicago Title In-surance Company records. (The land records of Chicago Title Insurance Company include maps and plats, recorded documents, and "tract book pages," which categorize land transfers by legal de-scription. Any subsequent reference to these records is hereafter cited in text as Chicago Title Insurance Company records.)

2. Statement of J. C. Chapeck, 20 January 1942, Harry A. Musham Collection, Notes on the Chicago Fire, Chicago Historical Society, hereafter cited in text as Statement of J. C. Chapeck; State-ment of Phillip J. Sharkey, 10 November 1939, Harry A. Musham Collection, Notes on the Chi-cago Fire, Chicago Historical Society, hereafter cited in text as Statement of Phillip J. Sharkey; "Origin of the Fire," supplement, p. [2].

3. "The Great Calamity of the Age!," *Chicago Evening Journal-Extra*, 9 October 1871, p. 1, here-after cited in text as "The Great Calamity of the Age!" The *Journal* later bragged that on October 9, while the city still burned, it was the one newspaper

FIGURE 47—VIEW OF THE O'LEARY HOME FROM THE SOUTHWEST. This photograph from a souvenir stereograph by Chicago photographer Joseph Battersby is a southwesterly view of the O'Leary and McLaughlin cottages. The animal (probably a steer or bull that may have been recruited from the nearby stockyards) that is tethered to what appears to be the remains of neighbor Anne Murray's house purports to be the culpable cow. (Chicago Historical Society ICHi-33547)

that managed to publish an issue: "On that day, the *Journal* was the only paper on the street with the news of the fire. Only the *Journal*, of all the newspapers in the city, went to press in a borrowed office, with smoke in the eyes of editors and printers and the fury of fire outside roaring its own story." This is not completely true. The *Tribune* printed pages two and three of its four page October 9 issue, but was unable to complete its press run because the fire melted the printing press rollers. At least one of the partial newspapers was saved, however, and it was later published in 1891 as a souvenir edition. See "Readers Bring Famous 'Extra' in to *Journal*," *Chicago Daily Journal*, 8 October 1921, p. 1, hereafter cited in text as "Readers

Bring Famous Extra"; "While the Fire Raged," *Chicago Sunday Tribune*, 1 February 1891, sec. 5, pp. 33–36, hereafter cited in text as "While the Fire Raged"; "The Great Fire," *Chicago Sunday Tribune*, 1 February 1891, sec. 2, p. 12.

4. Sawislak, pp. 43–48.

5. "Notes on the Great Chicago Fire of 1871," *Chicago Sunday Inter Ocean*, 4 October 1896, sec. 3, p. 28, hereafter cited in text as "Notes on the Great Chicago Fire of 1871"; Michael Ahern, "Mrs. O'Leary Cow Story Refuted by Old Reporter," *Chicago Daily Tribune*, 21 January 1915, sec. 2, p. 13, hereafter cited in text as "Mrs. O'Leary Cow Story Refuted by Old Reporter"; "A Snarling Dog," *Chicago Evening Journal*, 21 October 1871, p. [2].

FIGURE 48—LOOKING NORTH FROM THE RUINS OF THE O'LEARY BARN. **This photograph is supposedly a view from the O'Leary barn looking north towards Taylor Street. If this is so, then the debris in the foreground is all that remains of the famous barn. (Chicago Historical Society ICHi-02735)**

6. Michael Ahern, "Reporter of 1871 Fire Describes Blaze of Today," *Chicago Sunday Tribune*, 8 October 1911, sec. 1, p. [2], hereafter cited in text as "Reporter of 1871 Fire"; "Mrs. O'Leary Cow Story Refuted by Old Reporter," sec. 2, p. 13; "1871 Reporter," sec. 1, p. 3.

Ahern seems to imply in his 1915 article that not only did Haynie come up with the story of the cow and the lantern, but that Haynie's employer, the *Times*, printed it as well:

At the time of the fire I was police reporter for the morning *Republican*, which later became the *Inter Ocean*. Johnny English was the *Tribune*'s police reporter and Jim Haynie was on the *Times*. Both of them are dead. I am the only police reporter living who helped to cover the greatest fire in the world's history.

It was Jim Haynie, I think, who "faked" the story about the cow kicking over the lamp. No newspaper was printed the morning of Oct. 9, but when the papers were able to get out "extras" the cow and lamp story was given as the cause of the holocaust.

This is one more reason why Ahern's credibility is suspect. The *Times* did not issue its first post-fire newspaper until October 18, more than a week after the *Journal* published its account of the cow kicking over the lamp.

7. John Kelley to Jim [O'Leary?], 9 October 1911, Chicago Fire of 1871 Personal Narratives Collection, Chicago Historical Society; John Kelley to Patrick O'Leary, 2 March 1927, Chicago Fire of 1871 Personal Narratives Collection, Chicago Historical Society, hereafter cited in text as John Kelley 1927 letter; "While the Fire Raged," sec. 5, p. 33; "Reporter of 1871 Fire," sec. 1, p. [2]; "Michael Ahern Dies; Reporter in Fire of 1871," *Chicago Sunday Tribune*, 20 February 1927, sec. 1, p. 12. The two letters from John Kelley that are in the collections of the Chicago Historical Society are photocopies. Both of these letters have been transcribed. Although the typed transcriptions indicate that John Kelley's name was "John Kelly," the scrawled signatures on these photocopies possibly generations removed from the originals are inconclusive. *Chicago Tribune* newspaper articles from 1924 and

1925, however, disclose that "John Kelly's" name was actually John Kelley. See "Works Cited" for these articles' bibliographic information.

8. Perry R. Duis and Glen E. Holt, "Kate O'Leary's Sad Burden," *Chicago* 27 (October 1978), p. 222, hereafter cited in text as "Duis and Holt"; Tom Burnam, *The Dictionary of Misinformation* (New York: Thomas Y. Crowell Co., 1975), s.v. "Mrs. O'Leary's Cow"; Miller, p. 165; David Cowan, *Great Chicago Fires: Historic Blazes That Shaped a City* (Chicago: Lake Claremont Press, 2001), pp. [13], 20, hereafter cited in text as Cowan; Dr. Frederick C. Hanmore to the President of the Chicago Historical Society, 21 January 1938, Chicago Fire of 1871 Personal Narratives Collection, Chicago Historical Society; "History of the Conflagration," *New York Herald*, 11 October 1871, p. 5. This *New York Herald* account is dated October 10. The *Herald*'s Chicago correspondent probably read the *Journal*'s report of the fire on October 9, subsequently wrote his own account of the fire and managed to eventually wire it to New York on October 10, whereupon it was published the next day. Even though it seems clear that Hanmore was less than truthful with his son, in 1891 the *Tribune* claimed that "the story about the cow kicking over the lamp had been written and wired to New York by the *Herald* correspondent—not by Mr. English, who never believed the story and doesn't to this day." See "While the Fire Raged," sec. 5, p. 33.

9. "Readers Bring Famous Extra," p. [2]; Donald B. MacKenzie to Caroline McIlvaine, 10 October 1921, Chicago Fire of 1871 Personal Narratives Collection, Chicago Historical Society.

10. John J. McKenna, *Reminiscences of the Chicago Fire on Sunday Evening, October 9th 1871* (Chicago: Clohesey & Co., 1933), p. 6, hereafter cited in text as 1933 McKenna; Smith, pp. 22–25; Rosemary K. Adams, ed., "Remembering the Great Chicago Fire," *Chicago History* 25 (Fall 1996), p. 24. A slightly different version of John J. McKenna's *Reminiscences of the Chicago Fire* appears as a chapter in his book, *Stories by the Original "Jawn" McKenna from "Archy Road" of the Sun Worshipers Club of McKinley Park in Their Political Tales and*

M. Philyaw

FIGURE 49—JAMES "BIG JIM" O'LEARY, son of Patrick and Catherine O'Leary, always maintained that spontaneous combustion of hay caused the Chicago Fire. He was born in 1863 and grew up working in Chicago's stockyards. His large size earned him the nickname "Big Jim." In the early 1890s, he opened a saloon; a few years later, he built a palatial gambling hall and saloon on the city's South Side. Outside the building, a large electric sign bearing the name "O'Leary" winked steadily. Inside, one could bet on anything from the name of the next president to whether it was going to rain or shine the next weekend.

In 1935, a reminiscing *Tribune* reporter referred to O'Leary as "Chicago's greatest gambler." The newspaper article included O'Leary's philosophy of life: "There are three classes of people in the world—gamblers, burglars, and beggars. Nearly everybody gambles. Sometimes it's with money, sometimes it's with time, sometimes it's with jobs. Nearly every fellow is willing to take a chance. Other folks are burglars. They make their living by stealing. The second-story man, the safe cracker, and the dip [pickpocket] are not the only burglars. You'll find a lot of others in offices in [downtown Chicago]. A fellow that won't gamble or steal is a beggar."

Jim O'Leary died in 1925. He and his wife are buried next to his parents in a Chicago cemetery. (Drawing by Marshall Philyaw. Reproduced with permission of the *chicago Tribune*.)

Reminiscences (Chicago: John F. Higgins, 1918), pp. 143–59, hereafter cited in text as 1918 McKenna. Admittedly, perhaps McKenna is not suggesting that the children around DeKoven and Clinton streets made up the tale of the cow kicking over the lamp, only that they helped spread the story throughout the area. Nonetheless, the possibility that now-anonymous neighborhood children concocted the cow and lamp story remains a very plausible theory.

11. Catherine O'Leary, *Inquiry*, vol. [1], pp. 59–60, 66; Patrick O'Leary, *Inquiry*, vol. [1], p. 249; Catherine Sullivan, *Inquiry*, vol. [1], p. 117; Dennis Regan, *Inquiry*, vol. [1], pp. 121–22; Daniel Sullivan, *Inquiry*, vol. [1], pp. 254–56; "The Cow That Kicked Over the Lamp," *Chicago Tribune*, 19 October 1871, p. [2]; hereafter cited in text as "The Cow That Kicked Over the Lamp"; "How It Originated," p. [2]; "The Great Fire," *Chicago Tribune*, 24 November 1871, p. 6; "The Great Fire," *Chicago Tribune*, 5 December 1871, p. 2; "History of the Great Conflagration," *Chicago Tribune*, 19 November 1871, p. 7; "Chicago and the Great Conflagration," *Chicago Tribune*, 21 November 1871, p. 6; Musham, pp. 69–70. Carl Smith describes the creation of these "instant histories" in Smith, pp. 23–25.

12. "The Fire in Print," *Chicago Evening Journal*, 23 November 1871, p. 1, hereafter "The Fire in Print"; Sewell, pp. [7], 20–21; Andreas, vol. 2, p. 759; "New Books," *Chicago Republican*, 16 December 1871, p. [2], hereafter cited in text as "New Books"; "Chicago and the Great Conflagration," *Chicago Republican*, 25 December 1871, p. [4].

13. Colbert and Chamberlin, p. 201; Goodspeed, pp. 156–57; "Chicago and the Great Conflagration," *Chicago Tribune*, 17 December 1871, p. 4; "New Books," p. [2].

14. Andreas, vol. 2, pp. 709–10; "The Great Fire," *Chicago Evening Journal*, 12 December 1871, p. [4]; "Nobody to Blame," *Chicago Times*, 12 December 1871, p. 5, hereafter cited in text as "Nobody to Blame"; "The Great Fire," *Chicago Republican*, 12 December 1871, p. [4]; "City Intelligence," *Prairie Farmer* 42 (16 December 1871), p. 386; *1872 Report of the Board of Police*, p. 12; "Story of the Great Chicago Fire," sec. 3, p. 20; Sawislak, p. 46. Perhaps a hint of Williams' thoughts concerning the role of incendiaries in the spread of the fire is disclosed by his inquiry testimony: "We got there, and after we had been playing awhile, the whole garret was full of fire, and there was a kind of green and blue mass ran down out of that. I did not for two or three days find out what it was. They had all their telegraph fixings up there, so I made up my mind it was that. I did not know but what

somebody had been preparing that to burn." See Robert A. Williams, *Inquiry*, vol. [4], p. 268.

15. Musham, pp. [69], 99–100, 103, 158, 177; H. A. Musham to Walter Kogan, 10 October 1942, Harry A. Musham Collection, Notes on the Chicago Fire, Chicago Historical Society; William Musham, *Inquiry*, vol. [1], p. 6. For an example of Musham's patriarchal platitudes, consider this description of his father's steam engine, the *Little Giant*: "If the correct box had been struck these companies would have all been at the fire within five to ten minutes and would have put it out in short order. As it was, the *Little Giant*—and a little giant it turned out to be—worked all alone for about twenty minutes before another engine arrived ready for work." See Musham, pp. 161–62.

Paul M. Angle, former director of the Chicago Historical Society, termed Musham's work "masterly" and "definitive." See Angle, p. 12; Paul M. Angle, introduction to *The Great Chicago Fire of 1871* (Ashland: Lewis Osborne, 1969), p. 10. Angle, however, did have one criticism. In his introduction to Robert Cromie's book, *The Great Chicago Fire*, Angle wrote that "even [Musham's] excellent monograph left something to be desired, for the author was more concerned with the work of the fire department than with the fire as a community convulsion." See Cromie, p. x. Despite this minor criticism and Musham's aforementioned biases, his work remains an admirable account of the fire.

16. Musham, pp. 149–52, 156–57; "The Fire Investigation," *Chicago Evening Journal*, 25 November 1871, p. [4]; "The Great Fire," *Chicago Tribune*, 25 November 1871, p. 6; Catherine O'Leary, *Inquiry*, vol. [1], pp. 59–60.

17. Musham, pp. 150, 153; Robert S. Critchell, *Recollections of a Fire Insurance Man* (Chicago: privately printed, 1909), p. 81, hereafter cited in text as Critchell; "The Fire," *Chicago Times*, 18 October 1871, p. 1; *Reminiscences of Chicago During the Great Fire*, pp. xiv–xv; Goodspeed, p. 156.

18. "Mrs. O'Leary's Cow," *Chicago Daily Tribune*, 17 September 1894, p. 8, hereafter cited in text as "Mrs. O'Leary's Cow"; John Corrigan, "O'Leary Research Sheds New Light on Fire and Family," *Scéal* 4 (Fall 1986), p. 2; hereafter cited in text as *Scéal*; 1870 U.S. Census, Cook County, Illinois, Population Schedule, National Archives micropublication M593, roll 204, sheet 171, page 86, line 17; 1880 U.S. Census, Cook County, Illinois, Population Schedule, National Archives micropublication T9, roll 200, Supervisor's District 1, Enumeration District 197, sheet 26, page 302, line 12.

19. Sawislak, pp. 44–48, 294.

20. "Origin of the Fire," supplement, p. [2]. For an apparent reference to this man, see Untitled article, *Chicago Tribune*, 16 November 1871, p. 4: "We have still the O'Leary cow, the man with a pipe who passed through the O'Leary back-yard just before the fire...."

21. Chicago Title Insurance Company records; *Halpin's Seventh Annual Edition Chicago City Directory, 1864–5: Containing, Also, a Classified Business Register and City and County Record* (Chicago: T. M. Halpin & Co., 1864), p. 329; "Chicago's Forgotten House," sec. 1, p. 18; "Origin of the Fire," supplement, p. [2].

22. "Origin of the Fire," supplement, p. [2]; "How It Originated," p. [2]; "The Cow That Kicked Over the Lamp," p. [2].

23. Stephen W. Sears, "The Giant in the Earth," *American Heritage* 26 (August 1975), pp. 94–99, hereafter cited in text as "The Giant in the Earth"; Untitled article, *Chicago Times*, 19 November 1871, p. [2].

24. "The Giant in the Earth," p. 95; Jean Cochran, "Mrs. O'Leary's Delivery Boy Tells True Story of Great Fire," *Oak Leaves* (Oak Park, Ill.), 12 October 1939, pp. [3], 10; hereafter cited in text as "Mrs. O'Leary's Delivery Boy"; Jacob J. Schaller to H. A. Musham, 15 October 1939, Harry A. Musham Collection, Notes on the Chicago Fire, Chicago Historical Society.

25. H. A. Musham to Jacob J. Schaller, 14 October 1939, Harry A. Musham Collection, Notes on the Chicago Fire, Chicago Historical Society; "He Peddled Milk for Mrs. O'Leary; He's Sure Cow Started the Fire," *Chicago Herald-American*, [6 October 1939], Harry A. Musham Collection, Notes on the Chicago Fire, Chicago Historical Society; "Looks Like O'Leary Cow Must Take That Fire Rap," *Chicago Herald-American*, [8 October 1939], Harry A. Musham Collection, Notes on the Chicago Fire, Chicago Historical Society; "Historian Is Here for an Interview with Mr. Schaller," *Oak Leaves* (Oak Park, Ill.), 19 October 1939, p. 5, hereafter cited in text as "Historian Is Here for an Interview"; "Historian Comes to Village," *Oak Leaves* (Oak Park, Ill.), 26 October 1939, p. 63, hereafter cited in text as "Historian Comes to Village"; Statement of Jacob John Schaller, 17 October 1939, Harry A. Musham Collection, Notes on the Chicago Fire, Chicago Historical Society, hereafter cited in text as "Statement of Jacob John Schaller."

26. Statement of Jacob John Schaller; Dedmon, p. 261; "History Finds One Who Knew a Famous Cow," *Chicago Sunday Tribune*, [19 November 1939], Harry A. Musham Collection, Notes on the Chicago Fire, Chicago Historical Society.

27. Chicago Title Insurance Company records; E[lisha] Robinson, *Robinson's Atlas of the City of Chicago, Illinois* (New York: privately printed, 1886), vol. 1, plates 5 and 6, hereafter cited in text as *Robinson's Atlas*; Cromie, inside front cover; Colbert and Chamberlin, foldout map between pages [8] and 9, hereafter cited in text as Colbert and Chamberlin, foldout map; Andreas, vol. 2, pp. 705, 707; Musham, p. 91; *1870 City Directory*, p. 1089.

28. Catherine O'Leary, *Inquiry*, vol. [1], pp. 59, 77–78; "Statement of Jacob John Schaller." Mrs. O'Leary's testimony that she owned six cows and a calf is probably not inconsistent with her October 20 *Tribune* affidavit given before Michael McDermott in which she attests that she owned five cows and a horse. It appears that the cows and horse Mrs. O'Leary refers to in this affidavit were those animals killed in the fire and not the total number of animals she owned. See "How it Originated," p. [2]. Although Musham acknowledges that Schaller was incorrect in claiming that Mrs. O'Leary owned only one cow, the historian failed to question or even comment on this discrepancy. See Musham, p. 152.

29. Catherine O'Leary, *Inquiry*, vol. [1], pp. 59, 61; Patrick O'Leary, *Inquiry*, vol. [1], p. 249; Dennis Regan, *Inquiry*, vol. [1], pp. 121–22, 124; Daniel Sullivan, *Inquiry*, vol. [1], pp. 254–56.

30. *The New Encyclopædia Britannica*, 15th ed., s.v. "Food Processing: Dairy Products."

31. Chicago Title Insurance Company records; Lloyd Wendt and Herman Kogan, *Lords of the Levee* (Indianapolis: Bobbs-Merrill Co., 1943), pp. 11–12; *1870 City Directory*, p. 464; *1871 City Directory*, p. 517; *Merchants' Chicago Census Report, Embracing a Complete Directory of the City—Showing Number of Persons in Each Family, Male and Female—Birth Place and Ward Now Residing In* [Chicago: Richard Edwards, 1871], p. 617; *Robinson's Atlas*, vol. 1, plate 6.

32. Catharine McLaughlin, *Inquiry*, vol. [1], pp. 237–39. Chicago Title Insurance Company records indicate that Michael Coughlin owned 79 DeKoven Street until 1880. A search of the Chicago city directories from 1871 through 1880 reveals no "Schaller" or "Shaller" at this address. Jacob Schaller told Musham that his father's name was Jacob Andrew Schaller. From 1873 through 1880, these directories list a "Jacob A. Schaller" at "201 W. 16th," "117 W. 13th," and "146 W. 13th." These addresses are only a few blocks south of the O'Leary home. It is possible that even Schaller's story of renting from Michael Coughlin was a fabrication. Perhaps Jacob Andrew Schaller simply moved into the O'Learys' West Side neighborhood in 1873, whereupon young Jacob John Schaller

learned firsthand about the famous Mrs. O'Leary. These same city directories list no "Michael Coughlin" at 79 DeKoven Street until 1879. But the 1879 directory also indicates that "Frank Schallot" lived in the rear portion of the building at this address. Perhaps Coughlin was renting out the entire house until 1879, when he moved into the front part and rented out the rear to Mr. Schallot. If this were the case, then who was living at 79 DeKoven Street prior to the time Coughlin and Schallot moved in? The Schallers? See Chicago Title Insurance Company records; Lowe, p. 42; *Chicago & Vicinity 6-County StreetFinder* (n.p.: Rand McNally, 1995), p. 57 (Cook County), hereafter cited in text as *Chicago & Vicinity 6-County Street-Finder*; "Statement of Jacob John Schaller"; *The Lakeside Annual Directory of the City of Chicago, 1879: Embracing a Complete General and Business Directory, Miscellaneous Information and Street Guide* (Chicago: Donnelley, Gassette & Loyd, 1879), pp. 302, 951.

33. "Mrs. O'Leary's Delivery Boy," p. [3].

34. "The O'Leary Cow: Eye Witness in *Oak Leaves*," *Oak Leaves* (Oak Park, Ill.), 26 October 1939, p. [iii].

35. "Historian Is Here for an Interview," p. 5; Musham, pp. 150–52. Just as Musham obtained his interview, Jacob Schaller received his recognition, ill-gained though it was. The December 14, 1939, *Oak Leaves* featured an article about Schaller's upcoming golden wedding anniversary. It included the following sentence: "With publication of *Oak Leaves'* story regarding the origin of the great conflagration, cheerful, white haired Mr. Schaller suddenly became an important personage in his seventy-eighth year." See "The Schallers, Wed 50 Years, Won Fame by *Oak Leaves* Story," *Oak Leaves* (Oak Park, Ill.), 14 December 1939, p. 16; "Jacob Schaller 80; Recalls Chicago Great Fire," *Oak Leaves* (Oak Park, Ill.), 11 June 1942, p. 7; "J. J. Shaller [sic] Dies; Delivered Milk for Mrs. O'Leary," *Oak Leaves* (Oak Park, Ill.), 19 July 1945, p. 42; "J. J. Schaller, Mrs. O'Leary's Milk Boy, Dies," *Chicago Daily Tribune*, 18 July 1945, sec. 1, p. 3.

36. H. A. Musham, telephone call memorandum, 18 October [1939], Harry A. Musham Collection, Notes on the Chicago Fire, Chicago Historical Society; Mrs. O'Leary's Delivery Boy," p. 10. This telephone call memorandum is dated October 18. Although the year is not shown, it is undoubtedly 1939.

In the weeks after the fire, even the city's newspaper reporters, for all their sensationalism, never suggested that an intoxicated Mrs. O'Leary caused the fire. But perhaps other Chicagoans were not as gracious. In 1928, Mrs. Jennie E. Counselman reminisced about the fire to "members of the Women's Club." She, like Musham and Schaller, talked about an inebriated Mrs. O'Leary: "Another story of how the fire was started was that as Mrs. O'Leary was not a believer in prohibition and had taken several long pulls out of a dark bottle, that she herself, in her unsteady condition, kicked over the lamp." See Statement of Jennie E. Counselman, "Reminiscences of the Chicago Fire and Some of My Girlhood Days," March 1928, Chicago Fire of 1871 Personal Narratives Collection, Chicago Historical Society.

H. A. Musham made similar but even more ludicrous statements in a 1955 newspaper interview. Apparently relying on a letter he received in 1942 from F. H. Shults, Musham claimed that on the night of the fire, Mrs. O'Leary went down the street to the saloon owned by F. H. Shults's father, Frank Shults. This saloon was at the corner of DeKoven and Jefferson streets. She bought a can of beer, joked with the other customers, then left. Musham noted that "it was a warm evening, in the lower 70s," and then added: "Chances are she had a few swigs." See Jack Lind, "Fire? Blame Mrs. O'Leary, Not Her Cow," *Chicago Daily News*, 8 October 1955, sec. 1, p. 13; F. H. Shults to Col. H. A. Musham, 25 January 1942, Harry A. Musham Collection, Notes on the Chicago Fire, Chicago Historical Society, hereafter cited in text as F. H. Shults letter.

37. Musham, pp. 87–89; Andreas, vol. 2, pp. 703–04, 713; Cox and Armington, p. 197; "Story of the Great Chicago Fire," sec. 3, p. 20. For a comprehensive listing of all false alarms, fires and losses during this period, see *1872 Report of the Board of Police*, pp. 106–8.

38. "Story of the Great Chicago Fire," sec. 3, p. 20; "On the Defensive," p. 4; Andreas, vol. 2, pp. 704–07; William Musham, *Inquiry*, vol. [1], p. 29; Michael Sullivan, *Inquiry*, vol. [1], pp. 98–99; Christian Schimmals, *Inquiry*, vol. [1], pp. 131–33; Lewis Fiene, *Inquiry*, vol. [1], pp. 216–18; Sheahan and Upton, pp. 63–64; Luzerne, p. 66; Little and McNalis, pp. 99–100; "The Fire Fiend," p. [3]; Musham, pp. 89–94.

39. Little and McNalis, p. 99; Musham, p. 86; David Lewis to Richard F. Bales, 28 October 2001; Ken Little to Richard F. Bales, 31 October 2001.

40. "Story of the Great Chicago Fire," sec. 3, p. 20; Musham, p. 93; Christian Schimmals, *Inquiry*, vol. [1], pp. 134–36, 152–53; Andreas, vol. 2, p. 711.

41. Statement of F. L. J., "The Little Girl Who Should Have Been a Boy," n.d., appended to

Emma Hambleton to Mrs. William Harrison Lander, 11 October 1871, and Chalkley J. Hambleton to Emily Hambleton, 11 October 1871, Chicago Fire of 1871 Personal Narratives Collection, Chicago Historical Society; John P. Barrett to Albert D. Hager, n.d., John P. Barrett Collection, Chicago Historical Society, hereafter cited in text as John P. Barrett letter; Andreas, vol. 2, pp. 92–93; *1870 City Directory*, pp. 914–15; Goodspeed, pp. 117–18; Musham, pp. 84–86, 99–100; Cromie, p. 14; Robert A. Williams, *Inquiry*, vol. [4], p. 237.

42. "Story of the Great Chicago Fire," sec. 3, p. 20; Musham, pp. 85–86, Cromie, p. 14.

43. Mathias Schaefer, *Inquiry*, vol. [1], p. 5; Musham, pp. 99, 161; "Boring for Facts," *Chicago Tribune*, 19 November 1871, p. 6; "1871 Reporter," sec. 1, pp. 1, 3; Andreas, vol. 2, p. 711; Cromie, pp. 36–37; *1870 City Directory*, p. 915; Colbert and Chamberlin, foldout map.

44. Mathias Schaefer, *Inquiry*, vol. [1], p. 5; Musham, pp. 87, 100–102, 160–61; "Reporter of 1871 Fire," sec. 1, p. [2]; J. F. Cleveland, comp., *The Tribune Almanac and Political Register* (New York: Tribune Association, 1871), p. [14], hereafter cited in text as *Almanac*; Cromie, pp. 37–38; *1870 City Directory*, p. 915; Colbert and Chamberlin, foldout map.

45. "The Great Fire," *Chicago Tribune*, 24 November 1871, p. 6; "Setting Them Right," *Chicago Tribune*, 15 November 1871, p. 6, hereafter cited in text as "Setting Them Right." Although fifty people testified during the inquiry, the actual transcript contains the statements of only forty-nine people. A newspaper account of the last day of the investigation indicates that although a final witness testified, no one made a record of his testimony. See "The Great Fire," *Chicago Tribune*, 5 December 1871, p. 2.

46. Andreas, vol. 2, pp. 711–13; Musham, pp. 160–62, 179; Cromie, pp. 38–39; "Story of the Great Chicago Fire," sec. 3, p. 20; Miller, p. 146.

47. Little and McNalis, p. 100; Ken Little, co-author of *History of Chicago Fire Houses of the 19th Century*, interview by Richard F. Bales, 1 April 2001, hereafter cited in text as Ken Little interview; "The Great Fire," *Chicago Tribune*, 24 November 1871, p. 6.

48. Historian A. T. Andreas probably would have concurred with this assessment. In his *History of Chicago*, he notes that "the error in sounding Box 342 prevented at least four of the best engines, located in the district, [from] taking part in the work...." But he also comments that "it has been asserted that the engines were not judiciously posted on their arrival at the scene, but the fact is plain that the fire had assumed insuperable di-

mensions long before the greater number of engines arrived." He then adds one more observation: "It is easier to discover errors after they are committed than to avoid them in the excitement of a great peril." See Andreas, vol. 2, p. 713.

49. Andreas, vol. 2, pp. 711–13; "Reporter of 1871 Fire," sec. 1, p. [2]; "1871 Reporter," sec. 1, pp. 1, 3; "Story of the Great Chicago Fire," sec. 3, p. 20; William J. Brown to his sister [Sarah R. Hibbard?], 2 November 1871, Chicago Fire of 1871 Personal Narratives Collection, Chicago Historical Society, hereafter cited in text as William J. Brown letter, 2 November 1871. In a 1911 interview, Schaefer said nothing about Brown's refusal to strike Box 319. Instead, he appeared to admit some responsibility in allowing the fire to get out of control: "I had a spyglass raised to my eyes scanning the sky when I saw the light on the west side of the river. I rang up Brown and told him to strike box 342 at Canalport avenue and Halsted street. A few minutes later I discovered my mistake and notified Brown to give the right location. Valuable time had been lost, however, and the fire had a good headway before the mistake was rectified." See "Man in Tower at Fire of '71 Tells of Sighting Flames," *Chicago Sunday Tribune*, 8 October 1911, sec. 1, p. [2], hereafter cited in text as "Man in Tower." Post-fire Chicago newspapers contained many letters and editorials criticizing the fire department's performance on October 8–10. The public's opinion of the firemen's conduct and condition during the fire is discussed in Chapter 5.

50. Andreas, vol. 2, pp. 711–12; "Marks Anniversary of the Great Fire," *Chicago Sunday Record-Herald*, [8 October 1911], William J. Brown, Chicago Fire of 1871 Personal Narratives Collection, Chicago Historical Society, hereafter cited in text as "Marks Anniversary of the Great Fire"; "Man in Tower," sec. 1, p. [2]; "Reporter of 1871 Fire," sec. 1, p. [2]; "1871 Reporter," sec. 1, p. 1; Cromie, p. 36; Statement of James O. Brayman, "The Great Conflagration," 22 January 1880, Chicago Fire of 1871 Personal Narratives Collection, Chicago Historical Society; David Kenyon, *Inquiry*, vol. [2], pp. 117–18.

51. Andreas, vol. 2, pp. 711, 714–16; Musham, pp. 97–98, 100–[101], 158–60; "Reporter of 1871 Fire," sec. 1, p. [2]; "1871 Reporter," sec. 1, p. 3; "Man in Tower," sec. 1, p. [2]; *1870 City Directory*, pp. 282, 488; Chicago Title Insurance Company records; William J. Brown, *Inquiry*, vol. [1], p. 1; *Robinson's Atlas*, vol. 1, plate 6. (See also Appendix A, "What Really Happened at Bruno Goll's Drugstore?")

52. Musham, pp. [101], 159; Andreas, vol. 2, p. 711; *1870 City Directory*, p. 915; "The Great Fire,"

Chicago Evening Journal, 12 December 1871, p. [4]; William J. Brown, *Inquiry*, vol. [1], p. 1; James S. McQuade, ed., *A Synoptical History of the Chicago Fire Department from the Earliest Volunteer Organization Up to the Present Time...* (Chicago: Benevolent Association of the Paid Fire Department of Chicago, 1908), p. 48, hereafter cited in text as McQuade.

53. Musham, pp. 100, 102; Christian Schimmals, *Inquiry*, vol. [1], pp. 126–28; "Notes on the Great Chicago Fire of 1871," sec. 3, pp. 21, 28; Michael Ahern, "The Fire Fighters," (*Chicago*) *Daily Inter Ocean*," 9 October 1893, sec. 1, p. [2], hereafter cited in text as "The Fire Fighters."

54. Musham, pp. 102–04, 177; John Kelley, "Never Another '71 Fire, Says Retiring Chief," *Chicago Sunday Tribune*, 5 October 1924, sec. 1, p. 16; Christian Schimmals, *Inquiry*, vol. [1], pp. 141–46.

55. Musham, pp. 105, 177–78; Christian Schimmals, *Inquiry*, vol. [1], pp. 146–47; Andreas, vol. 2, pp. 711–13. H. A. Musham claimed that after the *Chicago* received the Box 342 alarm, the engine left its firehouse and drove to the corner of Forquer and Jefferson streets. This intersection was about two blocks northwest of the O'Leary barn. But after the steamer connected to a fireplug at the northwest corner, its hose burst. Musham maintained that although the firemen tried to patch the hose by wrapping it in blankets, their repairs were unsuccessful, and they could do nothing until they obtained another supply of hose. Although Schimmals testified about the hose bursting at the Saturday night fire and of a shortage of hose on Sunday night, he never said anything about hose problems disabling the *Chicago* when it first took a position near the O'Leary barn during the fire's earliest stages. Furthermore, not only does the transcript of Schimmal's testimony contain nothing concerning Benner's later allegations of negligence, Schimmal testified that "at half past four o'clock Box 28 [a false alarm] came in, and we just got back from that and got cleaned up, ready for another one, when the large fire broke out." See Musham, pp. 102–3, 177; Christian Schimmals, *Inquiry*, vol. [1], pp. 131, 35–36, 149, 152–54. (The *1872 Report of the Board of Police*, p. 108, indicates that the false alarm from Box 28 came in at 7:00 P.M. and not at 4:30.)

56. Musham, pp. 104–5, 177–78; Andreas,

vol. 2, pp. 712–13; Michael Sullivan, *Inquiry*, vol. [1], p. 80.

57. "Story of the Great Chicago Fire," sec. 3, p. 20; William S. Walker, "Description of the Great Fire," in *The Lakeside Memorial of the Burning of Chicago, A.D. 1871* (Chicago: University Publishing Co., 1872), pp. 22–23, hereafter cited in text as Walker; Andreas, vol. 2, p. 713; Cromie, pp. 30–31.

58. Andreas, vol. 2, p. 708; Catherine O'Leary, *Inquiry*, vol. [1], pp. 59, 76–78; Daniel Sullivan, *Inquiry*, vol. [1], pp. 259–61, 265; Catharine McLaughlin, *Inquiry*, vol. [1], pp. 242–43; Patrick O'Leary, *Inquiry*, vol. [1], pp. 247, 250–51; Dennis Regan, *Inquiry*, vol. [1], p. 122; "How it Originated," p. [2]; Cromie, p. 29.

59. George L. Barclay's *The Great Fire of Chicago!...* (Philadelphia: Barclay & Co., 1872), with its lurid illustrations, is probably the epitome of sensationalistic fire literature. For a discussion of this literary genre, see generally Smith, pp. 51–63. But as noted herein in chapters one and three, horrific stories of thieves and incendiaries gone amok were largely unfounded. Chicago newspapers were outraged at the exaggerations promulgated by the eastern press. One "instant history" appropriately sub-titled *The Horrors of Chicago* is a compilation of such sensational newspaper articles, many from New York City papers. See "Absurd Misstatements," p. [2]; "Atrocious Fabrications," p. [2]; *The Ruined City; or, The Horrors of Chicago* (New York: Ornum & Co., 1871), hereafter cited in text as *The Horrors of Chicago*. But see also Michael C. Hickey, *Inquiry*, vol. [2], pp. 165–67, 169–70, wherein a Chicago police captain testified at the inquiry investigation about allegedly observing two attempted lynchings.

60. "The Fire," *Chicago Times*, 18 October 1871, p. 1; "How They Look and Act," *Chicago Times*, 3 December 1871, p. [3], hereafter cited in text as "How They Look and Act."

61. Sawislak, pp. 44–46; Smith, pp. 51–55; Untitled article, *Chicago Tribune*, 27 November 1871, p. 2. Sawislak notes that the term "dangerous classes" first saw wide public usage after the publication of Charles Loring Brace's book, *The Dangerous Classes of New York and Twenty Years' Work Among Them* (New York: Wynkoop and Hollenbeck, 1872). See Sawislak, p. 293.

• *Chapter Three* •

Debunking Other Myths

We have had enough causes assigned for the Chicago conflagration.
—*Chicago Tribune*, November 16, 1871

The story of Mrs. O'Leary and her cow is one of the more enduring legends of Chicago history. After more than 130 years, school children still read about Mrs. O'Leary's cow kicking over the lantern and starting the Great Chicago Fire. But these students probably never learned that many possible causes of the fire (not just bovine intervention) have been suggested in the years following the blaze. Many theories were considered, even in the first few weeks after October 8, 1871. In fact, the *Chicago Tribune* commented on October 27 that "there have been not less than nine hundred causes assigned for the Chicago conflagration...." This chapter discusses and debunks just a few of the popular, and some not so popular, fire theories of both yesterday and today.[1]

Spontaneous Combustion of Hay

The spontaneous combustion of "green" hay in the O'Leary barn is one of the more unusual possible causes. In fact,

this was the theory of choice of picturesque James "Big Jim" O'Leary (Figure 49), who, years after the fire, complained: "That musty old fake about the cow kicking over the lamp gets me hot under the collar." O'Leary, the son of Patrick and Catherine, grew up to be a saloon owner and bookmaker. According to legend, he would accept a bet on anything from a presidential election to the weather.[2]

The odds that hay caused the fire initially seem to be in Jim O'Leary's favor. Spontaneous combustion is the process by which certain materials ignite without the application of exterior heat. In order for hay to self-combust, it must be moist. As the O'Learys' hay had apparently been delivered only the day before the fire, it might have been freshly cut when it was placed in the loft of the barn. Therefore, at first it seems reasonable to suggest that the newly harvested hay might have contained sufficient moisture for spontaneous combustion.[3]

But this is one wager that "Big Jim" undoubtedly lost. In 1871 the summer and fall had melted together into one long, continuous, simmering heat wave. As one contemporary observer wrote, "There had been a baking of earth, trees and dwellings, in the dry air of a rainless autumn, until everything had been cooked to the crisp, igniting point." So even if the hay had been cut just hours before delivery, it seems a virtual certainty that it was thoroughly dry even before it was placed in the barn. It would not have been susceptible to spontaneous combustion, as the microorganisms that initiate the process need at least 12 percent moisture to flourish.[4]

Prior to spontaneous combustion there is spontaneous heating. As the temperature of stored hay begins to rise and even before there is actual ignition, a great deal of smoke is produced. This smoke is accompanied by an irritating pungent odor that is not at all like the smell of smoke from a chimney or wood stove. This is because hay's combustion products include aldehydes and acrolein. Mrs. O'Leary milked her cows at four-thirty on the evening of October 8, just a few hours before the fire broke out. She later put her horse in the barn at about seven o'clock, less than three hours before the building erupted in flames. Had smoke and the distinctive odor of smoldering hay been present in the barn that day, surely Mrs. O'Leary would have noticed it, as the barn was a relatively small structure. And had she seen smoke or smelled burning hay, she certainly would have investigated immediately.[5]

Whether or not hay will self-ignite is somewhat dependent on the quantity stored. Generally speaking, the greater the amount of hay, the greater the likelihood of ignition. The other element of crucial importance is the ambient temperature, which is the temperature of the surrounding air. In general, the higher the temperature, the more likely the chance of self-ignition. The ideal conditions for spontaneous combustion of hay are a large body of moist hay and a high outside temperature. The larger quantities of hay provide greater insulation and thus reduce the rate of heat loss to the outside air. The rate of heat loss is also lessened if the outside air is already warm or hot. But if the quantity of hay is relatively small and dry, the temperature at the center of the pile (where it would be best insulated from the outside air) may never get high enough for the onset of spontaneous combustion. The temperature that October day was certainly warm, but with only about two or three tons of dry, not moist, hay in the loft, it is doubtful that the temperature of the hay ever reached the degree necessary for self-ignition.[6]

Finally, spontaneous combustion of hay is a slow chemical process that can take days or even weeks. As it appears that the hay had been delivered only the day before, it is unlikely that it would have been in the barn long enough to self-ignite.[7]

A Spark from a Chimney

The commissioners asked Mr. O'Leary during the inquiry: "Could sparks from a house south from your barn being driven by the wind get into your barn and into those shavings?" O'Leary was noncommittal, replying only that "I couldn't tell anything about that." Nonetheless, the Board of Police and Fire Commissioners suggested in their final report that the blaze might have been caused by "a spark blown from a chimney on that windy night...."[8]

But how many stoves would have been burning at that hour? There would have been no need for a heating fire on that warm October evening, and any cooking probably would have been completed hours ago. Although a spark might have fallen into some wood shavings earlier and smoldered before eventually catching fire (both doors of the barn were open at the time the fire broke out), certainly Mrs. O'Leary would have smelled the smoke when she went out to milk her cows that evening.[9]

Mrs. Anne Murray was the O'Learys' neighbor to the west. The O'Leary barn was located at the rear of their property, and it appears that Murray's house was near the front of her land, near DeKoven Street (Figure 50). This resulted in the Murray home and O'Leary barn aligning on a southwest-northeast diagonal (Figure 51). As the wind was blowing from the southwest to the northeast on the night of October 8, the most logical source of any possible spark would be the home of Mrs. Anne Murray.[10]

The Murray and O'Leary properties were each about one hundred feet deep. Could a chimney spark from Mrs. Murray's house travel sixty feet or more and eventually wend its way into the O'Leary barn next door? This does not appear likely. John D. DeHaan, author of *Kirk's Fire Investigation*, points out that although the updraft of large fires can loft flaming debris hundreds of yards, wind-blown sparks will normally not travel more than thirty or forty feet before dying out. With no independent evidence to support the theory that an ember from a chimney caused the fire, it must be discarded.[11]

FIGURE 50—SOUTHWESTERN VIEW OF THE O'LEARY AND MCLAUGHLIN HOMES AND THE REMAINS OF ANNE MURRAY'S HOUSE. Even though the wind was blowing from the south-southwest when fire broke out in the O'Leary barn, some buildings west of the O'Leary and McLaughlin houses, including the adjacent home owned by Anne Murray, were destroyed by the fire. The flames probably traveled along adjoining barns and fences to Murray's house.

This southwesterly view of the O'Leary and McLaughlin homes reveals that although the window of the O'Leary house has been boarded up, the McLaughlin windows are undisturbed. Perhaps there was either some minor damage or the window was covered up to prevent curiosity seekers from peering inside. (Chicago Historical Society ICHi-02737)

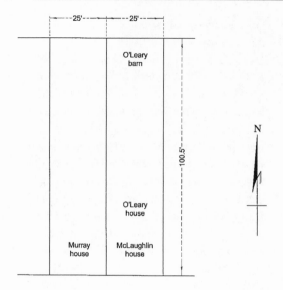

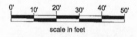

The Anne Murray and Patrick O'Leary Properties

October 8, 1871

FIGURE 51—THE ANNE MURRAY AND PATRICK O'LEARY PROPERTIES. **Although it is possible to pinpoint the location of the O'Leary barn and the O'Leary and McLaughlin cottages (Figure 54), the exact location and size of the Murray home is unknown. For this reason only the names of these structures have been shown on this diagram, but properly situated in relation to each other. It seems clear that the Murray home and the O'Leary barn were so far apart that a wind-blown spark from the Murray chimney would have died out before it reached her neighbors' barn. (Diagram by Douglas A. Swanson)**

Incendiaries

On October 23, 1871, the *Chicago Times* published a page-one confession allegedly written by a member of the Societe Inter-

nationale, which apparently was an off-shoot of the militant revolutionary organization, the Paris Commune of 1871. This particular communist claimed that he helped set the fire in order to burn the business section of Chicago and thus "humble the men who had waxed rich at the expense of the poor." Now burdened by a guilty conscience, this supposed perpetrator wanted to set the record straight.[12]

The *Chicago Evening Journal*'s reaction was immediate and to the point. In an editorial published the same day as the *Times* article, the *Journal* accused its morning rival of being a "pauper in brains" that "invented fiction." It proclaimed:

This whole Internationale yarn is a "mess of nonsense." No one who witnessed the progress of those terrible flames under the irresistible force of that heated wind—a hurricane of burning air and firebrands—a veritable sirocco—will attribute the work of destruction to petroleuse communists, or to any other cause except the force of that wind, fire-laden, against a mass of buildings that had been rendered as dry and inflammable as tinder-boxes by the protracted drouth and hot weather....[13]

The *Illinois Staats-Zeitung*, a local German newspaper, also criticized the *Times*. In a series of editorials, it denounced this confession as being "most ridiculous" and pointed out that because Chicago did not have as much labor conflict as more established industrial cities as New York or Boston, it would be an unlikely victim for such an act of terrorism. Commenting on the city's appetite for sensationalism—"So extraordinary an event must have an extraordinary cause"—the newspaper echoed the *Journal*'s call to demythologize the origin of the fire. It reminded its readers that fires were a daily occurrence in Chicago and that this disaster needed no special explanation.[14]

Authors Elias Colbert and Everett Chamberlin were also skeptical of the *Times'* tale of a Communist plot, and observed that "the motive for such a deed did not appear to be sufficient, nor was the story free from marks which betrayed its origin in the brain of a professional newspaper writer." But the two men did not ask the most obvious question: Why would the Societe Internationale, whose goal, according to the anonymous *Times* correspondent, was to destroy the city's business district and thus "elevate the workingmen to the level of the rich," start the fire many blocks from Chicago's downtown in what was obviously a "workingmen's" neighborhood?[15]

If an international conspiracy did not start the fire, what about a local one? That is, was the fire deliberately set or propagated by one or more arsonists? Many people were convinced that this was the case, as they saw buildings that were blocks ahead of the fire suddenly burst into flames. The press helped to popularize this theory, with numerous colorful stories of post-fire incendiaries torching the remaining structures of a defenseless city, its water mains now empty, dry, and useless. Consider the following "reports" that were published in the October 11 *Chicago Evening Journal*:

- "A boy attempted to help on the conflagration by igniting a clothes line saturated with kerosene and throwing it into a building on Thirty-second street. He received his deserts at the hands of the firemen, who saw the act, and 'now sleeps in the valley.'"
- "Bridget Hickey was arrested for setting fire to a barn in the rear of a house on Burnside street. By some mistaken idea of clemency, she was not hanged."

- "Two men, who were caught trying to set fire to the Jesuit Church, on the West Side, were disposed of without ceremony, and the lookers-on were pleased to say, Served 'em right."
- "At about 11 o'clock yesterday forenoon, a man also residing on Fourth avenue, caught a man in the basement of his house, number unknown, armed with hay and matches. He gave the alarm, and the incendiary was caught and stoned and battered to death. He lies on the avenue yet, near Fourteenth street."
- "Another man was shot last evening by a police officer, who detected him in the act of attempting to fire the Jesuit Church on Twelfth street."
- "An excited crowd gathered round the West Division Police Station, about 5 o'clock yesterday afternoon, intent upon making an application of lynch law to a man who was alleged to have tried to set fire to a house on Milwaukee avenue. Three or four ropes were flourished vigorously in the crowd, and several speeches were made by parties urging them to rescue the incendiary from the hands of the police, but the latter were firm, and at the last accounts the man was still a prisoner, in the cell."[16]

Although these tales of the shooting, stoning, and hanging of arsonists made for thrilling and titillating newspaper copy, the stories were nonetheless completely groundless. Buildings caught fire from convection whirls hurling burning brands far ahead of the advancing flames, not from the arsonist's torch. But as fire historians James W. Sheahan and George P. Upton so aptly observed, "The result was as if a corps of men were firing the city at various points simultaneously." And contrary to the lurid accounts of the Chicago newspapers and even the national press, General Sheridan reported to Mayor Mason on October 12 that "no authenticated attempt at incendiarism has reached me...." A month later, Thomas B. Brown, President of the Board of Police, reached a similar conclusion: "In our investigation, we were unable to find a single case of probable incendiarism during the whole time." With not even a shred of evidence to the contrary, this theory can be rejected—and besides, why would an incendiary set fire to a cow barn on DeKoven Street?[17]

McLaughlin Party Milk Thief

"There was one out of the party went in for to milk my cows." With these words, Mrs. O'Leary introduced into the inquiry record what the residents along DeKoven Street had been talking about almost since the fire began. That is, that on the evening of October 8, Mr. and Mrs. McLaughlin were hosting a party in honor of Mrs. McLaughlin's "greenhorn" brother, who had just come to America from Ireland. Someone from this party, seeking milk to make either punch or an oyster supper, crept into the O'Leary barn with a lamp or other light in order to surreptitiously milk one of the cows. Somehow the barn caught fire, and the rest is history.[18]

There are several variations of this story. In 1939 historian H. A. Musham interviewed one Phillip Sharkey, who claimed that on Monday morning, October 9, he and his father went to the O'Leary home, where Mrs. O'Leary told them what happened the day before:

There was [a] party in the front four rooms of the O'Leary house which was occupied by the McLaughlin family. Mrs. Catharine McLaughlin asked for some milk just before

the fire. Mrs. O'Leary said there was none on hand, but she could have it if she would go out and milk the cow herself, which Mrs. McLaughlin did.[19]

But Sharkey's story is obviously apocryphal. Mrs. O'Leary never mentioned this incident when she testified before the Board on November 24. Already being blamed for starting the fire, surely she would have done so if it were true.

In other versions of "the McLaughlin party theory," the "greenhorn brother" was actually a young girl; there were six people from Ireland, not just one; the party was a christening; and so on. But perhaps the most colorful account is the tale related by Mrs. Mary Callahan (Figure 52) that appeared on the front page of the September 26, 1903, Chicago Tribune. Professing to be one of the persons who attended the McLaughlin party, she maintained that while helping to make some tea, she discovered that her hosts had no milk. Callahan and three others quietly left the house and stole into the barn, carrying a lamp and a tin pail. While one of them, Denny Connors (Callahan maintained that he was the greenhorn cousin, not brother, of the McLaughlins), clumsily attempted to milk the cow, the lamp fell over and started the fire. Callahan and another girl screamed and ran towards the house. One of the others ran after them and admonished the girls to be quiet, explaining that the fire would be extinguished quickly. According to Callahan, she and the other girl resumed their dancing until Connors and a neighbor, "Denny Sullivan," came running in, shouting that the "house was all afire."[20]

Several elements common to both Callahan's story and Mrs. McLaughlin's inquiry testimony indicate that Callahan did attend the McLaughlin party. The commissioners questioned Mrs. McLaughlin extensively about who was at her home that

FIGURE 52—MARY CALLAHAN. On the evening of October 8, 1871, Mr. and Mrs. McLaughlin held a party for Mrs. McLaughlin's brother, who had just come to America from Ireland. Mrs. Mary Needham Callahan was one of the guests. In 1903, Callahan came forward with the apocryphal tale that she was in the barn when Denny Connors, the party's guest of honor, clumsily attempted to milk the cow. She maintained that somehow the lamp fell over, and the barn caught fire. (Drawing by Marshall Philyaw)

evening. One of the guests she named was "Mary Needham." This *Tribune* article discloses that Callahan was formerly known as Mary Needham. Mrs. McLaughlin told the commissioners that after the fire, Mary Needham went to either Michigan or Wisconsin. The *Tribune* indicates that Mary Callahan left the city for Sheboygan. Furthermore, the names of the other guests listed by McLaughlin are substantially the same as those noted by Callahan. Finally, both women tell of Mr. McLaughlin playing his fiddle for the guests.[21]

But a careful comparison of Calla-

han's account and Mrs. McLaughlin's inquiry testimony, which was given under oath, reveals serious discrepancies and indicates that little else of what Callahan said was true:

- Callahan claimed that Mr. McLaughlin played "Mrs. McLeod's reel, the blackbird and other tunes that started our feet pattering." She commented several times on the dances that she and her friends enjoyed throughout the evening. But Mrs. McLaughlin testified that her husband "played two times on the fiddle, that was all. There was one a brother of mine and another lady danced a polka. That is all that was played."[22]
- Contrary to Callahan, Mrs. McLaughlin testified that she did *not* make any tea or coffee that night:

  Q. Did you make any tea or coffee during the time?
  A. No sir. If I did, of course I should have started the stove. Not a mouthful of victuals ever came there that evening before God this day.[23]

- The commissioners asked Mrs. McLaughlin several times if anyone left her home that evening. Although her answers were somewhat inconsistent, it seems clear that half of her guests— four out of at least eight people—did *not* all suddenly leave her small house during the party.[24]
- Callahan stated that after the fire started, she went back into the house and continued dancing (presumably to the tune of Mr. McLaughlin's fiddle) with the other guests until Denny Connors and a neighbor came running in, shouting that the house was on fire. But Mrs. McLaughlin testified

that her husband had *stopped* playing half an hour *before* the fire began.[25]

• Several people, including Mr. and Mrs. O'Leary, testified at the inquiry about who and what they saw along DeKoven Street in those first few minutes as the fire consumed the barn and then spread to adjoining buildings. Although they mentioned seeing this neighbor, no one told of seeing Denny Connors.[26]

• Callahan alleged in the article that Mrs. O'Leary learned years later that the fire started when Callahan and the others slipped into the barn to steal milk. This is extremely doubtful. For the rest of her life O'Leary grieved about being blamed for starting it. It is incomprehensible that she would have remained silent after hearing about Denny Connors. If she had felt that there was any truth to the story, she undoubtedly would have come forward immediately to proclaim her innocence to the world. And even assuming that she was somehow coerced into quiet submission, surely her son James would not have followed suit. The ex-stockyards worker was called "Big Jim" for good reason and he hated the infamy the fire brought to the family name.[27]

• Mrs. McLaughlin testified that as many as three men left her home during the party. She identified them as Denny Connors, Willie Lewis, and Johnny Ryan. On the other hand, Callahan claimed that four people—herself, another woman named Alice Reilly, and two men, Connors and a man named Johnny Finnan—left the party.[28]

• Callahan implied that she and the others were able to sneak into the barn because its door was unlocked. But

Patrick O'Leary testified that the south door—the door that faced the O'Leary home—was actually nailed open so that it would not shut. Whether the door was locked or unlocked was irrelevant.[29]

One last question remains. Even though Mrs. McLaughlin testified under oath, is it possible that she was aware of people leaving her party to go to the barn, but that she lied to protect her guests? At first one might think so. Mrs. McLaughlin testified the day after Mrs. O'Leary did, and Mrs. McLaughlin partially confirmed O'Leary's suggestion that "there was one out of the party went in for to milk my cows." That is, Mrs. McLaughlin admitted—but only after being asked by the Board—that some guests apparently *did* leave the party during the course of the evening. The Board asked McLaughlin several times if any of her guests left her home that night. Her first response seemed evasive: "Of course I do not know that I could not say whether they did or not. If I was going dead 'fore God, I could not tell whether they went out or not." She later conceded that three young men did leave her house. Finally, when asked if anyone left her home to bring back refreshments, she again sidestepped: "No sir. There was no one left the house. Only one man went out and got a half gallon of beer or two half gallons, I don't know which." Were these conflicting statements deliberate lies?[30]

It seems unlikely that Mrs. McLaughlin lied to the commissioners in order to protect Ms. Callahan and company. Instead, she was probably simply nervous about speaking publicly and under oath before the numerous commissioners, fire officials, and reporters. Shortly after her questioning began, the commissioners asked McLaughlin, who was only the twelfth person to testify, the following question: "Will you give the names of all these persons who were there at the house that evening?" She was cooperative; not only did she give the Board their names, but when asked, she also told the commissioners where her guests lived and worked. Apparently Mary Callahan was the only one who had left the city. Incredibly, the commissioners never bothered to question these other people. But when Mrs. McLaughlin identified them, she would have had no way of knowing that they would never be called to testify. For this reason it is doubtful that she would have lied during her testimony, taking the chance that one of her guests might later contradict her or, even worse, attempt to falsely incriminate her.[31]

It seems evident that Mrs. Callahan made up the story about the hapless greenhorn and his fateful attempts at milking the O'Leary cow. By September of 1903, Denny Connors was deceased—she was quick to mention this—and so was unable to defend himself. Mrs. O'Leary was also dead. At the time Chicago was celebrating its centennial, one hundred years since the establishment of the first Fort Dearborn. As part of the festivities, the city was preparing to reenact its great fire by igniting "heaps of powder" at twenty-eight street corners in downtown Chicago. No doubt Mary Callahan, like Jacob Schaller years later, wanted to take advantage of the fire-related publicity and wheedle her way into the history books.[32]

Although Callahan's version of the "McLaughlin party" theory is just one of several that permeates Chicago Fire lore, it probably is the most detailed and descriptive. And at first the idea of someone sneaking into the barn to steal milk seems reasonable. After Mrs. O'Leary was questioned during the inquiry proceedings, the *Chicago Tribune* commented on her testimony:

[Mrs. O'Leary] heard that one of the neighbors was having a "social time" that evening, and that some of the gay company went into her barn to get some milk for an oyster stew—that is, to steal it by milking her cows while she was asleep with her children. It is not unlikely that the investigation will show that these social milk thieves, becoming alarmed at some noise, and fearing discovery, threw down their light and ran away, and thus kindled a conflagration that swept down two hundred millions of property.[33]

But all these "social milk thieves" stories have one common flaw: All fail to take into account the unique architecture of the O'Leary house and barn. Not only did Patrick O'Leary testify that both front and back barn doors were open at the time the fire started, he added: "The one next to the house is nailed up so it would not shut at all." A window in the north wall of his home faced this door, and no doubt this window was also open on that warm October evening (Figure 53). It is unlikely that *anyone* could leave unnoticed out of the small McLaughlin cottage, exiting through the front door that overlooked DeKoven Street—the only door to the McLaughlin home, as shown in Figures 37 and 47, and creep back past the O'Leary home, steal into the backyard, and slip into the barn to steal milk. Any lantern or light he carried or noise he or a bothered bovine made could be seen or heard from the O'Leary house, which, as shown in Figure 54, was less than fifty feet away.[34]

Several versions of this theory also include the discovery of a lamp in the blackened remains of the barn in the days after the fire. H. A. Musham interviewed Phillip Sharkey, who claimed he found the fragments of a lamp behind the carcass of a cow. Mr. S. H. Kimball wrote a letter to Caroline M. McIlvaine of the Chicago Historical Society in 1914; in the letter Kimball alleged that he found the bottom of a glass

FIGURE 53—PEOPLE GATHERED AROUND THE REAR OF THE O'LEARY HOME. This photograph of the rear of the O'Leary home reveals that the north window, as well as the west window, were boarded up after the fire.

Herman Kogan and Robert Cromie suggest that this throng of curiosity seekers is clustered around the remains of the famous barn. But the barn was next to the alley that ran along the rear of the O'Leary property. Instead, these blackened timbers are probably the remains of another building immediately adjacent to Mr. and Mrs. O'Leary's house.

Mrs. O'Leary was often the victim of spurious newspaper stories. *The New York Tribune*, for example, described the O'Leary home as "a warped and weather-beaten shanty of two rooms, perched on thin piles, with tin plates nailed half way down them like dirty pantalets." But this photograph clearly indicates that the lower portions of both homes were covered by boards, not tin plates, and that the boards extended all the way to the ground, not just halfway down. (Chicago Historical Society ICHi-02739)

lamp in the recess of a broken floorboard. Joseph Dushek, a neighbor of the O'Learys, was the most descriptive of his prize:

Just after the fire, while looking through the ruins of the O'Leary barn, I found an oil lamp, of the usual pattern, with a foundation-piece, about five and a half inches square, of brown stone or marble. The upright piece which set into it, and upon which

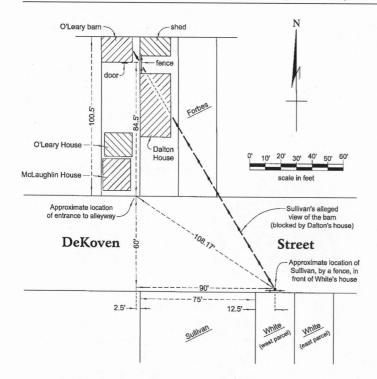

O'Leary barn — shed — fence — door — Forbes — O'Leary House — Dalton House — McLaughlin House — N — 100.5' — 84.5' — 0' 10' 20' 30' 40' 50' 60' scale in feet — Approximate location of entrance to alleyway — Sullivan's alleged view of the barn (blocked by Dalton's house) — **DeKoven** 60' — 108.17' — **Street** — Approximate location of Sullivan, by a fence, in front of White's house — 90' — 75' — 2.5' — 12.5' — Sullivan — White (west parcel) — White (east parcel)

O'Leary Property and Surrounding Area

October 8, 1871

FIGURE 54—O'LEARY PROPERTY AND SURROUNDING AREA. This diagram of the O'Leary neighborhood is based primarily on Chicago Title Insurance Company records, inquiry testimony, and post-fire photographs. It shows the O'Leary, Dalton, and Forbes properties on the north side of DeKoven Street and the Sullivan and White parcels on the south side of the street. Note that the O'Leary barn, located at the rear of their property, is less than fifty feet away from their home, which is in back of the McLaughlin house. Other information contained in this drawing is discussed in the following chapter. (Diagram by Douglas A. Swanson)

rested the oil-holder, was of brass. The foundation-piece, the upright, and the oil reservoir or holder, were all together. The oil-holder, however, had been broken. The globe and chimney were gone[35] (Figure 55).

Forensic scientist John D. DeHaan notes that Dushek's description of the lamp gives added credence to the "McLaughlin party" theory. He points out that

Mrs. O'Leary would have never kept such an ornate lamp in her barn, that it was more appropriate for use in a living room—such as Mrs. McLaughlin's living room. DeHaan's suggestion is thought-provoking, but as it seems evident that no "milk thief" caused the Great Chicago Fire, his observation, like the more dubious claims of Messrs. Sharkey, Kimball, and Dushek, can be discounted.[36]

Nighttime Smoker

"A smoker in the barn" has often been suggested as a possible cause of the Chicago Fire. As one might guess, there are also several variations of this theory.

Historian Frank Luzerne sets out one version in his history of the fire. He suggests that a smoker might have stepped inside the barn on that breezy Sunday evening to more easily light a pipe or cigar. He also comments that "a spark alighting on this tinder of hay and shingles, and fanned by the wind, would soon wrap the slight barn in flames."[37]

At the time the fire started, a wind of about twenty miles an hour was blowing, so at first Luzerne's suggestion seems to have

FIGURE 55—ALLEGED REMAINS OF THE O'LEARY LAMP. Joseph Dushek, a neighbor of the O'Learys, claimed that while looking through the ruins of the O'Leary barn, he found a broken oil lamp. Historian A. T. Andreas included a drawing of this lamp in his *History of Chicago*, and it is reproduced here courtesy of artist Marshall Philyaw.

the catch and unlock the door before entering the barn. Although the door facing the O'Leary home was nailed open, to use it one would have to step off the alley and walk around to the other side of the barn. This small dark building contained at least five cows and a calf, which was certainly a fetid combination on that hot summer night and one that would surely discourage even the most ardent windblown tobacco lover.[38]

In a story remarkably reminiscent of the Callahan Chronicles of just a few years earlier, the *Tribune* of October 9, 1921, again announced that the mystery of the cause of the Chicago Fire had been solved. This time the eyewitness was Mrs. Anton Axsmith. She claimed that on the day of the fire, she and her husband were visiting Mr. and Mrs. John Kokes, who lived on Taylor Street, across the

merit. But anyone walking along DeKoven Street would most likely shelter his match against a fence or house, rather than walk through a yard to the O'Leary barn, which was located in the rear of their property next to an alley. Granted, someone could have been strolling down the alley and stopped inside to light a pipe or cigar. But it appears that although the upper half of the barn door adjoining the alley was open, allowing for the full circulation of air, the lower half was shut and latched that evening. Any smoker would first have to locate

alley and almost directly opposite the O'Learys. While sitting in the Kokes' backyard, they saw six men behind the O'Leary home, drinking beer, smoking, and laughing. Eventually, she claimed, some of these men entered the barn, clambered into the hayloft, and fell asleep: "They had been smoking pipes and probably one of these, slipping into the hay, was the real cause of the start of the disaster."[39]

Axsmith, like Callahan, mixes a small amount of fact with apparently liberal doses of fiction. Although Mr. and Mrs.

Kokes did live across the alley and nearly opposite the O'Learys, the rest of her account is almost certainly fantasy. Neither the O'Learys nor Mrs. McLaughlin said anything about these men when questioned at the inquiry proceedings. Surely Mrs. O'Leary, already being blamed for causing the fire, would have mentioned them if they had been lounging in her yard all Sunday afternoon.[40]

Axsmith came forward with this information fifty years after the fire. Why did she wait so long? It should come as no surprise that Axsmith's account and a "Fire Day Program" detailing the events commemorating the fiftieth anniversary of the fire appear on the same newspaper page. Jacob Schaller used the forthcoming publication of Musham's book as his springboard to immortality. Most likely Axsmith used this anniversary in a similar fashion, fabricating her story during the celebration in hopes of carving out fame and glory from the fire[41] (Figures 56–57).

So if adult smokers did not cause the Chicago Fire, what about younger ones? Alfred T. Andreas suggests that "some boys were enjoying a moment of stolen pleasure in the barn, with pipes or cigars, and carelessly let fire fall among the inflammable substances on the floor." (A 1909 *Chicago Tribune* article offers a similar opinion, contending that boys, seeking to mix milk with a bottle of whiskey, dropped a lamp which started the fire.) At first these presumptions do seem reasonable. It is easy to imagine boys accidently starting a fire, panicking, and then running away without thinking of the consequences. But historian Harry A. Musham points out that because the fire started after dark, there would be no reason for boys to take the trouble to enter a barn to smoke when they could do so without fear of detection in the alley or behind a fence. There is no evidence at all that

youthful smokers (or drinkers) caused the fire, and so this theory can be rejected.[42]

A Gambler Named Louis M. Cohn

Alan Wykes suggests in his book *The Complete Illustrated Guide to Gambling* (1964) that the fire was caused by one Louis M. Cohn, who knocked over a lantern while playing craps in the O'Leary barn (Figure 58). Unfortunately, Wykes's brief account is short on details and long on anecdotes, adding that Cohn, apparently in an attempt to shift the burden of guilt, claimed that it was the cow that kicked over the lantern. Wykes does mention, however, that in 1944, two years after Cohn died, the dean of Illinois's Northwestern University received from Cohn's estate not only a bequest of thirty-five thousand dollars but also the full story of the "truth" about the fire.[43]

This "true" cause of the fire would probably still be known only to gambling aficionados were it not for the investigative efforts of Anthony DeBartolo, a freelance writer who penned two *Chicago Tribune* articles about Cohn in late 1997 and early 1998. DeBartolo's research clarified Wykes's tale of Cohn, craps, and the Chicago Fire. DeBartolo noted that when Cohn's bequest was handed over to Northwestern University, the school issued a press release, which included Cohn's assertion that on the night of the fire, he, Mrs. O'Leary's son, and several other boys were shooting dice in the hayloft of the famous barn. One of the boys (the release did not indicate it was Cohn) overturned the lantern, setting the barn on fire.[44]

DeBartolo interviewed Stanley K. Feinberg, the son of Judge Michael Feinberg, who was Cohn's friend and executor.

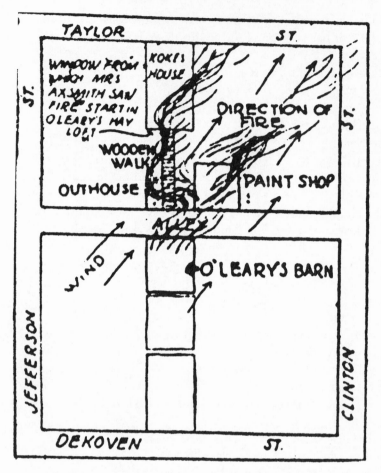

FIGURE 56—MRS. ANTON AXSMITH'S MAP OF THE O'LEARY NEIGH-
BORHOOD. Mrs. Anton Axsmith was probably lying when she
maintained that on the day of the fire, she saw several men
lounging in the O'Learys' back yard, drinking beer and
smoking. She alleged that some of these men entered the
barn, climbed into the hayloft, and fell asleep. Axsmith
suggested that one of their pipes slipped into the hay and
started the fire. But if the map that accompanied the 1921
Tribune story of her claim is accurate, then this drawing
may be a historically significant depiction of some of the
pre-fire improvements in the O'Leary neighborhood. The
caption below the drawing reads as follows: "The above di-
agram is drawn from information given by Mrs. A. Axsmith, who saw the fire start in
the O'Leary barn and who saw the drinking party making merry there. She says the
flames leaped across the alley to a paint shop and then to an outhouse and along a
wooden sidewalk to the [Kokes'] home, whence it spread rapidly."

How accurate is Axsmith's diagram? Andreas' *History of Chicago* includes a drawing of the O'Leary neighborhood as well, and it appears as Figure 57. Although this
map also discloses a paint shop north of the alley, Andreas depicts the shop as being
east of the location shown in Axsmith's diagram. John McGovern mentions a paint
shop in his novel *Daniel Trentworthy.* His description of the shop's location is consistent with Andreas' drawing.

Feinberg confirmed and
even expounded on the
contents of the press re-
lease, explaining that
Cohn told him several
times that on the night of
the fire, Cohn, one of
Mrs. O'Leary's sons, and
some other boys were
playing craps in the barn
when Mrs. O'Leary chased
them out. While running
away, they tipped over a
lantern. But was it spe-
cifically Cohn who top-
pled it? Feinberg indi-
cated that he never heard
Cohn admit that he
knocked it over, but that
whenever someone asked
Cohn if he did it, his
only response would be
"a knowing smile."[45]

A smile? Odds are
Cohn was laughing to
himself at how com-
pletely he had buffaloed
his friends. It is almost
certain that Cohn was
not rolling sevens on the
hayloft floor on the eve-
ning of October 8. Dur-
ing the inquiry investigation Mrs. O'Leary had
testified under oath that
her children were in bed

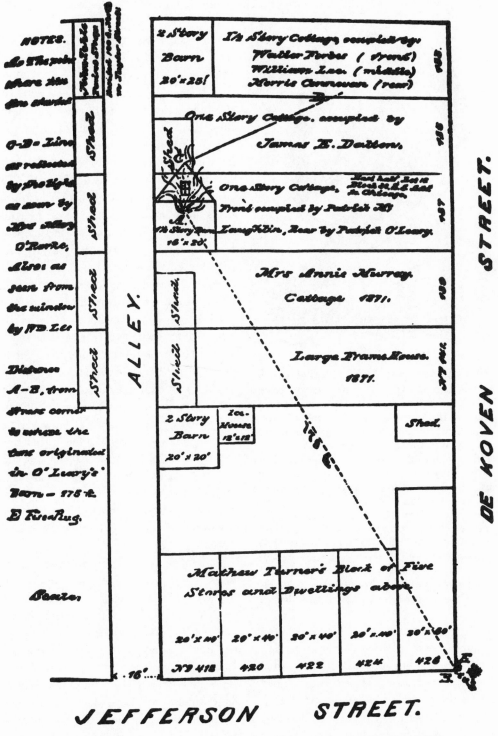

PLAT OF LOCALITY WHERE FIRE ORIGINATED.

FIGURE 57—A. T. ANDREAS' MAP OF THE O'LEARY NEIGHBORHOOD. This drawing of the O'Leary neighborhood originally appeared in A. T. Andreas' *History of Chicago*.

FIGURE 58—LOUIS M. COHN. Louis M. Cohn was a Chicago importer and world traveler who died in 1942. He maintained that on the night of the fire, one of Mrs. O'Leary's sons, some other boys, and he were playing craps in the barn when Mrs. O'Leary chased them out. While running away, they tipped over the lantern, starting the fire. A 1944 *Chicago Daily News* article reported that "Mr. Cohn never denied that when the other boys fled he paused long enough to scoop up the money." Cohn should have used that time to come up with a better story; there is not one piece of evidence that supports his claim. (Drawing by Marshall Philyaw, permission of *Chicago Tribune*)

when the fire broke out. Did she lie to the commissioners in order to protect her son from the ire of burnt-out Chicagoans? This is perhaps a reasonable conclusion, until one realizes that if Cohn's tale of dice on DeKoven Street is accurate, then it is also true that even though both Mrs. O'Leary and her son were present when the barn caught fire, neither made any attempt to extinguish the blaze and rescue the endangered cows. Instead, they merely went back

inside their home, leaving the animals to fend for themselves. The improbability of this scenario is obvious.[46]

Is it possible that Mrs. O'Leary chased the boys away, but she did not see them knock over the lantern as they ran from the barn? This would explain why she went back into her house, only later to discover the barn on fire. But assuming this to be the case, then one of two other assumptions must also be made. One, if she confronted her son after the fire and he told her that he did not tip the lantern over, then it seems likely that when she testified at the inquiry, she would have mentioned seeing these young dice throwers in her barn. However, her testimony includes no reference to them. Two, if her son later admitted to knocking the lantern over, it is possible, perhaps likely, that she would be unwilling to mention these boys when she testified, as she would not want to implicate her son in the fire's cause. However, it nonetheless seems equally likely that her son would have attempted to put out the flames or at least tried to rescue the animals after he struck the lantern; he would not have just quietly walked away and let his parents' barn and bovines go up in smoke.

Cohn's account raises other questions. There were at least two tons of hay in the loft of the O'Leary barn on the night of October 8. Did the loft contain so much hay that it would have been impractical for the boys to play craps there? Thanks to Patrick O'Leary's inquiry testimony, historians know the size of the barn. Barely larger than a shed (indeed, several firemen called it this during their own inquiry questioning), O'Leary indicated that it was twenty feet long, sixteen feet wide, and fourteen feet high. Unfortunately, little else is known about the barn or about the hay that was inside. How big was the barn's loft? Was the roof flat or sloped? If the latter, was there only one slope (shed roof) or two slopes (gable roof), and how severe was the pitch?[47]

Although Mrs. O'Leary testified that there were two tons of hay in the barn, her husband claimed that there were three tons. Who was right? The cubic footage of two (or three) tons of hay not only depends on the type of hay (some grasses and forage crops are heavier than others) but also on the moisture content (the greater the moisture level, the heavier the hay). Admittedly, historians may have information on these latter two considerations. One contemporary observer claimed that the hay allegedly delivered the day before was "timothy" hay, and this was confirmed years later by Mrs. O'Leary's son Jim. Because of the hot weather, surely the hay's moisture content was virtually nonexistent. But there is still the "compression factor." That is, as the loose hay was placed in the O'Leary barn (baled hay was not available in 1871), the upper layers of hay would compress the lower layers. Therefore, although the hay closest to the floor of the loft would be very compressed, the uppermost layer of hay would not be packed at all. Without knowing the height of the loft and the amount of hay in the loft, it would be impossible to determine the degree of hay compression. With more questions than answers, it is equally impossible to determine if the loft was completely full of hay.[48]

But even assuming that there was plenty of room in the barn for the boys to host their casino night, why would they want to? Why would the boys choose to play craps after dark in the sultry and stifling confines of a hay-filled loft, virtually under the eyes of Mr. and Mrs. O'Leary, when they just as easily could have played outside in the alley behind a fence? For that matter, there apparently was a vacant house across the alley, nearly opposite the O'Leary property. Boys in the neighborhood congregated there. If Cohn had been playing craps that night, it seems more likely that he was playing in this house or in a nearby shed. But no matter. After the fire, he continued the literary tradition established by Schaller, Callahan, and Axsmith and rewrote the history of October 8, 1871.[49]

Ultimately, just as in the earlier tales of these three revisionists, there is not one piece of evidence that supports Cohn's claim. The archives of the Chicago Historical Society contains several stories such as his, all written by people who maintained that they knew what caused the fire. Typical of these is the 1956 letter written by Mrs. August Ott in which she related a conversation between a shoe salesman and the owner of a Dixon, Illinois, shoe store. The owner told a story substantially similar to the Callahan version of the fire's cause, except that in this account the party guests were playing games instead of dancing. Almost as an afterthought, but clearly in an attempt to prove the veracity of her story, Mrs. Ott added: "The salesman said he did business with that man for years and knew him to always tell the truth." More than forty-five years later, the story is changed but the "proof" remains the same: Feinberg, in commenting on the accuracy of Cohn's account, points out that "looking him in the eye, I had no reason to doubt what he said. The man was not known to be a liar. He was quite a gentleman." But in all but one respect, Jacob John Schaller was probably a gentleman, too.[50]

A Comet, Not a Cow

Educational film director Mel Waskin contends in his book *Mrs. O'Leary's Comet* (1985) that a comet called Biela II caused not only the Chicago Fire but also huge conflagrations in Peshtigo, Wisconsin, and Manistee, Michigan. Although Waskin gets an "A" for originality, his work fails to pass serious muster as a well-reasoned treatise explaining the fire's cause.[51]

Waskin notes that fireman Michael W. Conway testified at the inquiry about seeing blue flames in basements. Conway also remarked that it appeared as if whiskey and alcohol were burning. Waskin suggests that cometary gases, which are heavier than air, settled in the basements and took fire. He adds that these gases are made up of methane and acetylene and that the components of these substances are similar to the chemicals that make up alcohol.[52]

But Waskin fails to mention that the commissioners implied that the blue color might have been caused by the burning of natural gas. Although this is possible, modern fire science indicates that the blue color was probably caused by the burning of carbon monoxide produced in the basements because of poor ventilation.[53]

Waskin points out that during the course of the fire, buildings would suddenly burst into flame. Fire would first begin eating away at the rear of these structures; then the fronts would explode without warning. He argues that this was caused by sparks and burning debris falling on buildings and igniting the cometary gases inside. On the other hand, one contemporary writer suggested that this was caused by burning brands falling through the skylights of buildings, setting fire to their contents. Again, fire science indicates the more likely cause—heat radiation. When a fire is burning in a portion of a building, the surfaces of any objects or materials that face the fire are heated by radiant heat. When the temperature of a surface reaches the ignition point of the object or material, the substance will burst into flame. In large fires the radiant heat of a burning building can even ignite adjacent buildings. Surely it was heat radiation and not cometary gases that caused these sudden eruptions of flame.[54]

Fire Marshal Williams indicated at the inquiry that initially he felt that his men could stop the fire's progress just a few blocks from the O'Leary barn—until St. Paul's Church, several blocks to the north, caught fire. Waskin contends that "what probably happened was that chunks of frozen gases broke away from the main body of Biela II and were heated to their gaseous states as they plunged through the atmosphere, fueling existing fires or igniting new ones."[55]

A more earthly cause is also the more likely. It was convection whirls, flinging flaming brands hundreds of feet ahead of the fire, that surely led to Williams' short-lived optimism. In fact, the fire marshal said as much in a letter to the *Chicago Tribune* published on November 17, 1871: "While we were working on the original fire, which was surrounded and under our control, the fearful gale which was raging at the time carried, not only sparks, but brands and pieces of boards on fire, the distance of two to four squares."[56]

Even Waskin's theories concerning the Wisconsin fires appear to be unsound. He notes that during the Peshtigo blaze, a rain of red-hot sand accompanied the firestorm. Where, asks Waskin, did this sand come from? Although there was sand on the beaches, he maintains that these lay to the East, and the wind was blowing from the West and the South. He concludes that the sand may have come from a comet, as sand is one of its elements.[57]

But Waskin fails to note that beaches were not the only source of sand in Peshtigo, that at least some of the roads were apparently covered with it. He also fails to consider the power of convection whirls. Stephen J. Pyne, author of the cultural history *Fire in America*, vividly describes them: "The turbulence from the violent convection was awesome. Winds of 60–80 mph uprooted trees like match sticks; a 1,000-pound wagon was tossed like a tumbleweed. Papers were lofted by the winds from Michigan across Lake Huron to Canada. The peculiar physics of mass fire had multiplied its fury into a maelstrom of energy equivalent to the chain reaction of a thermonuclear bomb. There was no defense for the populace but flight." The winds that could lift a wagon and uproot trees surely sucked up both beach and road sand into a hurricane of fire and hurled it upon Peshtigo's fleeing settlers[58] (Figure 59).

Waskin's book ultimately falls short because it fails to address even the basic questions relative to his theory. How could a comet streaking across the sky above Chicago go unnoticed by the city's 334,000 inhabitants? If this comet did strike Chicago, why didn't anyone report seeing it flash overhead or hearing an explosion when it struck the earth? The post-fire newspapers are silent as to any such extra-terrestrial visitor—until December 13, when the *Republican* reported that "a very brilliant meteor was seen at about 10:45 o'clock *last night* [emphasis added]." For these reasons, more than anything else, Mel Waskin's comet fails to shed any light on the cause of the Great Chicago Fire.[59]

Other Theories

Several other equally bizarre theories have been suggested since the fire burnt itself out on the prairies of nineteenth-century Chicago. Frank Luzerne wrote of three men who came to Chicago in March of 1871 to persuade the city authorities to purchase their carbonic acid gas fire extinguishing system. As the story goes, the men were initially told that their proposal would be favorably received and that the city would eventually accept it. Accordingly, they labored hard all through the summer, spending money and building an acid gas works. But in late September they learned that city officials had changed their minds and wanted nothing to do with the new extinguisher, refusing even to test it.

On Saturday, October 7, these three men passed through New York on their way home. At the depot, one of them remarked to a friend, "We have tried our best to do something for Chicago, she has kicked us out, and now she may bear the consequences." Twenty-four hours later, the entire world knew what these consequences were.[60]

Another story also involves three men—but these three were "trying out" a new terrier, hunting rats in the O'Leary barn, when one of them dropped a lighted match, starting the blaze. Another theory has a man wildly shouting during the fire, "I knew they would do it! I knew they would do it!" When asked to explain, the man replied, "The bloody Ku-Klux have done this, knowing us to have been extra loyal. They have burned our city, and it is useless for us to attempt to escape, for they will burn us up too!"[61]

Not surprisingly, other people felt that the destruction of Chicago was a punishment from on high. Some suggested that God destroyed Chicago because it was a wicked city, an 1871 Sodom and Gomorrah. Others apparently more in His inner circle knew a more specific reason for His wrath. Although some said that it was because Chicago had recently voted to allow saloons to be open on Sundays, others claimed that the fire was divine retribution

FIGURE 59—THE BURNING OF PESHTIGO, WISCONSIN. Marshall Philyaw's drawing of the Peshtigo Fire is based in part on the picture entitled "The Burning of Peshtigo" that originally appeared in the November 25, 1871, issue of *Harper's Weekly*. Mel Waskin, author of *Mrs. O'Leary's Comet*, maintains that a comet caused the Peshtigo, Wisconsin, fire (as well as the Chicago Fire), but it is more likely that the village was destroyed by a firestorm generated by the convection whirls of forest fires. Although the exact body count will never be known, it is likely that 1,200–1,300 people died horrible deaths in the Wisconsin fires (at least 600 people died in Peshtigo alone) and another 100–200 were killed the same day in the Michigan forest fires. But communications were primitive in the Wisconsin and Michigan wilderness (continuous forest fires throughout the summer had destroyed the one telegraph line leading into the Peshtigo area) and so it was Chicago, not Peshtigo, that first captured the nation's sympathies.

Father Peter Pernin was pastor of the Peshtigo Congregational Church in 1871. He published his "Eyewitness Account" of this disaster in 1874. Pernin wrote of "large wooden houses torn from their foundations and caught up like straws by two opposing currents of air which raised them till they came in contact with the stream of fire." Philyaw depicts the drama and imagery of these words in this drawing of Pernin's church being destroyed by fire and wind.

for the burning of Atlanta by Sherman's soldiers. (As the Rushville, Indiana, *Democrat* commented: "Chicago did her full share in the destruction of the South. God adjusts balances. Maybe with Chicago the books are now squared.")[62]

Chicagoans did not limit their improbable theories and wild conjectures to just the cause of the fire. Newspapers and books of the day even alleged that the blaze spread quickly because many of Chicago's buildings were built of what was described as "petroleum stone," or limestone allegedly impregnated with petroleum. This suggestion fell into disfavor when it was pointed out that the Second Presbyterian Church, the only building actually built of this material, withstood the fire better than many other stone structures.[63]

And that is how it has always been—more than one hundred years of suggestions, allegations, and speculation, ranging from the reasonable to the absurd. Through it all, though, the question has always remained: If a cow did not kick over a lantern, if hay did not spontaneously combust, if a comet did not veer off course—what, then, *did* cause the Great Chicago Fire? History books will indicate that the cause has never been determined. But these books fail to suggest that the story of the fire did not have to end with a question mark. Generations of school children did not have to grow up learning about the legend of Mrs. O'Leary's cow. Rather, they could have been reading in history class about how the fire *really* started.[64]

Notes

1. "How It Burned," *Chicago Tribune*, 27 October 1871, p. [2]; hereafter cited in text as "How It Burned."

2. "Mrs. O'Leary Cow Story Refuted by Old Reporter," sec. 2, p. 13; John Kelley, "O'Leary,

Who Would Bet on Anything, Dies," *Chicago Daily Tribune*, 23 January 1925, sec. 1, p. 1, hereafter cited in text as "O'Leary, Who Would Bet on Anything, Dies"; "Fifty Years Ago," *Chicago History* 1 (Fall 1971), p. 249, hereafter cited in text as "Fifty Years Ago"; Guy Murchie, Jr., "Linked to Chicago's Two Worst Fires—The Family O'Leary," *Chicago Sunday Tribune*, 31 March 1935, sec. 7, p. 10, hereafter cited in text as "Linked to Chicago's Two Worst Fires"; "O'Leary Defends Noted Cow," *Chicago Daily Tribune*, 30 November 1909, p. 3, hereafter cited in text as "O'Leary Defends Noted Cow"; Musham, p. 148.

3. Boyd Kidwell, "Make Hay, Not Fire," *Progressive Farmer* 111 (August 1996), p. [24], hereafter cited in text as "Make Hay, Not Fire"; Charles A. Browne, *The Spontaneous Combustion of Hay* (Washington, D.C.: United States Department of Agriculture, 1929), p. 11, hereafter cited in text as Browne; Lawrence T. Lorimer, ed., *Academic American Encyclopedia* (Danbury, Conn.: Grolier, 1995), s.v. "Spontaneous Combustion," by Stephen Fleishman; Michael Allaby, ed., *Illustrated Dictionary of Science* (Oxfordshire, England: Andromeda Oxford Limited, 1995), s.v. "Spontaneous Combustion"; *Kirk's Fire Investigation*, p. 117; "Linked to Chicago's Two Worst Fires," sec. 7, p. 10; Andreas, vol. 2, p. 714.

4. *Kirk's Fire Investigation*, p. 119; Walker, p. 23; John D. DeHaan to Richard F. Bales, 25 June 2000, hereafter cited in text as John D. DeHaan letter.

5. Catharine McLaughlin, *Inquiry*, vol. [1], p. 234; Patrick O'Leary, *Inquiry*, vol. [1], p. 251; John D. DeHaan letter; Browne, pp. 8, 22; "Make Hay, Not Fire," p. [24]; John D. DeHaan, author of *Kirk's Fire Investigation*, interview by Richard F. Bales, 1 October 2000, hereafter cited in text as John D. DeHaan interview; "How It Originated," p. [2]; *Kirk's Fire Investigation*, p. 122; Andreas, vol. 2, p. 701.

6. John D. DeHaan interview; *Kirk's Fire Investigation*, pp. 117–118, 121; John D. DeHaan letter; Catherine O'Leary, *Inquiry*, vol. [1], p. 59; Patrick O'Leary, *Inquiry*, vol. [1], p. 251; Brian Gray to Richard F. Bales, 7 December 1999; Browne, p. 11; Warren E. Roberts, "Early Log-Crib Barn Survivals," in *Barns of the Midwest*, eds. Allen G. Noble and Hubert G. H. Wilhelm (Athens: Ohio University Press, 1995), pp. 35–36.

7. John D. DeHaan letter; Andreas, vol. 2, p. 708; *Kirk's Fire Investigation*, pp. 120–21. Admittedly, it is not clear as to when the hay was delivered to the O'Leary barn. Andreas quotes Joseph Dushek, who maintained that "on Saturday, the day before the fire, I noticed a fine load of timothy

hay which was taken into the alley and unloaded into the O'Leary barn." This was confirmed by Jim O'Leary, who once reminisced, "The day before the fire—it was a Saturday—I helped the old gent [Patrick O'Leary] put in some timothy hay in the loft above the cow shed." But Jim O'Leary's recollections apparently changed over time. A 1909 *Chicago Tribune* article quoted him as saying that "the old man had put in a load of 'green' hay *a few days* before the fire." In a 1915 *Tribune* article, Michael Ahern indicated that Jim O'Leary had told him that the green hay had been placed in the loft *two weeks* before the fire [emphasis added]. See Andreas, vol. 2, p. 714; "Linked to Chicago's Two Worst Fires," sec. 7, p. 10; "O'Leary Defends Noted Cow," p. 3; "Mrs. O'Leary Cow Story Refuted by Old Reporter," sec. 2, p. 13.

8. "The Great Fire," *Chicago Evening Journal*, 12 December 1871, p. [4]; Patrick O'Leary, *Inquiry*, vol. [1], p. 252; Daniel Sullivan, *Inquiry*, vol. [1], pp. 263–64.

9. Patrick O'Leary, *Inquiry*, vol. [1], pp. 250–53; Daniel Sullivan, *Inquiry*, vol. [1], pp. 259–60.

10. Cox and Armington, p. 367; "Meteorological Observations by the United States Signal Corps, War Department, Chicago, Illinois, Register of Meteorological Observations Compiled Under the Direction of the Smithsonian Institution," Harry A. Musham Collection, Notes on the Chicago Fire, Chicago Historical Society, hereafter cited in text as "Meteorological Observations by the United States Signal Corps"; Chicago Title Insurance Company records; George Rau, *Inquiry*, vol. [1], p. 179; Catherine O'Leary, *Inquiry*, vol. [1], p. 62; Daniel Sullivan, *Inquiry*, vol. [1], pp. 259, 271–72; John D. DeHaan and Richard E. Tontarski, "The Great Chicago Fire of 1871: A Cause-and-Origin Examination of the Great Fire of 1871 (Was It Really the Cow?)," unpublished manuscript, August 1987, hereafter cited in text as De-Haan and Tontarski; Andreas, vol. 2, p. 717; Musham, pp. 95–96.

11. *Kirk's Fire Investigation*, p. 103; Chicago Title Insurance Company records.

12. "A Startling Story," *Chicago Times*, 23 October 1871, p. 1, hereafter cited in text as "A Startling Story"; Frank Jellinek, *The Paris Commune of 1871* (New York: Grosset & Dunlap, Universal Library, 1965), pp. [11]–16; Luzerne, pp. 185–96; Musham, p. 148; Smith, pp. 49–50.

13. "The Organ of the Petroleuse," *Chicago Evening Journal*, 23 October 1871, p. [2]; Untitled article, *Chicago Republican*, 10 November 1871, p. [2].

14. Sawislak, p. 47.

15. Sawislak, p. 47; Colbert and Chamberlin, p. 372; "A Startling Story," p. 1. "Petroleuse communists" were in the news at the time of the fire. See, e.g., "Women of the Commune," *Chicago Tribune*, 26 September 1871, p. [3]; David Lasswell, "Chicago Before the Fire: Some People, Places, and Things," *Chicago History* 1 (Fall 1971), pp. 200–2, hereafter cited in text as Lasswell.

16. Colbert and Chamberlin, p. 373; "Incendiaries Killed," p. 1; "Miscellaneous Items," *Chicago Tribune*, 12 October 1871, p. [3]; "Incendiary Fires," *Chicago Tribune*, 14 October 1871, p. 1, hereafter cited in text as "Incendiary Fires"; "Death to Incendiaries," *Chicago Evening Journal*, 11 October 1871, p. 1; Lasswell, pp. 200–2; Andreas, vol. 2, pp. 716, 757–58; Musham, pp. 140–41, Foster, pp. 27–28.

17. "A Defence of Fire Marshal Williams," *Chicago Tribune*, 28 November 1871, p. 6, hereafter cited in text as "A Defence of Fire Marshal Williams"; "Exaggerated Reports," *Chicago Evening Journal*, 16 October 1871, p. 1; "After the Great Fire," *Chicago Evening Journal*, 8 November 1871, p. [2]; Musham, pp. 135–36; Andreas, vol. 2, pp. 775, 780; Sheahan and Upton, pp. 66, 417; Cox and Armington, p. 368.

18. Catherine O'Leary, *Inquiry*, vol. [1], pp. 60–71 passim; Catharine McLaughlin, *Inquiry*, vol. [1], pp. 225, 241–42; Andreas, vol. 2, p. 701; Musham, p. 148; James A. Gavin to H. R. Clark, 23 March 1921, Chicago Fire of 1871 Personal Narratives Collection, Chicago Historical Society.

19. Statement of Phillip J. Sharkey.

20. John C. Miller, ed., "Mr. Ryan Sees Chicago Fire from DeKoven St.," *The West Side Historical Society Bulletin* 2 (April 1937), p. 2; Philip Kane to [Isaac Rosenfeld], 23 May 1956, Robert Allen Cromie Collection, Notes on the Chicago Fire, Chicago Historical Society; David Swing, *A Story of the Chicago Fire* (n.p.: H. H. Gross, 1892), pp. 11–12, hereafter cited in text as Swing; "Centennial Eve Reveals Truth of Great Fire," *Chicago Daily Tribune*, 26 September 1903, sec. 1, pp. 1–[2], hereafter cited in text as "Centennial Eve"; Mary Basich to Richard F. Bales, April 1998, hereafter cited in text as Mary Basich letter, April 1998; Paul T. Gilbert, "The Legend of Mrs. O'Leary's Cow," *Chicago Sun*, 24 July 1942, p. 9, hereafter cited in text as "The Legend of Mrs. O'Leary's Cow"; Edmund J. Rooney, Jr., "Mrs. O'Leary's Cow 'Exonerated,'" *Chicago Daily News*, 6 October 1962, sec. 1, p. 13; Musham, pp. 152–53; Mrs. Eda D. Hungerford to the Chicago Historical Society, 13 December 1922, Chicago Fire of 1871 Personal Narratives Collection, Chicago Historical Society. Mrs. McLaughlin never mentioned the name

of her "greenhorn" brother in her testimony. Although Callahan suggests that it was Denny Connors, the 1870 Chicago city directory and *Robinson's Atlas* indicate that a "Daniel Conners" lived half a block away at 120 DeKoven Street. See *1870 City Directory*, p. 179; *Robinson's Atlas*, vol. 1, plate 6.

21. "Centennial Eve," sec. 1, pp. 1–[2]; Catharine McLaughlin, *Inquiry*, vol. [1], pp. 225–28, 242.

22. "Centennial Eve," sec. 1, pp. 1–[2]; Catharine McLaughlin, *Inquiry*, vol. [1], p. 225.

23. Catharine McLaughlin, *Inquiry*, vol. [1], pp. 229–30.

24. Catharine McLaughlin, *Inquiry*, vol. [1], pp. 225, 228–30, 235–36, 241–42. Because of the poor penmanship of the transcript of Mrs. McLaughlin's testimony, it is impossible to determine the exact number of her guests. It is possible that "John Riley" and "Johnny Ryan" were one and the same person. But at least seven guests (and Mrs. McLaughlin's brother from Ireland) were crowded into the McLaughlin cottage on the night of the fire.

25. "Centennial Eve," sec. 1, p. [2]; Catharine McLaughlin, *Inquiry*, vol. [1], pp. 225–26.

26. Catherine O'Leary, *Inquiry*, vol. [1], pp. 60–63; Patrick O'Leary, *Inquiry*, vol. [1], pp. 245–47; Catherine Sullivan, *Inquiry*, vol. [1], pp. 115–17. Unfortunately, although Mrs. McLaughlin testified that "some persons came to the door and hollered 'fire,'" she did not indicate *who* these "persons" were. See Catharine McLaughlin, *Inquiry*, vol. [1], pp. 224, 230–31, 236.

27. "Centennial Eve," sec. 1, p. [2]; "Linked to Chicago's Two Worst Fires," sec. 7, p. 10; "Fire Alley Is Paved," *Chicago Daily Tribune*, 25 May 1894, p. 1, hereafter cited in text as "Fire Alley Is Paved"; "Fifty Years Ago," p. 249; "O'Leary Defends Noted Cow," p. 3; "O'Leary, Who Would Bet on Anything, Dies," sec. 1, p. 1.

28. Catharine McLaughlin, *Inquiry*, vol. [1], pp. 235–36; "Centennial Eve," sec. 1, p. [2]. Admittedly, McLaughlin's "Johnny Ryan" and Callahan's "Johnny Finnan" may be one and the same person. It is possible that either the *Tribune* or the inquiry shorthand reporter incorrectly transcribed the surname.

29. "Centennial Eve;" sec. 1, p. [2]; Patrick O'Leary, *Inquiry*, vol. [1], pp. 250, 252–53.

30. Catharine McLaughlin, *Inquiry*, vol. [1], pp. 223, 228–29, 235–36, 241; Catherine O'Leary, *Inquiry*, vol. [1], pp. 59, 67.

It is possible that historian A. T. Andreas believed that Mrs. McLaughlin knew who caused the fire, but that she lied to the commissioners. His

History of Chicago contains an extensive chapter entitled "The Burning of Chicago." He wrote the following in the chapter's introduction: "The precise cause of the fire is now a mystery, and must ever remain so, unless the knowledge at present withheld through fear or pride shall hereafter be revealed, as those who may know the cause *manifest a decided aversion* [emphasis added] to the subject. It is difficult to deal with people who can not be made to understand that accident is not crime, even when dreadful results ensue."

Andreas later detailed the reminiscences of some of the residents of DeKoven Street. He had this to say about Mrs. McLaughlin: "She was called upon by the compiler of this record, and asked to state what she knew about the origin of the fire. She *manifested so decided an aversion* [emphasis added] to being interviewed that little information was obtained. In fact, she threatened to 'prosecute' those engaged in writing the history, if her name were used."

Of all these residents, Mrs. McLaughlin was the only person that Andreas described as manifesting "so decided an aversion to being interviewed." Perhaps Andreas merely wrote these words in a fit of pique, angry at not being granted an interview. Or perhaps he was implying that Mrs. McLaughlin knew that one of her guests was in the barn that night. But in between two paragraphs describing the McLaughlin party, he slipped in a one-sentence editorial comment: "The evidence must stand as conclusive until, by confession of some one who has retained hidden knowledge, the truth is made known." Perhaps Andreas did believe that Mrs. McLaughlin knew who caused the fire. See Andreas, vol. 2, pp. 701, 708, 714; John Franch to Richard F. Bales, 28 November 1998; John Franch to Richard F. Bales, 30 November 1998.

31. Catharine McLaughlin, *Inquiry*, vol. [1], pp. 226–28; "How They Look and Act," p. [3]; "The Fire," *Chicago Times*, 26 November 1871, p. 1; "The Fire Investigation," *Chicago Evening Journal*, 25 November 1871, p. [4]. Why didn't the commissioners question the other guests? Is it possible that Mrs. McLaughlin told the Board that her guests left Chicago after the fire or were otherwise unavailable, but this testimony was never memorialized in the inquiry transcript? Although this possibility cannot be ruled out, note that in one other instance the calling of an additional witness *was* discussed during the proceedings and *was* preserved in the transcript. The following exchange took place during the questioning of Third Assistant Fire Marshal Mathias Benner about the possible bribery of firemen:

Q. Do you know of any other marshals that received any presents since this fire?

A. No sir, I do not.

Q. Did you hear how the money was divided? For my part, I would like to have the foreman of Ryerson's yard called here to testify in regard to this matter.

See Mathias Benner, *Inquiry*, vol. [4], pp. 184–85.

32. Andreas, vol. 1, pp. 79–80; "Centennial Eve," sec. 1, p. [2]; "Chicago's Day to Revere the Past," *Chicago Daily Tribune*, 26 September 1903, sec. 1, p. [2].

But there is one major difference between the competing claims of Callahan and Schaller. In telling her tale of the clumsy Denny Connors, Callahan (unlike Schaller) implicated third parties who could either confirm or deny her charges. She maintained that Denny Connors, Johnny Finnan, and Alice Reilly were in the barn with her when the cow upset the lamp. Although Connors was dead, she implied that Finnan was still alive and added that Alice Reilly lived on Chicago's Sixteenth Street. Why would she fabricate a story, knowing that Finnan or Reilly could easily refute her allegations? Perhaps she didn't care, thinking that it would be her word against theirs. It is possible she lied; perhaps Finnan and Reilly left the city after the fire or were deceased. Or perhaps she had already contacted them, and they had agreed to assume their roles as fictional witnesses to Connor's American milking debut in exchange for the chance to share the O'Leary limelight.

33. Untitled article, *Chicago Tribune*, 26 November 1871, p. 2. The October 5, 1971, *Wall Street Journal* refers to a 1924 *Chicago Tribune* interview with a Thomas O'Connor, who claimed that he was at the McLaughlin party and that a fellow guest named Mr. Quinlan went out to get the milk. Not surprisingly, neither Mrs. McLaughlin nor Mrs. Callahan mentioned these men in their statements about the party. See Jonathan R. Laing, "Mrs. O'Leary's Cow, Vilified for 100 Years, Maybe Wasn't Guilty," *Wall Street Journal*, 5 October 1971, p. 1, hereafter cited in text as "Mrs. O'Leary's Cow, Vilified for 100 Years, Maybe Wasn't Guilty."

34. Patrick O'Leary, *Inquiry*, vol. [1], pp. 250, 252–53.

35. S. H. Kimball to Caroline M. McIlvaine, 30 January 1914, Chicago Fire of 1871 Personal Narratives Collection, Chicago Historical Society; Statement of Phillip J. Sharkey; Musham, p. 153; *Reminiscences of Chicago During the Great Fire*, pp. xvi–xviii; Andreas, vol. 2, pp. 714–15; "Greatest Fire in History Sweeps Heart of Chicago; Loss Set

at \$196,000,000," *Chicago Evening Post*, 8 October 1921, Chicago Fire Edition, sec. 1, p. 3; *1870 City Directory*, p. 240. (With so many people finding so many pieces of The Lamp, one cannot help but think that if they had dug further into the barn's detritus, they would have also found charred splinters of The Cross.)

36. DeHaan and Tontarski; John D. DeHaan interview; John D. DeHaan letter.

37. Luzerne, pp. 91–92; Martha Murphy, "Mrs. O'Leary's Cow Slandered, Say Ex-Firemen," *Chicago Daily Tribune*, 5 October 1942, sec. 1, p. 14, hereafter cited in text as "Mrs. O'Leary's Cow Slandered"; John Kelley 1927 letter. It appears that Luzerne was an exception to many of the contemporary authors of fire histories. Sewell, Goodspeed, Sheahan and Upton, and Colbert and Chamberlin, undoubtedly hoping to capitalize on the nation's fascination with the fire, must have rushed their books to their respective publishers within weeks of the blaze, as their histories are all dated 1871. Luzerne's book is dated 1872.

38. "Meteorological Observations by the United States Signal Corps"; Cox and Armington, p. 367; Catharine McLaughlin, *Inquiry*, vol. [1], pp. 238–39; George Rau, *Inquiry*, vol. [1], p. 179; Daniel Sullivan, *Inquiry*, vol. [1], pp. 259–61, 271–72; Patrick O'Leary, *Inquiry*, vol. [1], pp. 250, 252–53; Catherine O'Leary, *Inquiry*, vol. [1], pp. 59, 77–78; "How It Originated," p. [2]; Andreas, vol. 2, p. 714.

39. "Beer, Not Milk, Caused Chicago Fire, New Story," *Chicago Sunday Tribune*, 9 October 1921, sec. 1, p. 3, hereafter cited in text as "Beer, Not Milk, Caused Chicago Fire"; Statement of Anton Axsmith, "The Chicago Fire of October 9th 1871," n.d., Chicago Fire of 1871 Personal Narratives Collection, Chicago Historical Society; Statement of Catherine Jefferson, [23 November 1932], Chicago Fire of 1871 Personal Narratives Collection, Chicago Historical Society; Oney Fred Sweet, "Mrs. O'Leary's Bossy Ruined His Night Off," *Chicago Sunday Tribune*, 6 October 1929, Metropolitan Section (SW), p. 1.

40. Chicago Title Insurance Company records.

41. "Fire Day Program," *Chicago Sunday Tribune*, 9 October 1921, sec. 1, p. 3.

42. Andreas, vol. 2, p. 701; Musham, p. 148; "New York Post Has Its Say as to O'Leary Cow," *Chicago Evening Post*, 8 October 1921, Chicago Fire Edition, sec. 3, p. 10; "O'Leary Defends Noted Cow," p. 3; "Kin of O'Leary Absolves Cow in Fire of 1871," *Chicago Sunday Tribune*, 8 October 1933, sec. 1, p. 4, hereafter cited in text as "Kin of O'Leary Absolves Cow in Fire of 1871"; Catharine

McLaughlin, *Inquiry*, vol. [1], pp. 231–32; Daniel Sullivan, *Inquiry*, pp. 271, 274. In his reminiscences, John J. McKenna combines two "cause of the fire" theories, recalling that "some of the boys said the gang was at the rear of the barn rushing the can and smoking cigars and left the lamp where the cow tipped it over; but that's a long time ago and has not been proven as yet." At first this comment seems inconsistent with his suggestion, discussed in chapter two, that children made up the story of the cow kicking over the lamp. But it is possible that this tale of youthful cigar smokers is just one of several stories concocted by neighborhood children in the first few hours after the fire. See 1933 McKenna, p. 6. ("Rushing the can" is apparently a slang expression for drinking beer. See "Kin of O'Leary Absolves Cow in Fire of 1871," sec. 1, p. 4; "Beer, Not Milk, Caused Chicago Fire," sec. 1, p. 3.)

43. Alan Wykes, *The Complete Illustrated Guide to Gambling* (New York: Doubleday & Co., 1964), pp. 146–47.

44. Anthony DeBartolo, "Who Caused the Great Chicago Fire?: A Possible Deathbed Confession," *Chicago Tribune*, 8 October 1997, sec. 5, pp. 1, 3; Anthony DeBartolo, "Odds Improve that a Hot Game of Craps in Mrs. O'Leary's Barn Touched Off Chicago Fire," *Chicago Tribune*, 3 March 1998, sec. 5, pp. 1, 3, hereafter cited in text as "Odds Improve"; "$35,000 Estate Goes Into Scholarships," *Chicago Sun*, 29 September 1944, p. 24; "Cohn Estate Turned Over to University," *Chicago Daily News*, 28 September 1944, sec. 1, p. 12, hereafter cited in text as "Cohn Estate Turned Over to University."

45. "Odds Improve," p. 3.

46. Catherine O'Leary, *Inquiry*, vol. [1], pp. 59, 66.

47. "The Great Fire," *Chicago Tribune*, 26 November 1871, p. 1; Catherine O'Leary, *Inquiry*, vol. [1], p. 59; Patrick O'Leary, *Inquiry*, vol. [1], p. 251; George Rau, *Inquiry*, vol. [1], p. 158; Lewis Fiene, *Inquiry*, vol. [1], p. 194; John Campion, *Inquiry*, vol. [3], p. 38; Mathias Benner, *Inquiry*, vol. [4], p. 126; Ingolf Vogeler, "Dairying and Dairy Barns in the Northern Midwest," in *Barns of the Midwest*, eds. Allen G. Noble and Hubert G. H. Wilhelm (Athens: Ohio University Press, 1995), pp. 105–6; H. Armstrong Roberts, *The Farmer His Own Builder* (Philadelphia: David McKay, 1918), pp. 146–48.

48. Andreas, vol. 2, p. 714; Catherine O'Leary, *Inquiry*, vol. [1], p. 59; Patrick O'Leary, *Inquiry*, vol. [1], p. 251; Robert Steinkamp to Richard F. Bales, 17 March 1998; Ingolf Vogeler to Richard F. Bales, 1 December 1997; Ingolf Vogeler to Richard F.

Bales, 23 January 1998; "Linked to Chicago's Two Worst Fires," sec. 7, p. 10.

Daniel Trentworthy is a novel centered around the Chicago Fire that John McGovern wrote scarcely a generation after October 8, 1871. Although it is fictional, McGovern alludes to Patrick O'Leary, James Dalton, and the other residents of DeKoven Street. The book contains a lengthy description of the O'Leary barn: "We have an inclosure fronting the alley, twenty feet; backing from the alley, sixteen feet.... Seven feet to the top of the lower floor; ten-foot side-boards along the alley, fourteen-foot side-boards along the inside; a roof that shall slant from the top of the fourteen-foot sideboards to the top of the ten-foot side boards at the alley; a floor above that partly covers the ground area; sideboards all around, that are nailed in perpendicular position; cleats over the joints of sides and roof; an eight-foot gate; an eight-foot board fence running forty feet to the rear of the cottage on both sides."

Remarkably, the barn's dimensions (sixteen feet wide, twenty feet long, fourteen feet high) are the same as noted by Patrick O'Leary in his inquiry testimony. McGovern's description is of a barn with a shed roof, i.e., a roof with only one plane or slope. Ironically, the May 25, 1894, *Tribune* includes a picture of "the shed built on the place where Mrs. O'Leary's stable stood." This building also has a shed roof. A drawing of the O'Leary barn, as described by McGovern, appears in Figure 60.

How realistic is this drawing? Is it possible that *Daniel Trentworthy* contains an accurate description of the O'Leary barn? Historians will probably never know, but it is clear that the book contains a good deal of fact as well as fiction. John McGovern, who was twenty-one years old at the time of the fire, had worked as typesetter, proofreader, and night editor at the *Tribune*. He later became an editorial writer for the *Chicago Herald* and then editor of the *Illustrated World's Fair*, a publication devoted to news of the Columbian Exposition. It appears that McGovern was concerned about including accurate background information in his book; not only does he mention such prominent Chicago Fire personages as Patrick McLaughlin and his wife's greenhorn brother, he also includes such obscure minutiae as the plat of subdivision lot number of the O'Leary property. McGovern's newspaper contacts might have given him access to the inquiry transcript which the Board noted in its final report was "on file for reference." He might even have been able to examine the inquiry diagrams that the commissioners referred to throughout the investigation—diagrams

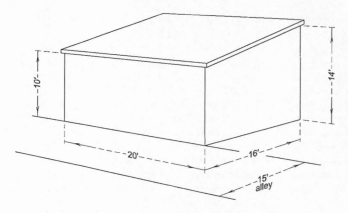

FIGURE 60—THE O'LEARY BARN, AS DESCRIBED BY JOHN MC-
GOVERN IN *DANIEL TRENTWORTHY*. **Although John Mc-
Govern's book *Daniel Trentworthy* is fictional, it does
include references to Patrick O'Leary and his neigh-
bors. This drawing of the O'Leary barn is based on
McGovern's lengthy description. Although histori-
ans will probably never know if McGovern's account
of the barn is accurate, it is consistent with Mr.
O'Leary's inquiry testimony. (Diagram by Douglas A.
Swanson)**

that possibly could have disclosed what the O'Leary
barn looked like. It seems at least possible that his
desire for accuracy might have led him to include
an exact description of the O'Leary barn in his
novel. See John McGovern, *Daniel Trentworthy: A
Tale of the Great Fire of Chicago* (Chicago: Rand,
McNally & Co., 1889), pp. 176–79, hereafter cited
in text as McGovern; Smith, p. 289; "Fire Alley is
Paved, p. 1, "The Great Fire," *Chicago Evening Journal*, 12 December 1871, p. [4].

49. Chicago Title Insurance Company rec-
ords; Daniel Sullivan, *Inquiry*, vol. [1], pp. 271–72,
274.

50. Mrs. August Ott to Isaac Rosenfeld, 23
June 1956, Robert Allen Cromie Collection, Notes
on the Chicago Fire, Chicago Historical Society;
"Odds Improve," p. 3. Mrs. Ott wrote Rosenfeld
that she read a letter to the editor in the *Daily
News* that recounted this conversation between the
shoe salesman and the shoe store owner. This story
is almost identical to William Parrett's account
that was published in the *Tribune* in 1921. Parrett
wrote a letter to the newspaper in response to an
article written by reporter Michael Ahern. Parrett,
a salesman, said in this letter that Thomas Southwell, who ran a shoe store, told him that he and
some other boys were in the O'Leary barn on the
night of the fire. Some of these boys started the
fire while milking the cow. In this version, however, Parrett sold fire extinguishers, not shoes, and

the shoe store was in Wenona, Illinois, not Dixon. Nonetheless, Southwell's story is obviously fabricated.
Southwell, like Jacob Schaller, assumed that Mrs. O'Leary owned only
one cow. Also, Southwell claimed that
Mrs. O'Leary invited him and the
other boys into the barn to milk the
cow. If this were true, surely Mrs.
O'Leary would have mentioned it
during the inquiry. See William Parrett, "Kicking Over the Cow Legend,"
Chicago Sunday Tribune, 16 October
1921, sec. 1, p. [8].

51. Mel Waskin, *Mrs. O'Leary's
Comet: Cosmic Causes of the Great Chicago Fire* (Chicago: Academy Chicago
Publishers, 1985), pp. 53–54, 143–44,
hereafter cited in text as Waskin; Paul
Galloway, "Mrs. O'Leary's Comet,"
Chicago Tribune, 13 December 1985,
sec. 5, pp. 1, 3, hereafter cited in text
as Galloway.

52. Waskin, pp. 122–23, 125;
Michael W. Conway, *Inquiry*, vol. [2],
pp. 11½–13; Michael C. Hickey, *In-
quiry*, vol. [2], pp. 152–53; Peter T.
Burtis, *Inquiry*, vol. [3], pp. 65–66; Robert A.
Williams, *Inquiry*, vol. [4], p. 268; "The Fire," *Chi-
cago Times*, 28 November 1871, p. [4]; "The Great
Fire," *Chicago Tribune*, 26 November 1871, p. 1.

53. Thomas Byrne, *Inquiry*, vol. [2], pp. 137–
39; "Story of the Great Chicago Fire," sec. 3, p. 20;
"On the Defensive," p. 4; "The Gas Works," p. 2;
"The Great Fire," *Chicago Evening Journal*, 29 November 1871, p. [4]; *Kirk's Fire Investigation*, pp.
84–85.

54. Waskin, p. 127; *Kirk's Fire Investigation*,
pp. 28–29; "A Defence of Fire Marshal Williams,"
p. 6; "Sky Lights and the Fire," *Chicago Evening
Journal*, 29 November 1871, p. [4]; Cox and Armington, p. 368.

55. Waskin, pp. 74, 127; Galloway, p. 3; Robert A. Williams, *Inquiry*, vol. [4], pp. 243–48 passim; "Story of the Great Chicago Fire," sec. 3, p. 20;
"On the Defensive," p. 4; Cromie, inside front cover.

56. Cox and Armington, p. 368; *Kirk's Fire
Investigation*, p. 28; "On the Defensive," p. 4; Andreas, vol. 2, pp. 725, 743; "A Defence of Fire Marshal Williams," p. 6.

57. Waskin, pp. 90, 143–44.

58. Colbert and Chamberlin, p. 491; Goodspeed, p. 552; Pyne, p. 206; Robert W. Wells, *Fire
at Peshtigo* (Englewood Cliffs, N.J.: Prentice-Hall,
1968), pp. 199–214 passim, hereafter cited in text
as Wells.

59. Lois Warburton, *The Chicago Fire* (San Diego: Lucent Books, 1989), p. [51]; "Chicago Condensed," *Chicago Republican,* 13 December 1871, p. [4]. So what did cause the Peshtigo Fire? The northeastern part of Wisconsin had been dotted with dozens of fires since September. By the first week of October, the situation had become a crisis, with even the Chicago newspapers running lengthy articles featuring headlines such as "Wisconsin Ablaze." Most of these fires had been set by farmers for the purpose of clearing land, but other fires had been started by hunters, lumberjacks, railroad workers, and locomotives. In his book *Fire at Peshtigo,* Robert W. Wells theorizes that on the night of October 8, winds fanned these small blazes into bigger ones. Heat radiation from these separate fires may have ignited nearby underbrush, logging debris, and other combustible material, creating even larger fires as the individual blazes merged together. Wells suggests that above the heavier, smoke-laden air of northeastern Wisconsin was a layer of colder air. This cold air mass initially suppressed the convection whirls that these original smaller fires generated, causing them to burn sluggishly. When the swirling, overheated air of the combined convection whirls finally broke through the blanket of cooler air above it, it was as if a giant furnace damper had been opened. The hot air rushed skyward and the colder air swept in from all sides towards the column of rising air. This updraft created a firestorm that ravaged approximately one thousand square miles. It incinerated the village of Peshtigo and other settlements and farms in both Wisconsin and Michigan. Wells, pp., 169, 190–91, 209–13; Stewart H. Holbrook, *Burning an Empire: The Story of American Forest Fires* (New York: Macmillan Co., 1943), pp. 69–73, hereafter cited in text as Holbrook; "Forest Fires in the West," *Harper's Weekly* 15 (November 25, 1871), p.1109, hereafter cited in text as "Forest Fires in the West"; Pyne, pp. [199]–206; Peter Pernin, *The Great Peshtigo Fire: An Eyewitness Account,* 2d ed. (Madison: State Historical Society of Wisconsin, 1999), pp. 7, 12, 60–61, hereafter cited in text as Pernin; "Peshtigo Blaze Classified As Rare Fire Storm," *Peshtigo Times* (Peshtigo, Wis.), Special Edition, 7 October 1998, sec. B, p. B-20; "The Fire in Kewaunee, Wis.," *Chicago Tribune,* 28 September 1871, p. [3]; "Fires," *Chicago Tribune,* 5 October 1871, p. [4]; "Wisconsin Ablaze," *Chicago Republican,* 5 October 1871, p. 1; "Fires in the Woods," *Chicago Tribune,* 6 October 1871, p. [2];

"Conflagrations," *Chicago Tribune,* 7 October 1871, p. 1; "The Wiscon[s]in and Michigan Fires," *Chicago Tribune,* 16 October 1871, p. [3]; "A Tempest of Fire," *Chicago Tribune,* 3 November 1871, p. 1.

60. Luzerne, pp. 184–85.

61. Cromie, p. 30; Goodspeed, p. 229; "The Legend of Mrs. O'Leary's Cow," p. 9. At the time of the fire, the press was writing about atrocities allegedly committed by the Ku-Klux. See, e.g., "Ku-Klux," *Chicago Tribune,* 23 September 1871, p. [2]; "The Ku-Klux Convictions," *Chicago Tribune,* 27 September 1871, p. [2].

62. Lloyd Lewis and Henry Justin Smith, *Chicago: The History of its Reputation* (New York: Harcourt, Brace and Co., 1929), pp. 134–35, hereafter cited in text as Lewis and Smith; Cromie, p. 278; Pierce, vol. 2, p. 477; "A Mystery Solved," *Chicago Tribune,* 13 December 1871, p. 4; Untitled article, *Chicago Tribune,* 16 November 1871, p. 4; Untitled article, *Chicago Tribune,* 25 November 1871, p. 4; "Doctors Disagree," *Chicago Evening Journal,* 20 November 1871, p. [4]; "Southern Feeling Toward Chicago," *Chicago Evening Journal,* 24 November 1871, p. [2]. The November 24, 1871, *Evening Journal* contained the following item: "One of the 'lost cause' adherents who lived on the line of Sherman's march to the sea, proposes a novel subscription for Chicago. He offers to give a hundred bundles of hay to the cow that kicked over the kerosene lamp in the stable on DeKoven Street!" See untitled article, *Chicago Evening Journal,* 24 November 1871, p. [2].

63. Colbert and Chamberlin, p. 372; Sheahan and Upton, pp. 277–80; "How It Burned," p. [2]; Goodspeed, pp. 225–26; "The Oil Stone Story," *Chicago Tribune,* 30 October 1871, p. 1; "An Architect's Opinions of the Fire," *Chicago Tribune,* 6 December 1871, p. 3; Untitled article, *Chicago Evening Journal,* 7 December 1871, p. [2]; "Fire Scraps," (*Chicago*) *Daily Inter Ocean,*" 9 October 1893, sec. 1, p. [2].

64. For a discussion of some of the lesser-known theories concerning the cause of the Chicago Fire, see "The Legend of Mrs. O'Leary's Cow," p. 9; Oney Fred Sweet, "Fighter of '71 Blames Fire on Cow's Ire," *Chicago Sunday Tribune,* 6 October 1929, Metropolitan Section (NW), p. 1. The October 21, 1871, *Chicago Times* sarcastically comments that "the fire has been entirely owing to the former existence of slavery in this country." See untitled article, *Chicago Times,* 21 October 1871, p. [2].

• *Chapter Four* •

The Real Cause

[Daniel Sullivan] went across the street and cried "fire" "fire," and went into O'Leary's barn, where he found the hay in the loft on fire. He then attempted to cut loose the cows and horse, but failed to save anything but a half burned calf. He then came to O'Leary's and found them out of bed. [Dennis Regan] alarmed them during his time at the barn.

—*Chicago Tribune*, October 20, 1871

On December 12, 1871, Chicago newspapers published the results of the Board of Police and Fire Commissioners' investigation into the "origin and spread" of the fire. The commissioners claimed in this report that they were unable to determine the fire's cause. But was this really the case? DeKoven Street residents Daniel Sullivan and Dennis Regan were two of the fifty witnesses who testified before these commissioners. A careful analysis of their testimony, together with information gleaned from Sullivan's sworn affidavit that was published in the *Chicago Tribune* more than a month before Sullivan testified, indicates that it is quite possible that the commissioners *could* have determined the cause of the fire. The conclusions drawn from the statements of Daniel Sullivan and Dennis Regan, who were neighbors of the O'Learys, cannot be brushed aside as easily as the claims of Jacob Schaller, Mary Callahan, and Louis Cohn.[1]

Daniel "Peg Leg" Sullivan and His Testimony

Daniel "Peg Leg" Sullivan lived across the street from the O'Learys at 134 DeKoven Street. He was nicknamed "Peg Leg" because of his wooden leg. (He apparently lost the original in a railroad accident.) Little is known of Sullivan other than that information contained in his inquiry testimony and in a few reminiscences. He was a drayman, or cart driver, by trade, and by 1871 he had worked at this profession for at least fifteen years. He must have been fairly successful, apparently delivering oil for a local oil company, as he owned five horses at the time of the fire. He was then about twenty-six years old.[2]

Daniel Sullivan testified before the commissioners and fire marshals on November 25, 1871. When the officials asked him, "Do you know anything about the origin of the fire Sunday night, October

8, that there was back of Leary's?" he replied:

> I went across the street over to Leary's and went in there. When I got into Leary's house, both him and his wife and three young ones was in bed. The youngest one and the oldest one was up. I asked what was the reason they went to bed so soon, and the old woman said she didn't feel very well. I stayed there, as near as I could think of it, very near an hour and maybe more.... I went out of [the] house, went across the street on the other side of the street where I lived myself—one lot east of me—and I stayed there a little while. There was a little house belonging to Leary that was in the front. There was a party there, and I stayed there as long as from about twenty minutes past nine to twenty-five minutes past nine. Said I, "It is time for me to go in and go to bed." Just as I turned around, I saw a fire in Leary's barn. I got up and run across the street and kept hollering, "fire, fire, fire." I couldn't run very quick. I could holler loud enough but could not run. At the time I passed Learys' house, there was nobody stirring in Learys' house. I made right straight in the barn, thinking when I could get the cows loose, they would go out of the fire. I knew a horse could not be got out of a fire unless he be blinded, but I didn't know but cows could. I turned to the left-hand side. I knew there was four cows tied in that end. I made at the cows and loosened them as quick as I could. I got two of them loose, but the place was too hot. I had to run when I saw the cows were not getting out. I was going along [the] right side of the wall. The boards were wet, my legs slipped out from me, and I went down. I stood up again, and I was so close to the wall, I could hold on to something and made for the door.[3]

Later in his testimony, Sullivan clarified his location, stating that he was sitting on the sidewalk, by a fence "at the head of White's house or head of his lot." William White did own land east of Sullivan's property; it was across the street, on the south side of DeKoven Street, and southeast of the O'Leary and McLaughlin homes. But in 1871 William White owned not one but two separate tracts of land. These two adjoining properties, a "west parcel" and an "east parcel," were each twenty-five feet wide. In front of which one did Sullivan sit? As explained in Appendix B and as illustrated in Figure 54, it was probably the "west parcel."[4]

Cracks in Sullivan's Testimony

Daniel Sullivan told the commissioners and marshals that he left the O'Leary home, walked across the street, and walked east, *past his own house*, to the property of William White. Although his testimony is unclear, it appears that he remained in front of White's house for as long as twenty or twenty-five minutes, sitting on the sidewalk by a fence, which was probably located along the front lot line between DeKoven Street and William White's property.[5]

Why did Sullivan do this? Why did Sullivan walk across the street, walk past his own home, and sit in front of White's house for what may have been almost half an hour? Mr. McLaughlin had played his fiddle during the party that evening, and some historians have suggested that Sullivan sat in front of White's home in order to enjoy the music. McLaughlin, though, played only two times, just long enough for Mrs. McLaughlin's brother to dance a polka. It seems doubtful that this music would have lasted twenty or twenty-five minutes. More conclusive is the fact that Mrs. McLaughlin testified at the inquiry that the fire started half an hour *after* her husband finished playing. Mrs. O'Leary's testimony indicates that she heard this music. Unfortunately, it does not confirm Mrs. McLaughlin's inquiry statement that her husband was not playing the fiddle when the fire started. On the other hand, O'Leary does not contradict McLaughlin either. When Mrs. O'Leary was asked if there was dancing "going on at the time the fire broke out," she merely replied, "I could not tell you, sir."[6]

Despite O'Leary's noncommittal answer, it does seem that Sullivan was not sitting in front of White's house in order to listen to the music. There would have been no reason for Mrs. McLaughlin to lie to the commissioners and marshals. In fact, it would have been in her best interests to tell the officials that the fire started *while* her husband was playing, as they might reasonably infer that her guests were inside the house enjoying the concert and not outside in the barn stealing milk.

One might think that Sullivan sat by White's fence in order to take in the festive sounds of the McLaughlin party emanating from their front door, which opened up onto a small wooden porch overlooking DeKoven Street (Figure 47). But if Sullivan had wanted to do this, he probably would have sat directly in front of the McLaughlin home or in front of his own house. He would not have crossed the street, walked past his own home, and sat down in front of a neighbor's house. The commissioners and marshals never asked Sullivan to explain why he chose to sit at this particular location.[7]

In fact, the fire officials failed to ask Sullivan several things. Sullivan said, for example, that after the fire broke out "everyone made an alarm...." The commissioners and marshals never asked him who "everyone" was so that these persons might be interviewed. Also, the transcript of the inquiry investigation and the *Tribune's* summary of the proceedings indicates that Mrs. McLaughlin was the second witness to testify on November 25 and that Sullivan was the fourth. After hearing Mrs. McLaugh-

lin's testimony about her party, the fire officials should have questioned Sullivan extensively about what he might have seen or heard that night. They should have asked Sullivan such questions as:

- "The porch of the McLaughlin cottage fronted on DeKoven Street. From your position across the street, how good a view did you have of this porch? If someone had left the home during the party, would you have been able to see this person leaving?"
- "Did you hear anyone walking around the McLaughlin home before the fire broke out?"
- "Mrs. McLaughlin has given us the names of the people who were at the party. Do you know any of these people? If anyone left during the party, would you have been able to recognize that person from where you sat across the street?"
- "What time did the music stop? Did it stop, as Mrs. McLaughlin testified, about half an hour before the fire started?"[8]

Instead, their questions were perfunctory at best. They merely asked Sullivan in very general terms if he saw anybody going in or out of the McLaughlins' house or going through the O'Learys' yard. These were vaguely leading questions, inviting answers limited to whether or not he had seen anyone *before* the fire started, thus leaving unasked the equally important question as to whether or not he had seen anyone go into the home or yard *after* the fire began. The officials' line of questioning probably stems from Mrs. O'Leary's earlier testimony in which she stated that Mrs. White told her that someone from the McLaughlin party entered the barn that evening to milk the cow:

[Mrs. White] said—the first she told me she mentioned a man was in my barn milking my cows. I could not tell, for I didn't see it. The next morning I went over there. She told me it was too bad for Leary to have all what he was worth lost. We did not know who done it. Said she some of the neighbors there was someone from the party went and milked the cows.[9]

Incredibly, the commissioners or marshals never asked Mrs. White to identify this man. In fact, the commissioners, who publicly declared that their mission was to investigate the cause of the fire, never even bothered to question Mrs. White at all during the course of their investigation! The fire obviously displaced thousands of people, but because Mrs. White lived on the south side of DeKoven Street, outside of the "burnt district," she was not one of them. But even if she were, the officials did not even bother to ask Mrs. O'Leary if Mrs. White was still in the area and whether or not she would be available to testify.[10]

Sullivan's Testimony Crumbles— He Could Not Have Seen the Fire

By utilizing Chicago real estate records, inquiry testimony, post-fire photographs, and other information from historical works on the fire, it is possible to graphically reproduce the O'Leary property and surrounding area. Even improvements such as an adjoining fence and various buildings have been located on this diagram with reasonable accuracy (Figure 54).

When one examines Sullivan's testimony through the lens of this diagram, several startling conclusions are revealed:

- Sullivan could not have seen the fire from his position in front of William White's house, as at least one neighboring home blocked his view.

Sullivan testified that while in front of White's house, "I saw a fire in Leary's barn." But Figure 54 discloses that this would have been impossible. Regardless of where Sullivan sat along the front line of White's two parcels, his view of the barn would have been completely blocked by the home of James and Catherine Dalton, located immediately east of the O'Leary and McLaughlin homes. Admittedly, Andreas comments that the Dalton house was built four feet off the ground on cedar posts. Although one might think that the area between the home and the ground was open, thus affording Sullivan a view of the burning barn, this was probably not the case. Post-fire pictures of the O'Leary property reveal that the McLaughlin house was also built several feet above the ground, but that the space between the home and the ground was completely covered by wooden boards (Figures 47 and 53). It seems likely that the Dalton house next door would have been similarly constructed. Also, if Sullivan had seen the fire only because of this open area, it is at least possible that he would have mentioned it during the inquiry proceedings. Finally, the Board of Police and Fire Commissioners commented after its investigation that in the O'Leary neighborhood, "wood shavings [were] piled in every form and under every house...." If there were shavings under the Dalton house, they probably would have blocked Sullivan's view of the barn.[11]

But even assuming that there was this open space, Walter Forbes' home, which was east of and next to the Dalton house, almost certainly would have obstructed Sullivan's view (see Appendix B). Finally, an eight-foot-high fence ran from Dalton's house to his shed, located at the rear of his property; this also may have blocked Sullivan's view of the barn.[12]

Had the fire started in the hay loft of

the barn and thus first broken through the roof, one might argue that perhaps Sullivan saw the fire above Dalton's house. However, Sullivan testified that when he entered the barn, the fire had not yet broken through the roof.[13]

Sullivan stated in a sworn affidavit that when he went into the O'Leary barn, "he found the hay in the loft on fire." This affidavit was published in the October 20, 1871, *Chicago Tribune* and is reprinted in Appendix C. Sullivan's comments were concerned with what and where the fire was burning when he entered the barn— that is, it was the *hay* in the *loft*. A few weeks later, though, when Sullivan testified at the inquiry, he completely changed his remarks concerning both elements of this affidavit—he told the Board and marshals that he did not know what was on fire, and he claimed that the fire was in the lower portion of the barn:

Q. [Now?] did I understand you to say that the fire was in the upper or lower portions of the barn when you went in?
A. In the lower portion.
Q. What seemed to be on fire?
A. I couldn't tell. I got excited.
Q. It was filled with fire?
A. It was all smoke and fire and flames.
Q. You could not tell whether the fire was above?
A. No, the fire was from below.[14]

Incredibly, the fire officials never questioned him about the inconsistencies between his earlier published affidavit and this testimony. In fact, they never questioned him about anything else, either. These questions and answers are the final statements made during Sullivan's questioning before the commissioners and marshals.[15]

Nonetheless, it seems almost certain that Sullivan did not see the fire above Dalton's house. Sullivan never claimed in either the affidavit or his testimony that when he first saw the fire, it had broken through the roof of the barn. Furthermore, it appears that Dalton's home was at least two stories high, so it was probably taller than the O'Leary barn which, according to Mr. O'Leary, was only fourteen feet in height.[16]

Dalton's house was one of the first buildings to be destroyed by the fire. It is possible that Forbes's home also burned down. One might be tempted to excuse the fire officials from failing to address the incongruity of Sullivan's testimony, as any buildings that blocked Sullivan's line of sight were not in existence at the time of the inquiry. Therefore, his claims as to seeing the fire from across the street could not be verified or challenged by the commissioners or marshals.[17]

It is quite likely, though, that on November 25, 1871, the day Sullivan testified, debris from the burned buildings still littered the area where the houses were, and thus the original locations of the buildings were probably still discernable (Figures 31, 47). Admittedly, post-fire cleanup in some parts of the city was immediate and swift. Gangs of laborers, hired to clear away the rubble from the areas destroyed by the fire, did yeomen's work in undertaking this urban renewal of Chicago. As William Brown wrote on November 2, 1871: "It is astonishing to take a walk through the 'burnt district' and look at the ruins; they seem to be alive and walking off, they disappear so *fast* [emphasis in original]." It appears, however, that Brown was writing about the North and South Sides of Chicago. It seems doubtful that workers were as diligent in the hardscrabble warrens of the city's West Side. The December 14, 1871, *Chicago Times*, for example, featured an article subtitled "Progress of Rebuilding in the Conflagration's Cradle." The author claimed that "the only sign of resurrection in the block between DeKoven and Forquer streets is a diminutive shanty, in which Mrs. O'Leary's famous bovine is supposed to be on exhibition."[18]

But even if the West Side laborers were every bit as industrious as their North and South Side brethren in carting away the fire's debris, this still does not excuse the commissioners and marshals. Throughout much of the investigation, and especially throughout Sullivan's testimony, the Board utilized detailed diagrams that indicated not only the location of destroyed buildings in the area, but even such minutiae as the location of the doors of said buildings. Consider, for example, the following exchange between the officials and fireman Lewis Fiene, who testified the same day as Sullivan:

Q. This is Jefferson Street? (Showing diagram)

A. Yes sir.

Q. This is DeKoven?

A. Yes sir.

Q. I presume here was located some buildings ("a"). Here was a small alleyway (marked "b") and here is an alley in the rear of this building (marked "c"). Which way did you go in from Jefferson Street?

A. We run up Jefferson Street and stopped about there (marked "d").[19]

The commissioners introduced Sullivan to these visual aids shortly after he began testifying:

Q. Suppose now that to be the barn (indicating on diagram). You say that when you went in, you knew the cows were at the west end of the barn?

A. Yes sir, four of them.

Q. About where was the door situated?

A. Here was the door, right within a little ways of this corner (a) and the horse stood in that end. The cows stood in the furthest corner. (b) On this end there was four cows tied. That was the west end of it.

Q. They were shut off into stalls?

A. No, only they were all tied, one by one by a rope.

Q. The door was here? (c)

A. The door was here (c). As I came in here, I went to the left where the four cows were tied. The two cows first, that is the two I got loose. They didn't get out. The flames were most through the barn altogether.[20]

There appears to be no explanation for the officials' failure to question Sullivan's testimony, as these diagrams certainly would have disclosed that he would have been unable to see the O'Leary barn from his position across the street.[21]

Sullivan obviously knew the location of the Dalton home. Surely he realized that it blocked his view of the barn. Why did he state that he was in front of White's house? Perhaps Sullivan did not know that the commissioners had prepared these diagrams. The inquiry transcript indicates that the Board did not use them during Sullivan's testimony until *after* Sullivan testified about sitting across the street. Also, debris from the burned homes might have been so pervasive (or non-existent) throughout the area that Sullivan may have simply failed to realize that the Dalton home (and very likely the Forbes house) would have blocked his line of sight.[22]

Is it possible that Sullivan saw the smoke of the burning barn rising above Dalton's house? If that were the case, then the location and height of these buildings would be irrelevant. But such a possibility seems unlikely. The 1871 *Tribune Almanac* reveals that the sun set at 5:31 P.M. on October 8, leaving in its wake a moonless autumn evening. At the time the fire started, therefore, there would have been no natural light by which Sullivan could have seen the smoke.[23]

What about artificial light? Although gas street lights were present in 1871, they probably did not illuminate Mrs. O'Leary's home. There were 533 miles of streets in Chicago at the time of the fire, but only 195 miles were lit by gas lamps, and it appears that there were only sixty miles of gas mains on Mrs. O'Leary's West Side. Post-fire photographs reveal that DeKoven Street was unpaved, apparently a dirt roadway (Figure 50). As this street was hardly Chicago's epicenter, it is doubtful that it was one of the fortunate avenues that enjoyed outdoor lighting. The O'Learys used wood, wood shavings, and coal for fuel, so gas service was probably not even available. It seems likely that on this dark evening the normal autumn haze, possibly augmented by drifting smoke from Saturday night's fire (the Lull & Holmes planing mill was only about ten blocks away, but admittedly north of the O'Leary home and thus upwind at the time their barn caught fire) would have made it difficult, if not impossible, for Sullivan to notice the smoke of the burning O'Leary barn. Most important, though, is the fact that Sullivan did not testify that he saw *smoke*; rather, he specifically stated at the inquiry that "just as I turned around, I saw a *fire* in Leary's barn. I got up and run across the street...." He later added that "the *fire* was breaking out the side of the barn *when I first saw it* [emphasis added]." Consequently, the suggestion that Sullivan spotted the smoke or even the glare of the burning O'Leary barn from in front of White's house appears to have little merit.[24]

Why Wasn't Sullivan Injured by the Flames?

- It is highly unlikely that Sullivan, in his attempt to extinguish the fire and rescue the animals, would have had the time to run across the street to the barn without being injured by the flames.

Sullivan testified that as he ran across the street, "I made right straight in the barn...." There was a small alleyway that ran along the east side of the O'Leary and McLaughlin homes back to the rear yard; it seems reasonable to assume that Sullivan would have run through this passageway to get to the barn, which was at the rear of the O'Leary property. Indeed, he indicated as much when he testified that "nobody made an alarm to wake Leary up until I passed through the lot." Therefore, from in front of White's house Sullivan would have run northwesterly across DeKoven Street to the entrance of this alleyway, then north between the O'Leary and Dalton properties to the barn (Figure 54). An analysis of the inquiry transcript and Chicago real estate documents reveals that the distance Sullivan allegedly ran was about 193 feet (see Appendix B).[25]

Sullivan admitted during the inquiry that he could not run very fast. In 1871 many Chicago streets were paved with either wooden blocks or stones. As previously mentioned, however, DeKoven Street was not one of them. Post-fire photographs of the O'Leary property indicate that an embankment and sidewalk were adjacent to this street (Figures 31, 50). It does not seem possible that Sullivan, hampered by his wooden leg, would be able to hobble 193 feet, which is more than one-half the length of a football field, over this rough terrain into a burning barn that was full of hay and wood shavings, struggle with animals, fall down, and still ultimately free a calf, without being injured. Andreas writes of how the fire advanced so rapidly, reaching and burning Dalton's house so quickly, that Dalton's mother-in-law, who was in the house at the time the fire broke out, was barely able to escape the home before two sides of the building crashed in. This seems to be consistent with Mrs. McLaughlin's testimony; she stated that when she heard people cry "fire," she went outside and saw that already both the barn and Dalton's home were on fire. The flames had traveled from the barn to the home via Dalton's shed and the fence that ran through the rear of Dalton's property:

Q. Where did the fire appear to commence?

A. It seemed to commence with Leary's barn. I knew the folks. When they came in and hollered, "fire," said that Leary's barn was on fire, and whether it was there that it commenced or not, I could not say.

Q. Did you get out immediately and look?

A. The very minute they hollered, "fire," I went out. I looked back and saw Leary's barn on fire and the back part of Mr. Dalton's house.[26]

On the other hand, Sullivan, who was not even in the barn when the fire started, was allegedly able to run to it and enter and exit unscathed. Although Sullivan's testimony appears to be somewhat implausible, the commissioners and marshals did not question it.

It is possible that Sullivan was well aware of just how improbable his testimony was. When the fire officials questioned Sullivan about the depth of the lots on De-Koven Street, he replied correctly that "the lot I live on is one hundred feet and six inches." Although Sullivan knew to the inch the length of his lot, he was wildly inaccurate when he testified that "I guess there was about twenty or twenty-five feet between Leary's house and the barn." On the other hand, Catharine McLaughlin testified that the distance was about forty feet; the accuracy of this figure was confirmed at the inquiry by the testimony of firemen George Rau and Lewis Fiene and later by the recollections of James Dalton. Post-fire photographs disclose that the McLaughlin home was built very close to the front lot line, with the O'Leary home directly behind it (Figures 31, 50). In order for Sullivan to be correct, the barn would have had to have been built in the middle of the O'Leary property and not adjacent to the rear alley. Sullivan, though, indicated during the inquiry that the barn was indeed built next to the alley when he referred to the back door of the barn as "going out to the alleyway." It would be tempting to conclude that he deliberately lied about the distance from the house to the barn because he was well aware of the disparity between his testimony and the actual likelihood of being able to run 193 feet into a burning barn and eventually leave without being burned. Granted, it is possible that Sullivan did not lie, that he was genuinely mistaken. Even so, it is clear that despite having diagrams or drawings of the O'Leary neighborhood, the commissioners and marshals did not question Sullivan's remark. Assuming that Sullivan's statement indicating "there was about twenty or twenty-five feet between Leary's house and the barn" was correctly memorialized into the transcript, then the lack of a response to Sullivan's remark represents just one more example of the fire officials' failure to comment on the incongruities of his testimony.[27]

Admittedly, Sullivan may have been

alluding to the distance between the O'Leary home and a shed that was located south of the barn. The O'Learys stored coal, wood, and wood shavings in it. Post-fire photographs indicate that this shed, like the barn, was destroyed by the fire (Figures 31, 50). Unfortunately, it is not clear where the shed was located. At first Sullivan testified that "there was a little shed outside right up against the barn. The south side of the barn, a little shed that was used to keep coal and things in." Later, though, he implied that the barn and shed were five feet apart:

Q. You say that at the end of this twenty-foot place, there was five feet more to that shed?

A. It was not the end of it. It was the side of it, the south side as you go into the yard.[28]

Perhaps this shed and the barn were about five feet apart. When Sullivan was asked, "Did the fire spread pretty rapidly from Leary's barn?" he replied, "Not very rapidly. The next thing that took afire was a barn at the west end of it." This was consistent with Mrs. O'Leary's earlier testimony:

Q. How many houses were on fire or sheds or barns at the time you first saw it?

A. At the time I first saw it, my barn was and Mrs. Murray's barn was afire and Mr. Dalton's little shed. That is all that was afire, I think, when I first saw it. I thought there was no more fire, only them places.[29]

Had the barn and shed abutted each other, surely the shed would have been the next structure to catch fire and not the barn of Mrs. Murray, who was the O'Learys' neighbor to the west. But on the other

hand, perhaps the shed and barn were such an integral unit that Sullivan and Mrs. O'Leary referred to both buildings as the collective "barn."[30]

Post-fire photographs also disclose the ruins of a possible third building, apparently constructed only a few feet from the O'Leary home (Figures 47, 50, 53). Some historians have mistakenly suggested that these blackened timbers were actually the remains of the O'Leary barn. But this conclusion is contrary to inquiry testimony—and surely the O'Learys would not have kept their odoriferous animals so close to their home[31] (Figure 61).

But what is ultimately significant is not the location of the various sheds and outbuildings on the O'Leary property. Rather, it is Sullivan's claim that the fire spread "not very rapidly." This statement appears to be inconsistent with Mrs. Mc-Laughlin's testimony about the progress of the fire, and it is certainly inconsistent with Andreas' comments about James Dalton's mother-in-law fleeing from Dalton's burning home. Did Sullivan purposely say this so that the commissioners and marshals would not question his somewhat unconvincing testimony of his hobbling across the street and his heroic efforts inside the O'Leary barn? If so, it appears that his ruse succeeded.[32]

Sullivan's Inconsistent and Questionable Testimony

• Sullivan's questionable inquiry statements concerning the O'Leary barn are not limited to his apparent inability to estimate distances. Even his testimony concerning the barn's contents is inconsistent with the statements of others who testified at the investigation.

FIGURE 61—O'LEARY AND McLAUGHLIN HOMES AND O'LEARY BARN. **This drawing entitled "Where Mrs. O'Leary Lived" appeared in the Rev. David Swing's 1892 booklet A *Story of the Chicago Fire*. One needs only to compare this sketch to photographs of the O'Leary and McLaughlin homes to realize that this picture is not historically accurate. Nonetheless, the drawing is significant because it depicts a small building (third from the left) built between the O'Leary home and the O'Leary barn. Figure 53, a photograph of the rear of the O'Leary cottage, appears to show the ruins of this structure.**

Mrs. O'Leary stated during the inquiry that she routinely threw wood shavings into her barn:

Q. Did you have any [shavings] packed in your barn?

A. Yes sir. I had some packed in my barn.

Q. How many, do you think?

A. When I used to clean out the barn, I used to throw in a little shavings.

Q. Did you use them for bedding?

A. Yes sir. Not so much for bedding. I used to clean out the places and take a dish full and throw it in along with the cows.

Her husband also indicated during the proceedings that shavings were stored in the barn, apparently on the right side. He stated that on occasion he would put them under the horse. But after Sullivan admitted that "I have been there in Leary's barn hundreds of times," he was immediately asked, "Do you recollect noticing at the right hand as you went in any quantity of shavings there?" He replied, "I didn't.... I never noticed shavings inside of the barn." Sullivan was never asked to explain the discrepancy between his testimony and that of Mr. and Mrs. O'Leary.[33]

- It is doubtful that Sullivan yelled "fire" as he ran to the barn.

Sullivan stated that he yelled "fire, fire, fire" as he ran; indeed, during the inquiry he even bragged of his "hollering" prowess. Despite his claim, neither Mr. and Mrs. O'Leary or even Sullivan's mother said anything during the inquiry about hearing his cries as he allegedly ran to the barn. The fiddle playing at the McLaughlin home had ended by this time, so surely Catharine McLaughlin would have heard him, but she also mentioned nothing. One would think that *someone* living along DeKoven Street would have heard Sullivan's cries—especially if the windows of his or her home were open at the time.[34]

So *were* the DeKoven Street windows open? Unfortunately, the inquiry transcript gives no clear answer. Charles H. French, a police sergeant, testified that the people on Canal Street "were very much excited there and had their windows open," implying that but for the fire, the windows of their homes would have been closed.[35] On the other hand, Thomas B. Burtis, Assistant Superintendent of the Chicago Gas Light & Coke Company, testified that when he arrived at the gas works, "I saw [Thomas Ockerby] had closed all the windows, apparently to keep the sparks out of the carpenter shop and the exhaust room and so forth, and I went into the condensing room and closed the windows."[36] Burtis' testimony suggests, of course, just the opposite—that had it not been for the fire, the windows of these buildings would have been open. It is therefore impossible to make any kind of conclusion based on the general tenor of the inquiry transcript.

Perhaps the answer to this question may be found, not in the inquiry, but in the 1871 meteorological observations. By 4:00 P.M. on October 8, the temperature had climbed to seventy-nine degrees. Because of the unseasonably high temperature that day, the windows of the homes along DeKoven Street surely *would* have been open that evening. One would think that if Sullivan had cried out, someone would have heard him. After all, James Dalton, the O'Learys' neighbor to the east, claimed (albeit apparently years after the fire) that on the night of the fire, at about 8:45 P.M., he heard a woman scream. Dalton maintained that he heard her through his west window. But the commissioners

and marshals never commented on the apparent failure of the O'Leary neighbors to hear Sullivan, nor did they ask any of these neighbors if they heard him as he ran by. The first words that Mrs. O'Leary spoke at the inquiry were: "I was in bed myself and my husband and five children when this fire commenced." But she also testified that she could hear the sounds of the McLaughlin party from her bedroom. The east wall of the O'Leary home fronted on the alleyway that ran back to the barn, and the door into their home was in that wall. There was a window in the north wall, the wall facing the back yard (Figure 53). Mrs. O'Leary never told the commissioners she was asleep when the fire broke out. Why didn't they ask her if she heard Sullivan as he ran to the barn?[37]

And the fire officials never asked the O'Learys if they heard the cries of their animals as the fire destroyed the barn. Sullivan testified that "the fire was breaking out the side of the barn when I first saw it." He testified that the fire was "in the lower portion" of the barn when he entered. He testified that "the barn was taken fire from the east end" and that a horse was tied up in that part of the barn. But how long had the fire been burning before it finally broke through the side of the barn? How much longer did it burn while Sullivan supposedly stumbled across DeKoven Street? Surely the cows, and especially the horse, all crazed with fear, would have made a racket that would have alarmed the O'Learys long before Sullivan allegedly came to their animals' aid. But just as the commissioners and marshals never asked the O'Learys if they heard Sullivan as he ran by their home and the McLaughlin house, they never asked the couple if they heard their cows and horse in the moments (if not minutes) before Sullivan supposedly made his dramatic entrance onto the O'Leary property.

Mr. O'Leary testified that "Dan Sullivan is the first that called me out of bed." After hearing Sullivan's testimony, the officials should have asked each other the obvious question: Why didn't the animals in the burning barn get the O'Learys out of bed before Dan Sullivan did?[38]

And *why* did Sullivan run by the Mc-Laughlin house? As he knew he could not run very fast, it seems odd that he ran past their house and into the O'Learys' back-yard. He testified that "there was a party there" at the McLaughlins, and so he knew there were people inside. It does not make sense that Sullivan would run past the McLaughlin home, past the O'Leary home, and back to the barn. Why didn't he simply hobble up the McLaughlin's front porch, throw open the door (although it was probably already open), and call for help? The Board never asked Sullivan this question.[39]

What Really Happened?

Consider a possible explanation for all of these inconsistencies:

• After Sullivan left the O'Leary home, he never went across the street to sit in front of White's house. This statement was merely a convenient alibi to explain where he was when the fire started. Instead, he went to the O'Leary barn, where he started the fire.

Sullivan indicated at the inquiry that he was never in the O'Leary barn on Sunday, October 8, prior to the fire. But perhaps he lied at the inquiry. Perhaps he went to the barn that evening to relax for a few minutes before going home. Sullivan testified, "I used to go in there every eve-

ning, because my mother keeps a cow herself, and I used to go in there and bring feed. I knew where the cows were. I have been there in Leary's barn hundreds of times." Because he had been in the barn so often, perhaps Sullivan (and the O'Learys) felt that he could enter and exit it with impunity, unlike the hypothetical "milk thieves" mentioned in the previous chapter. While inside, he dropped a match or pipe in some hay or wood shavings. The hay or shavings caught fire, and he immediately attempted to extinguish the blaze. The fire spread quickly, though, and Sullivan, realizing that his efforts were fruitless, abandoned these measures and turned instead to rescuing the trapped animals. He was able to untie only two of the cows until the flames forced him to flee for safety. While attempting to leave, he slipped on the floorboards and fell. Quickly getting up, he exited the barn and ran to the O'Learys' house in order to warn them of the fire. The neighborhood began to stir, even though only a few moments had passed since the fire started. This shorter and more realistic elapsed time is a distinctive difference between Sullivan's testimony and this theory.[40]

Two days later the fire was extinguished, but Sullivan needed only a fraction of that time to realize that he was responsible for leveling much of Chicago. For obvious reasons he was reluctant to admit his culpability, and so he lied to the marshals and commissioners about not being in the O'Leary barn on Sunday. But he also needed an alibi as to where he was from the time he left the O'Leary home until the time the fire broke out in their barn.

"I was sitting at the head of White's house or head of his lot" was that perfect explanation. As Sullivan lived nearby, the fact that he was in the immediate vicinity would arouse no suspicion. He could not state that he was closer, on the same side of the street but in front of his own home or the McLaughlin home, as anyone at the McLaughlin party could possibly contradict him, claiming that he was not in either place at the time the fire broke out. When the fire started the night was dark, and there was no moon yet in the evening sky. Therefore, it seems likely that someone standing on the McLaughlin front porch would not be able to see Sullivan if he were in front of White's house. On the other hand, it seems equally likely that despite the moonless night, he would have been seen if he were closer, across the street but in front of his own home or the McLaughlin home[41] (Figure 62).

Sullivan's probable fear of being seen by someone leaving the McLaughlin home is not unfounded. During the course of the festivities at the McLaughlin home, it would not be unreasonable for someone to step outside onto the porch for some fresh air or perhaps even to walk onto the sidewalk or street. Furthermore, on October 9 Mrs. White told Mrs. O'Leary about the possibility that someone from the McLaughlin party might have started the fire. Surely by November 25, the day Sullivan testified, Mrs. White's remark to Mrs. O'Leary that a guest might have left the party had become common knowledge. Indeed, the following excerpt from Mrs. McLaughlin's testimony suggests that as many as three men left her home that evening before the fire broke out. Sullivan could not risk these men challenging his alibi:

Q. You didn't tell the name of these persons who went out, if any. Who did, if anyone?
A. There was no one came out of my house during the fire.
Q. Previous to that time?

A. I do not know if the boys got in before the house got afire. I could not really say. I do not know whether they were in my house then or whether they got in before then or not. They came into the house and went back to save their things.
Q. Do you know whether they were in before or not?
A. No sir. I could not say.
Q. What three boys were these?
A. Denny Connors and Willie Lewis and Johnny Ryan. I think them is the three boys.
Q. Boys or young men?
A. Young men.[42]

Sullivan testified that he was sitting by White's fence; he was apparently sitting against it. People living along the south side of DeKoven Street would not be able to question this, as they would not be able to see him. Sitting in front of the fence, he would be hidden from view. Finally, as he was outside, in close proximity to the O'Leary barn, he would be able to claim that he noticed the fire from its inception.[43]

Sullivan's statements at the inquiry must have somehow been convincing, as he was never charged with causing the fire. Nonetheless, in many respects his testimony does not seem plausible. The commissioners and marshals never asked him why he walked past his own house and sat down. Despite having diagrams of the location of buildings in the neighborhood, they never asked him how he was able to see the barn from his position in front of White's house. The fire officials never asked him to explain the marked inconsistencies between his October 20 Tribune affidavit and his testimony. They never questioned how Sullivan was able to run approximately 193 feet into a burning barn

FIGURE 62—MAN STANDING IN FRONT OF THE O'LEARY AND MCLAUGHLIN HOMES. The McLaughlin home is the taller cottage in front, with the porch overlooking DeKoven Street. The O'Learys lived in the rear house. Daniel Sullivan testified at the inquiry that after leaving the O'Leary home, he went across the street and sat down. It is likely that guests leaving the McLaughlin party and walking onto this porch (the only exit) would have seen Sullivan if he had been sitting in front of his own home. This may be why he told the Board of Police and Fire Commissioners that he sat (out of sight) in front of William White's house, which was farther down the street.

The Dalton house, destroyed in the fire, was to the right, or east, of the O'Leary and McLaughlin cottages. As the O'Leary property was only twenty-five feet wide, it seems reasonable to assume that the alleyway between the O'Leary/McLaughlin and Dalton homes was through the set of two pillars closest to the O'Leary and McLaughlin houses. The unpaved road, dirt embankment, and raised sidewalk all indicate that it would have been difficult for Sullivan to run across the street, probably through this alleyway, to the burning barn. (Courtesy of the Illinois State Historical Library)

full of hay and wood shavings, struggle with animals, fall down, and eventually exit without being injured. Sullivan stated that he yelled "fire, fire, fire" as he ran to the barn. The neighbors who testified, including his own mother, said nothing during the inquiry about hearing these cries. The Board never questioned this either.[44]

What is perhaps most incongruous about Sullivan's testimony is his statement about coming home, having supper, and then visiting with the O'Learys for about an hour—*even though both Mr. and Mrs. O'Leary were in bed at the time!* Was Sullivan lying? His mother's inquiry testimony hints that he might have been, and offers a tantalizing glimpse of what at first appears to be a very plausible theory as to what might have really happened on DeKoven Street on October 8. She testified that on that evening, "one of my boys was out until it was after eight o'clock, and we didn't have supper until he came in.... I waited until he ate his supper, and we were talking. After that he went out. I was washing up my dishes. I hadn't them washed up when I saw the fire coming through the window." Mrs. Sullivan never identified which one of her three "boys" was out. It is tempting to conclude that it was Daniel, and that after he ate, he stepped outside and went directly to the O'Leary barn, where he started the fire. But Daniel claimed that after eating supper, he went to the O'Learys' home, not their barn: "I went into my own house and sat there a little while and eat my supper. I started right out about eight o'clock or as near as I could come to it. I went across the street over to Leary's and went in there." If Daniel Sullivan really did leave his mother's house and go directly to the barn, then he obviously lied about eating supper and visiting with the O'Learys for an hour.[45]

At first it appears that he was less than

truthful. Mrs. Sullivan testified that after her son left, she washed her dishes, but had not finished them when she saw the fire. It seems reasonable that Mrs. Sullivan would do her dishes immediately after supper, not an hour later, and so the relatively short elapsed time from when her son left her home to when she saw the flames is consistent with the theory that Daniel Sullivan ate, went to the barn, and started the fire. But on the other hand, it also seems reasonable that Sullivan would not clumsily lie at the inquiry about visiting the O'Learys, knowing that the couple might be asked to corroborate his testimony. Furthermore, perhaps the O'Learys eventually got out of bed and played the role of gracious (albeit probably reluctant) hosts for an hour. Finally, an analysis of inquiry testimony (see endnote) indicates that Daniel Sullivan was not the son who was eating supper with Catherine Sullivan that evening. Daniel probably did not even live with his mother, and so ultimately this theory fails to pass muster. Although Catherine Sullivan's testimony is unclear, it seems likely that she lived in a nearby home that her sons bought her, a house that was at least seventy-five feet east of Daniel's house, located at the southwest corner of DeKoven and Clinton streets. Daniel testified that "when I got through with my horses, *I went into my own house* and sat there a little while and eat my supper" [emphasis added]. On the night of October 8, Daniel Sullivan was probably having supper in this house and his mother was eating with one of her other sons in her home.[46]

But the following is uncontroverted: Mrs. O'Leary testified on November 24. Her husband was the third person to testify on November 25. Daniel Sullivan was the fourth. Neither O'Leary mentioned anything about Sullivan being at their home before the fire broke out. After hearing

Sullivan's testimony, it seems incredible that the commissioners and marshals did not immediately question Mr. O'Leary again in order to verify Sullivan's contention that he visited with the O'Learys for an hour, especially after Sullivan stated that the couple was in bed at the time. And at the very least it seems unusual that the Board did not ask Sullivan to explain an apparent inconsistency: His mother testified that "one of her boys" was out and did not come in until *after* eight o'clock, at which time he ate dinner and then left again. But Sullivan seemed to indicate that he had come home, eaten supper, and was out the door either at or even *before* eight o'clock! Why didn't the fire officials attempt to identify Mrs. Sullivan's nameless son, confirm that it was not Daniel, and ask to interview him in order to determine what he might have seen or heard that evening? But when Daniel Sullivan finished his stint before the commissioners and fire marshals on November 25, they questioned neither Mr. O'Leary nor Mrs. Sullivan. Instead, they chose to recall fireman Lewis Fiene, who was the first person interviewed that day. Fiene's additional testimony was of little, if any, value to the investigation.[47]

Was Dennis Regan an Accomplice?

It is possible that Dennis Regan, a laborer, might also have been responsible for causing the fire, or at least was in the barn when the fire started. Regan testified at the inquiry, and when the fire officials asked him if he knew anything about the "origin and commencement" of the fire, he replied:

All I know, I was into Mr. Leary's at half past eight, and I was talking to the man that was

in bed and his wife. I asked his wife what was the reason she went to bed. She told me she had a sore foot. I went away, so as the man was in bed. I went home. A short while after nine o'clock I heard one of the neighbors say Leary's barn was on fire. I jumped out of bed and went up there, and the barn was on fire and all the neighbors around it. I ran through the alleyway and tried to save his wagon in the alleyway but could not go near it. I went to work there to throw water on the house because the house was not insured or nothing. That is all I know about it.[48]

And historians know even less about Regan. Even his name seems shrouded in mystery. The *Chicago Tribune* of October 20, 1871, also mentions the appearance of Mr. Regan at the O'Leary property during the first few minutes of the fire, but refers instead to a "Denis Ryan." Andreas quotes this *Tribune* account, but changes the name to "Dennis Rogan" without comment. Musham summarizes Regan's inquiry testimony; citing Andreas, he too refers to "Dennis Rogan." "Dennis Ryan" was the eighth witness to testify before the Chicago Board of Police and Fire Commissioners. During his testimony he indicated that he lived at 112 DeKoven Street. This is the same address noted in the October 20 *Tribune* article. Chicago Title Insurance Company records for this parcel of land disclose that "Dennis Ryan" purchased this home in 1865, but that "Dennis Regan" mortgaged the property four years later. The 1870 Chicago city directory notes that "Dennis Regan" lived at this address. The *Chicago Evening Journal*, commenting on Regan's testimony at the inquiry, referred to him as "Dennis Reagan." Catherine Sullivan testified that her son and "a man called Dennis Regan" awakened the O'Learys when the fire broke out. Reporter Michael Ahern, reminiscing about the fire years later, referred to "Dennis Rogan, who resided at 112 De Koven street."[49]

Taken together, this evidence indicates that these different names all refer to the same person. Andreas appears to have initiated the use of the name "Rogan." The penmanship in the inquiry transcript is spotty; in many places the handwriting is almost illegible. Seeing a reference to "Dennis Regan," in, for example, Catherine Sullivan's testimony, it is possible that Andreas mistakenly read the name as "Dennis Rogan." Musham, probably relying on Andreas or Ahern, subsequently referred to the name as "Rogan."[50]

It appears that Dennis Regan was one of the first people to arrive at the O'Leary property after their barn caught fire. Accounts differ, however, as to whether it was Regan or Daniel Sullivan who first alerted the O'Learys. In two affidavits published in the October 20, 1871, *Chicago Tribune*, Mr. and Mrs. O'Leary and Daniel Sullivan all indicated that Regan alarmed the O'Learys on the night of the fire. But several weeks later, at the inquiry, both Mr. and Mrs. O'Leary testified that it was Sullivan who warned them. When Regan testified, he never mentioned anything about alarming the couple. The commissioners and fire marshals did not comment on this inconsistency. But Sullivan did state at the inquiry that while he was attempting to alert the O'Learys, "a man by the name of Regan came along." This was confirmed by Sullivan's mother, who testified at the proceedings that "my son and a man called Dennis Regan" warned the O'Learys. Furthermore, when Mrs. O'Leary was asked if she knew how the fire started, she replied, "I could not tell anything of the fire, only that two men came by the door." Finally, Mrs. McLaughlin also apparently saw these two men, as she testified at the inquiry that "I knew the *folks*. When *they* came in and hollered 'fire,' said that Leary's barn was on fire..." [emphasis added]. Based on these

various statements, it is reasonable to presume that the men Mrs. McLaughlin said she knew were Sullivan and Regan; it is also reasonable to conclude that any inconsistency in these accounts as to who alerted the O'Learys—Sullivan or Regan—is insignificant at best, as it appears that both men were outside the O'Leary home at the very early stages of the fire. But the marshals and commissioners never asked Mrs. McLaughlin to identify these men whom she said she knew, and that, it seems, is not reasonable.[51]

Regan lived a block east of the O'Learys, but on the opposite side of DeKoven Street. He testified that while in bed, he heard a neighbor say that the O'Leary barn was on fire. But because Regan and Sullivan warned the O'Learys of the fire, this neighbor must have discovered the fire even before the O'Learys themselves learned about it. Instead of either awakening the O'Leary household or attempting to put the fire out, this neighbor chose instead to run down the street. As this is very unlikely, it seems clear that this person (if he or she existed) should have been questioned during the inquiry. But the fire officials never even asked Regan who the neighbor was. Or perhaps the neighbor was never near the O'Leary barn. In those first moments after the fire started, did this person hear a general commotion a block away that alerted him? If so, why did this person hear it and no one else, not even the O'Learys? How could Regan be in bed, hear a neighbor's cries, get out of bed, run one block to the O'Leary home, and still be one of the first persons at the fire? The commissioners never asked Regan these questions.[52]

Regan stated at the inquiry that while "passing" the McLaughlin cottage, he heard music. This also appears unlikely, as Catharine McLaughlin, who testified only a day after Regan did, told the officials that the only music at the party was her husband's fiddle and that the fire started *after* her husband finished playing. True to form, the commissioners and marshals failed to question either Regan or McLaughlin about this marked inconsistency.[53]

Dennis Regan's testimony indicates that Sullivan was not the only visitor crowding the O'Leary house on the night of October 8. Regan testified that prior to the fire he too visited with the O'Learys at their home, and he also commented that they were both in bed at the time. Again, neither Mr. nor Mrs. O'Leary mentioned this while testifying, and again, the officials never questioned Regan about this. Furthermore, Sullivan's and Regan's inquiry comments indicate that they had apparently called on the O'Learys *at the same time.* But Regan never stated that Sullivan was with him at the O'Learys' home, and Sullivan did not mention that Regan was with him. The Board never asked Regan or Sullivan about this somewhat significant, if not bizarre, incongruity.[54]

Clearly Regan's story does not seem credible. Could he have caused the fire? Or was he in the barn when Sullivan started it? Sullivan testified that "I used to go in [the O'Leary barn] every evening, because my mother keeps a cow herself, and I used to go in there and bring feed." Perhaps Regan and Sullivan *were* both visiting the O'Learys. If so, did they leave the O'Leary home to go to the barn to bring feed to Catherine Sullivan's cow? Probably not; it is more likely that she kept her cow in one of the two barns on the Sullivan family property (see endnote). On the other hand, the following scenario is not at all implausible:[55]

Perhaps Sullivan and Regan left the O'Leary home together at about nine o'clock, walked into the O'Learys' backyard, and went directly to the O'Leary barn. Perhaps the two of them wanted to sit, relax, and talk for a few more minutes before going home. Despite the heat of that October evening, this would not have been unusual. As both barn doors were at least partially open, the doors faced north and south, and a wind was blowing from the south-southwest at about twenty miles an hour, there would have been a cross ventilation through the barn that evening. But although there was a breeze in the barn, there was probably no lamp. Mrs. O'Leary stated in her *Tribune* affidavit that she had no lamp in the barn that day or evening.[56]

Patrick O'Leary indicated during his testimony that the barn door next to the alley was in two sections, and that although the lower half was closed, the upper half was open. He testified that "there was no trouble in opening [the lower half]. There was only a little catch that you could shove in and out." Although a nighttime smoker would probably forego this closed lower door and the barn's dark, animal-filled environs in favor of a more inviting atmosphere, Sullivan was familiar with the barn. Having been inside "hundreds of times," he knew its doors, its interior, even its odors. Unlike a nocturnal smoker, Sullivan could confidently walk into the barn's open south door that faced the O'Leary home (or just as confidently work the latch that secured the lower half of the north door, the door adjacent to the alley). And although the O'Leary barn might have been a bit unpleasant for Daniel Sullivan and Dennis Regan, it was certainly comfortable enough to relax in for a few minutes before going home.[57]

While Sullivan and Regan rested in the barn, somehow the fire started. How did it happen? There are a number of possibilities:

- Perhaps Sullivan took out a pipe and after lighting it, tossed the match away, not realizing it was still lit.

- Sullivan told the commissioners and marshals that the barn had a board floor. Both Mr. and Mrs. O'Leary testified that wood shavings were in the barn. Sullivan testified that when he was in the barn, "the boards were wet, my legs slipped out from me, and I went down." Perhaps Sullivan was telling the truth. Perhaps Sullivan's peg leg slipped on the wet wood, causing him to stumble and drop his pipe into a pile of shavings.[58]
- Perhaps it was Regan who smoked, and although he was careful with the match, he was not so careful when he scraped out and discarded what he thought was dead pipe ash prior to tamping in fresh tobacco.
- Were they both at fault? While Sullivan was lighting his pipe, did Regan jostle him, causing Sullivan to drop the match into some loose hay or a pile of wood shavings?
- Perhaps Sullivan or Regan did bring a lamp into the barn, and a careless foot, not hoof, caused the fire.

Regardless of how the fire started, it is quite possible that they both walked into that barn at approximately nine o'clock on Sunday evening, October 8, 1871. About twenty minutes later they both ran out because the barn was ablaze, and the rest is Chicago history[59] (Figure 63).

This theory is consistent with Sullivan's and Regan's testimony. Sullivan suggested at the inquiry that he left the O'Leary home at about nine o'clock; Regan did not indicate what time he left, only that it was sometime after eight-thirty. Both Sullivan and Regan needed alibis, as both men chose to account to the Board for where they were from the time they left the O'Leary home to the time the fire started.

Sullivan told the fire officials that he walked across the street and sat in front of William White's house for about twenty or twenty-five minutes; as he turned around, ready to go home, he saw the fire. Regan testified that after going home, he heard a neighbor say the O'Leary barn was on fire "a short while after nine o'clock."[60]

This theory is also much more plausible than the suggestion that Sullivan left his home after eating supper and went directly to the O'Leary barn. As pointed out in Appendix A, it is virtually impossible to determine with certainty when the fire started. But the analysis in this appendix (which is not based on Sullivan's and Regan's testimony) also indicates that the fire started at about 9:20 P.M. Assuming that the O'Leary barn caught fire at about this time, it seems doubtful that Sullivan would have left his house at about eight o'clock, gone into the barn, and stayed there for one hour and twenty minutes until it caught fire. Even with cross ventilation, the barn surely would have been too hot and stifling for Sullivan to relax in for that length of time. But on the other hand, the barn would not have been that uncomfortable for Sullivan and Regan to sit in for a few minutes.[61]

Proponents of Regan's innocence and the truthfulness of his inquiry statements might point to a distinctive difference between Regan's and Sullivan's testimony. Although Sullivan indicated that he sat against a fence in front of White's home for as long as twenty or twenty-five minutes, he did not mention whether there was anyone else outside during this time, someone that the Board could have interviewed in order to determine the veracity of his statements. But Regan's alibi includes such references to third parties, and so his statements, unlike Sullivan's, could have been confirmed by the commissioners or the fire marshals.

FIGURE 63—DANIEL "PEG LEG" SULLIVAN AND DENNIS REGAN IN THE O'LEARY BARN. **This is an illustration of how the fire *might* have started in the O'Leary barn. Although purely conjecture, it is conjecture based on the inquiry testimony of Daniel Sullivan and Dennis Regan. Both men indicated during questioning that they were in the O'Leary home on the evening of October 8. Sullivan told the fire officials that he had been in their barn "hundreds of times." He also testified that the barn had a wooden floor and that the boards were wet. Perhaps the men left the O'Leary house together and walked to the barn to relax for a few minutes before going home. Did Sullivan's peg leg slip on the wet wood, causing him to stumble and drop his pipe into some hay or wood shavings? Or did he trip over Dennis Regan's feet? Perhaps Regan, relaxing against the wall of the barn, suddenly stretched out his legs as Sullivan hobbled by, causing him to lose his balance and fall. No one knows what really happened in the barn on October 8, 1871, but the evidence seems clear that the fire was *not* caused by Mrs. O'Leary's cow kicking over a lantern. (Drawing by Marshall Philyaw)**

They could have asked Regan to identify the neighbor who alerted him, and the Board could have questioned him. Regan testified that neighbors had gathered around the O'Leary barn when he arrived there. The officials could have asked Regan who they were and then interviewed them as well in order to determine if they saw Regan running from his house, down the

street, and to the barn, probably through the same alleyway Sullivan ostensibly ran through. One would think that if Regan caused the fire he, like Sullivan, would have given the commissioners and marshals an alibi that could not be verified by other parties. For example, Regan could have easily mirrored Sullivan's testimony by claiming that after he and Sullivan left the O'Leary home, they *both* walked across the street and sat down in front of White's house.[62]

But perhaps Regan simply wanted to distance himself from Sullivan. Perhaps it was Sullivan who caused the fire, so Regan, fearing "guilt by association," did not want to testify that he was with Sullivan prior to the time the fire started. And the fact that Regan's testimony might have been corroborated appears to be an argument of questionable value. If the commissioners or marshals had asked who alerted him, Regan could have replied that he did not recognize the person's voice and that he just assumed it was a neighbor. With all the commotion and confusion outside the burning O'Leary barn, it would not be unreasonable for the people milling around to not see Regan supposedly running through the alleyway. In any event, the fact that Regan's testimony might have been confirmed by third parties does not outweigh the dramatic incongruities in his statements. The inquiry transcript is in four volumes that total more than 1,100 pages. Regan's account consists of only four and one half pages, but these few pages contain inconsistencies that almost rival the discrepancies found in Sullivan's twenty-one and one half pages of testimony. Ultimately, the issue of third party corroboration of Regan's testimony speaks not so much to the possibility of Regan's innocence but instead to the fire officials' ineptitude in failing to effectively question him.

The evidence that most exonerates Mrs. O'Leary is in the final analysis the most damning to Sullivan and Regan. At the time the fire broke out, there was no reason for anyone to believe that it would be of any more consequence than the twenty-eight previous fires of that first week in October. Therefore, the person responsible for the fire would most likely, upon its inception, attempt to extinguish the fire or

save the O'Leary animals and property— this Sullivan and Regan did. Failing that, this person would next alert the O'Learys— this Sullivan and Regan did. Because of their incriminating behavior and because of their equally incriminating testimony, it seems reasonable to conclude that either Daniel "Peg Leg" Sullivan or Dennis Regan and not Mrs. O'Leary and her cow were responsible for the fire. The many inconsistencies in Sullivan's testimony create the proverbial smoking gun that almost assuredly links Sullivan to the fire's cause. The discrepancies in Regan's testimony are fewer but no less dramatic. If Sullivan lit a pipe or lantern that sparked the fire, then Regan was pounding on the O'Leary door with the matchbox in his back pocket. As the inquiry ground to a conclusion in early December of 1871, Sullivan and Regan surely went to sleep at night, content in the knowledge that they would never be charged with causing the Great Chicago Fire. An investigation that was halfhearted at best, bumbling at worst, had insured this. After the Police and Fire Commissioners issued their report, with no clear explanation for the fire's cause, Mrs. O'Leary became the fire's *cause célèbre* by default.[63]

Notes

1. "The Great Fire," *Chicago Evening Journal*, 12 December 1871, p. [4]; "Nobody to Blame," p. 5; "The Great Fire," *Chicago Republican*, 12 December 1871, p. [4]; "How It Originated," p. [2]. Inexplicably, "Daniel Sullivan" is referred to in this affidavit as "Dennis" and "Denis" Sullivan.

2. Daniel Sullivan, *Inquiry*, vol. [1], pp. 254, 271; Chicago Title Insurance records; "How They Look and Act," p. [3]; *1870 City Directory*, p. 801; *1871 City Directory*, pp. 194, 867, 1055–56; F. H. Shults letter; Statement of J. C. Chapeck; *Robinson's Atlas*, vol. 1, plate 6; 1870 U.S. Census, Cook County, Illinois, Population Schedule, National Archives micropublication M593, roll 204, sheet

174, page 87, line 26. The transcript of the Inquiry contains no mention of what Sullivan's peg leg was made of. The November 26, 1871, *Chicago Tribune* referred to his wooden leg, and although this is undoubtedly correct, it is not a necessary assumption. For example, in *Bloody Williamson*, an account of a 1922 southern Illinois labor massacre, historian Paul Angle noted that a "peglegged" strikebreaker had a cork leg. See "The Great Fire," *Chicago Tribune*, 26 November 1871, p. 1; Paul M. Angle, *Bloody Williamson* (New York: Alfred A. Knopf, 1952), p. 5.

3. Daniel Sullivan, *Inquiry*, vol. [1], pp. 254–57; see also "A Defence of Fire Marshal Williams," p. 6. As explained in Chapter Five, the various witnesses testified before the commissioners, Marshal Williams and the three assistant marshals, and newspaper reporters. But the transcript seldom indicates who questioned a witness during the course of an inquiry session. As a questioner might have been a fire marshal and not a commissioner, this chapter will usually refer to "officials" or "commissioners and marshals" instead of "the Board."

4. Daniel Sullivan, *Inquiry*, vol. [1], pp. 262, 264, 267; Chicago Title Insurance Company records.

5. Daniel Sullivan, *Inquiry*, vol. [1], pp. 255, 262, 264, 266–67; Kenneth Grenier, retired Survey Officer, Chicago Title Insurance Company; Charles O'Connor, retired Superintendent of Maps Department, City of Chicago; Nicholas Raimondi, co-owner of National Survey Service, Inc., interview by Richard F. Bales, 28 November 1995; Chicago Title Insurance Company records.

Sullivan testified that he left to go to the O'Leary home at about eight o'clock and stayed there for about an hour. He then went across the street and "stayed there as long as from about twenty minutes past nine to twenty-five minutes past nine." As he turned around, ready to go home, he saw the fire. Taken as a whole, his testimony seems to imply that he left the O'Leary home at about nine o'clock, walked across the street, and sat in front of White's house for twenty or twenty-five minutes, when he then saw the barn on fire. Or did Sullivan sit down in front of White's house for only five minutes, from 9:20 to 9:25? His subsequent testimony seems to confirm the former interpretation:

Q. You spoke of having been into Leary's and gone out of there a little while before.
A. I was into Leary's about eight o'clock and a few moments after, and from that until nine o'clock.

Q. Then you went out at that time?
A. Yes sir.
Q. The fire broke out about half past nine?
A. Yes sir, from twenty to twenty-five minutes past nine.

See Daniel Sullivan, *Inquiry*, vol. [1], pp. 261–62.

The *Chicago Tribune* summary of his testimony is also consistent with this interpretation: "Daniel Sullivan, of No. 134 DeKoven street, was in Leary's house about 8 o'clock in the evening, and remained there about one hour.... He left the house, and, while on the opposite side of the street, at twenty or twenty-five minutes past 9 o'clock, he saw fire in Leary's barn." See "The Great Fire," *Chicago Tribune*, 26 November 1871, p. 1.

Finally, his sworn statement published in the October 20 *Tribune* is in agreement: "[Daniel Sullivan] testifies that he was at Patrick O'Leary's house, No. 137 DeKoven street, on Sunday night the 8th, of October, 1871, from about 8½ to 9 o'clock at night, during which time Mr. O'Leary and wife were in bed, that he went a few lots east of O'Leary's on the opposite side of DeKoven street, until about half-past 9 o'clock, when he saw the fire." See "How It Originated," p. [2].

6. Catherine O'Leary, *Inquiry*, vol. [1], p. 65; Catharine McLaughlin, *Inquiry*, vol. [1], pp. 225–26; Kogan and Cromie, p. 50.

7. Catharine McLaughlin, *Inquiry*, vol. [1], p. 236.

8. Daniel Sullivan, *Inquiry*, vol. [1] p. 263; "The Great Fire," *Chicago Tribune*, 26 November 1871, p. 1.

9. Daniel Sullivan, *Inquiry*, vol. [1], pp. 262–63, 266–67; Catherine O'Leary, *Inquiry*, vol. [1], p. 69; "That Investigation on Kicks," *Chicago Evening Journal*, 11 November 1871, p. [4], hereafter cited in text as "That Investigation on Kicks."

10. Lowe, p. 42; "The Cause of the Fire," *Chicago Evening Journal*, 10 November 1871, p. [4], hereafter cited in text as "The Cause of the Fire"; "That Investigation," *Chicago Evening Journal*, 17 November 1871, p. [4]; "Board of Police," *Chicago Tribune*, 10 November 1871, p. 6; "The Great Fire," *Chicago Tribune*, 24 November 1871, p. 6; Chicago Title Insurance Company records; Andreas, vol. 2, pp. 714, 760; *Robinson's Atlas*, vol. 1, plate 6.

Catherine Sullivan's inquiry testimony at vol. [1], pp. 114–16, indicates that homes south of DeKoven Street, although not in the "burnt district," did at least catch fire despite the prevailing southwest winds. On the other hand, Patrick O'Leary's inquiry comments may be to the contrary:

Q. Did the fire burn any south of DeKoven Street? Did any building catch afire on the south side?
A. No, they didn't. It went very near it. The people were throwing water on top of their houses all the time.

See Patrick O'Leary, *Inquiry*, vol. [1], p. 248.
11. Daniel Sullivan, *Inquiry*, vol. [1], p. 256; Andreas, vol. 2, pp. 713–14, 717; Musham, p. 98; Perry R. Duis, *Challenging Chicago: Coping with Everyday Life, 1837–1920* (Urbana: University of Illinois Press, 1998), p. 99, hereafter cited in text as Duis; Chicago Title Insurance Company records; "The Great Fire," *Chicago Evening Journal*, 12 December 1871, p. [4].
12. Andreas, vol. 2, p. 715; Catharine McLaughlin, *Inquiry*, vol. [1], pp. 237–40; Chicago Title Insurance Company records; "Notes on the Great Chicago Fire of 1871," sec. 3, p. 21; George Rau, *Inquiry*, vol. [1], p. 164.
13. Daniel Sullivan, *Inquiry*, vol. [1], p. 258.
14. "How It Originated," p. [2]; Daniel Sullivan, *Inquiry*, vol. [1], pp. 258–59, 267, 274–75. The original transcript of the inquiry asks the question, "*How* did I understand you to say...?" This appears to be erroneous, and so the word has been changed to "now" in the text.
15. Sullivan claimed in his October 20 *Tribune* affidavit that when he went into the barn, "he found the hay in the loft on fire." But when the commissioners and marshals questioned him on November 25, they apparently ignored, forgot, or didn't read his earlier published comments, as they asked him if there was a hayloft in the barn. The men failed to notice that Sullivan sidestepped this question, dismissing it with the briefest of answers before steering the testimony away from him and onto a new topic that included "young scoundrels" as possible suspects in the fire's cause:

Q. (By Mr. Williams) How large was that barn of Mr. Leary's?
A. It was about twenty feet.
Q. There was a hay loft overhead?
A. There was, and at the same time there was a house full of shavings that fronted on Taylor Street that nobody, so far as I can understand, had been living in it for quite awhile. A good many of these young scoundrels living around the city used to make their home in it.

See "How It Originated," p. [2]; Daniel Sullivan, *Inquiry*, vol. [1], p. 271.
16. "How It Originated," p. [2]; John Dorsey,

Inquiry, vol. 2, p. 63; Patrick O'Leary, *Inquiry*, vol. [1], p. 251. But on the other hand, note the testimony of fireman George Rau, who stated during the inquiry that the height of the barn "was about sixteen to twenty feet, that is to the peak of the roof." George Rau, *Inquiry*, vol. [1], p. 164. See also Andreas, who claimed that the Dalton home was a "one story cottage." Andreas, vol. 2, p. 717.
17. Andreas, vol. 2, p. 714; Catherine Sullivan, *Inquiry*, vol. [1], p. 115; Lewis Fiene, *Inquiry*, vol. [1], p. 214; Catharine McLaughlin, *Inquiry*, vol. [1], pp. 224, 231, 233, 236, 239; Mathias Benner, *Inquiry*, vol. [4], p. 126; Cromie, p. 31; "Origin of the Fire," supplement, p. [2].
18. *The Great Conflagration: A Complete Account of the Burning of Chicago...* (Chicago: Western News Co., 1871), p. 85, hereafter cited in text as *The Great Conflagration: A Complete Account of the Burning of Chicago*; William J. Brown to his sister [Sarah R. Hibbard?], 20 October [18]71, Chicago Fire of 1871 Personal Narratives Collection, Chicago Historical Society, hereafter cited in text as William J. Brown letter, 20 October 1871; William J. Brown letter, 2 November 1871; "The Fire's Nursery," *Chicago Times*, 14 December 1871, p. 5, hereafter cited in text as "The Fire's Nursery"; "Out of the Ashes," *Chicago Tribune*, 25 November 1871, p. 1; "The North Division," *Chicago Times*, 21 October 1871, p. [2].
19. Lewis Fiene, *Inquiry*, vol. [1], p. 193.
20. Daniel Sullivan, *Inquiry*, vol. [1], pp. 260–61.
21. The present location of these diagrams is unknown.
22. "Origin of the Fire," supplement, p. [2]; Colbert and Chamberlin, p. 390; Goodspeed, pp. 158, 330–31; Daniel Sullivan, *Inquiry*, vol. [1], pp. 255–56, 260; Andreas, vol. 2, p. 754. A few days after the fire, a newspaper reporter made the following observation about De Koven Street: "On the south side of the street not a house was touched. On the north only one remained. All the rest were simply ashes. There were no piles of ruin here. The wooden hovels left no landmarks except here and there a stunted chimney too squat to fall." See Harold M. Mayer and Richard C. Wade, *Chicago: Growth of a Metropolis* (Chicago: University of Chicago Press, 1969), p. 107, hereafter cited in text as Mayer and Wade.
23. *Almanac*, p. [14]; Mathias Benner, *Inquiry*, vol. [4], p. 168.
24. Catherine O'Leary, *Inquiry*, vol. [1], pp. 59, 72–73; Patrick O'Leary, *Inquiry*, vol. [1], pp. 251–52; Daniel Sullivan, *Inquiry*, vol. [1], pp. 256, 267; Duis, pp. 98–99; Andreas, vol. 2, pp. 57–58, 701–2; Pierce, vol. 2, pp. 319–20; Lowe, p. 42; Cox

and Armington, p. 367; Musham, pp. 74, 87; *Eleventh Annual Report of the Board of Public Works, to the Common Council of the City of Chicago, for the Municipal, Fiscal Year Ending March 31, 1872* (Chicago: D. & C. H. Blakely, 1872), pp. 33–40. When *Chicago Evening Post* reporter Joseph E. Chamberlin covered the fire, he was not impressed with DeKoven Street: "I was at the scene in a few minutes. The fire had already advanced a distance of about a single square through the frame buildings that covered the ground thickly north of DeKoven Street and east of Jefferson—if those miserable alleys shall be dignified by being denominated streets." See Don Hayner and Tom McNamee, *Streetwise Chicago: A History of Chicago Street Names* (Chicago: Loyola University Press, 1988), p. 30, hereafter Hayner and McNamee. John Hay of the *New York Tribune* was even blunter in his comments: "I found De Koven street at last, a mean little street of shabby wooden houses, with dirty door-yards and unpainted fences falling to decay. It had no look of Chicago about it. Take it up bodily and drop it out on the prairie, and its name might be Lickskillet Station as well as anything else. The street was unpaved and littered with old boxes and mildewed papers, and a dozen absurd geese wandered about with rustic familiarity. Slatternly women lounged at the gates, and bare-legged children kept up an evidently traditional warfare of skirmishing with the geese." See Goodspeed, pp. 157–58; Mayer and Wade, p. 107; "That Cow," *Chicago Times*, 23 October 1871, p. [4].

25. Daniel Sullivan, *Inquiry*, vol. [1], pp. 256, 259, 263, 271–72; Catharine McLaughlin, *Inquiry*, vol. [1], pp. 237–39; George Rau, *Inquiry*, vol. [1], p. 179; Chicago Title Insurance Company records.

26. Catharine McLaughlin, *Inquiry*, vol. [1], pp. 224, 230–31, 236; Daniel Sullivan, *Inquiry*, vol. [1], pp. 256–57; Andreas, vol. 2, pp. 57–59, 714; Goodspeed, p. 158; George E. Harper, ed., *Chicago: City on Fire...* (Chicago: Chicago Association of Commerce and Industry, 1971), p. 54-F, hereafter cited in text as *Chicago: City on Fire.*

27. Daniel Sullivan, *Inquiry*, vol. [1], pp. 259, 268, 271–73; Catharine McLaughlin, *Inquiry*, vol. [1], pp. 238–39; George Rau, *Inquiry*, vol. [1], p. 179; Lewis Fiene, *Inquiry*, vol. [1], p. 207; Andreas, vol. 2, pp. 713–14; Chicago Title Insurance Company records; "Linked to Chicago's Two Worst Fires," sec. 7, p. 10.

28. Daniel Sullivan, *Inquiry*, vol. [1], pp. 265, 267–68; Patrick O'Leary, *Inquiry*, vol. [1], p. 251.

29. Daniel Sullivan, *Inquiry*, vol. [1], p. 269; Catherine O'Leary, *Inquiry*, vol. [1], p. 62.

30. Chicago Title Insurance Company records.

31. Kogan and Cromie, p. 181. Perhaps the fire officials are referring to this third building in this somewhat peculiar exchange of inquiry testimony with Daniel Sullivan:

Q. Was there any window at this end?
A. There was not, for the door was opening right into it.
Q. Which side of it was the door?
A. The south side of it.
Q. Out of the southeast corner of that shed (indicating on diagram), [illeg.] *the other shed*, or out of the barn [emphasis added]?

(Daniel Sullivan, *Inquiry*, vol. [1], p. 268.)

32. Daniel Sullivan, *Inquiry*, vol. [1], p. 269; Catharine McLaughlin, *Inquiry*, vol. [1], pp. 230–31; Andreas, vol. 2, p. 714.

33. Daniel Sullivan, *Inquiry*, vol. [1], pp. 264–65; Catherine O'Leary, *Inquiry*, vol. [1], pp. 73–74; Patrick O'Leary, *Inquiry*, vol. [1], pp. 251–53.

34. Daniel Sullivan, *Inquiry*, vol. [1], pp. 256, 267; Catharine McLaughlin, *Inquiry*, vol. [1], pp. 225–26; *Chicago: City on Fire*, p. 54-F.

35. Charles H. French, *Inquiry*, vol. [3], p. 304; Thomas B. Burtis, *Inquiry*, vol. [3], p. 77; Thomas Ockerby, *Inquiry*, vol. [4], p. 6.

36. The transcriber wrote of Ockerby closing the windows to keep the sparks "out of the carpenter shop and the exhaust room +c,..." probably using "+c" as a synonym for "and so forth."

37. Catherine O'Leary, *Inquiry*, vol. [1], pp. 59, 65; Catharine McLaughlin, *Inquiry*, vol. [1], p. 239; Andreas, vol. 1, p. [3]; Andreas, vol. 2, pp. 701, 710–11, 714; "Meteorological Observations by the United States Signal Corps." These observations indicate that by 11:00 P.M. the temperature had dropped to sixty-six degrees. Nonetheless, it still seems likely that the neighbors' windows would have been open at the time the fire started.

38. Patrick O'Leary, *Inquiry*, vol. [1], p. 246; Daniel Sullivan, *Inquiry*, vol. [1], pp. 258–61, 267, 275.

39. Daniel Sullivan, *Inquiry*, vol. [1], p. 255.

40. Daniel Sullivan, *Inquiry*, vol. [1], pp. 256–58, 261, 264. Some sources suggest that Sullivan might have crept into the barn to drink alcohol, hidden away from the eyes of either his disapproving mother or Mrs. O'Leary. There appears to be no evidence that supports this theory. See "Mrs. O'Leary's Cow, Vilified for 100 Years, Maybe Wasn't Guilty," p. 1; *Chicago: City on Fire*, pp. 56-F–57-F; Larry Weintraub, "Mrs. O'Leary's Cow Wins an Acquittal," *Chicago Sun-Times*, 2 September 1971, p. 3; Mike Royko, "Inside Story of Chicago Fire," *Chicago Daily-News*, 3 September 1971, sec. 1, p. 3.

41. Daniel Sullivan, *Inquiry*, vol. [1], p. 267; *Almanac*, p. [14].

42. Catherine O'Leary, *Inquiry*, vol. [1], pp. 67–69; Daniel Sullivan, *Inquiry*, vol. [1], p. 254; Catharine McLaughlin, *Inquiry*, vol. [1], pp. 235–36, 241–42.

43. Daniel Sullivan, *Inquiry*, vol. [1], pp. 262, 264.

44. Daniel Sullivan, *Inquiry*, vol. [1], pp. 256, 260–61, 268, 274; Lewis Fiene, *Inquiry*, vol. [1], pp. 193–95.

45. Catherine Sullivan, *Inquiry*, vol. [1], pp. 114–15; Daniel Sullivan, *Inquiry*, vol. [1], pp. 254–55. Like Mrs. O'Leary, Sullivan also gave a sworn statement before Michael McDermott that was published in the *Chicago Tribune* on October 20. In this affidavit Sullivan attested that he was at the O'Leary home on the night of the fire: "[Daniel Sullivan] testifies that he was at Patrick O'Leary's house, No. 137 DeKoven street, on Sunday night the 8th, of October, 1871, from about 8½ to 9 o'clock at night, during which time Mr. O'Leary and wife were in bed...." See "How It Originated," p. [2].

46. See Daniel Sullivan, *Inquiry*, vol. [1], p. 254. It is not clear from Catherine Sullivan's testimony if she lived by herself or with one or more of her three sons. Consider the following; all emphasis in this note is mine. At one point she testified that "I was in *my own basement* in the rear part of *my own building*, and *one of my boys was out* until it was after eight o'clock, and we didn't have supper until he came in. *We lived in the basement*...." But on the other hand, she later testified: "It was not a long time until *our own two houses* catched afire" and that "*all of my children was at home*. And what they began to do was to save *their own place*, of course."

The 1870 U.S. Census records initially suggest that she and her sons lived together. The following entries from the census form appear in a column titled "The name of every person whose place of abode on the first day of June, 1870, was in this family":

Sullivan Catherine
_____ Daniel
_____ Michael
_____ John

But the enumerator, or census taker, filled out this form on June 27, 1870, and Catherine Sullivan acquired another property, the southwest corner of Clinton and DeKoven streets, three months later, on September 26, 1870. Therefore, it is possible that Mrs. Sullivan lived with her sons until September 1870, when she acquired this parcel of land, which is probably the home Daniel

was referring to when he testified: "There were three of us boys there. My father was buried twenty-six or twenty-seven years, and my mother never put a stepfather over us, and all we earned we saved it and *bought a place for her*." This conclusion that she might have moved from one house to another house nearby would be consistent with her inquiry testimony: "I am living nine years *in that neighborhood*. See Catherine Sullivan, *Inquiry*, vol. [1], pp. 114–118; Daniel Sullivan, *Inquiry*, vol. [1], pp. 273–74; Chicago Title Insurance Company records; 1870 U.S. Census, Cook County, Illinois, Population Schedule, National Archives micropublication M593, roll 204, sheet 174, page 87, lines 25–28.

47. "The Great Fire," *Chicago Tribune*, 25 November 1871, p. 6; "The Great Fire," *Chicago Tribune*, 26 November 1871, p. 1; Catherine Sullivan, *Inquiry*, vol. [1], pp. 114–15; Daniel Sullivan, *Inquiry*, vol. [1], p. 254.

48. Dennis Regan, *Inquiry*, vol. [1], pp. 121–22; *1870 City Directory*, p. 683.

49. "How It Originated," p. [2]; Andreas, vol. 2, p. 709; Musham, p. 155; Dennis Regan, *Inquiry*, vol. [1], p. 121; Catherine Sullivan, *Inquiry*, vol. [1], p. 117; *1870 City Directory*, p. 683; Chicago Title Insurance Company records; "The Fire Investigation," *Chicago Evening Journal*, 25 November 1871, p. [4]; "Reporter of 1871 Fire," sec. 1, p. [2]; *Robinson's Atlas*, vol. 1, plate 6. For the sake of consistency, this book will refer to this O'Leary neighbor as "Dennis Regan," as set forth in the 1870 Chicago city directory and in his 1869 mortgage.

50. Catherine Sullivan, *Inquiry*, vol. [1], p. 117. It seems possible that at least some of these name variations (Dennis Ryan, Dennis Regan) resulted from the uncertain penmanship of the inquiry transcript. The writing on page 121 of the first volume of the transcript (see Dennis Regan, *Inquiry*, vol. [1], p. 121) suggests that "Dennis Ryan" was sworn prior to testifying, but the name could just as easily be construed as "Dennis Regan." This volume contains the testimony of the first fourteen people who testified. At some point, probably post-inquiry, someone listed the names of these fourteen witnesses on a flyleaf at the beginning of the bound pages. The eighth person to testify is shown as "Dennis Ryan," probably because of how the name appears at the top of page 121, which is the first page of his testimony. For this reason Dennis Regan's name is shown as "Dennis Ryan" on page 121 of the annotated transcription of his testimony that appears in Appendix D.

51. Daniel Sullivan, *Inquiry*, vol. [1], p. 257; Patrick O'Leary, *Inquiry*, vol. [1], p. 246; Catherine O'Leary, *Inquiry*, vol. [1], pp. 60–61; Catherine

Sullivan, *Inquiry*, vol. [1], p. 117; Catharine Mc-
Laughlin, *Inquiry*, vol. [1], pp. 224, 230; "How It
Originated," p. [2].

52. Dennis Regan, *Inquiry*, vol. [1], p. 122;
Robinson's Atlas, vol. 1, plate 6; *Chicago: City on Fire*,
p. 54-F.

53. Dennis Regan, *Inquiry*, vol. [1], pp. 121–
23; Catharine McLaughlin, *Inquiry*, vol. [1], pp.
223, 225–26. Why would Regan testify that he
heard music as he ran past the McLaughlin home,
when it appears that Mr. McLaughlin had already
stopped playing? Perhaps Regan heard McLaughlin's fiddle while Regan visited with the O'Learys
that evening. If he did, it is possible that Regan remembered hearing it when he testified on November 24, and so he indicated that he heard
music as he ran to the O'Leary house—not realizing that Mr. McLaughlin had stopped playing at
the time the fire broke out.

54. Dennis Regan, *Inquiry*, vol. [1], pp. 121–
22; Daniel Sullivan, *Inquiry*, vol. [1], pp. 254–55.

55. Daniel Sullivan and Dennis Regan both
testified that they were at Mr. and Mrs. O'Leary's
house on the evening of October 8. After Sullivan
and Regan left the O'Leary home, did they go to
the barn to deliver feed to Catherine Sullivan's
cow? Sullivan's testimony is ambiguous: "I wasn't
in Leary's barn at all on Sunday. I *used* to go in
there every evening, because my mother *keeps* a
cow herself, and I *used* to go in there and bring
feed. I knew where the cows were. I have been
there in Leary's barn hundreds of times [empha-
sis added]." Is Sullivan indicating that his mother
still "keeps" a cow in the O'Leary barn, but that
he no longer feeds it? Or is Sullivan implying that
his mother still owns a cow, but that she boards it
somewhere else, and that is why he no longer goes
to the barn? Recorded property deeds and inquiry
testimony suggest a probable answer.

Chicago Title Insurance Company records
disclose that at the time of the fire, Catherine Sullivan owned three contiguous half-lots on the
south side of DeKoven Street, almost directly opposite the O'Leary home. The west half-lot was
legally described as the west half of lot 18, the middle half-lot was the east half of lot 18, and the half-
lot on the east was the west half of lot 19 (Figure
64). She purchased all of lot 18 in 1864 and the
west half of lot 19 a year later. Sullivan must have
lived in a house on the west half of lot 19 (the east
half-lot) because he testified that after leaving the
O'Leary house, he went next to and east of his
home and sat in front of William White's house,
and William White owned the adjoining land to
the east, the east half of lot 19. Andreas states that
there was a "vacant lot" west of Sullivan's home;

this must have been the middle half-lot, the east
half of lot 18.

These title company records also indicate that
in September of 1870, Catherine Sullivan acquired
another tract of land, lot 21. This lot was also on
the south side of DeKoven Street, but seventy- five
feet east of where her son lived. Lot 21 was at the
southwest corner of DeKoven and Clinton streets.

As discussed in note 46 of this chapter, at the
time of the fire, Catherine Sullivan was probably
living in a house on lot 21. Daniel Sullivan testified
he had four of his horses in one barn and one
horse in another barn. If the east half of lot 18 (the
middle half-lot) was vacant, if Daniel Sullivan lived
on the west half of lot 19, (the east half-lot) and if
Mrs. Sullivan lived on lot 21, it is quite possible
that one of Daniel Sullivan's barns was on the only
remaining Sullivan parcel—the west half of lot 18,
or the west half-lot. So where was the other barn
located?

Catherine Sullivan testified that "I was in my
own basement in the rear part of my own building, and one of my boys was out until it was after
eight o'clock, and we didn't have supper until he
came in. We lived in the basement, for *we had a
horse building on the other side* [emphasis added]." Although Mrs. Sullivan's rationale for subterranean
living is confusing, if not impenetrable, it seems
reasonable to theorize that her home was on one
side of lot 21 and the second barn was on "the
other side" of this fifty-foot-wide lot.

It seems equally reasonable to conclude that,
although Daniel Sullivan was lying when he
claimed that he was not in the O'Leary barn that
Sunday, he was telling the truth when he testified
that he *used* to go to the barn to bring feed to his
mother's cow. Why would he lie about something
that could so easily be verified? He testified that he
and his brothers "bought a place" for their
mother. Daniel Sullivan probably *did* go to the
O'Leary barn to feed his mother's cow—until
Catherine Sullivan's sons bought her the house
and barn on lot 21 in September of 1870. With two
barns in the family, she would be able to keep both
her cow and her son's horses on her own property;
she would no longer have to board her cow in Mrs.
O'Leary's barn. And because Catherine Sullivan's
cow was not in the O'Leary barn on the night of
October 8, Daniel Sullivan and Dennis Regan
would not have gone to the barn to bring it feed
after they left the O'Leary home. See Daniel Sullivan, *Inquiry*, vol. [1], pp. 254–55, 264, 266–67,
270–71, 273–74; Dennis Regan, *Inquiry*, vol. [1], p.
121; Catherine Sullivan, *Inquiry*, vol. [1], pp. 114–15;
Robinson's Atlas, vol. 1, plate 6; Andreas, vol. 2, p.
715; Chicago Title Insurance Company records.

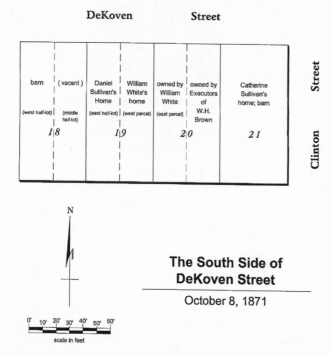

FIGURE 64—THE SOUTH SIDE OF DEKOVEN STREET. Catherine Sullivan owned several parcels of land on the south side of DeKoven Street. Inquiry testimony and Chicago Title Insurance Company records suggest that her son Daniel kept his horses in a barn on the west half of lot 18 and in another barn on lot 21, that he lived in a house on the west half of lot 19, and that his mother lived in a home on lot 21. (Diagram by Douglas A. Swanson.)

56. Daniel Sullivan, *Inquiry*, vol. [1], pp. 259–60; Patrick O'Leary, *Inquiry*, vol. [1], pp. 250, 252–53; "Meteorological Observations by the United States Signal Corps"; Cox and Armington, p. 367; "How It Originated," p. [2].

57. Daniel Sullivan, *Inquiry*, vol. [1], p. 264; Patrick O'Leary, *Inquiry*, vol. [1], pp. 250, 252–53.

58. Daniel Sullivan, *Inquiry*, vol. [1], pp. 257, 269; Patrick O'Leary, *Inquiry*, vol. [1], pp. 251–53; Catherine O'Leary, *Inquiry*, vol. [1], pp. 73–74.

59. It is also possible that Sullivan and

Regan left the O'Leary home at nine o'clock and decided to walk around the neighborhood before going home. Perhaps Sullivan, hampered by his peg leg, could not walk for very long before tiring. While passing through the alley that ran next to the O'Leary barn, he might have decided to rest inside for a few moments. As he and Regan relaxed in the barn, somehow the fire started.

60. Daniel Sullivan, *Inquiry*, vol. [1], pp. 254–56; Dennis Regan, *Inquiry*, vol. [1], pp. 121–22.

61. One might initially infer from Sullivan's testimony that he kept his horses in the O'Leary barn:

Q. Did the fire spread pretty rapidly from Leary's barn?

A. Not very rapidly. The next thing that took afire was a barn at the west end of it.

Q. Do you know when Dalton's house took fire?

A. I don't. I didn't keep account of it. I went and got my horses out.

But this does not appear to be the case. Sullivan's subsequent testimony indicates that he kept the horses in two other barns. See Daniel Sullivan, *Inquiry*, vol. [1], pp. 269–71.

62. Dennis Regan, *Inquiry*, vol. [1], p. 122; Daniel Sullivan, *Inquiry*, vol. [1], pp. 255–56.

63. "The Great Fire," *Chicago Tribune*," 5 December 1871, p. 2; "How It Originated," p. [2]; Daniel Sullivan, *Inquiry*, vol. [1], pp. 256–58; Dennis Regan, *Inquiry*, vol. [1], pp. 122, 124; Catherine Sullivan, *Inquiry*, vol. [1], p. 117; Patrick O'Leary, *Inquiry*, vol. [1], p. 246; Catherine O'Leary, *Inquiry*, vol. [1], pp. 60–61.

• *Chapter Five* •

The Inquiry—
Charade or Cover-Up?

The investigation now in progress, with a view to ascertain the origin of the Chicago fire, and the responsibility for its extensive spread, will, we hope, result in something tangible. Nevertheless, it must be admitted that very little satisfactory information has been obtained.

—*Chicago Tribune*, November 27, 1871

So *why* was the inquiry a disappointment? Didn't the Board of Police and Fire Commissioners realize there were serious discrepancies in the testimony of Sullivan, Regan, and other witnesses? Did it even care if there were? Did commissioners Thomas B. Brown, Mark Sheridan, Frederick W. Gund, and James E. Chadwick deliberately soft-pedal the investigation? Even worse, was there a conspiracy to frame Mrs. O'Leary? When Daniel Sullivan and Dennis Regan set fire to the O'Leary barn, did the Board watch from a grassy knoll across the street? Were eighteen and one-half minutes of Mrs. O'Leary's testimony quietly erased from the pages of the inquiry transcript? Any attempt to answer these questions must begin by taking the pulse of post-fire Chicagoans, a mood that would shift dramatically during the weeks after that memorable Sunday evening, just as the per-

sistent hot breezes of October 1871 finally yielded to the cold winds of December.[1]

The Firemen's Honeymoon

After the fire the stunned residents of Chicago began to dig themselves out of the blackened rubble that was only hours earlier their "Queen City of the West." During those first few days, concerns like food, shelter, missing family members, the financial condition of the local banks, and the payment of insurance losses weighed heavily on the minds of all Chicagoans, and it was these and other similar topics that crowded the pages of the newspapers during this immediate post-fire period.[2]

But even while writing about "Dora Wagner, 4 years old, missing," and that her "mother is at Mr. Theil's, 661 West Erie

139

street," the press did find the time and space to heap kudos on the fire department. The *Tribune* of October 11, for example, bragged that the men battled the fire with "extraordinary perseverance." The October 9 and 17 *Evening Journal* was similarly effusive. Even the normally carnivorous *Times* gushed in its first post-fire issue of October 18 how "in vain the fire laddies fiercely fought the approach of the conflagration." During this time there were no letters to the editor published in the major Chicago newspapers. Citizens clearly had more pressing and immediate worries than writing the local paper. But to the extent that the daily paper was a barometer of the general sentiment of the city, the public initially must have felt nothing but praise for the firemen who valiantly but unsuccessfully struggled to contain the fiery onslaught.[3]

But the honeymoon was short-lived. After the newspapers relocated their offices, purchased or borrowed equipment and supplies, and otherwise limped back to normal, they began to cast a more critical eye towards these heretofore lauded public servants. By October 20 the *Journal* was calling the fire department "demoralized and poorly-handled." On the following day the *Times* termed the fire marshal and commissioners "too imbecile" for not quickly authorizing James Hildreth to blow up buildings. This was clearly an unwarranted accusation, because in most instances the convection whirls would have blown flaming debris over any firebreak that Hildreth could have created. But this made little difference, for by now the handwriting was on the wall, albeit a toppled one, and fireman William J. Brown was reading it to his sister when he wrote her on October 20: "Among the news is the item of the bad feeling against the fire marshal and other heads of the city government; it is in every-

body's mouth and one hears of it everywhere...."[4]

The Controversy Continues

With each passing day, criticism of the fire department intensified. By October 24 the *Chicago Evening Journal* was suggesting that the fire spread out of control because "drunken and stupefied members of the Fire Department were the rule, and sober ones the exception." Other newspapers similarly criticized the police and fire commissioners. The *Tribune*, for example, referred to commissioner Frederick Gund as the man "under whose able administration Chicago burned up." The *Times* was even more uncharitable to fellow commissioner Mark Sheridan, describing him as "a bummer, a loafer, and a drunkard" and accusing him of "lying in the gutters in a state of beastly intoxication." How did the Board of Police and Fire Commissioners respond? On November 9, at one of the Board's semi-weekly meetings, the commissioners appointed some "special policemen," acknowledged the receipt of several thousand feet of hose, and decided to conduct an inquiry—but only to look into the cause of the fire. Left unsaid was any mention of investigating the fire department's handling of the blaze. They agreed to start the following morning.[5]

But they didn't start. For "want of witnesses," the commissioners postponed the investigation until the following day. But the inquiry didn't begin then, either. Reaction was swift and to the point from both the press and the public. In an anonymous letter published in the November 11 *Evening Journal*, an "Old Fireman" declared: "Let the investigation be thorough and complete, especially into the management, condition and conduct of the Fire Department, and the alleged incapacity of the Chief of that Department as exhibited on that terrible Sunday night." On November 14 the *Times* published a letter from a disgruntled "Taxpayer" who asked why the commissioners had not yet commenced the inquiry: "Is it because they are afraid that the evidence adduced at such a trial would not only convict [Marshal Williams] but also criminate themselves for employing a man so totally unfit to fill the very responsible position of chief of our fire department?" The *Tribune* jumped even farther into the fray by launching a series of hard-hitting interviews that could have inspired *Washington Post* reporters Bob Woodward and Carl Bernstein a century later. The newspaper articles were dubbed "Boring for Facts" and were the *Tribune*'s own investigation of "All the Fire Marshal's Men." The mission statement of the series (which the *Republican* derisively claimed was "more bore than facts") was aptly set forth in the first paragraph of the first article; it appeared on November 15, page one, column one: "The Board of Police and Fire Commissioners having failed in their duty to investigate and report to the public, whose servants they are, the origin and progress of The Great Fire, and the conduct of the Fire Department on the fatal night of October 9, a reporter of the *Tribune* was yesterday despatched to interview...."[6]

Fire Marshal Williams. First Assistant Fire Marshal Schank. Third Assistant Fire Marshal Benner. These and others were questioned by the *Tribune* in the next few days. Meanwhile, Board President Thomas Brown was assuring the public that the inquiry would begin as soon as witnesses could be gathered together and a course of action adopted. But several days passed with no further Board activity, and on November 21 the *Journal* joined the *Tribune* and *Times* in calling for an investigation

into not only the cause of the fire but also the performance of the firemen: "If, as is generally believed, the flames succeeded in getting the mastery of the Fire Department because of the drunkenness or inefficiency of its officers and employes, the fact ought to be established, or, if not a fact, disproved, by a thorough and searching investigation into all the circumstances of beginning and early stages of the conflagration." Finally, on the afternoon of November 23, after one more delay—it was supposed to start at ten o'clock that morning—the inquiry began. By this time new charges of misconduct were being leveled against the city's firefighters. Besides complaints of being drunk and incompetent, they were now also being accused of accepting bribes. Chicagoans claimed that during the fire they had to pay firemen money before these public servants would turn the hoses on their burning property. If citizens did not pay, the firemen left to find others (presumably wealthier or more desperate) who would. Apparently because of charges such as these, what was at first an investigation into the cause of the blaze had now expanded to include a review of the firemen's conduct on October 8–10. It appeared that the people and the press had not only spoken, they also had been heard.[7]

Optimism Changes to Criticism

This new and improved inquiry consisted of the interrogation of various alleged "witnesses." These people were questioned inside a small, chilly room at Chicago's second precinct police station. On that first day only two men were interviewed, firemen William J. Brown and Mathias Schaefer, but during the next two weeks many others were questioned. There were the obvious witnesses like Mr. and

Mrs. O'Leary, Dennis Regan, and Daniel Sullivan. But there were others not so prominently associated with the fire—men like Chalkley J. Hambleton, a lawyer, and William Fraser, who owned a bakery. By December 4, the last day of testimony, a total of fifty people would have taken their turns (some very reluctantly), sitting on the only cushioned chair in what was called "the captain's room," fielding questions posed by the four commissioners, the fire marshal, or his three assistants. After the first day, a shorthand reporter was also present to transcribe the questions and answers. Representatives of the press sat nearby to summarize each day's testimony for their respective papers and on occasion even to ask a witness a question.[8]

At first, some of these newspapers seemed to be at least guardedly optimistic about the inquiry. On the opening day of questioning the *Evening Journal* described it as the "long expected fire investigation." On the following day the *Republican* hailed the testimony of William J. Brown and Mathias Schaefer as the first step towards "brushing away the cobwebs that clothe the great conflagration, its origin and progress." After Mrs. O'Leary testified, the November 26 *Tribune* confidently predicted that the inquiry would eventually reveal that someone from the McLaughlin party caused the fire.[9]

The enthusiasm lasted only twenty-four hours. On November 27 the *Evening Journal* termed the investigation a "farce." The *Tribune* that day, although more tactful, did admit that to date "very little satisfactory information has been obtained," due in part, it seems, to the officials' propensity to interview firemen instead of tapping the recollections of private citizens who were at the fire from beginning to end. By the time the inquiry ended on December 4, even the *Tribune* was characterizing

testimony as "superfluously tedious, dry, uninteresting, and irrelevant." At the start of the investigation, this newspaper printed long and thorough summaries of each person's statements. But by the end of the inquiry, it was dismissing much of the testimony with just a few sentences and occasionally adding a sarcastic comment of its own: "George S. Dorset was driver of the fire escape. He did not know much about the fire, except that it was a pretty big one."[10]

On December 2, two days before the investigation ended, the *Evening Journal* claimed that "the Commissioners are sick of the whole thing." Was this true? Was the *Journal* correct? Had even the Board become disenchanted with the inquiry? Possibly yes; evidence of possible Board apathy is uncovered by comparing the Board's actions at the start of the inquiry to its behavior during the waning days of the investigation.[11]

As no stenographer was available on opening day to take down the statements of the first two witnesses, Commissioner Brown dutifully wrote out the details of their testimony. On the last day of the investigation, the Board met at two in the afternoon. A shorthand reporter was present but the final witness, the foreman of Ryerson's lumberyard, was not. By three o'clock he had not appeared, and so the Board dismissed the reporter. But after he left, the foreman arrived, and the officials questioned him. This time, though, it appears that none of the commissioners bothered to write down his statements. Although both the *Tribune* and *Evening Journal* of December 5 printed summaries of his testimony, the inquiry transcript contains no reference whatsoever. This is especially surprising, because only two days earlier an official had specifically requested that the foreman testify so that the witness could address concerns about the possible brib- ing of firemen. Perhaps this seemingly unas- suming incident is indicative of the Board's sentiments during the investigation's final days.[12]

Perhaps the commissioners *were* "sick of the whole thing." But *why* did the Board feel this way? What happened during those nine days of inquiry testimony? Even if the Board was simply unnerved by the press, this does not explain the commissioners' failure to determine the cause of the fire. In fact, one would think that after being in- cessantly browbeaten, the Board would have been spurred to draw a more positive conclusion other than "whether it origi- nated from a spark blown from a chimney on that windy night, or was set on fire by human agency, we are unable to deter- mine."[13]

Even stranger is the public's lack of re- action to the Board's tepid final report, which the *Evening Journal, Times* and *Re- publican* all published on December 12, just eight days after the inquiry ended (see Ap- pendix E). There were no editorials in these newspapers that blasted the commission- ers for their failure to ascertain the fire's cause. The *Times*, for all its criticism and sarcasm (e.g., repeatedly referring to the Board as the "Smelling Committee" in its articles about the inquiry), merely com- mented that "the conclusions that the com- missioners draw are worthy of attention, no doubt, but are given in a 'we-told-you- so' tone that might have been avoided." On December 30 the *Evening Journal* published a "chronological record of the more im- portant Chicago events" of 1871. Although this compilation contained such Chicago Fire minutiae as the date the courthouse bell was removed from the ruins (Novem- ber 2) and even noted the "close of the fire investigation" (December 4), it failed to recognize the December 12 publication of

the commissioners' report. During the final days of 1871, neither the *Times, Eve- ning Journal, Tribune*, nor *Republican* pub- lished even one "letter to the editor" from a concerned citizen, incensed or otherwise, commenting on the Board's findings or lack thereof. In short, over the course of twelve days the commissioners and mar- shals haphazardly interviewed fifty people, published an inconclusive report, and in the end, nobody cared. Why was the in- quiry conducted so poorly? Why didn't the Board's conclusions elicit a reaction?[14]

The report that was eventually issued by Messrs. Brown, Sheridan, and Chadwick (Mr. Gund having retired only days earlier) could have been a contender. It could have been a thoughtful analysis of the fire de- partment's performance on October 8–10. By exposing the many inconsistencies in Sullivan's and Regan's testimony, the re- port might have revealed the fire's cause. The Board's conclusions could have had the significance of Martin Luther's Ninety- five Theses, with Board president Thomas Brown nailing copies to firehouse doors throughout the city. Instead, Chicagoans had to settle for the Warren Report, for in presenting their findings, the commission- ers ignored key evidence and neglected to interview important witnesses. Further- more, a careful examination of the text of the transcript reveals other shortcomings as well:[15]

- Much of the information gleaned from the investigation was not pertinent to the origin of the fire and the fire department's handling of it.
- The commissioners and fire officials fre- quently asked inane questions. Dif- ferent witnesses were often asked the same irrelevant question.
- Board members and marshals asked leading questions that invited re-

sponses favorable to the fire department.

• The men asked questions when they already knew the answers.

• The fire officials often avoided controversial and potentially embarrassing answers, but were quick to comment on "safe" and mundane issues.

• The commissioners and marshals did ask some critical and thought-provoking questions, but they did so only occasionally and primarily towards the end of the investigation.

Irrelevant Information

Historian A. T. Andreas noted that the inquiry "produced a mass of irrelevant matter." But it was more than just a mass; it was the vast majority of the 1168 pages of testimony. Newspaper articles indicate that the public wanted answers to two fundamental questions: How did the fire start? Was the fire department lax in fighting the fire? The commissioners failed miserably in responding to the first question, and the inquiry transcript suggests that the commissioners neglected to deliver the answer to the second question as well.[16]

It is clear that the firemen were unable to extinguish the fire only hours after it started in the O'Leary barn. Not only were they exhausted from fighting the Lull & Holmes blaze of Saturday night, but convection whirls were hurling burning brands throughout this wooden city. For this reason it is perhaps more appropriate to phrase the second question as: Was the fire department lax in fighting the fire *at its inception?* The *Tribune* asked this in one of the most thoughtful articles that appeared in the immediate post-fire press. It was published on November 19, just a few days before the start of the inquiry. The article included an observation and comment that could have formed a policy touchstone that would have successfully guided the commissioners over the course of twelve days of inquiry proceedings:

> If any blame can attach to [the fire officials] in the premises, it is that they did not check the fire in the outset. After it had once gained headway, and fire and wind were acting together, Fire Marshal Williams and his assistants might as well have attempted to extinguish the sun as to master it.... If any investigation is to be had concerning their competency, that investigation should appertain to the commencement of the fire alone.[17]

But the commissioners and marshals did not concentrate their investigation on the fire's commencement. They should have grilled William Brown, the courthouse telegraph operator. Did he see the incipient blaze even before Mathias Schaefer called down to him? Was Brown really playing his guitar that evening, as his sister Sarah R. Hibbard later claimed, possibly fiddling while Chicago burned? Instead, the officials interviewed not one, not two, but three superintendents of the Chicago Gas Light and Coke Company, who droned *ad nauseam* about telescopic gas holders, coupling points, and gasometers.[18]

Mathias Schaefer, the courthouse watchman, testified that while on duty inside the cupola, two people, apparently visitors, questioned him about the courthouse clock. (Four-sided, a gift from the Astronomical Society, it had been installed just a few months earlier.) After talking with them, he lit his pipe and stepped outside; a walkway encircled the tower (Figure 13). He looked first to the east, and then, turning to the southwest, he saw the fire. In response to his testimony, the fire officials should have asked Schaefer how much time he spent speaking to these people. Did they distract him? Might he have seen the fire earlier if they had not been there?[19]

But it appears that the men did not ask Schaefer these and other crucial questions. But they did interview John Tolland, self-described "keeper of the lake tunnel." Tolland was stationed upon a forty-foot-high wooden crib that was sunk offshore in thirty feet of water. Chicago's water supply passed through the crib's sluices, then through a cylindrical tunnel, which was about five feet high, five feet wide, and under the lake bed, to the city's water works. As Tolland was two miles from land at the time the fire started, his testimony could not have been of any relevance. Indeed, Tolland himself appeared to grow exasperated at the officials' line of questioning. They repeatedly asked him to describe the nature of the flaming debris that rained onto his wooden island (Figure 65). Fearful for his life (at one point he remarked, "I would have sold out my chances between two and three o'clock for a dollar to any man that came along"), he finally replied, "A man placed in the predicament I was, he would not pay much attention how [the debris looked], so long as he saved his own place." But the marshals and commissioners ignored Tolland's sarcasm and continued to question him and then added six more pages to Andreas's already imposing "mass of irrelevant matter."[20]

The officials interviewed several firemen in order to learn why the fire spread out of control. But they could have questioned a myriad of other people. They could have interrogated Bruno Goll and William Lee in an attempt to determine if Goll really did turn in an alarm from his store. The officials could have questioned the residents of DeKoven and Taylor streets to find out why they apparently failed to set off an alarm at nearby fire alarm Box

295 (Figure 46). But the commissioners and marshals did not question any of these people. They did, though, interview police sergeant Louis J. Lull. They gave men like Lull free rein to prattle endlessly without simply answering the questions posed them. And so these witnesses told the Board everything they knew about the fire in apparent hopes of preserving their primarily insignificant recollections for posterity. And preserved for posterity they were—all 1168 pages.[21]

Ineffective and Indifferent Questioning

Some of the superfluous material that appears throughout the transcript is due to the many inane questions that the commissioners and fire marshals asked the witnesses. Occasionally they asked several witnesses the same ridiculous question. For example, Commissioner Brown asked fireman William Mullin, the fourth person to testify, "How much rain had we had for the last two or three months before that fire?" This question was clearly irrelevant to the proceeding. Nonetheless, Mullin was asked the question—and so was Mrs. O'Leary, policeman Michael C. Hickey, and firemen Michael Sullivan and Michael W. Conway.[22]

Once it was firmly established that the weather had been dry during the previous weeks, one could probably assume that Chicago's buildings were in a similar condition. But the questioners assumed nothing. They asked firemen Leo Meyers, William Musham, David Kenyon, and also Michael Hickey whether or not the buildings were dry. Musham was one of the first firemen to arrive at the burning O'Leary property. The officials asked him the direction the wind was blowing at the time, then subsequently asked four other

FIGURE 65—JOHN TOLLAND AND HIS WIFE ON THE WATER CRIB. The "crib" was a giant wooden pentagon-shaped box 40 feet high and 90 feet across. It was constructed in 1865 out of 675,000 feet of lumber and 200 tons of bolts and iron fastenings. After it was built on shore, it was floated two miles out into Lake Michigan, filled with 4,500 tons of stone, and sunk in 30 feet of water. Fresh lake water ran from the crib through a brick tunnel and an iron shaft to the city's water works and water tower and eventually distributed throughout the city's water mains. John Tolland and his wife were stationed on the crib on the night of October 8. In this drawing, Marshall Philyaw captures the drama and terror of Tolland's inquiry testimony as the couple fight for survival on top of their wooden island and against a background of a blazing city skyline. (Drawing by Marshall Philyaw)

witnesses—Mrs. O'Leary, Daniel Sullivan, Michael Sullivan, and fireman John Dorsey—the same question.[23]

The burning of St. Paul's Catholic Church was episodic in the fire saga. One would think that the commissioners and marshals knew where the church used to stand. But not only did they ask Michael Sullivan where it was located, they also asked fellow firemen Denis and Francis Swenie. Although Fire Marshal Williams testified during the inquiry that "I ran

around to the front of Bateham's mill," he asked James Hildreth, "That Bateham's mills stood where, between what streets?"[24]

The commissioners and fire officials posed other questions that were even more ridiculous, but at least the men asked them only once:

- "Was it pretty hot in the alley?"[25]
- "Was the air very warm?"[26]
- "Was the wind blowing pretty strong?"[27]
- "What effect had the wind upon your

stream at that time when you were throwing it directly in the eye of the wind?"[28]

- "Did the church burn down?"[29]
- "Suppose the water works hadn't burned. Would the fire have been as disastrous as it was?"[30]

And finally, the ultimate in idiocy:

- "It is dangerous to go near a falling wall without a fire hat?"[31]

With the commissioners, Fire Marshal Williams, and his assistant marshals asking questions such as these, it is understandable why the *Evening Journal* derisively commented on December 1:

> Some valuable information is being elicited by the "investigation" into the causes of the great fire. For example, one of the witnesses—a volunteer fireman—solemnly testifies that he heard Fire Marshal Williams exclaim, right in the midst of the excitement, "Charley, it's hot!" and that he thought the Fire Marshal spoke the truth. This valuable testimony will go far towards clearing up the mystery. It settles one stupendous fact that had been half-suspected before—to wit: that the fire was *hot!* Now if the "investigation" will only settle one other fact, it may adjourn—to wit: why it came to be so very hot.[32]

Not only did these men ask absurd and asinine questions, they sometimes added a leading tone that telegraphed favorable responses:

- "Could the fire have been started in any other place in the city where it had as good a field to make a big burn—spread over as much ground?"[33]
- "Was there any other place in the city more adapted to make a big burn than that was?"[34]
- "I should judge from what you saw of it,

it was a very difficult fire to combat with any fire department."[35]

- "Do you think you ever saw a fire move quite as rapidly as that did in Chicago before?"[36]
- "Of course all that was wearing upon the men, machinery, and everything else."[37]
- "Did it or not strike you, as soon as you found the water works were burned down, and the North Side well on fire, that it was a doomed district?"[38]
- "Do you think that the excessive work on Saturday night had anything to do with preventing the men from going to the fire Sunday night?"[39]

And then there were the questions that the officials not only asked, they also immediately answered:

- **Q.** On that block was there anything else besides mills and lumber?
  A. There was large frame buildings. I do not think there was a brick structure on the whole square.
  Q. A match factory?
  A. Yes sir.
  Q. Furniture factory in the rear of the mill?
  A. Yes sir.
  Q. Pretty extensive?
  A. Very extensive. I understand he used the whole west building for the furniture manufactory.
  Q. A lumber yard in the rear?
  A. A lumber yard in the rear also.[40]

- **Q.** During the time foreign engines were here, under whose orders were they acting?
  A. I could not state. I understand from Mr. Walter himself that he was over on the North Side giving them instructions.

Q. Of course they were in the immediate command of their chiefs and assistants who were there.[41]

- Q. What kind of a roof was there over there, the works there?
  A. I have been upon the tower there several times and I should judge it was one of those composition roofs—graveled.
  Q. Wood and composition, was it?[42]

- Q. That Bateham's mills stood where, between what streets?
  A. I ought to be able to state without a thought because I have passed by that a thousand [times] within two or three years.
  Q. Do you think between Mather and Harrison?
  A. Yes sir, I think that was it.
  Q. Just south of Harrison?
  A. Yes sir....[43]

- Q. What are the buildings just south of that?
  A. The main structure was wood.
  Q. I think you are mistaken on that.[44]

But the fire officials could not lob these grapefruit-sized softballs for all nine innings of the inquiry. Bribery, drunkenness, ineptitude—the public had demanded that these issues be addressed. When the commissioners and fire marshals questioned the witnesses on matters such as these, the responses sometimes proved embarrassing. But no matter. When this happened, these officials would often either ignore the reply or merely comment innocuously, steering the controversy aside. For example, the following excerpt from Mrs. McLaughlin's inquiry statements includes their reaction to her testimony concerning

the fire department's delay in arriving at the burning O'Leary barn:

- Q. About how long a time after you went outdoors and saw the barn on fire and Mr. Dalton's house did you see a fire engine come?
  A. I could not say. It was some minutes.
  Q. Do you know that it was five minutes?
  A. I think it was more, about ten minutes.
  Q. The time seems long at such times.[45]

When Daniel Sullivan echoed Mrs. McLaughlin's conclusion, the questioners likewise replied in a similar fashion:

- Q. Do you remember how long after you noticed this fire before any fire engines came on the ground?
  A. Well, it was quite a while.
  Q. Can you give a definite idea in minutes of the time?
  A. I should think, so far as my understanding goes, that it was from ten to fifteen minutes.
  Q. A minute would seem pretty long when you wanted help.[46]

While James Hildreth was describing his efforts to save the city by blowing it up, he indicated: "I was fatigued and had not had anything that night to eat. I drank more than the firemen did, for that matter...." This last remark, albeit revealing, was ignored by the marshals and the Board. Later, when specifically asked about possible firemen drunkenness, Hildreth replied, "No sir, never saw firemen work harder in my life." He then added, though, the cryptic comment: "There was, of course, when it got to be along toward morning." Rather than ask Hildreth to elaborate, the questioner immediately changed the subject.

Similarly, when witness Benjamin Bullwinkle revealed that private citizens, not firemen, were manning the fire hose of a steam engine, the reply was not, "Where were the firemen? Why weren't they at the engine?" Instead, the next question was, "Which way were they working?"[47]

But perhaps the most egregious example of fire official indifference occurred during the questioning of Marshal Williams. In the middle of a long monologue, he remarked that when the fire reached a point about 150 feet from where he lived, he thought he should rescue his wife. He did, but then also corralled at least one other fireman to help move his piano down the stairs. Before he was finished, he also attempted to save his carpet and stove. On the other hand, *Evening Journal* employees remained at their posts and struggled to publish a newspaper while the city burned around them. In an issue that commemorated the fiftieth anniversary of the fire, the paper reminisced: "As the printers set the type, each one knew that his family was homeless and in danger. But not one of the staff, from editor to galley boy, ran from his job."[48]

While the *Times* later gleefully trumpeted Williams's behavior in a headline, "He Tried to Save His Own Piano, in Preference to Preserving Chicago," the Board and the other marshals seemed oblivious to the import of Williams' conduct. Even after Williams disclosed this apparent bombshell, the commissioners and other officials let him ramble on for ten more pages of testimony. When they finally asked him a question, it was not a request to explain his actions. Instead, they asked him to "mention the cities that have sent engines or firemen here, if you can recollect them all."[49]

The Fire Officials' Selective Response

Perhaps the Board and the marshals did not deliberately ignore these controversial matters. Is it possible that the witnesses' long discourses prevented the officials from effectively examining them, that by the time the commissioners and marshals were able to respond, the opportunity to question had passed? Did the sometimes meandering testimony of these witnesses sidetrack the questioners and prevent them from remembering and focusing on issues?

This does not appear likely. The inquiry is replete with instances where the fire officials quickly interjected and commented on matters that were initially disclosed even days earlier. For example, Third Assistant Fire Marshal Mathias Benner's testimony consists largely of pages and pages of uninterrupted exposition. But when he remarked that William Musham, foreman of the steam engine *Little Giant*, had spoken to him when he was directing fire department operations on the city's South Side, the commissioners and other marshals immediately asked Benner if Musham had told him about the *Giant*'s stoker being absent, an incident that Musham had mentioned in his inquiry testimony a full eight days earlier. Why did these officials ask Mathias Benner about an absent fireman but fail to ask James Hildreth about drinking firemen? Did they deliberately concentrate their attention on innocuous issues and just as consciously ignore more important but potentially damaging matters? This exchange between Benner and the fire officials makes it clear that at least in this instance the Board and marshals were listening closely to Benner's rambling account:

- **Q.** Was the *Giant* working when you ordered her back on the South Side?
- **A.** No sir, because I had broken up that lead in consequence of the fire running across Wabash Avenue. We lost some few hundred feet of hose there; that was burned up on Wabash Avenue, corner of Van Buren. The engine at that time was in a pretty hot place when I ordered her away from there. The *Giant* was then, I think, on Van Buren Street just east of Wabash Avenue. I ordered that lead to be led up Michigan Avenue. Then, when Mr. Musham came to me and asked me what he was to do, that was just after my getting a report from the West Division about the condition of the fire there, and I sent the *Giant* over there.
- **Q.** Did he say anything about his stoker being absent?
- **A.** No sir.[50]

Previous pages detail the many inconsistencies in Daniel Sullivan's inquiry statements of November 25, inconsistencies that were either ignored or unnoticed by the commissioners and marshals. William Mullin, foreman of the steam engine *Illinois*, testified on November 24. He stated that when he arrived at the burning O'Leary property, he led in with his hose from Taylor Street, which was north of the fire. George Rau, foreman of the hook and ladder *Protection*, testified later that same day. Rau commented that he saw the *Illinois* come in on DeKoven Street, not Taylor Street, as Mullin indicated. Although the fire officials failed to recognize critical problems with Sullivan's inquiry statements, the following portion of Rau's testimony indicates that they were quick to correct Rau on the name of a street:

- **Q.** Did you see the *Illinois* stream?
- **A.** Yes sir.
- **Q.** Where was that?
- **A.** They came in on DeKoven Street.
- **Q.** Aren't you mistaken?
- **A.** No. I guess not.
- **Q.** I think you are.[51]

Thomas B. Burtis and Thomas Ockerby were both superintendents of the Chicago Gas Light and Coke Company, which had operations on both the North Side and the South Side of Chicago. Burtis testified on November 29, and Ockerby followed on December 2. Both spoke in excruciatingly mind-numbing detail about the operation of the company. During his testimony Burtis suggested that a North Side gas holder was heavier than one on the city's South Side. The questioners were quick to comment when Ockerby later claimed that the opposite was true:

- **Q.** I understand that, that your holders balance each other so that if there was a deficiency here, the gas flows in this direction, and if there is a deficiency on the other side, it flows over.
- **A.** These gas holders do not balance each other. I told you, sir. This one is the heaviest holder of the lot.
- **Q.** Was there not one on the North Side heavier than the South Side?
- **A.** No sir.
- **Q.** I understood Mr. Burtis to say so the other day.
- **A.** I cannot help what Mr. Burtis said, and I know more today about the management of gas holders in the last four years than any other man in the city, and I know that this gas holder is heavier than anything they have there.[52]

Mrs. O'Leary testified on November 24. When asked if Daniel Sullivan lived "opposite you on DeKoven," she replied that he lived "right across the road" and that he was a drayman. Catherine Sullivan appeared before the commissioners and fire marshals later that day. It is clear that these men remembered Mrs. O'Leary's testimony when they asked Mrs. Sullivan about her son:

• Q. Are you any relation to Mr. Sullivan who is a drayman and lives about opposite that fire?
  A. Yes sir. He is my son.[53]

Why is it that officials commented on Mr. Burtis' observations as to gas holders, but ignored Marshal Williams' disclosures about his efforts to save his piano, carpet, and stove? It appears that they were selective in many of their statements, that they would freely mention insignificant matters such as where Daniel Sullivan lived and what he did for a living, but quietly disregard controversial issues such as possible derelict firemen—or what Sullivan was doing on the night of October 8.[54]

A Different Line of Questioning

But the commissioners and fire officials occasionally threw the witnesses a hardball. As the inquiry wore on into December, the tenor of the investigation almost imperceptibly changed. The interrogation was never hostile, but it did eventually acquire an edge as the actions of the firemen, although not blatantly criticized, were questioned:

• Q. In your judgment, was there any possibility of stopping the fire on the West Side when you arrived there?

A. When I got there, I did not think the fire was going to get any further. It seemed pretty well dampened when I got there. I think the *Rehm* and our own engine could have taken care of the church if they had not let the fire come down from the other way on top of us. The church was all down.

Q. You think it was the neglect to protect the Canal Street line that led to the fire surrounding you?[55]

• A. After the fire struck the South Side, all the engines in the country could not save the city, in my opinion.

Q. But the limits of the fire might have been bounded?[56]

• Q. Did I understand you to say that at one time you could have done considerable work had you had short hooks with you?

A. Yes sir.

Q. Are you [aware?] that over [twelve?] months ago an order was passed by the Board, directing that the engines not immediately in connection with hook and ladder trucks to carry short hooks?[57]

• Q. How long were you engaged at the Rock Island depot there moving those cars?

A. I should judge it must have been three quarters of an hour to an hour.

Q. Did you consider that a part of your duty, to be moving cars there?

A. Yes sir. If them cars had caught fire, it would have swept clear across there.

Q. Suppose you had been giving your attention to getting some engines about there?

A. I had sent for some engines.

Q. Isn't it your duty to be about and see that they come?[58]

What caused this change in the tone of questioning? Why were the firemen no longer immune from criticism? There seem to be three possible reasons for the rips and tears in their heretofore impermeable shirts and jackets:

First, perhaps the local newspapers' constant criticism of the inquiry eventually galvanized the commissioners and fire marshals into a more aggressive style of questioning. But the press had criticized more than just the quality of the inquiry testimony. The November 27, 1871, *Evening Journal* also had condemned the officials for padding the witness list with firemen. This was apparently why James H. Hildreth, the thirty-fourth person to testify, was summoned to appear before the marshals and commissioners two days later. Sixteen others followed the ex-alderman before the investigation ended, and despite the *Journal's* concerns to the contrary, six of these were firemen. All sixteen, though, had very little to offer the investigation. For example, one questioner asked the thirty-eighth witness if he knew anything about the origin of the fire. This certainly would have been an appropriate question for William White or James Dalton. But the witness was neither White nor Dalton; it was Henry J. Hittorff, a South Side watchmaker and jeweler, whose testimony was useless in solving this nineteenth-century whodunit.[59]

Second, it appears from the post-fire newspapers that there was little love lost between Marshal Williams and some of his men. The *Republican* even suggested that firemen from the steam engine *Gund* disobeyed orders during the blaze and deliberately abandoned their engine, allowing it to burn up in the fire so that they could

"put up a job on the Chief Fire Marshal." Admittedly, the bent of many of the *Republican's* articles makes it clear that it was as much a pro–Williams paper as the *Times* was not. But even the *Tribune* noted, in summarizing the testimony of Francis T. Swenie, that when Williams cross-examined the fireman, "the replies tended to show that there was very little affection wasted between the two." And one of the more memorable passages from Swenie's inquiry comments includes a statement that provides a rather frank indication of how Marshal Robert "Bob" Williams felt about his first assistant John Schank: "I [Swenie] met Mr. Schank and I asked him why Bob was not getting the engines around to the other side of the fire. [Schank had apparently suggested that Williams do this.] He [Schank] told me that Bob told him to go to hell." With Marshal Williams a potential questioner of all the firemen who testified, as well as a possible target of any questions of assistant fire marshals John Schank, Lorens Walter, and Mathias Benner, one wonders why the inquiry testimony did not often degenerate into a state approaching raw acrimony instead of only occasionally slipping over into something slightly less than starched civility.[60]

Finally, the *Republican* suggests that the Board of Police and Fire Commissioners may have split into two separate factions: "A portion of the Board," as the newspaper succinctly concluded, "is disposed to investigate, and a portion aint; and that's the way the matter stands." Perhaps the former bloc might have been responsible for these sporadic lapses into something at least resembling incisive questioning. But with such eleventh-hour cross-examination being the exception rather than the rule, clearly these queries were too little and too late.[61]

Espionage at the Inquiry?

Newspaper reporters were present during the investigation to observe each day's testimony, which was later summarized for publication. But these accounts do not always mirror the transcript:

• According to the *Evening Journal* of November 25, Mrs. O'Leary testified that although she owned six cows, "she only saved a calf, which, however, afterward died from its injuries...." But the transcript of her testimony indicates that the calf lived: "Saturday morning I refused eleven dollars for the calf, and it was sold afterwards for eight dollars." Did the calf live or die? Which version is correct?[62]

• In commenting on Patrick O'Leary's inquiry testimony, the *Tribune* of November 26 observed that "he did not know how the fire started." The paper also quoted him as declaring, "If he was to be hanged for it he couldn't tell. He didn't blame any man in America for it." On the other hand, the transcript is silent about O'Leary not blaming anyone, only indicating, "If I was to be hanged for it, I don't know who done it." This newspaper article also contains a summary of Mrs. McLaughlin's testimony. According to the *Tribune*, Mrs. McLaughlin testified about how "boys could go into the alley near the barn, as there was nothing to prevent them." But the transcript discloses no such remark. Where did the additional statements of O'Leary and McLaughlin come from?[63]

• Although the November 29 *Tribune* claimed that fireman Alexander McMonagle knew that some frame buildings contained "engraver's rooms," this term is not found in the transcript of McMonagle's testimony.[64]

• Admittedly, the *Times* was renowned for its sarcasm and exaggeration. But for the most part, its summaries of each day's proceedings were fairly straightforward. The November 30 issue includes a comment by Commissioner Mark Sheridan on the scarcity of fire hose: "It was d—d strange where all the hose went to so very suddenly." But it was equally strange that this remark did not appear in the transcript.[65]

Although these differences are not substantive, they are apparent. J. L. Bennett, a court reporter, took down the testimony of the witnesses in shorthand. This was then transcribed into a final longhand format. Could Bennett have deliberately modified the transcript? Was he responsible for these differences? More importantly, could he have changed the questions and comments of the commissioners and marshals in a deliberate attempt to discredit the fire department? Is it possible that these officials *did* effectively interview such "important" witnesses as Daniel Sullivan and Dennis Regan, but that their testimony was later sabotaged?[66]

Not likely. First of all, the following excerpt from fireman Charles Anderson's inquiry statements indicates that pages of transcribed transcript were available for post-questioning examination. Surely someone reviewing these written reports would have spotted any significant inconsistencies between them and what was said at the inquiry:

Q. Had the *Giant* or *Chicago* got there then?

A. I saw nothing but ourselves. Our apparatus was the only apparatus I saw there, but the other man that works with me, Mr. Manwell, ran to the alley as it is customary with him, and he says when he went to the fire, the *Giant* was on the southeast corner of, I think, DeKoven and Jefferson streets, and they were leading in the hose, and he says there were three houses and two barns on fire then. That is what he told me today. *I was reading the evidence that was given yesterday* and he told me that [emphasis added].[67]

And although there were some discrepancies in this evidence, they were generally minor. Overall, the reporters' summaries of each day's testimony were consistent with the transcript. This is especially the case during the first few days of the inquiry, when key witnesses like Mr. and Mrs. O'Leary and Mrs. McLaughlin were interviewed. But as the days passed, and as these reporters realized that the proceedings were ineffectual, many of their summaries grew shorter as the newspapers reflected an increasing frustration with the administration and direction of the investigation: "All that the firemen thus far have done is to state that they were 'there,' did their best, saw very little, and were positive that every one was sober. Twenty or thirty large volumes might be filled up with such evidence, which does not amount to a 'hill of beans.'"[68]

It is possible that a disheartened press became careless and that newspaper reporters were responsible for many of these inconsistencies. The daily struggle to quickly summarize a day's worth of testimony into a few column inches might have been a factor as well. But it is also possible that J. L. Bennett was to blame. There is no evidence, though, of subterfuge on his part. If Bennett wanted to undermine the in-

quiry, there certainly would have been drastic, not minor, differences between the transcript and the newspaper accounts. Furthermore, his credentials were impeccable. He was a civil war veteran, rising to the level of captain before being discharged in 1865. He became an attorney in 1867, but finding the pace of a lawyer too slow for him, began to study shorthand. He soon was back in the courtroom, but this time as a stenographer. He also did reporting for many business conventions and worked for the *Tribune, Times,* and *Inter Ocean* covering various presidential campaigns. In 1882 he not only became president of the International Association of Shorthand Writers of the United States and Canada, but also was commander of Post 28, Grand Army of the Republic. If Bennett was at fault, surely it was not as a subversive, but as a harried recorder who occasionally failed to memorialize formal testimony or possibly even "off the record" observations.[69]

Although Bennett may have been the only shorthand reporter employed during the investigation, the different penmanship styles evidenced in the inquiry transcript suggest the possibility that several people transcribed the witnesses' testimony from shorthand into longhand.[70] Perhaps mistakes were made as these people struggled to read Bennett's notes. Or perhaps there were several shorthand reporters, and errors were made as each stenographer rushed to transcribe his notes for impatient commissioners and marshals. It is also possible that Bennett was the only court reporter and that after each day of testimony, he hastily transcribed his shorthand notes into longhand. Later, perhaps several people made a final version of Bennett's initial draft and while copying it made these mistakes. Regardless of the reason for these discrepancies, it seems clear that the Societe Internationale had not infiltrated

Chicago's second precinct police station and that there was no nefarious plot to discredit the fire department. There was no need to sabotage the inquiry transcript. It was evident from the daily newspaper articles recounting (and commenting on) the testimony of each witness that there were enough problems with the investigation.[71]

Putting It All Together

The *Evening Journal* was right. The inquiry was a farce. Charged with determining how the fire started and evaluating the fire department's conduct in fighting it, the marshals and commissioners failed on both counts. Why didn't they question important witnesses? Why did they neglect to effectively question the people they did interview?

The answer seems clear. They did not have to ask Daniel Sullivan why he was in front of William White's house on the night of October 8. Why should they attempt to determine the cause of the fire, when the city's newspapers had been telling Chicagoans for weeks that it was Mrs. O'Leary, her cow, and her lantern? Even before the inquiry began, Mrs. O'Leary had already been tried and convicted—but not by a jury of her peers, rather, by the press. The following comments appeared in the *Tribune, Evening Journal, Republican,* and *Times* in November of 1871, prior to and during the inquiry, but several weeks after the initial post-fire hysteria:

- On motion of the President [of the Board], it was resolved to commence investigating the origin of the fire of the 7th, and of the 8th and 9th days of October, this morning. The lady who owned that cow will be summoned to appear.[72]

- Mrs. O'Leary persists in denying the story about her cow having kicked over the lamp which set fire to Chicago. It is too late. She told the kicking story herself in the first place—it has become a fact in history—and she and all the cows on DeKoven street cannot now kick it over.[73]

- The Board of Police and Fire Commissioners met yesterday afternoon, to begin to investigate the origin of the great fire, which is so universally ascribed to a demoralized cow, a helpless lamp, and an industrious Irishwoman.[74]

- [The fire marshals] left Commissioner Chadwick and the reporters in the lurch staring at each other and wondering whether box No. 342 had any connection with another Irishwoman-cow-kerosene lamp-explosion.[75]

- Mrs. O'Leary, the owner of the cow, which, it was claimed, kicked over the lamp and started the fire, testified that she and her family—her husband and five children—were in bed, but not asleep, on that Sunday night.[76]

- Mrs. O'Leary affirms that she was in bed asleep when the fire broke out in her barn.... Oh, Mrs. O'Leary! Why will you persist in trying to kick over that kicking cow and lamp story?[77]

- No, no, Mrs. Leary, that game won't win. Your renowned cow *did* kick over that lamp filled with non-combustible kerosene, and you needn't deny it.[78]

- In conclusion, witnesses said it was impossible for [Mrs. O'Leary] to say positively which cow it was kicked over the lamp.[79]

These statements indicate that even before the inquiry began, Mrs. O'Leary was being blamed for starting the fire. For this reason it is doubtful that the fire marshals and the commissioners conspired to frame her. But did these men use its investigative mandate in an attempt to at least *dissuade* the public from believing that she and her cow caused the fire? No, it did not. But why not? Is it possible that they deliberately chose *not* to determine the cause of the fire? After all, if they *did* discover how the fire started, perhaps people would then stop wondering about the fire's origin and start asking other questions, such as, "Why did it take so long for the fire department to arrive at the O'Learys' burning barn?"

Then was it the press that plotted against Mrs. O'Leary? Although there is no evidence of any such collusion, anti–Irish sentiment was alive and well in post–Civil War Chicago. In 1865 the *Times* published a lengthy article entitled "The City: Squatter Settlements," stating that "these are the 'patches' where the sons of the Emerald isle have 'squatted,' built their seven-by-nine shanties, reared their offspring and bred their extensive droves of geese, hens, cows, dogs and cats." In 1868 the *Chicago Evening Post* complained that the Irish filled prisons, reform schools, and charitable institutions and remarked: "Scratch a convict or a pauper and the chances are that you tickle the skin of an Irish Catholic at the same time...." The *Tribune* evidenced a lesser but still noticeable degree of nativism in November 1871 when it commented on the inquiry testimony of Mrs. O'Leary, Mrs. McLaughlin, and Catherine Sullivan: "Considerable know-nothingism can be developed among the Irish, since none of the people in that vicinity have any idea of how long it was, or how far the fire had got, before the engines arrived." But this *Tribune* writer failed to mention that it was the firemen with the decidedly non–Irish names of William J. Brown and Mathias Schaefer

who may have been responsible for the engines' delay in the first place! In November and December of 1871, not one reader of the *Tribune, Evening Journal, Republican,* or *Times* spoke up against the native-born that controlled these newspapers by writing a letter to one of these papers' respective editors, protesting Mrs. O'Leary's treatment by the press and proclaiming her innocence.[80]

But not all Chicagoans abandoned Mrs. O'Leary. She did have one curious ally in fellow Irishman Michael McDermott, notary public and surveyor. In October he submitted her "statement and affidavit" (Figure 66, reprinted in Appendix C) to the *Tribune* in response to the "great want of charity in the epithets used by the *Times*...." In it, O'Leary revealed that she milked her cows at five o'clock in the morning and four-thirty in the afternoon and that she had no lamp in either her yard or her barn on the night of the fire. Although McDermott suggested in an accompanying letter that after Chicagoans read her statement, they would "look for the cause [of the fire] in other sources, and perhaps attribute it to the love of plunder, Divine wrath, etc.," it appears that his invitation evoked no response from a city already convinced that a cow caused a conflagration.[81]

Mrs. O'Leary couldn't write the *Tribune* to complain about how the *Times* and other papers portrayed her; apparently unable to write, she signed this affidavit with an "X." But there were plenty of other Chicagoans not so handicapped, and many of them took pens in hand and filled the newspapers with letters. But they did not write impassioned pleas of clemency for DeKoven Street's most famous resident. Instead, they wrote letters criticizing the firemen's conduct during the fire. The department clearly had an image problem, and as a result, the Board and fire marshals

HOW IT ORIGINATED.

Statements and Affidavits as to the Start-ing Point of the Great Fire.

To the Editor of The Chicago Tribune :

A great deal has been published respecting the origin of the great fire, which all reports have settled down on the head of a woman, or as the *Times* has it, an " Irish hag" of 70 years of age. Admitting for a moment that an Irish hag of 70 years was by an unforeseen accident the cause, yet there was a great want of charity in the epithets used by the *Times* of the 18th. The following facts are stubborn things, and will cause the public to look for the cause in other sources, and perhaps attribute it to the love of plunder, Divine wrath, etc.:

On last Sunday night I made my way to the O'Leary's house, yet standing, and there, at No. 137 DeKoven street, on the east ½ of Lot 12, in Block 39, School Section Addition to Chicago, found Dennis Sullivan, of No. 134, and Dennis Ryan, of No. 112, both of DeKoven street. There and then I took the annexed affidavits. The parties have been known to me personally for several years as of irreproachable character. Mrs. O'Leary is neither haggard nor dirty.

Patrick O'Leary and Catherine, his wife, being duly sworn before me, testify that they live at No. 137 DeKoven street, and own the lot and house in which they live: they had five cows, a horse and wagon, on all of which they had not one cent of insurance. She milked her cows at 4½ p. m. and 5 a. m., as Mrs. O'Leary peddled the milk. Mrs. O'Leary fed the horse beside the fence at about 7 o'clock p. m., and then put him in the barn. She had no lamp in the yard or barn that night or evening.

Patrick O'Leary testifies that he was not in the barn during that day or night; left the feed-ing of the cows and horse to his wife and daughter; that both were in bed when awakened by Denis Ryan, of No. 112 DeKoven street; that they have lost their barn, cows, horse and wagon.

Subscribed and sworn before me this 15th day of October, 1871.

his
PATRICK ⋈ O'LEARY,
mark.
her
CATHERINE ⋈ O'LEARY
mark.
MICHAEL McDERMOTT,

Notary Public for Chicago and City Surveyor.

Denis Sullivan being duly sworn before me testifies that he was at Patrick O'Leary's house, No. 137 DeKoven street, on Sunday night the 8th, of October, 1871, from about 8½ to 9 o'clock at night, during which time Mr. O'Leary and wife were in bed, that he went a few lots east of O'Leary's on the opposite side of DeKoven street, until about half-past 9 o'clock, when he saw the fire. He went across the street and cried "fire" "fire," and went into O'Leary's barn, where he found the hay in the loft on fire. He then attempted to cut loose the cows and horse, but failed to save anything but a half burned calf. He then came to O'Leary's and found them out of bed, Denis Ryan alarmed them during his time at the barn.

Subscribed and sworn to before me this 15th day of October, 1871.

his
DENIS ⋈ SULLIVAN.
mark.
MICHAEL McDERMOTT.

Notary Public for Chicago, and City Surveyor.

were at least unofficially charged with de-termining whether or not this public per-ception was justified.[82]

But these officials failed to meet this challenge. Chicagoans demanded that they *evaluate* the fire department. Instead, the inquiry transcript indicates that they chose to merely *exonerate* the department. If they had been sincerely interested in assessing the behavior of department personnel, they would have aggressively interrogated fire-men like Mathias Schaefer and William J. Brown. But their indulgent questions and ready acceptance of accommodating an-swers make it clear that the commissioners and marshals wanted to guide their fifty witnesses along a path of least resistance. Pressured by both the people and the press to investigate the fire, the men interviewed six DeKoven Street residents, eleven other private citizens, four policemen, two mem-bers of the Fire Insurance Patrol, and twenty-seven firemen, but the transcript of this inquiry indicates that the Board sleep-walked through the nine days of question-ing. The real mystery of the Chicago Fire is not its cause, but rather, *why* the fire officials chose to conduct their investiga-tion in this manner. The fire department valiantly fought the blaze, but in the end it was no match for the fire's Four Horsemen of fatigue, equipment breakdown, convec-tion whirls, and a burned-out waterworks. Surely an unbiased and independent in-quiry would have brought this out. From the beginning the public had clamored for

FIGURE 66—McDERMOTT LETTER AND O'LEARY AFFIDAVITS. These "statements and affida-vits" of Mr. and Mrs. O'Leary and city sur-veyor Michael McDermott were pub-lished in the October 20, 1871, issue of the *Chicago Tribune*. An annotated ver-sion appears in Appendix C. It appears that both O'Learys signed their affidavits with an "X."

such an investigation. Why didn't the fire officials give the city what it wanted?[83]

Because although the fire department deserved a collective "A" for its efforts, there may have been some below average grades on some of the firemen's individual report cards for "conduct":

• Was Mathias Schaefer remiss in not spotting the fire sooner from atop the courthouse?
• Did William J. Brown see the fire even before Mathias Schaefer called down to him? Was Brown negligent in not striking Box 319?
• Did Marshal Robert Williams abandon his duties when he stayed at his home to save his piano, carpet, and stove from the advancing flames?
• Were the firemen James Hildreth alluded to inebriated when they fought the fire?
• Was Christian Schimmals, foreman of the *Chicago* engine company, at fault for not cleaning and servicing his engine immediately after the Saturday night fire? Was the *Chicago* unprepared to fight the fire when it took its position at the corner of Jefferson and Taylor streets?

Perhaps these and other similar questions weighed on the fire officials' minds as they began to interrogate the first of the fifty witnesses. Possible fire department intoxication and incompetence was already on the minds of Chicagoans when the inquiry finally staggered to a start on the afternoon of November 23, 1871. Perhaps the Board did not *want* to conduct a thorough investigation, as any damaging testimony might further erode public confidence in the department. Although a diligent inquiry might have determined that Schaefer, Brown, and these other firemen were

not negligent, it appears that the Board did not want to take that chance. Instead, a mediocre investigation would insure that any and all skeletons would remain locked up in the fire stations' closets. The first witness was William J. Brown, and as he opened the door of the second precinct police station and walked inside on the afternoon of November 23, 1871, perhaps the board members and fire officials reviewed their game plan: The best way to win back the city's trust would be to get the inquiry over as soon as possible and issue an indecisive report. As Chicago's attention in the weeks that followed turned to rebuilding the city, its citizens would soon forget the newspapers' clarion calls for answers.[84]

It seems that the commissioners and marshals *were* more interested in public relations and in mending the department's battered and tattered reputation than in learning how their firemen measured up on that memorable Sunday evening of early October. Because in the wake of virulent public criticism, the officials folded. They should have demanded, for example, that James Hildreth explain his statement about drinking more than the firemen. Instead, concerned (if not consumed) only with damage control, they asked firefighters like Michael W. Conway, John Doyle and Nicholas Dubach innocuous questions that invited favorable responses:[85]

• "How was the air at that time?"[86]
• "Did you see any of the firemen intoxicated?"[87]
• "Was there any possibility of the firemen doing anything more to stop the progress of the fire?"[88]
• "Did the men all behave properly?[89]
• "Do you know of any money being offered to any firemen or anybody to move engines that night to play on any particular spot?"[90]

Satisfied with the answers to these and other equally transparent and vacuous inquiries, Commissioners Brown, Sheridan, and Chadwick went off to draw up its verdict. Encouraged by an acerbic press, the Board had spent weeks allowing Chicagoans to think that a West Side Irishwoman and her cow caused the fire. But now the investigation was over. The 50 witnesses had left. The commissioners had to face the realization that not only did they have no evidence that Mrs. O'Leary and her bovine companion were responsible for the blaze, they had no evidence of anything whatsoever. Consequently, the Board's decision was one of foregone conclusions. Honest, sober, and industrious firemen did all they could to contain the fire. Naturally, the report was inconclusive as to the cause, but it did shift blame away from Mrs. O'Leary. Once the newspapers printed the commissioners' findings on December 12, she was no longer appropriate fodder for the press' cannons, and so the inflammatory articles stopped. The *Tribune*, *Evening Journal*, *Republican* and *Times* published virtually nothing about Mrs. O'Leary and her cow in December after the Board's findings appeared in print.

But this was of little solace to Catherine O'Leary, as the damage to the family name had already been done. On the night of October 8, 1871, in a barn behind a tiny cottage on DeKoven Street, a cow, prodded by the Chicago press, kicked both a lantern and its owner into the history books. But Mrs. O'Leary wanted a rewrite of the first few pages, as she had a different story to tell. Unfortunately, she would quickly find out that no one wanted to listen to her. The history books were already going to press.[91]

Notes

1. When the investigation began Brown, Sheridan, Gund, and Chadwick were commissioners. Gund retired on December 4, the day the investigation ended, and was succeeded by Jacob Rehm. See Andreas, vol. 2, pp. 84, 86, 710; Flinn, pp. 123, 134; "The Fire Investigation," *Chicago Evening Journal*," 27 November 1871, p. [4]; "Police and Fire Commissioners," *Chicago Evening Journal*, 5 December 1871, p. [4]. (The Board's final report, with annotations, appears in Appendix E.)

2. Cromie, p. 1; "To the Homeless," *Chicago Tribune*, 11 October 1871, p. [2]; "Missing Persons," *Chicago Evening Journal*, 11 October 1871, p. 1; "Just and Generous," *Chicago Tribune*, 13 October 1871, p. [2]; "Condition of the Banks," *Chicago Tribune*, 11 October 1871, p. [2].

3. "List of Missing," *Chicago Tribune*, 11 October 1871, p. 1; "The West Side," *Chicago Tribune*, 11 October 1871, p. 1; "The Great Calamity of the Age!," p. 1; "The Fire Department," *Chicago Evening Journal*, 17 October 1871, p. 1; "The Fire," *Chicago Times*, 18 October 1871, p. 1.

4. "While the Fire Raged," sec. 5, p. 33; "Readers Bring Famous Extra," p. [2]; "Mistake," *Chicago Evening Journal*, 20 October 1871, p. 1; "The 'Blowing Up' Business," *Chicago Times*, 21 October 1871, p. [2], hereafter cited in text as "The Blowing Up Business"; William J. Brown letter, 20 October 1871.

5. "Liquor-Drinking Firemen," *Chicago Evening Journal*, 24 October 1871, p. [2], hereafter cited in text as "Liquor-Drinking Firemen"; "Gund," *Chicago Tribune*, 7 November 1871, p. 4; "The Man Gund," *Chicago Times*, 26 October 1871, p. [2]; Untitled article, *Chicago Times*, 26 October 1871, p. [2]; "The Chicago Fire Department," *Chicago Times*, 4 November 1871, p. [2]; Untitled article, *Chicago Times*, 6 November 1871, p. [2]; "Board of Police," *Chicago Tribune*, 10 November 1871, p. 6; "The Cause of the Fire," p. [4].

6. "Management of the Fire De[p]artment," *Chicago Evening Journal*, 11 November 1871, p. [2], hereafter cited in text as "Management of the Fire Department"; "That Investigation on Kicks," p. [4]; "Fire-Marshal Williams," *Chicago Times*, 14 November 1871, p. [4], hereafter cited in text as "Fire-Marshal Williams"; "Boring for Facts," *Chicago Tribune*, 15 November 1871, p. 1; "Chicago Condensed," *Chicago Republican*, 20 November 1871, p. [4]; Untitled article, *Chicago Times*, 15 November 1871, p. [2]; "Our Fire—Its Causes and Lessons," *Chicago Tribune*, 12 November 1871, p. 4, hereafter cited in text as "Our Fire—Its Causes and Lessons."

7. "Boring for Facts," *Chicago Tribune*, 15 November 1871, p. 1; "Boring for Facts," *Chicago Tribune*, 17 November 1871, p. 4; "That Investigation," *Chicago Evening Journal*, 17 November 1871, p. [4]; "Investigation Wanted," *Chicago Evening Journal*, 21 November 1871, p. 1; "That Investigation Again," *Chicago Evening Journal*, 23 November 1871, p. [4], hereafter cited in text as "That Investigation Again"; "That Investigation," *Chicago Evening Journal*, 24 November 1871, p. [4]; Untitled article, *Chicago Times*, 18 November 1871, p. [2]; Untitled article, *Chicago Times*, 21 November 1871, p. [2]; "The Fire Department," *Chicago Times*, 14 November 1871, p. 1; "The Fire," *Chicago Times*, 24 November 1871, p. [4]; "The Great Fire," *Chicago Tribune*, 24 November 1871, p. 6; "City Brevities," *Chicago Republican*, 18 November 1871, p. 1, hereafter cited in text as "City Brevities"; William Mullin, *Inquiry*, vol. [1], pp. 54–55; Leo Meyers, *Inquiry*, vol. [2], pp. 109–10; Mathias Benner, *Inquiry*, vol. [4], pp. 176–86 passim; Robert A. Williams, *Inquiry*, vol. [4], pp. 290–92; Michael W. Conway, *Inquiry*, vol. [2], pp. 25–30.

8. "The Fire," *Chicago Times*, 24 November 1871, p. [4]; "The Fire," *Chicago Times*, 26 November 1871, p. 1; "How They Look and Act," p. [3]; "The Great Fire," *Chicago Tribune*, 24 November 1871, p. 6; "The Great Fire," *Chicago Tribune*, 26 November 1871, p. 1; "The Great Fire," *Chicago Tribune*, 30 November 1871, p. 4; *1870 City Directory*, p. 914; "Important Order," *Chicago Republican*, 4 November 1871, p. [4]; "How Was It?," *Chicago Republican*, 24 November 1871, p. [4], hereafter cited in text as "How Was It?"; "How It Was," *Chicago Republican*, 25 November 1871, p. [4]; "The Smelling Committee," *Chicago Times*, 30 November 1871, p. [4]; "The Fire Investigation," *Chicago Evening Journal*, 25 November 1871, p. [4]; "The Fire Investigation," *Chicago Evening Journal*, 27 November 1871, p. [4]; "That Investigation Again," p. [4]; "The Great Fire," *Chicago Tribune*, 5 December 1871, p. 2; Chalkley J. Hambleton, *Inquiry*, vol. [2], p. 46; William Fraser, *Inquiry*, vol. [3], p. 238; James H. Hildreth, *Inquiry*, vol. [3], p. 128; William Mullin, *Inquiry*, vol. [1], p. 35; Francis T. Swenie, *Inquiry*, vol. [3], p. 177. William Musham was the third person to appear before the commissioners and marshals. He was the first person to testify on the second day of the investigation. The "question and answer" format of his testimony indicates that this was the first time a shorthand reporter was present at the hearing to take down a witness' statements, which were later transcribed into longhand. See William Musham, *Inquiry*, vol. [1], pp. 6–34. Newspaper articles indicate that, on occasion, not all commissioners and marshals were

present to interrogate a witness. The *Times*, in fact, seemed to take particular pains to point out what commissioners were not present during inquiry questioning or when one "finally" arrived. See, e.g., "The Great Fire," *Chicago Tribune*, 25 November 1871, p. 6; Untitled article, *Chicago Times*, 25 November 1871, p. [2]; "The Fire," *Chicago Times*, 26 November 1871, p. 1.

9. Untitled article, *Chicago Tribune*, 26 November 1871, p. 2; "How Was It?," p. [4]; "That Investigation Again," p. [4].

10. Untitled article, *Chicago Tribune*, 27 November 1871, p. 2; "Two Fire Items," *Chicago Evening Journal*, 27 November 1871, p. [2]; "The Fire Investigation," *Chicago Evening Journal*, 27 November 1871, p. [4]; "The Great Fire," *Chicago Tribune*, 25 November 1871, p. 6; "The Great Fire," *Chicago Tribune*, 2 December 1871, p. 4; "The Great Fire," *Chicago Tribune*, 3 December 1871, p. 4; "The Other Side," *Chicago Republican*, 30 November 1871, p. [4], hereafter cited in text as "The Other Side."

11. "That Investigation," *Chicago Evening Journal*, 2 December 1871, p. [4].

12. "The Great Fire," *Chicago Tribune*, 5 December 1871, p. 2; "That Investigation," *Chicago Evening Journal*, 5 December 1871, p. [4]; Mathias Benner, *Inquiry*, vol. [4], pp. 176–86 passim; "The Great Fire," *Chicago Tribune*, 24 November 1871, p. 6. It appears that the strain of adverse public opinion eventually forced Commissioner Thomas B. Brown to resign from the board. In a newspaper interview published on November 15, Brown told the *Tribune*: "Yes, I made up my mind to resign. To tell the truth, I'm tired of this business. The whole city is down on this board. They have an idea that everything has been mismanaged, and I am tired of it all." Brown stepped down on December 18. See "Setting Them Right," p. 6; "The Fire Department," *Chicago Tribune*, 17 November 1871, p. 3; "Brown's Valedictory," *Chicago Times*, 19 December 1871, p. 7.

13. "The Great Fire," *Chicago Evening Journal*, 12 December 1871, p. [4].

14. "The Great Fire," *Chicago Evening Journal*, 12 December 1871, p. [4]; "Nobody to Blame," p. 5; "The Great Fire," *Chicago Republican*, 12 December 1871, p. [4]; "1871," *Chicago Evening Journal*, 30 December 1871, p. [4]; "How They Look and Act," p. [3]; Untitled article, *Chicago Times*, 12 December 1871, p. 4. A review of the *Evening Journal*, *Tribune*, *Times*, and *Republican* from December 12, the day the Board's final report was published, through the end of the year discloses only three newspaper articles that were even mildly critical of the Board's findings. As noted in the text, the

December 12 *Times* remarked that the Board's conclusions were given in a "we-told-you-so" tone, the December 15 *Times* observed that the fire department "escaped censure by the board in summing up the result of their investigations," and the December 12 *Republican* included the following sarcastic comment: "The Fire Commissioners have reported that if the fire had occurred under more favorable circumstances, it would not have done so much damage. If the little dog hadn't fooled away his time, he would have had rabbit-hash for supper." See Untitled article, *Chicago Times*, 12 December 1871, p. 4; "Fires," *Chicago Times*, 15 December 1871, p. 2; "Personalities," *Chicago Republican*, 12 December 1871, p. [4].

15. Andreas, vol. 2, p. 86; "The Little Police Farce," *Chicago Republican*, 5 December 1871, p. [4]; "Police and Fire Commissioners," *Chicago Evening Journal*, 5 December 1871, p. [4]; "The Great Fire," *Chicago Evening Journal*, 12 December 1871, p. [4]. For an objective opinion of the Warren Commision—an opinion that parallels this chapter's assessment of the Board of Police and Fire Commissioners—see John Kaplan, "The Case of the Grassy Knoll: The Romance of Conspiracy," in *The Historian as Detective: Essays on Evidence*, ed. Robin W. Winks (New York: Harper & Row, 1968), pp. 371–419.

16. Andreas, vol. 2, p. 709; "That Investigation," *Chicago Tribune*, 14 November 1871, p. 4; "Boring for Facts," *Chicago Tribune*, 15 November 1871, p. 1.

17. "The Fire Marshal and His Assistants," *Chicago Tribune*, 19 November 1871, p. 2.

18. "Marks Anniversary of the Great Fire"; Cromie, p. 36; Peter T. Burtis, *Inquiry*, vol. [3], pp. 51–57; Thomas B. Burtis, *Inquiry*, vol. [3], pp. 81–92 passim; Thomas Ockerby, *Inquiry*, vol. [4], pp. 12–22 passim; Andreas, vol. 2, p. 711.

19. Cromie, pp. 36–37; Kogan and Cromie, pp. 10–11; Mathias Schaefer, *Inquiry*, vol. [1], p. 5; Colbert and Chamberlin, p. 154.

20. Andreas, vol. 2, pp. 66–68; Pierce, vol. 2, pp. 332–33; Cromie, pp. 125–26; Colbert and Chamberlin, pp. 155–59, 352; John Tolland, *Inquiry*, vol. [2], pp. 183–186.

21. Andreas, vol. 2, pp. 709, 711, 714; Louis J. Lull, *Inquiry*, vol. [4], pp. 89–117 passim.

22. William Mullin, *Inquiry*, vol. [1], p. 48; Catherine O'Leary, *Inquiry*, vol. [1], p. 72; Michael C. Hickey, *Inquiry*, vol. [2], p. 181; Michael Sullivan, *Inquiry*, vol. [1], p. 95; Michael W. Conway, *Inquiry*, vol. [2], p. 39.

23. Leo Meyers, *Inquiry*, vol. [2], p. 84; William Musham, *Inquiry*, vol. [1], pp. 18–19; David Kenyon, *Inquiry*, vol. [2], p. 126; Michael C. Hic-

key, *Inquiry*, vol. [2], p. 181; Catherine O'Leary, *Inquiry*, vol. [1], pp. 71–72; Daniel Sullivan, *Inquiry*, vol. [1], p. 264; Michael Sullivan, *Inquiry*, vol. [1], p. 84; John Dorsey, *Inquiry*, vol. [2], p. 80.

24. Michael Sullivan, *Inquiry*, vol. [1], pp. 96–97; Denis J. Swenie, *Inquiry*, vol. [2], p. 224; Francis T. Swenie, *Inquiry*, vol. [3], p. 181; Robert A. Williams, *Inquiry*, vol. [4], pp. 247–48; James H. Hildreth, *Inquiry*, vol. [3], p. 129.

25. Lewis Fiene, *Inquiry*, vol. [1], p. 197.

26. Thomas Byrne, *Inquiry*, vol. [2], p. 136.

27. George Rau, *Inquiry*, vol. [1], p. 176.

28. Charles Anderson, *Inquiry*, vol. [3], p. 109.

29. William Fraser, *Inquiry*, vol. [3], p. 242.

30. Robert A. Williams, *Inquiry*, vol. [4], p. 279.

31. Robert A. Williams, *Inquiry*, vol. [4], p. 292.

32. Untitled article, *Chicago Evening Journal*, 1 December 1871, p. [2], col. 2, third article. The *Journal* is probably referring to fireman Charles Anderson, who testified on November 29. See Charles Anderson, *Inquiry*, vol. [3], p. 101.

33. Leo Meyers, *Inquiry*, vol. [2], p. 100.

34. Leo Meyers, *Inquiry*, vol. [2], p. 101.

35. Chalkley J. Hambleton, *Inquiry*, vol. [2], p. 59.

36. George Rau, *Inquiry*, vol. [1], p. 175.

37. Mathias Benner, *Inquiry*, vol. [4], p. 122.

38. Lorens Walter, *Inquiry*, vol. [4], p. 205.

39. Robert A. Williams, *Inquiry*, vol. [4], p. 289.

40. Leo Meyers, *Inquiry*, vol. [2], p. 93.

41. Leo Meyers, *Inquiry*, vol. [2], p. 110.

42. Lorens Walter, *Inquiry*, vol. [4], pp. 201–2.

43. James H. Hildreth, *Inquiry*, vol. [3], p. 129.

44. Charles G. Wicker, *Inquiry*, vol. [4], p. 72.

45. Catharine McLaughlin, *Inquiry*, vol. [1], p. 233.

46. Daniel Sullivan, *Inquiry*, vol. [1], p. 265. Admittedly, the Board and marshals did not always ignore potentially embarrassing answers. For example, when the fire officials asked Mrs. O'Leary, "How long after you got outdoors was it before you saw the engine there?" she replied that "it was not very quick at all." Instead of blandly commenting, the men continued to ask her how much time elapsed before an engine arrived. Perhaps this was because unlike Mrs. McLaughlin or Daniel Sullivan, Mrs. O'Leary never gave a definite answer to the question. See Catherine O'Leary, *Inquiry*, vol. [1], pp. 75–77.

47. James H. Hildreth, *Inquiry*, vol. [3], pp. 152, 170–71; Benjamin Bullwinkle, *Inquiry*, vol. [3], p. 281.

48. Robert A. Williams, *Inquiry*, vol. [4], pp. 264–65; "Readers Bring Famous Extra," pp. 1–[2]. John J. Flinn indicates in his *History of the Chicago Police* that Chicago's policemen were as dedicated as the staff of the *Evening Journal*. "One hundred and fifty of the police force were left homeless and almost penniless by the fire. Most of these were on duty during the nights of October 8th, 9th and 10th, doing what little they could to assist the firemen, to help the distracted and fleeing people, to protect property and to keep the peace, while their own houses were being swept away, and their own families were being driven before the flames, to the lake side or the prairie." See Flinn, p. 125; see also Michael C. Hickey, *Inquiry*, vol. [2], pp. 161–62, who expressed similar sentiments about the police force.

49. "The Smelling Committee," *Chicago Times*, 4 December 1871, p. [3]; "Story of the Great Chicago Fire," sec. 3, p. 20; Robert A. Williams, *Inquiry*, vol. [4], pp. 264–275. Fireman John Doyle testified that he also left his post to look after his family. The Board and commissioners did not comment on his actions. See John Doyle, *Inquiry*, vol. [3], p. 10. On the other hand, Henry J. Hittorff's testimony was extremely critical of the fire department, and his remarks occasionally produced a lukewarm response. See Henry J. Hittorff, *Inquiry*, vol. [3], pp. 267–79 passim.

50. William Musham, *Inquiry*, vol. [1], pp. 30–31; Mathias Benner, *Inquiry*, vol. [4], pp. 175–76.

51. William Mullin, *Inquiry*, vol. [1], pp. 38–39; George Rau, *Inquiry*, vol. [1], p. 183.

52. Thomas B. Burtis, *Inquiry*, vol. [3], pp. 74, 83–85, 88–89; Thomas Ockerby, *Inquiry*, vol. [4], pp. 1, 36–37; Andreas, vol. 2, pp. 701–2.

53. Catherine O'Leary, *Inquiry*, vol. [1], pp. 59, 61; Catherine Sullivan, *Inquiry*, vol. [1], p. 114; "The Fire Investigation," *Chicago Evening Journal*, 25 November 1871, p. [4].

54. For another example of the Board's discriminating memory, see Michael W. Conway, *Inquiry*, vol. [2], pp. 1, 44–45. When Conway, pipeman of the steamer *Chicago*, testified on November 25 that his engine company did not have much hose, an official retorted, "I understood there was eighteen lengths [of hose]." This was an apparent reference to the previous day's testimony of Christian Schimmals, who was the foreman of the *Chicago*: "There was eighteen lengths [of hose] in our house in the basement...." See Christian Schimmals, *Inquiry*, vol. [1], pp. 126, 136.

55. Denis J. Swenie, *Inquiry*, vol. [2], p. 234.

56. Isaac L. Milliken, *Inquiry*, vol. [4], p. 88.

57. Mathias Benner, *Inquiry*, vol. [4], p. 166.

58. John Schank, *Inquiry*, vol. [4], p. 222.

59. "The Great Fire," *Chicago Tribune*, 30 November 1871, p. 4; Henry J. Hittorff, *Inquiry*, vol. [3], p. 267; "The Fire Investigation," *Chicago Evening Journal*, 27 November 1871, p. [4]. Appendix D includes a list of the fifty people who appeared before the commissioners. The names of the witnesses are shown in the order in which they testified. Also included are their occupations, if noted in the transcript, and the date they testified.

60. Francis T. Swenie, *Inquiry*, vol. [3], pp. 173, 175; Untitled article, *Chicago Republican*, 2 December 1871, p. [2], col. 1; "The Other Side," p. [4]; "The Great Fire," *Chicago Tribune*, 2 December 1871, p. 4; "Boring for Facts," *Chicago Tribune*, 17 November 1871, p. 4; "Boring for Facts," *Chicago Tribune*, 18 November 1871, p. 4; "How They Look and Act," p. [3]. For two vastly disparate opinions of Marshal Williams, compare "The Other Side," p. [4] with "Municipal Reconstruction," *Chicago Times*, 18 November 1871, p. [4]. Francis T. Swenie testified on December 1, and during questioning he related to the Board John Schank's claim that Marshal Williams told Schank to "go to hell." John Schank testified the following day, and Williams then asked Schank about this alleged incident:

Q. (By Mr. Williams) In evidence it was stated yesterday that you came to me and requested me to move the engines north of the fire, and I told you to go to hell. Have I ever given you such an answer as that?

A. I do not recollect that you ever told me anything of that kind.

See John Schank, *Inquiry*, vol. [4], pp. 207, 232–33.

61. "City Brevities," *Chicago Republican*, 15 November 1871, p. 1.

62. "The Fire Investigation," *Chicago Evening Journal*, 25 November 1871, p. [4]; Catherine O'Leary, *Inquiry*, vol. [1], p. 59.

63. "The Great Fire," *Chicago Tribune*, 26 November 1871, p. 1; Patrick O'Leary, *Inquiry*, vol. [1], p. 249.

64. See "The Fire Investigation," *Chicago Tribune*, 29 November 1871, p. 4.

65. "The Smelling Committee," *Chicago Times*, 30 November 1871, p. [4].

66. *Edwards' Chicago Directory: Fire Edition* (Chicago: Richard Edwards, 1871–72) p. 41, hereafter cited in text as *Fire Edition Directory*; William Mullin, *Inquiry*, vol. [1], p. 35; "How They Look

and Act," p. [3]; "The Great Fire," *Chicago Tribune*, 26 November 1871, p. 1; "Nobody to Blame," p. 5.

67. Charles Anderson, *Inquiry*, vol. [3], pp. 104–5.

68. The Fire Investigation," *Chicago Evening Journal*, 27 November 1871, p. [4].

69. A[lfred] T[heodore] Andreas, *History of Chicago: From the Earliest Period to the Present Time*, vol. 3, *From the Fire of 1871 until 1885* (Chicago: A. T. Andreas Co., 1886), p. 714, hereafter cited in text as Andreas, vol. 3.

70. In some instances, obvious differences in penmanship indicate that two different people transcribed the testimony of one witness into the final longhand version. See, e.g., Mathias Benner, *Inquiry*, vol. [4], pp. 150–51; Robert A. Williams, *Inquiry*, vol. [4], pp. 259–60.

71. The transcript of the inquiry discloses two basic types of discrepancies. The first type is a phrase or sentence that is in a newspaper's summation of a witness' testimony, but is either not shown in the transcript or appears in the testimony but in a substantially different rewording. For example, the *Evening Journal*, in commenting on the October 8 McLaughlin party, wrote that Mrs. O'Leary described the event as "a little bit of a shindy." This phrase does not appear in the transcript. See Untitled article, *Chicago Evening Journal*, 27 November 1871, p. [2]. According to the *Republican*, Denis J. Swenie's testimony indicated that "the foreman of the *Coventry* had a sick shoulder...." But the transcript suggests that Swenie merely said that the foreman "had just been hurt," nothing more specific. See "How Was It?," *Chicago Republican*, 29 November 1871, p. [4]; Denis J. Swenie, *Inquiry*, vol. [2], p. 223. This first type of inconsistency is probably the fault of the shorthand reporter.

The second type is a word that is either omitted from the transcript or appears in the testimony but is misspelled. See, e.g., Robert A. Williams, *Inquiry*, vol. [4], pp. 267–8: "I ordered the *Winnebago* to lead up their hose from where they were playing and *get on the of the building...*" [emphasis added]. It seems clear that at least one word is omitted between "the" and "of." Was Williams referring to the "front" of the building or the "rear" of the building? Or see James H. Hildreth, *Inquiry*, vol. [3], p. 135, wherein Marshal Williams asked Hildreth: "Did you notice whether that hose led from that building on the *cor* [emphasis added] of Madison and LaSalle?" It is obvious that Williams did not refer to the "cor" of Madison and LaSalle, but rather, to the "corner" of these two streets. This type of error is surely the fault of the person who transcribed Bennett's notes from shorthand to longhand.

72. "Board of Police," *Chicago Republican*, 10 November 1871, p. [2].

73. Untitled article, *Chicago Evening Journal*, 16 November 1871, p. [2].

74. "The Origin of the Fire," *Chicago Republican*, 11 November 1871, p. 1.

75. "That Investigation," *Chicago Evening Journal*, 24 November 1871, p. [4].

76. "The Great Fire," *Chicago Tribune*, 25 November 1871, p. 6.

77. Untitled article, *Chicago Evening Journal*, 27 November 1871, p. [2].

78. "Mrs. Leary's Cow," *Chicago Evening Journal*, 4 November 1871, p. [4], hereafter cited in text as "Mrs. Leary's Cow."

79. "The Fire," *Chicago Times*, 25 November 1871, p. [4].

80. Lawrence J. McCaffrey, "The Irish-American Dimension," in *The Irish in Chicago*, by Lawrence J. McCaffrey, Ellen Skerrett, Michael F. Funchion, and Charles Fanning (Urbana: University of Illinois Press, 1987), p. 8; Ellen Skerrett, "The Irish of Chicago's Hull-House Neighborhood," in *New Perspectives on the Irish Diaspora*, ed. Charles Fanning (Carbondale: Southern Illinois University Press, 2000), p. 211, hereafter Skerrett; Untitled article, *Chicago Tribune*, 27 November 1871, p. 2; Andreas, vol. 2, pp. 453, 490–501 passim; Andreas, vol. 3, pp. 695–704 passim; Samuel L. Brown, comp., *Surnames Are the Fossils of Speech* (privately printed, 1967), s.v. "Brown," "Schaefer," "Shaffer"; Patrick Hanks and Flavia Hodges, *A Dictionary of Surnames* (Oxford: Oxford University Press, 1991), s.v. "Brown," "Schäfer," "Schaffer"; C[harles] D. Mosher, *Mosher's 1876 Centennial Historical Album*, vol. 6, *Containing Photographs, Autographs and Biographies of the Chicago Bar* (privately printed, 1876), s.v. "Homer N. Hibbard"; C[harles] D. Mosher, *Mosher's 1876 Centennial Historical Album*, vol. 7, *Containing Photographs, Autographs and Biographies of Chicago Editors* (privately printed, 1876), s.v. "Wilbur F. Storey," "James W. Sheahan," "Andrew Shuman"; "The City: Squatter Settlements," *Chicago Times*, 7 August 1865, p. [3], hereafter cited in text as "The City: Squatter Settlements."

The day after the *Times* featured its article on "Squatter Settlements," it published an apology, stating that the story "would not have appeared had the manuscript passed through the hands of the responsible editor." Although the newspaper admitted that the printing of the article was an accident, the *Times* also angrily maintained that "we feel cordial contempt for those few individuals— those few Irishmen—who have made the publication of the article the occasion of discontinuing their subscriptions to the *Times*." The paper added that "it parts company with the disaffected with a great deal of pity for their unhappy feebleness." See untitled article, *Chicago Times*, 8 August 1865, p. [2].

81. "How It Originated," p. [2]; Andreas, vol. 2, pp. 708–9; Michael McDermott, *The Civil-Engineer & Surveyor's Manual* (Chicago: Fergus Printing Co., 1879), p. [3].

82. See, e.g., "Our Fire—Its Causes and Lessons," p. 4; "River Engines," *Chicago Tribune*, 18 November 1871, p. 4; "Management of the Fire Department," p. [2]; "Destroy to Save," *Chicago Evening Journal*, 23 November 1871, p. [2]; "Fire-Marshal Williams," p. [4]. Mrs. O'Leary was not alone in her inability to write. Sawislak notes that the Chicago Relief and Aid Society put approximately two hundred women to work in makeshift sewing factories. Most of these women were immigrants (predominantly Irish), and it appears that about one-third signed their payroll records with an "X" instead of a signature. See Sawislak, pp. 97, 311.

83. For further information concerning the names and occupations of the fifty witnesses, see Appendix D.

84. James S. McQuade's *A Synoptical History of the Chicago Fire Department* is for the most part a flattering chronicle, but even he comments that "the general tone of the report shows that its aim was to exonerate the fire department from responsibility, and to quiet the loud expressions of dissatisfaction with the department." See McQuade, p. 46.

85. James H. Hildreth, *Inquiry*, vol. [3], p. 152.

86. Michael W. Conway, *Inquiry*, vol. [2], p. 15.

87. John Doyle, *Inquiry*, vol. [3], p. 11. (Although questions directed at other witnesses concerned intoxicated "firemen," the transcriber wrote "foremen" here. As every engine company had a foreman, it is very likely that "foremen" is correct.)

88. John Doyle, *Inquiry*, vol. [3], p. 11.

89. Nicholas Dubach, *Inquiry*, vol. [3], p. 22.

90. Nicholas Dubach, *Inquiry*, vol. [3], p. 22.

91. Andreas, vol. 2, pp. 709–10. A review of the *Tribune, Evening Journal, Times,* and *Republican* from December 12, the day the Board's final report was published, through the end of the year reveals only four articles that even slightly disparaged Mrs. O'Leary or her cow, and all four were more sarcastic than vitriolic in nature. The December 19 *Journal* used the O'Leary cow to make a political analogy; the December 14 *Times* casually referred to the "diminutive shanty, in which Mrs. O'Leary's famous bovine is supposed to be on exhibition"; the December 28 *Times* noted the O'Leary barn in passing; and the December 16 *Tribune* mentioned Mrs. O'Leary and her cow in order to belittle author and lecturer George Francis Train. See Untitled article, *Chicago Evening Journal*, 19 December 1871, p. [2]; "The Fire's Nursery," p. 5; Untitled article, *Chicago Times*, 28 December 1871, p. 4; "George Francis Train and the O'Leary Cow," *Chicago Tribune*, 16 December 1871, p. 4, hereafter cited in text as "George Francis Train and the O'Leary Cow"; Cromie, pp. 8–9.

Mrs. O'Leary's Legacy

"Mrs. O'Leary" is a name inseparably associated with the great Chicago fire. In point of fact, it is riveted to the event just as the star is to the policeman, and any reference to one would be incomplete without some allusion to the other.
                                    —*Chicago Daily News*, 9 October 1886

Despite the numerous newspaper articles that suggested that the fire was the result of Mrs. O'Leary working overtime in her barn, it appears that Chicago did not retaliate against her for allegedly starting it. The most likely reason for her good fortune is that as the newspapers ceased sensationalizing the fire's origin, Chicagoans accepted her inquiry denial and agreed with the Board's final report and its indecisive findings. Also, in the days and weeks after the fire, articles in the city's newspapers indicate that Chicago was more interested in rebuilding, not retribution.[1]

But even though Mrs. O'Leary managed to avoid the wrath of the city, at least one person chose to jump into the limelight and onto the bandwagon formerly driven by Robert Critchell, Jacob Schaller, and Mary Callahan and contend that *Mr.* O'Leary was the subject of a "great hunt" after the fire. In 1927 Mrs. Nellie L. Hayes maintained in an obviously fictional *Tribune* account that *she* warned the couple of

their burning barn (Figure 67). Hayes claimed that after the fire, the O'Leary family, fearful of a lynch mob, hid for a week in her home. Her father helped spirit them away, with Mr. O'Leary (who people thought started the fire) disguised as a woman.[2]

But Mrs. Hayes' tale contradicts inquiry testimony, and it seems clear that she made up this story. She claimed that the O'Learys owned three cows, but Mrs. O'Leary testified that she owned six cows and a calf. Hayes contended that the fire "did not happen when the O'Learys were up anyway, for I had to tell them about the fire first." But neither O'Leary said anything during the inquiry about her warning them. Mrs. Hayes said that the McLaughlins were having a christening party for their "new baby" on the night of the fire. But Mrs. McLaughlin testified that the party was for her brother. Furthermore, when the Board asked McLaughlin if she had a family, she replied that she had "a

FIGURE 67—NELLIE L. HAYES. In 1927, Mrs. Nellie L. Hayes maintained that *she* (not Daniel Sullivan or Dennis Regan) warned the O'Learys about their burning barn. She claimed that after the fire, the O'Leary family, fearful of a lynch mob, hid in her home until her father helped them escape. There is no evidence that supports her story. (Drawing by Marshall Philyaw. Reproduced with permission of the *Chicago Tribune*)

child five years old." She said nothing about a baby.[3]

And why did Hayes wait more than fifty years before coming forward with her story? The *Tribune* unconvincingly reports that "she has kept still all these years for fear of starting a backfire of gossip and ill feeling somewhere." Predictably, this article was published on October 20, less than two weeks after the anniversary of the fire. Like others before her, it appears that Hayes wanted a chance at even fleeting fame by latching onto a Chicago Fire legend, but this time at the expense of the *other* O'Leary.[4]

Although Mr. O'Leary eluded a hanging, it appears that he and his wife did not escape the curiosity of the public. Post-fire photographs of their home and the Mc-Laughlin cottage reveal that although the windows of the McLaughlin house were undisturbed, those of the O'Leary residence were boarded up. As these photographs also disclose a large number of people milling about the yard, it seems probable that the windows were covered to discourage nineteenth-century *paparazzi* from peering inside[5] (Figures 50, 53).

The prying eyes of the idle curious must have soon become unbearable, for although the O'Learys did not sell their home until 1879, a review of Chicago city directories for the years 1872 through 1879 disclose no DeKoven Street listing for the couple after the 1872 directory entry. While possibly renting their property to boarders, they moved to a series of homes, eventually settling in on South Halsted Street on what was then the city's far South Side (Figures 68–69). But although Mrs. O'Leary may not have liked the stares of her neighbors, she tolerated the questioning of the press even less. She and her family hated newspaper reporters, and she refused to talk to them. But her physician, Dr. Swayne Wickersham, was not as averse, and in 1894 he spoke to a *Tribune* reporter about his famous patient:

It would be impossible for me to describe to you the grief and indignation with which Mrs. O'Leary views the place that has been assigned her in history. That she is regarded as the cause, even accidentally, of the great Chicago fire is the grief of her life. She is shocked at the levity with which the subject is treated and at the satirical use of her name in connection with it.... She admits no reporters to her presence, and she is determined that whatever ridicule history may heap on her it will have to do it without the aid of her likeness. Many are the devices that

FIGURE 68—PEOPLE IN FRONT OF AND ON TOP OF THE O'LEARY AND MCLAUGHLIN HOMES. In this photograph that appeared in the October 10, 1925, issue of the *Chicago Daily News*, more than a dozen people pose on the sidewalk, on a ladder, and even on the McLaughlin roof. The blurry picture reveals details not found in other photographs of the O'Leary and McLaughlin homes. An uneven boardwalk over the embankment along DeKoven Street leads up to the sidewalk; the alleyway between the O'Leary and Dalton properties is also paved with boards.

It seems incomprehensible that Mrs. O'Leary would allow these people in her yard, much less on her roof. It appears that the McLaughlins moved out of their rented cottage two days after the fire. If this photograph were taken shortly after October 8, 1871, it gives added credence to the theory that even though the O'Learys did not sell their property until December 1879, they too soon moved away to escape the multitudes of the curious. On the other hand, it is possible that this picture was taken years after the fire. Shortly after the O'Learys deeded their land to Anton Kolar and his wife in 1879, Kolar demolished both the O'Leary and McLaughlin houses and built a three-story brick home on the property (Figure 72). Perhaps Kolar and his friends posed for this picture shortly before they tore down the buildings. (Courtesy of the Illinois State Historical Library and with the permission of the Chicago Historical Society)

have been tried to procure a picture of her, but she has been too sharp for any of them. No cartoon will ever make any sport of her features. She has not a likeness in the world and will never have one.[6]

As Mrs. O'Leary would not give the press a story, it appears that when necessary the press would simply fabricate its own. This seems to be what happened when a *Chicago Daily News* reporter supposedly

FIGURE 69—VIEW FROM THE SOUTHWEST OF PEOPLE IN FRONT OF AND ON TOP OF THE O'LEARY AND MCLAUGHLIN HOMES. People have again posed on top of the O'Leary cottage. There is no sidewalk in front of what used to be Anne Murray's home, although a section of the wooden walkway lies nearby. Perhaps the sidewalk was ripped up by the firemen to use as fuel for the steam engines in a desperate attempt to save the Murray house from the flames. Christian Schimmals, foreman of the *Chicago* steam engine, testified at the inquiry that his engine "was worked from tearing up sidewalks and having men breaking wood for us."

This photograph may be the strongest evidence yet that the O'Learys vacated their home long before selling it in December 1879. Surely Mrs. O'Leary would not have allowed people to climb on top of her roof to have their picture taken. And surely the sidewalk would have been replaced years before the O'Learys sold their home. The May 25, 1894, *Tribune* claimed that "after the fire Mrs. O'Leary rebuilt and lived on the same spot several years and then sold the property to Anton Kohler." But although there is a DeKoven Street listing for Patrick and Catherine O'Leary in the 1872 Chicago city directory, there is no such listing for the years 1873 through 1879. The reason for this may be because the O'Learys moved away shortly after the fire, even before an upended section of wooden sidewalk was put back in place. (Chicago Historical Society ICHi-02738)

came to her South Side home 15 years after the fire. Although the O'Learys were not poor, this unknown scribe portrayed the family as if they had moved from DeKoven Street to Skid Row:

Her home is on 50th street, near Halsted, in a one-story frame house which stands in off the street and serves alike to accommodate an interesting family, consisting of the aged partner of her joys; a daughter, aged perhaps 18; one cow, and two dogs.... The house has no front door, in lieu of glass clothing is stuffed into two or three windows, and long before a stranger reaches the place the pungent odor of distillery swill and the effluvium of cows proclaim that old habits are strong with Mrs. O'Leary and that she is still in the milk business.... She wore a man's coat, the sleeves of which were tied about her neck. Her dress was patched in a good many places and the skirts were pulled up to give free play to her limbs, which were stockingless. On one foot she had a slipper, on the other she wore a man's boot. Back of her was her husband, who wore a straw hat, a flannel shirt, and a pair of jeans overalls, held in place by means of a single strap running diagonally across his shoulder. The girl had on a calico wrap, with the sleeves cut off at the elbow. The trio emerged from their living-rooms, which were adjoining those occupied by a cow, three or four pigs, and the two dogs.[7]

When the visitor introduced himself as a reporter, an elaborate scene of Rube Goldberg–like proportions unfolded. Mrs. O'Leary seized the hapless newspaperman and her husband struck him on the head. She then hurled a brick at him, but he was able to catch it and throw it at the two dogs that were bounding towards him, mouths gaping. Mr. O'Leary shouted to his daughter, "Hurry up there, Lizzie, and get me the revolver. I'll kill him!" but because O'Leary was a "very poor shot," the reporter lived to later write of his alleged adventures. He did not even bother to check first to see if the O'Learys had a daughter named "Lizzie" before relating his story to the public. Predictably, the 1870 and 1880 U.S. Census records indicate that the couple did not.[8]

Members of the press were not the only people who craved a piece of the O'Leary legend. P.T. Barnum wanted Mrs. O'Leary to tour with his circus, but when his agent dropped by to discuss the details, she reportedly chased him away with a broomstick. In the early 1890s one of the owners of the Chicago Fire Cyclorama, a 50-foot-high and 400-foot-long mural of beautifully detailed fire scenes, asked Mrs. O'Leary to endorse his enterprise. He agreed to pay her (she merely had to sit where she could be seen) and even offered to employ her husband as well. Although such a proposal would be eagerly accepted by many modern-day celebrities, Mrs. O'Leary was appalled by it. She replied that she was not in need of money, but that even if she were, there was not enough money in the world that would make her agree to do such a thing.[9]

The O'Learys continued to live as quietly as they could on Halsted Street, refusing to talk about the fire, even with their friends, and also refusing to capitalize on their unwanted notoriety. On September 15, 1894, Patrick collapsed suddenly on his front stoop and died (Figure 70). Less than a year later, on July 3, 1895, his wife passed away, also at home. Her obituary and death certificate stated that she died of "acute pneumonia," but her neighbors knew the real cause of death—they claimed that she died of a broken heart[10] (Figures 40, 71).

Although the Board of Police and Fire Commissioners vindicated Mrs. O'Leary, she has remained vilified by history. A writer for the *Chicago Evening Journal* wrote the following in 1871, but more than 130 years later, the words are just as timely:

> The story told that night, and before any one had the least idea that a great conflagration was in store, was caught up by the electric wires the next morning and flashed wherever telegraphy extends. Even if it were an absurd rumor, forty miles wide of the truth, it would be useless to attempt to alter "the verdict of history." Mrs. Leary has made a sworn statement in refutation of the charge, and it is backed by other affidavits; but to little purpose. She is in for it, and no mistake. Fame has seized her and appropriated her,

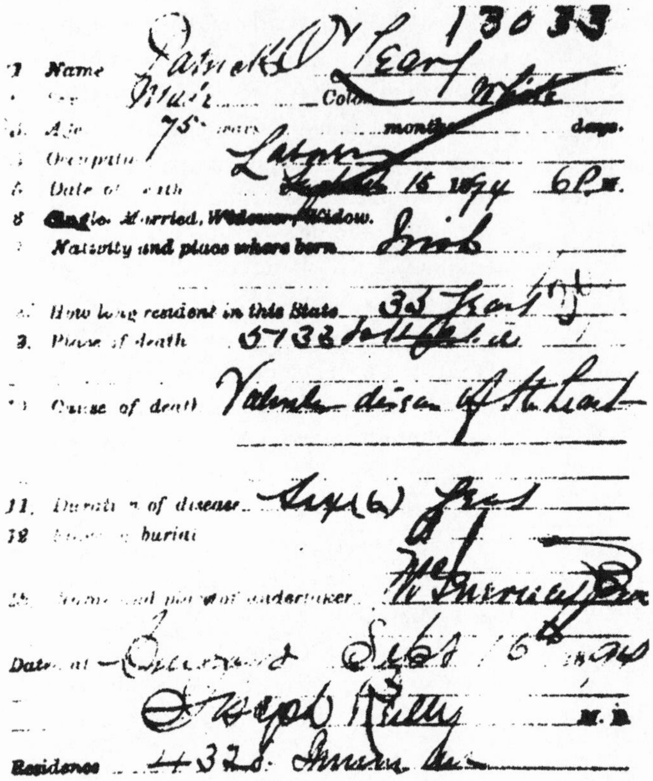
13033
Name Patrick O'Leary
Color White
Age 75 years ... months ... days.
Date of death ... 15 1894 6 P.M.
Single, Married, Widower, Widow.
Nativity and place where born Irish
How long resident in this State 33 Years
Place of death 5733 ...
Cause of death Valvular disease of the heart
Duration of disease Six (6) years
... burial
Name and place of undertaker ...
Dated at ... Sept 16th ...
... M.D.
Residence 4328 ...

FIGURE 70—PATRICK O'LEARY'S DEATH CERTIFICATE. **Mr. O'Leary's death certificate states that he died on September 15, 1894. This is confirmed by newspaper accounts of his death. But the O'Leary family monument (Figure 71) erroneously indicates that he died on September 5, 1894. (For privacy purposes, the place of burial has been removed from the certificate.)**

name, barn, cows and all[11] (Figures 72–74).

Notes

1. See, e.g., "The West Side," *Chicago Evening Journal*, 11 November 1871, p. [4]; "Common Council," *Chicago Republican*, 16 November 1871, p. [2]; "Real Estate," *Chicago Tribune*, 19 November 1871, p. 6; "Rebuilding," *Chicago Times*, 27 October 1871, p. [3]. John J. Flinn concurred with this assessment of post-fire Chicagoans' frames of mind, writing that "the people, while panic-stricken at first, very soon regained their composure and went about making the best of it, attending to their own business, and looking neither to the right nor to the left, but to the future, which looked bleak enough before the ashes cooled." See Flinn, p. 129.

2. "True Story of Chicago Fire Told at Last," *Chicago Daily Tribune*, 20 October 1927, sec. 3, p. 31, hereafter cited in text as "True Story of Chicago Fire Told at Last"; "The Legend of Mrs. O'Leary's Cow," p. 9.

3. "True Story of Chicago Fire Told at Last," sec. 3, p. 31; "The Legend of Mrs. O'Leary's Cow," p. 9; Catharine McLaughlin, *Inquiry*, vol. [1], pp. 223–25; Catherine O'Leary, *Inquiry*, vol. [1], pp. 59, 77–78. The 1870 census records indicate that Mrs. McLaughlin's child (a daughter named Mary Ann) was only two years old at the time the census was taken, or three years old when Mrs. McLaughlin testified. It does not seem likely that Mrs. McLaughlin would lie to the commissioners about the age of her daughter. But even if these census records are correct, a three year old child is hardly a "new baby." See 1870 U.S. Census, Cook County, Illinois, Population Schedule, National Archives micropublication M593, roll 204, sheet 171, page 86, line 15.

Opposite: FIGURE 71—THE O'LEARY FAMILY MONUMENT. **Patrick and Catherine O'Leary are buried in a Chicago cemetery with their son James and his wife Anna, who Mary Callahan claimed was the granddaughter of fiddler Patrick McLaughlin. The monument is impressive, standing ten feet high and topped with a draped urn, which is a symbol of death and mourning.**

Although the monument indicates that Patrick O'Leary died on September 5, 1894, his death certificate discloses that he died on September 15 of that year. The monument shows that Catherine O'Leary was 68 years old when she died. This is consistent with her death certificate (Figure 40). (Photograph by Robert A. Bales)

FIGURE 72—ANTON KOLAR HOME, CIRCA 1881. After the O'Learys sold their land to Anton Kolar and his wife in December 1879, the Kolars built a three-story home on the property. In 1881, the Chicago Historical Society placed a four foot by two foot white marble tablet into the front wall of the new house that read: "The Great Fire of 1871 originated here and extended to Lincoln Park." The slab is shown in this drawing of the Kolar home. The picture originally appeared in the booklet *The City That a Cow Kicked Over*, which was published circa 1881.

4. "True Story of Chicago Fire Told at Last," sec. 3, p. 31.

5. Kogan and Cromie, p. 180.

6. Chicago Title Insurance Company records; "Fire Alley Is Paved," p. 1; Mary Basich, descendant of Mrs. O'Leary, interview by Richard F. Bales, 2 February 1999; *Scéal*, pp. 2, 4; "Duis and Holt," pp. 222, 224; "Mrs. O'Leary Is Dead," *Chicago Daily Tribune*, 4 July 1895, p. 1, hereafter cited in text as "Mrs. O'Leary Is Dead"; *Edwards' Fifteenth Annual Directory of the Inhabitants, Institutions, Manufacturing Establishments and Incorporated Companies of the City of Chicago, Embracing a Complete Business Directory for 1872* (Chicago: Richard Edwards, 1872), vol. 15, p. 565. Although it appears that the O'Learys moved shortly after October 8, 1871 (Figures 68–69), one 1894 account claims that "after the fire Mrs. O'Leary rebuilt and lived on the same spot several years...." Historian John Corrigan suggests that the O'Learys remained on DeKoven Street until 1879, which was when they sold their property to Anton Kolar and his wife. See "Fire Alley Is Paved," p. 1; *Scéal*, p. 2; "Duis and Holt," p. 222; Chicago Title Insurance Company records; Henry Wood, "Mrs. O'Leary's Kin Spikes Story That Cow Started Fire," *Chicago Tribune*, 9 October 1969, sec. 1, p. 1.

The October 8, 1921, *Chicago Evening Post* states that "a Chicago fire version of 'The House That Jack Built' was exceedingly popular among the juvenile population of the city in the late '70s and the '80s." A published version of the poem includes drawings that depict Mrs. O'Leary as oafish and her home as dilapidated. The poem contains this indictment of Mrs. O'Leary, her house, and her cow: "This is the Hovel dingy and dreary,/ That sheltered the famous Mrs. O'Leary,/ That milked

FIGURE 73—STEAM ENGINE ON DEKOVEN STREET (1953). When Chicago observed the hundredth anniversary of its incorporation as a city in 1937, the Chicago Charter Jubilee Committee and the Chicago Historical Society placed a second marker on the front of the Kolar home. This bronze plaque was mounted directly below the white marble tablet that the historical society installed in 1881. Both monuments to the fire are clearly visible in this photograph, which was taken on October 9, 1953. In celebration of Fire Prevention Week (always held during the week of October 8), a horsedrawn steam engine saunters down DeKoven Street while spectators fill the front steps of the now aging Kolar house. In a ceremony conducted by the fire department and the Chicago Association of Commerce, the 1937 plaque was apparently removed from the building just minutes after this photograph was taken; the October 9 *Tribune* reported that "the metal plaque marking the site where Mrs. O'Leary's cow is said to have kicked over a lantern and started the great Chicago fire of 1871 will be removed from the building at 558 Dekoven st. at 10 A.M. today and turned over to the Chicago Historical society." (Chicago Historical Society ICHi-25941; photograph by Betty Hulett)

the Cow forlorn and weary,/ That kicked the Lamp, that started the/ Fire, that burned the City." See *The City That a Cow Kicked Over*, pp. [11, 13]; "Asks Version of Famous Verses of Chicago Fire," *Chicago Evening Post*, 8 October 1921, sec. 1, p. 1 (home page).

7. Chicago Title Insurance Company records; *Chicago & Vicinity 6-County StreetFinder*, p. 62 (Cook County); Mary Basich to Richard F. Bales,

July 1998; "Tales of the Great Fire," *Chicago Daily News*, 9 October 1886, p. 2, hereafter cited in text as "Tales of the Great Fire"; "Duis and Holt," p. 222.

8. "Tales of the Great Fire," p. 2; 1870 U.S. Census, Cook County, Illinois, Population Schedule, National Archives micropublication M593, roll 204, sheet 171, page 86, lines 16–21; 1880 U.S. Census, Cook County, Illinois, Population

FIGURE 74—1937 PLAQUE INSIDE THE FIRE ACADEMY. **When the Kolar home was slated for demolition in 1955 as part of a residential slum clearance project, the Chicago Historical Society tried to acquire the marble tablet that was placed in the front wall of the house in 1881. Unfortunately, the stone marker broke when the building came down. At the urging of Mayor Richard J. Daley, the Chicago Fire Academy was built on this site, and the 1937 bronze plaque, shown here, was placed on protective display on the first floor of the academy. The marker reads:**

Mrs. O'Leary's Home
On this site stood home and barn of Mrs. O'Leary where the Chicago Fire of 1871 started.
Although there are many versions of the story of its origin the real cause of the fire has
never been determined.

On the floor below the plaque is a Maltese cross that supposedly marks the location of the O'Leary barn. (Photograph by Richard F. Bales)

Schedule, National Archives micropublication T9, roll 200, Supervisor's District 1, Enumeration District 197, sheet 26, page 302, lines 11–15. John Corrigan writes that the O'Learys moved to a Halsted Street address in 1885. If this is correct, then this is one more indication that the 1886 *Daily News* interview is specious, as the reporter stated that the O'Learys lived on 50th Street. Also, 50th Street is hundreds of feet north of this Halsted Street location. Chicago Title Insurance Company records, however, indicate that no O'Leary owned this Halsted Street property until 1894, when Henry T. Higgins and Sarah Higgins conveyed it to Annie O'Leary, wife of James O'Leary. Furthermore, Chicago Title records are consistent with Chicago city directories. A review of these directories for the years 1885 through 1895 discloses only one entry for an O'Leary living at this Halsted Street address—the 1895 city directory. See *Scéal*, p. 2; Chicago Title Insurance Company records; [Charles] Rascher, *Rascher's Atlas of Chicago* (Chicago: Rascher Insurance Map Publishing Co., 1891), vol. 13, p. 29; Chicago Guarantee Survey Company records; Greg Hannon, president of Chicago Guarantee Survey Company, interview by Richard F. Bales, 19 July 2001; *The Lakeside Annual Directory of the City of Chicago, 1895: Embracing a Complete General and Business Directory, Miscellaneous Information, and Street Guide* (Chicago: Chicago Directory Co., 1895), p. 1314.

9. "Fire Alley Is Paved," p. 1; Swing, pp. [33], 36; Kogan and Cromie, p. 64; Smith, pp. 273, 377; "Duis and Holt," p. 222; "Linked to Chicago's Two Worst Fires," sec. 7, p. 10.

10. *Scéal*, p. 2; "Duis and Holt," p. 224; "Linked to Chicago's Two Worst Fires," sec. 7, p. 10; "Mrs. O'Leary's Cow," p. 8; "Mrs. O'Leary Is Dead," p. 1. Although Mrs. O'Leary refused to take advantage of her fame, the *Louisville Courier-Journal* urged her to do so, stating that "if you don't want to avail yourself of it, you ought to sell out to some more enterprising somebody that does. If you deserve to be called a citizen of Chicago, you would have had your cow photographed long before the fire was extinguished, and would have been selling the pictures all this time at twenty cents apiece. Dry up, or act like a woman of sense." See "Mrs. Leary's Cow," p. [4].

The O'Leary family monument indicates that Patrick O'Leary died on September 5, 1894. But the *Chicago Tribune* of Monday, September 17, 1894, states that Mr. O'Leary died on "Saturday evening." That previous Saturday was September 15, not September 5. September 5 was a Wednesday. Also, the *Tribune*'s obituary of Mrs. O'Leary noted somewhat indelicately that her husband "dropped dead Sept. 15 last." Patrick O'Leary's death certificate (Figure 70) confirms that he died on September 15 and that the information on the monument is incorrect. See "Mrs. O'Leary's Cow," p. 8; "Mrs. O'Leary Is Dead," p. 1.

11. "Origin of the Fire," supplement, p. [2]. This *Chicago Evening Journal* article included a final reference to Mrs. O'Leary: "She has won, in spite of herself, what the Ephesian youth panted after." This sentence is undoubtedly a reference to Colley Cibber's *The Tragical History of King Richard III*:

Th' aspiring youth, that fir'd the *Ephesian* dome,
Outlives, in fame, the pious fool that rais'd it.

See Colley Cibber, *The Dramatic Works of Colley Cibber, Esq...* (London: J. Rivington and Sons, 1777; reprint, New York: AMS Press, 1966), p. 341. For other references to this "Ephesian youth" analogy, see "George Francis Train and the O'Leary Cow," p. 4; "Mrs. Leary's Cow," p. [4]; see also Colbert and Chamberlin, p. 202: "The blame of setting the fire rests on the woman who milked, or else upon the lazy man who allowed her to milk. The name of this female we shall not hand down to posterity in these pages; for we have the familiar words of the poet to remind us that

'The ambitious youth who fired the Ephesian dome, Outlives in fame the pious fool that reared it.'"

Afterword

In 1920 the 18th Amendment ushered in Prohibition, a ban on the manufacture, transport, and sale of alcoholic beverages. Until this time Al Capone was little more than a two-bit hoodlum, distinguished only by the knife slashes on his face that earned him the nickname "Scarface." But Prohibition proved to be a golden opportunity for the underworld, giving birth to the legendary Gangster Era. Soon bootlegging and speakeasies, "beer wars" and protection rackets became the order of the day. There would be more than seven hundred gangland killings during the next thirteen years, and the soon-to-be infamous mobster would be linked to many of them.

Al Capone reportedly once complained, "They've hung everything on me except the Chicago Fire."[1] Though exonerated by time and circumstance (even Eliot Ness and his Untouchables could not prove that Capone, born in 1899, knocked over the lantern), no doubt the other reason why no one ever fingered "Big Al" is that Mrs. O'Leary had as firm a grip on the public's fancy as "Scarface" had on the City of Chicago. Even today, if a Chicagoan travels out of state or even out of the country and mentions the name of his hometown,

chances are he or she will be greeted by a response that includes one of three famous citizens: Al Capone (accompanied, of course, by the "rat-a-tat-tat" of a pantomimed machine gun), Michael Jordan, or Mrs. O'Leary's cow.

But Mrs. Eileen Knight, the granddaughter of Mrs. O'Leary, despised the infamy of the O'Leary legend. She saw how the press badgered her mother, Catherine O'Leary Ledwell, every October for an interview, just as it had harassed her grandmother years earlier. Newspapers and magazines would annually resurrect the pictures that depicted Mrs. O'Leary as old and churlish, and Mrs. Knight witnessed the pain and anguish that this caused her mother.

It has been more than 130 years since a fire that started in a barn on the West Side of Chicago spread out of control and eventually leveled much of the city. Catherine O'Leary, Catherine O'Leary Ledwell, and Eileen Knight represent three generations of O'Learys that have suffered the unwitting pen of a newspaper reporter. It was only one sentence, four lines of print in an otherwise innocuous article, but it was a sentence that changed their lives forever. It was a story that might have died with the fire's rain-soaked embers on the morning of October 10, 1871, had it not been fueled by the lies of Robert S. Critchell, Jacob John Schaller, Nellie L. Hayes, and others who couldn't resist a chance at the brass ring of fleeting fame—but at the expense of a family's reputation.[2]

I hope that I have laid bare the legend of Mrs. O'Leary and her cow and exposed its many fabrications and inconsistencies. I hope that in the future, history will show that the story of the cow kicking over the lantern is only a myth. And I hope that I have set the record straight and cleared the O'Leary name. Eileen Knight, Catherine O'Leary Ledwell, Mrs. O'Leary—and of course, her much-maligned bovine—deserve as much.

Notes

1. Melissa Burdick Harmon, "Badfella: The Life and Crimes of Al Capone," *Biography* 5 (May 2001), p. [116].

2. Nancy Knight Connolly, descendant of Mrs. O'Leary, interview by Richard F. Bales, 25 June 2001; Tom McNamee, "119 Years After the Fire, O'Learys' Hurt Smolders," *Chicago Sun-Times,* 7 October 1990, sec. 1, p. 4.

Questions, Mysteries, and Controversies

Now that our reporters have a little leisure for matters of secondary importance, for things more curious than essential....
—*Chicago Evening Journal*, October 21, 1871

In the chronicles of the Great Chicago Fire, the cause of the blaze is undoubtedly the ultimate "curious" mystery. But there are many other questions associated with the fire and its origin that are almost equally enigmatic. Although a few can be answered or explained, most of them cannot, but all afford a fascinating trip down the less-traveled byroads of the legend of the fire.

When Did the Fire Start?

Daniel Sullivan testified that he sat in front of White's house and "stayed there as long as from about twenty minutes past nine to twenty-five minutes past nine." As he turned around, he claimed that he "saw a fire in Leary's barn." Although the commissioners did not state in their final report that the fire started at this time, they did mention that "the fire was first discovered" by Sullivan "at not more than 20 to 25 minutes past 9 o'clock" as he sat on the south side of DeKoven Street. William Brown testified that he received Mathias Schaefer's Box 342 alarm at nine-thirty, and the Board also noted this in its findings. (The Board's final report appears in Appendix E.)[1]

The commissioners, though, failed to mention Schaefer's testimony concerning Brown's refusal to strike Box 319 and the resultant delay in firemen reaching the O'Leary property. Whether deliberately or not, the commissioners created the impression in their report that the fire department was, to quote Marshal Williams, "right on their taps and on it before it got started." They subtly intimated that Schaefer saw the fire minutes after it began and immediately called down to Brown, who promptly sounded the nine-thirty tocsin.[2]

But in his *History of Chicago* historian A. T. Andreas provides what initially appears to be compelling proof that the fire began much earlier, no later than 8:45 P.M. This evidence consists of the recollections of firemen and "the statements of citizens who witnessed the fire in its early stages." He notes, for example, that William Lee claimed that after he returned to his house after allegedly attempting to convince Bruno Goll to turn in a fire alarm, "the clock struck nine." Richard Riley, a railroad contractor, lived about three-and-one-half blocks from the O'Leary home. On the night of October 8 he was preparing for a train trip to St. Louis. Just as he prepared to walk out onto his front porch to meet the Canal Street omnibus that would take him to the train depot, he saw the fire. An examination of the Chicago & Alton Railroad timetable discloses that Riley's train was scheduled to leave Chicago at nine o'clock.[3]

By arguing that the fire began much earlier than 9:30 P.M., Andreas raises the curtain on a markedly different tableau of what happened that Sunday evening, one that potentially depicts the fire department in a much less favorable light. If the fire broke out at about 8:45 P.M. and not at nine-thirty, then what was Schaefer doing for forty-five minutes? Why did he wait for three quarters of an hour before calling down to Brown? Even worse, did the commissioners deliberately omit key testimony from their report in a calculated attempt to sanitize the public image of the fire department and make it appear that there was no delay in getting the steam engines to the O'Leary property?

Historians to date have unearthed no memorandum "From the Desk of Thomas B. Brown" or any other evidence that would indicate that the commissioners fraudulently massaged the inquiry's numbers with the intent to misrepresent their findings. Indeed, one could argue that they were only parroting the information that Daniel Sullivan and William Brown gave them, information that was essentially confirmed by others who testified, such as Dennis Regan, William Musham, and Michael Sullivan. But on the other hand, the Board did choose to ignore testimony concerning Brown's refusal to strike Box 319. The commissioners also failed to include in their report one possibly damaging inquiry statement of Mrs. O'Leary. When they asked her, "about what time did this fire break out?" she indicated that it was much earlier than when Sullivan allegedly saw it: "As near as I can guess, it was a little after nine o'clock." So when did the fire start? Was Andreas correct? Did the O'Leary barn ignite as early at 8:45 P.M.?[4]

The entire history of the Great Chicago Fire teems with contradictory information. This is especially obvious when attempting to reconcile the varying times associated with the first few minutes of the fire that are recounted in inquiry testimony and later reminiscences. For this reason, any attempt to determine when the blaze started must first begin by assuming that

at least a few basic facts (derived primarily from inquiry testimony) are true:

- William Brown testified that Mathias Schaefer called in the Box 342 alarm at 9:30 P.M.[5]
- William Musham, foreman of the *Little Giant* engine company, indicated that his company watchman saw the fire about one minute before the Box 342 alarm sounded. Musham testified that he immediately left the engine house and drove directly to the corner of DeKoven Street and Jefferson Street, a distance of five-and-one-half blocks (Figure 46). Although the commissioners stated in their final report that the *America* hose company arrived at the scene and was pumping water on the fire before any engine did, Andreas argues convincingly that the *Little Giant* was at work at least fifteen minutes before the *America* drove up. The Board implies in its report that it would take the *Giant* five minutes to drive from its engine house to the fire. Therefore, the *Giant* probably arrived at the blaze no later than 9:35 P.M.[6]
- Mrs. McLaughlin testified that after going outside and seeing the O'Leary barn and Dalton's house on fire, ten minutes elapsed until she saw a fire engine drive up. In all likelihood this engine was the *Little Giant*, which means that she went outside and saw the fire at about 9:25 P.M.[7]
- Mrs. O'Leary did not indicate in her testimony when she saw the fire, only when she thought the fire started. But because she and Mrs. McLaughlin lived only a few feet from each other and because both of them testified about people coming to their doors and warning them of the fire, they probably discovered the blaze at virtually the same time.[8]

If these assumptions are true, then Andreas' conclusion as to when the fire started may be erroneous. If the fire started at 8:45 P.M., it seems likely that the O'Learys or McLaughlins would have seen the blaze, smelled the smoke, or heard the cries of the horse and cows well before 9:25 P.M. Surely it would have taken just a few minutes for the barn and perhaps even the adjoining buildings to be completely engulfed in flames. Indeed, Catherine Sullivan suggests this in her inquiry testimony:

I was washing up my dishes. I hadn't them washed up when I saw the fire coming through the window. I said, "Good God, can the place be on fire?" I run through the rear, out to the gate, and at that time the second house was catching fire, and Leary's barn was afire, and Mr. Dalton's was afire at the same time.[9]

Then could Mrs. O'Leary be correct? If the fire did not start at 8:45 P.M., then did the barn ignite "a little after nine o'clock," perhaps 9:05 P.M., which would be twenty minutes later than what Andreas suggests? This is also doubtful, for the same reason—if the fire started at 9:05 P.M. it certainly would have been discovered before 9:25 P.M. Because it is likely that only minutes elapsed from the time Sullivan and Regan started the fire in the barn to when they attempted to rescue the animals and sound the alarm, it seems equally likely that Mrs. O'Leary and Mrs. McLaughlin would have seen the fire or heard the commotion only minutes after the barn caught fire.

So when *did* the Great Chicago Fire start? It is possible that the fire began at about 9:20 P.M. and that Mrs. O'Leary and Mrs. McLaughlin discovered it at 9:25 P.M. Because of contrary and conflicting information, the answer may never be known. But the key to uncovering the truth is not whether William Lee, Richard Riley, or Andreas' other "citizens who witnessed the fire" lied or misspoke. Rather, the answer will be found only by somehow sifting through the chaff of contradictions in hopes of finding those few kernels that can withstand historical scrutiny. Although William Brown claimed that he struck his first alarm at nine-thirty, perhaps one day historians will determine that James Hildreth was the one who was right—he testified that he heard an alarm and heard fire engines go by his home "not far from the neighborhood of nine o'clock."[10]

Did Blowing Up Buildings Help Prevent the Fire from Spreading?

James Hildreth told the commissioners at the inquiry that had it not been for the blowing up of buildings, "the fire would have continued." But some historians have questioned the effect and impact of his efforts. For example, although Hildreth bragged that "we could make an explosion as often as once in five minutes," fire historian H. A. Musham maintains that "attempts to demolish buildings had no effect whatsoever as it took at least an hour of preparation before the powder could be touched off and the buildings burned before this could be done."[11]

But it appears that Musham's conclusion was based on incomplete information. He cites the November 30, 1871, *Chicago Tribune*, which contains a long synopsis of Hildreth's inquiry testimony. The article includes this statement: "It would take an hour to lay powder to blow up a house." But Hildreth's actual inquiry comments clearly indicate that he was referring to his initial demolition efforts at the Union National Bank. Hildreth points out that the more he and his men worked, the more adept they became at their job:

Q. You had to carry the powder from Michigan Avenue?

A. Yes sir, kept the team off quite a long distance and carried the powder, but then we got it down so the men would have it at a minute's time. They got used to it, and would set down and smoke on a keg of powder to show you that if we had been as slow at Harrison Street as we were at Smith and Nixon's and the other places, the buildings would have burned down before we could have burned them up.[12]

Although contemporary author E. J. Goodspeed admits that in one area the use of powder helped to keep the fire from spreading, he also points out that after the Merchants' Insurance Company building was blown up, "a broad, black chasm was opened in the face of the street; but with as little attention to the space intervening as though it had only been across an ordinary alley, the arms of flame swung over the gap, and tore lustily at the rows of banking houses and insurance structures beyond."[13]

But writer A. T. Andreas cites another historian (probably James W. Sheahan, associate editor of the *Chicago Tribune*), who lauded the demolition work as a "salvation," contending, for example, that because buildings were destroyed at the corner of State and Harrison, on the city's South Side, "the fire was effectually checked, at least so far as the high-reaching, dangerous flames were concerned." The *Chicago Times* praised Hildreth's work even more fervently, declaring on October 21 that "there can be no doubt in the minds of those who were in a position to watch the progress of the great fire in the South division that it was only checked by the explosion of buildings." But *Times* owner Wilbur F. Storey clearly had an ax to grind with Chicago's administration, charging that "every department in the city and county government is to some extent responsible for the calamity that has come upon us," and he used it frequently in the immediate post-fire weeks to attack various city officials with razor-sharp commentary and criticism. Even Hildreth must have thought that to at least some degree the accolades that the *Times* directed at him and his assistants were as much a jab at the mayor and his minions as they were kudos for a job well done:

> The facts are that hours were wasted in this way, a few private citizens, led by Mr. Hildreth, assuming the duties of the officials who were too imbecile to discharge them, and even then consuming precious time, during which millions upon millions of property were destroyed, in striving to secure the authority which was necessary in order to proceed. Is not this showing a sufficient justification for the demand of the *Times* that all the present officials shall be incontinently swept from the board? Are not the mayor, the fire commissioners, and the fire marshal, to say nothing of the remoter responsibility of the other officials, answerable for criminal imbecility, incapacity, and neglect of duty?[14]

But even discounting the *Times'* biased opinion—and the sarcasm of the *Evening Journal*, which remarked that "next to the story of Cock Robin, we do not think there is a nursery story equal to the testimony of the Ex-Alderman"—Hildreth's sense of accomplishment was probably justified. Walls of fire in the business area (home to Goodspeed's Merchants' Insurance Company building) were fueled by densely packed, multi-storied buildings that towered so high no firebreak could have contained them. But Sheahan's corner of State and Harrison was south of the city's downtown, at the southern edge of the "burnt district" (Figure 75). Here the flames were less severe, and it was here that Hildreth was successful. Hildreth surely felt

vindicated when he opened the *Journal* on December 30, 1871, and read General Arthur C. Ducat's report to the fire insurance companies of Chicago. Ducat's suggestions include the following comments:

> The great fire has demonstrated new theories for the management of extensive conflagrations; for instance, the importance of having ready, at all times, the proper material for blowing up blocks of buildings, when the judgment of the Chief may dictate; men should be properly instructed in its use, and magazines for its storage should be constructed at different available points.[15]

Did Daniel Sullivan's Peg Leg Slip Between the Floorboards of Mrs. O'Leary's Barn?

Previous pages have detailed the various inconsistencies that are scattered throughout Daniel Sullivan's inquiry testimony. Ironically, what is perhaps the most interesting discrepancy concerning his statements is not what he said before the Board, but what he possibly did *not* say. The November 26, 1871, issue of the *Chicago Tribune* contained a report of Sullivan's inquiry statements of the previous day. The article indicates that the reason he slipped in the O'Leary barn was because "his wooden leg went between two boards, and he half fell over, catching himself on his sound leg. He caught hold of the wall and pulled himself out...." But this was not disclosed in the transcript of his testimony, which states only that "the boards were wet, my legs slipped out from me, and I went down. I stood up again...."[16]

Is it feasible that court reporter J. L. Bennett failed to properly transcribe this portion of Sullivan's account? This is a possibility; as mentioned in the previous chapter, a comparison of witnesses' testimony to newspaper summaries of their testimony suggest that this might have happened. Or did the *Tribune* embellish Sullivan's inquiry statements? This is also conceivable. But the strongest indication that Sullivan *did* tell the commissioners of his leg slipping between the floorboards would be if any other newspaper also mentioned it in its coverage of his testimony. Unfortunately, the summaries proffered by the *Times* and *Republican* do not include the story. Although the *Evening Journal*'s account of Sullivan's questioning does, it

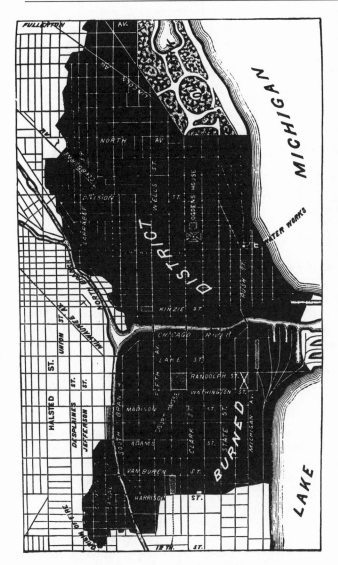

FIGURE 75—MAP OF THE BURNT DISTRICT. **The fire's origin is marked on this map of the burnt district in the lower left hand corner. Other landmarks on the map include the courthouse, the water works and the home of Mahlon Ogden. Remarkably, Ogden's palatial house on the city's North Side managed to escape the flames unscathed. (Chicago Historical Society ICHi-02870)**

is of no value, as it is not the report of an independent third party, but merely a word-for-word plagiarism of the *Tribune* version.[17]

Later so-called "reminiscences" embellish this 1871 *Tribune* account, contradict each other, and are otherwise completely useless. A 1942 *Tribune* article detailed the recollections of the members of the Retired Firemen's Association of Chicago, who claimed that the fire was started by hobos drinking and smoking in the barn. One ex-fireman recounted the story that on the day after the fire, Daniel Sullivan was using a crutch instead of his wooden leg. When the man (then about ten years old) asked Sullivan where the leg was, Sullivan led him to the remains of the O'Leary barn. There, stuck in the ruins, was the leg. Sullivan explained that "it caught in the rotten boards when I tried to chase the bums out."[18]

But only a few months earlier a Mr. J. C. Chapeck had recalled a completely different scenario, arguing that Sullivan "could not have lost his leg in the fire, as he had it the next day when he took his two wheel cart to the lake for water." (Chapeck also maintained that after the fire, Mr. and Mrs. O'Leary's sons told him that the blaze was caused by boys smoking clay pipes filled with corn silk near or behind the barn. Chapeck claimed that the O'Leary youths, fearing punishment, were afraid to tell the truth.)[19]

H. A. Musham puts even more spin on this infamous "slip and fall" case, asserting that Sullivan was forced to unfasten the leg and hobble out of the barn while holding onto a calf for support. Other histories of Chicago have also contained, in one form or another, the *Tribune*'s tale of Daniel Sullivan's wayward wooden leg. As to whether or not the story is true—this is just one of the many unsolved mysteries associated with the cause of the fire.

But one thing seems clear: if Sullivan did get his leg stuck between the floorboards, it appears even more likely that he would not have had sufficient time to do all that he testified he did without being injured by the fire.[20]

Who Screamed When the Fire Broke Out?

Andreas' *History of Chicago* includes the recollections of Mr. and Mrs. O'Leary's neighbor, James Dalton, who claimed that he "heard a woman's scream of terror" about ten minutes before his mother-in-law saw the reflected light of the fire shining on the cottage of Walter Forbes, which was immediately east of Dalton's home. Dalton, who heard the woman's voice through the west windows of his house, recalled that it came from the direction of the O'Leary property. H. A. Musham, seeing a chance to pull the noose even tighter around Mrs. O'Leary, pounced on Dalton's story (which was corroborated by Dalton's wife), and in a giant leap of faith and with no further evidence, declared that "the first thing that Mrs. O'Leary did, after the lamp was overturned, was to scream."[21]

Much of the lore of the Great Chicago Fire is apocryphal, and Dalton's tale of a voice in the night may be no exception. But assuming that his story is true, then who was it that screamed that evening? Could it have been Mrs. O'Leary?

Certainly not. Musham's bold and biased assertion to the contrary, Mrs. O'Leary can easily be omitted from any roundup of the usual suspects. As previously discussed, it is inconceivable that she would cry out but then turn her back on her burning barn and walk into her home. It would be tempting to accuse Mary Callahan, who alleged that after the lamp fell over, she and another girl screamed, but her story lacks credibility. As it appears that the interviews amassed in Andreas' *History* were gathered years after the fire (fireman Denis J. Swenie, for example, was questioned in June of 1885), it is possible that Dalton's memory may have been colored by the tincture of time, and what he described as a "scream of terror" was actually just a shout from one of Mrs. McLaughlin's partygoers.[22]

Dalton recalled hearing the scream *before* his mother-in-law saw the blaze. But perhaps the passing years may have distorted this recollection as well. This seems possible; as previously mentioned, there have been many contradictory reminiscences of details concerning the first moments of the fire. The woman may actually have cried out *after* the O'Leary barn was in flames. Perhaps Dalton heard Mrs. McLaughlin, who testified that "I just looked around and saw the blaze. I turned in and hollered to my brother to pick up my child...." Or perhaps he did hear Mrs. O'Leary. She stated at the inquiry that *after* she discovered her barn on fire, "I got frightened. I got the way I did not know when I saw everything burn up in the barn."[23]

Historians will probably never know who, if anyone, James Dalton heard that night. But if he did hear a woman scream minutes before a burning barn illuminated the evening sky, it was not Mrs. O'Leary. She was in bed, for the moment oblivious to what history had in store for her.[24]

Was Mrs. O'Leary Asleep When the Fire Broke Out?

In his *History of Chicago* Andreas comments on an alleged inconsistency in Mrs. O'Leary's inquiry testimony, noting that O'Leary supposedly testified that she and her family "were in bed, *but not asleep*, on that Sunday night. They knew nothing of the fire until Mr. Sullivan, a drayman, who lives on the south side of DeKoven Street, *awoke* them, and said their barn was on fire [emphasis in original]." In fact, Andreas even includes a footnote, remarking that "the discrepancy in this statement is not commented on by the commissioners, and must have been regarded (if it was noticed at all) as a lapsus linguæ, or an 'Irish bull.'" But the actual inquiry transcript indicates that Mrs. O'Leary never said this. On the other hand, the November 25, 1871, *Chicago Tribune* summary of her testimony suggests that she did; indeed, it is this *Tribune* account that is repeated virtually verbatim by Andreas.[25]

H. A. Musham, the consummate O'Leary-phobe, seized upon this alleged discrepancy, implying that she lied at the inquiry: "If the O'Learys were in bed and asleep at 8:30 P.M. and for the next half hour, they were certainly very good sleepers to sleep through a party, with fiddling and dancing going on within a few feet of them, and through all the noise and excitement attending the discovery of the burning of their barn." But although Musham cites the November 26, 1871, *Chicago Tribune* in his monograph as a reference for Mrs. McLaughlin's testimony about her party, he conveniently fails to mention that this same issue reported that there was very little "fiddling and dancing" at this party: "[Mr. McLaughlin] played two tunes on his fiddle, and one of the women danced a 'bout' and another a polka. That was all the dancing that was done."[26]

So is there any substance to this alleged inconsistency? Was Mrs. O'Leary asleep or awake when the fire broke out? An apparently legitimate interview published in the October 19, 1871, *Chicago Tribune* reveals that "she was asleep when the alarm was given, and was awakened by a neighbor, who rapped on the door and told her that the stable was on fire." Michael McDermott's "subscribed and sworn" *Tribune* affidavit was published the next day; in it Patrick O'Leary attested that his wife was "in bed when awakened by [Dennis Regan]." Granted, when the commissioners asked Mrs. O'Leary, "Were you and your family up when [the fire] broke out?" she replied only that "we were in bed" without adding that she was asleep. But a simple failure to mention that she was in bed and also asleep at the time the fire started is hardly a discrepancy.[27]

At one point during the inquiry, the commissioners asked Mrs. O'Leary about the McLaughlins:

Q. Do you know whether they were in bed?
A. I knew they were not in bed.
Q. How did you know that?
A. Because I could hear from my own bedroom. Could hear them going on. There was a little music there.[28]

So does Mr. O'Leary's sworn affidavit, which suggests that his wife was asleep when the fire broke out, contradict her inquiry testimony, which indicates that she heard the sounds of the McLaughlin party? Possibly—but possibly not. She might have been in bed and heard the music before falling asleep. But when the commissioners asked her if dancing "was going on at the time the fire broke out," she cryptically replied, "I could not tell you, sir." Does her answer indicate that she didn't know whether or not the guests were dancing because she was asleep? Or does it suggest that she was awake, but didn't know if the partygoers were dancing at the time the fire broke out? No one knows for sure.[29]

What Fire Company Was First on the Scene of the Fire?

Not surprisingly, there is conflicting inquiry testimony as to what fire company was first to arrive at the O'Leary barn and adjoining burning buildings. Like the supporters of rival politicians in the final days before a primary election, department personnel vied with each other in asserting or at least alluding to a belief that their company was number one:

- "I believe we were [the first engine to get there]."[30] (William Musham, foreman of the steam engine *Little Giant*)
- "Yes sir. [We were the first engine on the ground.]"[31] (William Mullin, foreman of the steam engine *Illinois*)
- "I was the only stream at the time on Taylor [Street] at the start of the fire."[32] (Christian Schimmals, foreman of the steam engine *Chicago*)
- "I am pretty sure there was no engine there then."[33] (George Rau, foreman of the hook and ladder *Protection*)
- "No engine appeared to be in sight, and we coupled onto the plug and led into the fire."[34] (Charles Anderson, driver of the hose cart *America*)

Despite these conflicting claims, there appear to be only two real contenders for the winner's circle: the steam engine *Little Giant* and the hose cart *America*. The commissioners maintained in their final report that the *America* was first at the scene, putting water on the fire before the arrival of any engine. In declaring the *America* the victor, they even managed to tweak the hose nozzles of the also-rans by adding that "two engines were located considerably nearer to the fire."[35]

But if the *America* won the gold medal, it did so with an asterisk next to its name. Historian A. T. Andreas argues in his *History of Chicago* that the *Little Giant* "sent the first stream, and had been at work at least fifteen minutes before the *America* arrived." Is Andreas correct? No one knows, and probably with good reason. The evening watchman at the *Little Giant*'s firehouse apparently saw the fire even before the Box 342 alarm came in, and the steam engine rushed to a hydrant at the corner of DeKoven and Jefferson streets, which was southwest of the O'Leary barn. Meanwhile, the *America* pulled up to the corner of Taylor and Clinton streets and took water from a hydrant that was northeast of the barn (Figure 10). With five or six buildings on fire by this time, it is very likely that at first both the *Little Giant* and the *America* fought the flames, each convinced that it was battling the blaze by itself. The *America*'s Charles Anderson concedes as much, admitting that "there might have been another stream on the other side of the barn, for aught that I know."[36]

Or perhaps, as Chicago Fire historian Robert Cromie suggests, the *Little Giant* was the first engine on the scene, but the *America* was the first piece of equipment to arrive. With William Musham indicating only that his *Little Giant* was the first engine there, and Charles Anderson remarking only that no engine appeared to be in sight when the *America* led in, Cromie's conclusion, although it straddles the fence, may be the best that history has to offer.[37]

Why Did Mathias Schaefer Call Down Incorrect Box Number 342?

William J. Brown and Mathias Schaefer were arguably two of the most important witnesses to speak before the commissioners. (This was probably why they were the first two people to testify.) But as previously described, Board President Thomas B. Brown unfortunately wrote down their remarks in affidavit form instead of in a verbatim "question and answer" format. Because of this, the details of their testimony are sketchy at best. Although it is not clear from William Brown's affidavit why he ignored Schaefer's request to ring a closer alarm box, the *Tribune* account of his testimony indicates that Brown felt that it would mislead or confuse the firemen. Similarly, Schaefer's affidavit does not reveal why he told Brown to strike the distant Box 342 in the first place—but neither do the *Tribune*, *Evening Journal*, *Times*, or *Republican* summaries of his testimony. The newspapers are merely consistent with Schaefer's affidavit, which indicates only the following:

When I saw [the fire], I run into the tower and whistled to the operator and told him to strike Box 342. This was my judgment. I then took my glass and looked in the direction of the fire again and immediately after this alarm [had?] been given, I whistled again to the operator and told him I had made a mistake, it ought to be 319, that would be nearer to it, but he said that the box struck was in the line of the fire, and he could not alter it now.[38]

"This was my judgment." But *why* was this Schaefer's judgment? What caused him to think that the fire was about one mile farther southwest than its DeKoven Street origin? Immediate post-fire newspapers offer no clue. Although the *Tribune*, for example, interviewed William Brown for one of its "Boring for Facts" articles, it never questioned Schaefer. But as the years passed, and as the memory of the fire grew dimmer and as its mythology grew brighter, the papers began to offer their own explanations for Schaefer's behavior. Quoting Third Assistant Fire Marshal Mathias Benner, Michael Ahern wrote in the October 9, 1893, issue of the *Inter Ocean* that "Schaefer, the watchman, could not be blamed much. The dull glare from the blazing ruins of the Saturday night fire was between him and DeKoven street. His vision was easily enough made farsighted." But Benner may have been mistaken. By playing "connect the dots" on the "burnt district" map that is found in almost any history of the fire, or on the diagram shown as Figure 76, drawing a line from the courthouse to the Saturday night ruins and a line from the courthouse to the O'Leary property, it seems clear that Schaefer had an unimpeded view of the burning barn from his perch in the cupola.[39]

By October 8, 1911, the ubiquitous Ahern had jumped ship from the *Inter Ocean* to the *Tribune*, and he was now claiming in a lengthy newspaper article that "there was a haze in the sky from the fire of the previous night and Schaeffer's vision was obscured." But the distance from the courthouse to the barn was a bit more than a mile, and it was another mile farther southwest to Box 342. Could this haze have caused Schaefer to overshoot his mark by almost 100 percent? Even historian H. A. Musham, whose admiration of firemen was only surpassed by his prejudice against Mrs. O'Leary, remarked that "an error of a mile in a distance of a mile and an eighth is too large, even under difficult conditions." Ironically, on the same page of this 1911 newspaper there is an article that details Schaefer's recollections of various "Incidents of the Great Blaze." Just as he did before the commissioners forty years earlier, Schaefer recounted his mistake but gave no reason as to why he blundered—possibly because he simply had no explanation for his error. Perhaps fireman Denis J. Swenie was speaking for Schaefer when he reminisced in 1893 about the fallibility of the department watchmen and alluded to the possibility that it was the concept of the lookout system that was flawed: "Generally the place the watchman thought the fire was at was

just where it wasn't. That was the trouble with the watchman system...." But no one really knows why Schaefer called down Box 342. The fireman died many years ago, and he apparently went to his grave, taking his secret with him.[40]

What Really Happened at Bruno Goll's Drugstore?

William Lee claimed that when he saw the O'Leary barn on fire, he ran to Bruno Goll's

FIGURE 76—MATHIAS SCHAE-FER'S VIEW OF THE O'LEARY BARN FROM THE COURT-HOUSE. **According to newspaper reporter Michael Ahern, Third Assistant Fire Marshal Mathias Benner maintained that Mathias Schaefer, fire department courthouse watchman, could not be blamed for misjudging the location of the burning O'Leary barn. Benner apparently believed that the still-glowing ruins of the Lull & Holmes planing mill fire were between the courthouse and the barn, which caused Schaefer to think that the fire was farther away than it really was. However, it appears that Benner was mistaken. Two sight lines drawn on this map of Chicago, one connecting the O'Leary barn and the courthouse and the other connecting the planing mill and the courthouse, indicate that Schaefer's view of the barn was not obstructed by the burning ruins of the planing mill. (Diagram by Douglas A. Swanson)**

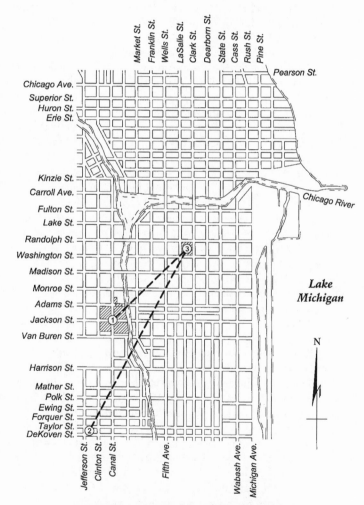

Mathias Schaefer's View of the O'Leary Barn from the Courthouse

October 8, 1871

1. Lull & Holmes planing mill (October 7 fire)
2. O'Leary barn
3. Courthouse

drugstore, intending to turn in an alarm. Box 296 was located on the exterior wall of the store (Figure 45). Lee later charged that not only did Goll refuse to give him the key to the box so that he could send the alarm, but that Goll would not turn it in either. Lee said that Goll told him that an alarm was not necessary, as a steam engine had just gone down the street on its way to the fire. On the other hand, Goll maintained that "despite all assertions or allegations to the contrary, he turned in two separate alarms of fire from the city fire alarm box then attached to his store...." Goll stated in an affidavit that at about nine o'clock a man ran into his store and asked him to turn in an alarm, adding that the fire was near the O'Leary house. At this time Goll turned in the first alarm. About ten minutes later, another man rushed into the store crying, "The fire is spreading very rapidly," and Goll turned in the second alarm. It is probably reasonable to assume that the first man who entered Goll's store was William Lee. Although the identity of the alleged second man is unknown, author H. A. Musham suggests that it was a neighbor of the O'Learys.[41]

Historians will probably never learn the name of this mysterious "second man." They will probably never know what really happened at Bruno Goll's drug store that night. Nonetheless, it is possible to piece together a reasonable conjecture of what transpired between Goll and Lee that evening. Courthouse telegraph operator William J. Brown stated in his inquiry testimony that Schaefer's Box 342 alarm came in at 9:30 P.M., which was *after* Goll's alleged two alarms, and that he received "no alarm whatever from boxes up to this time." Brown's affidavit indicates that neither of Goll's two alarms registered at the courthouse. Is it possible that Goll did not send them?[42]

Years after the fire, newspaperman Michael Ahern maintained that Goll did turn in the alarms, but that they failed to go through because the Saturday night fire knocked out some of the fire alarm telegraph lines. True to form, Ahern was probably mistaken, as the inquiry testimony of Marshal Williams and other firemen indicates that Goll's Box 296 was working later in the evening. Williams was one of the first firemen to arrive at the O'Learys' burning West Side neighborhood. Williams came in on Taylor Street, which was one block north of DeKoven. As the buildings on the north side of Taylor began to smoke, he realized that the fire was going to spread. He ran over to the *America* hose cart and asked Charles Anderson, its driver, to turn in a second alarm. Anderson replied, "I do not know how to turn in the second alarm," so Williams sent *America* foreman John Dorsey instead. Dorsey ran to Goll's drug store and turned it in. William J. Brown testified at the inquiry that at 9:40 P.M., which was less than an hour after Goll allegedly turned in his two alarms, he received an alarm from Box 296. This was undoubtedly Dorsey's. But more importantly—how could Brown receive *any* signal from the drug store if the telegraph lines were down? Musham suggests that a light wind might have swung the wires against a wall or against other wires, temporarily interrupting the circuit, but this theory seems ludicrous. Surely the fire department would not have tolerated so delicate a system.[43]

The system, delicate or not, was first installed in 1865. The original alarm boxes were known as "cranks," undoubtedly due to the crank that (according to directions) had to be turned "slowly and steadily about twenty-five times" in order to send an alarm. These boxes were notoriously unreliable, and in the summer of 1871 they were replaced with new automatic boxes that were operated by merely pulling down a hook. Musham suggests that the box outside Goll's drug store had not yet been converted to the new pull system, and that the undependable crank box may have failed to send Goll's two alarms to the fire department's central office at the courthouse.[44]

But Goll's drug store *did* have the new system. Dorsey testified at the inquiry that in sending the alarm, "I just opened the box and pulled down the hook—one of those things you pull down with your thumb." (As he did not wait to have Goll operate the box, Dorsey must not have been the unknown "second man," the person who asked Goll to send the second alarm.)[45]

Although no one knows for sure, it appears that Goll may have lied in his affidavit and that Lee was telling the truth. But why would Goll refuse to turn in Lee's alarm? Why would he later perjure himself in a sworn affidavit?

Andreas' *History of Chicago* suggests a possible answer. In discussing the Goll and Lee controversy, the historian includes the observations of the druggist's brother-in-law, Lewis Wesley Fick. Fick alleged that on the evening of October 8, Goll told him he had earlier turned in two alarms. But Fick also remarked that "Goll was always extremely cautious about turning in an alarm, lest he should call out the engines on a false alarm." Perhaps Goll did not believe William Lee when he came running into his store, asking for the key to the alarm box, probably telling Goll that the O'Leary barn was on fire. Lee claimed that Goll told him that the alarm was not necessary, as an engine had just gone down the street to the fire. Goll might not have even known where the engine was rushing to, but to appease Lee, told him that it was already en route to the blaze. Or if Goll did believe that the engine was headed for the burning barn, maybe he assumed that one engine was all that was needed; he did not want to be the person responsible for requesting unnecessary additional fire equipment. And finally, perhaps Goll was simply afraid of turning in a false alarm. Later, as the fire began to spread through the city's West Side, he realized his mistake. Fearful of being accused of allowing the fire to burn out of control, he quickly concocted the story of the "second man" and of turning in the two alarms.[46]

But if Goll *had* lied, one could not guess it from reading Andreas' account of the battle of words between Goll and Lee. William Lee was a blacksmith, a renter in one of the city's poorer neighborhoods, and an apparent member of Chicago's lower class. On the other hand, Bruno Goll was a local businessman and entrepreneur. In describing the incident, Andreas does not even pretend to be objective as he devotes hundreds of words to extolling Goll's virtues. He characterizes Goll's affidavit as being "most conclusive." The notary statement that accompanies it describes Goll as "a man in whose statements complete credibility can be placed, and whose veracity is thoroughly reliable." Finally, in the slim chance that the reader is not yet cheering for the unjustly maligned Goll, Andreas includes a short biography of the druggist, a biography in which Goll is lauded as "being of an enterprising character." In this conflict of honesty, ethics, and integrity titled *Bruno Goll vs. William Lee*, Lee was outclassed from the beginning.[47]

Were the Firemen Intoxicated As They Fought the Fire?

One of the threads that runs consistently through the pages of the inquiry transcript is the issue of whether or not the firemen were intoxicated as they fought the fire. This line of questioning was probably not unexpected, with the *Evening Journal* reporting as early as October 24 in an article entitled "Liquor-Drinking Firemen" that "there seems to be no question that a fire department, strictly trained to abstinence, would have saved our city as easily on Sunday night as on Saturday. The temptation which Saturday's exhaustion and Sunday's rest brought worked a world of mischief." Less than a month later, Alfred Sewell echoed this opinion (but more bluntly) in his book *The Great Calamity!*: "A drunken Fire Department is, in a measure, responsible for the destruction of Chicago."[48]

So were Sewell and the *Evening Journal* correct? Did Chicago burn because its firemen were lit? As expected, the facts are not as clear-cut as Sewell suggests.

Historians Elias Colbert and Everett Chamberlin maintained that in 1871, firemen would celebrate the successful culmination of their firefighting efforts by "a good thorough drunk." They claimed that because of the firemen's indulgence after the Saturday night fire at the Lull & Holmes planing mill, the department was not in the best condition for a second bout of fire fighting the following day. Instead, exhausted from work and hung over as well, the men labored "stupidly and listlessly."[49]

But if they did appear stupid and listless, it was probably not because of alcohol. Twenty-seven firemen testified at the inquiry. Ten of them indicated what time it was when they finally finished working at the Lull & Holmes fire, which started at about eleven o'clock Saturday night. All ten worked throughout the night, and seven men did not leave the planing mill until Sunday afternoon. Third Assistant Fire Marshal Mathias Benner testified that "a portion of the department [was] at work there about eighteen hours." Surely after battling this fire, the men would have been interested in only food and rest, not drink. The transcript of the inquiry certainly bears this out; fireman Leo Meyers' testimony is typical:

Q. Did you see any of the firemen or marshals intoxicated?

A. No sir.

Q. Did not visit any engine houses except your own on the Sunday after the Saturday night fire?

A. No. We worked around, did not get home until two or three o'clock in the afternoon from the Saturday night fire. The first thing we done, we laid down for a rest until [Box] 28 came in.

Q. There has been some charges made of carousing at the engine houses Sunday.

A. That is the first I am aware of it.[50]

But this is not to say that the firemen met the *Evening Journal*'s standard of a department that was "strictly trained to abstinence." James Hildreth testified that he "drank more than the firemen did," and at least one fireman, William Mullin, foreman of the steamer *Illinois*, admitted to drinking on the job. But Mullin was adamant that he knew of no intoxicated firemen:

Q. Did you have any liquor in your house on Sunday?

A. No sir.

Q. Don't allow it there?

A. No sir. Not known to me.

Q. You don't know that any of the men were in liquor on Sunday at all?

A. No sir. Might have had a glass of beer.

Q. If they had been intoxicated that day, would you have known it?

A. Certainly I would.

Q. Were they?

A. No.

Q. Do you know of any other company being intoxicated or any of the members of it or any of the officers?

A. I didn't see a man belonging to the fire department in my line so that he was not fit to attend to business.

Q. Do you know of any whiskey being passed about to any of the men during the progress of the fire?

A. Yes sir. I got two bottles of wine myself. It was sent to me by one of the men in the freight house. He came to me and asked me, "Will I fetch you a little brandy or something to drink?" Said I, "I haven't had anything to eat for a few days now, and I do not think I will take any of that. It is too heavy." Said he, "I will bring you a couple of bottles of wine." Said I, "I do not think that that will hurt me any. And a couple of bottles of cider."

Q. For you and your men?

A. Yes sir.

Q. None of your company got intoxicated upon it?

A. No sir.[51]

Perhaps the most celebrated example of public servant imbibing is the story recounted by one Alexander Frear, New York Commissioner of Emigration, Commissioner of Public Charities, and member of New York's state assembly. On October 8 he happened to be in Chicago, and his colorful account of fire and bedlam in the city's downtown, somewhat immodestly entitled "The Full Story of the Great Fire: Narrative of an Eye Witness," was published in the *New York World* a week later. Frear's article is memorable because of its graphic and sensational anecdotes. Unfortunately, many of these stories, with underlying morality themes of good and evil, seem apocryphal: the thieving ragamuffin, his pockets stuffed with gold-plated buttons and wearing white kid gloves, who was killed by a marble slab thrown from a window; the woman kneeling in the street, praying while holding a crucifix, her skirt burning, who was dashed to the ground by a runaway truck; the man who stood on a piano, declaring that the fire was the friend of the poor, preaching from his makeshift pulpit until an unappreciative member of his congregation threw a bottle at him and knocked him off. And finally, the story of several firemen from the *Little Giant* engine company, safely ensconced inside a restaurant: "One of them was bathing his head with whiskey from a flask. They declared that the entire department had given up, overworked, and that they could do nothing more."[52]

As one might expect, the inquiry testimony of *Little Giant* foreman William Musham and first pipeman John Campion contains no mention of this incident. But even assuming that Alexander Frear's story is true and that the men of the *Little Giant* did fall from grace and land on a barstool, it only indicates that the firemen were not teetotalers during the fire's rampage.

Frear's "Narrative of an Eye Witness" does not prove that when they eventually stood up, they were so inebriated that they could not perform their firefighting duties.

So if Alfred Sewell, the *Evening Journal*, Elias Colbert, and Everett Chamberlin were all mistaken, if Chicago's firemen were battling only the fire and not the effects of alcohol, then how did the allegations of drunkenness originate? There are five possibilities:

- After toiling all night at the Lull & Holmes fire, the men were exhausted from work and lack of sleep. Their eyes were red from the dust and cinders, and many of the firemen were almost blind. The men were laboring under the influence of fire and fatigue, not drink, but the physical effects were the same.[53]
- Upon seeing the firemen (many of whom were Irish), "listlessly" stumble about, late nineteenth-century xenophobia may have prompted Chicago journalists and authors to stereotype these firefighters as drunks.[54]
- Perhaps the firemen moved slowly only because their foremen weren't present to spur them on. That was the opinion of Denis J. Swenie, foreman of the steam engine *Gund*, when he testified at the inquiry:

  Q. Did you see any misbehavior on the part of the men or officers or any intoxication at the fire?
  A. No I did not. Some of the companies had no officers, and the men were very slow about moving.[55]

- As the engines raced through the streets en route to the fire, it is possible that a bystander might have mistaken the firemen's quick response for something less admirable. John R. Chapin of *Harper's Weekly* penned a thrilling eyewitness account for the October 28, 1871, issue: "Here comes a steamer! Back rushes the crowd, and four splendid horses, followed by an engine, whose driver was either wild with excitement or crazy drunk, dashed across the bridge, and, wheeling to the right, took up a position on the edge of the dock."[56]
- But what seems at first to be the strangest possibility is actually one of the most plausible. Both Marshal Robert A. Williams

and fireman Michael W. Conway testified about intoxicated civilians wearing fire hats. Naturally, these citizens were mistaken for firemen. As Conway explained to the commissioners:

Q. Did you see any of the men any the worse for liquor?
A. No sir, I didn't see a man that was intoxicated. I didn't see a member of the fire department—I saw men who had firemen's hats on that I knew personally were not firemen that were intoxicated.
Q. Where did they get these hats?
A. Came to hose carts standing on the street where they found them. One man took my hat and a policeman, I believe, shoved him in the river so he lost his hat. He was drunk and the supposition, I suppose, among the citizens was that he was a fireman.[57]

Fireman John Dorsey also testified about "leaving my two coats right by the fire" when he ran to turn in the alarm at Goll's drug store. He had apparently taken them off because of the heat. It seems likely that while firemen were preoccupied with fighting the fire, citizens would have been able to acquire coats as well as hats, thus nearly completing their feloniously acquired ensembles.[58]

It appears equally likely that while Chicago burned, only some of the city's firemen indulged themselves. Furthermore, the inquiry transcript indicates that none of these firemen drank heavily. Although the department ultimately failed to subdue the fire, this was not because alcohol hampered their job performance. Rather, it was due to the sheer magnitude of the blaze. Although Colbert and Chamberlin were surely wrong in their characterization of the firemen, they were certainly correct in describing the event of October 8–10, 1871, as "The Great Conflagration" and not merely as "The Great Chicago Fire." Michael W. Conway undoubtedly would have agreed with the authors' assessment. When he was asked during the inquiry whether or not the fire could be confined to the city's South Side, he replied, "I do not think it could have been stopped unless you picked it up and threw it into the lake." And surely telegraph operator George E. Fuller spoke for the entire department when he testified that he did not believe that the firemen had "time to become intoxicated. They had all they could do to save themselves and apparatus from being burned up."[59]

How Many Houses Were on the O'Leary Property?

Historians disagree on the physical nature of the O'Leary and McLaughlin houses. Did the two families share one building, with the McLaughlins living in the front half and the O'Learys occupying the rear portion, or did each family live in its own individual cottage?[60]

Post-fire pictures of the O'Leary property (e.g., Figure 62) suggest that there was only one house, and at first this conclusion appears to be consistent with the inquiry transcript. Consider, for example, the following exchange between the commissioners and Mrs. O'Leary:

Q. Was there any other family living in your house?
A. Yes sir. There was Mrs. Laughlin.
Q. How many rooms did they occupy?
A. Two rooms.
Q. Front rooms?
A. Yes sir.[61]

The questioning continued in much the same vein, with Mrs. O'Leary failing to comment on the Board's continued references to "the front part of the house" and "your part of the house." At one point, though, when asked about the McLaughlin party, she replied, "I could hear anything from our own bed to their rooms, because they pretty near joined together." Her remark implied that perhaps the buildings were not connected, but the Board failed to question it. But on the other hand, when a fire official asked fireman Lewis Fiene about the size of the O'Leary home, a questioner noted, "Well, it is built in house shape, in two sections." But this statement is somewhat inconsistent with Patrick O'Leary's testimony. When the commissioners asked O'Leary, "Didn't the firemen put water on your house during the fire?" he replied, "They did on the taller end."[62]

Mrs. McLaughlin's testimony initially seems as enigmatic as the O'Learys'. When asked if she owned the house in which she lived, she replied, "No sir. It was Pat Leary's house. I lived in the house the fire took place in. In the front of it. He lived in the rear part of it." But later she was asked, "Was there a door in your apartment leading back to the yard?" and her reply finally clarified the issue: "No sir. The whole house was by itself. It is separated between the houses." This was later confirmed by James Dalton: "O'Leary had two small cottages, one immediately behind the other, though practically attached." Even Daniel Sullivan's testimony was in agreement: "There was a little house belonging to Leary that was in the front. There was a party there...." It seems clear that there were two detached homes on the O'Leary property in October of 1871. Just as Patrick O'Leary indicated, the McLaughlin house was noticeably higher than the O'Leary cottage (Figure 62). Ironically, both buildings survived the fire.[63]

Notes

1. Daniel Sullivan, *Inquiry*, vol. [1], pp. 255–56, 266–67; William J. Brown, *Inquiry*, vol. [1], p. 1; "The Great Fire," *Chicago Evening Journal*, 12 December 1871, p. [4]; "The Great Fire," *Chicago Tribune*, 24 November 1871, p. 6.

2. William J. Brown, *Inquiry*, vol. [1], pp. 1–2; Mathias Schaefer, *Inquiry*, vol. [1], p. 5; Robert A. Williams, *Inquiry*, vol. [4], p. 288; "The Great Fire," *Chicago Evening Journal*, 12 December 1871, p. [4]; "The Great Fire," *Chicago Tribune*, 24 November 1871, p. 6.

3. Andreas, vol. 2, pp. 701, 710–19; *Robinson's Atlas*, vol. 1, plate 6.

4. William Musham, *Inquiry*, vol. [1], p. 8; Dennis Regan, *Inquiry*, vol. [1], p. 122; Michael Sullivan, *Inquiry*, vol. [1], pp. 79–80; Catherine O'Leary, *Inquiry*, vol. [1], p. 66.

5. William J. Brown, *Inquiry*, vol. [1], p. 1.

6. Andreas, vol. 2, pp. 709–12; "The Great Fire," *Chicago Evening Journal*, 12 December 1871, p. [4]; William Musham, *Inquiry*, vol. [1], pp. 6–7; Musham, pp. 86, [101].

7. Catharine McLaughlin, *Inquiry*, vol. [1], pp. 231, 233. Mrs. McLaughlin testified that ten minutes passed from the time she saw the O'Leary barn and Dalton's house on fire until she saw a fire engine. On the other hand, Andreas comments that "the writer of this record conversed with a number of Bohemians.... They also say that no

engine arrived until at least *fifteen minutes* after the fire began [emphasis added]." See Andreas, vol. 2, p. 716.

8. Catherine O'Leary, *Inquiry*, vol. [1], pp. 60, 66; Catharine McLaughlin, *Inquiry*, vol. [1], pp. 224, 230–31.

9. Catherine Sullivan, *Inquiry*, vol. [1], p. 115.

10. James H. Hildreth, *Inquiry*, vol. [3], pp. 123–24. The *Evening Journal* published a "chronological table of the Great Fire, showing the hours at which the buildings named were known to be in flames." This table indicates that the O'Leary barn burned at 9:30 P.M. See "Fire Chronology," *Chicago Evening Journal*, 18 November 1871, p. [4], hereafter cited in text as "Fire Chronology."

11. James H. Hildreth, *Inquiry*, vol. [3], pp. 155–57; Musham, p. 134.

12. "The Great Fire," *Chicago Tribune*, 30 November 1871, p. 4; James H. Hildreth, *Inquiry*, vol. [3], pp. 153–55.

13. Goodspeed, pp. 147, 171–72.

14. "The City Election," *Chicago Times*, 19 October 1871, p. [2]; "The Blowing Up Business," p. [2]; Andreas, vol. 2, pp. 495, 738–39; Sheahan and Upton, p. 1.

15. Andreas, vol. 2, pp. 728, 739, 754; *1870 City Directory*, p. 1038; Kogan and Cromie, pp. 33, 41; "All Around Town," *Chicago Evening Journal*, 2 December 1871, p. [4]; "Precautions Against Fire," *Chicago Evening Journal*, 30 December 1871, p. [3]; Musham, p. 134.

16. "The Great Fire," *Chicago Tribune*, 26 November 1871, p. 1; Daniel Sullivan, *Inquiry*, vol. [1], p. 257.

17. "The City," *Chicago Evening Journal*, 27 November 1871, p. [3], hereafter cited in text as "The City"; "The Fire," *Chicago Times*, 26 November 1871, p. 1; "Cow, or How?," *Chicago Republican*, 27 November 1871, p. [4]. In describing the *Journal*'s summary of Sullivan's testimony, the word "plagiarism" is not intended to be pejorative. In 1891, the *Tribune* recalled that after the fire the *Tribune* and *Journal* worked together for some time, with the *Tribune* printing its papers in the evening and letting the *Journal* use the *Tribune* presses and machinery in the afternoon. Perhaps this partnership extended to the sharing of stories. (On the other hand, the *Journal* remembered this act of kindness to the competition differently, reminiscing in 1921 that "until the *Tribune* was able to secure an office of its own, its morning editions were printed by the *Journal*'s courtesy.") See "While the Fire Raged," sec. 5, p. 33; "Readers Bring Famous Extra," p. [2].

18. "Mrs. O'Leary's Cow Slandered," sec. 1, p. 14.

19. Statement of J. C. Chapeck.

20. Musham, pp. 97, 129; Lewis and Smith, p. 123; Dedmon, p. 98; Longstreet, p. 123; Mary Basich letter, April 1998; "Kin of O'Leary Absolves Cow in Fire of 1871," sec. 1, p. 1.

21. Andreas, vol. 2, pp. 701, 714; Musham, pp. 96–97, 159.

22. Andreas, vol. 1, p. [3], vol. 2, pp. 701, 710–11, 713; "Centennial Eve," sec. 1, p. [2].

23. Andreas, vol. 2, p. 714; Catharine McLaughlin, *Inquiry*, vol. [1], p. 231; Catherine O'Leary, *Inquiry*, vol. [1], p. 60.

24. Catherine O'Leary, *Inquiry*, vol. [1], pp. 59, 66.

25. Andreas, vol. 2, p. 709; "The Great Fire," *Chicago Tribune*, 25 November 1871, p. 6.

26. Musham, pp. 155–56; "The Great Fire," *Chicago Tribune*, 26 November 1871, p. 1.

27. "The Cow that Kicked Over the Lamp," p. [2]; "How It Originated," p. [2]; Catherine O'Leary, *Inquiry*, vol. [1], p. 66.

28. Catherine O'Leary, *Inquiry*, vol. [1], pp. 64–65.

29. Catherine O'Leary, *Inquiry*, vol. [1], p. 65. Perhaps Mrs. O'Leary was not as cryptic and close-mouthed in the years after the fire. In 1894 her doctor told a *Tribune* reporter: "As [Mrs. O'Leary] has told me a thousand times, she was in bed asleep when the fire broke out...." See "Fire Alley Is Paved," p. 1.

30. William Musham, *Inquiry*, vol. [1], p. 8.

31. William Mullin, *Inquiry*, vol. [1], p. 41.

32. Christian Schimmals, *Inquiry*, vol. [1], p. 127.

33. George Rau, *Inquiry*, vol. [1], p. 176.

34. Charles Anderson, *Inquiry*, vol. [3], p. 100.

35. "The Great Fire," *Chicago Evening Journal*, 12 December 1871, p. [4]; Andreas, vol. 2, p. 709; Kirkland, pp. 728–29.

36. Andreas, vol. 2, p. 709; William Musham, *Inquiry*, vol. [1], pp. 6–8; Charles Anderson, *Inquiry*, vol. [3], pp. 99–100, 104–5, 112–13; *Robinson's Atlas*, vol. 1, plate 6; Musham, p. 86; "Story of the Great Chicago Fire," sec. 3, p. 20; "1871 Reporter," sec. 1, p. 3.

37. William Musham, *Inquiry*, vol. [1], p. 8; Charles Anderson, *Inquiry*, vol. [3], p. 100; Cromie, p. 33.

38. "The Great Fire," *Chicago Tribune*, 24 November 1871, p. 6; Musham, pp. 99–102; Mathias Schaefer, *Inquiry*, vol. [1], p. 5.

39. "Boring for Facts," *Chicago Tribune*, 19 November 1871, p. 6; Kirkland, p. 728; "The Fire Fighters," sec. 1, p. [2]; Herman Schell, Chicago Fire historian, interview by Richard F. Bales, 26

February 1998; Musham, pp. 159–61; Lowe, p. 42. The Saturday night fire at the Lull & Holmes planing mill burned an area bounded approximately by Adams Street, Van Buren Street, Clinton Street, and the Chicago River. See Figure 10; Andreas, vol. 2, p. 707; "The Fire Fiend," p. [3].

40. "Reporter of 1871 Fire," sec. 1, p. [2]; "Story of the Great Chicago Fire," sec. 3, p. 20; Kirkland, p. 728; *Chicago & Vicinity 6-County StreetFinder*, pp. 51, 57 (Cook County); Musham, pp. 99, 161, 179; "Man in Tower," sec. 1, p. [2].

41. Andreas, vol. 2, pp. 714, 716; Musham, pp. 97–98, 100, 158–59; *Chicago: City on Fire*, p. 11-F; *1870 City Directory*, p. 915.

42. William J. Brown, *Inquiry*, vol. [1], p. 1; Andreas, vol. 2, pp. 711, 716; Musham, pp. 159–60; "The Great Fire," *Chicago Evening Journal*, 12 December 1871, p. [4].

43. William J. Brown, *Inquiry*, vol. [1], p. 1; Charles Anderson, *Inquiry*, vol. [3], p. 100; Robert A. Williams, *Inquiry*, vol. [4], pp. 238–41; John Dorsey, *Inquiry*, vol. [2], p. 64; Musham, pp. 84–85; 160, 183; "1871 Reporter," sec. 1, p. 3; "Story of the Great Chicago Fire," sec. 3, p. 20; Lowe, p. 42; Andreas, vol. 2, p. 716.

44. Andreas, vol. 2, pp. 92–93; Musham, pp. 84–85, 159–60; John P. Barrett letter. Musham notes that "the following directions were given for operating crank boxes: Upon discovery of, or positive information on, a fire near your signal box, unlock the door and turn the crank slowly and steadily about twenty-five times; then wait a few moments, and if you hear no ticking in the box, or alarm on the larger bells, turn as before until you hear the alarm. Cease turning after the bells have struck." See Musham, pp. 84–85.

45. John Dorsey, *Inquiry*, vol. [2], p. 65.

46. Andreas, vol. 2, pp. 714, 716.

47. Andreas, vol. 2, pp. 714–16; Chicago Title Insurance Company records; *1870 City Directory*, p. 488; *1871 City Directory*, p. 542.

48. "Liquor-Drinking Firemen," p. [2]; "The Fire in Print," p. 1; Sewell, p. 79. References in the inquiry transcript to possible firemen intoxication include William Musham, *Inquiry*, vol. [1], pp. 31–32; George Rau, *Inquiry*, vol. [1], p. 173; John Schank, *Inquiry*, vol. [4], p. 227.

49. Colbert and Chamberlin, pp. 227, 370–71.

50. "The Fire Fiend," p. [3]; William Musham, *Inquiry*, vol. [1], p. 32; William Mullin, *Inquiry*, vol. [1], pp. 49–50; Michael Sullivan, *Inquiry*, vol. [1], pp. 98–99; Christian Schimmals, *Inquiry*, vol. [1], pp. 132–33; Lewis Fiene, *Inquiry*, vol. [1], pp. 216–18; Michael W. Conway, *Inquiry*, vol. [2], pp. 2–3, 24–26; Leo Meyers, *Inquiry*, vol. [2], p.

103; Denis J. Swenie, *Inquiry*, vol. [2], pp. 229–30; Mathias Benner, *Inquiry*, vol. [4], pp. 123–24; Robert A. Williams, *Inquiry*, vol. [4], p. 234.

51. James H. Hildreth, *Inquiry*, vol. [3], p. 152; William Mullin, *Inquiry*, vol. [1], pp. 52–54.

52. *As Others See Chicago*, pp. 191, 197–99, 201–02.

53. "The Fire Fiend," p. [3]; Luzerne, pp. [171]–72; "Story of the Great Chicago Fire, sec. 3, p. 20; Musham, p. 174; Robert A. Williams, *Inquiry*, vol. [4], p. 290.

54. Cromie, p. 49.

55. Denis J. Swenie, *Inquiry*, vol. [2], p. 222.

56. John R. Chapin, "Account by an Eye-Witness," *Harper's Weekly* 15 (28 October 1871), p. 1011, hereafter cited in text as Chapin.

57. Robert A. Williams, *Inquiry*, vol. [4], pp. 291–92; Michael W. Conway, *Inquiry*, vol. [2], pp. 25, 38–39.

58. John Dorsey, *Inquiry*, vol. [2], pp. 64–65.

59. Colbert and Chamberlin, p. 11; Michael W. Conway, *Inquiry*, vol. [2], p. 39; George E. Fuller, *Inquiry*, vol. [2], pp. 197–98.

60. As to whether the O'Leary and McLaughlin residences constituted one building or two, compare Sawislak, p. 43 and Duis and Holt, p. 220 (one building) with Musham, pp. 94–95 and Cromie, pp. 25–26 (two buildings). See also Untitled article, *Chicago Evening Journal*, 27 November 1871, p. [2]; "How They Look and Act," p. [3] (one building).

61. Catherine O'Leary, *Inquiry*, vol. [1], p. 64. See also the testimony of Catherine Sullivan, *Inquiry*, vol. [1], pp. 117–18:

Q. Did you know anybody living in Mr. Leary's house besides themselves?

A. Yes sir. A man by the name of Patrick McLaughlin.

62. Catherine O' Leary, *Inquiry*, vol. [1], pp. 65–67; Lewis Fiene, *Inquiry*, vol. [1], pp. 212–13; Patrick O' Leary, *Inquiry*, vol. [1], p. 248.

63. Catharine McLaughlin, *Inquiry*, vol. [1], pp. 223, 237; Daniel Sullivan, *Inquiry*, vol. [1], p. 255; Andreas, vol. 2, pp. 713–14. Other inquiry references to the number of houses on the O'Leary property include: Dennis Regan, *Inquiry*, vol. [1], p. 122 ("Do you know whether there was company in the front part of the house?"); Catharine McLaughlin, *Inquiry*, vol. [1], p. 234 ("I lived in the front of the house."); Daniel Sullivan, *Inquiry*, vol. [1], p. 262 ("There was a party in front of Leary's house."); Daniel Sullivan, *Inquiry*, vol. [1], p. 267 ("The party carrying [on] was in the front of Leary's house and in McLaughlin's.")

Behind the Conclusions

> [Daniel Sullivan] left the house, and, while on the opposite side of the street, at
> twenty or twenty-five minutes past 9 o'clock, he saw fire in Leary's barn. He ran
> across the street as fast as he could....
>
> —*Chicago Tribune*, November 26, 1871

Introduction

This book contains several conclusions concerning Daniel Sullivan and his activities on the night of October 8. Appendix B sets forth the bases for these conclusions. This appendix also includes an explanation and analysis of Figure 54, the diagram that depicts the approximate location of the O'Leary and McLaughlin homes, the O'Leary barn, and other improvements.

Determining Where Daniel Sullivan Sat in Front of White's Property

During the inquiry Daniel Sullivan testified that he sat by a fence "at the head of White's house or head of his lot." But in 1871 William White owned two contiguous parcels of land on DeKoven Street, a "west parcel" and an "east parcel." In front of which one did Sullivan sit?[1] Chicago real estate records indicate that Sullivan probably sat in front of White's "west parcel." The reasons are as follows:

• White was deeded the west parcel in 1864. He obtained the adjoining east parcel in 1870. Chicago city directories for the years

1866 through 1871 disclose, with one exception (1870), a William White living at a DeKoven Street address—130 DeKoven Street. Therefore, White was living across the street from the O'Learys (who lived at 137 DeKoven Street) prior to the time he was deeded the east parcel in 1870. But was he living on the west parcel? *Robinson's Atlas of the City of Chicago* depicts improvements on Chicago properties; it also includes the addresses and legal descriptions for these improvements. The west parcel is described in this atlas as 130 DeKoven Street.[2]

• At the inquiry Mrs. O'Leary was asked the following questions about Mrs. White and where she lived:

> Q. [Did Mrs. White live] next to Sullivan's?
> A. Yes sir.
> Q. Next east to Sullivan's?
> A. Yes sir.
> Q. One story or two?
> A. Two stories.
> Q. There is two two-story houses there right together?
> A. Yes sir.
> Q. She lives in the east one?
> A. Yes sir.

Chicago Title Insurance Company records indicate that the parcel adjacent to and east of Catherine Sullivan's property was White's west parcel.[3]

• Mr. O'Leary testified that the fire did not burn any buildings south of DeKoven Street. This is confirmed by maps of the "burnt district," the area burned by the fire, which indicate that DeKoven Street was the southern boundary of the fire. Although *Robinson's Atlas* is circa 1886, it is possible that the buildings on the south side of DeKoven Street are the same structures that existed prior to the fire. In any event, this atlas does indicate that the building on Catherine Sullivan's property and the building on the "west parcel" immediately to the east are quite close together.[4]

• Daniel Sullivan testified that he lived at 134 DeKoven Street and that he walked "one lot east of me." Although the word "lot" is a legal term, one might presume that Sullivan was actually referring to one of the half-lot parcels on which many of the houses in the block were built. *Robinson's Atlas* indicates that the half-lot parcel east of his mother's one-and-one-half lots was 130 DeKoven Street, the west White parcel.[5]

This analysis was necessary in order to compute the distance that Sullivan allegedly ran from in front of White's house to the O'Leary barn. It was helpful but not crucial in determining whether or not Sullivan could see the barn from where he sat across the street. Figure 54 discloses that even if Sullivan sat in front of a fence on White's east parcel, his view of the barn still would have been obstructed by Dalton's house.

Why Walter Forbes' House Would Have Blocked Sullivan's View of the Barn

H. A. Musham's monograph includes a diagram of the O'Leary neighborhood. Musham locates Walter Forbes' house on it with exacting accuracy. As depicted, the house clearly blocks Sullivan's line of sight. Unfortunately, Mus-

ham's reference material, now in the Research Center of the Chicago Historical Society, does not indicate the source of his conclusions relative to the location of Forbes' home. Although Andreas' *History of Chicago* contains a diagram of some of the properties along DeKoven Street, this "Plat of Locality Where Fire Originated" (Figure 57) does not disclose the exact location of Forbes' house. But Andreas specifically points out that Dalton's house was set back from the street, "leaving room for a contemplated front addition." Even if Forbes' house had been similarly constructed, a corner of it would have blocked Sullivan's view (Figure 77). But it probably was not set back this far from the street, for although Andreas also refers to Forbes' home, the historian is silent as to its location. It seems at least somewhat plausible that if Forbes' house had been set back as much as Dalton's house (and it appears that Dalton's house might have been set back as much as thirty-seven feet), Andreas would have commented on it. It is more likely that Forbes' home was located just a few feet back from the street, like the McLaughlin cottage (Figure 62). If this were so, Forbes' entire house (possibly two stories in height) would have certainly blocked Sullivan's line of sight (Figure 78).[6]

Determining the Distance That Sullivan Allegedly Ran to the Barn

The lots in the subdivision in which the O'Learys lived were all originally 50 feet wide and 118 feet deep. The O'Learys lived in Block 38 in this subdivision. As platted, DeKoven Street was forty feet wide. On July 30, 1855, the Common Council of the City of Chicago passed an ordinance that authorized the widening of DeKoven Street from 40 feet to 60 feet. Ten feet was acquired from lots on either side of the street. This resulted in a taking of ten feet from the front of what would eventually be the O'Leary property. On this same day another ordinance was approved, appropriating a 15-foot-wide strip of land in Block 38. This land was taken for use as an alley, running through the block in an east-west direction. Seven-and-one-half feet were taken from the rear of the future O'Leary parcel and other lots on DeKoven Street. Because of these ordinances, what ultimately became the O'Leary property was

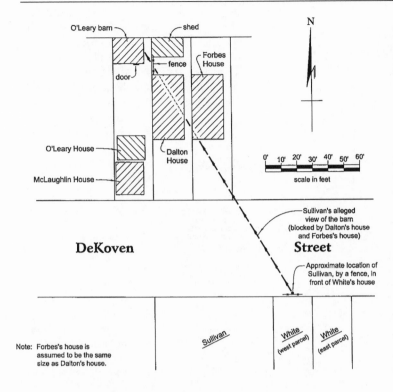

N

0' 10' 20' 30' 40' 50' 60'

scale in feet

O'Leary barn

shed

Forbes House

fence

door

O'Leary House

Dalton House

McLaughlin House

DeKoven

Street

Sullivan's alleged view of the barn (blocked by Dalton's house and Forbes's house)

Approximate location of Sullivan, by a fence, in front of White's house

Note: Forbes's house is assumed to be the same size as Dalton's house.

Sullivan

White (west parcel)

White (east parcel)

Daniel Sullivan's View of the O'Leary Barn
(Assuming Walter Forbes's house was set back from DeKoven Street)

October 8, 1871

FIGURE 77—DANIEL SULLIVAN'S VIEW OF THE O'LEARY BARN (ASSUMING WALTER FORBES' HOUSE WAS SET BACK FROM DEKOVEN STREET). **It is clear that the Dalton house would have blocked Daniel Sullivan's view of the barn from where he allegedly sat across the street. Although historians do not know the location or size of Walter Forbes's house, it seems equally clear that even if the Forbes house was set back as far as the Dalton house, a corner of Forbes's home would have nonetheless obstructed Sullivan's line of sight.** (Diagram by Douglas A. Swanson)

Andreas indicates on his aforementioned diagram that the barn was situated so that the twenty-foot length ran north-south. Musham, on the other hand, depicts the barn in his drawing so that its length ran east-west. Andreas describes in great detail the location of the improvements on the O'Leary and Dalton properties. This information, though, is contrary to his diagram, and suggests that the barn was probably oriented on an east-west axis, as delineated by Musham. Finally, in an exceptionally puzzling exchange of inquiry testimony, Daniel Sullivan also seems to imply, like Musham's diagram and Andreas' text, that the length of the barn ran from east to west, and thus the barn is shown accordingly in Figure 54:

Q. You say that at the end of this twenty-foot place, there was five feet more to that shed?
A. It was not the *end* of it. It was the *side* of it, the *south side* as you go into the yard [emphasis added].[8]

The distance from the DeKoven Street entrance of the passageway that was between the O'Leary/McLaughlin and Dalton homes to the front of the O'Leary barn can be calculated as follows:

100.5 feet = the length of the O'Leary property
−16.0 feet = the width of the barn
=84.5 feet

diminished from 118 feet in depth to 100.5 feet. There was now a widened DeKoven Street in front and a fifteen-foot alley that ran parallel to this street in the rear. The passageway that was east of the O'Leary and McLaughlin cottages ran north from and perpendicular to DeKoven Street.[7]

The O'Leary barn was located at the rear of their property, next to the fifteen-foot alley. Although it is clear that their barn was sixteen feet by twenty feet in size, the orientation of the barn on the O'Leary property is not so evident.

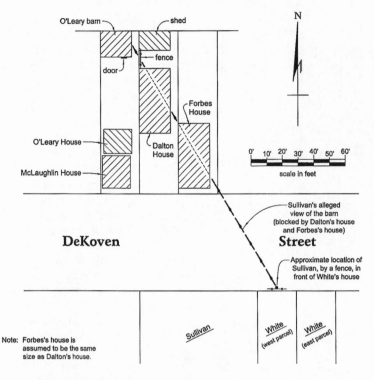

O'Leary barn ─╮   ╭─ shed

fence

door ─╯

─ Forbes
House

O'Leary House ─

─ Dalton
House

McLaughlin House ─

N

0' 10' 20' 30' 40' 50' 60'

scale in feet

─ Sullivan's alleged
view of the barn
(blocked by Dalton's house
and Forbes's house)

DeKoven   **Street**

─ Approximate location of
Sullivan, by a fence, in
front of White's house

Note: Forbes's house is
assumed to be the same
size as Dalton's house.

Sullivan   White
(west parcel)   White
(east parcel)

Daniel Sullivan's View of the O'Leary Barn
(Assuming Walter Forbes's house was close to DeKoven Street)

October 8, 1871

FIGURE 78—DANIEL SULLIVAN'S VIEW OF THE O'LEARY BARN (AS-
SUMING WALTER FORBES' HOUSE WAS CLOSE TO DEKOVEN STREET).
Walter Forbes' house was probably set back only a few feet
from DeKoven Street, just like the McLaughlin cottage next
door. If this were the case, Forbes' house would have certainly blocked Sullivan's view of the O'Leary barn. (Diagram
by Douglas A. Swanson)

The exact width and location of the passageway is not known. Nonetheless, reasonable
conclusions can be drawn from inquiry statements. While testifying, Mrs. O'Leary acknowledged that the passageway was "between the two
houses." Catharine McLaughlin concurred in
the following exchange of testimony:

Q. You had access to the yard through the nar-
row alley?
A. No sir.
Q. Ain't you the privilege of the yard?
A. Yes sir. From the division there was between
our house and Dalton's.

Q. You didn't live in the
front part of Mr. Dal-
ton's?
A. Mrs. Leary's.
Q. Between Mrs. Leary's
house and Dalton's
house?
A. There was a way to go
right through, a large
passage.
Q. Enough to roll in a
barrel of flour?
A. Yes sir, a good deal
wide.
Q. Between Mr. Dalton's
house and Mr. Leary's?
A. Yes sir.
Q. There is a fence be-
tween the two houses?
A. I could not tell whether
it was Mrs. Leary
or Dalton that owned
the fence.
Q. Was there a fence
there?
A. Yes sir. There was a
board fence going be-
twixt them.
Q. There was a little al-
leyway running along-
side of Mrs. Leary's
house going back to
the yard?
A. Yes sir.[9]

Based on Catharine
McLaughlin's statements,
this alleyway is estimated
to be at least five feet wide. As Dalton's house
was built on the west line of his land, this passageway would have burdened the east five feet
of the O'Leary property, which was twenty-five
feet wide.[10]

The distance from where Sullivan sat in
front of William White's house to a point due
west and directly opposite this passageway is
conservatively determined by measuring from
the midpoint of White's west parcel in a west-
erly direction to a point that is opposite the
middle of this five-foot alleyway. (Sullivan's location is presumed to be a point equidistant
from both sides of White's west parcel, and the

middle of the alleyway is presumed to be a point that is two-and-one-half feet west of the O'Leary-Dalton boundary line. See Figure 54.) Like the O'Leary and Dalton properties, the Forbes and White parcels were also twenty-five feet wide half-lots. The one-and-one-half lot tract owned by Catherine Sullivan was seventy-five feet wide.[11] With this information, the distance from where Sullivan sat to a point due west and directly opposite the O'Leary passageway can be computed as follows:

12½ feet = half the width of the White west parcel

75 feet = the entire width of the Catherine Sullivan tract

2½ feet = the approximate distance from the O'Leary-Dalton boundary line to a point opposite the presumed center of the passageway.

These figures, as shown in Figure 54, total 90 feet.

The estimated total distance that Sullivan claimed he ran can now be determined, using the Pythagorean Theorem (the square of the hypotenuse of a right triangle is equal to the sum of the squares of the other two sides, or $a^2 + b^2 = c^2$) to approximate the distance from where Sullivan sat in front of White's house to (along a northwesterly diagonal) the entrance of the passageway across the street:

a = width of DeKoven Street;
b = east-west distance from where Sullivan sat to a point opposite alleyway;
c = diagonal distance from where Sullivan sat to the entrance of the alleyway;
or,
$60^2 + 90^2 = c^2$;
or,
3600 + 8100 = 11700 (i.e., diagonal distance², or 108.17 feet).

Therefore, the approximate total distance that Sullivan allegedly traveled would be:

108.17 feet = the distance that Sullivan ran from in front of White's house to the entrance of the O'Leary passageway across the street

+ 84.5 feet = the distance from the entrance of this passageway to the front of the O'Leary barn

―――――――

= 192.67 feet

The barn door that Sullivan claimed he entered was located on the south wall of the barn, which faced the O'Leary home. As the door was located on the east, or right, side of this wall, it is reasonable to conclude that the door was nearly, but not exactly, opposite the alleyway. As one must assume that Sullivan did not continually run in a straight line towards the rear of the O'Leary property, but eventually at an angle to the left, towards the door of the barn, it would not be inappropriate to round off this distance to 193 feet.[12]

An Analysis of Figure 54

The map shown as Figure 54 depicts the dimensions of the O'Leary property and adjoining parcels. It also indicates the approximate location of improvements on these parcels.

The property boundary lines are drawn pursuant to pre-fire Chicago Title Insurance Company records. Inquiry testimony, post-fire photographs, and Andreas' *History of Chicago* were instrumental in locating the houses and other improvements within these boundary lines. (See Appendix F for specific citations to this reference material.) The location of the O'Leary and McLaughlin homes relative to the north and south O'Leary property lines appears to be especially accurate.

But in some cases assumptions had to be made. One is the size of the O'Leary and McLaughlin cottages. (Although Andreas memorializes James Dalton's recollections concerning the location of the two homes on the O'Leary property in his *History of Chicago*, the book fails to note their dimensions. Musham describes each house as being about thirty-six feet long and sixteen feet wide, but he cites no source for this statement.)[13] Another is the presumption that the McLaughlin home was constructed fairly close to the O'Learys' west property line. Although this is only a presumption, it seems plausible for these reasons:

- The alleyway (probably about five feet wide) that was between the O'Leary/McLaughlin and Dalton homes appears to have been located on the easterly five feet of the O'Leary property.
- The O'Leary and Dalton properties were only twenty-five feet wide.
- Post-fire photographs of the O'Leary and McLaughlin homes (Figures 53, 62) indicate that the O'Leary cottage was not directly in back of the McLaughlin house. Rather, the O'Leary home was north of but slightly east of the McLaughlin home. This resulted in the east line of the O'Leary home being that much closer to their east property line.
- James Dalton's home was located on the west line of his property.

Thus, in order for there to be a five-foot alleyway between the O'Leary home and the Dalton house, it seems likely that the McLaughlin home was very close to Mr. and Mrs. O'Learys' west property boundary line.[14]

Notes

1. Daniel Sullivan, *Inquiry*, vol. [1], pp. 255, 262, 264, 266–67; Chicago Title Insurance Company records.

2. Chicago Title Insurance Company records; 1866–1871 Chicago city directories; *Robinson's Atlas*, vol. 1, plate 6.

3. Catherine O'Leary, *Inquiry*, vol. [1], pp. 68–69; Chicago Title Insurance Company records.

4. *Robinson's Atlas*, vol. 1, plate 6; Andreas, vol. 2, pp. 714, 760; Lowe, p. 42; Patrick O'Leary, *Inquiry*, vol. [1], p. 248.

5. Daniel Sullivan, *Inquiry*, vol. [1], pp. 254–55; *Robinson's Atlas*, vol. 1, plate 6.

6. Musham, p. 98; Andreas, vol. 2, pp. 713–14, 717. In *Daniel Trentworthy*, John McGovern

describes Walter Forbes' house as "a two-story cottage; back of it a pretentious barn." See McGovern, p. 177.

7. Chicago Title Insurance Company records; Chicago Guarantee Survey Company records; Catharine McLaughlin, *Inquiry*, vol. [1], pp. 237–38; Catherine O'Leary, *Inquiry*, vol. [1], p. 65.

8. Andreas, vol. 2, pp. 713–14, 717; George Rau, *Inquiry*, vol. [1], p. 179; Musham, pp. 94–95, 98; Patrick O'Leary, *Inquiry*, vol. [1], p. 251; Daniel Sullivan, *Inquiry*, vol. [1], pp. 259, 267–68, 271–72. John McGovern writes in *Daniel Trentworthy* of Mr. O'Leary building "an inclosure fronting the alley, twenty feet; backing from the alley, sixteen feet." Although hardly conclusive, McGovern's description of the orientation of the O'Leary barn is consistent with Musham's diagram, Andreas' text, inquiry testimony and Figure 54. See McGovern, pp. 175–76.

9. Catherine O'Leary, *Inquiry*, vol. [1], p. 65; Catharine McLaughlin, *Inquiry*, vol. [1], pp. 237–38.

10. Andreas, vol. 2, p. 714; Chicago Title Insurance Company records. In *Daniel Trentworthy* John McGovern indicates that Patrick O'Leary's gate "shall open to the alley, "*from a pathway five feet wide* [emphasis added]." See McGovern, p. 176.

11. Chicago Title Insurance Company records.

12. Patrick O'Leary, *Inquiry*, vol. [1], pp. 252–53; Daniel Sullivan, *Inquiry*, vol. [1], pp. 256–61, 268–69.

13. Musham may have simply misinterpreted Andreas. Andreas recounts the reminiscences of James Dalton, who remembered this about the O'Leary and McLaughlin homes: "*The two* were thirty-six feet north and south ... [emphasis added]." More than fifty years later, Musham remarks that the O'Leary property consisted of "two small cottages, *each* about 36 feet long by 16 wide ... [emphasis added]. See Andreas, vol. 2, pp. 713–14; Musham, p. 94.

14. Chicago Title Insurance Company records; Catharine McLaughlin, *Inquiry*, vol. [1], pp. 237–40; Andreas, vol. 2, p. 714.

"How It Originated"— The McDermott Letter and the O'Leary and Sullivan Affidavits

Rightfully or wrongfully the great fire of Chicago, October 8, 1871, will go down to history as chargeable to one Mrs. Leary, a dairy-woman, living on De Koven street, between Canal and Jefferson streets.

—*Chicago Evening Journal*, October 21, 1871

Introduction

On October 15, 1871, Chicago surveyor Michael McDermott interviewed Mr. and Mrs. O'Leary and Daniel Sullivan. Their sworn affidavits, together with McDermott's opinion of Sullivan and the O'Learys and his thoughts on the origin of the fire, were published in the October 20 *Chicago Tribune* as a letter to the editor entitled "How It Originated." The entire text of the letter is reprinted in this appendix.

When Sullivan appeared before the Board of Police and Fire Commissioners on November 25, 1871, the commissioners apparently never realized that his inquiry testimony differed substantially from his sworn statements contained in this *Tribune* affidavit, even though McDermott's letter was published in the newspaper more than a month earlier:

• Sullivan stated in his affidavit that when he

went into the barn, the fire was in the building's loft. But when he testified, he claimed that as he entered the barn, the fire was in the barn's "lower portion."[1]

• Sullivan maintained in his affidavit that hay was on fire, but in his subsequent inquiry testimony he contended that he "couldn't tell" what was on fire.[2]

Inexplicably, McDermott refers to Daniel Sullivan as "Denis Sullivan" or "Dennis Sullivan" in his letter. McDermott corrected himself in his later *Recollections and Memoires*, which are also included in this appendix.

HOW IT ORIGINATED.

Statements and Affidavits as to the Starting Point of the Great Fire.

To the Editor of the Chicago Tribune:

A great deal has been published respecting the origin of the great fire, which all reports have settled down on the head of a woman, or as the *Times* has it, an "Irish hag" of 70 years of age. Admitting for a moment that an Irish hag of 70 years was by an unforeseen accident the cause, yet there was a great want of charity in the epithets used by the *Times* of the 18th.[3] The following facts are stubborn things, and will cause the public to look for the cause in other sources, and perhaps attribute it to the love of plunder, Divine wrath, etc.:

On last Sunday night I made my way to the O'Leary's house, yet standing, and there, at No. 137 DeKoven street, on the east ½ of Lot 12, in Block 38, School Section Addition to Chicago, found Dennis Sullivan, of No. 134, and Dennis Ryan, of No. 112, both of DeKoven street. There and then I took the annexed affidavits. The parties have been known to me personally for several years as of irreproachable character. Mrs. O'Leary is neither haggard nor dirty.

Patrick O'Leary, and Catherine, his wife, being duly sworn before me, testify that they live at No. 137 DeKoven street, and own the lot and house in which they live; they had five cows, a horse and wagon, on all of which they had not one cent of insurance. She milked her cows at 4½ P.M. and 5 A.M., as Mrs. O'Leary peddled the milk. Mrs. O'Leary fed the horse beside the fence at about 7 o'clock P.M., and then put him in the barn.[4] She had no lamp in the yard or barn that night or evening.

Patrick O'Leary testifies that he was not in the barn during that day or night; left the feeding of the cows and horse to his wife and daughter; that both were in bed when awakened by Denis Ryan, of No. 112 DeKoven street; that they have lost their barn, cows, horse and wagon.

Subscribed and sworn before me this 15th day of October, 1871.

his
PATRICK **X** O'LEARY.
mark.
her
CATHERINE **X** O'LEARY.
mark.
MICHAEL McDERMOTT,
Notary Public for Chicago and City Surveyor.

Denis Sullivan being duly sworn before me testifies that he was at Patrick O'Leary's house, No. 137 DeKoven street, on Sunday night the 8th, of October, 1871, from about 8½ to 9 o'clock at night, during which time Mr. O'Leary and wife were in bed, that he went a few lots east of O'Leary's on the opposite side of DeKoven street, until about half-past 9 o'clock, when he saw the fire. He went across the street and cried "fire" "fire," and went into O'Leary's barn, where he found the hay in the loft on fire. He then attempted to cut loose the cows and horse, but failed to save anything but a half burned calf. He then came to O'Leary's and found them out of bed. Denis Ryan alarmed them during his time at the barn.

Subscribed and sworn to before me this 15th day of October, 1871.

his
DENIS **X** SULLIVAN.
mark.
MICHAEL McDERMOTT,
Notary Public for Chicago, and City Surveyor.

Recollections and Memoires

Some time later McDermott penned (but apparently never published) his *Recollections and Memoires*. He included the following comments (lightly edited) to his *Tribune* statements and affidavits:

> The great fire of Chicago, Oct. 10, 1871, was supposed to have been caused by Mrs. Patrick O'Leary milking her cow with lamplight on De-Koven Street.
>
> I investigated the case thoroughly. Have witnesses sworn. The report published in the first issue of the Chicago Tribune after the fire. In the History of Chicago my account of the fire is taken "*as the most reliable*" [emphasis and quotation marks in original].
>
> I showed that O'Leary and wife were in bed. Dan Sullivan, a neighbor, lived across the street nearly opposite the O'Learys. Was in the house some and after going home sat on his doorstep a short time when he saw the fire and went back to alarm the O'Learys. No cow in the barn. *The authorities* know it was the work of an incendiary, that the fire was set in more places than one [emphasis in original].[5]

But there are numerous errors in McDermott's *Recollections*:

- His "report" did not appear in the first post-fire *Tribune*. That issue came out on October 11, and the *Tribune* did not publish his letter until October 20.
- Sullivan stated in his *Tribune* affidavit that after leaving the O'Leary home, "he went a few lots east of O'Leary's on the opposite side of DeKoven street...." He later testified that he sat in front of William White's house. Neither account suggests that he went home and "sat on his doorstep."[6]
- Mrs. O'Leary's inquiry testimony indicates that there *were* cows in the barn.[7]
- The Board's final report was published in the Chicago newspapers on December 12, 1871, and is reproduced in Appendix E. The commissioners did *not* conclude in this report that the fire was caused by an incendiary.

Notes

1. Daniel Sullivan, *Inquiry*, vol. [1], pp. 274–75.

2. Daniel Sullivan, *Inquiry*, vol. [1], p. 275.

3. "The Fire," *Chicago Times*, 18 October 1871, p. 1. McDermott is referring to the October 18, 1871, issue of the *Chicago Times*, which contained several unflattering (and untrue) comments about Mrs. O'Leary. For example, the newspaper referred to her as "an old Irish woman" and an "old hag" who was "70 years of age."

4. This statement appears to be contrary to the testimony of Patrick O'Leary, who indicated during the inquiry that the horse was tied outside. See Patrick O'Leary, *Inquiry*, vol. [1], p. 250.

5. Michael McDermott, *Recollections and Memoires*, n.d., p. 43, Chicago Historical Society.

6. Daniel Sullivan, *Inquiry*, vol. [1], pp. 255, 262, 266–67.

7. Catherine O'Leary, *Inquiry*, vol. [1], pp. 67, 69–70, 77–78; see also Daniel Sullivan, *Inquiry*, vol. [1], pp. 256–57, 259–61, 264.

Selections from the Transcript of the Inquiry into the Cause of the Chicago Fire and Actions of the Fire Department

The Board of Police and Fire Commissioner Chadwick commenced, yesterday, the investigation into the origin of the fire, and its progress, with a view to place the responsibility upon whom it belongs.

—*Chicago Tribune,* November 24, 1871

Introduction

In attempting to present a representative sampling of the inquiry testimony, I had to overcome two obstacles:

- How do I edit the occasional misspelled word, the more than occasional lack of punctuation, and other grammatical peculiarities, but still preserve the integrity of the transcript of the investigation?
- The four volumes of inquiry testimony contain the statements of forty-nine witnesses. As it is impossible to include all 1168 pages, how do I determine whose testimony should be included in this book?

Editing Guidelines

The transcript consists of oral testimony that was memorialized by a shorthand reporter and later transcribed into longhand. Because of this, these pages of cursive writing are at least two steps removed from what was said during the investigation. Consequently, the words on the pages of the transcript do not have the significance that is normally reserved for historical documents or letters. For example, it was appropriate for Matthew J. Bruccoli, editor of *F. Scott Fitzgerald: A Life in Letters,* to establish a ground rule in his book that "there are no silent deletions or revisions. The letters have been transcribed exactly as F. Scott Fitzgerald wrote them—with the exception of the few stipulated cases where words have been omitted." Similarly,

Joseph Blotner, editor of *Selected Letters of William Faulkner*, declared that "alterations have been kept to a minimum. Idiosyncratic punctuation, abbreviation, capitalization and the like have for the most part been retained, with changes made only for clarity."[1]

But the transcript is not significant for what was *written*. Its importance stems from what was *said*, and for this reason such strict editing practices are unnecessary. After all, James Hildreth did not tell the Board he "got upon Harrison St.," even though this is what the transcript indicates. Rather, he mentioned "Harrison *Street*" in his testimony. Similarly, the commissioners did not ask Patrick O'Leary where the fire "commenced Sunday night, *Oct* 8th." Instead, they asked him about the fire on "*October* 8th." For this reason I have chosen to edit the transcript pursuant to "The Modernized Method" that is set forth in *The Harvard Guide to American History*. I have drafted and adhered to the following editing guidelines with this method in mind.[2]

1. I have silently corrected the spelling, capitalization, and punctuation of the selected testimony. For ease of reading, I have added quotation marks where appropriate. I have eliminated all abbreviations. The witnesses occasionally mentioned the time of day, and these references have been reworded in a manner consistent with the rules set forth in *The Chicago Manual of Style*.[3]

2. If a word is omitted, but can be inferred with reasonable certainty, I have added the word to the testimony, but placed it in brackets.[4]

3. If a word is missing one to four letters or is otherwise imperfect or deficient, but it is clear what the word is, I have silently corrected it, using no brackets.[5]

4. If a word is almost illegible or otherwise questionable or ambiguous, and I can only decipher it with less than reasonable certainty, I have placed the word in brackets with a question mark.[6]

5. If a word is completely illegible, I have inserted [*illeg.*].[7]

6. If a word is missing and cannot be inferred, then [*blank*] is inserted.[8]

7. I have silently corrected obvious slips of the transcriber's pen.[9]

8. It is difficult to read the more than oc-

casional poor penmanship of the transcript. For example, while reading James H. Hildreth's testimony, I had trouble distinguishing between "in" and "on." It was hard to tell the difference between "run" and "ran" in Robert A. Williams's testimony. Rather than pedantically place these minor words in brackets or explain possible alternatives in endnotes, I have used my best efforts to silently decipher them.

9. In many instances throughout the transcript, there is no capital letter at the beginning of a sentence, no period at the end, and no comma or semi-colon in between. I have used my best judgment in attempting to determine the true meaning of a sentence and what each witness said. But in those cases where the moving or insertion of a comma or other punctuation mark could possibly alter the meaning of a sentence or phrase, I have left the passage intact.[10]

10. Finally, I have placed the page numbers of the transcript in brackets.

Choosing the Witnesses

I considered three factors in deciding whose testimony should be included in this appendix:

- Much of the inquiry material is (to use the *Tribune*'s words) "superfluously tedious, dry, uninteresting, and irrelevant." Any testimony included had to be at least somewhat engaging.[11]
- A witness's testimony had to relate to and complement the facts, theories, and conclusions presented in this book.
- The witnesses chosen had to represent a cross section of the forty-nine men and women whose testimony is memorialized in the inquiry volumes.

At times I weighed one factor more than the other. As the fire originated on DeKoven Street, I felt I had to include the testimony of all its residents, even though Catherine Sullivan's testimony, for example, is not particularly memorable. And although John Tolland's statements were important only to illustrate the rather dubious selection process the Board used in choosing witnesses, his harrowing story of survival two miles offshore in Lake Michigan, sandwiched between fire and water on a wooden island, is clearly a thrilling tale.[12]

More than half of the witnesses were firemen. Almost without exception their accounts were drab and tiresome, but in order to have a balanced representation, I needed to include the statements of several of them. William J. Brown and Mathias Schaefer were the first two witnesses the Board questioned. They were among the first people to see the fire break out in the O'Leary barn. The saga of their well-intentioned but unfortunate delay in striking Box 319 is crucial to any fire history. By questioning these men first, the commissioners and marshals must have recognized the significance of their testimony. But their statements are in affidavit form, and I also wanted to include a fireman's account that was transcribed in the more typical "question and answer" format. Such testimony more clearly reveals the interaction between the fire officials and the witness.[13]

Fire Marshal Robert A. Williams was the obvious choice. One can read how the commissioners and other marshals reacted (or more correctly, failed to react) to his offhand remarks about saving not only his wife but also his piano, carpet, and stove. One can marvel incredulously at the ridiculous questions the officials asked him, culminating in the absurd query, "Is it dangerous to go near a falling wall without a fire hat?" But on the other hand, his explanation for charges of possible firemen intoxication is certainly required reading, as it is lucid, reasonable, and thoughtful.

I chose James H. Hildreth, a private citizen, and Michael C. Hickey, a police captain, to offset Brown, Schaefer, and Williams. I discussed Hildreth's demolition efforts in the first chapter. Hickey worked with Hildreth in this endeavor, and it is interesting to compare the testimony of these two witnesses to see how each of them seems to emphasize his own role in saving the city. Although many of the 1168 pages of testimony are somniferous, Hickey's statements tend to be lively and colorful; his accounts of freeing the courthouse jail prisoners and of observing two attempted lynchings are especially gripping.

The Fifty Witnesses

The 50 people who appeared before the commissioners and fire officials are listed below in the order in which they testified. Also included are their occupations, if noted in the transcript, and the date they testified.[14]

#1—William J. Brown, courthouse telegraph operator, Thursday, November 23

#2—Mathias Schaefer, courthouse watchman, Thursday, November 23

#3—William Musham, foreman, Steamer *Little Giant* No. 6, Friday, November 24

#4—William Mullin, foreman, Steamer *Illinois* No. 15, Friday, November 24

#5—Mrs. Catherine O'Leary, Friday, November 24

#6—Michael Sullivan, foreman, Steamer *Waubansia* No. 2, Friday, November 24

#7—Catherine Sullivan, Friday, November 24

#8—Dennis Regan, laborer, Friday, November 24

#9—Christian Schimmals, foreman, Steamer *Chicago* No. 5, Friday, November 24

#10—George Rau, foreman, *Protection* Hook and Ladder No. 2, Friday, November 24

#11—Lewis Fiene, truckman, *Protection* Hook and Ladder No. 2, Saturday, November 25[15]

#12—Catharine McLaughlin, Saturday, November 25

#13—Patrick O'Leary, Saturday, November 25

#14—Daniel Sullivan, drayman, Saturday, November 25[16]

#15—Michael W. Conway, pipeman, Steamer *Chicago* No. 5, Saturday, November 25

#16—Chalkley J. Hambleton, lawyer, member of the Board of Education, Monday, November 27

#17—John Dorsey, foreman, *America* Hose Cart No. 2, Monday, November 27

#18—Leo Meyers, foreman, *Tempest* Hose Cart No. 1, Monday, November 27

#19—David Kenyon, second pipeman, Steamer *Chicago* No. 5, Monday, November 27

#20—Thomas Byrne, driver, Hose Elevator No. 2, Monday, November 27

#21—Michael C. Hickey, police captain, first precinct, Tuesday, November 28

#22—John Tolland, keeper of the lake tunnel, Tuesday, November 28

#23—George E. Fuller, night operator, fire alarm telegraph, Tuesday, November 28

#24—Denis J. Swenie, foreman, Steamer *Fred Gund* No. 14, Tuesday, November 28

#25—Alexander McMonagle, foreman, Steamer *Long John* No. 1, Tuesday, November 28

#26—Henry Ulrich, policeman, Tuesday, November 28

#27—John Doyle, engineer, Steamer *Jacob Rehm* No. 4, Tuesday, November 28

#28—Nicholas Dubach, foreman, Steamer *Economy* No. 8, Tuesday, November 28

#29—John Campion, first pipeman, Steamer *Little Giant* No. 6, Tuesday, November 28

#30—Peter T. Burtis, superintendent of the Chicago Gas Light and Coke Company, Tuesday, November 28

#31—Thomas B. Burtis, assistant superintendent of the Chicago Gas Light and Coke Company, Wednesday, November 29

#32—Charles Anderson, driver, *America* Hose Cart No 2, Wednesday, November 29

#33—John C. Schmidt, foreman, *Lincoln* Hose Cart No. 4, Wednesday, November 29

#34—James H. Hildreth, former alderman, Wednesday, November 29

#35—Francis T. Swenie, foreman, *Pioneer* Hook and Ladder No. 1, Friday, December 1

#36—William Fraser, bakery owner, Friday, December 1

#37—Charles G. Emory, member of the Fire Patrol, Friday, December 1

#38—Henry J. Hittorff, watchmaker and jeweler, Friday, December 1[17]

#39—Benjamin Bullwinkle, captain of the insurance patrol, Friday, December 1[18]

#40—George H. Dorsett, driver, *Pioneer* Hook and Ladder No. 1, Friday, December 1[19]

#41—Charles H. French, police sergeant, Saturday, December 2

#42—Thomas Ockerby, night superintendent of the "Gas Works," Saturday, December 2[20]

#43—Charles G. Wicker, Saturday, December 2

#44—Isaac L. Milliken, Saturday, December 2[21]

#45—Louis J. Lull, police sergeant, Saturday, December 2

#46—Mathias Benner, third assistant fire marshal, Saturday, December 2

#47—Lorens Walter, second assistant fire marshal, Saturday, December 2

#48—John Schank, first assistant fire marshal, Saturday, December 2

#49—Robert A. Williams, fire marshal, Saturday, December 2

#50—_____, foreman, Ryerson & Company lumberyard, Monday, December 4[22]

The Chicago Fire Department

Firemen William J. Brown and Mathias Schaefer and Fire Marshal Robert A. Williams referred to other firemen during their testimony. They also mentioned the names of steam engines and other fire equipment. A list of Chicago Fire Department personnel and fire company assignments is set forth in the department's "Pay Roll for the Month Ending October 31st, 1871." This payroll is reproduced below and is cited in this book as "1871 Pay Roll."

The various primary and secondary sources noted in this book spell the names of Chicago firemen in a myriad of different ways. Even the spelling of these names in the *1869 Report of the Board of Police* is not always consistent with the same names in the *1872 Report of the Board of Police*. Therefore, with one exception, the spelling of firemen's names below and throughout this book is in accordance with this payroll record. The one exception is the spelling of Mathias Schaefer's name. The October 1871 payroll lists his name as "Mathias *Schafer*." But it appears that both William Brown and Mathias Schaefer signed their respective inquiry affidavits. As Schaefer's affidavit is signed "Mathias *Schaefer*," the name is spelled accordingly in this book.

Unfortunately, the penmanship of this 1871 payroll is not always legible. H. A. Musham also includes this roster in his monograph, and on occasion the spelling of the firemen's names in his history is slightly different from the spelling shown below. This is probably because when necessary I consulted a Chicago city directory, a *Report of the Board of Police*, or Andreas' *History of Chicago* in an attempt to determine the correct spelling of a name.[23]

Chicago Fire Department

Robert A. Williams	Fire Marshal
John Schank	First Assistant Fire Marshal
Lorens Walter	Second Assistant Fire Marshal
Mathias Benner	Third Assistant Fire Marshal
Hiram Amick	Clerk
Gustavus Haenisch	Fire Warden, North Division
Benjamin F. McCarty	Fire Warden, South Division
William Horner	Fire Warden, West Division
John Desmond	Driver, Wagon No. 1
Ambrose N. Wilson	Driver, Wagon No. 2
George W. Weller	Driver, Wagon No. 3
Charles Evans	Driver, Wagon No. 4
Albin C. King	Driver, Supply Truck
John Toner	Hose Cleaner
Mathias Schaefer	Pipeman detailed as Watchman
Denis Deneen	Watchman

Fire Alarm Telegraph

Edward Bruce Chandler	Superintendent
John P. Barrett	Chief Operator
George Fuller	Operator
John F. Stevens	Operator
John Kennedy	Repairer
Frederick W. Gund	Repairer
William J. Brown	Repairer

Steamer Long John No. 1

Alexander McMonagle	Foreman
George W. Wagner	Pipeman
Andrew Coffey	Pipeman
William Flannery	Pipeman
Francis H. Butterfield	Pipeman
William F. Hendrickson	Watchman
Michael Kennedy	Driver
William E. Hand	Driver
Joseph L. Gilbert	Stoker
Timothy A. Moynihan	Engineer

Steamer Waubansia No. 2

Michael Sullivan	Foreman
Frederick Allen	Engineer
Michael Geimer	Pipeman
Peter Phelan	Pipeman
Theodore Lagger	Pipeman
Isaac M. Adler	Driver

William Otto	Driver
William A. McIntyre	Stoker
Patrick Kearns	Watchman

Steamer William James No. 3

John McLean	Foreman
Charles S. Petrie	Engineer
John Michael	Stoker
Henry Anderson	Pipeman
Rollin G. Harmon	Pipeman
Casper A. Charleston	Pipeman detailed as Watchman
James McNamara	Driver
George G. Seeber	Driver

Steamer Jacob Rehm No. 4

Gottfried Charlson	Foreman
John Doyle	Engineer
Charles Osborn	Stoker
Lewis Lawson	Pipeman
Lorenz Schnidt	Pipeman
George L. Taylor	Pipeman
Adam Breit	Driver
Frederick Varges	Driver
Olaf C. Johnson	Watchman

Steamer Chicago No. 5

Christian Schimmals	Foreman
Michael W. Conway	Pipeman
David B. Kenyon	Pipeman
Henry Welch	Pipeman
Conrad Ruhl	Pipeman
James McClellan	Driver
Charles H. Emery	Driver
Henry V. Coleman	Engineer
Charles Schroeder	Stoker
Ira Mix	Pipeman detailed as Watchman

Steamer Little Giant No. 6

William Musham	Foreman
John Campion	Pipeman
Frank R. Howard	Pipeman
Michael Dolan	Pipeman
William S. Dunham	Engineer
Joseph Lagger	Stoker
John Windheim	Driver
Calvin L. Cole	Driver
Joseph Lauf	Watchman

Steamer Liberty No. 7

Benjamin Rice	Engineer

Steamer Economy No. 8

Nicholas Dubach	Foreman
John C. Cooney	Engineer
Wallace T. Phelps	Stoker
Anthony Lagger	Pipeman
Nicholas Lewis	Pipeman
Joseph Stoltz	Pipeman
John Cook	Pipeman
Richard Stringer	Driver
John Mergenthaler	Driver
Charles Schank	Watchman

Steamer Frank Sherman No. 9

Joel A. Kinney	Foreman
John Holm	Engineer
George Leady	Stoker
Arthur E. Slocum	Driver
Claudius Blair	Driver
John M. Reis	Pipeman
John Fitzgerald	Pipeman
Christian Goodwin	Pipeman
Thomas Sanderson	Watchman

Steamer J. B. Rice No. 10

James J. Walsh	Foreman
Levi A. Forester	Engineer
Daniel H. O'Brien	Stoker
William H. Townsend	Driver
James A. Donegan	Driver
Joseph Burkhardt	Pipeman
Edwin Roberts	Pipeman
Patrick J. Ryan	Pipeman
Richard Fitzgerald	Pipeman
John Huhn	Watchman

Steamer A. C. Coventry No. 11

Lawrence J. Walsh	Foreman
John Lauf	Pipeman
Frederick Reis	Pipeman
Herman Baer	Pipeman
Daniel D. Healy	Pipeman
Francis R. Sowersby	Engineer
Charles H. Ripley	Stoker
John J. McClellan	Driver
Cornelius Casey	Driver
Thomas Melvin	Watchman

Steamer T. B. Brown No. 12

Frederick W. Taplin	Foreman
Joseph C. Pazen	Pipeman
James Cuddy	Pipeman
Joseph Casserly	Pipeman

Charles Pratt	Driver
Horace N. Ward	Driver
John E. Ferguson	Engineer
George R. Lathrop	Stoker
Michael S. Taplin	Watchman

Steamer A. D. Titsworth No. 13

Maurice W. Shay	Foreman
Alfred W. Pendleton	Pipeman
Peter Trainor	Pipeman
Francis B. Lane	Pipeman
Thomas Canty	Pipeman
John H. Manning	Engineer
William Olwell	Stoker
Myron Crum	Driver
Daniel Reardon	Driver
Alexander Reynolds	Watchman

Steamer Fred Gund No. 14

Denis J. Swenie	Foreman
Francis Paquin	Pipeman
Aaron Jansen	Pipeman
William R. Hoisington	Pipeman
John Farrell	Pipeman detailed as Watchman
Nicholas Weinand	Pipeman
John Berry	Engineer
Edmund Kaiser	Stoker
Peter Schnur	Driver
Daniel Daly	Driver

Steamer Illinois No. 15

William Mullin	Foreman
John Meyer	Pipeman
John O'Day	Pipeman
Francis Berry	Engineer
James Kingswell	Stoker
Norman T. Ormsby	Driver

Steamer Winnebago No. 16

John Dreher	Foreman
James F. Enright	Engineer
Patrick Crowley	Stoker
James Phillips	Driver
William Phillippi	Pipeman
James Young	Pipeman

Steamer R. A. Williams No. 17

Charles T. Brown	Foreman
John Cook	Pipeman
Arthur J. Calder	Pipeman

Daniel Toomey	Pipeman
Edward Ferris	Pipeman
Thad Healy	Engineer
John C. Strickler	Stoker
David Hyland	Driver
Patrick Lamey	Driver
Daniel O'Connell	Watchman

Pioneer *Hook and Ladder No. 1*

Francis T. Swenie	Foreman
Charles Miller	Truckman
Francis Flannigan	Truckman
John Gleason	Truckman
Patrick Dignan	Truckman
George H. Dorsett	Driver

Protection *Hook and Ladder No. 2*

George H. Rau	Foreman
Hugo Franzen	Truckman
Lewis Fiene	Truckman
John A. Cook	Truckman
Patrick Murtaugh	Truckman
James M. Houser	Driver

Rescue *Hook and Ladder No. 3*

John H. Green	Foreman
William Freise	Truckman
Thomas Maxwell	Truckman
Charles M. Duffy	Truckman
James Duff	Truckman
Norman N. Holt	Driver

Hook and Ladder No. 4

George Ernst	Foreman
Edwin Roberts	Truckman
Joseph O'Donohue	Truckman
Henry H. Breternetz	Truckman
Isaac G. Hallock	Driver

Tempest *Hose Cart No. 1*

Leo Meyers	Foreman
Paul Ditt	Hoseman
John George	Hoseman
John Fowler	Driver

America *Hose Cart No. 2*

John Dorsey	Foreman
David Manwell	Hoseman
Charles A. Anderson	Driver

John A. Huck *Hose Cart No. 3*

Mathew Schuh	Foreman
George Steurnegel	Hoseman
Joseph Freitsch	Hoseman
Peter Lawson	Driver

Lincoln *Hose Cart No. 4*

John C. Schmidt	Foreman
Edward Varges	Hoseman
John Hardell	Driver

Washington *Hose Cart No. 5*

James J. Grant	Foreman
Reuben A. Bunnel	Hoseman
Patrick Garrity	Driver

Douglas *Hose Cart No. 6*

Thomas Barry	Foreman
George H. Idell	Hoseman
Eugene Sullivan	Driver

Hose Elevator No. 2

James Enright	Foreman
Frank W. Locke	Truckman
Thomas Ryan	Truckman
Thomas Byrne	Driver

Understanding the Testimony

Throughout the inquiry transcript the O'Learys and those neighbors who testified not only refer to each other's homes and buildings, they also mention the improvements of other property owners along DeKoven Street. For example, consider this exchange between Mrs. O'Leary and the commissioners:

Q. How many houses were on fire or sheds or barns at the time you first saw it?

A. At the time I first saw it, my barn was and Mrs. Murray's barn was afire and Mr. Dalton's little shed. That is all that was afire, I think, when I first saw it. I thought there was no more fire, only them places. Then I catched one of the children and put him out on the sidewalk. I thought there was no more places on fire, only our places down there, and I saw Turner's big block on fire, and I thought there wasn't a touch on Turner's block until then. I saw the fire from the inside break out from Turner's block.[24]

To better understand these selections from the inquiry transcript, this book includes a map of the city block in which the O'Learys lived. Their name, the names of their neighbors, and the location and size of all these landowners' properties are indicated on this diagram, which appears in the book as Figure 79.

During the inquiry the witnesses alluded to dozens of people and places. Comprehensive annotations identify these otherwise obscure references. Where appropriate, these annotations also provide additional information about various incidents associated with the fire and its aftermath.

Introduction Notes

1. Matthew J. Bruccoli, ed., *F. Scott Fitzgerald: A Life in Letters* (New York: Charles Scribner's Sons, 1994), p. xvii; Joseph Blotner, ed., *Selected Letters of William Faulkner* (New York: Random House, 1977), p. xvii; "The Great Fire," *Chicago Tribune*, 26 November 1871, p. 1; "The Great Fire," *Chicago Tribune*, 5 December 1871, p. 2; "The Great Fire," *Chicago Evening Journal*, 12 December 1871, p. [4].

2. Frank Freidel, ed., *Harvard Guide to American History*, (Cambridge: Harvard University Press, Belknap Press, 1974), vol. 1, pp. 25–32; James H. Hildreth, *Inquiry*, vol. [3], p. 155; Patrick O'Leary, *Inquiry*, vol. [1], p. 244.

3. John Grossman, ed., *The Chicago Manual of Style*, 14th ed. (Chicago: University of Chicago Press, 1993), pp. 305–6; see, e.g., William J. Brown, *Inquiry*, vol. [1], p. 1 ("12½ o'clock" is changed to "12:30"); Catharine McLaughlin, *In-*

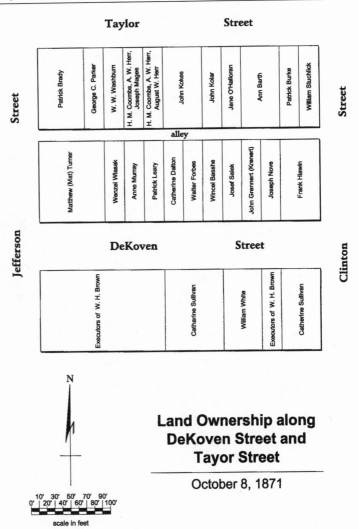

Land Ownership along DeKoven Street and Tayor Street

October 8, 1871

FIGURE 79—LAND OWNERSHIP ALONG DEKOVEN STREET AND TAYLOR STREET. The inquiry testimony that appears in Appendix D includes references to some of the people that lived near Mr. and Mrs. O'Leary. Chicago Title Insurance Company records reveal the names of all the parties who owned the various parcels of land in the O'Leary neighborhood at the time of the fire. These materials also indicate the location and size of all these landowners' properties. Figure 79 sets forth this information. (Diagram by Douglas A. Swanson)

quiry, vol. [1], p. 226 ("Geo Lewis" is changed to "George Lewis"); Patrick O'Leary, *Inquiry*, vol. [1], p. 244 ("Dont" is changed to "Don't"); William J. Brown, *Inquiry*, vol. [1], p. 1 ("+" is changed to "and"); William J. Brown, *Inquiry*, vol. [1], p. 2 ("staid" is changed to "stayed"), but see Andreas, vol. 2, p. 737, Colbert and Chamberlin, p. 403, and "Story of the Great Chicago Fire," sec. 3, p. 20, wherein this alternate spelling is used.

4. See, e.g., Robert A. Williams, *Inquiry*, vol. [4], p. 291: "And some them, perhaps having got burned out..." is changed to "And some [of] them, perhaps having got burned out...." The inference of an omitted word "with reasonable certainty" and subsequent insertion into the text of the transcripts occasionally entailed making difficult decisions. See, e.g., Michael C. Hickey, *Inquiry*, vol. [2], p. 156: "Ran up there and it was, and so right along just running around until the next afternoon." I almost revised this sentence by inserting [I went] before the words "right along." But because the transcript indicates that Hickey had uttered the word "ran" just seconds earlier and used the word "running" later in the sentence, I chose to insert "I ran" instead: "Ran up there and it was, and so [I ran] right along just running around there until the next afternoon."

5. See, e.g., James H. Hildreth, *Inquiry*, vol. [3], pp. 157–58: "I don't think it would have been a possibility to have *save* the Michigan Avenue Hotel or anything in that block" is silently changed to "I don't think it would have been a possibility to have *saved* the Michigan Avenue Hotel or anything in that block [emphasis added]."

6. See, e.g., Patrick O'Leary, *Inquiry*, vol. [1], p. 246: "I [turned?] in and put the children in the street as fast as I could."

7. See, e.g., Daniel Sullivan, *Inquiry*, vol. [1], p. 266: "That was the first [*illeg.*] I done."

8. See, e.g., Patrick O'Leary, *Inquiry*, vol. [1], p. 246: "Then you went to work to save your little [*blank*]?"

9. See, e.g., James H. Hildreth, *Inquiry*, vol. [3], p. 160: "I did did not have" is silently changed to "I did not have." See also James H. Hildreth, *Inquiry*, vol. [3], p. 162: "and if I could find a place where there were there were closets where I could put the powder into a small place..." is silently changed to "and if I could find a place where there were closets where I could put the powder into a small place...." See also Catherine O'Leary, *Inquiry*, vol. [1], p. 77, where Mrs. O'Leary was asked: "Can you give us an idea about how great a length of time *past* from your first hearing of the fire until you first saw the engine [emphasis added]?" Here I silently changed "past" to "passed."

10. For example, see Robert A. Williams, *Inquiry*, vol. [4], pp. 241–42. Here it is not clear what Williams is referring to when he comments, "I believe it is": "I do not think it was more than a minute-and-a-half before the whole center of the block back in the alley between Taylor and Forquer streets, I believe it is, the next street north of

that, they were all on fire." Similarly, see Robert A. Williams, *Inquiry*, vol. [4], p. 289: "There was a number of companies and *Titsworth* I think it was between four and five o'clock when I sent that company home." Ambiguous sentences such as these were left unedited.

11. "The Great Fire," *Chicago Tribune*, 3 December 1871, p. 4.

12. The testimony of some of the inquiry's first witnesses, including Mrs. O'Leary and other DeKoven Street residents, is summarized in Sheahan and Upton, pp. 419–439.

13. The November 24, 1871, *Republican* contains almost exact transcripts of the inquiry affidavits of William J. Brown and Mathias Schaefer. (In fact, the *Republican*'s account of the firemen's November 23 testimony is so similar to the actual affidavits, it was used to help decipher the penmanship of the originals.) The first paragraph of this newspaper article includes the following remark: "Below is given verbatim the testimony of two of the most important witnesses." This sentence suggests that the *Republican*'s report is a precise reproduction of what these firemen told the Board the previous day. The sentence (and the article) imply that the men were not questioned by the fire officials, but instead gave written statements which the newspaper then published.

This does not appear to be the case. The November 24 *Tribune* makes it clear that the men *were* questioned by the commissioners: "It was the intention to have a short-hand writer to take the evidence in full, but as one could not be procured, [Commissioner] Mr. Brown wrote the testimony in long-hand. *There were but two witnesses examined* [emphasis added]." Furthermore, the *Tribune*'s report of the previous day's proceedings contains information that does not appear in either the firemen's affidavits or the *Republican*'s article. This indicates that the *Republican*'s account is not a verbatim transcript of Brown's and Schaefer's statements. For example, the *Tribune*'s summary of Schaefer's testimony includes this sentence: "Some men had been fixing up the clock in the cupola and left a lot of shavings on the floor." If the *Republican*'s story had included a word-for-word transcript of Schaefer's testimony, this comment about shavings in the cupola would have appeared in the article. This newspaper's report of Schaefer's testimony, however, includes no such comment. See "How Was It?," p. [4]; "The Great Fire," *Chicago Tribune*, 24 November 1871, p. 6.

14. When the firemen testified before the Board and marshals, they invariably named their occupations and company assignments. These witnesses, however, did not always reply in a

uniform manner. For example, although Christian Schimmals testified that he was foreman of "*Chicago* Number 5," Michael W. Conway told the fire officials that he was a pipeman for the "steamer *Chicago*." I have listed the firemen's occupations and assignments in both this section (The Fifty Witnesses) and in the following section (The Chicago Fire Department) so that they are consistent with the 1871 Pay Roll. See Christian Schimmals, *Inquiry*, vol. [1], p. 126; Michael W. Conway, *Inquiry*, vol. [2], p. 1.

15. The transcript discloses that Lewis Fiene may have said that he was the "foreman" of this company. This is incorrect; George Rau was the foreman. Fiene probably did not misspeak. Instead, it appears that the transcriber made a mistake in noting that Fiene was the foreman. Both the *Tribune* and *Evening Journal* summaries of Fiene's testimony indicate that Fiene testified that he was a "truckman" with this company, and the 1871 Pay Roll lists this as his occupation. The penmanship of this portion of the transcript is poor. Although it is possible that Fiene said, "I am *fireman* of Hook and Ladder No. 2," this stilted interpretation can not be reconciled with the conflicting (and probably correct) newspaper summaries of his testimony. See Musham, p. 183; 1871 Pay Roll; "The Great Fire," *Chicago Tribune*, 26 November 1871, p. 1; "The Fire Investigation," *Chicago Evening Journal*, 25 November 1871, p. [4]; Lewis Fiene, *Inquiry*, vol. [1], p. 191.

16. The November 26 *Chicago Tribune* discloses that after Daniel Sullivan testified, Lewis Fiene was recalled for additional questioning. See "The Great Fire," *Chicago Tribune*, 26 November 1871, p. 1.

17. The inquiry transcript merely indicates that "H. J." Hittorff testified. The December 2 *Tribune*, however, noted that Hittorff's first name was "Henry," and so it is shown accordingly in this listing. See H. J. Hittorff, *Inquiry*, vol. [3], p. 267; "The Great Fire," *Chicago Tribune*, 2 December 1871, p. 4. See also the *1871 City Directory*, p. 433, which includes a listing for Henry J. Hittorff, a watchmaker.

18. Bullwinkle was head of the Fire Insurance Patrol. The inquiry testimony of Charles G. Emory, the thirty-seventh witness, indicates that Emory's "Fire Patrol" and Bullwinkle's "insurance patrol" were one and the same organization. See Andreas, vol. 2, p. 94; Andreas, vol. 3, pp. 461–65; Musham, p. 187; Charles G. Emory, *Inquiry*, vol. [3], p. 254.

19. The transcript indicates that it was "George S. Dorset," driver for the *Skinner*, who was the fortieth witness. Although the 1871 Pay

Roll does not list any fire department equipment named "Skinner," this is probably a reference to the *Skinner* hose elevator, an aerial ladder. The payroll does disclose a "George H. Dorsett" who was the driver for *Pioneer* Hook and Ladder No. 1. The payroll also notes that a "Francis Flannigan" was a driver for this company. As "George S. Dorset" testified that one of the members of his company was named "Flannigan," it seems almost certain that it was "George H. Dorsett" of the *Pioneer* Hook and Ladder No. 1 who testified and that the reference to the *Skinner* was in error. See George H. Dorsett, *Inquiry*, vol. [3], pp. 298, 301–2; 1871 Pay Roll; Little and McNalis, pp. 114, 128.

20. Ockerby worked for the Chicago Gas Light and Coke Company (commonly called the "gas works") on the city's South Side. See Thomas Ockerby, *Inquiry*, vol. [4], p. 1; Thomas B. Burtis, *Inquiry*, vol. [3], pp. 74, 76.

21. Although the transcript of Milliken's testimony does not indicate his occupation, the *Chicago Tribune* noted in its summary of his inquiry statements that he was an "ex–Police Justice." See "The Great Fire," *Chicago Tribune*, 3 December 1871, p. 4.

22. Although the lumberyard foreman testified, his testimony does not appear in the inquiry transcript. See "The Great Fire," *Chicago Tribune*, 5 December 1871, p. 2, which summarizes the testimony of this final witness. The article's final paragraph reads as follows: "This ends the investigation. The board have now all the testimony before them, and will after due deliberation and consultation, prepare a report upon it." This report appears in Appendix E.

23. See Musham, pp. 181–87.

24. Catherine O'Leary, *Inquiry*, vol. [1], pp. 62–63.

WILLIAM J. BROWN

[1] William. J. Brown, telegraph operator at the courthouse, being duly sworn on oath, declares that he went on duty at the central office at four o'clock Sunday evening, October 8, and remained on duty until 12:30 same evening. At 9:30 I received the alarm from watchman in the courthouse tower and others[1] for Box 342 in corner of Canalport Avenue and Halsted Street. I received no alarm whatever from boxes up to this time. Mathias Schaefer was the watchman on duty at that time. At 9:40

I received alarms from Boxes 293, 295, 296.[2] I supposed it to be for second alarm, but still I received no authorized signal. At 9:42 I asked the watchman if it was spreading. I then struck second alarm on my own judgment. The distance of the box first struck from the point the fire started at was about one mile in a southwesterly direction. Immediately after striking the first alarm, from my window I could only see the reflection of the fire. I cannot say exactly at what time I struck the third alarm, but I think it was about one hour after giving the first, receiving at that time signals from Boxes 293 and 296. I then struck third alarm on my own responsibility. Immediately after that the line opened, and no more alarms were received of any kind. I struck the second and third alarms both for Box 342. I was well satisfied that the fire was not in the neighborhood of Box 342 when I struck the third alarm, but [2] not receiving any authorized signal for striking any other box, I of course struck the same number as at first. About 11:15 the watchman ordered me to strike Box 287,[3] and I did so. I only struck one alarm for that. At 12:14 I received an alarm from Box 13, and I also struck this. This box is located at corner of Market and Madison streets. I struck no other alarms after this and was relieved from duty by George E. Fuller[4] at 12:30. I was so busy at my instruments that I did not have any time to see anything else until I was relieved from duty. I then went up on the cupola and helped put out a fire on the cupola. I then saw sparks and brands falling very thickly all about us. After assisting to put out the fire on the cupola, I left the building and went on the West Side to corner of Canal and Randolph streets and afterwards to the buildings that were on fire near the gas works.[5] I went in the alley in rear of Farwell's Dry Goods[6] storehouse on north side of Monroe. I stayed there a few minutes and then went out on Madison Street, got to Wells when I noticed the fire had jumped to rear of the Oriental Building[7] on LaSalle Street. I then went to the courthouse and went into our office on the third floor. I think this was about one o'clock. I stayed there until the fire drove us out of the building, I think about fifteen minutes. I then went to corner of Canal [3] and Randolph and watched the progress of the fire. When I observed the fire in the rear of the Oriental Building, I noticed that the wind was blowing very strong from the southwest, and the air was full of burning brands and sparks, and I had all I could do to keep my own clothes from burning. As I crossed back from the West Side on the Madison Street bridge, I went south on Market Street until I got to the alley between Madison and Monroe, and as I passed into that alley going east, I noticed an engine working, corner of Monroe and Market streets, but do not know what one it was. As I was in the alley, I saw her stream playing on Monroe Street. As I passed out of the alley going to the courthouse, I saw the *Coventry*[8] standing at the corner of LaSalle and Madison streets. I did not notice whether she was working or not. At this time I crossed back on the South Side over the Madison Street bridge. I did not notice the fire at any other point than in the vicinity of the gas works, but there was great quantities of fire flying in all directions. I did not see any other engines than those I have named as I went back to the courthouse. Do not know whether there was any other [*blank*] there or not. This information I received from the watchman in the tower satisfied me that the fire was not near this box the first alarm came from. No instruments were saved or any machinery were saved [4] out of the courthouse. I did not think the courthouse was going to burn until I saw it on fire and saw the men coming down from the cupola.

W. J. BROWN

William J. Brown Notes

1. The symbol "+c" was used here. This is probably a variation of the more formal abbreviation "&c." (See, e.g., Sheahan and Upton, p. 213; "City Brevities," p. 1.) Although this can mean "and so forth," it is also an abbreviation for "and others," and it appears that this use is what Commissioner Thomas B. Brown intended when he summarized William Brown's inquiry statements. But it is not clear who these "others" might have been. The *Chicago Tribune*'s account of Brown's testimony gives no indication. Sarah R. Hibbard, William Brown's sister, later claimed that she and a friend, Maggie Daily, were in the courthouse with Brown when the fire broke out and that Hibbard brought the blaze to her brother's attention. Perhaps these were the people to whom Brown was referring. Neither Hibbard nor Daily was

interviewed by the Board of Police and Fire Commissioners. See Stuart Berg Flexner, ed., *The Random House Dictionary of the English Language*, 2d ed. (New York: Random House, 1987), s.v. "Signs and Symbols: Miscellaneous," hereafter cited in text as *Random House Dictionary*; "The Great Fire," *Chicago Tribune*, 24 November 1871, p. 6; "Marks Anniversary of the Great Fire."

2. Fire alarm Box 293 was located at West Polk and Canal streets, Box 295 was at West Taylor and Desplaines streets, and Box 296 was at West Twelfth and Canal streets. See *1870 City Directory*, p. 915; *1871 City Directory*, p. 35.

3. Fire alarm Box 287 was at West Van Buren and Canal streets. See *1870 City Directory*, p. 915; *1871 City Directory*, p. 35.

4. George E. Fuller was a fire alarm telegraph operator. Fuller was interviewed by the *Chicago Tribune* as part of its "Boring for Facts" series. See Musham, p. 181; "Boring for Facts," *Chicago Tribune*, 19 November 1871, p. 6; *1871 Pay Roll*; *1870 City Directory*, p. 295; *1871 City Directory*, p. 339.

5. The South Side gas works, more formally known as the Chicago Gas Light and Coke Company, was located about twelve blocks north and three blocks east of the O'Leary barn, near the corner of Monroe and Market streets. See Musham, p. 111; Lowe, p. 42. For a history of the gas works, see Andreas, vol. 1, pp. 155–56; Andreas, vol. 2, pp. 701–2.

6. John Farwell's store containing "drygoods, woolens and notions" was at 106 to 112 Wabash Avenue. See *1870 City Directory*, p. 263; *1871 City Directory*, p. 307.

7. The Oriental Building was at 120 to 124 LaSalle Street, or the west side of LaSalle Street, between Washington and Madison streets. The November 24, 1871, *Chicago Republican* included an almost word-for-word duplicate of Brown's affidavit. But although the *Republican* claimed that the fire had jumped to the "roof by" the Oriental Building, the transcript indicates that it was the "rear of" this building that caught fire. See "How Was It?," p. [4]; *1870 City Directory*, p. 633; *1871 City Directory*, pp. 55, 691.

8. Brown is referring to the steam engine A.C. Coventry No. 11. See *1871 Pay Roll*.

MATHIAS SCHAEFER

[5] Mathias Schaefer, being duly sworn on oath, declares that he was the watchman of the courthouse cupola, and my duties there were

to look out for fires about the city and give notice of them to the telegraph operator below. I was on duty on the evening of October 8 and stayed until we were driven out by the fire. I was on the north side of the tower. There were two parties of [them?][1] on the tower and they called my attention to a light,[2] but I saw it was nothing but the West Side gas works.[3] Then I went inside. Then these parties came to the east door and asked me about the big clock. I was talking with them about the clock and then lit my pipe and stepped out on watch on the east side. I then, turning around towards the southwest, I saw the fire. When I saw it, I run into the tower and whistled to the operator and told him to strike Box 342. This was my judgment. I then took my glass and looked in the direction of the fire again and immediately after this alarm [had?] been given, I whistled again to the operator and told him I had made a mistake, it ought to be 319,[4] that would be nearer to it, but he said that the box struck was in the line of the fire, and he could not alter it now. The fire was not much when I gave the first alarm, but it spread very rapidly. The wind was blowing very strong at this time from the southwest. [6] I gave the operator information as to the progress of the fire every few minutes after the first alarm. I think it was about ten or fifteen minutes after the first alarm was given before the second alarm was struck, but I did not have any timepiece up there.[5] There was no third alarm struck from the courthouse bell. The operator told me he had struck the third alarm at the engine houses. My comrade[6] who watches with me came up about eleven o'clock. I stayed with him until, I should judge, about twelve o'clock, when I told him I would go down and see if the fire had crossed on the South Side. As I passed out of the courthouse yard at the southwest corner, I met Mr. Fuller, the telegraph operator. He said he was a little late, as he had been helping the *Long John* boys[7] light up hose at the fire.[8] I then went down LaSalle Street to Madison and west on Madison to near Market Street. The fire was then burning between Market and Franklin and Madison and Monroe streets. I stayed there about ten minutes and while there saw one engine and cart come over Madison Street bridge and saw them leading out hose.[9] I then went back to the courthouse and commenced ringing the bell pretty lively and continued to ring all the time until the fire drove us out.[10] With the exception of twice I went down on the roof and put out fire that had caught there. [7] There was a window in the southwest side of the tower under the balcony and the lights[11] of glass were all broken in this window and had been so ever since I had been there, and I am confident sparks and brands went through these broken windows under the roof and set fire to it. I was on the top of this roof putting out any fire that might catch there. There were four or five men in the tower assisting in keeping fires down on the balcony, but I was the only person that went down on the roof, as none of the others knew the way to get there. Before I left the courthouse and went down on Madison Street, the balcony had been on fire twice, and we beat it out. I think this was just after eleven o'clock, and I know it was before the fire had crossed to the South Side. I do not think it was more than half an hour after I gave the first alarm before the sparks began to fall about the courthouse. I am very sure before eleven o'clock I noticed a fire had started some distance north of the main fire, and I told the operator that another fire had started.[12] He asked me how far it was from the other fire, and I told him it was four or five blocks north. I then told him to strike Box 287,[13] which he did. I know this was before eleven o'clock because it was before my comrade came up, and he said [8] when he came up it was eleven o'clock. I noticed the second fire for which [he?] struck Box 287 was in some high building. Of course I could not tell what building it was. The first intimation I had that the fire was under the roof, I saw the smoke coming out of those broken windows under the balcony. When I noticed this, I went round on the north side of the tower and got into the dome about twenty-five feet below the top and hollered up to my partner that the courthouse was all on fire, and he came down at once, and as we came down the steps, the fire was blazing under them, and my partner had to jump down through it. I then came down into the operator's room, and the plastering was then dropping down in that room, and I could see the fire all above through the cracks of the plastering. I then came down outside and saw that the Evans Block[14] east of the Sherman House was on fire. I do not think it was more than seven to ten minutes after I came down before the

courthouse tower fell. As I came down out of the courthouse, I went down into the jail and told the keeper that the courthouse was all on fire and that he had better take care of the prisoners if he did not want them to burn. I then went out on Randolph [9] Street and saw Fire Marshal Williams and heard him tell the men of the *Economy*[15] engine to play on the Sherman House, and he asked me to give the boys a hand. I saw that the engine had up a pretty good stream, but the wind was blowing so strong that it did not get very high. I saw the foreman[16] and Mr. Lewis[17] were handling the engine, and I understood that the other men were attending to the hose.

MATHIAS SCHAEFER

Mathias Schaefer Notes

1. These two people may have been Sarah R. Hibbard, the sister of William Brown, and her friend Maggie Daily. Unfortunately, Commissioner Brown's penmanship is spotty at best, and it is not clear if this word is "them." Parties of "three" seems more appropriate, but this conclusion is contrary to the November 24, 1871, *Republican*, which indicates that the word is "them." It is also inconsistent with the 1911 reminiscences of Sarah R. Hibbard and Mathias Schaefer; neither Hibbard nor Schaefer suggested that six people were up in the courthouse tower on the evening of October 8. "See "Marks Anniversary of the Great Fire"; "Man in Tower," sec. 1, p. [2]; Cromie, pp. 36–37; "How Was It?," p. [4].

2. In her 1911 reminiscences, Sarah R. Hibbard claimed that she called her brother's attention to the fire half an hour before Schaefer signaled Brown to sound the alarm. See "Marks Anniversary of the Great Fire."

3. The West Side gas works was not the Chicago Gas Light and Coke Company, as its operations were on Chicago's North Side and South Side. Rather, it appears that Schaefer is referring to the People's Gas Light and Coke Company, a gas company located on the city's West Side. See Andreas, vol. 2, pp. 701–2.

4. Box 319 was at a police substation at Twelfth and Johnson streets. See Musham, p. 102; *1870 City Directory*, p. 915; *1871 City Directory*, p. 35; Flinn, pp. 115, 121.

5. Schaefer's opinion as to when the second alarm was struck is correct. Brown testified that he received Schaefer's signal for Box 342 at 9:30. At

9:42 he asked Schaefer if the fire was spreading and then struck a second alarm. See William J. Brown, *Inquiry*, vol. [1], p. 1; "Boring for Facts," *Chicago Tribune*, 19 November 1871, p. 6; "The Great Fire," *Chicago Tribune*, 24 November 1871, p. 6.

6. Schaefer's "comrade" was Denis Deneen, fire department watchman. See "The Great Fire," *Chicago Tribune*, 24 November 1871, p. 6; Musham, pp. 115, 181; Goodspeed, p. 118; 1871 Pay Roll.

7. The "*Long John* boys" are firemen from the Steamer *Long John* No. 1.

8. It is not clear what Schaefer meant in this statement about Fuller helping the firemen "light up hose." Perhaps he was helping the firemen handle the hose, thus making it "lighter." But the phrase is probably a derivation of the informal term "light out," meaning to move quickly. Marshal Williams, in fact, used the phrase "light out this hose" in his inquiry testimony. See Robert A. Williams, *Inquiry*, vol. [4], p. 241; "The Great Fire," *Chicago Tribune*, 24 November 1871, p. 6; *The American Heritage Dictionary of the English Language*, 3d ed., s.v. "light: light out," hereafter cited in text as *American Heritage Dictionary*.

9. "Lead," pronounced "leed," is both a noun and a verb. When Marshal Williams recounted a question in his own inquiry testimony, "who in the devil has cut off this lead?" and commented that "there were two leads," he was referring to a length of hose. One end of the hose is connected to the steam engine and the other end is attached to the nozzle. To "lead out hose" means to carry or stretch the hose from the steamer to the fire. See Ken Little to Richard F. Bales, 15 February 2001; Little and McNalis, p. 498; Robert A. Williams, *Inquiry*, vol. [4], pp. 241, 246.

10. Schaefer indicates that he rang the courthouse bell until the fire drove him out of the building. He seems to imply that the bell stopped ringing once he fled. This is not the case. As Schaefer and Denis Deneen left the courthouse, one of them set the machinery that would ring the bell continuously, and the bell rang until it finally crashed downward. The courthouse bell was not the only fire alarm bell in Chicago. In an interview with a *Tribune* reporter, George Fuller commented that while he was in the fire department office in the courthouse, he struck the "electric repeater" that rang the "outside bells." (This is an apparent reference to the other alarm bells scattered throughout the city.) As he left the building, he turned the repeater off. See Andreas, vol. [2], pp. 92–93, 719, 724–25; Luzerne, p. 94; Goodspeed, pp. 118–119; "Boring for Facts," *Chicago Tribune*, 19 November 1871, p. 6; Kirkland, p. 732; Musham, pp. 84–85.

11. The term "*lights* of glass" makes little sense, but this word does appear to be "lights" in the transcript, and this is confirmed by the *Times*' summary of Schaefer's testimony. See "The Fire," *Chicago Times*, 24 November 1871, p. [4].

12. This is a reference to the fire at St. Paul's Catholic Church. See "Boring for Facts," *Chicago Tribune*, 19 November 1871, p. 6; Musham, p. 105; Michael Sullivan, *Inquiry*, vol. [1], pp. 87–88; Cromie, pp. 56–59.

13. Box 287 was located at West Van Buren and Canal streets, about three blocks north and one block east of the church. See *1870 City Directory*, p. 915; *1871 City Directory*, p. 35; Musham, p. 105; Cromie, inside front cover. (Note that Musham's reference to Box "387" instead of "287" at page 105 of his monograph is a typographical error; no such box existed.)

14. Although the transcript indicates that Schaefer is referring to the "Evans" Block, and although this is confirmed by the report of his testimony that appeared in the November 24, 1871, *Chicago Republican*, the 1870 and 1871 Chicago city directories do not include an Evans Block in their listings of "Public Halls, Blocks, and Buildings." See "How Was It?," p. [4]; *1870 City Directory*, pp. 943–44; *1871 City Directory*, pp. 54–55.

15. This is a reference to the steam engine *Economy* No. 8. See 1871 Pay Roll.

16. Nicholas Dubach was the foreman of the *Economy*. See 1871 Pay Roll.

17. Nicholas Lewis was a pipeman for the *Economy*. A pipeman handles the fire hose. The nozzle at the end of the hose is called a "pipe." See 1871 Pay Roll; Ken Little interview; Little and McNalis, p. 498.

CATHERINE O'LEARY

[59]

November 24, 1871
Mrs. Catherine Leary sworn[1]
(5th witness)
Examination by Mr. Chadwick[2]

Q. What do you know about this fire?
A. I was in bed myself and my husband and five children when this fire commenced. I was the owner of them five cows that was burnt and the horse, wagon, and harness.[3] I had two tons of coal and two tons of hay. I had everything that I wanted in for the winter. I could not save five cents worth of anything out of the

barn, only that Mr. Sullivan got out a little calf. The calf was worth eleven dollars on Saturday morning. Saturday morning I refused eleven dollars for the calf, and it was sold afterwards for eight dollars. I didn't save one five cents out of the fire. [60]

Q. Do you know how the fire caught?

A. I could not tell anything of the fire, only that two men came by the door. I guess it was my husband got outside the door and he ran back to the bedroom and said, "Kate the barn is afire!" I ran out, and the whole barn was on fire. Well, I went out to the barn, and upon my word I could not tell any more about the fire. I got just the way I could not tell anything about the fire.

Q. You got frightened?

A. I got frightened. I got the way I did not know when I saw everything burn up in the barn. I got so excited that I could not tell anything about the fire from that time.

Q. Do you know the parties who first gave you the alarm? [61] Who told your husband that your house was on fire?

A. It was Mr. Sullivan gave the first alarm to me. The party were there. They were up but none of them didn't come and call for me. I was left in bed.

Q. Who is Mr. Sullivan?

A. He lives over there in DeKoven Street.

Q. Opposite you on DeKoven?

A. Yes sir, right across the road.

Q. What does he do?

A. He is a drayman. There was a party in the front of our place that night. I could not tell whether it was them made the fire or not. I didn't see it. I was in bed.

Q. When you first saw the fire, was there anyplace on fire but your own barn?

A. There was, sir. It was catched along down before [62] me. Mrs. Murray and Dalton have places was afire going together. The other side on Taylor Street and the rear of the alley. Both fires were going together.

Q. How many houses were on fire or sheds or barns at the time you first saw it?

A. At the time I first saw it, my barn was and Mrs. Murray's barn was afire and Mr. Dalton's little shed. That is all that was afire, I think, when I first saw it. I thought there was no more fire, only them places. Then I catched one of the children and put him out on the sidewalk. I thought there was no more places on fire, only our places down there, and I saw Turner's big block on fire, and I thought there wasn't a touch on Turner's block until then. I saw the fire from the inside break [63] out from Turner's block.

Q. Inside?

A. It was breaking out through the inside of Turner's block.

Q. Where was Turner's block located?

A. It was on Jefferson, a little west from us.

Q. (By Mr. Williams) A long row?

A. Yes sir.

Q. On the corner?

A. Yes sir. I thought there was not a touch of fire at all, only where we were and Mrs. Murray's barn and Mr. Dalton's barn. I thought there wasn't any fire any other place until I saw the fire in Turner's block. Over at least two story houses next to Mrs. Murray there wasn't but one window burning at that time. That catched from Mrs. Murray's house one window. When I saw Turner's block going, I gave up all hope.

Q. (By Mr. Chadwick) You thought your house was to burn then? [64]

A. Yes sir. Then the men went and fixed two washtubs at both hydrants. There is a hydrant in front of our place and a hydrant in front of Mrs. Murray's.[4] They set two washtubs and then began to put water on the little house. And everything was gone, only the little house and they made for that and kept it wet all through until the fire was gone.

Q. Is that your house?

A. Yes sir. They kept water on it until the fire went out. We had plenty of water until the fire was done.

Q. Was there any other family living in your house?

A. Yes sir. There was Mrs. Laughlin.

Q. How many rooms did they occupy?

A. Two rooms.

Q. Front rooms?

A. Yes sir.

Q. Do you know whether they [65] were in bed?[5]

A. I knew they were not in bed.

Q. How did you know that?

A. Because I could hear from my own bedroom. Could hear them going on. There was a little music there.

Q. They had a little party there?

A. Yes sir. Her husband was a fiddler.

Q. They had dancing there?

A. They had.

Q. Some company?

A. Some company. I could not tell how many were there.

Q. That was going on at the time the fire broke out, that dance, was it?

A. I could not tell you, sir.

Q. Did you hear any of these people from the front part of the house passing to the back end of the dwelling, pass back and forth in the alley between the two houses?[6]

A. I didn't indeed. [66]

Q. You did not hear them at all passing that night?

A. No sir. I did not indeed.

Q. How many does your family consist of?

A. I have got five children and myself and my husband.

Q. Any grown-up children?

A. There is one of them fourteen years the oldest.

Q. A boy or girl?

A. A girl.

Q. About what time did this fire break out?

A. As near as I can guess, it was a little after nine o'clock.

Q. Were you and your family up when it broke out?[7]

A. We were in bed.

Q. Were all the members of your family in bed?

A. All in bed.

Q. Had any of you been to this party in [the] front part of the house?

A. No sir.

Q. None of you?

A. No sir. We were not there. [67]

Q. Had any of the people who were at the party been in your part of the house?

A. No sir. There was not any of them there.

Q. You could simply hear the music and they were having a jolly time?

A. I could hear anything from our own bed to their rooms, because they pretty near joined together.

Q. Have you heard from any person who was there, anything in relation to anybody's going out to the barn with a light?

A. Yes sir. I have heard of it. I have heard from other folks.

Q. Who did you hear anything in regard to it from?

A. I heard from other folks. I could not tell whether it is true or not. There was one out of the party went in for to milk my cows.

Q. Who did you hear say that? [68]

A. I heard it the next day from some of the neighbors.

Q. Do you remember who it was?

A. Yes sir.

Q. Who was it?

A. I heard it by a lady who lives up close by us.

Q. What was her name?

A. Mrs. White.

Q. Where does Mrs. White live?

A. Across the way from us.

Q. On DeKoven Street?

A. Yes.

Q. Nearly opposite your house?

A. Yes sir.

Q. Opposite to Sullivan's house does she live?

A. Well, the same way.

Q. Is it towards the lake?

A. Yes sir.

Q. Next to Sullivan's?

A. Yes sir.

Q. Next east to Sullivan's?

A. Yes sir.

Q. One story or two?

A. Two stories. [69]

Q. There is two two-story houses there right together?

A. Yes sir.

Q. She lives in the east one?

A. Yes sir. She said—the first she told me she mentioned a man was in my barn milking my cows. I could not tell, for I didn't see it. The next morning I went over there. She told me it was too bad for Leary to have all what he was worth lost. We did not know who done it. Said she some of the neighbors there was someone from the party went and milked the cows.[8]

Q. Did they state who the person was?

A. No sir. They did not.

Q. What did they want the milk for?

A. Some said it was for oysters. I could not tell anything, only what I heard from the outside.

Q. Had these persons in your [70] house been in the habit of getting milk there before if they wanted it?

A. No sir. I never saw them in my barn to milk my cows.

Q. Have you heard from anybody who was at the party? Any statement of that kind?

A. I did not.

Q. You haven't heard from anybody a statement as to who did go to the barn, have you?

A. Someone they said was from the party went to the stable.

Q. Did they tell how?

A. I asked the lady myself and she said no. There was no one there.

Q. Did you have any talk with Mrs. Laughlin about it?

A. I did.

Q. What did she say about it?

A. She said she never was in the stable.[9]

Q. Did she deny that any- [71] body went from her house?

A. She did, sir. She said she had no supper that night. She said her man had supper to a relation and to her brother.[10]

Q. Had no coffee or oysters?

A. Had no coffee or oysters.

Q. Was there any other party in the neighborhood that you know of?

A. No sir. Well, there was always music in saloons there Saturday night. I do not know of any other.

Q. This was Sunday night.[11]

A. This was Sunday night.

Q. Is Mrs. Laughlin living in the house now?

A. No sir. She moved out of it.

Q. At the time you went outdoors, you say there were other buildings on fire beside your barn?

A. Yes sir. There was.

Q. From what direction was the wind blowing? [72]

A. The wind blowed every way. You could not tell one way more than the other way. The fire went just the same as you would clap your two hands together.

Q. Did the fire go very fast?

A. Yes sir. You would hear the roar of the fire like cannon. The [roar?][12] of the fire, you never heard such a thing.

Q. Do you think the wind blowed turned towards Turner's block?

A. It is not the way the wind blowed at all, sir.

Q. What was the character of the buildings about there?

A. All frame buildings, nothing there, only frame buildings.

Q. Had there been any rain of any account for a long time before that?[13]

A. Not for a very long time before that, sir.

Q. Do you know whether the tenants of the houses about there were in the habit of [73] getting shavings from the planing mills to burn?

A. There was shavings in every house there.[14]

Q. Put them in the house?

A. Yes sir.

Q. Almost every house?

A. Yes sir.

Q. They got them because they were cheaper fuel than they could get anywhere else?

A. Yes, there were shavings in every house. That I can say.

Q. In some houses large quantities of them?

A. Yes sir.

Q. Did you have any packed in your barn?

A. Yes sir. I had some packed in my barn.

Q. How many, do you think?

A. When I used to clean out the barn, I used to throw in a little shavings.

Q. Did you use them for bedding?

A. Yes sir. Not so much for bedding. I used to clean out [74] the places and take a dish full and throw it in along with the cows. [75]

Q. (By Mr. Brown) After you discovered the fire, can you state whether there was any engine on the ground or how soon after did you discover one?

A. The first engine I seen playing, it was on Turner's block.

Q. How long after you got outdoors was it before you saw the engine there?

A. I could not tell you exactly.

Q. Was it a very long time or very quick?

A. It was not very quick at all.

Q. Can you give some idea about how soon it got there?

A. Before I seen any engine there, our

barn was pretty near burned down. The engine might be there unknown to me.

Q. Did you see the engine or did you first see it when [76] they began to play water?

A. I did see the first playing of water on Turner's block.

Q. That is the first you saw of the engine?

A. Yes.

Q. (By Mr. Williams) Is there a fire hydrant for an engine to take water in the corner of Jefferson and DeKoven?

A. Yes sir.[15]

Q. Did you see any engines standing there?

A. I did, sir.

Q. How soon was that engine at that hydrant?

A. I could not tell.

Q. About five minutes after you got out of bed?

A. I do not know. I wasn't five minutes after I got out of bed. I didn't get out in front. I went to the rear to see if I could save anything, because there was a new wagon standing in the rear of the alley between our place and Taylor. I [77] went out to see if we could save the wagon. The other side was going just as well as our place, and we could not save the wagon.

Q. Both sides of the alley were on fire?

A. Both sides of the alley were on fire.

Q. Can you give us an idea about how great a length of time passed from your first hearing of the fire until you first saw the engine?

A. I could not, sir. The engine might be there unknown to me—I got so excited. All I had was there in that barn. I did not know the fire was down until the next day.

Q. Had you any insurance upon your barn and stock?

A. Never had five cents insurance—I had these cows, one of them was not in the barn that [78] night. It was out in the alley. That one went away. I could not get that one. My husband spent two weeks looking for it and could not find it anywhere in the world. I could not get five cents. I had six cows there. A good horse there. I had a wagon and harness and everything I was worth, I couldn't save that much out of it (snapping her finger), and upon my word I worked hard for them.[16]

Catherine O'Leary Notes

1. Different sources have spelled the name of Patrick O'Leary's wife as either "Catherine" or "Catharine." Chicago Title Insurance Company records indicate that when the O'Learys sold their home in 1879, the deed was executed by "Catherine" O'Leary. But this evidence is not conclusive, as both of the O'Learys were apparently unable to write. Neither party signed this deed; they merely placed an "X" next to their names, which appear to have been written in by the person who prepared the document (Figure 80). This "signature by mark" is consistent with the way the couple signed their affidavit that was published in the *Chicago Tribune* on October 20, 1871 (Figure 66). What does appear to be the final authority, though, is the O'Leary family tombstone, which indicates that her name was spelled "Catherine" (Figure 71). Consequently, this spelling is used throughout this book.

The surname "Leary" is equivalent to the name "O'Leary." The particles "O" and "Mc" on Irish names were often dropped during this time period. In fact, Mr. O'Leary was described in his 1879 deed as "Patrick O'Leary alias Patrick Leary." See "Kate! The Barn is Afire!," *Chicago History* 1 (Fall 1971), p. 216, hereafter cited in text as "Kate! The Barn Is Afire!"; *1870 City Directory*, p. 486; *1872 City Directory*, p. 565.

2. Board of Police and Fire Commissioner James E. Chadwick.

3. The original transcript referred to a "horse wagon and harness," with no comma between the first two words, implying that Mrs. O'Leary owned only a wagon (that was pulled by a horse) and a harness. But towards the end of her testimony (page 78) Mrs. O'Leary told the Board that she had "a good horse there. I had a wagon and harness...," and so the comma has been inserted.

4. In 1871, fire hydrants in Chicago were usually at street intersections and sometimes also in the middle of the subdivision blocks, but again in the right-of-way. They were generally at least three hundred feet apart. Therefore, Mrs. O'Leary's statement that "there is a hydrant in front of our place and a hydrant in front of Mrs. Murray's" at first seems puzzling. (Mrs. Anne Murray was the O'Learys' next door neighbor to the west.) Mary Callahan also referred to two hydrants in a 1903 *Tribune* article, but she claimed that they were both in the O'Leary yard. The following comment appeared in a possibly legitimate interview with Mrs. O'Leary that was published in the October 19, 1871, *Tribune*: "When asked how her house, which is not even scorched, was saved, she replied that

there was a hydrant on each side of it, and a hundred of her friends filled buckets with water and threw it on the sides and roof of the building." Perhaps Mrs. O'Leary was referring in this interview to fire hydrants that were at either end of her block. *Robinson's Atlas* (1886) notes that there was a hydrant at the southwest corner of DeKoven and Jefferson streets and a hydrant at the northeast corner of DeKoven and Clinton streets. Although this interpretation of Mrs. O'Leary's statement is possible, it is more likely that the hydrants she referred to in both her testimony and in this alleged *Tribune* interview were actually wells or pumps and not the conventional fire hydrants to which fire equipment could connect. Bessie Louise Pierce, for example, used this alternate meaning of the word "hydrant" in her *History of Chicago* when describing the problems of supplying water to the public in the 1860s: "Chicago housewives sometimes found it almost impossible to keep small fish from squirming out of the hydrant into their cooking receptacles, providing many a dish with an unwanted piscatorial flavor." Also, as noted in Appendix A, the steam engine *Little Giant* was the first fire engine to arrive at the fire. Foreman William Musham testified that he drove to the hydrant at the southwest corner of DeKoven and Jefferson streets. If there were a closer fire hydrant in front of the O'Leary or Murray homes, surely Musham would have driven to that hydrant. (Throughout Musham's testimony the term "plug" is used instead of "hydrant.") See *Robinson's Atlas*, vol. 1, plate 6; Ken Little to Richard F. Bales, 30 December 2001; "Centennial Eve," sec. 1, p. [2]; "The Cow That Kicked Over the Lamp," p. [2]; William Musham, *Inquiry*, vol. [1], pp. 7–9; Pierce, vol. 2, p. 333; Duis, pp. 98, 323.

5. As Mrs. O'Leary had already testified

about the McLaughlin party and that those in attendance "were up" (p. 61), there seems to be little reason to ask this question.

6. This is probably a reference to the alleyway that ran between the O'Leary and Dalton houses.

7. Mrs. O'Leary's first statement at the inquiry (p. 59) was that she and her family were in bed when the fire started. Again, there does not seem to be any reason to ask this question.

8. The punctuation and wording of this somewhat ambiguous sentence is shown exactly as the sentence appears in the transcript.

9. Did Mrs. O'Leary believe Mrs. McLaughlin? It is possible that in later years Mrs. O'Leary thought that the McLaughlins did cause the fire. In 1894, her physician, Dr. Swayne Wickersham, made this statement to a *Tribune* reporter: "As [Mrs. O'Leary] has told me a thousand times, she was in bed asleep when the fire broke out, and the blaze was occasioned by her tenants, the Laughlins, breaking into her stable and attempting to milk her cow." See "Fire Alley Is Paved," p. 1.

But on the other hand, did Mrs. O'Leary's descendants grow up thinking that Daniel Sullivan was the culprit? In 1933, the *Chicago Tribune* interviewed Catherine O'Leary Ledwell, the daughter of Mr. and Mrs. O'Leary. She discounted the "McLaughlin party" theory, suggesting instead that the fire was caused by "young bloods" in the neighborhood drinking beer in the barn and carelessly tossing a cigar butt into the hay. But the *Tribune* also apparently interviewed Mrs. Rose O'Connell, who allegedly was a neighbor of the O'Learys seventeen years after the fire, and Mrs. O'Connell offered another theory as to the cause of the fire. O'Connell insisted that she overheard Mr. O'Leary give "the true story of the origin and that is that the milking was done by 'Pegleg'

Opposite: FIGURE 80—1879 DEED FROM O'LEARY TO KOLAR. **Mr. and Mrs. O'Leary sold their DeKoven Street property in December 1879 to Anton and Anna Kolar for $1150. Their deed, shown here, was recorded with the official records of Cook County on January 2, 1880. It describes Patrick O'Leary as "Patrick O'Leary alias Patrick Leary." This is consistent with his 1870 and 1872 Chicago city directory listings, which also refer to him as "Patrick Leary." (Inexplicably, there is no listing for the O'Learys in the 1871 directory.) Both Mr. and Mrs. O'Leary were apparently unable to write. Neither one signed this deed; instead, Patrick O'Leary put a small "X" by the words "his mark" and his wife placed a similar "X" by the words "her mark."**

The O'Learys were not alone in their inability to sign their names. In her book *Smoldering City: Chicagoans and the Great Fire, 1871–1874*, historian Karen Sawislak notes that the Chicago Relief and Aid Society employed approximately 200 "sewing women," paying them 83 cents a day to produce clothing and bedding for distribution to fire victims. Payroll records indicate that most of these women were immigrants (predominantly Irish). Sawislak comments that many of them were unable to write, "marking their 'X' instead of a signature roughly one-third of the time."

Sullivan, who gave the alarm." The *Tribune* then added a possibly revealing postscript: "Mrs. Ledwell refused to discuss the theory." But Mrs. Eileen Knight, the granddaughter of Mrs. O'Leary, was not as reticent as Mrs. Ledwell, her mother. In 1971, the *Wall Street Journal* related her thoughts on the cause of the fire: "The family knew that Peg Leg did it…. They kept it quiet because Peg Leg would have been lynched if the truth was known." See "Kin of O'Leary Absolves Cow in Fire of 1871," sec. 1, p. 4; "Mrs. O'Leary's Cow, Vilified for 100 Years, Maybe Wasn't Guilty," p. 1.

10. It appears that Mrs. O'Leary means that Mrs. McLaughlin did not *cook* supper on Sunday evening, as Mrs. McLaughlin's testimony indicates that she did have supper that night: "I didn't cook a bit from noontime Sunday until Tuesday evening. I will tell you how it happened. We were invited to supper at Mr. Talbot's [on Sunday night]." See Catharine McLaughlin, *Inquiry*, vol. [1], p. 229.

11. There is little punctuation in much of the transcript. This is especially true with question marks. Although it is possible that this sentence was in the form of a question, there was no question mark in the original text.

12. The transcriber inexplicably crossed out what appears to be the correct word "roar" and inserted "roll" instead.

13. There seems to be no reason for asking Mrs. O'Leary this question.

14. A month before Mrs. O'Leary testified, the *Tribune* reported that the city's Common Council adopted a resolution "favoring an ordinance for the purpose of prohibiting the storing of shavings in any barns, wood-sheds and cellars, and the indiscriminat usee [sic] or burning of the same." See "Common Council Meeting," *Chicago Tribune*, 24 October 1871, p. 1. Both Patrick O'Leary and Daniel Sullivan commented about this apparently widespread use of shavings as fuel. It seems possible that this ordinance was proposed in direct response to these practices. See Patrick O'Leary, *Inquiry*, vol. [1], pp. 251–52; Daniel Sullivan, *Inquiry*, vol. [1], pp. 266, 271.

15. Mrs. O'Leary's answer is consistent with *Robinson's Atlas*, which also indicates that there is a hydrant at this intersection. See *Robinson's Atlas*, vol. 1, plate 6.

16. Mrs. O'Leary testified at page 59 that she owned "five cows that was burnt," a horse, and a calf. Here she claims that she owned six cows and a horse. Can these statements be reconciled? How many animals did she own at the time of the fire?

It appears that she owned six cows, a horse, and a calf. That is, she owned a horse, five cows that were in the barn and were burnt in the fire,

the calf that Sullivan rescued, and a sixth cow that was in the alley that evening, went away when the fire broke out, and could not be found later.

CATHERINE SULLIVAN

[114]

November 24, 1871
Catherine Sullivan sworn[1]
(7th witness)
Examined by Mr. Brown[2]

Q. Where do you live?

A. On the south side of DeKoven Street, right where that fire commenced.[3]

Q. What is your husband's name?

A. Haven't got a husband.

Q. Are you any relation to Mr. Sullivan who is a drayman and lives about opposite that fire?[4]

A. Yes sir. He is my son. I'm a widow more than twenty-six years.

Q. Do you know anything about the commencement of that fire on October 8th?

A. No sir. I could not tell you anything about that fire.

Q. Just tell us what you first saw of it.

A. I was in my own basement in the rear part of my own building, and one of my boys was out until it [115] was after eight o'clock, and we didn't have supper until he came in. We lived in the basement, for we had a horse building on the other side. I waited until he ate his supper, and we were talking. After that he went out. I was washing up my dishes. I hadn't them washed up when I saw the fire coming through the window. I said, "Good God, can the place be on fire?" I run through the rear, out to the gate, and at that time the second house was catching fire, and Leary's barn was afire, and Mr. Dalton's was afire at the same time. Mr. Dalton's house was between Clinton and Mr. Leary's. Then Forbes was next to that. So I could not tell anymore about it, but I heard the people say that they woke them up, that the Learys were in bed. I got so excited in a minute. It was not a long time until [116] our own two houses catched afire. We had no assistance, only the men that gathered around, took their pails, and assisted us.[5] Anything further than that I could not say about the fire. I never took out as much as I could fix upon my fingers. I was pretty near out of my senses. I was just from the rear of the fire to the front, and that was all I was doing. I got kind [of] out of my head. In the house the carpenter had been working in it, and we could not get near it on the outside. It was newly painted just fresh.[6] There was nothing troubled me from that time out. I was just silly. I was [illeg.] [going?] around. I didn't take out only the clothes I had on my back. I could not get any information of that fire.

Q. Your son was at home at that time?[7]

A. Yes sir, all of my children [117] was at home.[8] And what they began to do was to save their own place, of course. A man from Sebor Street came and took their horses out of the barn and took them along.

Q. Do you know who waked up [the] Learys folks?

A. I heard it was my son and a man called Dennis Regan. I heard them say so.

Q. Do you know anything about there being a gathering of people in that vicinity that night?

A. Yes sir. I could not tell you anything about it, only just as I heard from the neighbors. Just inquired about it the same as anybody else to see how it took fire. The next day or the day after we could not get any information about it, only just as somebody told.

Q. Did you know anybody living in Mr. Leary's house beside themselves?

A. Yes sir. A man by the name [118] of Patrick McLaughlin.

Q. You don't know whether he had any company there that night?

A. I could not tell. It is just as I tell you. I was in the rear part of my own place and didn't pay any attention to anything, only to my own business. I am living nine years in that neighborhood.[9] There was buildings across the street. I did not know the people.

Q. Are you acquainted with Mr. McLaughlin and Mrs. McLaughlin?

A. I do.

Q. Have you had any talk with them since the fire?

A. No sir. They were people that I never had any conversation with. A woman like me has plenty to do to take care of her own place.

Q. Could you tell whether the fire ap-

peared to commence in [119] the barn or in the house?

A. I heard it was in Mr. Leary's barn.

Q. Could you tell yourself?

A. I could not tell myself, only as I heard from others. I was surprised when a policeman called for me.[10]

Q. How soon after you saw the fire did you see any engines on the ground?

A. Upon my word, it was a good while. I couldn't exactly tell the time. And upon my word, everyone was crying out for the engines. What was keeping them? That is all I could tell about it. I didn't look at a clock or watch or anything of that sort. Only just as I am telling you. I got so much excited, I thought the world was on fire.

Q. Do you know that two-story new building?

A. Yes sir. I do.

Q. There wasn't any stream put on that house?

A. [120] No sir. Not a stream put on that.

Catherine Sullivan Notes

1. Chicago Title Insurance Company records indicate that Mrs. Sullivan originally took title to her properties as both "Catharine" Sullivan and "Catherine" Sullivan. As her estate was later probated as "Catherine" Sullivan, her name is spelled "Catherine" throughout this book.

2. Commissioner Thomas B. Brown.

3. Various sources have spelled the name of the street on which the O'Learys lived as either "De Koven" (with a space after the first syllable) or "DeKoven." In their book *Streetwise Chicago*, authors Don Hayner and Tom McNamee point out that this street was named after banker John DeKoven, and so the street is called "DeKoven" throughout the text. See Hayner and McNamee, p. 30. (Generally speaking, the spelling of all streets noted herein is in accordance with Hayner and McNamee's book. Streets mentioned in quoted material that are spelled contrary to *Streetwise Chicago* retain their original spelling.)

Ironically, the Chicago Fire Academy now stands on the site of the O'Leary home. See "Where City Learned a Lesson, Firemen to Study Theirs," *Chicago Daily News*, [24 February 1959], p. 34, Harry A. Musham Collection, Notes on the Chicago Fire, Chicago Historical Society, hereafter cited in text as "Where City Learned a Lesson"; "Kate! The Barn Is Afire!," p. 219; Kogan and

Cromie, p. 227; Ross Miller, *American Apocalypse: The Great Fire and the Myth of Chicago* (Chicago: University of Chicago Press, 1990), p. 149; hereafter cited in text as *American Apocalypse*.

4. This question as to whether or not Catherine Sullivan is related to Daniel Sullivan probably stems from Mrs. O'Leary's earlier testimony. See Catherine O'Leary, *Inquiry*, vol. [1], p. 61. One historian, citing an anonymous descendant of the O'Learys, wrote that Sullivan was a boarder of the O'Learys. This is incorrect. See *Chicago: City on Fire*, p. 57-F.

5. As maps of the "burnt district" indicate that the fire did not destroy houses south of DeKoven Street, these men must have been able to extinguish the burning Sullivan homes. See, e.g., Lowe, p. 42.

6. See Daniel Sullivan, *Inquiry*, vol. [1], p. 273, where Daniel Sullivan stated: "I knew that mother was building a new house." Perhaps this is the house that his mother is referring to in her testimony. In this regard, see chapter four, note 46.

7. Even though Mrs. Sullivan had just testified (p. 115) that her son left her house shortly before she saw the fire, the commissioners and marshals failed to ask Mrs. Sullivan the name of this son so that they could question him to determine what he might have seen. As Mrs. Sullivan had previously told the officials that "one of my *boys* was out," these men would have had no reason to silently assume that this son was Daniel.

8. The 1870 Census indicates that Catherine Sullivan had three sons: Daniel, Michael, and John. All were draymen. See 1870 U.S. Census, Cook County, Illinois, Population Schedule, National Archives micropublication M593, roll 204, sheet 174, page 87, lines 26–28.

9. Actually, Catherine Sullivan may have lived in the neighborhood only seven years. Mrs. Sullivan owned three parcels of land between Jefferson Street and Clinton Street. All of them fronted DeKoven Street. In 1864, she was deeded lot 18 in a subdivision of Block 38 of School Section Addition to Chicago. In 1865 she acquired the west half of lot 19, which was east of lot 18. In 1870 she was deeded lot 21, which was located at the southwest corner of DeKoven and Clinton streets and seventy-five feet east of the west half of lot 19. See Chicago Title Insurance Company records; Figure 63.

10. Mrs. Sullivan is probably referring to a policeman coming to her house and asking her to testify at the investigation.

DENNIS REGAN

[121]

November 24, 1871
Dennis Ryan[1] sworn
(8th witness)
Examination by Mr. Brown

Q. Where do you live?
A. DeKoven Street.
Q. What number?
A. 112.[2]
Q. What is your business?
A. Laborer.
Q. Was that between Clinton and Jefferson?
A. Between Canal and Clinton.
Q. On the north or south side of the street?
A. On the south.
Q. Your place did not burn?
A. No sir.
Q. Do you know anything about this fire? About the origin of it and commencement of it?
A. All I know, I was into Mr. Leary's at half past eight, and I was talking to the man [122] that was in bed and his wife.[3] I asked his wife what was the reason she went to bed. She told me she had a sore foot.[4] I went away, so as the man was in bed. I went home. A short while after nine o' clock I heard one of the neighbors say Leary's barn was on fire. I jumped out of bed and went up there, and the barn was on fire and all the neighbors around it.[5] I ran through the alleyway and tried to save his wagon in the alleyway but could not go near it. I went to work there to throw water on the house because the house was not insured or nothing. That is all I know about it.
Q. Do you know whether there was company in the front part of the house?
A. Yes sir. There was company there.
Q. How did you know that? [123]
A. Because I was passing and heard the music.[6]
Q. Dancing?
A. I didn't hear any dancing. I was told dancing was there.
Q. You didn't go in there at all?
A. No sir.

Q. You don't know who were there yourself, do you?

A. I don't know.

Q. Have you heard since anybody say they were there?

A. No, I did not know who was there or not, only I was told there was a dance there. I heard the music.

Q. (By Mr. Sheridan)[7] Nobody told you who the parties were that were there at the time?

A. No sir. I don't know who was there or not.

Q. (By Mr. Chadwick) Do you know who lived there?

A. Yes.

Q. Who was it?

A. McLaughlin, fiddler.

Q. (By Mr. Sheridan) You stayed [124] up, of course, while the fire was in that vicinity?

A. I stayed there so long as I could hold a pail of water to the house because the man was not insured.

Q. (By Mr. Chadwick) Which house do you speak of?

A. Mr. Leary's. I done as much as I could and tried to save that.

Q. (By Mr. Sheridan) About how long was it from the time you heard that the fire had started there until you saw the first engine?

A. I could not tell you. I only went to bed about nine o'clock.

Q. How long after you saw the fire was it until you knew of an engine being in the vicinity? A fire engine.

A. It looks to me about a quarter of an hour.

Q. (By Mr. Chadwick) Did they come down on DeKoven Street?

A. I didn't see any of them [125] going on DeKoven Street. Only I saw one in front of Mr. Leary's house and one on Taylor Street.

Q. (By Mr. Williams) Was the wind blowing hard at that time?

A. Yes sir. The wind was blowing awful hard.

Q. Did you see many sparks drifting away with the wind?[8]

A. There was no end of the sparks going.

Dennis Regan Notes

1. "Dennis Ryan" is just one of the several aliases for "Dennis Regan." It appears that the transcriber wrote that "Dennis Ryan" was sworn, but a careful examination of the penmanship indicates that the name could be interpreted very easily as "Regan."

2. On occasion, twentieth-century references to Chicago Fire landmarks on DeKoven Street will refer to street addresses that are different from those mentioned in this book. See, for example, "Where City Learned a Lesson," p. 34, which indicates that the site of the O'Leary home was at 558 DeKoven Street and not 137 DeKoven Street. See also "Chicago's Forgotten House," sec. 1, p. 18. In 1908 (later amended in 1909 and 1910), the Chicago City Council passed an ordinance that changed the street address numbering system. This ordinance created new addresses for many of Chicago's buildings. For example, what was originally Regan's 112 DeKoven Street address became 521 DeKoven Street. See House Number Ordinance, "New & Old House Numbers, City of Chicago," Bureau of Maps and Plats, Department of Public Works, City of Chicago. For a comprehensive history of the ordinance, see Hayner and McNamee, pp. xiv–xv, 149–50.

3. When Patrick and Catherine O'Leary were questioned by the commissioners, neither one mentioned Regan's nocturnal visit.

4. Historians A. T. Andreas and James S. McQuade both comment that if Mrs. O'Leary had a sore foot, she probably would not have been in the barn milking her cow that evening. See Andreas, vol. 2, p. 708; McQuade, p. 44. During the inquiry, Mrs. O'Leary told the fire officials repeatedly that she was in bed when the fire broke out. She never mentioned, however, that she was in bed because she had a sore foot. In fact, she never said anything at all about her foot. See Catherine O'Leary, *Inquiry*, vol. [1], pp. 59, 61, 66, 67.

5. The commissioners never asked Regan who these neighbors were. On the other hand, they asked Mrs. McLaughlin to "give the names of all these persons who were there at the house that evening." See Catharine McLaughlin, *Inquiry*, vol. [1], p. 226.

6. Regan could not have heard the music as he ran past the O'Leary house. Mrs. McLaughlin testified the day after Regan did, and she told the commissioners and marshals that the music *ended* about one-half hour *before* the fire started. The fire officials never questioned Mrs. McLaughlin about this inconsistency, nor did they recall Regan and

ask him to explain this apparent falsehood. See Catharine McLaughlin, *Inquiry*, vol. [1], pp. 225–26.

7. Commissioner Mark Sheridan.

8. Perhaps a fire official, thinking that a wayward chimney spark might have caused the fire, asked this question. The Board commented on this possibility in its final report: "Whether [the fire] originated from a spark blown from a chimney on that windy night, or was set on fire by human agency, we are unable to determine." See "The Great Fire," *Chicago Evening Journal*, 12 December 1871, p. [4].

CATHARINE McLAUGHLIN

[223]

Catharine McLaughlin sworn
November 25, 1871
(12th witness)

Q. Where do you live?

A. DeKoven Street, 137.

Q. Do you own the house?

A. No sir. It was Pat Leary's house. I lived in the house the fire took place in. In the front of it. He lived in the rear part of it.

Q. The fire took place in the barn in the rear of that?

A. Yes sir. They say so now.

Q. Are you still living there?

A. No sir. I left there two days after the fire. As soon as I got a place to go, I left.

Q. What is your husband's name?

A. Patrick McLaughlin.

Q. What is his business?

A. He used to work on the railroad. He is working in a foundry on Canal Street now.

Q. Have you a family?

A. Yes sir. A child, five years old, the twenty-third of [224] February.

Q. Do you know anything about the time the fire commenced on the night of October 8th?

A. No sir. I do not know anything about the fire more than you. Some persons came to the door and hollered "fire," and just when they came there, I went and opened the door and turned and looked back in Leary's yard and heard them holler and say that Pat Leary's barn

was on fire.[1] I went out and saw that Pat Leary's barn was on fire and Mr. Dalton's house. I went in and told my brother to pick up my child; and he took one armful of my clothes across the road; and as I went over across the road, I fainted and did not know anything more about the fire. I never went back again to bring a thing out.

Q. How many people were there [225] in your apartment at the time the fire commenced?

A. To the best of my knowledge, I think there was seven or eight boys and two girls. There was a greenhorn brother of mine there—

Q. You mean a man just come from Ireland?

A. Yes sir. And Sunday evening and of course the cousins and neighbors of mine came in to see him.

Q. You had seven or eight persons beside your own family?

A. Yes sir.

Q. Men and women?

A. Only two girls.

Q. Did you have music there that evening?

A. Yes sir. My husband played two times[2] on the fiddle, that was all. There was one a brother of mine and another lady danced a polka. That is all that was played.

Q. That was all that you had time to play before the fire?

A. No sir. The fire, so far as [226] I can think, was not for a half hour afterward. My husband didn't feel very well. He was not up all day. He got up about half past eight o'clock. I called him up. He was just after going to bed.

Q. Will you give the names of all these persons who were there at the house that evening?

A. Dan Talbot. There was George Lewis. Talbot lives on Jefferson Street, corner of Jefferson and Bunker.

Q. What is his business?

A. Works on the boats. I do not know what he does do.

Q. What is the name of the second one?

A. George Lewis. He lives on Polk Street. I could not tell whereabouts on Polk, up near Aberdeen some place.

Q. What business does he do?

A. Engineer in a coffee mill.

Q. Whose coffee mill?

A. I really could not tell. I don't know what street it is on. I think it is [227] McLaughlin or Coughlin.[3]

Q. On the West Side or South?

A. On the South.

Q. Is he working there now?

A. I do not know whether he is working. They got burned down there. I do not know whether they are built up or not yet.

Q. Who is the next?

A. Johnny Stanley.

Q. Where does he live?

A. I really don't know where he lives. Someplace up on Eighteenth Street. I do not know the number or the name of the street.

Q. What is his business?

A. Carpenter, I guess.

Q. What is the next?

A. There was John Riley.

Q. Where does he live?

A. He boards over on Fourth Avenue. I think it is there he boards.

Q. What is his business?

A. He was a carpenter. I do not know whether he is now or not. [228]

Q. What is the next?

A. Richard Russell.

Q. What business does he do?

A. Does nothing now. He is sick since the fire.

Q. Where does he live?

A. Forquer Street, between Desplaines and Halsted.[4]

Q. Who else?

A. I guess that is all.

Q. Who were the women?

A. Alice Riley and Mary Needham. She is not here now; she is in Michigan.[5]

Q. Where does Alice Riley live?

A. On the West Side someplace. I do not know where.

Q. A sister of this John Riley, a carpenter?

A. First cousin of his. She is an acquaintance of mine these three years.

Q. Did any of this party go out of your house during the evening?

A. Of course I do not know that I could not say whether they did or not. If I was going dead 'fore God, [229] I could not tell whether they went out or not.

Q. Did you go out yourself?

A. No sir, I didn't since nightfall. Just at nightfall I went out.

Q. Did you have anything to eat or drink there?

A. No sir, not a bit. I didn't cook a bit from noontime Sunday until Tuesday evening. I will tell you how it happened. We were invited to supper at Mr. Talbot's.

Q. Sunday night?

A. Yes sir. My husband went to bed Sunday night on account of being up two nights before and didn't get up till half past eight, and I didn't get supper for him. I hadn't a fire in the stove from Sunday at two o'clock until Monday till three or four.

Q. You don't know whether any of these persons went outdoors for any purpose during the time that this [230] company was there?

A. No sir.

Q. Did you make any tea or coffee during the time?

A. No sir. If I did, of course I should have started the stove. Not a mouthful of victuals ever came there that evening before God this day.

Q. Were these parties at your place at the time the fire broke out?

A. Yes sir. They were in there in my house at the time the fire broke out.

Q. None of them had gone home at that time?

A. No sir.

Q. Where did the fire appear to commence?

A. It seemed to commence with Leary's barn. I knew the folks.[6] When they came in and hollered, "fire," said that Leary's barn was on fire, and whether it was there that it commenced or not, I could not say.

Q. Did you get out immediately [231] and look?

A. The very minute they hollered, "fire," I went out. I looked back and saw Leary's barn on fire and the back part of Mr. Dalton's house.

Q. Can you tell about what part of the barn took fire?

A. I could not tell. I didn't mind that. I just looked around and saw the blaze. I turned in and hollered to my brother to pick up my child, and I went across the street and fainted.[7] I could not tell anymore.

Q. Did you hear or know or believe any

particular thing connected with the fire or the origin of it?

A. No sir. I do not nor do I believe that hardly anyone living can tell how it commenced.

Q. Were there any other places where boys or grown-up people congregated that night in that vicinity? [232]

A. No sir.

Q. Were boys in the habit of congregating in a barn in the vicinity, do you know?[8]

A. No sir. I did not hear it. I will tell you how it is. There is a kind of open place there and there was two barns there.

Q. How long had you lived there?

A. I lived there two years, I guess, and one month. This November was two years.

Q. You got along pleasantly with Mrs. Leary?

A. Yes sir. An honester woman I never would ask to live with.

Q. Did your husband help to keep down the fire on Mrs. Leary's house?

A. Yes sir. He did all night. He got a cold too, and the boys [helped] with keeping it down. There was six or seven working on the house.

Q. Did you see any fire engines come to the place? [233]

A. Yes sir. I did.

Q. Did any of them play on Mrs. Leary's house?

A. They did once or twice, to the best of my knowledge, twice.

Q. At the time you went outdoors, did you notice the fire engines?

A. No sir. There was an engine in a few minutes, corner of Jackson and DeKoven.[9]

Q. About how long a time after you went outdoors and saw the barn on fire and Mr. Dalton's house did you see a fire engine come?

A. I could not say. It was some minutes.

Q. Do you know that it was five minutes?

A. I think it was more, about ten minutes.

Q. The time seems long at such times.

A. Yes sir. It seems long and seems short. One gets frightened and doesn't know how it goes.

Q. Do you know anything more about this fire? [234]

A. No sir. I do not.

Q. Anything of interest or information in the management of it?

A. No sir. I know no more of it.

Q. Do you know whether Mrs. Leary was ever in the habit of going in their barn after night?

A. No sir. I really do not know. I lived in the front of the house. They might or they might not. I was never in the habit of going back in the night.

Q. Did Mrs. Leary generally do the milking?

A. Yes sir. Mrs. Leary used to do the milking about five o'clock.[10]

Q. Did ever any of your family help her?

A. No sir. I had no one to help her out myself that night. I never put my hand near a cow in my life. I am going nine years in America and have never [235] milked a cow since I have been here.

Q. You didn't tell the name of these persons who went out, if any. Who did, if anyone?[11]

A. There was no one came out of my house during the fire.[12]

Q. Previous to that time?

A. I do not know if the boys got in before the house got afire. I could not really say. I do not know whether they were in my house then or whether they got in before then or not. They came into the house and went back to save their things.

Q. Do you know whether they were in before or not?

A. No sir. I could not say.

Q. What three boys were these?[13]

A. Denny Connors[14] and Willie Lewis and Johnny Ryan.[15] I think them is the three boys.

Q. Boys or young men? [236]

A. Young men.[16]

Q. Did I understand you to say there was a porch on the back side of the house that you could go back and look out?[17]

A. I lived five or six steps going up in the doorway. In front there was a little partition you could stand and look back just back of the door.

Q. You went out to the end of that porch and looked back?

A. I went and looked over the side. It was a kind of a little stoop.

Q. Which way did you look?

A. I looked straight. I heard them holler "fire" and I saw Leary's barn blazing, and part of Mr. Dalton's house was burning at that time.

Q. You hadn't seen any firemen about there at that time?

A. No sir. There was no one that I could see at that [237] time.

Q. Hadn't heard anybody break down the fence in that back yard?

A. No sir, not one. In fact, they could break down all the fences in the world after I looked the second time and saw the fire and I not know it.

Q. Was there a door in your apartment leading back to the yard?

A. No sir. The whole house was by itself. It is separated between the houses.

Q. You had access to the yard through the narrow alley?

A. No sir.

Q. Ain't you the privilege of the yard?

A. Yes sir. From the division there was between our house and Dalton's.

Q. You didn't live in the front part of Mr. Dalton's?

A. Mrs. Leary's.

Q. Between Mrs. Leary's house and Dalton's house? [238]

A. There was a way to go right through, a large passage.

Q. Enough to roll in a barrel of flour?

A. Yes sir, a good deal wide.

Q. Between Mr. Dalton's house and Mr. Leary's?

A. Yes sir.

Q. There is a fence between the two houses?

A. I could not tell whether it was Mrs. Leary or Dalton that owned the fence.

Q. Was there a fence there?

A. Yes sir. There was a board fence going betwixt them.

Q. There was a little alleyway running alongside of Mrs. Leary's house going back to the yard?

A. Yes sir.

Q. About how far from the house was Mrs. Leary's barn?

A. I really could not say.

Q. As near as you could guess.

A. I guess it must be over forty feet. I could not tell you. I think it must be about forty feet or [239] more, that is, from the entrance off the street to where the barn was.[18] Her door reached out upon the side of Mr. Dalton's fence, I might say.[19]

Q. Did you say that Mr. Dalton's house was on fire?

A. Yes sir. The back part of their house. The summer kitchen.

Q. Was their barn on fire, too?

A. I did not see their barn. They had no barn.[20] Mr. Forbes had a barn back of that.

Q. Mr. Forbes's house was on the other side of Leary's house?

A. Mr. Dalton, who is next to Leary's, and Forbes next to that.

Q. I suppose this was Leary's house and that Dalton's house? (a)

A. Yes sir.

Q. Was there an alleyway between them?

A. Yes sir.

Q. On the line of which house [240] was this fence?

A. It was on Dalton's.

Q. In the line with the side of Dalton's house?

A. Yes sir.

Q. There was no fence on this side of Leary's house?

A. No sir.[21]

Q. Where did you go when you left the house?

A. That morning?

Q. That evening. After the alarm of fire, did you leave the house?

A. Yes sir. I went right across the road.

Q. To Mrs. Sullivan's?

A. No sir. I went across the road where there was a vacant lot. We all went there.[22]

Q. You stood there and watched the fire?

A. Of course I didn't watch the fire. I wasn't able.

Q. You fainted?

A. Yes sir. I didn't take anything out of my house, only one armful of clothes. They brought them out, of [241] course. They were not much good to me when they did bring them. They were all broken and torn.

Q. You say the engine was stationed here on this corner of the streets? (i)

A. Yes sir. It was stationed on the corner near Turner's building.

Q. You are quite certain that no person left the house to bring in refreshments of any kind?

A. No sir. There was no one left the house. Only one man went out and got a half-gallon of beer or two half-gallons, I don't know which.[23]

Q. Did you hear anything said by the parties about having an oyster supper that night at your house?

A. Yes sir. I heard a report about it.

Q. Did you hear it that night?

A. No sir, not a word. There **[242]** was no talk of oysters.

Q. Did you hear anything said about going out to get milk for the purpose of making milk punch?

A. No sir. That is a thing I never had in my life in my house. No kind of liquor or whiskey.

Q. You said a man did go out and get a half-gallon of beer?[24]

A. Yes sir.

Q. And brought it in?

A. Yes sir, and brought it right in.

Q. Once or twice?

A. Upon my word, I could not say. I know he brought one half-gallon into the house. I do not know but he did twice. I am not sure.

Q. What is the girl's name that has gone to Michigan?

A. Mary Needham. She has gone to Michigan or Wisconsin, I don't know which.

Q. Do you know of your **[243]** own knowledge whether Mrs. Leary saved anything out of her barn?

A. No sir. To my own knowledge she didn't save anything out of her barn excepting a calf.

Q. Alive?

A. Alive, and one cow was out. She was not in the barn. I do not know whether she is sickly or not. She was saved.

Q. Have they found that cow yet?

A. I don't know anything about that.

Catharine McLaughlin Notes

1. Both here and on pages 230–31 and 236, Mrs. McLaughlin refers to "persons," "them," and "they" warning her of the fire. But the commissioners never asked her who these people were, even though they were obviously at the fire during its very early stages.

2. This word has traditionally been construed as "tunes." See "The Great Fire," *Chicago Tribune*, 26 November 1871, p. 1; Sheahan and

Upton, p. 425; "Kate! The Barn Is Afire!," p. 218. But the transcript indicates that this interpretation is incorrect and that the word is actually "times."

3. The "Street and Avenue Guide" in the *1870 City Directory* does not list any Chicago street with the name of "McLaughlin" or "Coughlin." But this same reference discloses that William F. McLaughlin was a proprietor of the Union Coffee & Spice Mills. See *1870 City Directory*, pp. 533, 945, 984.

4. Richard Russell was a laborer who boarded at 206 Forquer Street. See *1870 City Directory*, p. 711.

5. Mary Needham was the maiden name of Mrs. Mary Callahan. See "Centennial Eve," sec. 1, p. [2]. Sidney Gay, a former director of the Chicago Relief and Aid Society, claimed that of the 100,000 people left homeless by the fire, "20,000 probably left the city in the course of a few days." See Sheahan and Upton, pp. 318–19; Sawislak, p. 83.

6. Earlier, while questioning Mrs. McLaughlin, the commissioners and marshals had methodically asked her about every person at her party. But here, when she testified that "I knew the folks" who warned her about the fire, the officials failed to ask her who these "folks" were.

7. James Dalton claimed that he heard a woman scream about ten minutes before his mother-in-law saw the fire. Perhaps it was Mrs. McLaughlin who screamed. Perhaps he heard Mrs. McLaughlin "holler" to her brother. See Andreas, vol. [2], pp. 701, 714.

8. Daniel Sullivan later testified about a vacant house on Taylor Street frequented by "young scoundrels living around the city." See Daniel Sullivan, *Inquiry*, vol. [1], pp. 271–72, 274.

9. Although Mrs. McLaughlin allegedly testified that the engine was at the corner of Jackson and DeKoven streets, the *Chicago Tribune*'s summary of her testimony indicates that she said that the engine was at the corner of Jefferson and DeKoven streets. As Jackson was parallel to and perhaps a mile north of DeKoven, the *Tribune* account is undoubtedly correct. See "The Great Fire," *Chicago Tribune*, November 26, 1871, p. 1; Lowe, p. 42. The steamer *Little Giant* No. 6 was probably the first engine to reach the fire. Foreman William Musham testified that he drove to the corner of DeKoven and Jefferson streets. See William Musham, *Inquiry*, vol. [1], p. 7.

10. See also "How It Originated," p. [2], and reproduced at Appendix C: "[Mrs. O'Leary] milked her cows at 4½ P.M. and 5 A.M., as Mrs. O'Leary peddled the milk."

11. The commissioners and marshals had previously asked Mrs. McLaughlin twice if anyone had left her home that evening. (See pages 228–29 and 229–30.) The officials must have found her answers to be inconclusive, because now they ask her a third time.

12. Mrs. McLaughlin earlier claimed on pages 228–29 that she did not know if any of her guests left her home that evening. But here she qualifies this earlier statement, indicating only that no one left *during the fire*. Upon further questioning (page 235), she admits that three of them did leave, but does not know if they returned "before the house got afire." But even this statement contradicts her testimony on page 230, where she told the commissioners and marshals that "[her guests] were in there in my house at the time the fire broke out."

13. Although Mrs. McLaughlin had just told the fire officials that "I do not know if the boys got in before the house got afire," she did not mention how many boys were outside. But here she is asked to identify these "three boys." How did the Board know that *three* boys left her home? Perhaps the transcriber omitted this fact from the transcript.

14. Denny Connors was probably Mrs. McLaughlin's "greenhorn brother" from Ireland. See "Centennial Eve," sec. 1, p. [2]. However, the *1870 City Directory* (but not the *1871 City Directory*) notes a "Daniel Conners" who boarded just a few houses away at 120 DeKoven Street. See *1870 City Directory*, p. 179.

15. When the fire officials asked Mrs. McLaughlin on page 226, "Will you give the names of all these persons who were there at the house that evening?" she failed to mention Willie Lewis and Johnny Ryan. (Although she did not name Denny Connors either, she had earlier referred to him on page 225.) The commissioners and marshals did not ask her why she did not originally name Lewis and Ryan as having attended her party.

16. How many guests were in the McLaughlin home on the night of the fire? According to Mrs. McLaughlin, ten people attended her party: Dan Talbot, George Lewis, Johnny Stanley, John Riley, Richard Russell, Alice Riley, Mary Needham, Denny Connors, Willie Lewis, and Johnny Ryan. Mary Callahan's version of the McLaughlin guest list includes only eight people: George Lewis, Will Lewis, John Finnan, John Hanley, John Reilly, Alice Reilly, Denny Connors, and herself. (However, the penmanship of the transcript of Mrs. McLaughlin's testimony is very poor. It is possible that "John Riley" and "Johnny Ryan" were one and the same person.) Mrs. McLaughlin's testimony includes the names of the streets where

many of her guests lived. An examination of the *1870 City Directory* and the *1871 City Directory* reveals only one name—Richard Russell—as living on the appropriate street identified by McLaughlin. See "Centennial Eve," sec. 1, pp. 1–[2]; Catharine McLaughlin, *Inquiry*, vol. [1], pp. 226–228, 235; *1870 City Directory*, p. 711; *1871 City Directory*, p. 775.

17. There is no earlier reference to Mrs. McLaughlin supposedly telling the commissioners and marshals about a porch on the back side of the house. Post-fire photographs of the O'Leary home (see, e.g., Figure 53) indicate that there was no back porch on either the McLaughlin or O'Leary homes.

18. The one doorway into the O'Leary home was located on the east side of the house and towards the north, or rear (see Figure 37). Mrs. McLaughlin's estimate of the distance between this entrance and the barn was apparently a very good guess; after the fire James Dalton recalled that the distance from the north end of the O'Leary home to the barn was "about forty feet." John McGovern described the O'Leary barn in *Daniel Trentworthy* and then mentioned "an eight-foot board fence running forty feet to the rear of the cottage on both sides." See Andreas, vol. 2, p. 714; McGovern, p. 177.

19. Figure 37, which is an eastern view of the O'Leary home, shows this door. Andreas' *History of Chicago* discloses that an eight-foot-high fence ran from the back of James Dalton's house to his shed, which was at the rear of his property. As shown in Figure 54, this fence may have blocked Daniel Sullivan's view of the O'Leary barn from where he allegedly sat across the street in front of William White's house. Mrs. McLaughlin's testimony suggests that another fence ran from the front of Dalton's house towards DeKoven Street, along the alleyway between the Dalton and O'Leary properties. As Dalton's house was set back from the street, this fence would have run past the doorway of the O'Leary home. See Andreas, vol. 2, p. 714.

20. Although Dalton may not have had a barn, he did have a shed at the rear of his property. Like his house, it was built on the west line of his land. See Andreas, vol. 2, p. 714.

21. Compare this testimony to "Notes on the Great Chicago Fire of 1871," sec. 3, p. 21, which describes the O'Leary property as follows: "High wooden sheds and fences adjoined the lot." But this 1896 newspaper article does not claim that the lot was bounded by fences on all sides, only that "fences" adjoined the lot. Therefore, the article may not be inconsistent with Mrs. McLaugh-

lin's reply, as her statement indicates only that
there was no fence on one particular side of the
O'Leary house. Furthermore, it appears that information in this newspaper article may have been
lifted from Andreas' *History of Chicago* and carelessly reworded. Andreas' original statement reads
as follows: "High wooden fences ran from the barn
to sheds on contiguous lots...." See Andreas, vol.
2, p. 708.

22. It appears that Catherine Sullivan owned
this vacant lot. See Andreas, vol. 2, p. 715; Chicago
Title Insurance Company records; Figures 63, 79.

23. Mrs. McLaughlin is again questioned as
to whether or not anyone left her home, and she
again gives an inconclusive answer. At first she
states that "no one left the house," but in the next
sentence she changes her testimony, claiming that
"only one man went out."

24. Frank Shults had a saloon at the northeast corner of DeKoven and Jefferson streets. It
was probably part of the aforementioned "Turner's
building." Robert Cromie implies that this beer
might have come from Shults' saloon. See Figure
79; Andreas, vol. 2, p. 716; F. H. Shults letter;
Cromie, p. 27; Musham, p. 98; *1871 City Directory*,
p. 1086; *Robinson's Atlas*, vol. 1, plate 6.

PATRICK O'LEARY

[244]

November 25, 1871
Patrick Leary sworn
(13th witness)
Examination by commissioners

Q. Where do you live?
A. DeKoven Street.
Q. The house that wasn't burnt?
A. Yes sir.
Q. On the north side of DeKoven Street,
fronting south?
A. Yes sir.
Q. What is the number?
A. 137.
Q. Do you know anything about the fire?
Where it commenced Sunday night, October
8th?
A. No. I do not, more than a man that
never saw it.
Q. Don't you know where it began?
A. No sir. I could not tell.
Q. Whose building did it begin in?

A. That is more than I can tell because I
was in bed when the fire commenced.
Q. What was the progress of [245] the
fire when you first saw it? How far had it burned?
A. It was my own barn.
Q. Any other building on fire?
A. That is more than I can tell because it
was lighting so strong when I got up.
Q. Was there anybody else's house on fire
when you got up?
A. No sir.
Q. Dalton's?
A. No sir.
Q. Do you know whether it was on fire or
not?
A. No sir. I couldn't tell anything about it.
The fire was too strong when I got [up]. The fire
was too strong when I got up.
Q. Didn't you get up on top of your house
and try to protect it?
A. Yes sir. But this barn was burned
down. The whole inside was burned out.
Q. Just state what you did as soon as you
found out that your barn was on fire. [246]
A. Dan Sullivan is the first that called me
out of bed,[1] and I saw my own barn burning
and couldn't get near it. I [turned?] in and put
the children in the street as fast as I could. That
is all I have to say about the fire.
Q. Didn't you do anything else?
A. Then when I had the children out, I
went and was pouring water on my own little
house until one o'clock at night.
Q. It didn't take you long to take the children out?
A. Not very long.
Q. Then you went to work to save your
little [blank]?
A. Yes sir.
Q. When you went and put water on, was
there any building on fire?
A. Yes sir. The whole block from that to
Jefferson.
Q. How many buildings should you think
there was on fire then? [247]
A. Be—That is more than I can tell. I will
tell you the reason why. I commenced to get the
children out, and I couldn't see anything but
the fire.
Q. Just about the time you began to put
water on with the buckets, did you see any engines playing on the fire?

A. No engines didn't play a bit. I can't tell the reason why only one little [splash?] they gave on it. The people came and asked me what company I was insured in. I said I wasn't insured in any company, and damned a stream did they put on it. It was burning in spite of the whole of it, only just they were quenching the other houses as fast as they could. Of course there was an engine there. I couldn't tell what time she came there. They gave it two or three [248] splashes.

Q. They were trying to put the fire out in other buildings.

A. Yes sir. They were.

Q. Doing their best to stop the fire.

A. Yes sir. I suppose so. They didn't trouble me much. They didn't help me anyway. My little shanty wasn't worth much. They didn't care much about it.

Q. Did the fire burn any south of De-Koven Street? Did any building catch afire on the south side?

A. No, they didn't. It went very near it. The people were throwing water on top of their houses all the time.

Q. Did your house catch fire?

A. Yes sir. Even the rafters were burning.

Q. Didn't the firemen put water on your house during the fire?

A. They did on the taller end.[2] [249]

Q. They probably saw that your house was not in much danger.

A. Yes sir. They had enough that could be saved. My house wasn't worth much anyway.

Q. Don't know anything about how the fire commenced?

A. No sir. I do not know anything about it.

Q. Do you have, in consideration of all the circumstances, any belief of how the fire commenced?

A. No sir. If I was to be hanged for it, I don't know who done it.

Q. What time did you go to bed that night?

A. The woman went to bed between eight and half past eight, as near as I could judge.

Q. Did you get to bed before her?

A. I did. I was in bed before her.

Q. Was you asleep when the alarm was given? [250]

A. I was indeed. If I was up sooner, I

could save my horse, too. There was no trouble in saving them. They were tied outside;[3] the two doors were open. There was only three feet of a door. I cut half of it off.

Q. About half the door was open?

A. Yes sir.

Q. The lower half was closed?

A. No, that is more than I can tell. There was nothing in, only a little thing. Anybody could put his hand in and open it. The outside door was nailed back. I wanted to give the horse and cows all the air I could.

Q. Do you mean the back door?

A. Yes, it was but three feet high. There was no trouble in opening it. There was only a little catch that you could shove in and out. The one next to the house is nailed up so it would not shut at all.

Q. You had room for how [251] many cows and horses in the barn?

A. I had nine cows there last winter and a horse and all their feed.

Q. Where did [you] put the feed?

A. I had three or four barrels just inside the door so I keep it handy to them.

Q. Was it a one-story or two-story barn?

A. Fourteen feet high, twenty feet long.

Q. Did it have any loft to it?

A. Yes sir, and three ton of hay in it.

Q. How wide was it?

A. 16 feet wide.

Q. Did you have any kindling wood, shavings, or anything of that kind?

A. Yes sir. I had shavings in the shed and coal and wood and everything.

Q. Do you use shavings for bedding?

A. No sir. I used to put a little under the horse.

Q. Was any others about there in the habit of having shavings around their places for kindling? [252]

A. I suppose they had.

Q. Wasn't it very much the habit of people about there to get shavings from the planing mill to burn?

A. Of course. Everyone used to get them there at that time. I saw lots of people going along with bags of shavings.

Q. Did the wind blow pretty strong?

A. It did blow very strong at the time.

Q. The fire went very rapidly, didn't it?

A. Indeed, it went out of my sight anyway

because when I was helping folks, I did not know how fast it went.

Q. Could sparks from a house south from your barn being driven by the wind get into your barn and into those shavings?

A. I couldn't tell anything about that.[4]

Q. What way was the south face of your barn constructed?

A. The door was open all the [253] time.

Q. Which side of the door as you went in from the house was the shavings?

A. The right hand side.

Patrick O'Leary Notes

1. Although O'Leary testified that "Dan Sullivan" called him out of bed, he had earlier claimed in a sworn affidavit that "Denis Ryan" awakened him. This affidavit was published in the *Tribune* on October 20, about five weeks before O'Leary testified, and is reprinted in Appendix C. The commissioners never commented on this inconsistency. See "How It Originated," p. [2].

2. Although O'Leary's statement suggests there was only one house on his property, inquiry testimony and later reminiscences indicate that the O'Leary and McLaughlin homes were actually two separate houses but very close together. (For further information, see "How Many Houses Were on the O'Leary Property?" in Appendix A.) The McLaughlin home faced DeKoven Street, and the O'Leary house was in back of it. Post-fire photographs reveal that the McLaughlin house was noticeably taller than the O'Leary home. See, e.g., Figure 62.

3. The "they" that O'Leary is referring to is possibly his horse and also a cow. See Catherine O'Leary, *Inquiry*, vol. [1], pp. 77–78. Although Patrick O'Leary implies that the horse was tied outside, his wife indicated in her statement to Michael McDermott (see Appendix C) that she fed her horse outside at about 7:00 P.M. and then put him in the barn. Daniel Sullivan's testimony also suggests that the horse was inside the barn at the time of the fire. See "How It Originated," p. [2]; Daniel Sullivan, *Inquiry*, vol. [1], pp. 260–61.

4. It appears that Anne Murray, O'Leary's neighbor to the west, couldn't tell anything about sparks drifting into the barn, either. Although her home was immediately southwest of the barn and thus directly upwind, the fire officials failed to interview her during the investigation and ask her if she had been using her stove on the night of the fire. But perhaps the reason Anne Murray was not questioned during the inquiry was that she was

no longer living in the area. Post-fire photos indicate that her home was destroyed by the fire. (But on the other hand, Mrs. McLaughlin testified that she left her home two days after the fire, and the Board was somehow able to find her.) See Catherine O'Leary, *Inquiry*, vol. [1], pp. 63, 71; Catharine McLaughlin, *Inquiry*, vol. [1], p. 223; Figures 47, 50.

DANIEL SULLIVAN

[254]

November 25, 1871
Daniel Sullivan sworn
(14th witness)

Q. Where do you live?

A. 134 DeKoven Street.[1]

Q. What is your business?

A. I drive dray. I am a drayman in this city for the last fifteen or sixteen years.[2] I guess the number is one hundred and thirty six, now.[3]

Q. Do you know anything about the origin of the fire Sunday night, October 8, that there was back of Leary's?

A. All I know about it I will tell to you with a good free will. When I got through with my horses, I went into my own house and sat there a little while and eat my supper. I started right out about eight o'clock or as near as I could come to it. I went across the street over to Leary's and went in there. When I got into Leary's house, both [255] him and his wife and three young ones was in bed. The youngest one and the oldest one was up. I asked what was the reason they went to bed so soon, and the old woman[4] said she didn't feel very well. I stayed there, as near as I could think of it, very near an hour and maybe more.[5] At that very time, he ordered the youngest one and the oldest one to bed, said that the little girl should be up early in the morning. I went out of [the] house, went across the street on the other side of the street where I lived myself—one lot east of me—and I stayed there a little while. There was a little house belonging to Leary that was in the front. There was a party there, and I stayed there as long as from about twenty minutes past nine to twenty-five minutes past nine.[6] [256] Said I, "It is time for me to go in and go to bed." Just as I turned around, I saw a fire in

Leary's barn. I got up and run across the street and kept hollering, "fire, fire, fire." I couldn't run very quick. I could holler loud enough but could not run. At the time I passed Leary's house, there was nobody stirring in Leary's house. I made right straight in the barn, thinking when I could get the cows loose, they would go out of the fire.[7] I knew a horse could not be got out of a fire unless he be blinded, but I didn't know but cows could. I turned to the left-hand side. I knew there was four cows tied in that end. I made at the cows and loosened them as quick as I could. I got two of them loose, but the place was too hot. I had to run when I saw the cows **[257]** were not getting out. I was going along [the] right side of the wall. The boards were wet, my legs slipped out from me, and I went down.[8] I stood up again, and I was so close to the wall, I could hold on to something and made for the door. Just as I got to the door, there was a Goddamned big calf come along, and the back of the calf was all afire, and Christ, I thought it was time I got out of the yard, and I got out of the yard. As I got out of the yard, I had hold of the calf by a rope. The calf was all burnt. I stood and looked back at the fire as a dog will look when he is licked with a rope. I stood by Leary's house, and they were in bed. A man by the name of Regan came along. I was hollering and shoving in the door when **[258]** Leary came out. He had nothing on but his pants and his shirt, and this is the way he done. He put up his hands and scratched his head same's he had a foot of lice in it. He went in and called his wife and she came out and just clapped her hands together that way (indicating).

Q. Did you see any other building on fire?

A. Not at the very same time I got into Leary's barn.

Q. How long before some of them caught?

A. The fire having broke out through Leary's barn at that time—

Q. It was in Leary's barn?

A. It was in Leary's barn.

Q. Hadn't broke out of the roof, you mean?

A. No sir, it had not.

Q. Where did it appear to be?

A. To the best of my knowledge, so far as I could understand it, the barn was taken fire **[259]** from the east end.

Q. That would be the right-hand side as you went into the door?

A. Yes sir. There was a horse tied near the door. There was a cow tied near the other corner, the mother of this calf that I brought out of the fire. The flames were right through the barn as I got into it. That back door of the barn was open as I was going into the lot. The door was same as you put sticks across to keep children from going down any high stairway. At that time there was nobody made any alarm to wake up Leary.

Q. When you went in from the yard, did you find the door leading from the yard into the barn open?

A. Yes sir.

Q. Were these bars there?

A. The bars, sir, was at the back door going out to the alleyway. The door towards **[260]** the house was wide open.

Q. Was the flames on your right hand side as you went in?

A. The best I could tell, it looked on my right. This was where the horse was tied and one cow, the mother of this calf, but the whole flames was through the barn as I got into it.

Q. Suppose now that to be the barn (indicating on diagram). You say that when you went in, you knew the cows were at the west end of the barn?

A. Yes sir, four of them.

Q. About where was the door situated?

A. Here was the door, right within a little ways of this corner (a) and the horse stood in that end. The cows stood in the furthest corner. (b) On this end there was four cows tied. That was the west end of it.

Q. They were shut off into stalls?

A. No, only they were all **[261]** tied, one by one by a rope.

Q. The door was here? (c)

A. The door was here. (c) As I came in here, I went to the left where the four cows were tied. The two cows first, that is the two I got loose. They didn't get out. The flames were most through the barn altogether.

Q. When you went in, you found the fire on your right hand?

A. Yes sir, as near as my judgment could go. I got kind [of] excited. I don't believe that there was anything between the horse and cow that was tied at that end, and I know that the calf that I brought out of the fire, I know that calf was tied the same day at the head of the cow, which was a cow that he hadn't owned over a month before that, that he paid fifty or sixty dollars for.

Q. You spoke of having been into Leary's and gone out of [262] there a little while before.

A. I was into Leary's about eight o'clock and a few moments after, and from that until nine o'clock.

Q. Then you went out at that time?

A. Yes sir.

Q. The fire broke out about half past nine?

A. Yes sir, from twenty to twenty-five minutes past nine.

Q. You said you went out on the sidewalk in front of your own place?

A. I went across the street from Leary's place. I lived on the other side of the street from Leary.

Q. Did you stand there?

A. I sat down on the sidewalk, a big high sidewalk that was there. There was a great big high fence not as high as that door. I sat down by that.

Q. You spoke of a party?

A. There was a party in front of Leary's house.

Q. At any time after you left [263] Leary's before you saw the fire, did you see anybody going out and in there?

A. Upon my word and honor, I didn't. I wasn't thinking of it. I know that everyone made an alarm, but nobody made an alarm to wake Leary up until I passed through the lot.

Q. Have you arrived in your own mind to any conclusion from the circumstances which you saw about that fire as to how that thing took fire?

A. I haven't, because I will tell you the reason why. If I had seen any sign of the fire, I wouldn't let the fire go far.

Q. Since that time thinking the matter over, comparing all the circumstances which you are acquainted with, have you arrived at any conclusion at all yourself?

A. I have not.

Q. You don't recollect of noticing any chimney or fire about there? [264]

A. There was not.

Q. You would not have been likely to have seen it?

A. There was not. I was sitting on the sidewalk. The corner of the fence where I was sitting down was coming out about two feet further than where my back was.

Q. In what direction was the wind blowing at that time?

A. As far as I could understand, the wind was blowing fair from the south. It might not be right straight south. It might be a little southwest.

Q. Was you in Leary's barn on Sunday before dark?

A. I wasn't in Leary's barn at all on Sunday. I used to go in there every evening, because my mother keeps a cow herself, and I used to go in there and bring feed. I knew where the cows were. I have been there in Leary's barn hundreds of times.

Q. Do you recollect noticing at [265] the right hand as you went in any quantity of shavings there?

A. I didn't, because I tell you because there was a little shed outside right up against the barn. The south side of the barn, a little shed that was used to keep coal and things in. It was built right up as high as the roof of the barn, but I never noticed shavings inside of the barn.

Q. Do you remember how long after you noticed this fire before any fire engines came on the ground?

A. Well, it was quite a while.

Q. Can you give a definite idea in minutes of the time?

A. I should think, so far as my understanding goes, that it was from ten to fifteen minutes.

Q. A minute would seem pretty long when you wanted help.

A. I didn't leave very long for I tell you, for fear anything might catch my own [266] place. I shoved out five horses there through an alley. That was the first [illeg.] I done. I lost about a hundred and twenty-five dollars worth of harness. I know the end I [illeg.] in two houses got afire, and we saved them by the help of people. There were people that lived east of Leary's house. A lot of Bohemian women. When the fire broke through, there was more shavings than a man could haul on his back in two months. East of Dalton's, nearer to Clinton.

Q. (By Mr. Williams) As a general thing all around in that vicinity, there is more or less shavings?

A. Yes, more or less. Anything more than that, I could not tell.

Q. Did you at the time you stood there at the sidewalk before the fire broke out, did you notice anyone going through Leary's yard?

A. Upon my word, I didn't. I was about two lots east of Leary's [267] barn or three. I was sitting at the head of White's house or head of his lot.

Q. You was on the other side of the street?

A. I was on the other side of the street, same as if I was seated on the other side of the street here, but the party carrying [on] was in the front of Leary's house and in McLaughlin's.

Q. Did you see anybody going in or out of there?

A. I didn't take any notice because if I had and saw anything like that, the fire would not go so far. But the fire was breaking out the side of the barn when I first saw it. I hollered as hard as I could holler, and I can holler pretty loud when I am outside.

Q. You say that at the end of this twenty-foot place, there was five feet more to that shed?[9]

A. It was not the end of it. It was the side of it, [268] the south side as you go into the yard. I guess there was about twenty or twenty-five feet between Leary's house and the barn.

Q. This shed runs in this way? (d)

A. Yes sir. The shed was right there.

Q. Was there any open windows in the shed in which he kept his coal and wood and shavings?[10]

A. The most I ever see in it anytime I went in there, they would have about a half a barrel full of shavings or a bag full and that is all.

Q. Was there any window at this end?

A. There was not, for the door was opening right into it.

Q. Which side of it was the door?

A. The south side of it.

Q. Out of the southeast corner of that shed (indicating on diagram), [illeg.] the other shed, or out of the barn? [269]

A. It run pretty near the whole length of the barn where they used to keep their wood

and coal, just as you was going into the barn on the right hand side. The fire was inside of the barn. It was not in the shed. It was not in the shed at all. It was in the barn.

Q. What was in the barn to burn? Would not the boards be rather damp and moist?

A. I suppose at the place they used to give hay to their cows and horse, there might be just the hay or something get right down where they stood.

Q. Was it a board floor?

A. It was a board floor.

Q. Did the fire spread pretty rapidly from Leary's barn?

A. Not very rapidly. The next thing that took afire was a barn at the west end of it.[11]

Q. Do you know when Dalton's house took fire? [270]

A. I don't. I didn't keep account of it. I went and got my horses out.

Q. Did you see the first engine when it came there?

A. As far as I can understand, it was from ten to fifteen minutes after I hollered "fire" before I saw the engine.

Q. How many buildings were on fire?

A. I do not recollect.

Q. Was there more than one or two?

A. There might be two barns on fire.

Q. Do you know whether there was more or less?

A. Well b'God, I could not tell, it might be more and it might be less. I know two was afire.

Q. During this time before the engines had arrived, had you succeeded in getting your horses out from your barn?

A. I hadn't the whole of them out. I had two out. I had [271] a black horse I drive myself and a big roan horse.

Q. Did you have somebody assisting you?

A. I hadn't them all together. I had four in one barn and one in another barn. I had a black horse that I drive myself and another horse. I took him out and a big roan horse with him.

Q. (By Mr. Williams) How large was that barn of Mr. Leary's?

A. It was about twenty feet.[12]

Q. There was a hay loft overhead?

A. There was, and at the same time there was a house full of shavings that fronted on

Taylor Street that nobody, so far as I can understand, had been living in it for quite awhile.
A good many of these young scoundrels living
around the city used to make their home in it.

Q. Did he have a barn in the rear of it?

A. Yes sir. Back up to Leary's [272] barn.[13]

Q. How wide was that alley?

A. I do not know. It might be fourteen or
fifteen feet.[14]

Q. The barn was in the rear of this house?

A. Yes sir.

Q. Right on the line?

A. Yes sir. It was not a barn. It was a big
shed.

Q. Was there any door opening into the
alley?

A. I cannot tell you. I know the barn was
opening [going?] out of the house. Washburn's
house was right opposite Leary's.[15]

Q. The alleys were not wide?

A. Not very wide. It is a fifteen-foot alley
on the side I live on or a sixteen-foot. I guess the
alley was the same width there.[16]

Q. Taylor Street is next north of DeKoven?

A. Yes sir.

Q. What street is next?

A. Forquer. [273]

Q. Then what?

A. Ewing.

Q. Then Mather?

A. No, then comes Polk Street, then
comes Mather Street, then comes Sebor, then
comes Harrison.

Q. The blocks there are quite short, aren't
they?

A. Not very short. I can tell how many
lots there are in the block I live in.

Q. What is the depth there?

A. The lot I live on is one hundred feet
and six inches.[17]

Q. Do you know of anybody going to the
box to turn the alarm?

A. No sir, I do not. All I know about it I
have told you. I tried to save my own things. I
knew that mother was building a new house. Father wasn't alive. There were three of us boys
there. My father was buried twenty-six or
twenty-seven years, and my mother never put a
stepfather over us, and all we earned we saved
it and bought [274] a place for her.

Q. This is Washburn's house? (m)

A. The shed run on the edge of the alley.

Q. Did you say that shed was filled up
with trash?

A. No, I did not say anything like it. I did
not say so. I said there was nobody living in
Washburn's house.

Q. You say these vagrant boys that were in
the habit of living about there were in the habit
of congregating in that house?

A. Yes sir. That is what I heard.

Q. Was it in the house or shed?

A. I heard them say it was in the house.

Q. Was the house open so that they could
get in?

A. I believe so. The house has been quite
awhile so, nobody living in it.

Q. [Now?] did I understand you to [275]
say that the fire was in the upper or lower portions of the barn when you went in?

A. In the lower portion.

Q. What seemed to be on fire?

A. I couldn't tell. I got excited.

Q. It was filled with fire?

A. It was all smoke and fire and flames.

Q. You could not tell whether the fire was
above?

A. No, the fire was from below.

Daniel Sullivan Notes

1. Sullivan's address of 134 DeKoven Street
was on the south side of the street. Curiously, the
1871 Chicago city directory, which contains pre-fire
information, indicates that Daniel Sullivan lived
at 135 DeKoven Street and not at number 134.
This is incorrect. 135 DeKoven Street was on the
north side of the street and was the address of
James Dalton, whose house was directly east of the
O'Leary and McLaughlin homes. See *1871 City Directory*, pp. 244, 867; Andreas, vol. 2, p. 713; *Robinson's Atlas*, vol. 1, plate 6; Chicago Title Insurance
Company records; Daniel Sullivan, *Inquiry*, vol.
[1], p. 262.

2. Sullivan may have been a drayman for
Chase, Hanford & Co., an oil company. See F. H.
Shults letter; Statement of J. C. Chapeck; *1870
City Directory*, p. 1069; *1871 City Directory*, pp. 194,
1055–56.

3. Sullivan appears to be referring to a house
address—136 DeKoven Street. *Robinson's Atlas* discloses that the DeKoven Street property addresses
were numbered ascendingly from east to west.
Does Sullivan's statement indicate that after the
fire he moved into another house immediately

west of his home at 134 DeKoven Street? As discussed in chapter 4, note 55, Catherine Sullivan owned three half lots on the south side of DeKoven Street and west of William White's home. Figure 63 indicates there was a vacant parcel west of Sullivan's house and possibly a barn west of that. Perhaps there was also a house on this "barn" parcel. But on the other hand, *Robinson's Atlas* indicates that there was no 136 DeKoven Street address. Instead, all three of these Sullivan properties had the same address—134 DeKoven Street. See *Robinson's Atlas*, vol. 1, plate 6.

4. Contrary to Sullivan's testimony, Mrs. O'Leary was *not* an old woman. Is Sullivan consciously distancing himself from Mrs. O'Leary, allying with the sentiment expressed by the October 18 *Times*, published about five weeks earlier, which also called her an old woman? See "The Fire," *Chicago Times*, 18 October 1871, p. 1.

5. Neither Patrick O'Leary nor his wife mentioned Sullivan's visit when they were questioned by the Board.

6. A. T. Andreas or one of his employees must have interviewed Daniel Sullivan while Andreas was researching his *History of Chicago*. The historian made the following comment in his book concerning the time the fire started: "Mr. Sullivan's statement before the commissioners places the time at about 9:30. He now says 'about nine o'clock.'" See Andreas, vol. 2, p. 708.

7. Catharine McLaughlin was the second person to testify on Saturday, November 25. Daniel Sullivan was the fourth. During inquiry questioning, Mrs. McLaughlin indicated that the O'Learys' door opened out into the alleyway that ran between the O'Leary and Dalton properties. Sullivan testified that from his alleged position across the street, he ran across the street and kept hollering "fire, fire, fire," ran past the O'Leary home, and "made right straight in the barn." His testimony suggests that he ran through this alleyway, as he told the fire officials (p. 263) that "nobody made an alarm to wake Leary up until I passed through the lot." Also, this alleyway would have been the quickest route to the barn (see Figure 54). It would appear that a "hollering" Sullivan ran within a few feet of the O'Learys' doorway. If this were so, why didn't the O'Learys testify that they heard him? After questioning both Mrs. McLaughlin and Daniel Sullivan on the same day, why didn't the fire officials recall Mrs. McLaughlin and ask her if she heard Sullivan as he allegedly ran by? At the very least, why didn't the commissioners and marshals question Sullivan further about his dubious testimony? See Catharine McLaughlin, *Inquiry*, vol. [1], p. 239;

"The Great Fire," Chicago Tribune, 26 November 1871, p. 1.

8. Although Sullivan testified that he slipped on the wet boards and fell, he said nothing about his peg leg slipping between the boards, as the November 26 *Tribune* indicates. See "The Great Fire," *Chicago Tribune*, 26 November 1871, p. 1.

9. There is no earlier reference to "this twenty-foot place." Although the commissioners and marshals may be referring to a diagram with a labeled dimension of twenty feet (see, for example, Daniel Sullivan, *Inquiry*, vol. [1], pp. 260–61, 268, 274), the transcript of Sullivan's testimony contains no reference to "five feet" up to this point.

10. This question appears to be in reference to Patrick O'Leary's earlier testimony: "I had shavings in the shed and coal and wood and everything." See Patrick O'Leary, *Inquiry*, vol. [1], p. 251.

11. Sullivan appears to be referring to Anne Murray's barn. See, e.g., Mrs. O'Leary's testimony: "At the time I first saw [the fire], my barn was [afire] and Mrs. Murray's barn was afire and Mr. Dalton's little shed." On the other hand, both Catherine Sullivan and Catharine McLaughlin indicated during the inquiry that the first buildings they saw on fire were the O'Leary barn and Dalton's house; neither one mentioned Mrs. Murray's barn. Patrick O'Leary testified that because "the fire was too strong when I got up," he couldn't tell if Dalton's house was on fire or not. Mr. O'Leary told the fire officials about seeing his own barn afire, but also said nothing about Mrs. Murray's barn. See Catherine O'Leary, *Inquiry*, vol. [1], p. 62; Catherine Sullivan, *Inquiry*, vol. [1], p. 115; Catharine McLaughlin, *Inquiry*, vol. [1], p. 231; Patrick O'Leary, *Inquiry*, vol. [1], p. 245.

12. The transcript indicates that Sullivan described the size of the barn as simply "about twenty feet." The *Tribune* summary of Sullivan's testimony, however, suggests that Sullivan told the fire officials that the barn was sixteen feet by twenty feet and fourteen feet high. This is consistent with Patrick O'Leary's testimony concerning the barn's dimensions. See "The Great Fire," *Chicago Tribune*, 26 November 1871, p. 1; Patrick O'Leary, *Inquiry*, vol. [1], p. 251.

13. A. T. Andreas' "Plat of Locality Where Fire Originated" (Figure 57) seems to be consistent with Sullivan's testimony, as it shows a shed across the alley from the O'Leary barn. On the other hand, Mrs. Anton Axsmith's diagram of the O'Leary neighborhood discloses a wooden walk opposite the barn (Figure 56).

14. Sullivan is correct. Chicago Title Insurance Company records indicate that the alley was

fifteen feet wide. Strangely, the *Chicago Tribune* account of his testimony suggests that he described the alley as being "about twelve feet wide." See "The Great Fire," *Chicago Tribune*, 26 November 1871, p. 1.

15. Sullivan is incorrect. Chicago Title Insurance Company records disclose that Sullivan is undoubtedly referring to the property of "W. W. Washburn." Washburn's property was *not* "right opposite" the O'Leary house. Rather, it was across the alley but fifty feet to the west (Figure 79).

16. Sullivan makes a very good guess. Chicago Title Insurance Company records disclose that the alley in back of his house was 15.5 feet wide.

17. Daniel Sullivan is exactly correct. Chicago Title Insurance Company records reveal that Catherine Sullivan's one-and-one-half lots were originally 118 feet deep. In 1855, the north ten feet of her land was taken for the widening of DeKoven Street. In this same year, the south 7.5 feet of the Sullivan property (together with the north eight feet of the adjoining land to the south) was taken to create an alley that was 15.5 feet wide. Therefore, in 1871 the Sullivan property was 100.5 feet deep.

MICHAEL C. HICKEY

[140]

Michael C. Hickey sworn[1]
November 28, 1871
(21st witness)

Q. Are you a member of the police department?

A. Yes sir.

Q. What is your position?

A. Captain of police.

Q. What precinct?

A. First precinct.

Q. Do you know anything about the origin and progress of the fire, October 8 and 9? What did you first see of it?

A. The first I saw the fire was on the West Side—the second precinct.

Q. At what time?

A. I think that was about nine o'clock. I think it was somewhere in that neighborhood. I am not positive as to the exact time.

Q. Where were you when you saw it?

A. I was at home getting supper.

Q. That was where? [141]

A. I was at 318 Calumet Avenue.

Q. What did you do?

A. I heard the alarm from the Cottage Grove station.[2] The fire bell gave the alarm. I started out to the door and waited a moment, and I heard a general alarm given. I started for the city as quick as I could. I got to the old Bridewell[3] where our police station was, and I went in as quick as possible and ordered every man that was there to turn out and go to the West Side fire. They had all done so, for I gave them orders in the evening at roll call in case of fire. I talked to the superintendent in regard to it, and he gave me orders to take every available man I had to whichever side of the river the fire might occur. We talked it over on Sunday on account of the Saturday night fire. We talked the matter over, and he told me he wanted me to turn out every man I had in case of emergency to any side of the river that a fire might [142] occur. I went over on the West Side. I forget what street it was. I went on Canal Street until I got pretty near where the fire was. I think I was there but a very short time when I met Captain Miller.[4] I joined Captain Miller and told him I was ready to render him any assistance I could with my men. So we placed the men all around everywhere we thought they could be of any use and went along every place we could to try and help the fire department. We tore down several old sheds to try and stop the fire in the rear with some firemen. We helped all we could and tried to get people out of houses and tried to get furniture saved and tried to get them from getting killed or hurt until the fire reached—I think it was Van Buren Street, or pretty near Van Buren Street.

Q. Across Canal?

A. Yes sir.

Q. Where was the fire burning at that time? [143]

A. The fire was burning north. The fire was two blocks or three blocks south of Van Buren, I forget now which, and it was burning north all the time. I was there before St. Paul's church took fire. I think I spoke to the chief engineer. He was very busy at the time. I told him the cupola of the church was afire. He immediately got an engine, I think, or a hose onto the church, but it went very quick. It did not last any time. I also spoke to him about somebody giving me the information. I think it was Captain Miller. Said I, "There is a match factory directly north of the church.[5] That is going to make an awful fire if it gets there," and I think the chief made the remark to me, "I know it, and we must try to do something," or words to that effect, and at that time, I think, or not very long after, another fire took place in a wooden frame building that was north of the church.

Q. Did the fire appear to eat its **[144]** way regularly to that?

A. No sir, it jumped. The church took fire, and I think the biggest portion of the fire was at the block south of there, working its way north.

Q. You know it was separated some distance by buildings not burning?

A. Yes sir.

Q. Do you know the exact distance?

A. It may be but a block; it may be more. At the time the church caught fire, I know that I ran down where the buildings were on fire. I ran north to St. Paul's. I know we ran some distance to get to St. Paul's church when the cupola took fire. I remember there was an old gentleman who owned some buildings directly west of St. Paul's church come to me and asked me if I would not speak to the chief engineer to play on the buildings and to try and save them if possible. I told him he had better see the chief himself—that there the chief was. **[145]** He had better see him himself. After that church got afire, we went down to the next street and went down to the planing mill. The fire ran along the street. I know Captain Miller and myself took some men into Bateham's planing mill and tried to put out cinders that were falling there pretty thick and over the sidewalk. Then there was a rush out on Canal Street. There was some trouble on Canal Street in a saloon there, and Captain Miller and I went out there with some men and tried to stop a quarrel on Canal Street. They were gutting a saloon there—trying to take everything out of it. We went along before the fire, trying to keep things clear until we got to Van Buren Street. In Van Buren Street I do not know whether it was the first engineer or somebody else said, "You had better send some men in this building and try and keep the fire off." Sergeant Lull[6] was there, I think, **[146]** and I told him and five or six men to try and keep the sparks off, if possible.

Q. Which side of Van Buren Street was that?

A. I think the south side of Van Buren Street. I was under the impression it was the south side. I may be mistaken. And the men remained there until they were driven off by the heat. A little while after—I cannot tell how long—somebody hallooed, "The South Side is on fire! There is a fire on the South Side!" and I think I run up until I got sight of the fire. I got one or two officers—officer Morgan[7] was one of them. Said I, "You go and get all the South Side men you can get hold of and get them on the South Side as quick as possible." At that time, if I am not mistaken, Van Buren Street bridge was on fire. We could not get across Adams Street or Van Buren Street and had to run to Madison Street. We ran as fast as we could **[147]** to Madison Street, and as we crossed the bridge, I looked and said, "The gas factory is on fire!" We ran up Market Street until we came to Monroe and found it was Powell's factory.[8] The fire was then just extending the other side of Monroe Street.

Q. Was it extending south of Monroe?

A. It crossed the street there, and I saw that there was three or four houses on fire there at the same time, and this tar material in the yard of Powell's was burning very fast, and the old buildings there were burning pretty fast.

Q. Were his works extensive?

A. No sir, not very. It was a kind of yard or shed there.

Q. Do you know whether he had large or small quantities of this roofing material?

A. Not from my own knowledge I do not know. I understood there was quite a lot of it in there. They generally bought, I believe, the tar from the gas company and used it for streets **[148]** and for this composition roofing. I ran clear around and somebody says, "The Armory is on fire!" I turned back and ran through and got around to the Armory. The hose tower room was on fire as I got around.

Q. There was a tower there where they hung hose—a room where they stored old hose?

A. Yes sir. Then the fire extended in that patch—a lot of wooden buildings on Monroe Street or Quincy Street. The fire then extended south into that patch.[9]

Q. What do you call that patch?

A. It was a combination of wooden buildings.

Q. (By Mr. Williams) Was that row between the Armory and Wells Street?

A. No, it was north of Adams Street. That was on fire. The fire extended across Adams Street into Mr. Ogden's property there.[10] When I got around, the fire got into the Armory. It went right through, and just as I got in west of the Armory, the maga- [149] zine, I should judge, exploded and made quite an explosion. Then the cry was, "The gas house was going to be blown up!" and people were running in every direction and said, "Get out of the way, the gas house will be blown up in a moment!"

Q. Did you see the gas works on fire?

A. A portion of it was on fire. The retort works was on fire after that. The purifying house was on fire. I was there when that exploded. I was on Adams Street near Fifth Avenue when that exploded.

Q. That purifying house around on Monroe Street?

A. Yes sir.

Q. Do you know what management was had about the gas that was manufactured there? What disposition was had of it?

A. Whatever amount of gas was on hand was in the holder.

Q. Did you notice it being up pretty well?

A. I thought it was up to a considerable height. Of course [150] all the gas that had been consumed the fore part of the evening reduced it down from its general height. As the gas is consumed through the city, the holder goes down with the pressure. I heard somebody say—I could not tell positively who it was—it was all safe now; the gas had been allowed to escape. There was such confusion! Men, women, and children hollering and yelling and drawing out their things—the streets were just perfectly thronged with these human beings trying to get out of these patches, and they were all hollering and running in every direction. It was nothing but excitement. Then Monroe Street took fire and was burning right along. The wind was blowing very strong from the southwest. It was blowing very strong, [151] and I got around on Fifth Avenue and come down and headed off the fire there to see what the result was on the corner of Monroe and Fifth Avenue, and everything seemed to be on fire both sides of the street. I got down to Monroe Street, and pretty much all those buildings on Fifth Avenue were

on fire. I ran down to Madison Street and came back on the other side as quick as I could. I got down on Monroe Street towards LaSalle, and all the buildings on both sides of Monroe Street were on fire between Wells and LaSalle Street, and there was a mass of people there trying to get things out of the buildings.

Q. Had the Bryan Block[11] got afire then?

A. No sir. I am speaking of between Fifth Avenue [152] and LaSalle Street.

Q. Had that building on the corner of Monroe and LaSalle took fire?

A. No, the fire hadn't reached there then. It was working off towards Mr. Otis's building,[12] more towards Madison Street at that time.

Q. Was there much wind?

A. Considerable, and the wind seemed to increase. As the fire increased, the wind seemed to increase. It increased more and more after that. I went right onto LaSalle Street.[13] I went down to Madison Street and the buildings in the rear—it got into Madison Street from the wooden buildings in the rear. Everything was burning that way.

Q. Did you notice whether there was any buildings on fire in the basements before the roof burned or the upper portions? [153]

A. I think I noticed one building on LaSalle Street between Washington and Madison; if I don't mistake, the building was burning underneath in the basement. I think there was one building burning there, but the buildings were burning from the rear. The first thing I observed when I got around to the Board of Trade[14]—I went on Clark Street and came around on Washington Street—I saw the tower of the courthouse was on fire. I went right along to LaSalle Street. The buildings on LaSalle Street were on fire. I went around in front of the courthouse—on the north side of the courthouse. The courthouse was pretty well on fire. The roof was all afire. I went to the jail door; I think there was some parties wanted me [154] to go to the jail door and try and have the prisoners let out. I went to the jail door and spoke to Eddy Longley.[15] Said I, "Who is here?" Said he, "I am." Said I, "The courthouse is on fire. It won't be five minutes before this roof will go in." I spoke a few words to him, and he came out and looked around and spoke a few words more. They were hollering over to the Sherman House.[16] I ran across the square, and there was a lot of people at the corner of the Sherman House on Clark Street. They asked me what I thought. I said, "You had better get out of here." I went back and they were hollering to let out the prisoners. I went back and said, "Mr. Longley, you had better let them out." Said he, "I hate to take the respons- [155] ibility." I said, "I will take the responsibility."[17] We were about two minutes talking there before the bell came down.[18] Said I, "You had better get them out as quick as you can." Said he, "What will you do?" Said I, "I have got seven or eight men with me. Take the murderers and get them over to the North Side." Said he, "What will we do with the rest of them?" Said I, "You can't take them now." The flames were coming down there and sparks as thick as snow. You couldn't hardly escape them anywhere. Men were running with their coats burning. We let out the prisoners, and the fire struck the Sherman House and the blocks along there, and there was some hollering again that Lake Street was on fire. I went down onto Lake Street, [156] and there was a fire on Lake Street. We hardly got down to Lake Street when somebody else hollered that there was a fire on Dearborn Street. Ran up there and it was, and so [I ran] right along just running around there until the next afternoon. Everything was on fire. Every place you turned was on fire.

Q. Do you know of any explosion of gas mains or anything that appeared like it?

A. I heard the explosion of the purifying house. I paid more attention to that. Our attention was called to it at the time by somebody hollering that the gas house was going to be blown up.

Q. Did you notice the "manholes"[19] of the sewers, the covers to them, as to whether any of them were burned underneath? [157]

A. I haven't paid particular attention to that. I know there was a good many of them burned on the top next day. I saw they were very dangerous, a good many of them burned.

Q. (By Mr. Williams) Did you see any of them blown off?

A. I do not remember.

Q. What did you do with the prisoners in the Armory?[20]

A. We turned them out.

Q. All of them?

A. Every one. And only got out by the skin of our teeth ourselves.

Q. Did you save anything?

A. We saved our books, saved the telegraph instrument—that they saved when the bridge took fire. They got that apart and sent it out. We saved our books and the greater portion of what deposits we had there for the prisoners. The prisoners we all let go. Most of the men [158] lost their clothing there. I had twenty-nine men, I think, burned out and most of them lost every bit of uniform they had.

Q. Did you have a large quantity of small arms?

A. We had seven hundred stand of arms set away in boxes. We had six pieces of artillery with all the equipments. They were in the Bridewell.

Q. Where were they stored at the time?

A. The guns we had taken to the Bridewell and put in under a shed there. The harness was in the artillery room hung up on a hook. The small arms were in boxes stored away. These hadn't been moved. They were all lost.

Q. Do you know what became of the artillery?

A. The artillery was burned [159] up. The woodwork of it was all burned up at the Bridewell. Every bit of it.

Q. What became of the guns, the cannon?

A. Sometime after, I don't know exactly how long, but [it] may be two weeks or it may be more or it may be less, I was going over from the Central Station[21] to my station; and I saw three or four men coming along with a very large truck; and they had five pieces, I think, of artillery on the truck. I stopped them on the street. I looked at them and said, "Those are our guns from the Armory." I spoke to the men and said, "Hold on, my friends; I want to see you. Where did you get these?" He said, "I got them out of the old Bridewell." I said, "By what authority have you taken them?" and he told me, "The [160] comptroller." Said I, "That is not right exactly." Said he, "If you doubt my word, I will show you the order." And he pulled out his order and showed it to me.

Q. Did the order show that they were sold?

A. The order showed they were sold to the Northwestern Manufacturing Company.[22]

Q. By the comptroller?

A. Yes sir. The small arms were in boxes in the artillery room in the old Armory. With all our stationery—and everything connected—desks and everything else all stood in one room and the room locked up. All our stationery for the next six months. Everything we had that could not be moved to the Bridewell we had that stowed away in a room and the room locked up. All the bedding, [161] pretty much of all the police department were burned up there—a great portion of their bedding.

Q. Was the police force in good order, doing all the service they could during the fire?

A. Yes sir. I never saw men that worked any better than they did and worked while a greater portion of them were burned out and did not know where their families were for two or three days after.[23] They lay on the floor for two or three nights with no cover, until we went up and got some government blankets, and they used them for the balance of the time, I think two weeks, lying on the floor, and done duty all the time, those that could. There was four or five men wounded. One got his leg broken or sprained. [162] There was another man got his finger bit. There was four or five disabled for some time after.[24]

Q. Do you think there was any extraordinary visitation of thieves from abroad during the fire?

A. I shouldn't wonder but there was a good many, but I think they left mighty quick. They saw things were getting very hot. Saw the citizens were going to get the law in their own hands. I think a good many of them "lit out"[25] as soon as they found what was going on.

Q. Do you know of any occasions of violence towards parties, lynching or anything of that kind, any authentic cases?

A. Yes. There was a matter that occurred on the corner of Washington early in the morning—Washington and Wabash [163] Avenue. That was the morning of the fire. There was a lot of thieves who were stealing this property on Wabash Avenue through the wholesale stores there. They were fetching it along in loads. It was the opinion of everybody that we would save that portion of the city over there south of Washington Street. We went to work and put this property into Mr. Farwell's store.[26] I should judge it was several thousand dollars worth. We took it off them and there was quite a crowd of citizens there tried to take it away from them, and we fought them there nearly half an hour.

About that time Mr. Mason's son[27] came to me and asked me where the chief engineer was.[28] Said I, "I have not seen the chief engineer all this morning." [164] Said he, "Do you know where he is?" Said I, "I do not. I cannot tell where he is." Said he, "We want to blow up some buildings here. We have got some powder here, and father sent me here, and he wants these buildings blown up." Said I, "It is the duty of the chief engineer. I have no power to do it. If I do it, I am responsible. I don't hesitate to do anything I can, but I don't want to take the responsibility." He said, "I will go back and see my father again." He went away and came back again and said, "Father says that you go and do it, and he would hold you harmless." Said I, "If he says so, I will do it." Said he, "How will you go about it?" Said I, "I have got two or three policemen here, and Mr. Hildreth was standing by, [165] and said he, 'I will assist you.'" Said I, "Have you got any fuse?" Said he, "No, we haven't got a bit of fuse." Said I, "Where can we get some?" Said he, "I don't know. The places where fuse was sold are all burned up. I do not know how we can manage without fuse." Well, we went off and got some wicking and substituted that for fuse. We got some powder. It came up by way of Michigan Avenue in a fire wagon. One of the firemen had it, and it was covered with tarpaulins, wet. I told them they had better keep it on the lake shore, and keep it out of the way as far as possible. About that time, the citizens found out it was powder in the wagon, and they went for the driver, a young man in the fire department, and they were going [166] to lynch him and hang him to a big telegraph post there, and some man came to me. I ran back, and two or three of them had hold of him by the neck and were marching him off. They asked him, "Where are you going with that powder?" Said he, "Captain Hickey and the mayor sent it there." They said, "Damn Captain Hickey and the mayor!" I got there, and we stopped them. Said I, "If you will go about your business, we will try and do some good." So I got him away and told them what it was for. Told them we were trying to save some property if we could not do any better. We got into a building, got some seven or eight kegs of powder on the floor, and we got this wick attached to it and [167] got some rubbish and piled it right onto this powder, and by that time the roof was on fire. At this time the house was all deserted, and we got on the other side of the street and went and kept the crowds back. They were running towards this building where we were going to blow up. That was one of the lynching cases.

Q. Did you succeed in blowing up the building?

A. We blowed up a portion of it.

Q. Did it blow up before the fire got down to it?

A. It did.

Q. Which building was that?

A. Directly north of Kinsley's eating house.[29]

Q. On Wabash Avenue?

A. Yes sir.

Q. The one at the corner of Randolph Street?

A. No, Washington, north of [168] that. Then we went directly across the street, north of the Second Presbyterian Church,[30] and after consulting a little while, we thought we had better blow up that building and see if we could not save Drake and Farwell's block there.[31] So we went in there.

Q. A drug store?

A. No sir. It was a boot and shoe store, I think. By George, I was so excited from one thing and another that I could not tell what was in half the stores. It was the building north of the Second Presbyterian Church fronting on Dearborn Park and on Wabash Avenue. We had some trouble there in getting people out of the house. There was a portion of that building blown up.

Q. How much powder did you put in? [169]

A. We put in from seven to eight kegs of powder in some of them.

Q. Where did you put the powder in?

A. On the first floor and put some rubbish around it. But it was working uphill without fuse.

Q. Did the wick answer the purpose?

A. It did, but it was very slow and was uncertain. You might go and set it, and then it would go out. It went out once or twice, at least once, and we had to go back and set it on fire again. It was very uncertain and very dangerous. You could not tell the moment you would be blown up. You might wait an hour, and per-

haps by the time you got inside of the door, away went the whole building. One other thing that I remember in regard to lynching [170] was a man on the corner of Harrison and Clark Street, a peaceable man, a man I knew and a good citizen. About five hundred people got around him. That was two nights after the fire, I think it was. They licked him on the start and got together to lynch him on a lamppost. He went in an alley to draw water. We brought him to the station, and there was about five hundred people followed him up. We got him to the station. It was little Mc[*illeg.*].[32]

Q. What was his business?

A. He has been connected with the press.[33] We got him away from them. They were trying to hang him to a lamp post.[34] They were perfectly loony, didn't seem to have any sense or any reason at all. They thought he was trying to set fire to [*blank*].[35] [171]

Q. How many of your men of the first precinct were burned out?

A. I think it was twenty-nine.

Q. How did the fire department behave during that fire? Did you see any of the officers or men intoxicated?

A. I saw all of the marshals on this side of the river. I saw Marshal Schank on the other side of State the next day and the day after.[36] I forget whether I saw the Chief Engineer or not. I may have seen him, but I don't recollect it.

Q. When was that?

A. That was the day of the fire.

Q. On Monday?

A. On Monday.

Q. Where were you stationed?

A. I was everywhere where I thought I could do any good during the fire.

Q. As to that day during the fire, where was your place of operations? [172]

A. In the South Division. Altogether I was from Dearborn Street to Wabash Avenue and State. I was all along. Through every place that I could go that I could get around.

Q. That was rather in the rear of the fire?

A. Working against the fire, yes sir.

Q. You say you saw the chief and talked with him on Sunday night on the West Side?

A. Yes sir.

Q. You saw Mr. Schank?

A. I saw all the marshals there, I think, every one of them.

Q. (By Marshal Williams) Did you see a stream on the Sherman House front?

A. I think I did if I remember, but there was so much hallooing and screaming and excited people and trying to get people away from the fire and trying to get the prisoners out of the jail, that [173] I really can't remember.

Q. The prisoners all ran towards Clark Street?

A. Yes sir. Some without coats and some with blankets around their necks. I remember one of them, the blanket took fire on his back, and the blanket was on fire when he crossed the square. Another gentleman got his coat on fire on the corner. I ran for him and tried to put out the fire.

Q. You didn't see any drunken firemen or anything disorderly in the fire department during the time?

A. I didn't. I saw the firemen doing all they could under the circumstances. I think it was a matter of impossibility to stop that fire when it once got on Monroe Street. I think there was nothing could stop it but Providence alone. After it got so furious, there was no handling [174] of it. I have seen men taken at the corner of Clark and Randolph Street coming around that corner there, and the wind would take them fifty feet before they could get on their feet. You could not stand the heat. The wind would burn your face, alone. The wind grew stronger around that corner. Around the courthouse it seemed to be worse than any other place I could see.

Q. Did you see any person perish in consequence of the fire?

A. I do not remember of seeing any person perish. They told me on Lake Street when I got around there that there was a man supposed to be perished on Randolph between Dearborn and Clark. The howling of the wind, the hallooing of people, and screaming around that corner was the most [175] horrible thing that ever I heard in my life or anybody else will ever hear. You could not hear yourself with the howl of the wind and the howling of the flames. You could not imagine what a scene there was there. It was the most terrible and horrible sight I ever saw in my life. That was right around the Sherman House corner. There may be several things that have passed my memory. There was so much excitement, but when my memory is refreshed in regard to it, I can state.

Q. Do you know anything about the letting off of gas in the gas house?

A. Nothing from my own knowledge. But what I have heard.

Q. (By Mr. Schank) When that gas exploded, did it make a great report or raise the building any?

A. It was an adjoining build- [176] ing. It was not the main building of the gas house. It was the purifying house fronting on Monroe Street.

Q. Did it raise that building any?

A. It knocked the building all to pieces there. I didn't see it immediately after, but I saw afterwards. Where the gas is manufactured, it goes right into this purifying house. It is purified there, and then there is another lead that lets it into the holder. Then it is purified in the holder and goes into the street.

Q. Where does the residue of this purifying go? In the sewer?

A. No sir. It is carted off into the street. It is purified with lime, and that is carted off into the street after they get through with it.

Q. Use it for filling the streets?

A. Yes sir. [177]

Q. There is a gas tar that is frequently sold?

A. It is separated in the factory where the gas is made. It runs through a large pipe where there is a washer that washes the gas and separates the gas and tar. That runs out into the tar holder, where it is pumped out afterwards and put into barrels while the gas goes off into another part, where it is purified and then it is let into the holder.

Q. When passing into the gasometer after the last process, does it not go through water?

A. No sir, I think not.

Q. There is a basin of water under?

A. That is for the holder. When the gas is made, it goes into the holder, goes up the pipe higher than the water which lays in the bottom.

Q. How is that water led off?

A. The holder comes down every night.

Q. Where does this water that [178] is [in] the base of the gasometer go to?

A. That I could not tell.

Q. Your police station or armory has been on the opposite side of the street from the gas works?[37]

A. Yes sir.

Q. Have you ever experienced difficulty from the escape of gas from their gas house through their sewer into yours so as to render it unhealthy for men to remain there?

A. Yes sir.

Q. How was that?

A. The only way we can account for that is this: The main sewer runs down Adams Street to the bridge. There is a sewer runs out of the gas house and from the Armory, and both empty into the main sewer down Adams Street, and when there is wind from the Northwest, it blowed that all up into the Armory where we had **[179]** no stench trap to stop it and could not have under the circumstances because of the amount of soil that passed through there.

Q. Was that little or of considerable magnitude?

A. It has been of considerable magnitude and has been a great nuisance. Complained of for the last seven or eight years.

Q. Then there must have been something in the nature of the gas, pure or impure, to escape from the gas house into the sewer?

A. Certainly there was very much. The washings of the gas are always going right through the sewer, I suppose.

Q. You have seen most of the fires that have occurred in Chicago for the last twenty odd years. I would ask you from your great experience what you thought of the possibility of stopping this fire **[180]** in its earliest stages?

A. I do not know. I think myself I saw the fire department do all they could in regard to it. Used all [exertions?] I thought to try to stop it. I wasn't at all points where the fire was, and I couldn't be a judge. I thought from the way the men worked, they were doing the best they could.

Q. Did it move more rapidly than any fire you ever saw before or not?

A. Yes sir, it did. More than any fire I ever saw in the world. The West Side was a [siphon?] to the South Side. It went from that Armory to LaSalle Street in less than no time. I never saw anything that went so quick. There was a portion of the time, too, on the West Side that it went very rapidly there.

Q. On which side was the most **[181]** combustible material, the South or West?

A. From where the fire took place in both places, I don't think there was but very little

difference. I wasn't so very well acquainted with the West Side, but I noticed they were all wooden buildings there and manufacturing establishments of some kind or nature. I did not notice many brick buildings in the neighborhood or many stone structures. And the South Side where it took fire there—excepting the Armory and gas house, they are pretty much all wood there. That is in that certain neighborhood there.

Q. Was all that woodwork dry, unusually so?

A. Yes sir, very dry.

Q. How long had we been without rain to any extent?

A. I hadn't noticed much rain **[182]** for two or three months before.

Michael C. Hickey Notes

1. At the time of the fire, Michael Hickey was captain of the first precinct. In 1873, he resigned from the force, apparently amidst charges of corruption. The Board of Police found him innocent and ordered him reinstated. Later, similar charges were brought against Hickey, but he was again vindicated. In 1875, he was promoted to General Superintendent of Police, and Hickey remained at this position until he was removed by Mayor Carter H. Harrison in 1878. See Flinn, pp. 123, 142–43, 147, 150, 165, 189–90, 205.

2. The police substation for the first precinct was on Cottage Grove Avenue. See *1870 City Directory*, p. 914; *1871 City Directory*, p. 34; Flinn, pp. 119–20, 493.

3. The Bridewell was originally a prison and was located at the northwest corner of Polk and Wells streets. At the time of the fire, however, the Bridewell was home to the first precinct police station, as the precinct's usual headquarters at the Armory building, which was at the southwest corner of Franklin and Adams streets, was then undergoing repairs. See *1871 City Directory*, pp. 34, 54; Andreas, vol. 1, p. 204; Andreas, vol. 2, pp. 84, 730; Flinn, pp. 99, 132, 478; John Moses and Joseph Kirkland, eds., *History of Chicago, Illinois* (Chicago: Munsell & Co., 1895), vol. 1, p. 259; Duis, pp. 337–38.

4. George Miller was a police captain at the second precinct station. See *1870 City Directory*, p. 914; *1871 City Directory*, p. 629; Flinn, p. 120.

5. This match factory was probably the Garden City Match Factory, located at 316-318 South Clinton Street. See *1870 City Directory*, pp. 300,

1059; "Boring for Facts," *Chicago Tribune*, 15 November 1871, p. 1; *Robinson's Atlas*, vol. 1, plate 3.

6. Louis J. Lull was a sergeant at the first precinct station. See *1870 City Directory*, pp. 509, 914; *1871 City Directory*, p. 566; Flinn, pp. 120, 123. Lull was the forty-fifth witness to testify during the inquiry investigation.

7. James Morgan was a first precinct police officer. See *1870 City Directory*, p. 585; *1871 City Directory*, p. 641.

8. In the Board's final report (see Appendix E), the commissioners noted that "Powell's roofing establishment" adjoined the gas works. The formal name was probably Powell, Getchell & Co. See "The Great Fire," *Chicago Evening Journal*, 12 December 1871, p. [4]; *1870 City Directory*, pp. 1096–97.

9. This was probably the infamous "Conley's Patch," which was on the city's South Side near Adams and Wells streets (Figures 5, 10).

10. "Ogden" was a famous Chicago name. Mahlon D. Ogden lived on the city's North Side in a palatial home that is now the site of the Newberry Library. Although his house was in the "burnt district," it survived the flames (Figure 75). Ogden's good luck angered his less fortunate neighbors. He and his family received threats for weeks afterwards, and Hermann Raster, editor of a German newspaper (the *Illinois Staats-Zeitung*), even wrote that "this house must be confiscated for the shelterless, or the condition will become general that the rich Yankeedom wants to reconstruct Chicago as a Yankee city, at the cost of poor Germans and Scandinavians. Also for another reason—hundreds of those who have lost everything have become half insane, and have only one thought that all should be equal in misfortune. How if one of these unfortunates, with the idea of compensating an injustice of fate, were to put the burning torch to the millionaire Ogden's house?" William B. Ogden was not only the first mayor of Chicago, he was one of its leading citizens. Both Ogdens had been partners in the real estate firm of Ogden, Sheldon & Co., although William Ogden had retired prior to 1871. William Ogden was twice cursed by fire on October 8 of that year. He was president of the Peshtigo Company, which owned 160,000 acres of Wisconsin pine trees. William Ogden allegedly lost $3,000,000 worth of property in the Chicago and Peshtigo fires. See Mayer and Wade, p. 15; Andreas, vol. 2, pp. 569, 759; Pierce, vol. 2, p. 478; Pierce, vol. 3, p. 100; Wells, p. 142; Colbert and Chamberlin, p. 341; *1870 City Directory*, p. [992]; Kogan and Cromie, p. 176; Miller, pp. 160–62; Sawislak, pp. 310–11; "The Story of Peshtigo," *Chicago Tribune*, 31 October 1871, p. 2.

11. The Bryan Block was at the northwest corner of LaSalle and Monroe streets. See Sheahan and Upton, p. 146; *1871 City Directory*, p. 54.

12. The Otis building was at the southwest corner of State and Madison streets. See *1870 City Directory*, p. 944; *1871 City Directory*, p. 55.

13. There are numerous references in the transcript to firemen going "on to" certain streets. Although this original document indicates that the men are going "on to" the street, the intent was probably that they are going "onto" the street from an outside position, and hence in this context the word "onto" is used throughout these excerpts from the transcript. See *American Heritage Dictionary*, s.v. "on, onto."

14. The Board of Trade was in the Chamber of Commerce building, which was at the southeast corner of LaSalle and Washington streets. See Andreas, vol. 2, pp. 352–53, 357–58, 368–69.

15. Ed "Eddy" Longley was a deputy sheriff and jail keeper. See "The Debtors," p. 3.

16. The Sherman House was a hotel that was built in 1836–37 by Francis C. Sherman, who later became mayor of Chicago. It was located at the corner of Clark and Randolph streets. See Andreas, vol. 2, pp. 502–3.

17. Hickey's account of "taking responsibility" is consistent with Andreas' *History*: "Captain Hickey, seeing that there was no hope of saving the building, ordered the cells to be unlocked...." See Andreas, vol. 2, p. 725. But Hickey's testimony seems to be slightly at odds with Longley's version of these events. An interview with Longley appeared in the December 4, 1871, *Chicago Tribune*. It reads in part:

REPORTER: Had you received any orders to release the prisoners?

LONGLEY: Yes, I got an order from Mayor Mason. Here it is.

SHERIFF: Release all prisoners from the jail at once, keeping them in custody if possible.

R. B. MASON, Mayor.

Almost as soon as I commenced to let the men out, the policemen came in. My idea was to secure the murderers first and send them out. When I saw the officers I unlocked the cells of the murderers, and of Jack White, the confidence man, and delivered them to the officers, telling George Hutchinson, a Deputy Sheriff, to take charge, and see that they were locked up in the Huron Street Station.

See "The Debtors," p. 3. Mason's letter recently resurfaced, is now in the collections of the Chicago Historical Society, and is shown as Figure

81. It appears to be unique, being correspondence that was written *during* the fire and not afterwards. For more information concerning the letter, see Mark LeBien, "Fragile Note Illuminates City's Great Fire," *Chicago Tribune*, 2 October 1998, sec. 1, pp. 1, 24, hereafter cited in text as "Fragile Note Illuminates City's Great Fire."

18. Hickey is referring to the courthouse bell falling.

19. The quotation marks around "manholes" appear in the original transcript.

20. Even though the police department's first precinct had vacated the Armory because of building repair work, perhaps prisoners were still being held there. Or perhaps the questioner and Hickey are referring to the first precinct's present location in the Bridewell as the Armory. Flinn notes, for example, that even though the headquarters of the second precinct was eventually moved from the corner of Union and Madison streets to the Desplaines Street station, "it was always known by the old name of the 'Union street station.'" See Flinn, pp. 119–20. At the time of the fire, there were twenty-five prisoners in the Bridewell. Andreas comments that when the building caught fire, not every prisoner was eager to escape: "The keeper opened the door, and bade them run for their lives. They obeyed with fleetness—all save one, who was lying on the floor, stupidly drunk. The keeper could not rouse him." See Andreas, vol. 2, p. 730.

21. The "Central Station" was the headquarters of the police department. Prior to the fire it was in the basement of the west wing of the courthouse. After the fire, because the courthouse was destroyed, the headquarters was moved to the Union Street police station, also known as the second precinct police station. The inquiry investigation was conducted at this station, which, as noted above in note 20, was located at the corner of Union and Madison streets. See *1870 City Directory*, p. 914; *1871 City Directory*, p. 34; Flinn, pp. 119–120, 127–28, 132, "The Great Fire," *Chicago Tribune*, 26 November 1871, p. 1; "The Smelling Committee," *Chicago Times*, 29 November 1871, p. [4]; "How They Look and Act," p. [3].

22. The Northwestern Manufacturing Company hosted the auction of the courthouse bell. (Figure 14)

23. While the police force was working, Marshal Williams was rescuing not only his wife but also his piano, carpet, and stove. See Robert A. Williams, *Inquiry*, vol. [4], pp. 264–65.

24. Post-fire newspapers do reveal a few police improprieties. The October 27 *Evening Journal* and *Republican* reported that two sergeants were

ordered to return "rewards" for recovering civilians' personal property. These incidents prompted the Board of Police and Fire Commissioners to issue a notice prohibiting policemen from accepting presents in exchange for any police service. Four days later, the *Journal* reported that an officer was dismissed from the force for "dishonorably taking possession of some property belonging to a Mr. Moore, during the fire...." See "Police and Fire Commissioners," *Chicago Evening Journal*, 27 October 1871, p. [4]; "Police and Fire Commissioners," *Chicago Evening Journal*, 31 October 1871, p. [4]; "Fire and Police," *Chicago Republican*, 27 October 1871, p. [4]; "Fire and Police," *Chicago Republican*, 31 October 1871, p. [4].

25. The quotation marks around "lit out" are in the original transcript.

26. This store was probably the dry goods store of John V. Farwell & Co., located at 106-112 Wabash Avenue. See *1870 City Directory*, pp. 1002–3.

27. Roswell B. Mason was mayor of Chicago at the time of the fire. His son was Roswell H. Mason. See Andreas, vol. 2, pp. 51, 725.

28. The "chief engineer" Hickey is referring to is probably Ellis S. Chesbrough, Chicago's City Engineer from 1861 to 1871. Chesbrough designed Chicago's sewerage and water systems. Historian A. T. Andreas claims that he "stands among the world's great civil engineers." See Andreas, vol. 2, pp. 56, 65; *1871 City Directory*, pp. 34, 195; Hugo S. Grosser, *Chicago: A Review of its Governmental History from 1837 to 1906* (privately printed, 1906), pp. [28, 45–46], hereafter cited in text as Grosser.

29. This "eating house" was probably the restaurant of H. M. Kinsley, 93 Wabash Avenue. See *1870 City Directory*, p. 1095; *1871 City Directory*, p. 1077.

30. The Second Presbyterian Church was at the northeast corner of Wabash and Washington streets, on Chicago's South Side. See *1870 City Directory*, p. 932; *1871 City Directory*, p. 43.

31. The Drake and Farwell Block was at the corner of Wabash Avenue and Washington Street. See Colbert and Chamberlin, p. 289.

32. The *Times* described this incident as follows: "A man went into an alley to urinate when he was set upon by a crowd of people and pounded with stones and sticks, and abused shamefully; they threatened to hang him to lamp posts, and would have done so had he not been rescued by the police." See "The Smelling Committee," *Chicago Times*, 29 November 1871, p. [4].

33. The *Times* commented that "this gentleman is well known among journalists as having at one time been the publisher of a newspaper, after

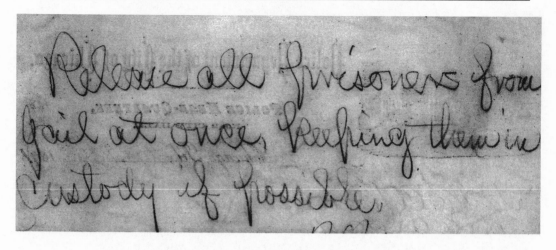

FIGURE 81—MAYOR MASON'S LETTER ORDERING THE RELEASE OF THE PRISONERS. **This letter from Mayor Roswell B. Mason was apparently written to Ed "Eddy" Longley, Deputy Sheriff and jail keeper. Although Longley had the note in his possession at the time of the fire, Mason, possibly realizing its significance, must have reacquired it later, as the letter thereafter remained in the Mason family until 1998, when it was given to the Chicago Historical Society. It reads: "Release all prisoners from jail at once, keeping them in custody if possible."**

Longley released 143 prisoners from the courthouse jail cells. He commented that after they were freed, "They were all perfectly wild, and yelled as if they were exercising their lungs for the last time; running hither and thither, as if they did not know what to do. It was the greatest excitement I ever saw." (Chicago Historical Society P&S-1998.137)

that a reporter on the *Evening Post*, and subsequently a solicitor of advertisements." See "The Smelling Committee," *Chicago Times*, 29 November 1871, p. [4].

34. Michael Hickey told the fire officials that he interrupted two attempted hangings, but General Sheridan's October 17 report to Mayor Mason appears to contradict Hickey's testimony: "I respectfully report to your Honor the continued peace and quiet of the city. There has been no case of violence since the disaster of Sunday night and Monday morning. The reports in the public press of violence and disorder here are without the slightest foundation. There has not been a single case of arson, hanging or shooting—not even a case of riot or street-fight. I have seen no reason for the circulation of such reports." See Andreas, vol. 2, pp. 776, 780.

On the other hand, John J. Flinn wrote in his *History of the Chicago Police* that "exaggerated reports of disorder, tumult, riot, loss of life, lynchings, etc., were sent out by excited or unscrupulous newspaper correspondents for a week after the fire.... That a number of persons met death at the hands of excited citizen-policemen is most probably true, but that the number exceeded, or even

reached, half a dozen, all told, is very improbable." See Flinn, pp. 129–30.

Can the disparate views of Sheridan and Flinn be reconciled? Probably not. But Hickey might have been telling the truth. It is possible that the attempted lynchings he witnessed never escalated into "riots or street-fights" and so were never reported to General Sheridan.

35. Hickey testified about two attempted lynchings. The first apparently took place on Michigan Avenue. The second was at the corner of Harrison and Clark streets. The *Chicago Republican* wrote of an alleged third incident, but this time the unsuccessful hanging was on LaSalle Street. Hoping to halt the spread of the flames, a young man procured a keg of powder and entered the basement of a store "with the intention of blowing the building to atoms." Some citizens saw him "in the very act of applying the match" and mistook him for an incendiary. The men were "dragging a cowering victim to the nearest lamppost" when Hickey stopped them. It appears that Hickey failed to mention this third attempted hanging when he testified before the fire officials. But Hickey testified on November 28. The *Republican* reported this incident the next day, and its

article included this statement: "Capt. Hickey is the medium through which the unknown young man's exploits and hair-breadth escapes have come to the ear of the Board of Police and Fire Commissioners." Perhaps Hickey did tell the Board on November 28 of this third attempted hanging. Although it is possible that the shorthand reporter failed to memorialize Hickey's comments, it seems equally possible that this story was an "off the record" statement made to the Board either before or after Hickey's formal inquiry testimony. See "A Narrow Escape," *Chicago Republican*, 29 November 1871, p. [4].

36. Hickey is testifying that he saw First Assistant Fire Marshal John Schank on the other side of State *Street*.

37. The Armory was located at the southwest corner of Franklin and Adams streets. The South Side facility of the Chicago Gas Light and Coke Company was originally on Monroe Street (a street parallel to and one block north of Adams) near Market Street, but the works was later extended south to Adams Street. Thus, the Armory was on the south side of Adams Street, and the gas works was across the street on the north side. See Andreas, vol. 2, p. 702; Flinn, p. 99; Cromie, inside front cover; *1870 City Directory*, p. 943; *1871 City Directory*, p. 54.

JOHN TOLLAND

[183]

John Tolland sworn[1]
November 28, 1871
(22nd witness)

Q. What is your business?

A. I am keeper of the lake tunnel.

Q. Stationed where?

A. Stationed on Lake Michigan, two miles and seven feet from the water works.

Q. In an easterly direction?[2]

A. In an easterly direction.

Q. Who else lives upon the crib besides yourself?

A. My wife.

Q. Do you know anything about the origin or the progress of the fire of October 8th and 9th?

A. I know nothing about the origin of the fire or the progress of the fire. All I know is that the sparks came out there between eleven and three o'clock Monday morning.

Q. How is that crib made?

A. Made of oak plank to within six feet from the surface of the water, and over that [184] up thirty feet it is two-inch pine plank covered with shingle.

Q. When did you first notice the fire?

A. I noticed the flame of the fire sometime Sunday evening. I could not say precisely the hour—sometime after nine o'clock or between eight and nine. I noticed the fire to the southwest.

Q. You say sparks came out there to your crib?[3]

A. Yes sir.

Q. About when did they begin to come?

A. About half past eleven.

Q. What quantities did they come in?

A. They came ranging from three to six inches in size—pieces of boards.

Q. Did they injure the roof there?

A. I would have sold out my chances between two and three o'clock for a dollar to any man that came along. [185]

Q. Describe particularly what they did do.

A. They lit on the south side of the crib. Sparks lit there, and I had to take up six pails and a broom and wet them and swept them off from that time until four o'clock Monday morning.

Q. Did you have all you could do?

A. Yes sir, all I could possibly attend to.

Q. Did your wife assist you?

A. I made her go to bed at eleven o'clock. I did not want to scare her, and I wanted to stick to the crib as long as I could. There was a heavy sea at the time, and I could not have saved her if we had had to leave.

Q. How large were these sparks?

A. Ranging from three to six inches, I should say.

Q. Could you tell what the material was, whether it was [186] roofing?

A. No sir, I did not pay any particular attention that way.

Q. Were they board or felt?

A. They seemed like boards and pieces of pine. A man placed in the predicament I was, he would not pay much attention how they were, so long as he saved his own place.

Q. Where was that fire at the time these sparks began to come?

A. I could not say very well. It seemed to

be all a bank of smoke in the air. I could not pay any attention to where the fire was.

Q. The closest point from which sparks could have come from was at least two miles?

A. The way the wind was blowing it could have brought them further than that.

Q. Was the wind blowing hard? **[187]**

A. Yes sir. From the southwest it was blowing a good eight knot breeze right along there—over eight knots. I should judge it was nearly equal to a line of three miles that the sparks came from. If the crib had ever taken fire, you would have been worse off for water than you was with the water works stopped.

Q. Do you know what time the water works took fire?

A. No sir. I was busy on the roof. I could not tell the exact time. It was sometime in the morning. I came down and saw the current in the tunnel was stopped, and I told my wife the water works was burned.

Q. About what time was that?

A. I could not say. I did not pay very particular attention. I was so busy on the roof.

Q. Did you feel any effects of the heat out there? **[188]**

A. Well, you could not feel the effects of the heat. You could feel the effects of the smoke. You can smell it now when the wind blows from the west. You can smell Chicago pretty strong with the smoke.[4]

John Tolland Notes

1. Contemporary sources spell this witness' surname in several different ways. The inquiry transcript clearly identifies him as "John Tolland," and his name is spelled accordingly in this book. The *Tribune's* summary of his testimony, however, refers to him as "John Lolland." The *Times* calls him "John Tollen," "John Tolby," and "John Tolly," and the *Republican* identifies him as "John Talmed." The *Evening Journal* refers to this witness as "John Follam," and the 1870 Chicago city directory includes a listing for "Follen James, wks. waterworks." See "The Fire Investigation," *Chicago Tribune*, 29 November 1871, p. 4; "The Smelling Committee," *Chicago Times*, 29 November 1871, p. [4]; "How Was It?," p. [4]; "How They Look and Act," p. [3]; "The Fire Investigation," *Chicago Evening Journal*, 28 November 1871, p. [4]; *1870 City Directory*, p. 281.

2. Every Chicagoan knows that Lake Michi-

gan laps the eastern shores of the city. As the water crib was two miles offshore, the importance and necessity of this question seems somewhat questionable.

3. Sparks traveled even farther than the crib. Historian Frank Luzerne wrote that "a man was plowing up at Evanston [Evanston, Illinois, a city north of Chicago], and that's 10 or 12 miles, and he saw sparks falling all around him...." See Luzerne, pp. 173–74.

4. For a colorful account of Tolland's fiery travails, see Colbert and Chamberlin, p. 352.

JAMES H. HILDRETH

[123]

November 29, 1871
J. H. Hildreth sworn[1]
(34th witness)

Q. Your name?

A. James H. Hildreth.

Q. Your residence?

A. 574 Halsted Street.

Q. You have been an alderman in the city?

A. Yes sir.

Q. Will you tell us if you know anything about the origin of the progress of the fire that commenced on October 8th? If you do not know anything in regard to the inception of the fire, tell us when you first knew of it and what you saw and did in your own way.

A. As to the origin, I certainly could not say.

Q. When did you first become aware of there being a fire?

A. I could not tell, exactly. It was not far from the neighborhood of nine o'clock. I had retired and hearing the alarm and the **[124]** alarm and the engines go by and seeing the light shining through my window, I got up, dressed myself, and went to the fire. I found it in DeKoven Street where the fire started. I pushed myself through the [crowd?] and got in where the fire was. It was then in four or five buildings, maybe more. I could not tell exactly how many buildings were afire, but there were four or five buildings on fire at the time. I stood and saw the [firemen?] work. The wind was blowing a pretty good gale, and I was of the opinion after while that the fire was going north faster than the department was putting it out. There was a man with me by the name of Mc[*illeg.*][2] who was in business on the South Side who was burned out, and I remarked to him that I wished that I could go and see the commissioners or the fire marshal, that the fire was getting away from them faster than they were aware of, I guessed. Started in search of them [125] and found the fire marshal and said to him that the fire was going away from him faster than he was putting it out, and he would have to resort to some other method or else there was no knowing where the fire would stop. The marshal said that he was doing everything he could do in every way, shape, and manner. I then said that it would be a good idea to place the engines north of the fire and fight it up, and the marshal then said the sparks was carrying the fire beyond him, and as fast as he would get one fire put out, another one would start with the wind. For that reason, I remarked that it would be well to place the engines north, to take them out of there and give so much [*illeg.*] the flames and then burn down. With that, the marshal left and went about his business. Afterwards, I met Mr. Locke, the assistant engineer, and I said to him, "Locke, we are going [126] to have the biggest fire that we ever had in Chicago unless we go to work and tore down these buildings. Blow them up or something else. It is going to be a hard matter to put them out. If you will come with me to the fire marshal," said I, "perhaps you bring one of the city officials. Perhaps it might encourage him more and he would take the responsibility upon himself."

Q. Mr. Locke was the name?[3]

A. Yes sir, he is the assistant engineer of the city.[4] Locke said he would go as soon as he went to see about a fire plug somewhere. He went a short distance and came back, and we went to the fire marshal, Mr. Williams, and then had some conversation in regard to tearing down the buildings, blowing them up, and so forth. The marshal felt as though the blowing up of the buildings was a matter that he did not understand. In fact, as near as I could infer, he did not have the power[5] nor the means to do it with, and I remarked [127] to him that I would get the powder, if necessary. I also stated to him that he had power to [control?] the people or do as he chose and if he would give me the power, that I would get a thousand men to go through and tear down the buildings. The

marshal said, "Get your powder, then," and I started and got the powder, went down on the South Side, got this new insurance wagon.

Q. Dan Bullwinkle?[6]

A. I do not know his name.

Q. (By Mr. Williams) Let me ask you one question. When you started for the powder, about where was the fire then?

A. It had not got into Bateham's mills. There might have been a corner of Bateham's mills on fire. It might be possible that there was fire there, but I was on Canal Street. It was in the locality of Bateham's mills at that time where I last spoke to you in regard to it at the time I left. I think that was the locality. What reminds me very strongly of that point [128] was there was an engine placed at the plug at Bateham's mills, and fire caught in some planks right by the engine, and I tried very hard to get the engine out, to uncouple it, and burned my [hair?] and eyes and moustache and finally told the driver to pull off and the driver did so.

Q. Was that engine on Canal Street?

A. Yes sir, right at Bateham's mills.

Q. That would indicate that the mills were on fire.

A. The mills were not afire, but the fire had caught under some planks.

Q. Burning pretty lively?

A. There was a pile of planks there two or three feet high that was scattered across.

Q. In the street?

A. Yes sir, in the gutter, and they caught underneath, and the engine was right close to the end of this plank.

Q. (By a reporter)[7] What was this engine?

A. The *Gund*, I think.[8] I am not really certain, but I give it as [129] my best belief that it was the *Gund* engine.

Q. (By Mr. Williams) That Bateham's mills stood where, between what streets?

A. I ought to be able to state without a thought because I have passed by that a thousand [times] within two or three years.

Q. Do you think between Mather and Harrison?

A. Yes sir, I think that was it.

Q. Just south of Harrison?

A. Yes sir, generally known as Bateham's red mills. Well, I went to the wagon and asked for the captain. This man said, "I am the captain." I said to him, "I want your wagon to go

and get powder. You can do more good," said
I, "than you can with your Babcocks."[9] Said he,
"I am ready to go." We started and went down
State Street and Water and broke in the powder magazines there on both sides of the street.
Some on the east side and some on the west
side and took all there was. We had considerable delay there in getting [130] fuse. A man
put his head out of the window and wanted to
know what we were doing, and I told him and
asked him to come down and let us into the
store to get fuse, that if he did not, I should
break in the door. He remarked that he did not
have anything to do with it. I told him of the
necessity, that we were compelled to get the
fuse, that we should have it. He took a great
deal of time in getting dressed; I don't know
why. After while he came down, and it took him
a long time to get the fuse. Finally, we got it
and started back. I got as far as Madison Street
bridge or nearly at the bridge, and we saw the
fire was on the South Side. Became somewhat
alarmed at that. Took our powder and started
back to the courthouse and put it in the police
department in the basement.

Q. The trial room, was it not?

A. We put it in there, and I said to Locke,
"Now come and let us go and find the commissioners [131] or the fire marshal." We started
and went to the West Side. The wagon went a
short distance with us, and then we went afoot,
traveled all around the fire in hopes of finding
one of the commissioners or all of the commissioners or the marshal. Either one, for I had
seen Sheridan and Brown at the fire, and Commissioner Brown passed right by me. I could
not have told for a certainty that it was Sheridan, only someone told me that "there goes
Sheridan," and I turned around and supposed
it to be Sheridan from sight.

Q. General Sheridan?

A. No sir. Commissioner Sheridan. I was
informed that all the commissioners were on
the ground. We went completely around the
fire. Then we started to go to the South Side,
thinking it possible that the commissioners had
gone to the South Side and the marshal. And
we crossed on Adams Street bridge, and there
was a report that the gas works were going to
blow up, [132] and there was a general stam-
pede, and we stampeded with the rest. Then we
went back and went across Madison Street

bridge. Said I, "We will go to the courthouse.
The probabilities that they have gone then there
to determine upon some course, and we will be
there with them to use the powder as they may
direct." We started and went to the courthouse
and did not find them there. I inquired if the
commissioners had been there and was told
that they had not. I inquired if the mayor had
been there and was informed that he had not,
but on turning to go out, the mayor came in.
Then I entreated the mayor to take some course
that would help to stop the progress of the fire,
that the mayor should write an order calling
upon the people. That was his first order, a sort
of an order or proclamation or a call, and soon
afterwards his son came in with Judge Fuller—
is not that his [illeg.]?

Q. No. Miller? [133]

A. Miller it is. The mayor submitted the
document to Judge Miller, and he suggested
that that was under the direction of the fire
marshal, so the mayor wrote another order and
copied it and asked who would see that it was
carried out. I said, "I will, give it to me quick."
I grabbed it and went to the fire marshal. I
found the fire marshal on LaSalle Street between Madison and Washington, in the alley.

Q. What was this order?

A. An order to assist under the directions
of the fire marshal in adopting such measures
as he might direct. I took the order to the fire
marshal, and we went around on the northwest
corner of Madison and LaSalle and stepped
into the awning of the door, and I read the
order to him and remarked, "That gives you all
the power that you want. Now," said I, "you
know the engines cannot stop the fire, and we
may stop it by blowing buildings on some [134]
given line." Well, the marshal did not go. I
could not tell exactly what his reply was. Something in regard to the engine or the fire or something. I could not say what it was authorita-
tively, but at all events I left the marshal then
and went around to the courthouse, and while
the mayor was writing the order, I was hurrying
him to write as fast as he possibly could, thinking that by being expeditious in the matter, we
might blow down the buildings on the south
side of Madison Street and not allow it to get
into the large buildings.

Q. That was the second order?

A. I think the mayor wrote three orders

and copied the third one. He wrote three, I think, and copied the third. [135]

Q. (By Mr. Williams) Let me ask you one thing. At the time you saw me with the order direct from the mayor, was not the Oriental Building then on fire?[10]

A. I wouldn't say that it was. I should judge from the circumstance of your being there with the engine, I should think that it was.

Q. (By Mr. Williams) Did you notice whether that hose led from that building on the corner of Madison and LaSalle?

A. No, I could not tell that.

Q. (By Mr. Williams) Did you notice another engine at the corner of Washington and LaSalle?

A. No, I couldn't tell. My only thought was to find you, and I was not looking for an engine or hose or anything. [136]

Q. (By Mr. Williams) I had just come out of the Washington Street [front?] with the Congress.[11]

A. You were engaged there somehow with the hose. You were with the engine or men or something. I couldn't tell anything about the direction you came from. The fire was blowing, and sparks and everything were flying, and my eye was in such a condition that it would prevent my observation. It was my hope to get him from there quick enough to get in the south side of Madison Street and blow up the buildings across there and not let it get into the big buildings. And Judge Miller remarked, "Do something in the name of God!" or something like that, to save those big buildings. I went up after leaving the marshal and said, "The marshal is attending to his engines and," said I, "We must take some steps immediately," and [137] I called Judge Miller out, called the mayor out and, said I, "The fire is coming right over here now and," said I, "I fear it is too late now but," said [I], "I think it is better we should commence in this building." That was the Union National Bank.[12] Said [I], "I think it would [be] better that we should commence there, and I think we shall be able possibly to stop it at this point." The mayor remarked, "Go on and do something." I went on, had a great deal of hard work to get men to carry powder; in fact, could not until I got Sergeant Lull, and he took a squad of police and made them carry it in under the bank and he stayed there with me,

and I burst in the kegs of powder with my boot for I didn't have anything else and strewed them out. I had quite a large quantity in there and touched it off and left. [138] Then the sergeant took the police again and carried the powder around under Smith and Nixon's building.[13] We got into a bakery there, had a great deal of trouble there in getting it off. [139]

Q. Did it explode in the bank?

A. Yes sir.

Q. What effect did it have?

A. Blew right through. Rushed right straight through. The room was so large that it would almost [be] impossible to blow it down.[14]

Q. (By Williams) Did not blow any of the walls down?

A. No sir, didn't throw any out on the north side. I don't know what it might have done on the east side.

Q. (By Mr. Williams) Was the courthouse on fire at that time?

A. I judge not; it might have been. If it was not, it was [a] very short time afterwards. It was not afire at the time when we took the powder out. When we went into the Union National Bank, I know it was not afire then. It was afire when we first got down there.

Q. (By Mr. Williams) Did you see the big bell fall? [140]

A. No sir. Saw nothing of the kind.

Q. (By Mr. Williams) Did you see my driver anywhere around on Clark and Washington Street?

A. No sir. I was on Clark and Washington. That is where I put the powder, in Smith and Nixon's building. And stayed there until it blew up, for I couldn't get away for some time.

Q. (By Mr. Williams) I want to know how long it was because my driver stayed there while you were going in Mr. Smith and Nixon's building to blow up, and he drove off for fear it would knock down the building, and when he drove away, the bell fell.

A. There was no wagon. I stayed around in each place where the powder was placed to keep the people away. In fact, stayed closer than anyone else, mostly. [141]

Q. Where did you put the powder in?

A. Into a bakery. It had the appearance of being a bakery. You might find it [if you?] wanted to know anything about it. It had the appearance of being a bake shop. Sergeant Lull was with me there and stayed with me until I started to run. Then we had used all the powder we had. The mayor afterwards said he had sent to Brighton and got some more powder.[15] His son came to me in the morning at the corner of Wabash Avenue and Washington and said there was a large supply of powder coming and that the mayor, his father, wanted leave to take charge of it—said it would be there within a few minutes. I assented to it and said all right. The powder came in very soon, and I placed the powder in a building on the northwest corner of Washington and [142] Wabash Avenue and also on the northeast corner in a large building that was there.

Q. There was a church on the corner, was there not?

A. This was not. That old spotted church[16] is on the corner, but this was a little off the corner in a drug store—no, not in the drug store, but next to it. That we took the powder, for they told us in the drug store that they were filled up with oils and so forth, and the fire would only ignite to make the fire stronger, and on that I was prevailed upon not to put it in there, but went into the next basement north. I didn't stop to see what it was.

Q. A boot and shoe establishment?[17]

A. I think not. I have an idea it was a millinery establishment next to this paint or drug store or whatever it was, and I came out and the [143] powder wagon had gone away. We then went south. I started for the wagon. A funny man named Herman[18] [found?] me when the wagon went south with the powder. I started after the wagon and I met David A. Gage[19] and I remarked that I was glad to see him and asked him to come and consult with me as to a line to blow up, that I was going to blow up somewhere in the locality. We were then about Terrace Row[20] on Michigan Avenue or Congress Street. It was at about Congress Street, and he said, "Go on, Hildreth. I will be with you just as quick as [I] find my wife, but go on." I started around and got to the corner of State and Harrison Street and there made up my mind what line to blow up, right along up in that line. Just then, fortunately, I got considerable assistance. A man by the name of Mahoney,[21] [144] Munn and Scott's foreman at the City Elevator,[22] and Driscoll, a police officer,[23] came and two brothers of mine and three

men who were working for me. I didn't have much trouble after that.

Q. Sergeant Hood?[24]

A. And Sergeant Hood. These men that I spoke of were men who took right hold and carried out. Then after I took hold of, Commissioner Sheridan came. I first saw him there. Then he gave me the first encouragement I got. I felt before that I was trespassing, rather presuming, taking more upon myself than I had authority to do, but Sheridan told me to go in, that buildings were coming down very nicely, and we could not ask to have them fall better than they did. The powder took very good effect. We blew from State Street and Harrison to the church that stands [145] there on Wabash Avenue to Congress Street on the west side of Wabash Avenue. Then on the north side of Congress Street to Michigan Avenue and as far as the buildings went. While there on Congress Street, Mr. Benner, one of the fire marshals, came and wanted me to go down to Terrace Row to blow up down there in the alley. I started to go there and found that the fire had crossed the alleys and got into the sheds and barns there, and I said, "No! I cannot. I must go on with what I have commenced," and went back and went to blowing up on the north side of Congress Street. After blowing on the north side of Congress Street, the heat had set fire to the cornice of the brick block, in the southeast corner of Harrison Street and Wabash Avenue; and then there were a great many to advise, some to blow up the whole block, [146] some to go north to Harrison and blow; but after a little thought, I went to work and blew up in the center. At the same time Mr. Sheridan got an engine in the back, so I was told. I couldn't swear it was Commissioner Sheridan, but whoever it was, they had got the hose leading up back, but I was told at the time that Commissioner Sheridan was getting an engine there, and I was guided by that fact somewhat. The hose would not lead around to the front side of the building. The hose would only lead to the alley east of the building, the alley between the Michigan Avenue Hotel[25] and this brick block. It came in back there, I believe there is an alley, and I went into the center of the building and blew up the center of the building. There I had to blow three times before I finally separated it. [147] Then I put into the first floor from the basement, and the walls seemed to be very strong some way, or the powder didn't have good effect; I don't know how it was, but I blew there once and then put in two kegs the second time, and that settled all the walls and separated, with the exception of the roof that covered the two houses in the center of the block. That had blown down from the powder and the roof was still standing, supported by a cinder wall. It seems that there was four corners of brick wall some way or another that supported the center of that roof, and I climbed up over the rubbish. Before I went up on the rubbish, I asked the fireman, whoever it was on the hose, how he could handle that roof best, with it smashed down or get his stream right over the roof. He said his stream couldn't **[148]** go over the roof, and he could handle it better if it was down. Then I took a keg of powder into the roof and leveled the roof at that point. In the meantime, General Sheridan had gone to work after, in my judgment, the fire was beyond all doubt checked at that time, and he was tearing down a block south. Colonel Hough's[26] house was where he was engaged tearing down, and while I was engaged at this brick block, three different men came to me with messages from Mayor Mason, from General Logan,[27] and from General Sheridan, to come to Harrison Street with the powder, that he wanted to blow up that way. When the third man came, I replied to him in a rather____[28] "probably not," as respectfully as I would under other circumstances, but at all events, it was to the effect that I should continue where I was. **[149]** I went there and found Colonel Hough was engaged on a roof in pulling down his own house, and as I was informed, General Sheridan was at the other corner with an axe cutting, and there I took Colonel Hough by the shoulder and pulled him off from his roof and remarked that it was useless to destroy any more property, that the fire was already stopped.

Q. Was that the deacon or the colonel? There is two brothers.

A. It was the [pork packer?].

Q. One is white-haired?

A. That is the man I know as Colonel Hough.

Q. The Colonel is as white as snow.

A. This is his brother, then; this is the one I've always known as Colonel Hough for

the last ten years. Colonel Hough joined with me then in stopping them from pulling down the house. Commissioner **[150]** Sheridan came along then and joined in getting the men away from there and getting them down and drawing debris of the building that had been blown up out in the street so there would not be so much matter to burn. About this time, a report came from the church. We were going to blow it up, and we had five kegs of powder in there to do so. Then the minister[29] came in there, and if his praying would have only done as much good to the general cause as it did, it would do a great of good for he did beg. At this time Commissioner Sheridan came along and said, "[Henry?],[30] give them the last hope. They made good promises to fight the fire and give notice that the fire got so strong they couldn't put it out." At the same time, the fire was in the back window of the church coming **[151]** through, that was the understanding, and afterwards the report came that the church had [*blank*] and they wanted to have it blown up. Somebody came down, I don't know who it was, and commissioners and myself went and examined the church and came to the conclusion that the church was all right, and it was better to let it stand.[31] That ending the blowing up that was done on the South Side, in fact, all I knew of [*blank*] [being?] blown up, but afterwards I went with a wagon load of powder on the North Side, thinking there might be a possibility of doing some good there.

Q. The powder ran out about that time?

A. I believe you had sent for about one hundred kegs.

Q. And you went up there for it?

A. No, not that time. I think I saw the order afterwards that you had given for one hundred barrels, and you came to me and said **[152]** there would be plenty of powder. That was the understanding I was working upon. I started to the North Side with a wagon of powder and had to cross the bridge at Ogden Slip,[32] I think it was, and then across North Avenue bridge, and the fire then reached as far as North Avenue on Clark Street. When I got there, I could see where the fire was. I then made an effort, although not a very strenuous one, to get the people to take hold and try to stop the fire where I thought I could do, but I couldn't get them to do it. And I was fatigued and had not had anything that night to eat. I drank more than the firemen did, for that matter,[33] and I tried with a great many, maybe twenty or thirty men, to get them to stop and assist in blowing up the buildings, to stop the fire on a line that was feasible to me at that time, but could not get them to stop, [153] and there was no one with me but a driver and a young man whose name I do not know, but who worked faithfully on the South Side helping to blow up. Further than that, I don't know I can say anything. I couldn't get them to stop on the North Side anyway. I grabbed hold of them, took right hold of them with more force than I would if I'd been sheriff, for that matter, and made them, but they would leave me just as quick as I would take my hand off them and cut. The word "powder"[34] was a terror to them. They could not stand the word "*powder.*"[35]

Q. I would like to ask you if you think the explosion at the Union National Bank or Smith and Nixon's or Brown and Mathews[36] or Hotchkiss Eddy's[37] had the effect of stopping the progress of the fire?

A. I do not think that it did.

Q. Did not have any effect on it? [154]

A. No sir, I don't think it did. I think at that time, in fact, I would almost say for a certainty that it did not because it did not have system enough.

Q. It did not have sufficient force?

A. What I mean to say is there was not system enough to carry it out as efficiently as it might have been done. It would take an hour to get powder into a building and get men around. It was almost impossible to get men around to do it. You could not get them to do it. And in carrying it myself, coals would light upon the barrels and upon myself.

Q. How did you manage to carry them?

A. Put our coats on them if we had time, if not, without. At that point I think that beyond all question, if there had been powder in the city where it could have been used and men to have taken hold of it thoroughly and [155] go on as we did when we got upon Harrison Street because we could make an explosion as often as once in five minutes.

Q. You had to carry the powder from Michigan Avenue?

A. Yes sir, kept the team off quite a long distance and carried the powder, but then we got it down so the men would have it at a minute's time. They got used to it, and would set down and smoke on a keg of powder to show you that if we had been as slow at Harrison Street as we were at Smith and Nixon's and the other places, the buildings would have burned down before we could have burned them up. I will say that going into Pat O'Neill's building,[38] we had to shut the back door to keep the fire out of the room where the powder was. The fire was in the back rooms. We had no time to lose. The fire was then in some buildings on Congress Street, [156] and then it was the same way, and in one building on Wabash Avenue between Congress Street and Harrison, the fire was so strong, and I was so long in the building that my brother crossed the street, thinking that I had suffocated and was going into the building to take me out. At the same time, the powder was in there when the fire was so strong.

Q. Did you have some fuse with you?

A. Yes sir. At the building at the northwest corner of Washington and Wabash Avenue, I made a fuse out of some paper; and then on the northeast corner, I made a fuse in the same way with paper, and sprinkled powder on it and lit the paper and stopped until I saw it burn and then ran. That I felt more danger in than in anything else I did.

Q. What in your judgment would have been the result if that [157] line of buildings on State, along Harrison to Wabash Avenue, and thence north to Congress Place, had not been blown down?

A. I think that is self-evident of itself. If you went through and noticed the buildings, that notwithstanding, the buildings were thrown flat to the ground, and the flames and everything were smothered together in the debris. It was almost impossible to keep the place from catching afire as it was. The people, after the buildings were thrown down, seemed to take vigor and threw pails of water and threw dirt and stopped it from catching. My opinion would be beyond all question that the fire would have continued. I do not know to what extent. I know this, that we could not have stopped the fire on Congress Street and even on the north side of Congress Street by the leveling of these buildings if we could not have blown down that [tailors'?] buildings.[39] I don't think it [158] would have been a possibility to have saved the Michigan Avenue Hotel or any-thing in that block. I don't think there would have been a chance.

Q. Do you recollect a pile of lumber that was right at the end of the Terrace Block and [stashed?] away out into the middle of the street, consisting of long joists? Do you recollect that catching on fire at one time and spreading across rapidly to [the] Michigan Hotel?

A. I don't really remember about [it]. I couldn't say of my own knowledge. If this was while we were at work there in those buildings, [in?] as quick as I got out of the building, I sat down until the explosion was made, for I was real tired and only looked at the building itself; but I've got a faint idea or something or other about there being a pile of lumber there and heard something about the lumber being afire; but I don't **[159]** exactly remember, just of my own personal knowledge of seeing it.

Q. These buildings which you blew up in the nighttime in the vicinity of the courthouse. I suppose you took some precaution to see that the people were out of there.

A. I don't think there was a building blown up that there was anybody blown up in. You say "powder!"[40] and they left. You could not get them to stay around. Anyway, there was a good deal of precaution taken in that respect about getting the people out, and it was circu-lated fast enough that they were blowing up buildings, and that seemed to go faster than the fire.

Q. (By Mr. Williams) Have you any recol-lection of the time we were talking by the *John*'s house[41] about making a commencement in blowing up that corner bank, but to be careful and have all the people out upstairs? Did not you **[160]** send two policemen through there to see if there were anybody up there?

A. Yes sir, that precaution was taken. I know when we came there, there was plenty of time, and I also asked Sergeant Hood.

Q. And you started to the courthouse to get the powder?

A. Yes sir.

Q. (By Mr. Williams) And I started for the *America* engine[42] to send her away from that plug because if you blew up the [blank],[43] it would blow up the engine and kill the men. You only put powder in that building once?

A. That is all.

Q. In any of these buildings, did you find where you put powder in the lower stories that it threw the debris sideways or into the air?

A. I will tell you with regard to putting it into the lower basement. I did not have **[161]** as good an effect in the buildings where there is a basement and the first floor from the base-ment. It seemed as there was not powder enough, for the powder could not burn and have so strong an effect to level the building thoroughly; but after three or four explosions, I put it into the floor above the basement in-stead of going down into the basement. The same as if in this building, I would place pow-der on this floor and not in the cellar. In that case the brick in some instances would throw out a little, but the buildings seemed to fall right in together. They fell right in and smoth-ered right down. Seemed as though it would lift it up and then fall right in. You could see that anytime before they commenced to clear up the debris. There was but very little, even on the sidewalks. It all seemed to fall right together. **[162]**

Q. I suppose you blew up some wooden houses, did you not?

A. I guess so; I forget about the wooden houses, too; the buildings would smash right down together. Some of the buildings were bet-ter constructed towards falling than others.

Q. How much powder did you put into Raster's building?[44]

A. I couldn't remember how many kegs. There was four or five kegs followed me into any building I went into; and if I could find a place where there were closets where I could put the powder into a small place, two kegs would be as good as five in such a room; and I was governed by the experience that I had that two would be as good as five.

Q. How many buildings do you think you blew up?

A. Really, I couldn't tell you, maybe thirty or forty. I couldn't tell you how many there **[163]** were. I have never taken pains to count up or form an idea. You can form as good an idea as I can myself from knowing the line that was blown. I can tell you that precisely.

Q. Were any buildings blown up south of the line where you blew?

A. No sir.

Q. Was there anybody else or any other

company engaged in blowing up buildings that you are aware of in the South Division?

A. I'll venture to say there was not. General Sheridan made an effort while we were engaged on Congress Street to get some powder from under the wagons to blow up just a block in the rear of where we were blowing, and the man that was put in charge of it, and whose charge I had every confidence that the wagons would not go away, would [164] not let anybody get to the powder.

Q. (By Mr. Sheridan) Do you recollect what I said to you when you were starting from the corner of Harrison and Wabash Avenue to go on the west line of Wabash Avenue to blow up? You and your brother were together.

A. Well, I rather think that conversation that took place with you in regard to blowing up on the west side of Wabash Avenue took place in the church.

Q. Just at the corner of the church.

A. I am of the opinion that it was directly after the interview had taken place between the minister and ourselves. It was directly after that, but I would be of the opinion that it was inside of the church, but there may be a possibility of our walking out of the church.

Q. (By Mr. Sheridan) We came out on the corner. Do you recollect what was said? There was some talk of suing the city for the buildings that were blown up and of [course?] if I should [165] refresh your memory possibly you could recollect. I said, "Henry, you take care of the powder brigade. Go on, but do not blow up anything unless it is absolutely necessary to be blown up to preserve other property."

A. Yes sir, that is very distinct as far as the conversation about blowing up and not blowing up anything further than was necessary is concerned. I felt that upon myself in doing what I was doing, I was very careful in doing what I did. The only encouragement that I had from any authority after I had left Mayor Mason and the courthouse and he said to go into the Union National Bank. I had not, as I remarked, and he said, "Go on, I am glad you are at work." Then I afterwards met Sheridan and Sheridan rather gave me encouragement enough so that I did not feel as though I was doing it myself.

Q. Did I not tell you that I had a conversation with the mayor, [166] George W. Gage,[45]

Mr. Hayes,[46] and others and they all conceded that it was a matter of necessity?

A. I do not remember about that.

Q. (By Mr. Sheridan) The utmost care you are certain used that nothing not absolutely necessary to be blown up in order to preserve other property was blown?

A. Certainly not. The fact is patent as you will see that there was not a building blown down that might have been left.

Q. (By Mr. Sheridan) You recollect that I said I would stay at the church while you went north?

A. Yes sir.

Q. And I would take charge and see when it became absolutely necessary. The crowd around there were excited and wanted the church blown down.

A. That was the universal cry of everyone there, to blow up the church and it was very reluctantly that the powder was taken out. That was the only trouble that I had with the men in obeying orders or complying with [167] any request that made—to take the powder out of the church. Policeman Driscoll worked like a demon. It was a credit to the man to do as he did and he would have had a good excuse to go away.

Q. If we had yielded to the clamor of the crowd at the church, would not the Methodist Episcopal Church have been blown down?

A. Certainly. We went and examined the walls when the people that were around there were calling to blow it down, and the men carrying powder were, too. There was not a man but what said, "Blow 'er! Goddamn it, blow 'er!" One man in particular, a man for whose judgment I have great respect, said, "The church is not any better than any other building. Blow 'er and stop the fire! We have commenced it. Blow 'er!" Then Mr. Sheridan and myself went and looked at the thickness of the walls, and then he made the remark I have stated before that [168] he would stay there. He said, "give her the last hope and go on, and I will stay here and take charge and inform you if it is necessary to blow up."[47] There was word afterwards that Sheridan had left.[48]

Q. You did succeed in stopping one man, Colonel Hough,[49] from destroying his own house?

A. Yes sir, he will state it himself right

before you, if it is necessary, that I took right hold of his collar and took him off from the rope. There was fifty or a hundred men on the rope, tearing down his own building, and we had stopped the fire entirely to show you how strong this belief was and the effect we were having in blowing down the buildings. The people around were at work, and there were fifty or a hundred men on a rope, and that rope was hitched on the southwest corner of the house, and Mr. Hough was on the rope. I saw him at it and was informed that [169] General Sheridan was at the other corner chopping, and a man who was General Sheridan's agent in this matter was assisting Sheridan in it. This was after the fire was all stopped on Harrison Street east and on the north side of Congress Street the buildings were all leveled down to the ground and the only danger that could be perceptible by my own ideas was of this brick building and then the moment we got separated and this stream was in back there there was no more danger than at any ordinary small fire.[50] Where the fire was just starting and there was an engine was there to put it out, still they were engaged after this under the directions of General Sheridan in tearing down Mr. Hough's house and were going to tore down through north. Mr. Hough said, "If the tearing of my building is going to save the rest, tear it down and I will help to do it." That is what he said, and he was engaged [170] in doing it.

Q. (By Mr. Schank) Do you recollect what engine that was there?

A. No, I do not. It might have been the *Titsworth*[51] that I saw on that locality, but I could not tell you what engine it was.

Q. But up to that time people were very reluctant to do anything?

A. Very reluctant. We could not get them to do anything. I think we could have blown down that [tailors'?][52] building still further north if it had been absolutely necessary and then got hold with ropes and taken it away; we might, by blowing down the whole brick block, there might have been even a possibility of stopping it, but it is a great question.

Q. Did you during that night or day see any improprieties about the firemen? Drunkenness or anything of that kind?

A. No sir, never saw firemen work harder in my life. There was, of course, when it got to be along [171] toward morning.

Q. Did anyone tell you or communicate to you that when the powder came in, I had gone to the North Side?

A. I think you told me yourself that you had sent for more powder, and it would be there, and I left this man Mahoney to take charge of the powder and stay at that place and not leave it. He is a very trusty man, a man who would be like the boy that stood on the burning deck. You could not drive him from his post, and it was from that that it troubled General Sheridan to get the powder away from him. General Sheridan went to him and failed to get the powder himself and took some man with him. I judge from the description that it was Mr. Stearns.[53] He failed to get it and afterwards went to get a policeman and demanded it, and Mahoney very quietly took his revolver out of his pocket [172] and told them that if they took any powder, it would be after he emptied that revolver, and he was the man that would do it. Afterwards I think he abused General Sheridan because he would not carry powder. I had just sent for some five kegs of powder, and Mahoney told Sheridan that if he wanted to assist, there was a way that he could do it. The General wouldn't do it. Sheridan wanted to know if he knew who he was, and Mahoney said that he did not care a damn. He could not have the powder.[54]

Examination adjourned to December 1st, 1871, ten A.M.

James H. Hildreth Notes

1. The summary of Hildreth's testimony that appeared in the November 30, 1871, *Tribune* included the following introductory comments: "It was stated that this gentleman was in the sergeants' room, and a messenger was despatched to find him. He had considerable objection to be interviewed by the city authorities and reporters. The Commissioners told him that they were accused of hearing only the Fire Department, and would like to hear his statement. He said if there was any liability he would speak out. He was then sworn, and made the following statement." See "The Great Fire," *Chicago Tribune*, 30 November 1871, p. 4.

2. The November 30, 1871, *Tribune* referred to this man as "McClelland." See "The Great Fire," *Chicago Tribune*, 30 November 1871, p. 4. It does not appear that this is the same person that

Michael C. Hickey rescued from a hanging. See Michael C. Hickey, *Inquiry*, vol. [2], p. 170.

3. Mr. Locke's full name was Joseph A. Locke. See *1871 City Directory*, p. 557; Cromie, p. 47.

4. Locke was Assistant Engineer in the Water Department. See "The Water Supply," *Chicago Tribune*, 15 October 1871, p. [4], hereafter cited in text as "The Water Supply."

5. The transcript clearly indicates that Hildreth is referring here to "power" and not "powder."

6. The questioner is probably referring to "Ben Bullwinkle" and not "Dan Bullwinkle." Captain Benjamin B. Bullwinkle was the Superintendent of the Fire Insurance Patrol. This group was organized by the Chicago Board of Underwriters on October 2, 1871, only days before the fire. It was not under the corporate control of the fire department. Bullwinkle was the thirty-ninth person to testify at the inquiry. The *Chicago Republican* may have been alluding to this insurance wagon when it wrote that while the city was in flames, the insurance patrol charged private citizens a fee to move their belongings to safety: "It is said that, during the recent fire, the plunder wagon *alias* [emphasis in original] the Fire Insurance Patrol wagon realized very handsomely on $5 per trunk. Will Mr. Bullwinkle please rise to explain in the premises?" See "Chicago Condensed," *Chicago Republican*, 21 November 1871, p. [4]; Andreas, vol. 2, p. 94; Andreas, vol. 3, p. 462; Musham, pp. 183, 187. Bullwinkle commented on these charges during the inquiry investigation:

Q. (By Williams) Did you haul any trunks that night?

A. Yes sir, we hauled one or two trunks.

Q. Did you get any present?

A. I admit to getting a present of five or ten dollars for a trunk that I saved. I did not charge anybody any such price at all. It was voluntarily given to me. It was divided between the men. They were burned out and had no place to go.

Q. You didn't take the trunk expecting to have any pay when you took it?

A. I never dreamed of anything of the kind. Moreover, the trunk was thrown into our wagon. I did not know it was there till afterwards. If I had known the trunk belonged to the character it did, I should have thrown it out.

Q. That money was very acceptable, was it?

A. It was at that time, yes sir. None of us had a cent, no place to eat, we were living on a church at that time. I lost everything, house

and home, and the men the same way, no place to go. Those that lived on the North Side were burned out, had no place to go to and the same on the South Side. We were left on charity, going to church to get our meals at that time.

See Benjamin Bullwinkle, *Inquiry*, vol. [3], pp. 296–97. For Chicagoans' reminiscences of Bullwinkle, see Herma Clark, "When Chicago Was Young," *Chicago Sunday Tribune*, 9 February 1941, sec. 7, p. 2; Herma Clark, "When Chicago Was Young," *Chicago Sunday Tribune*, 23 February 1941, sec. 6, p. 8; Herma Clark, "When Chicago Was Young," *Chicago Sunday Tribune*, 2 March 1941, sec. 7, p. 5.

7. The December 3, 1871, *Chicago Times* indicates that "representatives of the press" were present while inquiry witnesses were interviewed. Hildreth's testimony suggests that not only were reporters present, they were also allowed to ask questions. See "How They Look and Act," p. [3].

8. Steamer *Fred Gund* No. 14. See 1871 Pay Roll.

9. A Babcock was a type of fire extinguisher. See "The Babcock Fire Extinguisher!," *Chicago Tribune*, 7 October 1871, p. 1; "The Babcock," *Chicago Tribune*, 19 November 1871, p. 7; *1870 City Directory*, p. 1013; *1871 City Directory*, p. 1016.

10. The Oriental Building was on the west side of LaSalle Street between Washington and Madison streets. See *1870 City Directory*, p. 944.

11. Williams's statement is ambiguous. At first it appears that he is referring to Congress Street. (See, e.g., Hildreth's testimony at page 143.) But Congress Street was parallel to and six blocks south of Washington Street. Sheahan and Upton's *The Great Conflagration*, Colbert and Chamberlin's *Chicago and the Great Conflagration*, and Goodspeed's *History of the Great Fires in Chicago and the West*, all contain comprehensive lists of principal buildings destroyed by the fire. None of the lists includes a "Congress Building." See Lowe, p. 42; Sheahan and Upton, pp. 146–51; Colbert and Chamberlin, pp. 288–98; Goodspeed, pp. 395–97.

12. The Union National Bank was located at the southwest corner of LaSalle and Washington streets. See Sheahan and Upton, p. 151. The December 1 *Chicago Evening Journal* commented somewhat sarcastically on Hildreth's bank-related exploits: "It appears that ex–Alderman Hildreth was the man who blew up buildings with powder, during the late fire, to check the conflagration. He says he and those helping him thus blew up thirty or forty buildings on the South Side. Among those

he tried to explode, but couldn't, was a bank. This speaks well for the bank. The ex–Alderman is entirely satisfied that it is folly for anybody to try to 'burst up' a Chicago bank. It can't be done—not even with powder." See untitled article, *Chicago Evening Journal*, 1 December 1871, p. [2], col. 2, fourth article.

13. Smith & Nixon's Hall was a theater located at the southwest corner of Washington and Clark streets. See Andreas, vol. 2, p. 611.

14. On December 2, 1871, the *Evening Journal* commented again on Hildreth's testimony: "Ex-Alderman Hildreth, in testifying before the Board of Police and Fire Commissioners, in regard to the part he took in blowing up buildings, said he attempted to blow up [the Union National Bank], and kicked in the heads of *five* [emphasis in original] kegs of powder, but the explosion was not a success, the room was too large. Now we learn from those connected with the bank who were there, that no such attempt was made as is described by the florid ex–Alderman, and what is more, he could not have reached there at the time he states if he had tried it with 'five kegs of powder.' We are aware that Hildreth did a good deal of blowing at the time referred to, but, like the wonderful exploit he describes, 'it was not a success.'" See "Not Much of a Blow," *Chicago Evening Journal*, 2 December 1871, p. [4]; *1870 City Directory*, p. 958; *1871 City Directory*, p. 981.

15. The Hazard Powder Company was located in the village of Brighton, about seven or eight miles from the fire. See Colbert and Chamberlin, p. 251; Pierce, vol. 2, p. 92; "Tales of the Great Fire," p. 2; Andreas, vol. 2, p. 735.

16. Robert Cromie maintains that the "spotted church" got its name from the mottled appearance of the stone used in its construction. See Cromie, p. 210.

17. This question concerning a "boot and shoe establishment" is clearly a reference to Michael Hickey's prior testimony. See Michael C. Hickey, *Inquiry*, vol. [2], p. 168.

18. This is probably not Hermann Raster, editor-in-chief of the German newspaper *Illinois-Staats Zeitung*. The *Times* of October 20 identifies this person as "a young man named Herman, a nephew of A. H. [*illeg.*]." See "The Gun-powder Plot," p. [3].

19. David A. Gage was Chicago City Treasurer in 1871. After the fire, he was appointed treasurer of the General Relief Committee—or as more colorfully described in Andreas' *History of Chicago*, "the treasurer and custodian of the world's contributions to the sufferers by the fire." Gage was not reelected city treasurer in 1873, and

auditors later discovered that he had embezzled over $500,000 in municipal funds. But there must have been early indications of improprieties. On October 28, 1871, the *Republican* reported that "there are anxious inquiries concerning Mr. David Gage's use of the city funds since he has been Treasurer. Will he rise to explain?" See *1871 City Directory*, pp. [33], 341; Andreas, vol. 2, p. 768; Andreas, vol. 3, p. 845; Sawislak, pp. 267, 352; Pierce, vol. 3, p. 343; Grosser, pp. [51–52]; Untitled article, *Chicago Republican*, 28 October 1871, p. [2].

20. Terrace Row was located on the west side of Michigan Avenue between Van Buren and Congress streets. It consisted of a connected block of eleven row houses or town houses. The matching homes were solid brick, faced with carved limestone, and four stories high. All were destroyed in the fire (Figures 82–83). See Kogan and Cromie, pp. 17–18; Pierce, vol. 2, p. 140; Lasswell, pp. 196–97; Miller, p. 158; Lowe, p. 42; Andreas, vol. 2, pp. 733, 739.

21. Munn & Scott's foreman was Cornelius Mahoney. See *1870 City Directory*, p. 543; *1871 City Directory*, p. 600. Cromie erroneously refers to the foreman as "Edward Mahoney." See Cromie, p. 216.

22. Munn & Scott was a grain elevator company owned by Ira Y. Munn and George L. Scott. By 1871 Chicago was a leader in the bulk grain trade, with fifteen elevators and a total storage capacity of 11,375,000 bushels. These elevators would receive grain from railroad cars, canal boats in the Illinois and Michigan Canal, and ships along the Chicago River. A train or ship would come up to one side of an elevator, and the grain would be pumped from the train or ship into the elevator and then poured out into other railroad cars or boats waiting on the opposite side of the elevator. Munn & Scott's City Elevator was located along the Illinois and Michigan Canal and the tracks of the Chicago and Northwestern Railway Company. The elevator had a storage capacity of 1,200,000 bushels. It was not destroyed by the fire. See Andreas, vol. 2, pp. 134, 373–76; Kogan and Cromie, p. 18.

23. John Driscoll was a first precinct policeman. See *1871 City Directory*, p. 276.

24. Edward Hood was a sergeant in the first precinct police station at the time Michael Hickey was captain. Cromie refers to him as Edward "Wood," a mistake surely due to the poor penmanship of the transcript. See Flinn, p. 134; Cromie, p. 216; *1871 City Directory*, p. 443.

25. The Michigan Avenue Hotel opened to the public in 1870 and was located a block south of Terrace Row at the southwest corner of Michigan

FIGURE 82—TERRACE ROW; PRE-FIRE. Terrace Row was the epitome of residential elegance in pre-fire Chicago. Located on Michigan Avenue, it offered an unobstructed view of Lake Michigan. Terrace Row's residents were among the wealthiest in the city. They included ex–Lieutenant Governor William Bross, who was part owner of the *Chicago Tribune*, and Jonathan Young Scammon, a founder of the Chicago Historical Society, the Chicago Academy of Sciences, and the Chicago Astronomical Society. (Chicago Historical Society ICHi-32477)

Avenue and Congress Street. After John B. Drake watched his hotel, the Tremont House, go down in flames, he happened to walk by the Michigan Avenue Hotel. With the fire burning across the street, but taking the chance that the hotel would be spared, Drake went inside and offered to buy the building. The offer was accepted, and Drake handed over one thousand dollars as a down payment. Drake's luck later turned. First Assistant Fire Marshal John Schank and the steam engine *T.B. Brown* No. 12 managed to keep the flames at bay. (Hildreth claimed that the blowing up of buildings also helped save the hotel.) After the fire Drake came back with the balance of the purchase price. Legend has it that when the proprietor refused to close the deal, Drake left and returned a few moments later with several friends. Drake laid a watch on the table and told the man that he wanted possession in five minutes or else the man would be thrown in the lake. Drake took possession, presumably within the requisite five minutes, and renamed the hotel the Tremont House after his ruined building. See Kogan and Cromie, p. 113; Cromie, pp. 219, 261; Andreas, vol. 2, pp. 502, 508–09; Miller, pp. 158, 162; John Schank, *Inquiry*, vol. [4], pp. 217–19; James H. Hildreth, *Inquiry*, vol. [2], pp.157–58; 1871 Pay Roll; Musham, p. 181; "Tremont House," *Chicago Times*, 19 October 1871, p. 1.

26. The *Tribune*'s summary of Hildreth's testimony refers to Hough as "O. M. Hough." But in an October 15 article about a meeting of the members of the Board of Trade, the *Tribune* mentions a "Colonel R. M. Hough." The 1870 Chicago city directory includes a listing for a bank messenger named "R. M. Hough" who boarded at 360 Wabash

Avenue. The 1871 directory notes that an "O. S. Hough" lived at 360 Wabash Avenue. Charles G. Wicker testified that "Mr. Hough is on the corner of Harrison and Wabash, that they begun to tear down...." The *Robinson's Atlas* indicates that the northeast corner of Harrison and Wabash is 360 Wabash Avenue. Chicago Title Insurance Company records disclose that "Oramel S. Hough" owned the lot at this northeast corner. The 1869 city directory confirms that "O. S. Hough" is "Oramel S. Hough." Although Oramel S. Hough owned and lived at this property, Colonel R. M. Hough also lived there; therefore, it is possible that Colonel R. M. Hough is the man Hildreth is referring to through-

FIGURE 83—TERRACE ROW AND GRAIN ELEVATORS; PRE-FIRE. The left side of this pre-fire (circa 1868) photograph of Michigan Avenue, looking north from Congress Street, offers another view of Terrace Row. On the right side, far in the background, are two grain elevators. (Chicago Historical Society ICHi-04438)

out his testimony and that his house was at 360 Wabash Avenue. Andreas indicates that during the Civil War, the 67th Illinois infantry regiment was commanded by Colonel Rosell M. Hough and that both he and Oramel S. Hough were involved in various facets of Chicago business since 1839. R. M. Hough retired from the packing firm of Jones, Hough & Co. in 1868. Perhaps he continued to work even after formal retirement; this would explain the 1870 Chicago city directory bank messenger listing. See "The Great Fire," *Chicago Tribune*, 30 November 1871, p. 4; "Board of Trade," *Chicago Tribune*, 15 October 1871, p. [4]; Chicago Title Insurance Company records; Andreas, vol. 2, pp. 227, 338–39; [*Edwards' Twelfth Annual Directory of the Inhabitants, Institutions, Incorporated Companies, and Manufacturing Establishments of the City of Chicago, Embracing a Complete Business Directory for 1869*] (Chicago: Richard Edwards, 1869), vol. 12, p. 428; *1870 City Directory*, p. 398;

1871 City Directory, p. 447; Charles G. Wicker, *Inquiry*, vol. [4], p. 63; *Robinson's Atlas*, vol. 1, plate 7.

27. General John A. Logan, Civil War hero and later United States senator. See Andreas, vol. 2, pp. 168–69.

28. This line is in the original transcript.

29. H. A. Musham maintains that this minister was the Reverend Simon McChesney of the Wabash Avenue Methodist Episcopal Church. But on the other hand, the 1871 Chicago city directory and Robert Cromie both indicate that R. M. Hatfield was the minister of this church. Andreas is of little help, noting that "in 1870, Rev. Mr. Hatfield again became pastor, and was succeeded in 1871, by Rev. S. McChesney." See Musham, p. 134; *1871 City Directory*, p. 43; Cromie, pp. 216–17; Andreas, vol. 2, p. 426.

30. Although the transcriber's handwriting is difficult to decipher, it appears that he or she

wrote "Harry" here. If so, this is very likely a mistake. Apparently James H. Hildreth was known informally by his middle name. However, the following listing for Hildreth in the 1870 Chicago City Directory (confirmed by the 1871 directory) indicates that this name was "Henry" and not "Harry": "Hildreth Henry, alderman, r. 574 S. Halsted." Also, the *Chicago Republican*'s summary of Hildreth's testimony refers to him as "Hank Hildreth." See *1870 City Directory*, p. 382; *1871 City Directory*, p. 429; "Among Ashes," *Chicago Republican*, 30 November 1871, p. [4], hereafter cited in text as "Among Ashes."

31. Both Musham and Cromie claim that this church was the Wabash Avenue Methodist Episcopal Church. Hildreth also refers to the Methodist Episcopal church in his testimony at pages 167–68. Musham maintains that this church was at the northeast corner of Wabash Avenue and Harrison Street. However, as mentioned above in note 26, Oramel S. Hough owned the land at this intersection. The 1870 Chicago City Directory states merely that the "Wabash Avenue" Methodist Church was at the "Corner Harrison street." Other directories contain similar inconclusive entries. But Chicago Title Insurance Company records and Andreas's *History of Chicago* indicate that the church was at the northwest corner of this intersection. After the fire, the post office was moved to this church, as it survived both the flames and Hildreth, who agreed to "let it stand." See Musham, p. 134; Cromie, pp. 216–17; *1870 City Directory*, p. 931; Andreas, vol. 2, pp. 389–90; Andreas, vol. 3, p. 791; Chicago Title Insurance Company records.

32. Andreas mentions the "Ogden Slip" when describing how Isaac N. Arnold, one of Chicago's early settlers and leading citizens, and his family fled their burning home: "The air was full of cinders and smoke; the wind blew the heated sand worse than any sirocco. Where was a place of refuge? William B. Ogden had lately constructed a long pier, north of, and parallel with, the old United States pier, which prolonged the left bank of the river out into the lake, and this had been filled with stone, but had not been planked over; hence, it would not readily burn. It was a hard road to travel, but it seemed the safest place; and Mr. Arnold and his children worked their way far out upon this pier. With much difficulty, the party crossed from the Ogden slip, in a small row-boat, and entered the light-house, where they, with Judge Goodrich, Edward I. Tinkham, and others, were hospitably received." See Andreas, vol. 2, p. 748; see also Goodspeed, p. 385; Smith, 82.

33. The *Republican*'s summary of that por-

tion of Hildreth's testimony concerning his drinking more than the firemen is as follows; emphasis is in the original: "[Hildreth] was very tired himself, having *eaten nothing* and drunk more, probably, than the firemen did; witness thought that the explosion in the Union National Bank, Smith & Nixon's, or at Brown & Matthew's, did not check the fire any...." This newspaper account is significant because not only does it suggest that the inquiry transcript is an accurate account of what Hildreth said, it also indicates that the Board did not interrupt Hildreth after this remark and ask him for further explanation. But the importance of Hildreth's comment was not lost on the *Republican*. Its article describing his testimony included this lengthy, sensational, and boldfaced subtitle that was surely a precursor to the headlines of today's grocery store tabloids: "The Fire Investigation—Hank Hildreth—What He Knows About Blowing Up Buildings—Phil. Sheridan, and How He Behaved—Who Was Drunk?—The Inside History." See "Among Ashes," p. [4].

34. The quotation marks around "powder" do not appear in the original transcript.

35. The emphasis on "powder" and the quotation marks around it are in the original.

36. Brown & Mathews were tailors at 93 Wabash Avenue. See *1870 City Directory*, p. 121.

37. Hotchkiss, Eddy & Co. was a wholesale firm that sold hats, caps, and furs. It was located at 114 and 116 Wabash Avenue. See Colbert and Chamberlin, p. 298; *1871 City Directory*, p. 1028.

38. Patrick O'Neill owned the building at the southeast corner of Harrison and Dearborn streets. Goodspeed claimed that "O'Neil's brick block was blown up by powder, and prevented the further spread in that direction." See Chicago Title Insurance Company records; Goodspeed, p. 147.

39. Although the transcriber wrote "Taylors" here, it seems likely that Hildreth is referring to the "tailors'" buildings (or building?) of John H. Brown and George W. Mathews. See *1870 City Directory*, p. 121. (A similar reference is at page 170 of Hildreth's testimony, but there the transcriber wrote the singular "building." Hildreth had previously mentioned "Brown and Mathews" at page 153 of his testimony.)

40. The exclamation point appears in the original transcript; the quotation marks around "powder" are added.

41. The firehouse of the steam engine *Long John* No. 1. See 1871 Pay Roll.

42. This is apparently a reference to *America* Hose Cart No. 2. Marshal Williams' testimony is curious, however, in that he is referring to the

America as an engine and not as a hose cart. The Chicago Fire Department did not have an *America* steam engine. See 1871 Pay Roll, Musham, pp. 181–87.

43. The word "engine" was originally written here but crossed out.

44. At first this also appears to be a reference to newspaper editor Hermann Raster. However, this is probably not the case. The *Staats Zeitung* building was at 104 Madison Street, which was between Dearborn and Clark streets. Although this building was destroyed by the fire, it was several blocks north of the area blown up by Hildreth. Hermann Raster lived at 600 North Dearborn Street, but again, this was north of the area where Hildreth was working. See *1870 City Directory*, pp. 678, 783, [913], 1066; *1871 City Directory*, pp. 740, 847, 1054; Sheahan and Upton, p. 149; Lowe, p. 42; Jim Murphy, *The Great Fire* (New York: Scholastic, 1995), pp. 98–99; Sawislak, p. 75; *Robinson's Atlas*, vol. 3, plate 21.

45. George W. Gage was a former alderman and one of the founders of the Chicago Relief and Aid Society. This organization was incorporated in 1857; its purpose, as described by Andreas, was to aid in "the general relief of the needy." On October 13, 1871, just days after the fire was extinguished, Mayor Mason transferred the task of municipal relief from the General Relief Committee to this society, proclaiming that "I have deemed it best for the interest of the city to turn over to the Chicago Relief and Aid Society all contributions for the suffering people of this city." But tales of inefficiency, favoritism, dishonesty, and fraud soon surfaced, and in a litany of editorials, articles, and letters, the *Chicago Republican* attacked the society. Typical of these is the following allegation that compared the Executive Committee of the Relief and Aid Society to Tammany Hall, the Democratic machine that ruled New York City under the infamous William M. "Boss" Tweed: "We accuse [the Executive Committee] here, public[l]y, in the face of the whole country whose bounty they have squandered, in the presence of their helpless wards whose interests they have betrayed, of acting as dishonorably as Tweed, Sweeny and the arch-thieves of the broken Tammany ring could have done, and now proceed to proof." See Andreas, vol. 2, pp. 49–50, 670; Sawislak, p. 81; *Report of the Chicago Relief and Aid Society*, p. 121; "The Relief Funds," *Chicago Republican*, 22 November 1871, p. [2]; "Public Opinion," *Chicago Republican*, 23 November 1871, p. [2]; Untitled articles, *Chicago Republican*, 23 November 1871, p. [2], col. 1, first, fourth, and sixth articles; Untitled article, *Chicago Republican*, 27 November 1871, p. [2]; "Opening

Fire," *Chicago Republican*, 2 December 1871, p. [4]; "Wirt's Work," *Chicago Republican*, 2 December 1871, p. [4]; Untitled article, *Chicago Republican*, 2 December 1871, p. [2], col. 2; "Indorsed," *Chicago Republican*, 4 December 1871, p. [4]; "Public Opinion," *Chicago Republican*, 4 December 1871, p. [2]. For a critical look at the Chicago Relief and Aid Society, see Sawislak, pp. 69–119 passim; Smith, pp. 64–77. For a more sympathetic view, see Elisabeth Kimbell, "We Could Not Do Without the Chicago Fire...," *Chicago History* 1 (Fall 1971), pp. 220–231.

46. "Mr. Hayes" is probably Samuel S. Hayes, who was also one of the founders of the Chicago Relief and Aid Society. After the fire, Hayes drafted a proclamation that informed Chicagoans of what was being done for the sufferers. See Andreas, vol. 2, pp. 105, 670, 763–64; *Report of the Chicago Relief and Aid Society*, pp. 15–16; "Common Council," *Chicago Republican*, 15 November 1871, p. [2]. The proclamation read as follows:

PROCLAMATION.

WHEREAS, In the providence of God, to whose will we humbly submit, a terrible calamity has befallen our city, which demands of us our best efforts for the preservation of order and the relief of suffering:—

Be it known, That the faith and credit of the city of Chicago are hereby pledged for the necessary expenses for the relief of the suffering.

Public order will be preserved. The police and special police now being appointed will be responsible for the maintenance of the peace and the protection of property.

All officers and men of the Fire Department and Health Department will act as special policemen without further notice.

The Mayor and Comptroller will give vouchers for all supplies furnished by the different relief committees.

The headquarters of the City Government will be at the Congregational Church, corner of West Washington and Ann Streets.

All persons are warned against any act tending to endanger property. Persons caught in any depredation will be immediately arrested.

With the help of God, order and peace and private property will be preserved.

The City Government and the committee of citizens pledge themselves to the community to protect them, and prepare the way for a restoration of public and private welfare.

It is believed the fire has spent its force, and all will soon be well.

R. B. MASON, *Mayor.*
GEORGE TAYLOR, *Comptroller.*
(By R. B. MASON.)

CHARLES C. P. HOLDEN, *President Common Council.*
T. B. BROWN, *President Board of Police.*

October 9, 1871, 3 P.M.

47. Andreas writes that "it was [at the Wabash Avenue Methodist Church] that Mark Sheridan made his famous stand against the fire to save the church." Perhaps this comment is the "famous stand" to which Andreas is referring. See Andreas, vol. 2, p. 390.

48. Third Assistant Fire Marshal Mathias Benner testified that at one point a turret on the northeast side of the church was on fire, but because "solid masonry" was beneath the turret, the fire could do no harm. Both Benner and Hildreth apparently then left the area, Hildreth to the North Side and Benner to the corner of Congress Street and Michigan Avenue just two blocks away to the northeast. This may be why neither man told the Board how William Haskell, a former professional gymnast who had served as a Union scout during the Civil War, allegedly extinguished this fire and saved the church. Haskell first clambered up a ladder to the roof of the church. He carried a rope with him to haul up water, which was provided by a bucket brigade that formed a line to the lake. Throwing water on the rocks of the turret to cool them (the inside of this tower was on fire), he then climbed the side of the turret to the top, which was one hundred feet from the street. By now his clothes were smoldering; nonetheless, he managed to lower himself into the tower and put out the fire. See Mathias Benner, *Inquiry*, vol. [4], pp. 162–63; James H. Hildreth, *Inquiry*, vol. [3], pp. 150–52, 168; Cromie, pp. 220–22; Lowe, p. 42.

49. Colonel "Hough" is referred to as "Huff" and "Hull" on pages 168 and 169 of Hildreth's testimony. This appears to be an obvious error and has been silently corrected.

50. As Harrison Street is an east-west street, it is not clear what the phrase "this was after the fire was all stopped on Harrison Street east" means. This ambiguous sentence is shown exactly as it appears in the transcript.

51. Steamer *A.D. Titsworth* No. 13. See 1871 Pay Roll.

52. Although the transcriber wrote "Taylors" here, it seems likely that Hildreth is again referring to "tailors'."

53. "Mr. Stearns" is probably Colonel M. C. Stearns. Colbert and Chamberlin wrote of the personal experiences of Horace White, editor of the *Tribune*, who commented: "At what time the effort was first made to reach this magazine, and bring powder into the service, I have not learned, but I

know that Colonel M. C. Stearns made heroic efforts with his great lime wagons to haul the explosive material to the proper point." This is probably the "Mr. Stearns" to whom Hildreth is referring. See Colbert and Chamberlin, pp. 246, 252.

54. General Sheridan would soon have more important things to worry about than powder. The fire was barely extinguished before newspapers began reporting stories of criminals and incendiaries stalking what was left of the streets of Chicago. On October 11, 1871, Mayor Mason, concerned about an outbreak of lawlessness, transferred absolute police authority to the general. Sheridan ordered that a regiment of volunteers be formed. On the night of October 21, Thomas W. Grosvenor, the city's prosecuting attorney, was walking home after visiting a friend. He was stopped about two blocks from his house by a twenty-year-old college student named Theodore Treat, who was one of these volunteers. Treat told him to halt, but Grosvenor ignored him, kept walking, and recklessly told Treat to "go to hell and bang away." Treat fired his rifle and killed Grosvenor.

In an editorial the next day, the *Times* angrily protested Sheridan's presence in the city: "It is reported that General Sheridan is the generalissimo whom the valiant college boys have regarded as the authority for their lawless proceedings. Who is General Sheridan? Is he some imperial satrap in whose favor the city of Chicago or the state of Illinois have abdicated their functions? Who gave General Sheridan authority to put muskets in the hands of a parcel of crack-brained college boys?" The Board of Police held a special meeting on October 21. The Board drafted a letter to the mayor, suggesting that the presence of armed military forces patrolling the streets was "a nuisance fraught with evil consequences" and that all but "regular troops" should be relieved of further duty in the city. On October 24, the military was withdrawn and the volunteers were disbanded.

But as the troops moved out, a sense of uneasiness moved in, and on October 28 a number of leading Chicagoans wrote Sheridan and asked him to send four companies of United States Infantry, to be stationed at or near the city until the threat of "riotous proceedings" passed. Sheridan did not hesitate to comply with this request. The *Evening Journal* heartily approved, editorializing "that the people of Chicago have a right to the security which the presence of these troops affords them, no one with a grain of sense will pretend to question." But Illinois Governor John M. Palmer was opposed to the return of military troops to Chicago. By this time, Palmer had investigated the Grosvenor killing, and on October 28 he wrote

Attorney General Washington Bushnell and charged that the actions of Mayor Mason and General Sheridan were illegal in that they had suspended the laws of the State of Illinois and the U.S. Constitution in favor of the law of military force. He added one final note: "I have to request that you, in conjunction with the State's attorney of the Seventh Judicial Circuit, will bring all the facts before the grand jury of Cook County, in order that all persons concerned in the unlawful killing of Thomas W. Grosvenor may be brought to speedy trial."

Two days later Governor Palmer wrote to Charles H. Reed, state's attorney for the Seventh Judicial Circuit: "The matter has occasioned me a great amount of anxiety; and after the most mature reflection, I am forced to the conviction that the indictment against Treat, the person who inflicted the wounds upon him, should also include Philip H. Sheridan...." Although an inquest was held and a coroner's jury determined Grosvenor's death to be a homicide, it appears that no further action was taken against either Treat or Sheridan.

Sixteen years later, John J. Flinn published his *History of the Chicago Police.* Flinn was generally charitable in his assessment of these citizen patrols, but even he concluded the following: "Undisciplined, inexperienced, panicky and inclined to look with suspicion upon every stranger who came along, they served to increase rather than to diminish the alarm of honest people in many quarters." (Figure 84) See Cromie, pp. 270–76; Andreas, vol. 2, pp. 773–80; "Shocking Calamity," *Chicago Tribune,* 22 October 1871, p. 1; "The Grosvenor Tragedy," *Chicago Tribune,* 23 October 1871, p. 1; "The Grosvenor Tragedy," *Chicago Tribune,* 24 October 1871, p. 1; "The University Assassins," *Chicago Times,* 22 October 1871, p. [2]; "The Grosvenor Homicide," *Chicago Times,* 24 October 1871, p. 1; "Sheridan's Indictment," *Chicago Times,* 4 November 1871, p. 1; Untitled article, *Chicago Times,* 4 November 1871, p. [2]; "United States Troops in Chicago," *Chicago Evening Journal,* 2 November 1871, p. 1; "Fire Mayor of Chicago Built Many Railroads," *Chicago Evening Post,* 8 October 1921, Chicago Fire Edition, sec. 4, p. 18; Colbert and Chamberlin, pp. 398–99; Manly W. Mumford, *The Old Family Fire* (Evanston, Ill.: Chicago Historical Bookworks, 1997), pp. 16–17; Sawislak, pp. 55–63, 297–99; Flinn, p. 126; *1871 City Directory,* p. [33].

ROBERT A. WILLIAMS

[234]

December 2nd, 1871
Robert A. Williams sworn
(49th witness)

Q. What do you know about the origin and progress of the fire of October 8th and 9th?

A. I do not know anything about the origin. The first I knew of it was when the alarm came in. I was then abed. I would state on Saturday night I did not go home until seven o'clock in the morning.[1] Box 7 came in.[2] I went down and put out some fire that was on top of the old wooden elevator on the bank of the river just east of Lake Street bridge.[3] From there I went home and went right to bed. I slept from that to a quarter past two o'clock. I did not have any breakfast. I got up after my wife came from church and washed my face, put on some clean clothes, and went downstairs and ate some dinner. There was an [235] old lady called to see us. I went downstairs and stayed there for three quarters of an hour. I left her along with my wife, hitched up my horse, thinking that I would take a drive over to the old battleground,[4] see what engines were working, and also to the different engine houses to see what was wrong with them and get ready in case of another breeze. I went to the *John's* house and got my horse and buggy and started. I went over there, and before I went away I sent the *Titsworth* home. I did not see any use of keeping them there. I thought these men at the coal piles ought to shovel them to one side.[5] I then went home and took supper, and after supper I told my wife that I wanted to go over to Mr. Benner's.[6] We started to go over. I told her I would not stay twenty minutes. [236] I started out and crossed Franklin Street on Randolph just west of the courthouse, and Box 28,[7] I believe it was, came in. "There," said I, "There is just my luck." I left my wife on the sidewalk. Said she, "I won't go over; I will go back home." I ran along Randolph Street and met my wagon opposite the west wing of the courthouse. I went to Box 28. It did not amount to anything.[8] I came home again. The wind was blowing terribly hard. I had to pull my hat down on my head two or three times. I went back home and

FIGURE 84—GUARDING THE RUINED CITY. Alfred R. Waud's sketch of a rather formidable armed sentry confronting two trembling passersby amidst a bleak landscape of fire ruins is actually a portrait of Waud and Ralph Keeler. Keeler explains the story behind the drawing: "After passing the whole day collecting these sketches of Chicago on its first Sabbath after its dreary week of disaster, we were hurrying to catch the nine o'clock train for St. Louis.... We had little time to lose, and were walking as fast as we could through the burnt district, watching the grand effects upon the ruins of the distant coal piles towering and glaring upon the night, like volcanoes, when we heard a very loud and imperious 'Halt! Who goes there?' Turning suddenly in the direction of the startling sound, we became unpleasantly aware of a bayonet gleaming right in front of us, and of a soldier behind it. We explained our case to him ... and finally reached the depot just in time for the train." Here Waud masterfully juxtaposes the billowing coat, stern gaze, and rugged stance of the larger-than-life sentry with the timorous Waud and Keeler to create a superlative study of contrasts. (Chicago Historical Society ICHi-02990)

went upstairs and told my wife, "I am going to bed early. I feel as though I had got to be out between this and morning, the way the wind is blowing."[9] I got my fire clothes and laid everything down, ready to jump into them, and went to bed. My wife was sitting up reading and, [237] said I, "I either wish you would go to bed or close the door so I can go to sleep," so she got up and shut the door between our room and the sitting room. So I got to sleep and was asleep when the alarm came in. My wife had just come to bed. I got the very first tap of the gong, and at the same time my wife hit me with her elbow and said, "Robert! Fire!" I got up and dressed and went down and I could see a light. Said I, "There is no use of my running to meet the wagon. We have got to go to the West Side, and I will just stand here until the wagon comes along." I did not count what box it was from the gong. I can dress and get out faster than 342 comes in. I knew the driver always got the location of the box before he started. I jumped into the [238] wagon, and we crossed over Randolph Street bridge and went right to Desplaines Street. I was busy pulling on my rubber coat and buttoning it up and did not pay any attention when we came to Harrison Street, did not think we were so near Harrison Street until we turned the corner and had gone perhaps fifty feet. Said I, "We have gone out of the way. We ought to go up Desplaines Street." Said I, "We cannot go along Union Street; it don't run through." I went through to Halsted and went to Taylor. Said I, "Haul off here," and he hauled off and went onto Taylor and Jefferson.[10] I jumped out of the wagon and ran in on Taylor Street. I there saw—there was a vacant lot in there—I saw a hose in there, when I ran into that and saw it was the *America* hose. There was the rear end of two buildings on Taylor Street [239] facing north that were afire then, and there were two barns and a lot of little outhouses and fences, and I don't know what. There was a regular nest of fire. Said I, "Hang on to her, boys," just like that. I saw two men at the pipe.[11] I ran east of Clinton Street to see if there was anything else coming in. I had a very good time getting in there. I did not see anything else coming in to go there, and I came back again. When I came back, I still encouraged the boys. Said I, "Hang on to her, boys; she is gaining on us." I went out again and went

through Taylor, thought to get around on the west side of it and see if there was a vacant place through and whether it was going to run along on us, and just at that the *Illinois*[12] led in. I saw Mullin.[13] Said I, "Where is your water, Bill?" Said he, "It is coming, sir, coming." [240] He started back as fast as he could run along Taylor Street, and before he could find the engine they had let their water on, and he came back again. I took hold, the *Illinois* being short of men, and helped the men with their pipe, and it was very warm. I helped them in from Taylor Street to the rear and go in far enough so we could turn the pipe and strike the rear of the building. The building faced north. "Now," said I, "Hang on to her here." Bill said, "Marshal, I don't believe we can stand it here." Said I, "Stand it as long as you can." I then ran out and got around to the east side of these buildings on fire and saw the *America* hose. I saw then the buildings on the north side of Taylor Street were smoking and just ready to ignite. I ran in and, said I, "You go and [241] turn in the second alarm. This is going to spread." The driver said, "I do not know how to turn in the second alarm." Said I, "You go, Dorsey."[14] Said I, "Charley,[15] lead the pipe out of here; these buildings to the north side are going to burn." There were some outsiders there, and I said, "Please help light out this hose." Before we got it out on Taylor Street and had a chance to wet the front buildings on the north side of Taylor Street, the water was cut off. Said I, "Who in the devil has cut off this lead?" The foreman, I think it was, said he did. Said I, "Put it on again." So he put it onto his engine; and when I saw it in there, I started back; and before I got back, the houses were all afire, some four or five of them on the north side of Taylor Street. I do not think it was more than [242] a minute-and-a-half before the whole center of the block back in the alley between Taylor and Forquer Street, I believe it is, the next street north of that, they were all on fire.[16] The *Chicago*[17] led in there in the meantime. I jumped over her and [ought?] to have put her in before. She had got in when I went back. She led in there, and she led in north of Taylor Street, in between some buildings and back in there to the rear end of the buildings facing the south. The *Illinois* went to playing there on Taylor Street, but there were so many buildings on fire in the rear, in the center of that block, and it was running through to-wards Canal Street, and I ran back again and ran through. Thinks I, "There might be some other engines coming in on the east." There was some other engine; I did not know what it was—there was so [243] much smoke and dust, but they were leading in from Canal Street. I cannot tell what steamer it was. There was so much smoke and sparks that it was utterly im-possible to see a man half the time. We got four streams on Ewing Street, and there we thought we could stop it. They then came and said the church was afire.

Q. How many blocks away was the church?

A. Ewing—then there is Polk and For-quer—I should [blank] there were three of those blocks between us and the church.[18] I told George Rau, the foreman of Hook and Ladder 2,[19] "Go and put up your longest ladder." The wind was blowing so hard, I knew I could not throw a stream up to where it was on fire. Said I, "You go and put up a ladder, and I will get a stream down there just as quickly as I can." I started down and saw an engine [244] up that way, that was the Rehm,[20] and when I got down there, they took the plug on the opposite cor-ner, that was the south side of Forquer Street. The church was on the north side, corner of Clinton. In the meantime, Mr. Swenie[21] had come in there and wanted to know what I wanted him to do. That is the foreman of the Gund. Said I, "Go to work on the nearest build-ings you can." Said he, "All but one plug is taken up, and I have not hose enough to lead from any plug I can get at." Of course I could not run away, as the fire was going, to hunt up a plug and to hunt up hose.[22] Said I, "Do the best you can, Denis," and he went down and according to his testimony, he saw the Rehm and supposed they were going to form into line to-gether.[23] I went down there, and when I went down, I [245] saw the long ladder thrown down and broken in two halves, so I could not get the stream up. It appeared they had got it so it appeared to be put out, and the first thing I knew, it seemed to burst out between the ceil-ing and the roof. The Gund had then come around and got to work on Bateham's plug and led in on Mather Street from Canal. The smoke was very thick there. I do not know what com-pany it was. I went back through there. It was very warm there between the buildings on the

south side of Mather Street and the church. I saw it was the Gund Company. Said I, "Denis, cannot you work in north of this? I am afraid it is going to get ahead of us in there." Said he, "I think if we could get up on that flat roof there, we could switch it both ways." Said I, "if you can [246] get up there, see." He went and came back and said they could get up on the flat roof, and they went up there. There was a stream there. I saw he was doing very well. I came back to the Rehm. There were two leads. The boys' coats were burning in some places. I said, "Boys, hang to it or you will have to pull the engine away just as soon as it falls; it will be all right as soon as the first breeze is over."[24] Just at that time the steeple dropped right down. There was another lead. I do not know what pipe it was on the north side of it. The Rehm had out two leads, and there was another stream; I do not know whether it was the Williams[25] or not, but I think it was. She led from the west side of the fire. There was a drug store on the opposite side of the street, and we had hard [247] work to keep it out of that drug store. It was on fire sev-eral times, but we made out to keep it out. The next thing I knew, they came and told me Bate-ham's mill was on fire. I saw Mr. Schank some-time about that time, and said he, "Do you know the fire is getting ahead of you?" Said I, "Yes, it is getting ahead of me in spite of all I can do." I ran along north from the church. I told the Rehm, "You will have to go away from here, or you won't be able to pull out." So they left that plug. They had a door up to keep the heat away.[26] So I ran north. I found the wooden building belonging to the match factory was all aflame. The brick building was smoking very badly. Coming north of that, I found that the lumberyard just north of the match factory was on fire, and I [248] ran around to the front of Bateham's mill and passed through and passed the front shop, and they had two leads in there. I went in there, but the fire was coming down thicker than any snowstorm you ever saw, and the yard between the two mills was all filled with shavings, and chunks of fire came in of all sizes, from the length of your arm down to three inches. Leo Meyers was in there, and I said, "It is gone, sure." Said he, "I am afraid it is." I said, "If it has got to go, we will try and cut it off at Harrison Street." I ran north, and just as I was going out, the Gund engine was pulled away from the plug. There was some fire on the side-walk amongst a lot of lumber that was piled there. I was very well aware that the way the wind was blowing, it wouldn't be more than [249] two minutes before they would be driven out. I told the boys to get north of the fire. While they were going back, I met some po-licemen on Harrison Street. I said, "Shove down this office." I thought I would get that lumber office down, and with [Keeler's?] brick on the opposite corner, we would be pretty sure to cut if off there. They didn't succeed in shov-ing that over. The mill was then on fire. It was terribly hot. Set fire to the three-story boarding house and saloon between Bateham's and the wood yard, and when that got on fire, it was so high it threw out a terrific heat. They stopped and set their engine to work there, but I said, "You'll hardly get to work before you'll have to move. You had better go north and lead up this way and [illeg.] it." They led up north of Van Buren. The *John* had gone north to the plug that was in [250] the center between Harrison and Van Buren. Then [the] *Gund* went and took the corner of Van Buren and Canal and led one stream up this way, the other around this way (indicating). But before they got to work, the fire was then down about the center, started a new fire about the center of the block between Harrison and Van Buren. I was with the *John's* lead, was in with Alec.[27] He says, "Robert, we can't stay long here." Said I, "Hang on as long as you can." Said he, "I'll hang on as long as I can, but I can't hang any longer." Said I, "Get your horses around so as to be ready to pull away." They hung so long they hadn't time to do anything but disconnect the suction[28] and pull the hose and suction and all north on Van Buren Street. They pulled to Lull & [251] Holmes planing mill where it burned the night before. Alec was running to get a length of hose and had a length on his shoulder when he saw the fire on the South Side and dropped the hose and said, "Robert, the fire is on the South Side." Said I, "The devil it is." Said he, "You look." I did. Said I, "Go for it. I'll be there in a minute. You go to work." I then turned around and told Mr. Swenie, said I, "Denis, if you don't get the engine away, you'll lose her."[29] There was a crowd of outsiders around there. Said I, "Gentlemen, won't you help get that engine away and pull this hose back?" It was so hot a

man couldn't hang on to it. Before that, I saw Captain Hickey and Sergeant Lull and told them, "I wish you'd send some of your men [252] up on that large roof and keep the sparks off, and I think by keeping the sparks off, that with this brick building on the south side of Van Buren, we will be able to check it and save that row." I then turned around and told him to move the engine or he would lose it. I then pumped on a hose cart there, I think the *Wash-ington*, and rode towards the South Side.

Q. Was the lumber office on the corner burning?

A. Yes sir.

Q. On the south side of Van Buren?

A. Yes sir. I saw there was no salvation for the engine, that she couldn't stay there. It was a terrible fire that was coming down at the time. I then pumped on the hose cart and crossed to the South Side.

Q. Over Van Buren Street bridge?

A. No sir. We crossed over Madison Street. [253] The viaduct at Adams had been burned.[30] It wasn't safe to drive over with an engine or hose cart. I tried to pass the *John* as I drove on the [mesh?] of the bridge to get ahead of them, but there was a team in the way, so I had to allow them to pass over first. Didn't get ahead of the *John* at all. She went to Monroe Street. We passed by the *John* there. I went to Adams Street. I found the fire was this side. Somebody told me there was a fire south of the Armory, but I didn't pay any attention to that fire south of the Armory because I saw this was the way the wind was blowing, the fire being north of Adams Street. I ran around again to Monroe Street and came in down Market Street, and the cart drove through to Wells Street and gave the *John* the hose. Schank said [254] the *John* was there and had no hose. That is the first the *John* got to work there. I ran around, and the *Economy* was working. It wasn't, I guess, but about a minute-and-a-half until the *Brown's*[31] lead came in there on Monroe Street. When I went down, I ran in and saw the east part of the gas works was on fire. I ran down that place that ran down into the yard from Monroe Street. I saw some men in there to work. When I was running down in there, somebody hollered to me to come out of there, "You'll be blown to pieces!" I thought as long as they were in there, I'd take my chances. I ran down to get north of the fire. The fire was very warm, and men were running around there and hiding themselves. Thinks I, in case of explosion, I won't put my [255] men down in there. The fire was beating each way. It was all afire clear through there. There was heaps of empty barrels that burned worse than powder. It burned as quick as powder. It was terrible there, and the wind was blowing so we could not touch the cornice. The barn of the "Merchants Union"[32] was burning north side of Monroe Street. The cornice got afire, and we couldn't reach it. The next thing I saw, the fire had gone clear north between Monroe and Madison Street. I ran east towards Wells Street, and there somebody told me, "The fire is running down Wells Street between Monroe and Madison Street." I ran through to Wells and ran back again.

Q. The Express barn was east of Wells, wasn't it?

A. No sir. The Express barn was west of Wells. It was somewhere along about where Franklin Street [256] would be if it went through. I ran back and told the *Economy* to get in north of the fire. I then started and ran down Monroe Street to Market, down Market to Madison, and down Madison. It was all on fire there then. I saw the fire north of Madison Street. I sent to the *Economy* to come down there. I sent her to the plug at the corner of Washington Street. When I got down there, the *Coventry* had already come to the corner of Madison and LaSalle. Said I, "Hurry up, boys; it is all afire back of this Oriental Building."

Q. Was the fire north of Madison Street?

A. Yes sir.

Q. Whereabouts?

A. Right in the rear of the Oriental Building. I broke out some glass in the basement in an office. I don't know whose office it was and didn't care. I broke out the window and [257] got inside. I pulled up the bolt and opened it so the men could go through the back door, and I got the boys through into an [a rear?] way, I think, perhaps eight or ten feet or maybe twelve feet in the back of the building.[33] I got the boys back there and we turned our stream up. We couldn't throw it ten feet from the pipe. It was all cut down. The wind was blowing so fearfully hard.[34] I told them to hold on there. I then went into the street and found the *Economy*. They were "leading up"[35] in the Oriental

Building. I told them, "I don't want you here." We went down on Washington Street on the corner, and I led them through the first stairway into LaSalle Street. The next place I saw them was out on the street. I went around to see what the *Coventry* was doing. When I went there, I met Mr. Hildreth, and he told me, "You have got [258] to throw the engines to one side and commence blowing up." Said I, "Have you got powder?" He said, "I have." Said I, "I don't know where to commence." I knew the fire was running to that new building of Greenebaum's south of the Metropolitan Hotel[36] and also on the east side; it was coming down through there, and the blowing up of buildings there wouldn't amount to anything. There was chunks of fire blowing over us then, of all lengths and all sizes. It was blowing a block ahead of us. I said, "Take that bank on the corner.[37] Be sure you have people out before you do it." The next thing I saw, Mr. Hildreth was in there. Said I, "There's the courthouse on fire." I ordered the *Economy* down to the corner of LaSalle and worked along on the front of the Sherman House and these other buildings. I ran back again. [259] Mr. Hildreth ran to the courthouse. I ran to Madison Street. Then the flames were rolling down over the Oriental Building clear over the *John*'s house. I ran back and said, "Boys, you'll have to get away from here," and only for Bullwinkle's[38] men we never would have got away from there. It was Bullwinkle's men that broke the taper[39] off, and there wasn't enough of their own men there— the others were in the alley, and they had just passed into the street. [260] I told them to go down to the corner of Randolph Street to the Sherman House plug, and they started down Madison Street, and I supposed were going around there. They got as far as the corner of Washington and found they couldn't do any good on account of the taper. They drove away from there, and I didn't know where the fellows had gone. I went back and helped the *Economy* lead out their hose. There was only two men on it. I asked the driver and somebody else to help lead the hose down. They hadn't hose enough. Just then Swenie drove up with his hose and cart. Said I, "Have you any hose, Denis?" He said, "Yes, I have." "Give the *Economy* two lengths," said I. He done so. The *Washington* hose cart[40] [261] came around the corner of

Randolph, and I jumped on the cart and drove around to the *Titsworth*'s house to see what had become of the *Coventry* engine. I wanted them there because things were getting on fire in Miller's jewelry store.[41] They said there had been one engine there, but it had gone away. I then went away, and when I got back, Miller's jewelry store was all on fire. There was a piece of board, seemed to be three or four feet long; I do not know whether it came from the courthouse or the Board of Trade—it lit on the old *Tribune* row, the other side of Clark Street, from the Sherman House, and that was all on fire. The *Economy* then went down to the corner of LaSalle, I think, and [262] Lake Street. The fire had jumped over the Sherman House and got in the wooden buildings facing on Lake Street. I started for the West Side to see if I couldn't get an engine or two, but I couldn't see any engine except the *Illinois*. The rest were away at the south of the fire. I thought I had better go back and see there. Maybe some of them have rolled in there. I went back, and after I got back, somebody said the fire had crossed to the North Side, and the water works was on fire. I couldn't hardly believe it. Then I knew if the water works were on fire, there was no hopes of saving anything. I hadn't then any hopes of saving anything from the courthouse down. When I heard the water [263] works was afire, I took and jumped in my wagon and drove over to the North Side far enough to see that it was so, and then I gave up all hopes of being able to save much of anything. I came back again, and by that time the *Williams* had got to playing down on Lake Street, corner of Wells, and I got the *Chicago* and sent her down to Schuttler's corner.[42] The fire then was running through right into Gale's drug store.[43] I sent her down and led in the rear first until it caught fire. Then led down LaSalle Street and got the *Williams* to lead up Wells Street, thinking I might throw the fire off northeast; but it wasn't long before the fire rolled out of the front of Gale's drug store, right almost across the street; and the fire seemed to be [264] further along this way, three or four buildings, in the basement. I then made up my mind it was time for me to get my wife out.

Q. That was about opposite to where you boarded?

A. Gale's was about 150 feet east of where I boarded.[44] I ran up and found Mrs. Highland

there, and they had got out some of her things. Said I, "You go away from here and let everything go." Captain Miller was there and two or three others. One of the men belonging to the *Long John* was there. He said he had been told that the *Long John* was burned up. Said I, "Will you help take down this piano of mine?" Went up there and the boys were going to take it out just as it was. I commenced unscrewing the legs. When they got that out of the room, thinks I, I will try and save this carpet. Then [265] the glass began to crack in the windows. I had a new stove that cost me forty-six dollars. I tumbled that on the floor and went downstairs with the carpet. When I got down to the foot of the stairs, somebody or other grabbed the carpet and took it away. I went halfway up the first story again. It was getting so hot I thought I wouldn't go. That was all I got of my things.[45] The *Chicago* then had led back and was playing upon some wooden buildings, trying to keep it from crossing the street, but the fire had then got into a large block there, and I knew there was no use at all of trying to do anything. The *Chicago* then went back to work at the corner of Randolph and Market streets, and I was down on Lake Street and South Water. She moved away from there. I don't [266] know where she went. I saw the *Williams* down there and the *Winnebago*,[46] and somebody came to me and said the fire was going to cross to the West Side at the foot of Washington Street. There was big piles of coal on fire right on Market Street. I drove around there and found the *Chicago* there and this new engine of *Richards*,[47] and they didn't have enough hose to wet down the back of those buildings. I said, "How much hose have you got, *Chicago*?" They told me they had a reel. Nearly a full reel of hose. I thought I would let the *Richards* engine put on two lengths more and keep that from burning. That is the elevator at the foot of Washington Street.[48] The *Chicago* went to the North Side. I saw the buildings were all burning on the south [267] bank of the Chicago River. The *Winnebago*, while I was over to the West Side, went to the North Side, and the *Williams* went to the West Side and led her hose across Lake Street bridge. I went over to the North Side, and the *Winnebago* was working from the plug at the corner of Kinzie and Wells and was playing on the building that the Northwestern Railroad offices were in.[49] As soon as I reached the ground, some of the officers there came to me and said, "Here, Marshal Williams, if you want to do us any good, save our depot. It has got on fire and will you save our depot?" It had a very heavy cornice on the south side. I ordered the *Winnebago* to lead up their hose from where they were play-ing and get on the [268] [*blank*] of the build-ing and throw up some water there on the south side, but the *Winnebago* was getting out of water, and I led them right up alongside and put the pipe over a kind of balcony. We got there, and after we had been playing awhile, the whole gar-ret was full of fire, and there was a kind of green and blue mass ran down out of that. I did not for two or three days find out what it was. They had all their telegraph fixings up there, so I made up my mind it was that. I did not know but what somebody had been preparing that to burn.[50] I guess it must have been the chemicals of the telegraph.[51] The *Winnebago* was doing well there. It would probably have burned the roof pretty badly; but we would have [269] got it out; but the water gave out, and before we could get—I then went and sent the *Coventry* engine to play on it; but it got such a start; and before we could get a second stream on from the *Winnebago*, it had got to burning pretty badly and got to burning in the Hatch House.[52] At the same time, they were hoisting up the *Chicago's* pipe and playing on the east elevator. As soon as the Hatch House got to burning, I then thought of [Haney's?] shop. All the machinery of the *James* and *Liberty* was in there.[53] I ran around there and King[54] was there on the street. I got him to back up and got a lot of men around there to take hold and carry out all the machinery of the *James* and *Liberty* and put it in the wagon and carried it [270] away. [Haney's?] shop was on fire and John Murphy's shop was on fire. The elevators had caught fire, and the boys had hard work to get their machines away from the dock. I do not know exactly where they did go and locate. It was up towards Kinzie Street bridge, I think. My eyes were so full of dirt and dust that I couldn't see. Thinks I, I will have to go and fix myself up a little. I started for the West Side and went and got a pair of gog-gles and then went over to the Babcock arrange-ment to see about some Babcocks. Thought per-haps I might possibly make good use of them as the water works were gone. I went over and

told them to get every machine they had—these four-wheeled machines—so we could use them in case of fire on the West Side. I then went back to the [271] West Side and [Ches-brough?][55] had been there and left word that he wanted me to go and pump in the mains.[56] There was some engines coming in from Mil-waukee, and they were scattered around, and there was men coming to me to get engines to play on this coal pile and that safe and that vault. I was completely tired out and wet to the skin. I jumped in my wagon and drove up to where my wife was and changed my clothes and drank a cup of tea and had two bites of bread, and I couldn't swallow it. Then I went up on the North Branch and got the *Coventry* and put her across the river and led up there where there was a pile of tan bark burning.[57] It was near some bridge. I have forgotten what bridge it was. I was pretty [272] well racked. I was tired out. I had ordered the *America* Hose to go and get hose where the fire was up by Ewing Street. I then came down to the *Williams's* house. There was a dozen companies to be seen to there. There was companies come in, and they had to be taken care of and had to have something to eat and wanted horses and so forth, and they kept me busy the biggest part of the time. The *Long John* had come to me and reported "out of order." Said I, "What is the matter?" [Alec re-plied,] "She won't draft water."[58] Said I, "What are you going to do? Where is the engineer?"[59] [Alec replied,] "Don't know where he is. He is tired out." Said I, "Keep yourself in readiness. Keep the men together. If there is a fire on the West Side, she can form in line and work," and Alec went to bed. [273] The same with the rest of them. They were lying all around there. Along in the evening, I received word that there was some engines wanted up on the North Side. The Bloomington engine was up there working, and one or two others; and I sent word to the *Rehm* to go over there; but when we got up where the fire was, we only had half enough hose to reach there. We got a hook and ladder [that?] was there and pulled down a building that was then burning, and one or two others, and we got the fire out. It come on rainy, and the Bloomington company—when they got that out and a lot more up along the street—I do not know what street it is—put out all the fire along there that was dangerous—the Bloomington company wanted to go home. I believe they were ta- [274] ken to the *Chicago*'s house. I am not positive whether the *Chicago* or *James*. It came on raining that night, and I didn't get to bed until about three o'clock in the morning. I hadn't been to bed, I think an hour, when they came in and said there was some Cincinnati or Pittsburgh engines here, what to do with them. I was so sleepy and tired out; I did not know what to tell them. I hadn't got completely to sleep again when I was waked up by something else. I got up then. It was along about nine o'clock, I think. I heard that alderman Walsh,[60] ex-alderman now, was blowing about my not setting the *John* to work. I saw Alec and said, "Is that engine in working order? Will she draft water?" Said he, "They reported to me that she wouldn't [*illeg.*]." Said I, "I understand I am [275] catching about it, and when the council meet, they are going to slaughter me. You must get your engine around and have her fixed." I took and sent her down to the river to see if she would draft. She worked there until the afternoon, and then I sent her to the South Side, and as soon as I knew they wanted the *Skinner*[61] over there, I sent her over. As far as I know of any engine from the South Side on the West Side, the *Long John* was the only one.[62]

Q. Mention the cities that have sent engines or firemen here, if you can recollect them all.

A. Aurora, one.[63] Springfield, one. Milwaukee, three. Pittsburgh sent three, Allegheny sent two, Cincinnati sent three, Bloomington sent one. We had to go and get something for these men to [276] eat. They were coming in, and we had to get a place for them to sleep. We had to keep engines pumping in the mains; and as soon as these foreign engines would find that they had to go to pumping in the mains, they didn't like it; and there was a good deal of coaxing done, and a good deal of running around to do to get them to do anything.[64]

Q. Out of the many engines that arrived from outside cities, do you know of any that were sent in the South Division to pump in the mains?

A. Yes sir. There was one of the Milwaukee engines sent over south.

Q. To pump in the pipes?

A. I don't know what for. She went over to the South Side. There was one thing I omit-

ted in my testimony. I went to the West Side and sent the *Illinois* down [277] to protect the Pittsburgh and Fort Wayne Freight Depot[65] there along the river. That elevator got on fire, and I sent her down there.[66] The Detroit engines played a good deal upon safes.[67]

Q. Why I ask this was because on Thursday, when Mr. Hoyne's barn caught fire,[68] I could find no engines nearer than the round house. The *John*, I believe, was the only one that was on service that time in the South Division.

A. There was two of them gave out. The *Waubansia* and the *Rice*.[69] It wasn't but a day or two until the *Titsworth* gave out. The Cincinnati engines didn't stay here. They loaded their engines Tuesday night. The Cincinnati engines led across the river on coal piles on the west shore. The *Titsworth* engine was working on Jefferson Street on the West Side and then [278] she went to the South Side and the engine went ahead and the cart [went?][70] to follow, when they got their hose taken up but they couldn't get through.[71] They went as far as on South Water Street. There was no fire there yet, but the fire was falling so thick, they could not get south there. They took and turned around and went to the North Side across Wells Street bridge and across Kinzie Street bridge and around to Halsted Street and over to the West Side, and the engine went down to the corner of State and Washington streets, and the foreman said he thought if they had had about four engines there, they could have saved property. When he was asked, "Did the wind blow hard?" he said it blowed so hard he couldn't stand on his feet. Now, if he had had a dozen engines, he [279] couldn't have thrown a stream up to stop that fire. That was the big trouble in the whole fire. The stream was cut away.

Q. Suppose the water works hadn't burned. Would the fire have been as disastrous as it was?

A. If the water works hadn't burned, I feel confident that we would have saved a great portion of the North Side.

Q. How with the South Side?

A. I do not think we would have saved a great deal of the South Side, that lower part of the city. I wasn't up in the south part because when the fire run down through by the courthouse, it cut me off.

Q. From the testimony that has been given here, if the water hadn't given out early in the morning, would or would not a large portion of that that was burned on the South Side after that time been [280] saved?

A. I presume from what testimony I have heard, that they were badly crippled around Van Buren and Harrison streets and around there. I have been talking with several of the foremen, and they tell they were doing well, but when the water gave out, they couldn't do anything but take it through from Jackson running off down that way. The way that the wind was blowing the fire, I do not think you could have saved any of it.

Q. How were the water works roofed?

A. It was a wooden roof covered with felt, I believe. I never was on the top. I have understood it was this common felt roofing.[72]

Q. Was there any appliances there at the water works for protecting themselves in case of fire? [281]

A. Not that I know of. I always supposed there was, until after the fire. In fact, I never knew so much about it until last Sunday. They wanted a well pumped out—

Q. State whether or not you have been keeping engines at the water works for the purpose of keeping them from burning.

A. I went there to see whether the engine would lift water that distance and found she was working and had got very near as low as they wanted it. I got to talking with the assistant engineer,[73] and he said they hadn't anything there to force water. Said I, "I always supposed you had."

Q. Plug pressure is how much?

A. I do not know what pressure it would have there by the works. There was a great deal; of the time, we didn't have more than thirteen to nineteen pounds [282] pressure.

Q. State whether or not you have been keeping an engine there for the purpose of protecting it.

A. Since putting on the new roof, we have kept an engine there.

Q. What engine is that?

A. One belonging to Mr. Silsby,[74] a rotary engine shipped here from Quincy.[75] We had another engine there, a New York engine, but had to send her home. When they were sent home, we sent this rotary up there, and she remains there yet. I am satisfied that if the water works hadn't burned, the fire wouldn't have got west

of Wells Street. I do not think that the Galena Depot[76] would have burned and the Hatch House. I know it wouldn't at that time if the water hadn't given out. But when the elevators got [283] on fire, I don't know but it might have burned then, because that threw a terrible heat out, and they were so high[77] (Figure 85). Several things have been recommended a great many times. I have recommended that fire hydrants be put in outside the sidewalk and a pipe run into the river three feet below the surface where an engine could come up and attach, for the reason that I never could get on the dock to put our suctions in the river.[78] The fire department always has been crippled by that. Mr. Harris[79] used to complain of it when he was chief, and it has been bad all along.

Q. Would floating engines upon the river been beneficial?

A. The first year I was appointed fire marshal, I had a talk with the Board and recommended to get one [284] if we couldn't get any more for an experiment, and the Board did ask for an appropriation, I believe it was twelve thousand dollars for a floating fire engine, as it was suggested by some of the Board to have a fire engine, and it could be towed by a tug, but I told them it would have power enough to propel itself and work the streams.

Q. The plan recommended by the Board was to have a regular floating engine capable of throwing a dozen streams?

A. Yes sir. Throw any number of streams they saw fit to put on and have a reel or two on the deck, so if the fire was the second square from the river, you could take a run of hose right out. Also, to have a place for that boat to lie and have the telegraph located there on the dock, so the [285] boys could get the alarm and have them remain on the boat.[80]

Q. How long have you ever known the Chicago River to be frozen up so as to prevent the passage of the river?

A. I have seen some winters that the river had been closed up perhaps near three months. Not as a general thing.

Q. As a general thing, about how long a time?

A. Perhaps two months. We have some winters that are open, that wouldn't be as long as that, and even then that floating engine, you could locate it when she was to be ice bound

FIGURE 85—BURNING GRAIN ELEVATORS AT THE MOUTH OF THE CHICAGO RIVER. **Marshall Philyaw's nighttime scene of burning grain elevators along the Chicago River is based in part on a drawing that appeared in the October 28, 1871, issue of *Harper's Weekly*. John R. Chapin, a *Harper's* artist, wrote of seeing "an elevator towering one hundred and fifty feet in the air, which had withstood the fire of the night before, but which was now a living coal, sending upward a sheet of flame and smoke a thousand feet high." Marshal Williams expressed similar but less eloquent thoughts during his inquiry testimony, noting that the burning elevators "threw a terrible heat out, and they were so high."**

where the most dangerous fires were likely to be, and then she would be in good use.

Q. Do you consider that Chicago has had a large enough fire department to protect a city built in the combustible manner that Chicago has been? [286]

A. I do not think Chicago has had a sufficient number, although we have had good success in putting out fires. I do not think there is any city in the world that has had better success in putting out fires. We haven't had but very few fires that have been disastrous up to this fire, and if we had had all the fire departments in the world here, I don't think it could have been prevented.

Q. Our population was about the same as St. Louis, was it?

A. Yes sir.

Q. It was larger than Cincinnati?

A. Yes sir, I think so.

Q. What is the number of engines in St. Louis?

A. I do not know how many engines they run in St. Louis. St. Louis has got a different city to fight fires in from what Chicago is. The city is more compact and the build- [287] ings are nothing like as high. The majority of St. Louis is lower buildings.

Q. Are their water works elevated so as to give a heavy pressure?

A. I believe so. I never visited their water works. When I was there last spring, I hadn't time.

Q. Has Cincinnati more or less engines than Chicago?

A. She has, I believe, twenty-one engines, if I don't mistake.

Q. Aren't their engines very much more powerful than ours?

A. I do not know for that. There are some of them that are.

Q. Do you think they are an advisable kind of an engine for us to use?

A. No sir, I don't. I think a lighter engine is preferable. There are places where those large engines come in very well. Where you want a large quantity of water. You take ninety-nine [288] out of every hundred fires and a light engine is better, gets around faster and strike it before it gets the start of you. That is the only secret in putting out fires. If a fire gets the start of you, you have got to work very hard. One thing I would state. One great reason that the Chicago department has had such good success as they have had in this wooden city—it is nothing more or less—they have been right on their taps and on it before it got started.[81] With the class of buildings we have got here in Chicago, the streets filled up and low wooden buildings set upon posts and some as high as nine, ten, and eleven feet, some three or four. Sidewalks you can go in below at one corner and walk clean through a whole square. Once in a while there [289] would be a rough board partition there and wide cracks that you could run your fingers through.

Q. Do you think that the excessive work on Saturday night had anything to do with preventing the men from going to the fire Sunday night?

A. I think the men were fatigued and tired out, a great many of them from Saturday night. There was a number of companies and Titsworth I think it was between four and five o'clock when I sent that company home.[82] That company hadn't been home but a few hours before they had to pull out again. There was hook and ladders, too, that had been to work there pretty much the whole day, and after they went home, they hadn't been long at home when it seems Mr. Schank got [290] them down there to [overhaul?] some lumber. They were on their

way home when Box 28 came in, and then this large fire started.

Q. You went about, went to several houses?

A. Yes sir.

Q. Did you see any intoxication?

A. No sir, I didn't see any firemen who were intoxicated. I saw some people who said they were intoxicated, but the men were completely tired out. Their eyes, some people to look at them would say, "That fellow has been drinking," or "He looks pretty hard." There wasn't one of them that I could see was intoxicated. There might have been some of them had taken a drink. They all seemed to be ready for duty, but in rather poor shape. Seemed as though they had been to work pretty hard. I saw some citizens that were [291] pretty well set up and hanging around the engine houses. For instance, up here in the Chicago[83] and the hook and ladder and unless you was acquainted, you wouldn't know whether they were members of the company or not, and it is pretty hard after a fire to say to citizens and some [of] them, perhaps having got burned out and others of them very well acquainted with some of the fire department, and if they happened to come around there and got a little more in than what they ought to have, it is pretty hard to take him by the collar and say, "Get out of here." On the Saturday night fire I will state I took away from two different parties that were not members of the fire department—took fire hats away from them. [292] They were badly intoxicated.[84]

Q. How did they get those hats?

A. I do not know. When you get a hot fire, a great many of the boys won't put them on. The leather draws the heat, and a great many will put on a slouch hat in preference to a fire hat. I always wear a fire hat and would like that the men would for this reason. You don't know who are firemen and who are not. You don't know whether it is your own men or outsiders. If a man hasn't a fire hat on, he might pass you by in the same alley, and you couldn't hardly tell who it was.

Q. It is dangerous to go near a falling wall without a fire hat?[85]

A. Yes sir, dangerous where there is bricks and others falling.[86]

Q. Have you formed any [293] estimate as to the loss of property in consequence of the fire?

A. No sir, I have not.

Q. As to the number of buildings?

A. The number of buildings we haven't got at.

Q. (By Mr. Benner) Did you know what time the *Titsworth* went up to the *Economy's* house?

A. I did not. I do not know what time the *Economy* left the lower portion of the fire and come up south.

Q. (By Mr. Schank) You made the statement, one, that you didn't see me at the west side of the fire.

A. Yes sir.

Q. (By Schank) Don't you recollect of seeing me and my asking you to change the engines?

A. I have no recollection of seeing you at all at that **[294]** fire. I might have seen you; I cannot recollect.

Q. (By Schank) You don't recollect that I spoke to you?

A. I have no recollection of seeing Mr. Benner but once. I met Mr. Walter[87] on the south side of the fire when I was on Taylor Street. I saw Mr. Walter quite often. When I went to the South Side, I sent a man around to tell Walter to send us some more engines if he could.

Adjourned to Monday morning at ten o'clock.[88]

Robert A. Williams Notes

1. Williams is undoubtedly referring to the Lull & Holmes planing mill fire of Saturday night. His testimony indicates that he was at this fire all night and did not get home until seven o'clock Sunday morning.

2. Box 7 was located on the city's South Side at the corner of Lake and Market streets. See *1870 City Directory*, p. 914.

3. The *1872 Report of the Board of Police* (pp. 106–8) contains a detailed table that indexes all fires that broke out in the month of October 1871. The categories for the table are: Date, Time, Street and Number, Class of Building, Owner, Occupant, Use, Cause, Loss, and Insurance. This elevator fire does not appear on the list.

4. The "old battleground" is undoubtedly a reference to the site of the Lull & Holmes planing mill fire of the night before. Today firemen use the term "fire ground" when referring to a previous fire. See Ken Little interview.

5. Williams is probably referring to still-burning stockpiles of coal at the Lull & Holmes planing mill. Coal stored along the Chicago River and in people's homes continued to burn long after the fire. Daniel Goodwin's reminiscences of the Chicago Fire include this recollection: "The daily drives from my lakeside home to the city and back were very desolate. Several days after the fire the coal stored in the hundreds of former homesteads burst into glowing flames, and many of them lasted for weeks.... After sunset, through the fall and early winter, we drove through the waste of ashes with no gas lights; but the whole road was lighted by the blue flames from the hard coal fires." See Kogan and Cromie, p. 108; "The Fire Department," *Chicago Evening Journal*, 23 November 1871, p. [4]; Mathias Benner, *Inquiry*, vol. [4], pp. 181–82; William Gallagher letter; Daniel Goodwin to Mr. [George M.] Higginson, February 1895, Chicago Fire of 1871 Personal Narratives Collection, Chicago Historical Society, hereafter cited in text as Daniel Goodwin letter. Daniel Goodwin's letter was in response to Higginson's request "to note some recollections of the Chicago Fire." In Higginson's own fire narrative, he expressed an interest in collecting and preserving the personal histories of those who had suffered but survived the fire. See Statement of George M. Higginson, "Account of the Great Chicago Fire of October 9, 1871," June 1879, Chicago Fire of 1871 Personal Narratives Collection, Chicago Historical Society.

6. Mathias Benner, Third Assistant Fire Marshal. See 1871 Pay Roll.

7. Box 28 was located at Twelfth and Clark streets, on Chicago's South Side. See *1870 City Directory*, p. 914.

8. Williams' fire at Box 28 that "did not amount to anything" was a false alarm that was called in at seven o'clock Sunday evening. See *1872 Report of the Board of Police*, p. 108.

9. At this time the wind was probably blowing at about twenty miles an hour from the south-southwest. See "Meteorological Observations by the United States Signal Corps"; Cox and Armington, p. 367.

10. The corner of Taylor and Jefferson was immediately northwest of the O'Leary barn. See Figure 10.

11. The "pipe" is the nozzle at the end of the fire hose. See Ken Little to Richard F. Bales, 15 February 2001.

12. Steamer *Illinois* No. 15. See 1871 Pay Roll.

13. William Mullin, foreman of the Steamer *Illinois* No. 15. See 1871 Pay Roll.

14. John Dorsey, foreman of *America* Hose Cart No. 2. See 1871 Pay Roll.

15. "Charley" is Charles A. Anderson, driver for *America* Hose Cart No. 2. See 1871 Pay Roll.

16. The punctuation and wording of this somewhat ambiguous sentence is shown exactly as the sentence appears in the transcript.

17. Steamer *Chicago* No. 5. See 1871 Pay Roll.

18. It appears that Williams is mistaken as to both the location of Forquer Street and also the number of blocks between him and the church. From Taylor Street north the streets are Forquer, Ewing, Polk, and Mather. St. Paul's Church was at the corner of Mather and Clinton streets. Thus, Forquer Street was south of Ewing, not north, as Williams seems to indicate. Also, there were only two blocks between his Ewing Street location and the church, not three. See *1870 City Directory*, p. 928, Figure 10.

19. *Protection* Hook and Ladder No. 2. See 1871 Pay Roll.

20. Steamer *Jacob Rehm* No. 4. See 1871 Pay Roll.

21. Denis J. Swenie, foreman of the Steamer *Fred Gund* No. 14. See 1871 Pay Roll.

22. The punctuation and wording of this somewhat ambiguous sentence is shown exactly as the sentence appears in the transcript.

23. Marshal Williams is referring to a fire-fighting tactic that is used when the nearest supply of water is farther away than the amount of hose carried by an engine company. Assume, for example, that the nearest hydrant is one thousand feet from the fire. The 1871 hose carts that accompanied steam engines carried six hundred feet of hose. The first steamer would connect to the hydrant, and its hose cart would lead out six hundred feet of hose towards the fire and connect to a second steamer. The hose cart of the second steamer would lead out four hundred feet of hose to the fire. The first steam engine would pump water to the second engine, which would pump water to the fire. This relaying of water from one engine to another is also called "going in line." This procedure was used in the area of Harrison Street and Wabash Avenue (the southeastern corner of the burnt district), where water was relayed from Lake Michigan through three steam engines in order to fight the fire. See Ken Little to Richard F. Bales, 15 February 2001; Musham, pp. 81, 132; Denis J. Swenie, *Inquiry*, vol. [2], pp. 205, 229; Michael W. Conway, *Inquiry*, vol. [2], pp. 4–5; John Schank, *Inquiry*, vol. [4], pp. 215–17; "Story of the Great Chicago Fire," sec. 3, p. 20; "The Great Fire," *Chicago Evening Journal*, 12 December 1871, p. [4]; Lowe, p. 42.

An engine company consisted of a steamer and a hose cart. As noted above, these hose carts carried six hundred feet of hose. The Chicago Fire Department also had six other hose carts that were not assigned to steam engines. These were the *Tempest, America, John A. Huck, Lincoln, Washington,* and *Douglas*. Although the hose apparatus of these hose carts was the same as on the engine company carts, these six carts carried only five hundred feet of hose. This was possibly because the engine companies were composed of more men than the separate hose cart companies—enough men to handle more than one hose line. See *1869 Report of the Board of Police*, pp. 58–66 passim; *1872 Report of the Board of Police*, pp. 74–84 passim; 1871 Pay Roll; Ken Little to Richard F. Bales, 18 December 2001; Leo Meyers, *Inquiry*, vol. [2], p. 100.

24. This sentence originally contained confusing punctuation: "I said 'Boys, hang to it, or you will have to pull the engine away; just as soon as it falls it will be all right, as soon as the first breeze is over.'" The sentence, as amended, is probably what Williams said.

25. Steamer *R. A. Williams* No. 17. See 1871 Pay Roll.

26. Charles Anderson, driver for the *America* hose cart, graphically testified during the inquiry about the futility of using a door as a shield against the fire's heat: "[David Manwell] remained there alone for a minute, and there a man by the name of Charles McConners came and helped me, and he says, "Charley, this is hot." I said, "It is, Mac," and he stayed with me perhaps a minute and could not stay any longer, apparently, and started off, and about a minute afterwards he came with a door and put it in front of me toward the fire. Thinks I, I have it now; I can stand it a considerable time, and he could not stand there with the door, I do not suppose, more than half a minute, and he let go the door, and it dropped down, and it was all ablaze, and my clothes began to smoke, and my hat began to twist on my head...." It was apparently this incident on which the *Chicago Evening Journal* later sarcastically commented, noting that the fact that the fire was hot "will go far towards clearing up the mystery [of the cause of the fire.]" See Charles Anderson, *Inquiry*, vol. [3], pp. 99–102; Cromie, p. 42; 1871 Pay Roll; Untitled article, *Chicago Evening Journal*, 1 December 1871, p. [2], col. 2, third article.

27. Alexander McMonagle, foreman of the Steamer *Long John* No. 1. See 1871 Pay Roll.

28. In 1871 steam engines had an inflexible rubber suction hose that connected the steamer to the hydrant. See Ken Little interview.

29. For an itemized listing of the losses sustained by the fire department as a result of the fire, see "Police and Fire Losses," *Chicago Evening*

Journal, 27 October 1871, p. [4]; *1872 Report of the Board of Police,* p. 17. The two lists are not identical. For example, although the *Journal* reported that the loss of the *Long John* fire station and contents was $14,000, the *1872 Report of the Board of Police* noted this loss to be $23,298.36. Because the latter set of figures was apparently prepared months after the *Journal's*, it is probably more accurate.

30. In 1870, viaducts were constructed across Halsted Street, West Indiana Street, and West Adams Street. See Grosser, p. [47].

31. Steamer *T.B. Brown* No. 12. See 1871 Pay Roll.

32. The quotations marks around "Merchants Union" are in the original. This name is probably a reference to the American Merchants Union Express Company. Although Williams indicates that its barn was on Monroe Street, its offices were at the northwest corner of Lake and Dearborn streets. Express companies were an alternative to the U.S. mail. For example, this advertisement for another express company appeared in the *1870 City Directory:* "Baggage and Goods of all kinds called for and delivered to any part of the City or Hyde Park. Teams leave the office for each division of the City at 10 A.M. and 2 and 5 P.M. Hyde Park, 2 P.M. daily. We guarantee the prompt and safe delivery of all goods entrusted to us, and at prices much below usual rates." See Andreas, vol. 2, pp. 126–27; *1870 City Directory,* pp. 43, 1009; *1871 City Directory,* p. 1012.

33. The punctuation and wording of this somewhat ambiguous sentence is shown exactly as the sentence appears in the transcript.

34. On November 15, 1871, the *Chicago Tribune* inaugurated its "Boring for Facts" series of articles on "the origin and progress of The Great Fire, and the conduct of the Fire Department on the fatal night of October 9...." The first article included an interview with Marshal Williams. At one point he indicated that "the wind was blowing so heavy at the time that the water would not go ten feet from the nozzle of the pipe. We could not strike a second story window." See "Boring for Facts," *Chicago Tribune,* 15 November 1871, p. 1.

35. The quotation marks around "leading up" are in the original.

36. The Metropolitan Hotel was located at the southwest corner of Randolph and Wells streets. The Greenebaum Building was immediately south and adjacent to the hotel on Wells Street. (As shown in *Robinson's Atlas,* Wells Street was also known as Fifth Avenue.) See *1870 City Directory,* p. 567; *1871 City Directory,* p. 623; Robinson's *Atlas,* vol. 3, plate 2; Hayner and McNamee, p. 132.

37. This bank was the Union National Bank. See James H. Hildreth, *Inquiry,* vol. [3], page 137.

38. This is probably a reference to Benjamin B. Bullwinkle of the Fire Insurance Patrol.

39. The engine's hard rubber suction hose that connected the steamer to the hydrant was about four or five inches in diameter. As it had to connect to a two-and-one-half inch port on the hydrant, a reducer, or "taper," was used. See Ken Little interview.

40. *Washington* Hose Cart No. 5. See 1871 Pay Roll.

41. Miller's jewelry store was at the southeast corner of Clark and Randolph streets. When the prisoners were let out of the courthouse, a few of them ran across Clark Street to the store. Although some accounts have the prisoners breaking into the establishment, Mrs. A. H. Miller later wrote in her *Reminiscences* that her husband invited the prisoners to take the store's goods, believing that it was better to do that than to let the items burn up in the fire. See Charles H. French, *Inquiry,* vol. [3], p. 314; "Mama" [Gookins?] to "Lizy" [Gookins?], 13 October 1871, Chicago Fire of 1871 Personal Narratives Collection, Chicago Historical Society, hereafter cited in text as Gookins letter; Mrs. A. H. Miller, *Reminiscences of the Chicago Fire of 1871,* (privately printed, n.d.), pp. 3, 10; "Absurd Misstatements," p. [2]; Foster, p. 29.

42. This is probably a reference to the wagon works of Peter Schuttler, located at the southwest corner of Randolph and Franklin streets, on Chicago's South Side and on the western edge of the burnt district. The December 15, 1871, *Republican* noted that "Peter Schuttler's new building, a large wagon manufactory 200 × 50 feet, of brick and four stories in height, will be located on the northeast corner of Clinton and Monroe streets." See *1871 City Directory,* p. 1109; "Chicago Condensed," *Chicago Republican,* 15 December 1871, p. [4]; Lowe, p. 42; *Fire Edition Directory,* p. 138.

43. Williams is probably referring to the drug store of Gale & Blocki, 202 Randolph Street. See *1871 City Directory,* pp. 342, 1009.

44. Williams boarded at 213 Randolph Street. See *1871 City Directory,* pp. 886, 953.

45. Marshal Williams volunteered this information. Perhaps he did so in response to criticism from the press, such as this comment that appeared in the *Times* on November 22, only ten days before he testified: "If the man called Fire Marshal Williams can get time from the difficult labor of proving his wonderful and unprecedented generalship in fighting the Chicago conflagration, he should state whether the report is or is not true that, when he discovered that his boarding-house

was in danger he left his post of duty, employed a team, and spent two or three hours in transporting his own private effects beyond the reach of danger. Was or was not that the exploit in which he exhibited the greatest generalship?" See untitled article, *Chicago Times*, 22 November 1871, p. [2].

46. Steamer *Winnebago* No. 16. See 1871 Pay Roll.

47. Fireman Michael W. Conway also referred to the *Richards* engine in his testimony. This fire engine, however, is not noted in Musham's monograph as being one of the city's steamers, nor is it listed in the 1871 Pay Roll. Rather, this was undoubtedly the fire engine of the Richards Iron Works, 47-55 South Jefferson Street. The *Chicago Tribune* of October 28, 1871, contained a letter to the editor that read in part as follows: "The undersigned deem it their duty, as well as an act of justice to the Richards' Iron Works, to place on record the important service rendered by their new steam fire engine, during the late conflagration." See "Justice Rendered," *Chicago Tribune*, 28 October 1871, p. [4]; "Fire and Police," *Chicago Republican*, 27 October 1871, p. [4]; Michael W. Conway, *Inquiry*, vol. [2], p. 19; *1870 City Directory*, p. 691; *1871 City Directory*, p. 752; "The City," p. [3].

48. The 1871 Chicago city directory indicates that the Illinois River Elevator was located at the "foot W. Washington" Street. This was probably where Washington Street intersected the Chicago River. This grain elevator was not destroyed by the fire. See Andreas, vol. 2, p. 373; *Robinson's Atlas*, vol. 3, plate 2; *1871 City Directory*, p. 1012.

49. The Chicago & Northwestern Railway passenger station was at the southwest corner of Kinzie and Wells streets. See *Robinson's Atlas*, vol. 3, plate 2.

50. Williams appears to be alluding to a possible incendiary.

51. The Tribune summary of Williams' testimony provides a better explanation as to the possible nature of these chemicals: "While working there he [Williams] saw a great blue mass rolling down on them, which he subsequently found out to be chemicals from the telegraph battery." See "The Great Fire," *Chicago Tribune*, 3 December 1871, p. 4.

52. This is probably a reference to Hatch's Hotel, which was located at 29 North Wells Street. The *Chicago Republican* of Christmas Day, 1871, however, made a passing reference to the "Scene at Harry Hatch's" (which apparently was a clothing store) in its gossip column, "Chicago Condensed." See Andreas, vol. 2, p. 505; "Chicago Condensed," *Chicago Republican*, 25 December

1871, p. [4]; "The Clothing Trade," *Chicago Tribune*, 17 December 1871, p. 7.

53. Steamer *William James* No. 3; Steamer *Liberty* No. 7. See 1871 Pay Roll.

54. This is probably Albin C. King, driver of the fire department supply truck. See 1871 Pay Roll.

55. This is probably a reference to Ellis S. Chesbrough, City Engineer.

56. After the water works was destroyed, there was no longer a constant supply of water being pumped into the city's water mains. The only water remaining was the so-called "dead" water still left in the mains, and once that was gone, Chicago was virtually helpless in its fight against the fire. So steam fire engines and railway locomotives were used to pump water from the Chicago River and Lake Michigan into the mains in an attempt to replenish the city's water supply and thus ease the concerns of its citizens.

Although the *Tribune* maintained that this water was "suitable for general domestic purposes," it appears that drinking the water prompted an outbreak of diarrhea and "gastric irritation." Residents were urged to boil or filter the water or treat it with alum before drinking it. It seems that Chicagoan William Gallagher failed to heed this advice. In a letter dated October 17, 1871, he explained the water problem to his sister: "You see, when the supply of water failed, the steam fire engines were set to work to pump water from the river into the pipes, so that in case fire broke out there might be some water to draw on. Now, the river is moderately sluggish and dirty considering that all the sewers empty into it, and so the water in the pipes was rather foul. Well! Last Thursday they had succeeded in getting one of the engines at the Water Works repaired and commenced supplying us with water from the lake as usual. Instead of letting the foul water run off, it was forced along, and mingling with the pure lake water came on the table everywhere, and everybody drank. As a result, everybody is sick, not severely, but ailing, and with most of us it takes the form of a very weakening diarrhea. The pure water, however, has now reached us and we anticipate no further trouble." See William Gallagher letter; "The Water We Drink," *Chicago Tribune*, 19 October 1871, p. [2]; "Miscellaneous Items," *Chicago Tribune*, 12 October 1871, p. 1; "The Water Works," *Chicago Tribune*, 13 October 1871, p. [2]; "All Around Town," *Chicago Evening Journal*, 27 October 1871, p. [4]; "The Water Supply," p. [4]; Francis T. Swenie, *Inquiry*, vol. [3], p. 204; Mathias Benner, *Inquiry*, vol. [4], pp. 182–83; John Schank, *Inquiry*, vol. [4], pp. 215–16; Colbert and Chamberlin, p. 396.

57. Frank J. Loesch mentioned the term "tan bark" in his *Personal Experiences During the Chicago Fire*: "Only a day or two before the fire the son of the owner of a residence had recovered from an attack of typhoid and the tan bark had been removed from the street." See Loesch, p. 21. The inquiry contains other references to this term. Denis J. Swenie testified that while near a tannery, he helped extinguish a fire in some tan bark, and Michael W. Conway told the fire officials that he "worked on" a pile of tan bark on the city's North Side. See Denis J. Swenie, *Inquiry*, vol. [2], pp. 221–22; Michael W. Conway, *Inquiry*, vol. [2], p. 33; "Chicago Losses," *Chicago Evening Journal*, 20 November 1871, p. [3].

58. To "draft water" means to take the steam engine's suction hose and place it into a pond, lake, river, or other water source and draw water from it. See Ken Little interview; John Schank, *Inquiry*, vol. [4], p. 215.

59. Timothy A. Moynihan was the *Long John*'s engineer. See 1871 Pay Roll.

60. This is a reference to David Walsh. Andreas' *History of Chicago* indicates that he was an alderman in the following years: 1863, 1864, 1867, 1868, and 1869. See Andreas, vol. 2, pp. 49–50.

61. This is a reference to the *Skinner* Patent Hose Elevator, an aerial ladder that could be raised to a height of eighty-four feet. As the name "hose elevator" implies, this aerial ladder had a small movable platform on which a fireman could stand with a hose line, directing water into the upper floors of a burning building. See Little and McNalis, pp. 114, 128.

62. The *Long John*'s firehouse was on LaSalle Street between Washington and Madison streets, on Chicago's South Side. See Little and McNalis, pp. 6–7; *1870 City Directory*, p. 914; *1871 City Directory*, p. 34.

63. Although the *Tribune* of October 11, 1871, indicates that Aurora sent three engines, it appears that Marshal Williams is correct in claiming that the city sent only one engine. See "Items in General," *Chicago Tribune*, 11 October 1871, p. 1; "The Aurora Firemen," *Chicago Tribune*, 23 November 1871, p. 4, hereafter cited in text as "The Aurora Firemen"; "The Foreign Firemen," *Chicago Republican*, 24 November 1871, p. [4], hereafter cited in text as "The Foreign Firemen."

64. On November 19, 1871, the *Tribune* accused the Milwaukee; Janesville, Wisconsin; and Aurora, Illinois fire companies of accepting offers of money in exchange for turning their hoses on favored properties. The following day, the *Tribune* claimed that before the Aurora firemen returned home, thirteen of them took overcoats from the

relief supplies already donated by other cities. These two newspaper articles prompted an angry rebuttal from S. B. Sherer, Aurora's First Assistant Fire Marshal, which the *Tribune* published on November 23, and the Aurora Committee on Fire and Water passed a resolution to "ascertain all the facts in the case and have them as prominently and extensively published as the scandalous reports have been." By November 24, the *Tribune* had backed down and apologized to the Milwaukee firemen, writing that the charges were "wholly unfounded" and "destitute of foundation" and that "the article was inserted in the absence, and without the knowledge, of the responsible editor of the *Tribune*." The December 13 *Tribune* contained a similar apology to the Aurora firemen. The newspaper extended the olive branch to the Janesville fire department on December 16. See "Unparalleled Meanness," *Chicago Tribune*, 19 November 1871, p. 6; "Justice Rendered," *Chicago Tribune*, 20 November 1871, p. 6; "The Aurora Firemen," p. 4; "The Milwaukee Firemen," *Chicago Tribune*, 24 November 1871, p. 3; Untitled article, *Chicago Tribune*, 13 December 1871, p. 4; "The Janesville Firemen," *Chicago Tribune*, 16 December 1871, p. 4; "Greedy of Gain," *Chicago Republican*, 20 November 1871, p. [4]; "The Foreign Firemen," p. [4]; "L'Amende Honorable," *Chicago Republican*, 24 November 1871, p. [2]; Untitled article, *Chicago Republican*, 25 November 1871, p. [2], col. 1, fourth article; Untitled article, *Chicago Republican*, 25 November 1871, p. [2], col. 1, fifth article; Aurora Committee on Fire and Water Resolution on Tribune Slander of Fire Department, 20 November 1871, Aurora (Illinois) Regional Fire Museum.

65. The Pittsburgh, Fort Wayne & Chicago Railway freight depot was located at the corner of Stewart Avenue and 18th Street, on the city's West Side, just west of the Chicago River. See *1870 City Directory*, p. 659; *Chicago & Vicinity 6-County StreetFinder*, p. 57 (Cook County).

66. Andreas lists all the Chicago elevators and the railroad or waterway via which these elevators received their grain shipments. The Pittsburgh, Fort Wayne & Chicago Railway is not shown on this list. See Andreas, vol. 2, p. 373.

67. When the safes were opened up after the fire, the hot contents would sometimes burst into flames upon being exposed to the air. Consequently, the fire engines sprayed water on the safes in an attempt to cool them down prior to being opened. See Statement of Charles Elliott Anthony, "Experiences of the Anthony Family During the Great Chicago Fire October 8 and 9, 1871," n.d., Chicago Fire of 1871 Personal Narratives Collection, Chicago Historical Society; Goodspeed, p.

364; Kogan and Cromie, p. 139; Andreas, vol. 2, pp. 630, 722, 759; "The Ruins," *Chicago Tribune*, 12 October 1871, p. 1, hereafter cited in text as "The Ruins"; "Stories of the Big Fire," p. 13; Herman Kogan and Lloyd Wendt, *Chicago: A Pictorial History* (New York: Crown Publishers, Bonanza Books, 1958), p. 127, hereafter cited in text as Kogan and Wendt.

Shortly after the fire, the West Chicago Park Commissioners commissioned architect William Le Baron Jenney to design a monument to the fire that would be constructed in Central Park (later renamed Garfield Park) out of ruined safes and other fire relics. The public was asked to donate safes; the name of each donor would be inscribed on a metallic plate and fastened to each safe. (As these safes did not pass through the fire unscathed, it is perhaps understandable why the name of each safe maker would not be similarly displayed.) Jenney suggested a 120-foot-tower, capped by a spherical safe, and surrounded by broken columns (Figure 86). The commissioners accepted this proposal but later rejected it, deciding that "something more monumental in character was desirable." The October 28, 1872, *Tribune* contained a lengthy description of Jenney's second proposed monument. The newspaper indicated that "the design now adopted contemplates a total height of 125 feet. The base is a Gothic circular arcade, composed of twelve groined arches, resting on a raised platform of thirty-six feet diameter.... The spire of the monument is composed of safes contributed by the Chicago merchants; the whole terminated by a Gothic column surmounted by a female figure holding aloft, in both hands, a flaming torch, emblematic of destruction by fire." Although the cornerstone for this monument was

laid on October 30, 1872, it was never completed, and the site was eventually razed in 1882. Chicago would wait more than seventy years before it commissioned another fire memorial. In the 1950s, the city built the Chicago Fire Academy, a training school for firemen, on the O'Leary property and other land along DeKoven Street. Egon Weiner's metal sculpture of a flame stands in the academy's courtyard (Figure 87). See "Chicago Condensed," *Chicago Republican*, 25 November 1871, p. [4]; "Chicago Condensed," *Chicago Republican*, 29 November 1871, p. [4]; "The Fire Monument," *Chicago Evening Journal*, 14 December 1871, p. [4]; "The Safe Monument," *Chicago Tribune*, 25 November 1871, p. 6; "The Fire Monument," *Chicago Tribune*, 28 October 1872, p. 7; "The Fire Monument," *Chicago Tribune*, 31 October 1872, p. 3; "Those Roasted Safes," *Chicago Times*, 15 December 1871, p. 3; "OK Sale of 1st Ward Land to Industry," *Chicago Daily Sun-Times*, 10 July 1956, p. 3, hereafter cited in text as "OK Sale of 1st Ward Land to Industry"; Gerald A. Danzer, *Public Places: Exploring Their History* (Walnut Creek, Calif.: Sage Publications, AltaMira Press, 1997), pp. 77–86; *American Apocalypse*, pp. 146–49; Pierce, vol. 3, p. 18; Andreas, vol. 3, p. 179; Kogan and Cromie, p. 227; *Third Annual Report of West Chicago Park Commissioners for the Year Ending February 29, 1872* (Chicago: Chicago Legal News Co., n.d.), pp. 35–36.

68. This is probably a reference to a fire breaking out in Hoyne's barn on *Friday*, October 13. The October 14 *Tribune* reported that "a barn in the rear of No. 270 Michigan avenue, owned by Thomas Hoyne, and occupied by Jul[i]us Bauer & Co., dealers in pianos, caught fire at half-past 3 o'clock yesterday afternoon. An alarm was promptly

Opposite: FIGURE 86—WILLIAM LE BARON JENNEY'S FIRST PROPOSED CHICAGO FIRE MONUMENT. This appears to be architect William Le Baron Jenney's drawing of his first proposed Chicago Fire monument, as his name is in the lower right-hand corner of the picture. The words "To be erected at Central Park West Chicago" are in the lower left-hand corner. This drawing appeared in the 1872 book *The Lakeside Memorial of the Burning of Chicago,* A.D. *1871* with this caption: "Fire Monument, to Be Built of Safes and Columns Taken from the Ruins." The February 1872 issue of *The Land Owner: A Journal of Real Estate Building & Improvement* described this proposed fire monument in great detail: "The base of the monument will be formed of sculptured stone.... The body of the monument will be composed of safes and vault doors.... The base is square, the lower course of safes, a Greek cross; the body square, thus leaving shelves on which are placed relics, such as capitals of columns, urns, and sculptured ornaments from doorways, cornices, etc. A circlet of broken iron columns surrounds the body of the monument, which tapers gradually towards the top, which is formed by a large Corinthian column, surmounted by a little spherical safe, at a height of over one hundred feet." The diminutive figures standing to the left illustrate the height of the proposed monument. (Chicago Historical Society ICHi-32209)

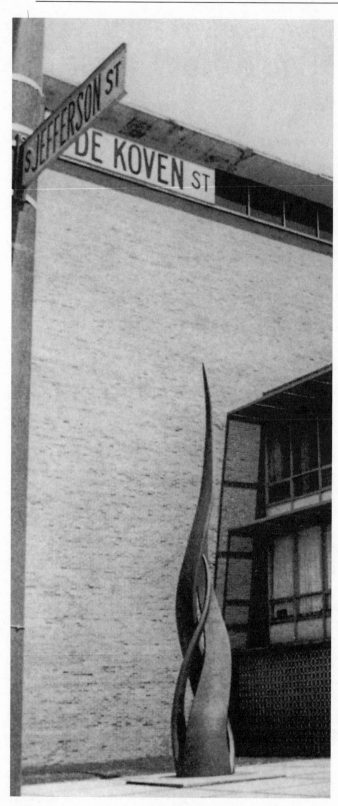

given, a bucket brigade was organized, and water in abundance was obtained from the lake. Everybody worked with a will, and the flames were subdued after about $200 damage had been done. No explanation regarding the origin of the fire was given; no one seemed to know anything about it, the general impression being that it was the work of an incendiary." Hoyne's Chicago Fire reminiscences suggest that a fire department steam engine eventually arrived to help extinguish the blaze; however, this fire is not listed in the table of fires contained in the 1872 *Report of the Board of Police*. See "Incendiary Fires"; "Musical Instruments," *Chicago Evening Journal*, 13 November 1871, p. [3]; Andreas, vol. 2, pp. 595, 737–38; Alexander McMonagle, *Inquiry*, vol. [2], p. 252; Sheahan and Upton, pp. 353–54; Colbert and Chamberlin, p. 298. The possible incendiary nature of this fire was alluded to in the following letter dated the same day of this fire: "We are at Mr. Philpot so far and safe, but as the city is full of incendiaries, no knowing how long we can remain

FIGURE 87—CHICAGO FIRE ACADEMY FLAME MONUMENT. **Egon Weiner's metal flame sculpture stands in the Chicago Fire Academy's courtyard near the corner of DeKoven and Jefferson streets. Some Chicago Fire references imply that this column of fire marks the exact location of the famous barn. This may be due to the inscription around the base of the sculpture, which reads: "Here Began the Chicago Fire of 1871." But the diagram shown as Figure 79 shows the location of the O'Leary property in relation to Jefferson Street, and it suggests that the barn was at least one hundred feet east of this sculpture—or very close to the Maltese Cross referred to in Figure 74. (Chicago Historical Society ICHi-34617; photograph by Elisabeth Kimbell)**

so.... This afternoon Mr. Tom Hoyne's stable on Michigan Avenue was set on fire, and we came near another fearful conflagration." See Gookins letter.

69. Steam engines *Waubansia* No. 2 and *J. B. Rice* No. 10. See 1871 Pay Roll.

70. It appears that the transcriber blindly adhered to the shorthand reporter's symbols and characters and not to what made sense or was grammatically correct. Although "went" appears to be correct, and although the transcriber originally wrote the word "went" in the inquiry transcript, he or she apparently crossed out the last two letters "nt" and inserted the letters "re," resulting in the following: "we^re~nt~," or "were." See also Catherine O'Leary, *Inquiry*, vol. [1], p. 72, where the transcriber, referring to the "roar" of the fire, crossed out the word "roar" and replaced it with "roll."

71. Except for the possible correction of the word "went," the punctuation and wording of this somewhat ambiguous sentence is shown exactly as the sentence appears in the transcript.

72. After the fire, Judge Lambert Tree recalled that "when I arrived at the building where my office was located, the roof and cupola of the Court-house were already beginning to burn; several other buildings south and west of the Court-house were in flames, and the air was full of sparks, cinders, and pieces of flaming felt torn from the roofs of the houses, and being carried in a northeasterly direction by the wind, which was blowing a gale." The *Tribune* commented that "this tarred paper, when once kindled and torn off by the wind, flew over the city in myriads of fireballs, igniting without fail whatever it lighted upon. It is doubtful whether, after the wind itself, any one cause is more blamable for the spread of the conflagration than this sort of roofing." See *Reminiscences of Chicago During the Great Fire*, pp. 92–93; Untitled article, *Chicago Tribune*, 18 November 1871, p. 4.

73. The 1871 Chicago City Directory indicates that Joseph A. Locke was the Assistant Engineer for the Board of Public Works. See *1871 City Directory*, p. 557; see also James H. Hildreth, *Inquiry*, vol. [3], pp. 125–26.

74. Horace C. Silsby was one of the founders of the Silsby Manufacturing Company of Seneca Falls, New York. The Silsby Company manufactured steam engines; an example of a Silsby engine is shown at Figure 88. The *Waubansia* No. 2 was also a Silsby engine. See *1872 Report of the Board of Police*, pp. 16, 30; Little and McNalis, pp. 11, 42; William T. King, *History of the American Steam Fire-engine* (n.p., 1896; reprint, Chicago: Owen Davies, 1960), p. 21.

75. The town of Quincy, Illinois, was one of several communities that sent fire engines or other fire apparatus during the fire. See *1872 Report of the Board of Police*, pp. 15–16.

76. This is probably a reference to the depot of the Galena & Chicago Union Railroad Company. A drawing of "The Old Galena Depot" appears in Andreas, vol. 2, p. 133. This railroad merged with the Chicago & Northwestern Railway Company in 1864. The new company retained the name "Chicago & Northwestern Railway Company." See Andreas, vol. 2, pp. 133–35.

77. It probably was not just the heat and height of a burning grain elevator that was of concern to Marshal Williams, as it appears that such fires were difficult to put out. The October 12, 1871, *Tribune* recounted that "another engine was near the Central Elevator, playing upon an immense hill of wheat, which was in Elevator A, and which was bursting out in little puffs of smoke all over its surface. It cannot be very easily extinguished, and all that is to be expected is that it will gradually moulder away." See "The Ruins," p. 1. Years later Chicagoan Daniel Goodwin expressed similar thoughts when he recalled that "the grain in the burned elevators was on fire for months." See Daniel Goodwin letter.

78. A few of Marshal Williams' recommendations and comments are found in the *1869 Report of the Board of Police*, pp. 16–23. They include the following observation: "Although this department has repeatedly suggested that more rigid laws be passed, and more power be given this department to regulate the construction of buildings, too little attention has been paid to these suggestions, and the result is well known."

79. Uriah P. Harris was William's predecessor. Harris was extremely popular; Andreas wrote that "if the boys ever had an idol to whom they bowed down and whom they worshiped, that idol was U. P. Harris. One secret of his popularity was his personal magnetism, by which he gained many friends and which he seemed to instill into the natures of those under him, so that, when his eye was upon them, they fought the flames like valiant soldiers." Harris retired from active service in 1868 and died in June 1871. See Andreas, vol. 2, pp. 91–92; Little & McNalis, p. 36.

80. Williams appeared before the Board and fire officials on December 2, and although he testified about several of the improvements that he had recommended prior to the fire, he did not comment during his testimony on his department's lack of fire hose. He was not as reserved in his lengthy letter to the *Chicago Tribune* that was published fifteen days earlier on November 17:

"One other circumstance that has greatly crippled our Fire Department, is the scanty supply of hose purchases from year to year.... I have always failed to obtain the amount of hose I have asked for from time to time, as in the case of the present year I requested 15,000 feet, which was small enough an amount for the number of fires we are having in Chicago (amounting to nearly 700 during the last year). Instead of allowing me the full amount, I was cut down one-third, and allowed 10,000 feet." See "On the Defensive," p. 4. But as noted in chapter one, fireman Leo Meyers expressed a completely different opinion when he testified: "It has been the remark that we had better facilities for the last three or four years for the extinguishment of a fire than we ever had before in Chicago. It has been a usual remark through the department that our facilities were better for extinguishing fires." See Leo Meyers, *Inquiry*, vol. [2], pp. 99–100.

81. In his history of the fire, Robert Cromie quotes Williams' statement about the fire department being "right on their taps and on it before it got started," but then adds a postscript: "Out of charity or tact, [Williams] made no mention of how the mix-up in alarms had prevented the department from doing just that on October 8." See Cromie, pp. 280–81.

82. The punctuation and wording of this somewhat ambiguous sentence is shown exactly as the sentence appears in the transcript.

83. This appears to be an ambiguous reference to the steam engine *Chicago* and not the city of Chicago.

84. Frank Luzerne's history of the fire includes an interview with Marshal Williams that originally appeared in the *Chicago Evening Mail*. In the interview Williams adamantly denied that his firemen were drunk and vehemently defended his men: "But bless your soul (and here the Marshal got interesting, not to say excited, and raised up on his elbow and threatened the reporter's nose with his finger) the heat was awful; 'twas like hell, and the firemen's eyes were red with the dust and fire, so that many of them were most blind. The hair was scorched off their faces, and they stuck to their machines like bull dogs, and worked them till they couldn't stand it any longer. Yes, sir, and they did stagger, for they were clean beat, and many of them, had to go home for the exhaustion from the heat. They were tired, too, from the fire of the night before, and then to give the same men such a long pull again, why, an iron man couldn't have stood it." See Luzerne, pp. [171]–72.

85. This question appears to be especially inane in light of the following news item that was published in the *Evening Journal* only twelve days

before Williams testified: "This forenoon another accident happened, owing to the falling of a brick wall—portions of the ruins of a building on State street, near the corner of Randolph. Two men were seriously injured. Their names are James Rosener, of No. 334½ Twenty-fifth street, and O. Peterson, of No. 21 Hubbard street. The men were conveyed to their respective homes, where medical aid was summoned. It is high time that the city authorities should take steps toward pulling down the dangerous ruins." See "Two More Men Hurt," *Chicago Evening Journal*, 20 November 1871, p. [4].

The danger of these ruins is horrifically illustrated in the reminiscences of Martin Stamm. Stamm was pastor of Chicago's First Evangelical Church at the time of the fire, and in his remembrances, written in the 1920s, he told of almost being killed by a falling wall: "One of the men glanced casually across the street and observed that the wall swayed slightly and that we were all in the greatest danger if it fell out towards us, as we would be covered. He called out, 'Gentlemen, we are all in danger of our lives.' We all looked up at the dangerous wall. At the same moment each of us recognized our danger, leaped up, and fled in all directions. I ran south on Dearborn Street. I never ran in all my life as at that moment. Fortunately, I reached the south end of that wall, perhaps 20–25 feet beyond, when it fell with the sound of thunder behind me and completely covered the street. Whatever living thing had not excaped [sic] was destroyed." See Kathy Ranalletta, ed., "'The Great Wave of Fire' at Chicago: The Reminiscences of Martin Stamm," *Journal of the Illinois State Historical Society* 70 (May 1977), pp. 149, [155].

But perhaps the city's firemen had devised their own means of at least minimizing the perils of falling walls. In 1893, while reminiscing about the Chicago Fire, Denis J. Swenie told a reporter about one recent close escape: "'You see I was up an alley sort of blocked in each side by the fire,' he said. 'The wall of the burning building started to fall. I saw the thing coming, but I couldn't get out at the side, and if I ran straight out I'd have got that wall on my neck good and hard, and I didn't want it. So I turned and charged the wall as it fell, meaning to break through. I would have got a bit scorched in the fire, but that was better than getting smashed. If that wall hadn't been so thundering thick I'd have been all right, but I only got half way through when the wall came down. I got my share of it, but wasn't hurt....'" See "Story of the Great Chicago Fire," sec. 3, p. 20.

86. The transcriber wrote "when there is bricks +c falling," apparently using "+c" as a synonym for "and others." See *Random House Dictionary*.

87. Lorens Walter, Second Assistant Fire Marshal. See 1871 Pay Roll.

88. Although the proceedings were adjourned to the following Monday, the transcript contains no further testimony. Marshal Williams was the forty-ninth person to appear before the Board and fire officials. Although the foreman of Ryerson & Co.'s lumberyard, the fiftieth and final witness, testified Monday afternoon, it appears that no one made a record of his statements. See "The Great Fire," *Chicago Tribune*, 5 December 1871, p. 2.

"After the Inquiry"—
The December 12, 1871,
Report of the Board of
Police and Fire Commissioners

The report of the board of police and fire commissioners, embodying the results
of the investigation into the late fire, is about such a document as was to be expected....

—*Chicago Times*, December 12, 1871

Introduction

On December 12, 1871, the *Evening Journal, Republican*, and the *Times* all published the
results of the Board's investigation. A. T. Andreas later included the commissioners' findings in his *History of Chicago*. The Board's conclusions, as they appeared in the *Evening Journal*,
are reproduced verbatim in this appendix.[1]

In their report the commissioners first discussed the history and progress of the fire. Although they were charged with determining the
fire's cause, the men devoted just four sentences
to how the fire might have originated, concluding in the third paragraph only that they
didn't know how it started. They were also expected to review the firemen's conduct during
the fire. Again, the commissioners dismissed
this in only a few sentences, sentences that were
as laudatory as the third paragraph was inconclusive.

The rest of their report is largely devoted
to finger pointing and exculpation. For example, the commissioners observed that "the
Board of Police have year by year, in annual reports to the Mayor and Common Council, endeavored to point out the great defects in the
manner in which our city was being built up.
We advised and entreated to have much greater
fire limits established.... We reported Mansard
roofs and tar roofs to be unsafe...."

On December 2, even before the investigation had ended, the *Chicago Evening Journal*
wrote: "In what particular good the inquiry has
resulted; it would be hard to decide." The *Journal* could have republished these words on December 12.[2]

THE GREAT FIRE.

Report of the Board of Police and Fire Commissioners of Their Investigation of the Origin and Spread of the Great Fire.

An Official History.

The Board of Police and Fire Commissioners have at last promulgated the results of their investigation into the origin and spread of the great fire. It reads as follows:

"The Board of Police, as required by law, have investigated the origin of the fire of October 8 and 9. We have heard the sworn testimony of fifty-one witnesses,[3] and had the same taken down by a stenographer, and subsequently transcribed. As written out it fills about 900 pages of foolscap paper. As a large part of this testimony was published in the daily papers as it was taken from day to day, and as the original is on file for reference, we deem it unnecessary to recapitulate the evidence to any great extent, but proceed to give the results of our investigation briefly, and place it on record.

The Board find that the fire originated in a two story frame barn in the rear of No. 137 DeKoven street, the premises being owned by Patrick Leary. The fire was first discovered by a drayman by the name of Daniel Sullivan, who saw it while sitting on the sidewalk, on the south side of DeKoven street, and nearly opposite Leary's premises. He fixes the time at not more than 20 to 25 minutes past 9 o'clock when he first noticed the flames coming out of the barn.

There is no proof that anybody had been in the barn after nightfall that evening. Whether it originated from a spark blown from a chimney on that windy night, or was set on fire by human agency, we are unable to determine. Mr. Leary, the owner, and all his family, prove to have been in bed and asleep at the time. There was a small party in the front part of Leary's house, which was occupied by Mr. McLaughlin and wife, but we failed to find any evidence that anybody from McLaughlin's part of the house went near the barn that night.

The first information received by the Fire Department came from the alarm struck in the fire-alarm office at 9:30. The alarm sounded box 342, at the corner of Canalport avenue and Halsted street, a point in the direction of the fire, but a mile beyond it. There was no signal given from any box to the central office, but the box was given by Mathias Shaffer, from the Court House cupola, he being the night watchman on duty at the time, and having sighted the fire. There was no signal given from any box by anybody until after the Fire Department had arrived and turned in the second and third alarms. If any person set the fire, either by accident or design, he was careful not to give any alarm. The nearest engine house was six blocks distant from the fire; the next nearest one was about nine blocks away. The nearest hose house was located about eleven blocks from the fire, and at this hose house the watchman had seen the fire before the alarm was given from the Court House, and the company was on their way to the fire before the box was struck. In consequence of this early sighting the fire, the hose company, the America, ran eleven blocks and attached their hose to the fire plug, and got water on the fire before any engine did, although two engines were located considerably nearer to the fire. It would require five minutes for the nearest engine to go to the fire, a distance of six blocks. From three to five minutes more would be required in which to unreel and lay out the hose, make connections with the fire plug and get to work. Intelligent citizens who lived near the place of the fire testify that it was from ten to fifteen minutes from the time that they saw the fire before any engines came upon the ground. It is proved that the engines repaired to the fire, after getting the alarm, with their usual celerity. When they arrived there from three to five buildings were fiercely burning. The fire must then have been burning from ten to fifteen minutes, and with the wind then blowing strongly from the southwest and carrying the fire from building to building in a neighborhood composed wholly of dry wood-buildings, with wood shavings piled in every form and under every house, the fire had got under too great headway for the engines called out by the first alarm to be able to subdue it.

Marshal Williams and Third Assistant Marshal Benner arrived upon the ground soon after the engines and at once saw that the fire could not be stopped without more engines, and Marshal Williams at once ordered the second, and soon after, the third, alarm to be turned in; but this only caused the distant engines to come. Many valuable minutes must elapse before they could reach the fire and get to work, and before this could be accomplished the strong wind had scattered the fire into many buildings, all as dry as tinder, and spread it over so large an area that the whole department, though working with their utmost energy, were unable to cut it off, or prevent the wind, which soon became a gale, from carrying burning shingles and boards over their heads, and setting buildings on fire far away from the main fire.

After it got into the high church at the corner of Clinton and Mather streets, and thence into the match factory and Bateham's mills and lumber, it got beyond the control of the Fire Department. About this time it crossed the river, between Van Buren and Adams streets, by means of flying brands, and set fire to Powell's roofing establishment, adjoining the gas works. Before this time, the watchman in the Court House cupola had twice extinguished the fire which had caught from brands carried by the wind into the Court House balcony from the West Side, a distance of a mile.

At 11 o'clock the keeper of the crib of the lake tunnel, being located two miles from the shore and three miles from the fire, found the sky full of sparks and burning brands, and from 11:30 till morning, he testified, worked with all his might to prevent the wooden roof of the crib from burning up and destroying himself and wife. From Powell's roofing establishment the progress of the fire was rapid and terrific, sweeping everything in its course. The engines had all been working on the West Side, and they could not reel 600 feet of hose each, and cross the river and get to work soon enough to prevent its spreading, literally, on the wings of the wind. Blowing up buildings in the face of the wind was tried, and without any benefit. The Court House and water works, though a mile apart, were burning at the same time. Gunpowder was used in blowing up buildings, with good effect, the next day, in cutting off the fire at the extreme south end of it, and preventing its backing any further. After the water works burned, the firemen could do little good with their engines, except on the banks of the river. They had lost 7,500 feet of hose, and one steam

fire engine. Two more engines had been in the repair shop and were partially destroyed, so that after 11 o'clock on Sunday night we had but fourteen engines in the service, and after daybreak had but about one-half of our hose remaining. This would not admit of an engine conveying water very far from the ruins. The firemen and their officers were sober and did all that men could do. They worked heroically to save the property of others when their own homes were burning and their families were fleeing from the flames. A large part of the Department had worked at the large fire on Saturday night and Sunday, till 3 o'clock in the afternoon—eighteen hours' steady work—and they were nearly exhausted when this fire commenced, but they responded to this call with alacrity, and worked with all their remaining energy.

We believe that had the buildings on the West Side, where the fire commenced, been built of brick or stone, with safe roofing, and the buildings need not have been fire-proof, that the fire could have been stopped without doing great damage, and certainly would not have crossed the river. After it did cross, the wooden cornices, wooden signs of huge size, the cupolas, and the tar and felt roofs which were on most of the buildings, caused their speedy destruction, and aided greatly in spreading the conflagration.

The single set of pumping works upon which the salvation of the city depended were roofed with wood, had no appliance by which water could be raised to its own roof in case of fire, and was one of the earliest buildings to burn in the North Division. The Board of Police have year by year, in annual reports to the Mayor and Common Council, endeavored to point out the great defects in the manner in which our city was being built up. We advised and entreated to have much greater fire limits established before such an immense amount of combustibles were piled around the heart of the city. We reported Mansard roofs and tar roofs to be unsafe; that the water supply was insufficient; that our fire hydrants were twice too far apart[4]; that we ought to have fire department cisterns at the intersection of the streets, so that we should always have water at fires; that we ought to have floating fire engines with powerful pumps in the river and thus enable the firemen to wet down 1,500 feet on either side of the river or its branches; that wooden cornices are an abomination; that the Holly system of pumping the water and sending it through the pipes with a pressure of forty pounds on ordinary occasions, with power to increase it to one hundred pounds in case of a fire, would give us four sets of pumping works in the different parts of the city, and not leave us to the mercy of chance or accident to a single set.[5]

We showed that the four sets of Holly works could be built for less than one year's interest on the cost of the present water works, and when built would admit of the dispensing with every engine in the Fire Department where the water was in the street, allowing us to get rid of most of the horses and all of the engines of the department, and reducing the number of men one-half, saving two-thirds of the expense of the Fire Department, and making it as efficient as it would be now with 100 steam fire engines.

None of these things were noticed by the Mayor, Common Council or the newspapers, no heed being paid to our suggestions so far as any change or improvement of our plan of extinguishing fires was concerned, the only thing we could do was to ask for an increase of the engine companies, so that we might be prepared as well as possible to contend with the great fires to which we were and still are liable.

Our engines have always been too few in number, and too far apart. The fire department should be very much enlarged, and the system of putting out fires by steam fire engines should be abandoned. If the citizens don't believe this now, they will after the next great fire sweeps out of existence the greater portion of the wooden city which now remains.

If we had had floating steam pumps of large capacity in the South Branch the fire would not probably have crossed to the South Side. If we could have had cisterns in the streets, we could have saved all of the North Division, north of Chicago avenue and west of Clark street, and all the southeast part now included in the burnt district of the South Division.

Evidence was given of money having been paid by citizens to some of our own firemen, but we can find no evidence that any of them worked during the fire with any idea of receiving any pay for their labor upon any property. The money paid was merely a testimonial of respect for the firemen and acknowledgment in a substantial form of services rendered by the firemen, many of whom had periled their lives to save the property of citizens and lost their own homes while doing so. No money was paid them until weeks after the fire, and was a surprise to the firemen who received it. The Fire Department received all the aid from firemen of nearly every city far and near that could be rendered, but they all came and brought their apparatus and worked with a will, and placed us under a load of obligation which we can never repay.

The area burned over by this fire is about 2,050 acres, divided among the three divisions as follows: About 160 acres in the West Division; nearly 500 acres in the South Division, and upward of 1,400 acres in the North Division.[6] The total loss of property burned is estimated at about $200,000,000. The number of buildings burned is between 17,000 and 18,000; the number of lives lost at the fire is supposed to have been about 200, although the Coroner as yet, has found but 117 bodies of persons lost at the fire.

T. B. BROWN,
MARK SHERIDAN,
J. E. CHADWICK,
Commissioners.

Notes

1. "The Great Fire," *Chicago Evening Journal*, 12 December 1871, p. [4]; "The Great Fire," *Chicago Republican*, 12 December 1871, p. [4]; "Nobody to Blame," p. 5; Andreas, vol. 2, pp. 709–10. Strangely, these four published reports are not identical; there are a few minor but nonetheless distinct differences between them. Although the *Evening Journal*, for example, notes that the wind carried "burning shingles and *boards*" over the firemen's heads, the *Republican* mentions "burning shingles and *brands* [emphasis added]." The last sentence of the *Journal*'s account concludes with "although the Coroner as yet, has found but 117 bodies of persons lost at the fire." Andreas, however, ends his version by stating "although the coroner has as yet found but one hundred and seventeen bodies in the ruins." The *Journal* and *Times* indicate that Commissioners Brown, Sheridan, and Chadwick

FIGURE 88—STEAM ENGINE AND CREGIER FIRE HYDRANT. Robert Cromie indicates in his book *The Great Chicago Fire* that the hydrants on Chicago's West Side might have been the older churn-shaped wooden hydrants and not the more modern cast iron models. But Ken Little, co-author of *History of Chicago Fire Houses of the 19th Century*, suggests that the fire hydrants near the O'Leary home may have been the newer "Cregier" hydrants. These hydrants were designed by DeWitt C. Cregier, chief engineer of the city's water works at the time of the fire, and patented in 1861.

This photograph (circa 1862–64) is of a steam engine on State Street, south of Lake Street, on Chicago's South Side, spewing debris into the air while connected to a single port Cregier hydrant. The picture aptly illustrates Cromie's description of steamers rushing toward a fire at full gallop:

> Clouds of steam, smoke, and cinders chuffed noisily from the boiler stacks, while a path of gleaming clinkers marked their wake. A contemporary story was told of two Irishmen, lately arrived in this country and staying overnight at a hotel. One was awakened by fire bells, and reached the window in time to see two steamers round the corner. He shook his companion. "Pat, wake up!" he shouted. "They're moving hell! Two loads have gone by already!"

The steam engine shown in Figure 7 was manufactured by the Amoskeag Manufacturing Company. On the other hand, the steamer in this photograph is a Silsby-style engine, made by the Silsby Manufacturing Company. Note the streetcar in the background and the ice on the rail of the steam engine. (Special Collections and Preservation Division, Chicago Public Library)

FIGURE 89—CREGIER FIRE HYDRANT. **Cregier hydrants were in use in Chicago for 100 years. Chicago Fire Department historian Ken Little recalls seeing a photograph of Chicago's Camp Douglas, the U.S. military camp, that disclosed a Cregier hydrant in the midst of Civil War prisoners of war. A drawing of a Cregier hydrant next to some North Side fire ruins appears in Andreas'** *History of Chicago.* **Ken Little took this picture of a double port Cregier hydrant sometime in the late 1950s. (Photograph by Ken Little)**

signed the report, Andreas maintains that Brown, Sheridan, and Gund signed it, and the *Republican* lists Brown, Sheridan, Gund, and Chadwick as the authors.

2. "That Investigation," *Chicago Evening Journal,* 2 December 1871, p. [4].

3. Actually, only fifty people testified.

4. Ironically, it appears that there were plenty of hydrants near Mrs. O'Leary's barn. *Robinson's Atlas* (1886) discloses hydrants in the O'Leary neighborhood at these locations: the southwest corner of DeKoven and Jefferson streets, the northeast corner of DeKoven and Clinton streets, and the northeast corner of Taylor and Jefferson streets. See *Robinson's Atlas,* vol. 1, plate 6; Figures 88, 89, 90.

5. Birdsill Holly of Lockport, New York, invented the Holly Fire Protection System in 1863. It consisted of a series of pumps powered by either water turbines, steam engines or water from a reservoir. A pressure regulator maintained a constant water pressure in the mains. The Holly system eliminated the need for steam fire engines. In case of fire, firemen would connect their hose to the hydrant and open a valve. The pressure regulator would respond to the drop in water pressure by raising the pressure and increasing the water supply. The City of Chicago never did adopt the Holly pumping system, although the Board may have suggested it again after the fire. In the 1880s railway magnate George M. Pullman built the company town of Pullman on four thousand acres south of Chicago. As the town was privately owned, it provided its own fire protection, and the town used the Holly system.

Birdsill Holly's invention was not without its faults. As the Holly system depended on continuous water pressure in the mains, a water main break could potentially wash out a street and undermine building foundations. See David Lewis to

FIGURE 90—THE GRAPHIC DRAWING OF FIREMEN. Entitled "The Burning of Chicago—Firemen at Work," this drawing of firemen fighting the fire originally appeared on the cover of the October 21, 1871, issue of The Graphic, a London illustrated weekly newspaper. In his book The Great Chicago Fire, Robert Cromie indicates that the fire hydrants on the West Side might still have been the older "churn-shaped wooden ones." Such a hydrant is shown in this picture. The sign on the building reads "W. D. Baker Engraver." Baker's establishment was on the corner of Randolph and Clark streets, on the city's South Side.

As depicted in this drawing, in 1871 the firefighter's uniform consisted of shirt, pants, a leather helmet, and leather cavalry-style boots that extended to just below the knees. When necessary, firemen also wore a woolen jacket similar to a navy pea jacket. But it was surely too warm for a jacket on the night of the fire. John Dorsey, foreman of the America hose cart company, testified at the inquiry, "I came back to the fire. I was after leaving my two coats right by the fire. The chief told me to run away. I was just pulling them off at the time; we could not keep them on...."

Richard F. Bales, 8 August 2001; Ken Little to Richard F. Bales, 14 August 2001; Little & McNalis, pp. 448–49; Bessie Louise Pierce, *A History of Chicago*, vol. 3, *The Rise of a Modern City, 1871–1893* (New York: Alfred A. Knopf, 1957), p. 159, hereafter cited in text as Pierce, vol. 3; *As Others See Chicago*, pp. 244–45.

6. Although the *Evening Journal* and *Times* note the total acreage of the burnt district to be "about 2,050 acres," the *Republican* and Andreas indicate the amount to be about 2,150 acres. But as all four sources allocate the burnt acreage identically throughout the three divisions, it appears that about 2,050 is the final report's correct number. (160 acres in the West Side and 500 acres in the South Side and 1400 acres in the North Side total 2060 acres.) On the other hand, the Chicago Relief and Aid Society claimed that the total acreage of the burnt district, including streets, was 2,124 acres, or nearly three and one-third square miles. See *Report of the Chicago Relief and Aid Society*, p. 10.

Sources Consulted for Photographs, Drawings, and Diagrams

This work is just issued from the press. It [is] a book of 528 pages of print, besides 36 illustrations,—the latter including a first-class map of the city....
—*Chicago Tribune*, December 17, 1871

Introduction

There are 90 photographs, original drawings, and diagrams in this book. In most cases, the captions for the photographs and drawings include information that is not otherwise noted in the text. For this reason, the sources for virtually all captioned material are listed in this appendix in note format.

Many of these illustrations are from sources that no longer enjoy copyright protection and are now in the public domain. Examples include the 1871 auction advertisement for the remains of the courthouse bell (Figure 14) and the drawing of Mary Callahan (Figure 52) that originally appeared in the September 26, 1903, *Chicago Tribune*. Bibliographic information for these illustrations is nonetheless included in this appendix.

Graphic artist Douglas A. Swanson drew all the diagrams in this book. They are based on several different primary and secondary references. Where appropriate, the source or sources for each diagram are shown in this appendix.

Artist and history buff Marshall Philyaw is responsible for all of the original drawings. The portraits are based on period newspaper photographs and pictures of the actual people. See, for example, the drawings of Michael Ahern (Figure 36) and Jim O'Leary (Figure 49). A few of the original "scene" pictures have been slightly enhanced. For example, an 1866 engraving of Lake Michigan's water crib served as a preliminary reference for Philyaw's dramatic depiction of John Tolland's inquiry testimony (Figure 65). The drawings of the Peshtigo Fire (Figure 59) and the burning grain elevators (Figure 85) are based in part on 1871 illustrations that originally appeared in *Harper's Weekly*.

Although the drawings of Conley's Patch (Figure 5), firemen attempting to extinguish the fire at the O'Leary property (Figure 12), and Daniel Sullivan and Dennis Regan in the barn (Figure 63) are based on conjecture and are somewhat fanciful, they are all grounded in historical fact. The references for Philyaw's drawings, as well as the sources for any additional caption information, are noted below.

Although almost all of Philyaw's drawings are of illustrations that are in the public domain, in a few instances a drawing was made of copyrighted material. In those cases permission to reproduce the illustration was obtained and credit is given in the caption that accompanies each drawing. Marshall Philyaw can be contacted at 1405 Beverly Drive, Round Lake Beach, Illinois 60073.

Figure 1—Map of Chicago showing the three divisions
Grosser, p. [39].

Figure 2—Wood's museum, pre-fire
Andreas, vol. 2, pp. 607–9; Kogan and Cromie, p. 13; Duis, p. 206; Robert Cromie, *The Great Chicago Fire*, illustrated ed. (Nashville: Rutledge Hill Press, 1994), p. 16, hereafter cited in text as Cromie, illus. ed.; Mayer and Wade, p. 104; *1871 City Directory*, p. 55.

Figure 3—Corner of Lake Street and Wabash Avenue, pre-fire
1870 City Directory, p. 1009; Robert A. Williams, *Inquiry*, vol. [4], p. 255.

Figure 4—Lake Street, pre-fire
Kogan and Cromie, p. [41].

Figure 5—Conley's Patch, pre-fire
Dedmon, p. 32; Sheahan and Upton, p. 74; "The City: Squatter Settlements," p. [3]; *Chicago Tribune*, "The Great Conflagration," 11 October 1871, p. 1; "Fire Alley Is Paved," p. 1; Kogan and Cromie, p. 16; Michael C. Hickey, *Inquiry*, vol. [2], p. 148; Duis, p. 187.

Figure 6—Fire Marshal Robert A. Williams
Andreas, vol. 2, p. 92.

Figure 7—Steamer *Little Giant* No. 6
1869 Report of the Board of Police, pp. 36–[37]; *1872 Report of the Board of Police*, pp. 38–[39]; Musham, p. 82.

Figure 8—*Tempest* Hose Cart No. 1
1869 Report of the Board of Police, pp. 58–59, 64–66; *1872 Report of the Board of Police*, pp. 74–[75]; Ken Little to Richard F. Bales, 5 June 2001; Leo Meyers, *Inquiry*, vol. [2], p. 81; Musham, p. 81; 1871 Pay Roll.

Figure 9—*Pioneer* Hook and Ladder No. 1
Little and McNalis, pp. 9, 80; *Fire Edition Directory*, p. [228]; *1870 City Directory*, p. [350]; Francis T. Swenie, *Inquiry*, vol. [3], pp. 173, 214–15; *1869 Report of the Board of Police*, pp. 54–55; Ken Little to Richard F. Bales, 15 January 2002; George Rau, *Inquiry*, vol. [1], p. 166; David Lewis, curator of the Aurora Regional Fire Museum, interview by Richard F. Bales, 30 January 2002.

Figure 10—Chicago Fire Landmarks
Cromie, inside front cover; Lowe, p. 42; Andreas, vol. 2, p. 707.

Figure 11—October 8, 1871, *Tribune* article about the Lull & Holmes planing mill fire
"The Fire Fiend," p. [3].

Figure 12—O'Leary barn on fire
Kogan and Cromie, pp. 50–51, 180–81; Christian Schimmals, *Inquiry*, vol. [1], p. 151; Dennis Regan, *Inquiry*, vol. [1], pp. 122, 124; Catharine McLaughlin, *Inquiry*, vol. [1], pp. 225, 237–38; Catherine Sullivan, *Inquiry*, vol. [1], p. 116; Daniel Sullivan, *Inquiry*, vol. [1], p. 257.

Figure 13—Courthouse, pre-fire
Kogan and Cromie, p. 10; Colbert and Chamberlin, pp. 153–54; Andreas, vol. 2, p. 66.

Figure 14—Auction advertisement of the courthouse bell
"The Co[urt] House Bell," *Chicago Tribune*, 17 December 1871, p. 7; "Auction Sales," *Chicago Times*, 16 December 1871, p. 8; Cook County (Illinois) Courthouse Bell Collection, Chicago Historical Society; "The Court House Bell," *The Land Owner: A Journal of Real Estate Building & Improvement* 4 (February 1872), p. 16.

Figure 15—Advertisement for the miniature courthouse bells
"The Court House Bell," *The Land Owner: A Journal of Real Estate Building & Improvement* 4 (February 1872), p. 16.

Figure 17—Courthouse on fire
"The Tornado of Fire," *Frank Leslie's Illustrated Newspaper* 33 (28 October 1871), pp. 101–2; "Atrocious Fabrications," *Chicago Tribune*, 19 October 1871, p. [2].

Figure 18—Wood's museum on fire
"Fire Chronology," p. [4]; Duis, p. 219; Cromie, illus. ed., p. 16.

Figure 19—Courthouse ruins; view along Randolph Street
Sheahan and Upton, p. 100; Kogan and Cromie, pp. 126–27; *Reminiscences of Chicago During the Great Fire*, p. xxiv; Lowe, p. 42; Herman Kogan, "Grander and Statelier Than Ever...," *Chicago History* 1 (Fall 1971), p. 236.

Figure 20—The "Horrors of Chicago"
The Horrors of Chicago, cover; Michael C. Hickey, *Inquiry*, vol. [2], pp. 169–70.

Figure 21—Chicago Fire sensationalism
The Horrors of Chicago, pp. [9]–10.

Figure 22—Mayor Roswell B. Mason
Untitled article, *Chicago Times*, 19 October 1871, p. [2]; "An Old Granny," *Chicago Times*, 19 October 1871, p. [2]; Andreas, vol. 2, p. 51; Sawislak, p. 126; Luzerne, p. [53].

Figure 23—General Philip H. Sheridan
Kogan and Cromie, p. 194; Andreas, vol. 2, pp. 383–84, 775.

Figure 24—Demolished building
Kogan and Cromie, p. 81; James H. Hildreth, *Inquiry*, vol. [3], pp. 123–72 passim.

Figure 25—Water tower and water works, pre-fire
Sheahan and Upton, pp. 34–37; Andreas, vol. 2, pp. 68–70; Kogan and Cromie, p. 43.

Figure 26—Fleeing from the burning city
Kogan and Cromie, p. 85; "When Chicago Burned," *American Heritage* 14 (August 1963), pp. 2, 54, 57, hereafter cited in text as "When Chicago Burned."

Figure 27—Fleeing the North Side; near the water tower
Andreas, vol. 2, pp. 740–54 passim.

Figure 28—Letter and illustration by Justin [Butterfield]
Justin [Butterfield] to [Philip Prescott], 19 October [1871], Chicago Fire of 1871 Personal Narratives Collection, Chicago Historical Society; Frederick M. Bradley to Mr. Charles Dewey, 11 December 1969, Chicago Fire of 1871 Personal Narratives Collection, Chicago Historical Soci-

ety; *Reminiscences of Chicago During the Great Fire*, p. 105; Andreas, vol. 2, pp. 744–45.

Figure 29—People gathered around the water tower; post-fire
Kogan and Wendt, pp. 129, 142; Kogan and Cromie, p. 208.

Figure 30—Chicago Fire ruins; view of Pine Street (now Michigan Ave.) from the top of the water tower
Cromie, p. [249]; Cromie, illus. ed., pp. 190–91; Andreas, vol. 2, pp. 373–74.

Figure 31—Southeastern view of the O'Leary and McLaughlin homes
"Origin of the Fire," supplement, p. [2].

Figure 32—A sympathetic interpretation of Mrs. O'Leary in the barn; drawing by the Kellogg & Bulkeley Company
"The Great Calamity of the Age!," p. 1; Kogan and Cromie, p. 52; Andreas, vol. 2, p. 715.

Figure 33—A not-so-kindly Mrs. O'Leary with rats, a chicken, and a cat; drawing by L. V. H. Crosby
Kogan and Cromie, p. 53.

Figure 34—Mrs. O'Leary and menagerie in the barn; drawing by W. O. Mull
Kogan and Cromie, p. 53.

Figure 35—October 9, 1871, *Chicago Evening Journal*
"The Great Calamity of the Age!," p. 1.

Figure 36—Michael Ahern
"Reporter of 1871 Fire," sec. 1, p. [2]; "Mrs. O'Leary Cow Story Refuted by Old Reporter," sec. 2, p. 13.

Figure 37—O'Leary home; from John J. McKenna's book
1918 McKenna, p. [143]; Chicago Title Insurance Company records; Catharine McLaughlin, *Inquiry*, vol. [1], p. 239.

Figure 38—First page of Mrs. O'Leary's inquiry testimony
Catherine O'Leary, *Inquiry*, vol. [1], p. 59.

Figure 39—Robert S. Critchell
Critchell, frontispiece, pp. 73–74, 80–81.

Figure 40—Catherine O'Leary's death certificate
"The Fire," *Chicago Times*, 18 October 1871, p. 1.

Figure 41—Newspaper advertisement of the Phenix Insurance Company and Robert S. Critchell
Critchell, pp. 73–74, 80–81; "Insurance," *Chicago Tribune*, 13 October 1871, p. [3].

Figure 42—Harry A. Musham and Jacob John Schaller
"Historian Comes to Village," p. 63.

Figure 43—Jacob John Schaller/Harry A. Musham telephone message
Harry A. Musham Collection, Notes on the Chicago Fire, Chicago Historical Society.

Figure 44—Mathias Schaefer
"Reporter of 1871 Fire," sec. 1, p. [2].

Figure 45—Bruno Goll's drugstore; fire alarm box 296
Chicago: City on Fire, p. 11-F; Andreas, vol. 2, pp. 711, 714, 716.

Figure 46—Location of fire companies and fire alarm boxes in the O'Leary neighborhood
Musham, pp. 97, [101]; Little and McNalis, pp. 12, 34–35; *1870 City Directory*, p. 915; *1871 City Directory*, p. 35; Lowe, p. 42; Andreas, vol. 2, p. 716; Ken Little to Richard F. Bales, 16 December 2000; Ken Little to Richard F. Bales, 7 January 2001. (Note: Although H. A. Musham indicates that the *Little Giant* Engine Company was located on Maxwell Street between Jefferson and Clinton streets, this is incorrect. The *Little Giant* was not at this location until 1913.)

Figure 47—View of the O'Leary home from the southwest
"Kate! The Barn Is Afire!," p. 217; Kogan and Cromie, p. 180.

Figure 48—Looking north from the ruins of the O'Leary barn
Kogan and Cromie, p. [118].

Figure 49—James "Big Jim" O'Leary
"O'Leary, Who Would Bet on Anything, Dies," sec. 1, p. 1; *Scéal*, p. 2; "Linked to Chicago's Two Worst Fires," sec. 7, p. 10.

Figure 50—Southwestern view of the O'Leary and McLaughlin homes and the remains of Anne Murray's house

Daniel Sullivan, *Inquiry*, vol. [1], p. 264; Catherine O'Leary, *Inquiry*, vol. [1], pp. 62–64, 71; Catharine McLaughlin, *Inquiry*, vol. [1], pp. 223, 237; Chicago Title Insurance Company records; Cox and Armington, p. 367; "Meteorological Observations by the United States Signal Corps"; "Notes on the Great Chicago Fire of 1871," sec. 3, p. 21; Andreas, vol. 2, p. 708.

Figure 51—The Anne Murray and Patrick O'Leary properties
Chicago Title Insurance Company records; George Rau, *Inquiry*, vol. [1], p. 179; Daniel Sullivan, *Inquiry*, vol. [1], pp. 259, 271–72; Andreas, vol. 2, pp. 713–14, 717; Skerrett, p. [205].

Figure 52—Mary Callahan
"Centennial Eve," sec. 1, p. [2]; Catharine McLaughlin, *Inquiry*, vol. [1], p. 225.

Figure 53—People gathered around the rear of the O'Leary home
Kogan and Cromie, p. 181; Goodspeed, pp. 157, 161; *The Great Conflagration: A Complete Account of the Burning of Chicago*, p. 85; Andreas, vol. 2, p. 717.

Figure 54—O'Leary property and surrounding area
Chicago Title Insurance Company records; Catharine McLaughlin, *Inquiry*, vol. [1], pp. 237–40; Catherine O'Leary, *Inquiry*, vol. [1], pp. 65, 68; Patrick O'Leary, *Inquiry*, vol. [1], pp. 250–53; George Rau, *Inquiry*, vol. [1], p. 179; Daniel Sullivan, *Inquiry*, vol. [1], pp. 258–67, 269, 271–72; Kogan and Cromie, pp. 50–51, 180–81; Andreas, vol. 2, pp. 713–14, 717; Musham, pp. 94–95, 98; various Chicago city directories; Chicago Guarantee Survey Company records; Kenneth Grenier, retired Survey Officer, Chicago Title Insurance Company; Charles O'Connor, retired Superintendent of Maps Department, City of Chicago; Nicholas Raimondi, co-owner of National Survey Service, Inc., interview by Richard F. Bales, 28 November 1995.

Figure 55—Alleged remains of the O'Leary lamp
Andreas, vol. 2, pp. 714–15; *1870 City Directory*, p. 240.

Figure 56—Mrs. Anton Axsmith's map of the O'Leary neighborhood
"Beer, Not Milk, Caused Chicago Fire," sec. 1,

p. 3; Andreas, vol. 2, p. 717; McGovern, pp. 177–78.

Figure 57—A. T. Andreas' map of the O'Leary neighborhood
Andreas, vol. 2, p. 717.

Figure 58—Louis M. Cohn
"Cohn Estate Turned Over to University," sec. 1, p. 12; "Odds Improve," sec. 5, p. 1.

Figure 59—The burning of Peshtigo, Wisconsin
Holbrook, pp. 64, 71–73; Wells, pp. 168–69, 191; "Forest Fires in the West," pp. 1104–5, 1109; "The Fires in the Woods," *Chicago Tribune*, 7 October 1871, p. [2]; Pernin, pp. 13, 24, 54.

Figure 60—The O'Leary Barn, as described by John McGovern in his novel *Daniel Trentworthy*
McGovern, pp. 176–77; Patrick O'Leary, *Inquiry*, vol. [1], p. 251.

Figure 61—O'Leary and McLaughlin homes and O'Leary barn
Swing, p. 10.

Figure 62—Man standing in front of the O'Leary and McLaughlin homes
Catharine McLaughlin, *Inquiry*, vol. [1], pp. 223, 237–39; Catherine O'Leary, *Inquiry*, vol. [1], p. 65; Daniel Sullivan, *Inquiry*, vol. [1], pp. 255–56, 262, 264, 266–67; Musham, p. 98; Andreas, vol. 2, p. 717; Chicago Title Insurance Company records.

Figure 63—Daniel "Peg Leg" Sullivan and Dennis Regan in the O'Leary barn
Daniel Sullivan, *Inquiry*, vol. [1], pp. 254–55, 257, 264, 269; Dennis Regan, *Inquiry*, vol. [1], pp. 121–22.

Figure 64—The South Side of DeKoven Street
Chicago Title Insurance Company records; Catherine Sullivan, *Inquiry*, vol. [1], pp. 114–17; Daniel Sullivan, *Inquiry*, vol. [1], pp. 254–55, 262, 265–67, 271, 273–74; Andreas, vol. 2, p. 715; *Robinson's Atlas*, vol. 1, plate 6.

Figure 65—John Tolland and his wife on the water crib
Mayer and Wade, p. [97]; Andreas, vol. 2, p. 67; Colbert and Chamberlin, pp. 155–59; Cromie,

p. 125; Goodspeed, pp. 85–107; Sheahan and Upton, pp. 33–34.

Figure 67—Nellie L. Hayes
"True Story of Chicago Fire Told at Last," sec. 3, pp. 31, 42.

Figure 68—People in front of and on top of the O'Leary and McLaughlin homes
Caroline M. McIlvaine, "The Great Chicago Fire of 1871," *Chicago Daily News*, 10 October 1925, photogravure section, p. [2]; Chicago Title Insurance Company records; "Chicago's Forgotten House," sec. 1, p. 18; "Fire Alley is Paved," p. 1; Catherine O'Leary, *Inquiry*, vol. [1], p. 71; Catharine McLaughlin, *Inquiry*, vol. [1], p. 223.

Figure 69—View from the southwest of people in front of and on top of the O'Leary and McLaughlin homes
"Fire Alley Is Paved," p. 1; Christian Schimmals, *Inquiry*, vol. [1], p. 151; *1872 City Directory*, p. 565.

Figure 70—Patrick O'Leary's death certificate
"Mrs. O'Leary's Cow," p. 8; "Mrs. O'Leary Is Dead," p. 1.

Figure 71—The O'Leary family monument
Gertrude Jobes, *Dictionary of Mythology Folklore and Symbols* (New York: Scarecrow Press, 1962), vol. 2, s.v. "Draped urn"; "Centennial Eve," sec. 1, p. 1.

Figure 72—Anton Kolar home, circa 1881
The City That a Cow Kicked Over, p. [30]; "Chicago's Forgotten House," sec. 1, p. 18; Kogan and Cromie, pp. 226–27; Chicago Title Insurance Company records; Andreas, vol. 2, p. 717.

Figure 73—Steam engine on DeKoven Street (1953)
Kogan and Cromie, pp. 226–27; "Recall Great Chicago Fire in Rites Today," *Chicago Daily Tribune*, 9 October 1953, sec. 3, p. 3; "A Factory Will Mark the Spot," *Chicago Daily News*, 2 October 1954, Roto[gravure], p. 4; "Chicago's Forgotten House," sec. 1, p. 18.

Figure 74—1937 plaque inside the fire academy

Little and McNalis, p. 35; Kogan and Cromie, p. 227; "OK Sale of 1st Ward Land to Industry," p. 3; "Fire Landmark Comes Down," *Chicago Sunday Sun-Times*, 4 December 1955, sec. 1, p. 5; "Fire at the O'Leary Homesite," *Chicago Daily Sun-Times*," 24 November 1955, p. 8; H. Maxson Holloway, Assistant Director, Chicago Historical Society to Chief of Police, Maxwell Street Station, 1 September 1955, "Chicago Fire of 1871: O'Leary Family," Clipping File, Chicago Historical Society.

Figure 79—Land Ownership along DeKoven Street and Taylor Street
Chicago Title Insurance Company records.

Figure 80—1879 deed from O'Leary to Kolar
Sawislak, pp. 97, 311; *1870 City Directory*, p. 486; *1872 City Directory*, p. 565; Chicago Title Insurance Company records.

Figure 81—Mayor Mason's letter ordering the release of the prisoners
"The Debtors," p. 3; "Fragile Note Illuminates City's Great Fire," sec. 1, p. 1.

Figure 82—Terrace Row; pre-fire
Kogan and Cromie, p. 17.

Figure 83—Terrace Row and grain elevators; pre-fire
Kogan and Cromie, p. 18.

Figure 84—Guarding the ruined city
Kogan and Cromie, p. 195; "When Chicago Burned," pp. 58–59.

Figure 85—Burning grain elevators at the mouth of the Chicago River
Chapin, pp. 1010, 1013; Robert A. Williams, *Inquiry*, vol. [4], pp. 282–83; *American Apocalypse*, p. [14].

Figure 86—William Le Baron Jenney's first proposed Chicago Fire Monument
"The Chicago Fire Monument," *The Land Owner: A Journal of Real Estate Building & Improvement* 4 (February 1872), p. 27; *The Lakeside Memorial of the Burning of Chicago, A.D. 1871* (Chicago: University Publishing Co., 1872), frontispiece.

Figure 87—Chicago Fire Academy flame monument
Chicago Title Insurance Company records, "Kate! The Barn Is Afire!," p. 219; Cowan, p. 21; *American Apocalypse*, p. 149.

Figure 88—Steam engine and Cregier fire hydrant
Little and McNalis, p. 4; Cromie, pp. 13–14, 17; Andreas, vol. 2, pp. 59–60; *1870 City Directory*, p. 193; *1871 City Directory*, p. 232; *1872 Report of the Board of Police*, p. 16.

Figure 89—Cregier fire hydrant
Little and McNalis, p. 331; Ken Little to Richard F. Bales, 27 December 2001; Ken Little to Richard F. Bales, 4 January 2002; Andreas, vol. 2, pp. 301, 743.

Figure 90—*The Graphic* drawing of firemen
Cromie, p. 17; John Dorsey, *Inquiry*, vol. [2], pp. 61, 65; Ken Little to Richard F. Bales, 21 December 2001; *1870 City Directory*, pp. 60, 1007; *1871 City Directory*, pp. 93, 1012; *Robinson's Atlas*, vol. 3, plate 1; "The Burning of Chicago," *The Graphic* 4 (October 21, 1871), p. [385]; Andreas, vol. 2, p. 489.

Annotated Bibliography

Books

INTRODUCTION

Although most of my research involved primary materials, I did utilize many secondary sources. I have briefly annotated those books that were especially interesting, useful, or otherwise important to any study of the fire. Obviously, the lack of an annotation is not an overt criticism of the work. Although some books and other works mentioned in this bibliography did not contain certain bibliographic information, I was sometimes able to obtain that material through other means. In those instances that additional information is shown in brackets.

Allaby, Michael, ed. *Illustrated Dictionary of Science*. Oxfordshire, England: Andromeda Oxford Limited, 1995. S.v. "Spontaneous Combustion."

The American Heritage Dictionary of the English Language. 3d ed. S.v. "light: light out."

Andreas, A[lfred] T[heodore]. *History of Chicago: From the Earliest Period to the Present Time*. Vol. 1, *Ending with the Year 1857*. Chicago: A. T. Andreas Co., 1884.

_____. *History of Chicago: From the Earliest Period to the Present Time*. Vol. 2, *From 1857 Until the Fire of 1871*. Chicago: A. T. Andreas Co., 1885. The "Burning of Chicago" section is eighty pages long. Written several years after the fire, Andreas's account is an objective observation that avoids the platitudes and histrionics found in the "instant histories" that were written in the weeks after October 8, 1871. This volume was also helpful in providing background information for many of the annotations to the inquiry transcript selections in Appendix D.

_____. *History of Chicago: From the Earliest Period to the Present Time*. Vol. 3, *From the Fire of 1871 Until 1885*. Chicago: A. T. Andreas Co., 1886.

Angle, Paul M., ed. *The Great Chicago Fire*. Chicago: Chicago Historical Society, 1946. A collection of annotated letters written in the aftermath of the fire.

_____. Introduction to *The Great Chicago Fire of 1871*. Ashland: Lewis Osborne, 1969. A reprint of three illustrated articles that originally appeared in *Harper's Weekly* on October 28, 1871, and November 4, 1871.

Barclay, George L. *The Great Fire of Chicago!...* Philadelphia: Barclay & Co., 1872. A sensational instant history of the fire that includes graphic depictions of the hanging and braining of thieves and incendiaries.

Blanchard, Rufus. *Discovery and Conquests of the North-West, with the History of Chicago*. Wheaton, [Ill.]: R. Blanchard & Co., 1879.

Blatchford, M[ary] E[mily], and E[liphalet] W[ickes]. *Memories of the Chicago Fire*. Privately printed, 1921. A so-called "personal history" of Chicago Fire reminiscences.

Brown, Samuel L., comp. *Surnames Are the Fossils*

of Speech. Privately printed, 1967. S.v. "Brown"; "Schaefer"; "Shaffer."

Browne, Charles A. *The Spontaneous Combustion of Hay.* Washington, D.C.: United States Department of Agriculture, 1929.

Burnam, Tom. *The Dictionary of Misinformation.* New York: Thomas Y. Crowell Co., 1975. S.v. "Mrs. O'Leary's cow."

Chicago & Vicinity 6-County StreetFinder. N.p.: Rand McNally, 1995.

Cibber, Colley. *The Dramatic Works of Colley Cibber, Esq....* London: J. Rivington and Sons, 1777; reprint, New York: AMS Press, 1966.

The City That a Cow Kicked Over. Chicago: A. H. Andrews & Co., n.d. A forgettable poem about the Chicago Fire. As one of the verses includes a reference to the courthouse bell "where ten short years ago she fell," the book appears to have been written in about 1881. The poem also refers to the miniature courthouse bells and suggests that the O'Leary cow started the fire. Ironically, this booklet contains an advertisement for the fire insurance company of "R. S. Critchell & Co." (See Critchell, Robert S., infra.) A slightly different version of the poem was published in the October 8, 1921, *Chicago Evening Post.*

Cleveland, J. F., comp. *The Tribune Almanac and Political Register.* New York: Tribune Association, 1871.

Colbert, Elias Colbert, and Everett Chamberlin. *Chicago and the Great Conflagration.* Cincinnati: C. F. Vent, 1871. An instant history of the fire.

Cowan, David. *Great Chicago Fires: Historic Blazes That Shaped a City.* Chicago: Lake Claremont Press, 2001. A chronicle of more than thirty "great" Chicago fires, including the fire of October 8–10, 1871.

Cox, Henry J., and John H. Armington. *The Weather and Climate of Chicago.* Chicago: University of Chicago Press, 1914. An invaluable resource for 1871 weather information.

Critchell, Robert S. *Recollections of a Fire Insurance Man.* Chicago: Privately printed, 1909. Critchell claims that Mrs. O'Leary told him that the story of the cow kicking over the lantern was true.

Cromie, Robert. *The Great Chicago Fire.* New York: McGraw-Hill Book Co., 1958. A popular account of the fire that is based in part on the inquiry transcript.

_____. *The Great Chicago Fire.* Illustrated ed. Nashville: Rutledge Hill Press, 1994. An illustrated edition of Cromie's 1958 history of the fire.

Danckers, Ulrich, and Jane Meredith. *A Compendium of the Early History of Chicago to the Year 1835 When the Indians Left.* River Forest, Ill.: Early Chicago, 1999. An encyclopedia of early Chicago history.

Danzer, Gerald A. *Public Places: Exploring Their History.* Walnut Creek, Calif.: Sage Publications, AltaMira Press, 1997. This book details the story of the proposed fire monument of ruined safes and other fire relics. It features a picture of William Le Baron Jenney's second proposed design of this monument.

Dedmon, Emmett. *Fabulous Chicago.* New York: Random House, 1953.

DeHaan, John D. *Kirk's Fire Investigation,* 4th ed. Upper Saddle River, N.J.: Prentice-Hall, 1997. This fire investigation textbook was essential for debunking the "comet" and "spontaneous combustion of green hay" theories.

Duis, Perry R. *Challenging Chicago: Coping with Everyday Life, 1837–1920.* Urbana: University of Illinois Press, 1998. A social history of how the lower and middle classes handled life in Chicago.

[*Edwards' Twelfth Annual Directory of the Inhabitants, Institutions, Incorporated Companies, and Manufacturing Establishments of the City of Chicago, Embracing a Complete Business Directory for 1869*]. Vol. 12. Chicago: Richard Edwards, 1869. Edwards's various directories include an alphabetized listing of individuals and businesses, city and county information, and a business directory of Chicago's trades and professions. (As both an actual directory and a microfilmed edition lacked the title page, the bibliographic information for this directory is only assumed and is therefore noted in brackets.)

Edwards' Thirteenth Annual Directory of the Inhabitants, Institutions, Incorporated Companies, and Manufacturing Establishments of the City of Chicago, Embracing a Complete Business Directory for 1870. Vol. 13. Chicago: Richard Edwards, 1870.

Edwards' Fourteenth Annual Directory of the Inhabitants, Institutions, Incorporated Companies and Manufacturing Establishments of the City of Chicago, Embracing a Complete Business Directory for 1871. Vol. 14. Chicago: Richard Edwards, 1871.

Edwards' Fifteenth Annual Directory of the Inhabitants, Institutions, Manufacturing Establishments and Incorporated Companies of the City of Chicago, Embracing a Complete Business Directory for 1872. Vol. 15. Chicago: Richard Edwards, 1872.

Edwards' Chicago Directory: Fire Edition. Chicago: Richard Edwards, 1871–72.

Einhorn, Robin L. *Property Rules: Political Economy in Chicago, 1833–1872*. Chicago: University of Chicago Press, 1991.

Eleventh Annual Report of the Board of Public Works, to the Common Council of the City of Chicago, for the Municipal, Fiscal Year Ending March 31, 1872. Chicago: D. & C. H. Blakely, 1872.

Flexner, Stuart Berg, ed. *The Random House Dictionary of the English Language*. 2d ed. New York: Random House, 1987. S.v. "Signs and Symbols: Miscellaneous."

Flinn, John J. *History of the Chicago Police*. Chicago: Police Book Fund, 1887; reprint, Montclair, N.J.: Patterson Smith Publishing Corp., 1973. A study of Chicago's police and urban life that was useful in annotating the inquiry testimony of Michael C. Hickey and James H. Hildreth.

Foster, Thomas D. *A Letter from the Fire*. Cedar Rapids, Iowa: Privately printed, 1949. A colorful and descriptive personal history by an eyewitness to the fire.

Freidel, Frank, ed. *Harvard Guide to American History*. Vol. 1. Cambridge: Harvard University Press, Belknap Press, 1974. This book contains guidelines used in editing the Appendix D selections from the transcript of the inquiry.

Full Account of the Great Fire in Chicago. Racine, [Wis.]: Wm. L. Utley & Son, 1871. A compilation of newspaper articles.

Goodspeed, E[dgar] J[ohnson]. *History of the Great Fires in Chicago and the West....* New York: H. S. Goodspeed & Co., 1871. An instant history of the fire.

The Great Conflagration: A Complete Account of the Burning of Chicago.... Chicago: Western News Co., 1871. An instant history that includes a "business directory and list of the principal business houses in their present locations."

Grosser, Hugo S. *Chicago: A Review of Its Governmental History from 1837 to 1906*. Privately printed, 1906. The title page of this book indicates that Grosser was Chicago's "city statistician." He compiled much of this book from official documents. It is an excellent resource for statistical information.

Halpin's Seventh Annual Edition Chicago City Directory, 1864–5: Containing, Also, a Classified Business Register and City and County Record. Chicago: T. M. Halpin & Co., 1864.

Hamilton, H. R. *Footprints*. Chicago: Lakeside Press, 1927.

Hanks, Patrick, and Flavia Hodges. *A Dictionary of Surnames*. Oxford: Oxford University Press, 1991. S.v. "Brown"; "Schäfer"; "Schaffer."

Hayner, Don, and Tom McNamee. *Streetwise Chicago: A History of Chicago Street Names*. Chicago: Loyola University Press, 1988. This encyclopedia of explanations for Chicago street names also includes a discussion of the city's new and old street numbering systems.

Holbrook, Stewart H. *Burning an Empire: The Story of American Forest Fires*. New York: Macmillan Co., 1943.

Howard, Robert P. *Illinois: A History of the Prairie State*. Grand Rapids, Mich.: William B. Eerdmans Publishing Co., 1972.

Jellinek, Frank. *The Paris Commune of 1871*. New York: Grosset & Dunlap, Universal Library, 1965.

Jobes, Gertrude. *Dictionary of Mythology Folklore and Symbols*. Vol. 2. New York: Scarecrow Press, 1962. S.v. "Draped urn."

King, William T. *History of the American Steam Fire-engine*. N.p., 1896; reprint, Chicago: Owen Davies, 1960.

Kirkland, Joseph. *The Story of Chicago*. Vol. 1. Chicago: Dibble Publishing Co., 1892.

Kogan, Herman, and Robert Cromie. *The Great Fire: Chicago 1871*. New York: G. P. Putnam's Sons, 1971. This is a comprehensive collection of pre-fire and post-fire photographs and drawings. Each picture is accompanied by equally comprehensive text. Some of these pictures appear in *The Great Chicago Fire and the Myth of Mrs. O'Leary's Cow*, and some of the captions for these pictures contain information from Kogan and Cromie's work.

Kogan, Herman, and Lloyd Wendt. *Chicago: A Pictorial History*. New York: Crown Publishers, Bonanza Books, 1958.

The Lakeside Annual Directory of the City Of Chicago, 1879: Embracing a Complete General and Business Directory, Miscellaneous Information and Street Guide. Chicago: Donnelley, Gassette & Loyd, 1879.

The Lakeside Annual Directory of the City of Chicago, 1895: Embracing a Complete General and Business Directory, Miscellaneous Information, and Street Guide. Chicago: Chicago Directory Co., 1895.

Lewis, Lloyd, and Henry Justin Smith. *Chicago: The History of Its Reputation.* New York: Harcourt, Brace and Co., 1929.

Little, Ken, and John McNalis. *History of Chicago Fire Houses of the 19th Century.* Privately printed, 1996. This 545 page heavily illustrated history contains information on fire houses and fire companies that appears to be unavailable elsewhere.

Loesch, Frank J. *Personal Experiences During the Chicago Fire, 1871.* Chicago: Privately printed, 1925. A post-fire personal history.

Longstreet, Stephen. *Chicago: 1860–1919.* New York: David McKay Co., 1973.

Lorimer, Lawrence T., ed. *Academic American Encyclopedia.* Danbury, Conn.: Grolier, 1995. S.v. "Spontaneous Combustion," by Stephen Fleishman.

Lowe, David, ed. *The Great Chicago Fire: In Eyewitness Accounts and 70 Contemporary Photographs and Illustrations.* New York: Dover Publications, 1979. A reprint of Mabel McIlvaine's *Reminiscences of Chicago During the Great Fire.*

Luzerne, Frank. *The Lost City! Drama of the Fire-Fiend!...* New York: Wells & Co., 1872. A not quite instant history of the fire.

Maclean, Norman. *Young Men and Fire.* Chicago: University of Chicago Press, 1992.

Mayer, Harold M., and Richard C. Wade. *Chicago: Growth of a Metropolis.* Chicago: University of Chicago Press, 1969. A historian and a geographer collaborate on a one-volume pictorial history of Chicago that suggests how the city expanded and explains why it looks the way it does.

McCaffrey, Lawrence J. "The Irish-American Dimension." In *The Irish in Chicago,* by Lawrence J. McCaffrey, Ellen Skerrett, Michael F. Funchion, and Charles Fanning, pp. [1]–21. Urbana: University of Illinois Press, 1987. A sweeping account of the Irish immigrants' "turbulent pilgrimage through American history."

McDermott, Michael. *The Civil-Engineer & Surveyor's Manual.* Chicago: Fergus Printing Co., 1879.

McGovern, John. *Daniel Trentworthy: A Tale of the Great Fire of Chicago.* Chicago: Rand, McNally & Co., 1889. A novel about the fire.

McIlvaine, Mabel, ed. *Reminiscences of Chicago During the Great Fire.* Chicago: Lakeside Press, 1915. A series of essays that illustrate how the fire affected Chicago's upper class. To read how the lower class fared, see Karen Sawislak's book *Smoldering City: Chicagoans and the Great Fire, 1871–1874,* infra.

McKenna, John J. *Stories by the Original "Jawn" McKenna from "Archy Road" of the Sun Worshipers Club of McKinley Park in Their Political Tales and Reminiscences.* Chicago: John F. Higgins, 1918. A slightly different version of McKenna's *Reminiscences of the Chicago Fire on Sunday Evening, October 9th 1871,* infra, appears as a chapter in this book.

_____. *Reminiscences of the Chicago Fire on Sunday Evening, October 9th 1871.* Chicago: Clohesey, 1933. A personal history of recollections about the fire.

McQuade, James S., ed. *A Synoptical History of the Chicago Fire Department from the Earliest Volunteer Organization Up to the Present Time....* Chicago: Benevolent Association of the Paid Fire Department of Chicago, 1908. An illustrated fire department history.

Merchants' Chicago Census Report, Embracing a Complete Directory of the City—Showing Number of Persons in Each Family, Male and Female—Birth Place and Ward Now Residing In. [Chicago: Richard Edwards, 1871].

Miller, Mrs. A. H. *Reminiscences of the Chicago Fire of 1871.* Privately printed, n.d. Post-fire reminiscences of the widow of the owner of Miller's jewelry store. This booklet was written in 1902 or after, as it is "dedicated to the memory of my husband, A. H. Miller, 1828–1902." Carl Smith suggests that "Mrs. Miller's *Reminiscences* is one of the few memoirs, certainly one of the very few published, that depict the fire as the source of sustained personal misfortune." See Smith, p. 306.

Miller, Donald L. *City of the Century: The Epic of Chicago and the Making of America.* New York: Simon & Schuster, 1996. This history of Chicago contains an extensive section on the fire that is distinguished by endnotes citing the letters and reminiscences contained in the "Chicago Fire of 1871 Personal Narratives Collection" of the Chicago Historical Society.

Miller, Ross. *American Apocalypse: The Great Fire and the Myth of Chicago.* Chicago: University of Chicago Press, 1990. A social and cultural history of the rebuilding of post-fire Chicago.

_____. *The Great Chicago Fire,* paperback ed. Urbana: University of Illinois Press, 2000. The paperback edition of *American Apocalypse.*

Moses, John, and Joseph Kirkland, eds. *History of Chicago, Illinois.* Vol. 1. Chicago: Munsell & Co., 1895.

Mosher, C[harles] D. *Mosher's 1876 Centennial Historical Album.* Vol. 6, *Containing Photographs, Autographs and Biographies of the Chicago Bar.* Privately printed, 1876. S.v. "Homer N. Hibbard."

Mosher, C[harles] D. *Mosher's 1876 Centennial Historical Album,* Vol. 7, *Containing Photographs, Autographs and Biographies of Chicago Editors.* Privately printed, 1876. S.v. "Wilbur F. Storey," "James W. Sheahan," "Andrew Shuman."

Mumford, Manly W. *The Old Family Fire.* Evanston, Ill.: Chicago Historical Bookworks, 1997. This short biography of Mayor Roswell B. Mason by one of his descendants includes references to family legends and transcripts of family letters.

Murphy, Jim. *The Great Fire.* New York: Scholastic, 1995. This history of the fire for young adults is distinguished by a series of maps that highlight the spread of the flames.

Musham, H[arry] A[lbert]. "The Great Chicago Fire, October 8–10, 1871." *Papers in Illinois History and Transactions for the Year 1940.* Springfield: Illinois State Historical Society, 1941. This is the first scholarly history of the fire; unfortunately, it is marred by the author's obsession with proving that Mrs. O'Leary and her cow started it. Nonetheless, Musham's monograph is still an excellent Chicago Fire reference. The information contained in the various appendices is especially useful. Appendix A, for example, is a roster of fire department personnel and fire companies.

The New Encyclopædia Britannica. 15th ed. S.v. "Food Processing: Dairy Products."

Pernin, Peter. *The Great Peshtigo Fire: An Eyewitness Account,* 2d ed. Madison: State Historical Society of Wisconsin, 1999. Father Peter Pernin was the parish priest for Peshtigo, Wisconsin, at the time of the Peshtigo Fire. Father Pernin's account of the fire was originally published in 1874. This 1999 edition includes a foreword by Stephen J. Pyne, author of *Fire in America,* infra, an introduction and epilogue by William Converse Haygood, former editor of the *Wisconsin Magazine of History,* comprehensive endnotes, and a bibliography of selected references.

Pierce, Bessie Louise. *A History of Chicago.* Vol. 2, *From Town to City, 1848–1871.* New York: Alfred A. Knopf, 1940. Unlike Andreas' *History,* Pierce's three-volume history of Chicago contains hundreds of useful footnotes.

_____. *A History of Chicago.* Vol. 3, *The Rise of a Modern City, 1871–1893.* New York: Alfred A. Knopf, 1957.

_____, ed. *As Others See Chicago: Impressions of Visitors, 1673–1933.* Chicago: University of Chicago Press, 1933. A collection of the diaries, letters, and magazine articles of the many visitors to Chicago "who looked around with wonder, or amusement, or disgust, and then went home and wrote about it."

Pyne, Stephen J. *Fire in America: A Cultural History of Wildland and Rural Fire,* paperback ed. Seattle: University of Washington Press, 1997. Pyne integrates the history of fire with ecology, agriculture, logging, and resource management. He includes a vivid description of the Peshtigo fire and the other Wisconsin fires of 1871.

Rascher, [Charles]. *Rascher's Atlas of Chicago.* Vol. 13. Chicago: Rascher Insurance Map Publishing Co., 1891. In 1908 Chicago's City Council passed an ordinance that changed its street address numbering system. The ordinance created new addresses for many of Chicago's buildings. This atlas was essential in locating the post-fire (and pre–1908) Halsted Street residence of Mr. and Mrs. O'Leary.

Report of the Board of Police in the Fire Department, to the Common Council of the City of Chicago: For the Year Ending March 31st, 1869. Chicago: Illinois Staats-Zeitung, 1869. This report includes statistical information on Chicago's firemen and fire equipment and suggestions from both Marshal Williams and the Board of Police on making the city safer from fires.

Report of the Board of Police, in the Fire Department, to the Common Council of the City of Chicago: For the Year Ending March 31st, 1872. Chicago: Hazlitt & Reed, 1872. Fire Marshal Williams reports to the Board of Police his thoughts and conclusions concerning the Chicago Fire and the conduct of his department.

Report of the Chicago Relief and Aid Society of Disbursement of Contributions for the Sufferers by the Chicago Fire. Cambridge, [Mass.]: Riverside Press, 1874. More than four hundred pages tell how the Chicago Relief and Aid Society helped Chicago's destitute and homeless. The book includes such minutiae as exhibits detailing the number of houses constructed by the Shelter Committee and the various furnishings (e.g., stoves, tables, chairs) that were given to Society applicants for use in these houses. The work lists no author, but historian Joseph Kirkland credits former society director Sidney Gay with writing the book. See Kirkland, vol. 1, p. 342; Sawislak, p. 83.

Roberts, H. Armstrong. *The Farmer His Own Builder.* Philadelphia: David McKay, 1918.

Roberts, Warren E. "Early Log-Crib Barn Survivals." In *Barns of the Midwest,* eds. Allen G. Noble and Hubert G. H. Wilhelm, pp. 24–39. Athens: Ohio University Press, 1995.

Robinson, E[lisha]. *Robinson's Atlas of the City of Chicago, Illinois.* Vols. 1, 3. New York: Privately printed, 1886. These volumes of maps disclose the legal descriptions and common addresses of Chicago properties.

The Ruined City; or, The Horrors of Chicago. New York: Ornum, 1871. A compilation of sensational newspaper articles that were published on October 9–12, 1871.

Sawislak, Karen. *Smoldering City: Chicagoans and the Great Fire, 1871-1874.* Chicago: University of Chicago Press, 1995. A history of the aftermath of the Chicago Fire in which the author suggests that the fire highlighted the social and economic differences of a culturally diverse community.

Sewell, Alfred L. *The Great Calamity!...* Chicago: Privately printed, 1871. The first instant history of the Chicago Fire.

Sheahan, James W., and George P. Upton. *The Great Conflagration....* Chicago: Union Publishing Co., 1871. An instant history of the fire.

Skerrett, Ellen. "The Irish of Chicago's Hull-House Neighborhood." In *New Perspectives on the Irish Diaspora,* ed. Charles Fanning, pp. 189–222. Carbondale: Southern Illinois University Press, 2000. This history of Mrs. O'Leary's West Side neighborhood also appears in the Summer 2001 issue of *Chicago History,* the magazine of the Chicago Historical Society.

Smith, Carl. *Urban Disorder and the Shape of Belief: The Great Chicago Fire, the Haymarket Bomb, and the Model Town of Pullman.* Chicago: University of Chicago Press, 1995. This Chicago history contains rich and exhaustive content notes that provide a wealth of information.

Swing, David. *A Story of the Chicago Fire.* N.p., H. H. Gross, 1892. A booklet that includes the story of the Chicago Fire Cyclorama, a twenty-thousand-square-foot canvas illustrating the burning of Chicago.

Szucs, Loretto Dennis. *Chicago and Cook County: A Guide to Research.* Salt Lake City: Ancestry, 1996. This indispensable research guide includes a section on "The Chicago Fire and Property Records."

Third Annual Report of West Chicago Park Commissioners for the Year Ending February 29, 1872. Chicago: Chicago Legal News Co., n.d. This report contains a photograph of the fire relics (including 219 safes) that were collected and deposited in Central Park in contemplation of the construction of a Chicago Fire monument. The report also contains a photograph of William Le Baron Jenney's second proposed design of this monument.

Vogeler, Ingolf. "Dairying and Dairy Barns in the Northern Midwest." In *Barns of the Midwest,* eds. Allen G. Noble and Hubert G. H. Wilhelm, pp. 99–124. Athens: Ohio University Press, 1995.

Walker, William S. "Description of the Great Fire." In *The Lakeside Memorial of the Burning of Chicago, A.D. 1871,* pp. 22–39. Chicago: University Publishing Co., 1872. This book contains a number of essays that are categorized under such topics as "Before the Fire" and "Burning of the City." Included in the book are several photographs. Although most of these photographs are of destroyed buildings, one of them is a picture of William Le Baron Jenney's first proposed fire memorial (Figure 86).

Warburton, Lois. *The Chicago Fire.* San Diego: Lucent Books, 1989.

Waskin, Mel. *Mrs. O'Leary's Comet: Cosmic Causes of the Great Chicago Fire.* Chicago: Academy Chicago Publishers, 1985. A comet supposedly caused the fire.

Wells, Robert W. *Fire at Peshtigo.* Englewood Cliffs, N.J.: Prentice-Hall, 1968. A history of the Peshtigo, Wisconsin, fire.

Wendt, Lloyd, and Herman Kogan. *Lords of the Levee.* Indianapolis: Bobbs-Merrill Co., 1943. A biography of John "Bathhouse John" Coughlin and Michael "Hinky Dink" Kenna, two infamous Chicago aldermen. Jacob Schaller claimed that at the time of the fire, he lived in a home owned by the father of John Coughlin. This book reveals the father's first name.

Wykes, Alan. *The Complete Illustrated Guide to Gambling.* New York: Doubleday & Co., 1964.

Newspapers

INTRODUCTION

Most of the newspaper articles noted below do not disclose the authors' names. Many of the articles are untitled, and some of the articles that do have titles share the same title with other articles of a different date and/or newspaper. (See, for example, the many articles entitled "The Great Fire.") Therefore, all articles are indexed first by newspaper and then listed chronologically. Many of the 1871 newspapers did not include page numbers. Citations to articles on such pages include the page numbers in brackets.

Chicago Tribune

"Our Next Public Improvement." *Chicago Tribune,* 10 September 1871, p. [2]. This pre-fire article criticizes Chicago's flimsy building construction.

"Ku-Klux." *Chicago Tribune,* 23 September 1871, p. [2]. A lengthy series of short articles that describe Ku-Klux activities throughout the South.

"Women of the Commune." *Chicago Tribune,* 26 September 1871, p. [3]. The trial of "petroleuse communists."

"The Ku-Klux Convictions." *Chicago Tribune,* 27 September 1871, p. [2]. Eight people are convicted of conspiracy in North Carolina.

"The Fire in Kewaunee, Wis." *Chicago Tribune,* 28 September 1871, p. [3]. A Wisconsin resident opines that the northern half of Kewaunee County is in flames.

"Fires." *Chicago Tribune,* 5 October 1871, p. [4]. The writer suggests that "the fires which are now prevailing in the six or seven northeastern counties of Wisconsin have never had a parallel since the settlement of this country."

"Fires in the Woods." *Chicago Tribune,* 6 October 1871, p. [2]. A comprehensive article that details the fiery destruction of property in Wisconsin, including homes in Peshtigo.

"The Babcock Fire Extinguisher!" *Chicago Tribune,* 7 October 1871, p. 1. An ad for the Babcock fire extinguisher.

"Conflagrations." *Chicago Tribune,* 7 October 1871, p. 1. The *Tribune* reports from Green Bay, Wisconsin, that "the fires in the woods and swamps north and west of this point are still raging. Nothing will check the flames, but a heavy rain, and there are [n]o signs of that. The telegraph lines are destroyed. Thousands of square miles of territory in this State and on the Michigan peninsula are burned over or are burning."

"The Fires in the Woods." *Chicago Tribune,* 7 October 1871, p. [2]. Fires raging in the woods threaten the town of Peshtigo; the fires cover three thousand square miles; the telegraph line south of Peshtigo is destroyed.

"The Fire Fiend." *Chicago Tribune,* 8 October 1871, p. [3]. A lengthy account of the Lull & Holmes planing mill fire of Saturday night, October 7.

"Condition of the Banks." *Chicago Tribune,* 11 October 1871, p. [2]. The *Tribune* is initially optimistic about the financial condition of Chicago's banks.

"Incendiaries Killed." *Chicago Tribune,* 11 October 1871, p. 1. A list of incendiaries allegedly killed for practicing their craft.

"Items in General." *Chicago Tribune,* 11 October 1871, p. 1. Various news items about the fire.

"List of Missing." *Chicago Tribune,* 11 October

1871, p. 1. A listing of men, women, and children missing after the fire.

"Scenes on Wabash Avenue." *Chicago Tribune,* 11 October 1871, p. 1. The *Tribune* describes Wabash Avenue on Monday, October 9, as being like "the retreat of a routed army."

"The Great Conflagration." *Chicago Tribune,* 11 October 1871, p. 1. The fire attacks Chicago's South Side.

"To the Homeless." *Chicago Tribune,* 11 October 1871, p. [2]. Information on where those rendered homeless by the fire can seek relief.

"The West Side." *Chicago Tribune,* 11 October 1871, p. 1. The beginning of the fire.

"Miscellaneous Items." *Chicago Tribune,* 12 October 1871, p. 1. Among other matters, the article discusses how river water is used to replenish the city's water supply.

"Miscellaneous Items." *Chicago Tribune,* 12 October 1871, p. [3]. A boy is arrested for attempting to set a building on fire; a tug boat captain attempts to steal the trunk of a man left homeless by the fire; and other "scenes and incidents in the burnt districts."

"The Ruins." *Chicago Tribune,* 12 October 1871, p. 1. A description of post-fire Chicago.

"Insurance." *Chicago Tribune,* 13 October 1871, p. [3]. An advertisement for Robert S. Critchell's insurance company.

"Just and Generous." *Chicago Tribune,* 13 October 1871, p. [2]. The *Tribune* believes that a larger amount of insurance claims will be paid than was first thought.

"The Water Works." *Chicago Tribune,* 13 October 1871, p. [2]. The post-fire condition of the water works.

"Incendiary Fires." *Chicago Tribune,* 14 October 1871, p. 1. The *Tribune* comments on how incendiaries should be punished; a listing of incendiary incidents.

"Board of Trade." *Chicago Tribune,* 15 October 1871, p. [4]. This article includes a reference to "Colonel Hough," whom James H. Hildreth mentioned in his testimony.

"Preparing for the Next Fire." *Chicago Tribune,* 15 October 1871, p. [2]. Why the city burned; how to prevent another fire.

"The Water Supply." *Chicago Tribune,* 15 October 1871, p. [4]. Rebuilding the water works.

"The Wiscon[s]in and Michigan Fires." *Chicago Tribune,* 16 October 1871, p. [3]. A graphic description of the Peshtigo fire.

"Absurd Misstatements." *Chicago Tribune,* 19 October 1871, p. [2]. New York newspapers print false and exaggerated stories.

"Atrocious Fabrications." *Chicago Tribune,* 19 October 1871, p. [2]. Eastern newspapers print fabricated stories of mayhem.

"The Cow That Kicked Over the Lamp." *Chicago Tribune,* 19 October 1871, p. [2]. An interview with Mrs. O'Leary.

"The Water We Drink." *Chicago Tribune,* 19 October 1871, p. [2]. A doctor cautions Chicagoans to boil or filter their drinking water.

"Erroneous Impressions." *Chicago Tribune,* 20 October 1871, p. [2]. The wind carries burning brands for long distances, thus creating new fires.

"How It Originated." *Chicago Tribune,* 20 October 1871, p. [2]. Post-fire newspapers published interviews with Mrs. O'Leary that were apparently fabricated. This interview, however, appears to be genuine. In this letter Michael McDermott memorializes the statements of Patrick O'Leary, Catherine O'Leary, and Daniel (alias "Denis") Sullivan.

"The Jail and Criminals." *Chicago Tribune,* 20 October 1871, p. [2]. The prisoners are released from the courthouse jail.

"What Remains of the City," *Chicago Tribune,* 20 October 1871, p. 1. A summary of Chicago's losses.

"Shocking Calamity." *Chicago Tribune,* 22 October 1871, p. 1. The story of Theodore Treat shooting and killing Colonel Thomas W. Grosvenor.

"The Grosvenor Tragedy." *Chicago Tribune,* 23 October 1871, p. 1. The coroner begins an inquest into the Grosvenor killing.

"A Marvellous Achievement." *Chicago Tribune,* 23 October 1871, p. 1. An interview with John G. Shortall, who tells how he saved Shortall & Hoard's real estate records.

"Common Council Meeting." *Chicago Tribune,* 24 October 1871, p. 1. The Common Council passes an ordinance that prohibits the storing of wood shavings.

"The Grosvenor Tragedy." *Chicago Tribune,* 24 October 1871, p. 1. The coroner concludes his inquest into the Grosvenor killing.

"How It Burned." *Chicago Tribune,* 27 October 1871, p. [2]. Different theories as to how the fire started.

"Justice Rendered." *Chicago Tribune,* 28 October

1871, p. [4]. This article includes a reference to the *Richards* fire engine.

"The Oil Stone Story." *Chicago Tribune*, 30 October 1871, p. 1. Stone buildings were destroyed by the fire because they were made of "stone heavily charged with petroleum."

"The Story of Peshtigo." *Chicago Tribune*, 31 October 1871, p. 2. A lengthy article detailing the horrors of the Peshtigo Fire.

"Working Up the Details." *Chicago Tribune*, 2 November 1871, p. 1. An eastern newspaper sensationalizes the fire.

"Correcting False Impressions." *Chicago Tribune*, 3 November 1871, p. [4]. The city of Buffalo acknowledges that the post-fire stories of incendiarism, pillage, and murder that the Eastern newspapers print are false.

"A Tempest of Fire." *Chicago Tribune*, 3 November 1871, p. 1. A vivid description of the Peshtigo Fire; the author suggests that "the storm that burst upon Peshtigo with such terribly destructive force was but a whirlwind of great power," or convection whirl.

"Gund," *Chicago Tribune*, 7 November 1871, p. 4. Criticism of Commissioner Gund.

"Board of Police." *Chicago Tribune*, 10 November 1871, p. 6. The Board of Police and Fire Commissioners decides to investigate the cause of the fire.

"Our Fire—Its Causes and Lessons." *Chicago Tribune*, 12 November 1871, p. 4. A letter to the editor that is critical of the fire department.

"That Investigation." *Chicago Tribune*, 14 November 1871, p. 4. The *Tribune* asks the commissioners when the inquiry investigation will start.

"Boring for Facts." *Chicago Tribune*, 15 November 1871, p. 1. Interviews with fire marshals Robert Williams and Mathias Benner.

"Setting Them Right." *Chicago Tribune*, 15 November 1871, p. 6. Thomas B. Brown announces his resignation from the Board of Police and Fire Commissioners.

Untitled article. *Chicago Tribune*, 16 November 1871, p. 4. A listing of some of the suggested causes of the fire.

"Boring for Facts." *Chicago Tribune*, 17 November 1871, p. 4. An interview with Assistant Fire Marshal John Schank.

"The Fire Department." *Chicago Tribune*, 17 November 1871, p. 3. Commissioner Brown announces his resignation.

"On the Defensive." *Chicago Tribune*, 17 November 1871, p. 4. A lengthy letter to the editor by Marshal Robert Williams.

"Boring for Facts." *Chicago Tribune*, 18 November 1871, p. 4. An interview with fireman "Sandy" Shay, foreman of the steam engine *A. D. Titsworth* No. 13.

"River Engines." *Chicago Tribune*, 18 November 1871, p. 4. A letter to the editor that is critical of the fire department.

Untitled article. *Chicago Tribune*, 18 November 1871, p. 4. An editorial commenting favorably on a proposed fire ordinance.

"The Babcock." *Chicago Tribune*, 19 November 1871, p. 7. An article about the Babcock fire extinguisher.

"Boring for Facts." *Chicago Tribune*, 19 November 1871, p. 6. An interview with fireman William Brown.

"The Fire Marshal and His Assistants." *Chicago Tribune*, 19 November 1871, p. 2. Thoughtful observations concerning the fire officials and the inquiry investigation.

"History of the Great Conflagration." *Chicago Tribune*, 19 November 1871, p. 7. The *Tribune* comments on the instant history written by James W. Sheahan and George P. Upton.

"Real Estate." *Chicago Tribune*, 19 November 1871, p. 6. A discussion of the proposed new fire ordinance and how it will affect the rebuilding of Chicago.

"Unparalleled Meanness." *Chicago Tribune*, 19 November 1871, p. 6. Fire companies from other cities came to Chicago to help fight the fire. The *Tribune* accuses these fire companies of accepting bribes.

"The Gas Works." *Chicago Tribune*, 20 November 1871, p. 2. A letter to the editor by Peter T. Burtis, Superintendent of the Chicago Gas Light and Coke Company, in response to Marshal Robert Williams's *Tribune* letter of November 17.

"Justice Rendered." *Chicago Tribune*, 20 November 1871, p. 6. The *Tribune* accuses an Aurora, Illinois, fire company of unprofessional conduct.

"Chicago and the Great Conflagration." *Chicago Tribune*, 21 November 1871, p. 6. The *Tribune* praises the instant history written by Colbert and Chamberlin.

"The Aurora Firemen." *Chicago Tribune*, 23 November 1871, p. 4. The Aurora, Illinois, fire department denies the *Tribune*'s charges of misconduct.

"The Great Fire." *Chicago Tribune*, 24 November 1871, p. 6. The inquiry investigation starts; a summary of testimony.

"The Milwaukee Firemen." *Chicago Tribune*, 24 November 1871, p. 3. The *Tribune* apologizes for falsely accusing the Milwaukee and Aurora, Illinois, fire companies of extorting money from citizens in exchange for saving their property.

"The Great Fire." *Chicago Tribune*, 25 November 1871, p. 6. A summary of inquiry testimony that includes the testimony of Mrs. O'Leary and Dennis Regan.

"Out of the Ashes." *Chicago Tribune*, 25 November 1871, p. 1. A comprehensive article on the progress of the rebuilding on Chicago's South Side that includes a listing of property addresses, owners, and nature of the new improvements.

"The Safe Monument." *Chicago Tribune*, 25 November 1871, p. 6. The proposed monument to the fire.

Untitled article. *Chicago Tribune*, 25 November 1871, p. 4. A discussion of southern sentiment towards Chicago.

"The Great Fire." *Chicago Tribune*, 26 November 1871, p. 1. A summary of inquiry testimony that includes the testimony of Daniel Sullivan.

Untitled article. *Chicago Tribune*, 26 November 1871, p. 2. The *Tribune* suggests that the fire was caused by "social milk thieves" from the McLaughlin party.

Untitled article. *Chicago Tribune*, 27 November 1871, p. 2. The *Tribune* is dissatisfied with the progress of the investigation and critical of Mrs. O'Leary and her neighbors.

"A Defence of Fire Marshal Williams." *Chicago Tribune*, 28 November 1871, p. 6. A lengthy letter to the editor that defends Marshal Robert Williams.

"The Fire Investigation." *Chicago Tribune*, 29 November 1871, p. 4. A summary of inquiry testimony.

"The Great Fire." *Chicago Tribune*, 30 November 1871, p. 4. A summary of inquiry testimony.

"The Great Fire." *Chicago Tribune*, 2 December 1871, p. 4. A summary of inquiry testimony.

"The Great Fire." *Chicago Tribune*, 3 December 1871, p. 4. A summary of inquiry testimony.

"The Debtors." *Chicago Tribune*, 4 December 1871, p. 3. An interview with "Eddy" Longley, the courthouse jail keeper.

"The Great Fire." *Chicago Tribune*, 5 December 1871, p. 2. A summary of the inquiry testimony of the foreman of Ryerson & Co.'s lumberyard. The Board's shorthand reporter did not transcribe the testimony of this last witness and so his testimony does not appear in the inquiry transcript.

"An Architect's Opinions of the Fire." *Chicago Tribune*, 6 December 1871, p. 3. A discussion of the "oil stone" or "petroleum stone" theory as to why the fire spread so quickly.

"A Mystery Solved." *Chicago Tribune*, 13 December 1871, p. 4. The possibility that the fire was the result of "Divine displeasure."

Untitled article. *Chicago Tribune*, 13 December 1871, p. 4. The *Tribune* apologizes to the Aurora, Illinois, firemen.

"George Francis Train and the O'Leary Cow." *Chicago Tribune*, 16 December 1871, p. 4. A satirical article about Mrs. O'Leary and her cow.

"The Janesville Firemen." *Chicago Tribune*, 16 December 1871, p. 4. A letter to the editor asks the *Tribune* to retract its statements concerning firemen misconduct.

"Chicago and the Great Conflagration." *Chicago Tribune*, 17 December 1871, p. 4. The *Tribune* gives a positive review to Colbert and Chamberlin's book, *Chicago and the Great Conflagration*.

"The Clothing Trade." *Chicago Tribune*, 17 December 1871, p. 7. This article includes a reference to "Hatch & Co." (Marshal Williams mentioned the "Hatch House" in his testimony.)

"The Co[urt] House Bell." *Chicago Tribune*, 17 December 1871, p. 7. The courthouse bell is sold at auction.

"Bell Relics." *Chicago Tribune*, 22 December 1871, p. 2. Courthouse bell "charm relics" for sale.

"Anniversary of the Great Fire." *Chicago Daily Tribune*, 9 October 1872, pp. [5]–13. An extensive article about Chicago before, during, and after the fire. Nine pages are devoted to such diverse topics as real estate, the theater, banking, rebuilding, and relief efforts.

"The Fire Monument." *Chicago Tribune*, 28 October 1872, p. 7. A lengthy description of the fire monument.

"The Fire Monument." *Chicago Tribune*, 31 October 1872, p. 3. The cornerstone of the fire monument is laid.

"The Great Fire." *Chicago Sunday Tribune*, 1 February 1891, sec. 2, p. 12. Looking back at the Chicago Fire.

"While the Fire Raged." *Chicago Sunday Tribune*, 1 February 1891, sec. 5, pp. 33–36. Reminiscences of *Tribune* employees, including Johnny English.

"City Wrapped in Angry Flames." *Chicago Daily Tribune*, 9 October 1893, sec. 3, pp. [18]–19. A story of the fire that includes a variety of statistics, such as number of acres burned, number of people left homeless by the fire, and summaries of losses.

"Story of the Great Chicago Fire as Told by the Men Who Fought It." *Chicago Daily Tribune*, 9 October 1893, sec. 3, p. 20. Reminiscences of firemen.

"Fire Alley Is Paved." *Chicago Daily Tribune*, 25 May 1894, p. 1. Mrs. O'Leary's doctor talks about his famous patient; the alley that runs along the rear of the O'Leary property is graded and paved.

"Mrs. O'Leary's Cow." *Chicago Daily Tribune*, 17 September 1894, p. 8. The obituary of Patrick O'Leary.

"Mrs. O'Leary Is Dead." *Chicago Daily Tribune*, 4 July 1895, p. 1. The obituary of Mrs. O'Leary.

"Centennial Eve Reveals Truth of Great Fire." *Chicago Daily Tribune*, 26 September 1903, sec. 1, pp. 1–[2]. Mrs. Mary Callahan claims that Denny Connors started the fire.

"Chicago's Day to Revere the Past." *Chicago Daily Tribune*, 26 September 1903, sec. 1, p. [2]. Chicago celebrates its centennial.

"O'Leary Defends Noted Cow." *Chicago Daily Tribune*, 30 November 1909, p. 3. "Big Jim" O'Leary claims that the fire was caused by the spontaneous combustion of green hay and not by two boys who wanted milk to mix with whiskey.

Ahern, Michael. "Reporter of 1871 Fire Describes Blaze of Today." *Chicago Sunday Tribune*, 8 October 1911, sec. 1, p. 1–[2]. Reminiscences of reporter Michael Ahern.

"Man in Tower at Fire of '71 Tells of Sighting Flames." *Chicago Sunday Tribune*, 8 October 1911, sec. 1, p. [2]. Reminiscences of fireman Mathias Schaefer.

Ahern, Michael. "Mrs. O'Leary Cow Story Refuted by Old Reporter." *Chicago Daily Tribune*, 21 January 1915, sec. 2, p. 13. Reminiscences of reporter Michael Ahern.

_____. "1871 Reporter Writes Story of Great Fire." *Chicago Sunday Tribune*, 9 October 1921, sec. 1, pp. 1, 3. Reminiscences of reporter Michael Ahern.

"Beer, Not Milk, Caused Chicago Fire, New Story." *Chicago Sunday Tribune*, 9 October 1921, sec. 1, p. 3. Mrs. Anton Axsmith claims that the fire was probably caused by a man dropping his pipe in the O'Leary's hayloft. The article includes a crude map of the O'Leary property and the land immediately to the north (Figure 56).

"Fire Day Program." *Chicago Sunday Tribune*, 9 October 1921, sec. 1, p. 3. The program for the celebration of the semi-centennial of the fire.

Parrett, William. "Kicking Over the Cow Legend." *Chicago Sunday Tribune*, 16 October 1921, sec. 1, p. [8]. A shoe store owner claims that neighborhood boys who were attending a party near the O'Leary home started the fire while they were milking the cow.

Kelley, John. "Never Another '71 Fire, Says Retiring Chief." *Chicago Sunday Tribune*, 5 October 1924, sec. 1, p. 16. John C. McDonnell, First Assistant Fire Marshal, talks about whether or not there could be another "great Chicago fire."

_____. "O'Leary, Who Would Bet on Anything, Dies." *Chicago Daily Tribune*, 23 January 1925, sec. 1, p. 1. The obituary of "Big Jim" O'Leary.

"Michael Ahern Dies; Reporter in Fire of 1871." *Chicago Sunday Tribune*, 20 February 1927, sec. 1, p. 12. The obituary of Michael Ahern; he is described as the last surviving reporter who covered the Chicago Fire.

"True Story of Chicago Fire Told at Last." *Chicago Daily Tribune*, 20 October 1927, sec. 3, pp. 31, 42. Mrs. Nellie L. Hayes claims that she first warned the O'Learys about the fire; she suggests the fire was caused by the McLaughlins.

Sweet, Oney Fred. "Fighter of '71 Blames Fire on Cow's Ire." *Chicago Sunday Tribune*, 6 October 1929, Metropolitan Section (NW), pp. 1, 4. Discussion of some of the lesser-known theories concerning the cause of the fire.

_____. "Mrs. O'Leary's Bossy Ruined His Night Off." *Chicago Sunday Tribune*, 6 October 1929, Metropolitan Section (SW), pp. 1, 3. Reminiscences of fireman George Leady.

"Kin of O'Leary Absolves Cow in Fire of 1871." *Chicago Sunday Tribune*, 8 October 1933, sec. 1, pp. 1, 4. Mrs. Catherine O'Leary Ledwell, the daughter of Mr. and Mrs. O'Leary, suggests that the fire might have been caused by young men drinking beer in the hayloft of the barn.

Murchie, Guy, Jr. "Linked to Chicago's Two Worst Fires—The Family O'Leary." *Chicago Sunday Tribune*, 31 March 1935, sec. 7, p. 10. The story of "Big Jim" O'Leary.

Clark, Herma. "When Chicago Was Young." *Chicago Sunday Tribune*, 9 February 1941, sec. 7, p. 2. Reminiscences about Captain Benjamin Bullwinkle of the Fire Insurance Patrol.

_____. "When Chicago Was Young." *Chicago Sunday Tribune*, 23 February 1941, sec. 6, p. 8. Reminiscences about Captain Benjamin Bullwinkle of the Fire Insurance Patrol.

_____. "When Chicago Was Young." *Chicago Sunday Tribune*, 2 March 1941, sec. 7, p. 5. Reminiscences about Captain Benjamin Bullwinkle of the Fire Insurance Patrol.

Murphy, Martha. "Mrs. O'Leary's Cow Slandered, Say Ex-Firemen." *Chicago Daily Tribune*, 5 October 1942, sec. 1, p. 14. Ex-firemen claim the fire was caused by bums drinking and smoking in the barn.

"J. J. Schaller, Mrs. O'Leary's Milk Boy, Dies." *Chicago Daily Tribune*, 18 July 1945, sec. 1, p. 3. The obituary of Jacob John Schaller.

"Recall Great Chicago Fire in Rites Today." *Chicago Daily Tribune*, 9 October 1953, sec. 3, p. 3. The 1937 Chicago Fire plaque is removed from the Kolar house.

Wood, Henry. "Mrs. O'Leary's Kin Spikes Story That Cow Started Fire." *Chicago Tribune*, 9 October 1969, sec. 1, p. 1. Descendants of Mrs. O'Leary want to "set the story straight and destroy the myth."

Galloway, Paul. "Mrs. O'Leary's Comet." *Chicago Tribune*, 13 December 1985, sec. 5, pp. 1, 3. Mel Waskin maintains that a comet caused the fire.

Parsons, Christi. "Historian Finds a New Suspect for Chicago Fire." 7 January 1997, *Chicago Tribune*, sec. 1, pp. 1, 14. New evidence un-

covered by Richard Bales incriminates Daniel "Peg Leg" Sullivan in the cause of the fire.

Mills, Steve. "Uncowed Aldermen Clear Mrs. O'Leary in 1871 Fire." *Chicago Tribune*, 7 October 1997, sec. 2, p. 8. Chicago aldermen exonerate Mrs. O'Leary and her cow.

DeBartolo, Anthony. "Who Caused the Great Chicago Fire?: A Possible Deathbed Confession." *Chicago Tribune*, 8 October 1997, sec. 5, pp. 1, 3. The possibility that Louis M. Cohn caused the fire.

_____. "Odds Improve That a Hot Game of Craps in Mrs. O'Leary's Barn Touched Off Chicago Fire." *Chicago Tribune*, 3 March 1998, sec. 5, pp. 1, 3. Further discussion concerning Louis M. Cohn as the cause of the fire.

LeBien, Mark. "Fragile Note Illuminates City's Great Fire." *Chicago Tribune*, 2 October 1998, sec. 1, pp. 1, 24. Story of the note that Mayor Roswell B. Mason wrote during the fire, ordering that the prisoners be released from the courthouse jail.

Chicago Evening Journal

"The Great Calamity of the Age!" *Chicago Evening Journal—Extra*, 9 October 1871, p. 1. While Chicago is still burning, the *Journal* writes that the fire was caused "by a cow kicking over a lamp in a stable in which a woman was milking."

"Death to Incendiaries." *Chicago Evening Journal*, 11 October 1871, p. 1. A listing of supposed incendiaries caught and killed.

"Missing Persons." *Chicago Evening Journal*, 11 October 1871, p. 1. A list of people missing after the fire.

"A Lowly Monument of the Fire." *Chicago Evening Journal*, 13 October 1871, p. [2]. The O'Leary home is a monument to the place where the fire began.

"Exaggerated Reports." *Chicago Evening Journal*, 16 October 1871, p. 1. Newspapers of other cities publish rumors and exaggerated reports.

"Sharks Among Us." *Chicago Evening Journal*, 16 October 1871, p. [2]. A condemnation of unscrupulous express men and draymen.

"The Fire Department." *Chicago Evening Journal*, 17 October 1871, p. 1. A tired fire department, a high wind, and combustible buildings caused the fire to spread out of control.

"Mistake." *Chicago Evening Journal*, 20 October 1871, p. 1. The *Journal* calls the fire department "demoralized and poorly-handled."

"Origin of the Fire." *Chicago Evening Journal*, 21 October 1871, supplement, p. [2]. An interview with Mrs. O'Leary.

"A Snarling Dog." *Chicago Evening Journal*, 21 October 1871, p. [2]. A criticism of the *Times*.

"The Organ of the Petroleuse." *Chicago Evening Journal*, 23 October 1871, p. [2]. A criticism of the *Times*' story of the Societe Internationale.

"Liquor-Drinking Firemen." *Chicago Evening Journal*, 24 October 1871, p. [2]. The belief that many firemen were intoxicated during the fire.

"All Around Town." *Chicago Evening Journal*, 27 October 1871, p. [4]. A complaint that the city's water mains were never sufficiently flushed after being filled with river water.

"Police and Fire Commissioners." *Chicago Evening Journal*, 27 October 1871, p. [4]. Policemen are ordered to return "rewards" for recovering civilian property.

"Police and Fire Losses." *Chicago Evening Journal*, 27 October 1871, p. [4]. A statement of the losses sustained by the police and fire departments as a result of the fire.

"Police and Fire Commissioners." *Chicago Evening Journal*, 31 October 1871, p. [4]. A police officer is dismissed for stealing during the fire.

"United States Troops in Chicago." *Chicago Evening Journal*, 2 November 1871, p. 1. The *Evening Journal* approves of the return of U.S. troops to Chicago.

"Mrs. Leary's Cow." *Chicago Evening Journal*, 4 November 1871, p. [4]. The *Louisville Courier-Journal* argues that Mrs. O'Leary should capitalize on her fame.

"After the Great Fire." *Chicago Evening Journal*, 8 November 1871, p. [2]. The editor of the *Cincinnati Daily Commercial* writes that the stories of massacred incendiaries and hanged thieves are false.

"The Cause of the Fire." *Chicago Evening Journal*, 10 November 1871, p. [4]. The police and fire commissioners decide to investigate the cause of the fire.

"Management of the Fire De[p]artment." *Chicago Evening Journal*, 11 November 1871, p. [2]. An "old fireman" writes the *Journal*, hoping that the inquiry into the origin of the fire will also include an investigation into the management, condition, and conduct of the fire department.

"That Investigation on Kicks." *Chicago Evening Journal*, 11 November 1871, p. [4]. The investigation into the cause of the fire and the actions of the fire department is postponed.

"The West Side." *Chicago Evening Journal*, 11 November 1871, p. [4]. The progress of rebuilding on Chicago's West Side.

"Musical Instruments." *Chicago Evening Journal*, 13 November 1871, p. [3]. An advertisement disclosing the post-fire address of Julius Bauer & Co. (Marshal Williams testified that "Mr. Hoyne's barn caught fire." The barn at this address was apparently rented to Julius Bauer & Co.)

Untitled article. *Chicago Evening Journal*, 16 November 1871, p. [2]. Mrs. O'Leary's cow is blamed for starting the fire.

"That Investigation." *Chicago Evening Journal*, 17 November 1871, p. [4]. The investigation into the start of the fire will soon begin.

"Fire Chronology." *Chicago Evening Journal*, 18 November 1871, p. [4]. A table of when Chicago's principal buildings were overtaken by the flames.

"Chicago Losses." *Chicago Evening Journal*, 20 November 1871, p. [3]. A statement of the losses of the tanners and the hide and leather dealers.

"Doctors Disagree." *Chicago Evening Journal*, 20 November 1871, p. [4]. The sins of Chicagoans caused the fire.

"Two More Men Hurt." *Chicago Evening Journal*, 20 November 1871, p. [4]. Men are hurt by falling ruins.

"Investigation Wanted." *Chicago Evening Journal*, 21 November 1871, p. 1. The *Journal* calls for an investigation into the cause and circumstances of the fire.

"Destroy to Save." *Chicago Evening Journal*, 23 November 1871, p. [2]. A letter to the editor argues that the fire would not have spread if the firemen had torn down wooden buildings.

"The Fire Department." *Chicago Evening Journal*, 23 November 1871, p. [4]. Coal piles by the water works are still burning.

"The Fire in Print." *Chicago Evening Journal*, 23 November 1871, p. 1. The *Journal* comments

"That Investigation Again." *Chicago Evening Journal*, 23 November 1871, p. [4]. The inquiry is postponed.

"Southern Feeling Toward Chicago." *Chicago Evening Journal*, 24 November 1871, p. [2]. Commentary on the southern press rejoicing over the fire.

"That Investigation." *Chicago Evening Journal*, 24 November 1871, p. [4]. The inquiry investigation begins; a summary of testimony.

Untitled article. *Chicago Evening Journal*, 24 November 1871, p. [2]. A southerner offers to reward Mrs. O'Leary's cow.

"The Fire Investigation." *Chicago Evening Journal*, 25 November 1871, p. [4]. A summary of inquiry testimony, including the testimony of Mrs. O'Leary.

"The City." *Chicago Evening Journal*, 27 November 1871, p. [3]. A summary of inquiry testimony, including the testimony of Daniel Sullivan.

"The Fire Investigation." *Chicago Evening Journal*, 27 November 1871, p. [4]. Criticism of the inquiry investigation to date; a summary of a previous day's testimony.

"Two Fire Items." *Chicago Evening Journal*, 27 November 1871, p. [2]. Criticism of what appears to be the inquiry testimony of fireman Michael W. Conway.

Untitled article. *Chicago Evening Journal*, 27 November 1871, p. [2]. Criticism of Mrs. O'Leary for claiming that she was in bed when the fire broke out.

"The Fire Investigation." *Chicago Evening Journal*, 28 November 1871, p. [4]. A summary of inquiry testimony.

"The Great Fire." *Chicago Evening Journal*, 29 November 1871, p. [4]. A summary of inquiry testimony.

"Sky Lights and the Fire." *Chicago Evening Journal*, 29 November 1871, p. [4]. A reader argues in a letter to the editor that burning brands breaking through skylights caused the interiors of buildings to catch fire.

Untitled article. *Chicago Evening Journal*, 1 December 1871, p. [2], col. 2, third article. Criticism of the investigation.

Untitled article. *Chicago Evening Journal*, 1 December 1871, p. [2], col. 2, fourth article. Sarcastic article about James Hildreth's failure to blow up a bank.

"All Around Town." *Chicago Evening Journal*, 2 December 1871, p. [4]. The *Journal* ridicules Hildreth's inquiry testimony.

"Not Much of a Blow." *Chicago Evening Journal*, 2 December 1871, p. [4]. The *Journal* claims that Hildreth did not attempt to blow up the Union National Bank.

"That Investigation." *Chicago Evening Journal*, 2 December 1871, p. [4]. Criticism of the investigation.

"Police and Fire Commissioners." *Chicago Evening Journal*, 5 December 1871, p. [4]. Commissioner Gund retires.

"That Investigation." *Chicago Evening Journal*, 5 December 1871, p. [4]. The foreman of Ryerson & Co.'s lumberyard is the last person to testify at the investigation.

Untitled article. *Chicago Evening Journal*, 7 December 1871, p. [2]. The fire allegedly spread because buildings were made of "bituminous limestone containing an oily substance."

"The Great Fire." *Chicago Evening Journal*, 12 December 1871, p [4]. The *Journal* publishes the final report of the Board of Police and Fire Commissioners.

"The Fire Monument." *Chicago Evening Journal*, 14 December 1871, p. [4]. Description of the proposed safe monument.

Untitled article. *Chicago Evening Journal*, 19 December 1871, p. [2]. The *Journal* uses Mrs. O'Leary and her cow to make a political comment.

"1871." *Chicago Evening Journal*, 30 December 1871, p. [4]. A listing of the principal events of 1871.

"Precautions Against Fire." *Chicago Evening Journal*, 30 December 1871, p. [3]. General Arthur C. Ducat presents a report to the fire insurance companies of Chicago.

"Helped to Save Records of Real Estate from Fire Half a Century Ago." *Chicago Daily Journal*, 8 October 1921, p. [2]. Chicago Title and Trust employee recalls rescuing the abstract books of Shortall & Hoard from the fire.

"Readers Bring Famous 'Extra' in to Journal." *Chicago Daily Journal*, 8 October 1921, pp. 1–[2]. The *Journal* reminisces about its famous issue of October 9, 1871.

Chicago Times

"The City: Squatter Settlements." *Chicago Times*, 7 August 1865, p. [3]. A lengthy article, decidedly anti–Irish in tone, describing some of the "patches" or poorer living areas in Chicago.

Untitled article, *Chicago Times*, 8 August 1865, p. [2]. The *Times* apologizes for publishing its article on "Squatter Settlements" the previous day.

"The Fire." *Chicago Times*, 18 October 1871, pp. 1, [4]. The *Times*'s published its first post-fire paper on October 18; this article contains the oft-cited story that Mrs. O'Leary started the fire in retaliation for being taken off the city's relief rolls.

"The City Election." *Chicago Times*, 19 October 1871, p. [2]. Criticism of elected officials.

"An Old Granny." *Chicago Times*, 19 October 1871, p. [2]. Criticism of Mayor Mason.

"Titles to Property." *Chicago Times*, 19 October 1871, p. [2]. The *Times* calls for legislation to address the problem caused by the destruction of Chicago's official land records.

"Tremont House." *Chicago Times*, 19 October 1871, p. 1. John Drake buys the Michigan Hotel.

Untitled article. *Chicago Times*, 19 October 1871, p. [2]. Criticism of Mayor Mason.

"The Gun-powder Plot." *Chicago Times*, 20 October 1871, p. [3]. The story of James Hildreth's efforts at blowing up buildings.

"The 'Blowing Up' Business." *Chicago Times*, 21 October 1871, p. [2]. The *Times* criticizes the mayor, fire commissioners, and fire marshal; it praises James Hildreth.

"The North Division." *Chicago Times*, 21 October 1871, p. [2]. Rebuilding on the North Side.

Untitled article. *Chicago Times*, 21 October 1871, p. [2]. A tongue-in-cheek suggestion that "the fire has been entirely owing to the former existence of slavery in this country."

"The University Assassins." *Chicago Times*, 22 October 1871, p. [2]. In a thundering editorial, the *Times* speaks out against General Sheridan and the "schoolboy vigilance committee" that patrols the streets of post-fire Chicago.

"A Startling Story." *Chicago Times*, 23 October 1871, p. 1. The Societe Internationale caused the Chicago Fire.

"That Cow." *Chicago Times*, 23 October 1871, p. [4]. An alleged interview with Patrick O'Leary, the husband of Mrs. O'Leary.

"The Grosvenor Homicide." *Chicago Times*, 24 October 1871, p. 1. The conclusion of the coroner's inquest into the killing of Thomas Grosvenor.

"The Man Gund." *Chicago Times*, 26 October 1871, p. [2]. Criticism of Commissioner Frederick W. Gund.

Untitled article. *Chicago Times*, 26 October 1871, p. [2]. Criticism of Commissioner Mark Sheridan.

"Rebuilding." *Chicago Times*, 27 October 1871, p. [3]. The immediate rebuilding of Chicago.

"The Chicago Fire Department." *Chicago Times*, 4 November 1871, p. [2]. Criticism of the Board of Police and Fire Commissioners.

"Sheridan's Indictment." *Chicago Times*, 4 November 1871, p. 1. Governor Palmer's letter to Attorney General Washington Bushnell concerning the Grosvenor killing.

Untitled article. *Chicago Times*, 4 November 1871, p. [2]. The *Times* supports Governor Palmer in his handling of the Grosvenor killing.

Untitled article. *Chicago Times*, 6 November 1871, p. [2]. Criticism of Commissioner Mark Sheridan.

"The Fire Department." *Chicago Times*, 14 November 1871, p. 1. Criticism of the fire marshals.

"Fire-Marshal Williams." *Chicago Times*, 14 November 1871, p. [4]. A letter to the editor that criticizes Marshal Williams.

Untitled article. *Chicago Times*, 15 November 1871, p. [2]. Criticism of the fire marshals and the commissioners.

"Municipal Reconstruction." *Chicago Times*, 18 November 1871, p. [4]. Criticism of the fire marshals and the commissioners.

Untitled article. *Chicago Times*, 18 November 1871, p. [2]. Allegations that citizens had to pay money to firemen before the firemen would do their jobs.

Untitled article. *Chicago Times*, 19 November 1871, p. [2]. The *Times* comments on the large quantities of courthouse bell relics.

Untitled article. *Chicago Times*, 21 November 1871, p. [2]. Allegations that citizens had to pay firemen in order for the firemen to do their jobs.

Untitled article. *Chicago Times*, 22 November 1871, p. [2]. The *Times* asks if Marshal Williams left his post during the fire.

"The Fire." *Chicago Times*, 24 November 1871, p. [4]. The inquiry investigation begins; a summary of inquiry testimony.

"The Fire." *Chicago Times*, 25 November 1871, p. [4]. A summary of inquiry testimony, including the testimony of Mrs. O'Leary.

Untitled article. *Chicago Times*, 25 November 1871, p. [2]. Criticism of Commissioners Gund and Sheridan.

"The Fire." *Chicago Times*, 26 November 1871, p. 1. A summary of inquiry testimony, including the testimony of Daniel Sullivan.

"The Fire." *Chicago Times*, 28 November 1871, p. [4]. A summary of inquiry testimony.

"The Smelling Committee." *Chicago Times*, 29 November 1871, p. [4]. A summary of inquiry testimony.

"The Smelling Committee." *Chicago Times*, 30 November 1871, p. [4]. A summary of inquiry testimony.

"How They Look and Act." *Chicago Times*, 3 December 1871, p. [3]. Although this article satirizes some of the inquiry witnesses, including Mr. and Mrs. O'Leary and Daniel Sullivan, it also includes what appears to be an accurate description of the room in which the investigation was held.

"The Smelling Committee." *Chicago Times*, 4 December 1871, p. [3]. A summary of inquiry testimony.

"Jottings About Town." *Chicago Times*, 7 December 1871, p. [4]. The *Times* comments on fire relics; they are vials containing chips of the courthouse bell.

"Nobody to Blame." *Chicago Times*, 12 December 1871, p. 5. The final report of the Board.

Untitled article. *Chicago Times*, 12 December 1871, p. 4. The *Times* criticizes the Board's final report.

"The Fire's Nursery." *Chicago Times*, 14 December 1871, p. 5. The progress of rebuilding in the burnt district on Chicago's West Side.

"Fires." *Chicago Times*, 15 December 1871, p. 2. The *Times* comments that the fire department escaped censure by the Board when it issued its final report.

"Those Roasted Safes." *Chicago Times*, 15 December 1871, p. 3. Details plans of the proposed safe monument.

"Auction Sales." *Chicago Times*, 16 December 1871, p. 8. An advertisement indicating that the remains of the courthouse bell will be sold at public auction.

"Brown's Valedictory." *Chicago Times*, 19 December 1871, p. 7. Thomas B. Brown leaves the Board of Police and Fire Commissioners.

"Jottings About Town." *Chicago Times*, 21 December 1871, p. 7. Sarcastic comments directed towards the *Tribune*.

Untitled article. *Chicago Times*, 28 December 1871, p. 4. A ship crossing the Atlantic Ocean on October 12, 1871, is enveloped in a cloud of smoke and ash that allegedly came from the fire.

"How Many Perished." *Chicago Times*, 30 December 1871, p. 3. This article attempts to estimate the number of people killed in the fire; it also includes a list of missing persons.

Chicago Republican

"Wisconsin Ablaze." *Chicago Republican*, 5 October 1871, p. 1. This front page article vividly describes how fire was rampaging through Northeastern Wisconsin even before the Peshtigo Fire of October 8.

"Fire and Police." *Chicago Republican*, 27 October 1871, p. [4]. A summary of a meeting of the Board of Fire Commissioners. The article mentions the *Richards* fire engine and reports on Board action relative to policemen taking money for services rendered during the fire.

Untitled article. *Chicago Republican*, 28 October 1871, p. [2]. The *Republican* questions Treasurer David Gage's use of city funds.

"Fire and Police." *Chicago Republican*, 31 October 1871, p. [4]. Possible policemen misconduct.

"Important Order." *Chicago Republican*, 4 November 1871, p. [4]. This article identifies the location of the second precinct police station.

"Board of Police." *Chicago Republican*, 10 November 1871, p. [2]. The Board resolves to commence investigating the fire.

"Common Council." *Chicago Republican*, 10 November 1871, p. [2]. A resolution is passed authorizing the sale of the courthouse bell.

Untitled article. *Chicago Republican*, 10 November 1871, p. [2]. Condemnation of the *Times* for publishing its article about the Societe International.

"The Origin of the Fire." *Chicago Republican*, 11

November 1871, p. 1. The Board postpones the inquiry proceedings.

"City Brevities." *Chicago Republican*, 15 November 1871, p. 1. Criticism of the inquiry investigation.

"Common Council." *Chicago Republican*, 15 November 1871, p. [2]. A letter from Charles Holden, President of the Common Council, outlines relief efforts.

"Common Council." *Chicago Republican*, 16 November 1871, p. [2]. Chicago is rebuilding.

"City Brevities." *Chicago Republican*, 18 November 1871, p. 1. Criticism of the "somnolent" Board for failing to investigate the cause of the fire.

"Chicago Condensed." *Chicago Republican*, 20 November 1871, p. [4]. Criticism of the *Tribune*'s "Boring for Facts" series.

"Greedy of Gain." *Chicago Republican*, 20 November 1871, p. [4]. The *Republican* echoes the *Tribune*'s charges of misconduct on the part of fire companies from Milwaukee; Janesville, Wisconsin; and Aurora, Illinois.

"Chicago Condensed." *Chicago Republican*, 21 November 1871, p. [4]. The *Republican* questions the conduct of Benjamin Bullwinkle of the fire insurance patrol.

"The Relief Funds." *Chicago Republican*, 22 November 1871, p. [2]. Criticism of the Chicago Relief and Aid Society.

"Public Opinion." *Chicago Republican*, 23 November 1871, p. [2]. Criticism of the Chicago Relief and Aid Society.

Untitled articles, *Chicago Republican*, 23 November 1871, p. [2], col. 1, first, fourth, and sixth articles. Three short disparagements of the Chicago Relief and Aid Society. For example: "Yes, my son, he is an idiot, a boor and a thief; but he is a cousin of mine, and we will make him a clerk in the Relief Society at two dollars a day and all he can steal."

"L'Amende Honorable." *Chicago Republican*, 24 November 1871, p. [2]. The *Republican* commends the "foreign" fire companies of Milwaukee and Aurora, Illinois.

"How Was It?" *Chicago Republican*, 24 November 1871, p. [4]. A summary of inquiry testimony.

"The Foreign Firemen." *Chicago Republican*, 24 November 1871, p. [4]. A lengthy defense of the Aurora, Illinois, and Milwaukee fire companies against charges of misconduct.

"Chicago Condensed." *Chicago Republican*, 25 November 1871, p. [4]. A solicitation for ruined safes for the fire memorial.

"How It Was." *Chicago Republican*, 25 November 1871, p. [4]. The Board meets "in the same old bedroom" to conduct its investigation; a summary of inquiry testimony.

Untitled article. *Chicago Republican*, 25 November 1871, p. [2], col. 1, fourth article. The *Republican* criticizes the *Tribune* for its articles concerning the misconduct of the foreign fire companies. The paper claims that the *Tribune* retracted its statements when threatened with a libel suit.

Untitled article. *Chicago Republican*, 25 November 1871, p. [2], col. 1, fifth article. The *Republican* criticizes the *Tribune* for its articles concerning the misconduct of the foreign fire companies. The paper questions the *Tribune*'s explanation that the "slanders were inserted by an irresponsible party in the absence of a competent editor."

"Cow, or How?" *Chicago Republican*, 27 November 1871, p. [4]. A summary of inquiry testimony.

Untitled article. *Chicago Republican*, 27 November 1871, p. [2]. Criticism of the Chicago Relief and Aid Society.

"Chicago Condensed." *Chicago Republican*, 29 November 1871, p. [4]. The *Republican* asks when the Chicago Fire safe monument will be built.

"How Was It?" *Chicago Republican*, 29 November 1871, p. [4]. A summary of inquiry testimony.

"A Narrow Escape." *Chicago Republican*, 29 November 1871, p. [4]. Captain Michael C. Hickey allegedly rescues a citizen from being hanged.

"Among Ashes." *Chicago Republican*, 30 November 1871, p. [4]. A summary of inquiry testimony.

"The Other Side." *Chicago Republican*, 30 November 1871, p. [4]. The *Republican* criticizes the Board and defends Marshal Williams.

"Opening Fire." *Chicago Republican*, 2 December 1871, p. [4]. Criticism of the Chicago Relief and Aid Society.

Untitled article. *Chicago Republican*, 2 December 1871, p. [2], col. 1. The *Republican* questions the conduct of the rank and file firemen.

Untitled article. *Chicago Republican*, 2 December 1871, p. [2], col. 2. Criticism of the Chicago Relief and Aid Society.

"Wirt's Work." *Chicago Republican*, 2 December 1871, p. [4]. Criticism of the Chicago Relief and Aid Society. (Wirt Dexter was chairman of the society's Executive Committee.)

"Indorsed." *Chicago Republican*, 4 December 1871, p. [4]. Criticism of the Chicago Relief and Aid Society.

"Public Opinion." *Chicago Republican*, 4 December 1871, p. [2]. Criticism of the Chicago Relief and Aid Society.

"The Little Police Farce." *Chicago Republican*, 5 December 1871, p. [4]. Commissioner Gund retires.

"Common Council." *Chicago Republican*, 6 December 1871, p. [3]. This article describes the combustible nature of pre-fire Chicago.

"The Great Fire." *Chicago Republican*, 12 December 1871, p. [4]. Publication of the Board's final report.

"Personalities." *Chicago Republican*, 12 December 1871, p. [4]. The *Republican* sarcastically comments on the Board and its final report.

"Chicago Condensed." *Chicago Republican*, 13 December 1871, p. [4]. A meteor is seen over Chicago.

"Chicago Condensed." *Chicago Republican*, 15 December 1871, p. [4]. The relocation of Peter Schuttler's wagon works.

"New Books." *Chicago Republican*, 16 December 1871, p. [2]. A review of two books on the fire.

"Chicago Condensed." *Chicago Republican*, 23 December 1871, p. [4]. This article mentions the miniature courthouse bell fire relics.

"Chicago Condensed." *Chicago Republican*, 25 December 1871, p. [4]. A comment concerning Harry Hatch's establishment. (Marshal Williams mentioned the "Hatch House" in his testimony.)

"Chicago and the Great Conflagration." *Chicago Republican*, 25 December 1871, p. [4]. Chicago Fire books by Sheahan and Upton and Colbert and Chamberlin will be published shortly.

Chicago Daily News

"Tales of the Great Fire." *Chicago Daily News*, 9 October 1886, p. 2. A history of the fire on its fifteen year anniversary.

"Stories of the Big Fire." *Chicago Daily News*, 9 October 1896, p. 13. Reminiscences of private citizens.

McIlvaine, Caroline M. "The Great Chicago Fire of 1871." *Chicago Daily News*, 10 October 1925, photogravure section, p. [2]. A pictorial history of the fire. These numbered pictures were printed by the *Daily News* as a "Radio Photologue" so that its readers could follow a radio presentation by Miss Caroline M. McIlvaine, librarian of the Chicago Historical Society. The article notes that Miss McIlvaine "will trace the course of the fire from the personal narratives of sufferers collected by the historical society soon after the disaster."

Drury, John. "Chicago's 'Forgotten House.'" *Chicago Daily News*, 14 April 1939, sec. 1, p. 18. A history of the O'Leary property.

"Cohn Estate Turned Over to University." *Chicago Daily News*, 28 September 1944, sec. 1, p. 12. A press release indicating that the $35,000 estate of Louis M. Cohn was turned over to Northwestern University.

"A Factory Will Mark the Spot." *Chicago Daily News*, 2 October 1954, Roto[gravure], p. 4. The Anton Kolar home is scheduled for demolition.

Lind, Jack. "Fire? Blame Mrs. O'Leary, Not Her Cow." *Chicago Daily News*, 8 October 1955, sec. 1, p. 13. H. A. Musham disparages Mrs. O'Leary.

Rooney, Edmund J., Jr. "Mrs. O'Leary's Cow 'Exonerated.'" *Chicago Daily News*, 6 October 1962, sec. 1, p. 13. Philip M. Kane combines elements of several fire theories into one, claiming that the O'Learys had a party in their barn and that ashes dropped from a clay pipe started the fire.

Royko, Mike. "Inside Story of Chicago Fire." *Chicago Daily-News*, 3 September 1971, sec. 1, p. 3. Famed Chicago columnist Mike Royko comments on the Chicago Association of Commerce and Industry's conclusion that "Peg Leg" Sullivan caused the fire.

Chicago Evening Post

"Aged Employe Tells of Saving Title Records." *Chicago Evening Post*, 8 October 1921, sec. 1, p. [13]. The story of how an employee of Chicago Title and Trust Company helped save land records from being destroyed by the fire.

"Asks Version of Famous Verses of Chicago Fire." *Chicago Evening Post*, 8 October 1921, sec. 1, p. 1 (home page). This article contains the verses to a poem that suggests that the fire started when Mrs. O'Leary's cow kicked over the lantern.

"Fire Mayor of Chicago Built Many Railroads." *Chicago Evening Post*, 8 October 1921, Chicago Fire Edition, sec. 4, p. 18. A laudatory biography of Mayor Roswell B. Mason that suggests that Mason was correct in transferring police authority of the city to General Sheridan in the aftermath of the fire. (This "Chicago Fire Edition" of the October 8, 1921, issue of the *Chicago Evening Post* contains a wide variety of articles about the fire.)

"Greatest Fire in History Sweeps Heart of Chicago; Loss Set at $196,000,000." *Chicago Evening Post*, 8 October 1921, Chicago Fire Edition, sec. 1, pp. 3–4. This article describes the poem that begins with "One dark night, when people were in bed" as "a ballad that used to be sung before the day of jazz." This account of the fire also includes Mr. S. H. Kimball's story of finding a fragment of a lamp in the ruins of the O'Leary barn.

"New York Post Has Its Say as to O'Leary Cow." *Chicago Evening Post*, 8 October 1921, Chicago Fire Edition, sec. 3, p. 10. The suggestion that the fire was caused by boys smoking in the barn, spontaneous combustion, or incendiaries.

Chicago Inter Ocean

Ahern, Michael. "The Fire Fighters." (*Chicago*) *Daily Inter Ocean*, 9 October 1893, sec. 1, p. [2]. Firemen reminisce about the fire and why it spread out of control.

"A City Laid Waste." (*Chicago*) *Daily Inter Ocean*, 9 October 1893, sec. 1, pp. 1–[2]. The story of the fire.

"Fire Scraps." (*Chicago*) *Daily Inter Ocean*, 9 October 1893, sec. 1, p. [2]. A discussion of the oil stone theory.

"Notes on the Great Chicago Fire of 1871." *Chicago Sunday Inter Ocean*, 4 October 1896, sec. 3, pp. 21, 28. An extensive article that discusses the impact of the fire and how it affected (among other elements of Chicago) the newspapers, shipping, and even theaters.

Chicago Sun-Times

"Fire at the O'Leary Homesite." *Chicago Daily Sun-Times*, 24 November 1955, p. 8. The Chicago Plastering Institute sets the Kolar home afire.

"Fire Landmark Comes Down." *Chicago Sunday Sun-Times*, 4 December 1955, sec. 1, p. 5. The Kolar home is demolished.

"OK Sale of 1st Ward Land to Industry." *Chicago Daily Sun-Times*, 10 July 1956, p. 3. Mayor Richard J. Daley calls for the construction of a fire department training academy on the O'Leary property.

Weintraub, Larry. "Mrs. O'Leary's Cow Wins an Acquittal." *Chicago Sun-Times*, 2 September 1971, p. 3. The Chicago Association of Commerce and Industry concludes after four months of research that "Peg Leg" Sullivan caused the fire. (See Harper, George E., ed. *Chicago: City on Fire...*, infra.)

McNamee, Tom. "119 Years after the Fire, O'Learys' Hurt Smolders." *Chicago Sun-Times*, 7 October 1990, sec. 1, p. 4. Descendants of Mrs. O'Leary still feel the pain of the O'Leary legend.

Oak Leaves (Oak Park, Ill.)

Cochran, Jean. "Mrs. O'Leary's Delivery Boy Tells True Story of Great Fire." *Oak Leaves* (Oak Park, Ill.), 12 October 1939, pp. [3], 10. Jacob John Schaller tells *Oak Leaves* that Mrs. O'Leary told him that the fire started when her cow kicked over the lantern.

"Historian Is Here for an Interview with Mr. Schaller." *Oak Leaves* (Oak Park, Ill.), 19 October 1939, p. 5. Harry A. Musham meets Jacob J. Schaller.

"Historian Comes to Village." *Oak Leaves* (Oak Park, Ill.), 26 October 1939, p. 63. This photograph of Harry A. Musham and Jacob Schaller is reproduced as Figure 42.

"The O'Leary Cow: Eye Witness in *Oak Leaves*." *Oak Leaves* (Oak Park, Ill.), 26 October 1939, p. [iii]. Jacob Schaller writes a letter to *Oak Leaves*, thanking the paper for printing his story about Mrs. O'Leary.

"The Schallers, Wed 50 Years, Won Fame by Oak Leaves Story." *Oak Leaves* (Oak Park, Ill.), 14 December 1939, p. 16. Jacob Schaller wins fame with his tale of how the Chicago Fire started.

"Jacob Schaller 80; Recalls Chicago Great Fire."

Oak Leaves (Oak Park, Ill.), 11 June 1942, p. 7. This article about Jacob Schaller's eightieth birthday celebration includes a reference to "Mr. Schaller's authentic account of how the fire started."

"J. J. Shaller [*sic*] Dies; Delivered Milk for Mrs. O'Leary." *Oak Leaves* (Oak Park, Ill.), 19 July 1945, p. 42. The obituary of Jacob Schaller.

Other Newspapers

"History of the Conflagration." *New York Herald*, 11 October 1871, p. 5. This is the first post-fire issue of the *New York Herald* that mentions the story of the cow kicking over the lantern.

"Marks Anniversary of the Great Fire." *Chicago Sunday Record-Herald*, [8 October 1911], William J. Brown, Chicago Fire of 1871 Personal Narratives Collection, Chicago Historical Society. A photocopy of this newspaper article was filed with the historical society's personal narratives collection of William J. Brown. A notation on the photocopy indicates that it was from the October 8, 1911, issue of the *Chicago Sunday Record-Herald*, but the article could not be located on the 1911 microfilm reel of this newspaper. The article contains the reminiscences of Sarah R. Hibbard, sister of William J. Brown.

Gilbert, Paul T. "The Legend of Mrs. O'Leary's Cow." *Chicago Sun*, 24 July 1942, p. 9. A discussion of some of the more obscure theories as to how the fire started.

"$35,000 Estate Goes Into Scholarships." *Chicago Sun*, 29 September 1944, p. 24. A news release concerning the estate of Louis M. Cohn.

Laing, Jonathan R. "Mrs. O'Leary's Cow, Vilified for 100 Years, Maybe Wasn't Guilty." *Wall Street Journal*, 5 October 1971, p. 1. A discussion of some of the more popular theories as to the fire's cause. Mrs. Eileen Knight, Mrs. O'Leary's granddaughter, is quoted as saying that "the family knew that Peg Leg did it."

Belluck, Pam. "Barn Door Reopened on Fire After Legend Has Escaped." *New York Times*, 17 August 1997, p. 10. Story of Richard Bales's theory concerning the cause of the fire.

"Peshtigo Blaze Classified as Rare Fire Storm." *Peshtigo Times* (Peshtigo, Wis.), Special Edition, 7 October 1998, sec. B, p. B-20. This article explains how the Peshtigo Fire evolved from a number of small forest fires into a horrific fire storm. It was published in a commemorative issue of the *Peshtigo Times*. This newspaper contains many other detailed articles on all aspects of the disaster.

Periodicals

Adams, Rosemary K., ed. "Remembering the Great Chicago Fire." *Chicago History* 25 (Fall 1996), pp. 24–39. A heavily illustrated article that contains first-hand accounts of Chicagoans who lived through the fire.

Bales, Richard F. "Did the Cow Do It? A New Look at the Cause of the Great Chicago Fire." *Illinois Historical Journal* 90 (Spring 1997), pp. 2–24. Richard Bales' initial findings concerning the cause of the Chicago Fire.

"The Burning of Chicago." *The Graphic* 4 (October 21, 1871), pp. [385], 390. A London newspaper writes about the fire.

Chapin, John R. "Account by an Eye-Witness." *Harper's Weekly* 15 (28 October 1871), pp. 1010–13. An artist details his observations of the fire.

Chicago Title and Trust Co.: The First 150 Years. Privately printed, [1997]. A commemorative brochure relating the history of Chicago Title and Trust Company.

"City Intelligence." *Prairie Farmer* 42 (16 December 1871), p. 386. The Board's final report.

Corrigan, John. "O'Leary Research Sheds New Light on Fire and Family." *Scéal* 4 (Fall 1986), pp. 1–2, 4. *Scéal* is the newsletter of the Chicago Irish Folklife Society. This issue contains a comprehensive article about the O'Leary family.

"The Chicago Fire Monument." *The Land Owner: A Journal of Real Estate Building & Improvement* 4 (February 1872), pp. 21, 27. The story of the first proposed Chicago Fire monument that is to be built out of ruined safes and other fire debris.

"The Court House Bell." *The Land Owner: A Journal of Real Estate Building & Improvement* 4 (February 1872), p. 16. An advertisement for the miniature court house bells.

"A Dairy Tale." *People* 48 (22 September 1997), p. 155. The story of Richard Bales' research into the cause of the Chicago Fire.

Duis, Perry R., and Glen E. Holt. "Kate O'Leary's Sad Burden." *Chicago* 27 (October 1978), pp. 220–22, 224. The life of Mrs. O'Leary after the fire.

"Fifty Years Ago." *Chicago History* 1 (Fall 1971), pp. 245–49. Jim O'Leary claims the fire was caused by the spontaneous combustion of green hay.

"Forest Fires in the West." *Harper's Weekly* 15 (November 25, 1871), pp. 1104–5, 1109. This article contains a double-page illustration of "The Burning of Peshtigo."

Harmon, Melissa Burdick. "Badfella: The Life and Crimes of Al Capone." *Biography* 5 (May 2001), pp. [100]–103, [115]–[116], 118. Al Capone reportedly once complained, "They've hung everything on me except the Chicago Fire."

Harper, George E., ed. *Chicago: City on Fire....* Chicago: Chicago Association of Commerce and Industry, 1971. An illustrated history of the fire that includes the theory that Daniel "Peg Leg" Sullivan might have caused it.

"Kate! The Barn Is Afire!" *Chicago History* 1 (Fall 1971), pp. 216–19. This article contains portions of Mrs. O'Leary's inquiry testimony.

Kidwell, Boyd. "Make Hay, Not Fire." *Progressive Farmer* 111 (August 1996), p. [24]. An article about the dangers of spontaneous combustion of hay.

Kimbell, Elisabeth. "We Could Not Do Without the Chicago Fire..." *Chicago History* 1 (Fall 1971), pp. 220–31. The story of the Chicago Relief and Aid Society.

Kirkland, Joseph. "The Chicago Fire." *The New England Magazine*, n.s., 6 (August 1892), pp. [726]–42. A lengthy article containing reminiscences of the fire.

Kogan, Herman. "Grander and Statelier Than Ever..." *Chicago History* 1 (Fall 1971), pp. 236–44. Chicago's recovery from the fire.

Lasswell, David. "Chicago Before the Fire: Some People, Places, and Things." *Chicago History* 1 (Fall 1971), pp. 196–203. What Chicago was like before October 8, 1871.

Miller, John C., ed. "Mr. Ryan Sees Chicago Fire from DeKoven St." *The West Side Historical Society Bulletin* 2 (April 1937), pp. 1–2. The reminiscences contained in this Chicago neighborhood historical society newsletter include the claim that a man with a peg leg caused the fire.

Ranalletta, Kathy, ed. "'The Great Wave of Fire' at Chicago: The Reminiscences of Martin Stamm." *Journal of the Illinois State Historical Society* 70 (May 1977), pp. 149–60. Many Chicago Fire personal histories were written by members of Chicago's upper class and native-born. But Martin Stamm was a German immigrant and church pastor, and so his reminiscences have special significance.

Sears, Stephen W. "The Giant in the Earth." *American Heritage* 26 (August 1975), pp. 94–99. The story of the Cardiff Giant.

"The Tornado of Fire." *Frank Leslie's Illustrated Newspaper* 33 (28 October 1871), pp. 101–5. This New York newspaper contains a rather sensational account of the fire.

"When Chicago Burned." *American Heritage* 14 (August 1963), pp. 2, 55–61. The on-the-spot drawings and prose of artist Alfred R. Waud and writer Ralph Keeler, employees of *Every Saturday* magazine, who traveled to Chicago to cover the fire.

Collections—Personal Narratives, Chicago Historical Society

INTRODUCTION

This extensive collection contains two types of primary source materials. The first is letters that were written in the days and weeks after the fire. The second includes personal reminiscences of eyewitnesses that were written years later. Historians Carl Smith and Karen Sawislak both comment that members and employees of the Chicago Historical Society made several efforts in the years following the fire to encourage eyewitnesses to record their experiences. (See Smith, p. 288; Sawislak, p. 291.) Some of these narratives were later published in fire histories, most notably the Chicago Fire chapter in volume two of A. T. Andreas' *History of Chicago* and the 1915 Lakeside Classic book *Reminiscences of Chicago During the Great Fire*.

Statement of Anthony, Charles Elliott, "Experiences of the Anthony Family During the Great Chicago Fire October 8 and 9, 1871," n.d., Chicago Fire of 1871 Personal Narratives Collection, Chicago Historical Society.

Statement of Axsmith, Anton, "The Chicago

Fire of October 9th 1871," n.d., Chicago Fire of 1871 Personal Narratives Collection, Chicago Historical Society.

Bigelow, Joel to S. and O. Bigelow, 10 October 1871, Chicago Fire of 1871 Personal Narratives Collection, Chicago Historical Society.

Bradley, Frederick M. to Mr. Charles Dewey, 11 December 1969, Chicago Fire of 1871 Personal Narratives Collection, Chicago Historical Society. Bradley's letter and the letter from Justin [Butterfield] to his "chum," infra, are stored together at the historical society. Bradley's letter indicates that Justin's friend was Philip Prescott.

Statement of Brayman, James O., "The Great Conflagration," 22 January 1880, Chicago Fire of 1871 Personal Narratives Collection, Chicago Historical Society.

Brown, William J. to his sister [Sarah R. Hibbard?], 20 October [18]71, Chicago Fire of 1871 Personal Narratives Collection, Chicago Historical Society.

Brown, William J. to his sister [Sarah R. Hibbard?], 2 November 1871, Chicago Fire of 1871 Personal Narratives Collection, Chicago Historical Society.

[Butterfield], Justin to [Philip Prescott], 19 October [1871], Chicago Fire of 1871 Personal Narratives Collection, Chicago Historical Society.

Statement of Counselman, Jennie E., "Reminiscences of the Chicago Fire and Some of My Girlhood Days," March 1928, Chicago Fire of 1871 Personal Narratives Collection, Chicago Historical Society.

Statement of F .L. J., "The Little Girl Who Should Have Been a Boy," n.d., appended to Emma Hambleton to Mrs. William Harrison Lander, 11 October 1871, and Chalkley J. Hambleton to Emily Hambleton, 11 October 1871, Chicago Fire of 1871 Personal Narratives Collection, Chicago Historical Society.

Gallagher, William to his sister [Isabel], 17 October 1871, Chicago Fire of 1871 Personal Narratives Collection, Chicago Historical Society.

Gavin, James A. to H. R. Clark, 23 March 1921, Chicago Fire of 1871 Personal Narratives Collection, Chicago Historical Society.

Goodwin, Daniel to Mr. [George M.] Higginson, February 1895, Chicago Fire of 1871 Personal Narratives Collection, Chicago Historical Society.

[Gookins?], "Mama" to "Lizy" [Gookins?], 13 October [1871], Chicago Fire of 1871 Personal Narratives Collection, Chicago Historical Society.

Hanmore, Dr. Frederick C. to the President of the Chicago Historical Society, 21 January 1938, Chicago Fire of 1871 Personal Narratives Collection, Chicago Historical Society.

Helmer, Bessie Bradwell to Caroline M. McIlvaine, 7 October 1926, Chicago Fire of 1871 Personal Narratives Collection, Chicago Historical Society.

Statement of Higginson, George M., "Account of the Great Chicago Fire of October 9, 1871," June 1879, Chicago Fire of 1871 Personal Narratives Collection, Chicago Historical Society.

Hungerford, Mrs. Eda D. to the Chicago Historical Society, 13 December 1922, Chicago Fire of 1871 Personal Narratives Collection, Chicago Historical Society.

Statement of Jefferson, Catherine, [23 November 1932], Chicago Fire of 1871 Personal Narratives Collection, Chicago Historical Society. Although these reminiscences are undated, they are appended to a letter dated November 23, 1932, and thus this date is noted in brackets.

Kelley, John to Jim [O'Leary?], 9 October 1911, Chicago Fire of 1871 Personal Narratives Collection, Chicago Historical Society.

Kelley, John to Patrick O'Leary, 2 March 1927, Chicago Fire of 1871 Personal Narratives Collection, Chicago Historical Society.

Kimball, S. H. to Caroline M. McIlvaine, 30 January 1914, Chicago Fire of 1871 Personal Narratives Collection, Chicago Historical Society.

Lott, Charles R. to the Chicago Historical Society, 7 October 1926, Chicago Fire of 1871 Personal Narratives Collection, Chicago Historical Society.

MacKenzie, Donald B. to Caroline McIlvaine, 10 October 1921, Chicago Fire of 1871 Personal Narratives Collection, Chicago Historical Society.

Moore, Del to [her father and mother], 14 October 1871, Chicago Fire of 1871 Personal Narratives Collection, Chicago Historical Society.

Statement of Tree, Lambert, "The Experience of Lambert Tree and the Several Members of

His Family during the Great Chicago Fire of Sunday and Monday Oct. 8th and 9th 1871," n.d., Chicago Fire of 1871 Personal Narratives Collection, Chicago Historical Society. Judge Lambert Tree's reminiscences are undated. But George M. Higginson of the historical society added a note after Tree's signature, indicating that Tree delivered the manuscript to him "about a month ago." Higginson's postscript is dated March 1, 1880. Tree's recollections are reprinted in Mabel McIlvaine's *Reminiscences of Chicago During the Great Fire* and A. T. Andreas' *History of Chicago*.

Collections—Chicago Fire of 1871, Chicago Historical Society

"Transcript of Inquiry into Cause of Chicago Fire and Actions of Fire Department Therein." [1871], Chicago Fire of 1871 Collection, Chicago Historical Society. These four bound volumes contain the statements of 49 of the 50 people who testified during the inquiry investigation into the cause of the Chicago Fire and the conduct of the firemen who fought the fire.

Collections—Chicago Fire Department, Chicago Historical Society

Pay Roll for the Month Ending October 31, 1871, Chicago Fire Department Collection, Chicago Historical Society. This listing of fire department employees and their job assignments is reprinted in Appendix D.

Collections—Harry A. Musham Collection, Notes on the Chicago Fire, Chicago Historical Society

This collection is an invaluable resource for the student of the Chicago fire. Musham was an indefatigable researcher, and his files contain a myriad of newspaper clippings, letters, and reminiscences. Although Musham was careful to include the publication information with every newspaper article he amassed, occasionally a Chicago newspaper article could not be independently located on the appropriate newspaper microfilm reel. This was probably because the article that Musham saved was not

from the same edition as the newspaper that was microfilmed. These articles are shown as being part of the Musham collection and the dates of the articles appear in brackets.

Musham interviewed several people while researching his monograph, "The Great Chicago Fire, October 8–10, 1871," and the summaries of these interviews are also included in this collection.

Statement of Chapeck, J. C., 20 January 1942, Harry A. Musham Collection, Notes on the Chicago Fire, Chicago Historical Society.

"He Peddled Milk for Mrs. O'Leary; He's Sure Cow Started the Fire." *Chicago Herald-American*, [6 October 1939], Harry A. Musham Collection, Notes on the Chicago Fire, Chicago Historical Society.

"History Finds One Who Knew a Famous Cow." *Chicago Sunday Tribune*, [19 November 1939], Harry A. Musham Collection, Notes on the Chicago Fire, Chicago Historical Society.

"Looks Like O'Leary Cow Must Take That Fire Rap." *Chicago Herald-American*, [8 October 1939], Harry A. Musham Collection, Notes on the Chicago Fire, Chicago Historical Society.

Meteorological Observations by the United States Signal Corps, War Department, Chicago, Illinois, Register of Meteorological Observations Compiled Under the Direction of the Smithsonian Institution. Harry A. Musham Collection, Notes on the Chicago Fire, Chicago Historical Society.

Musham, H. A. to Jacob J. Schaller, 14 October 1939, Harry A. Musham Collection, Notes on the Chicago Fire, Chicago Historical Society.

Musham, H. A., telephone call memorandum, 18 October [1939], Harry A. Musham Collection, Notes on the Chicago Fire, Chicago Historical Society. This memorandum is reproduced as Figure 43.

Musham, H. A. to Walter Kogan, 10 October 1942, Harry A. Musham Collection, Notes on the Chicago Fire, Chicago Historical Society.

Schaller, Jacob J. to H. A. Musham, 15 October 1939, Harry A. Musham Collection, Notes on the Chicago Fire, Chicago Historical Society.

Annotated Bibliography

Statement of Schaller, Jacob John, 17 October 1939, Harry A. Musham Collection, Notes on the Chicago Fire, Chicago Historical Society.

Statement of Sharkey, Phillip J., 10 November 1939, Harry A. Musham Collection, Notes on the Chicago Fire, Chicago Historical Society.

Shults, F. H. to Col. H. A. Musham, 25 January 1942, Harry A. Musham Collection, Notes on the Chicago Fire, Chicago Historical Society.

"Where City Learned a Lesson, Firemen to Study Theirs." *Chicago Daily News*, [24 February 1959], p. 34, Harry A. Musham Collection, Notes on the Chicago Fire, Chicago Historical Society.

Collections—Robert Allen Cromie Collection, Notes on the Chicago Fire, Chicago Historical Society

Mr. Isaac Rosenfeld was supposed to be the author of *The Great Chicago Fire*. He had started researching the book and had solicited the public for information, but he died suddenly of a heart attack in 1956 before he was able to finish it. Robert Cromie completed the research and wrote the book, which was published under his own name. What is described herein as Cromie's reference materials are in the Research Center of the Chicago Historical Society.

Although Robert Cromie's Chicago Fire material includes several letters, almost all are meandering second-generation reminiscences of dubious value. But Cromie indexed his research on hundreds of four-inch by six-inch index cards, and these cards form the core of a comprehensive reference collection.

Unfortunately, Cromie's book is a popular account of the fire that contains no footnotes or endnotes. His cards contain a wealth of information, but many times the citations to his sources are cryptic at best.

Kane, Philip to [Isaac Rosenfeld], 23 May 1956, Robert Allen Cromie Collection, Notes on the Chicago Fire, Chicago Historical Society.

Ott, Mrs. August to Isaac Rosenfeld, 23 June 1956, Robert Allen Cromie Collection, Notes on the Chicago Fire, Chicago Historical Society.

Miscellaneous Collections, Chicago Historical Society

Barrett, John P. to Albert D. Hager, n.d., John P. Barrett Collection, Chicago Historical Society. John P. Barrett became superintendent of the Fire Alarm Telegraph in 1876. Albert D. Hager was named secretary and librarian of the Chicago Historical Society in 1877.

Cook County (Illinois) Courthouse Bell Collection, Chicago Historical Society.

Holloway, H. Maxson, Assistant Director, Chicago Historical Society to Chief of Police, Maxwell Street Station, 1 September 1955, "Chicago Fire of 1871: O'Leary Family," Clipping File, Chicago Historical Society.

McDermott, Michael, *Recollections and Memoires*, n.d., Chicago Historical Society.

Collections—Newberry Library, Chicago, Illinois

Illinois. Cook County. 1870 U.S. Census, Population Schedule. Micropublication M593, roll 204. Washington: National Archives.

Illinois. Cook County. 1880 U.S. Census, Population Schedule. Micropublication T9, roll 200. Washington: National Archives.

Correspondence to the Author

Basich, Mary to Richard F. Bales, April 1998.

Basich, Mary to Richard F. Bales, July 1998.

DeHaan, John D. to Richard F. Bales, 25 June 2000.

Franch, John to Richard F. Bales, 28 November 1998.

Franch, John to Richard F. Bales, 30 November 1998.

Gray, Brian to Richard F. Bales, 7 December 1999.

Lewis, David to Richard F. Bales, 8 August 2001.

Lewis, David to Richard F. Bales, 28 October 2001.

Little, Ken to Richard F. Bales, 16 December 2000.

Little, Ken to Richard F. Bales, 18 December 2000.

Little, Ken to Richard F. Bales, 7 January 2001.

Little, Ken to Richard F. Bales, 15 February 2001.

Little, Ken to Richard F. Bales, 5 June 2001.

Little, Ken to Richard F. Bales, 14 August 2001.

Little, Ken to Richard F. Bales, 31 October 2001.

Little, Ken to Richard F. Bales, 21 December 2001.

Little, Ken to Richard F. Bales, 27 December 2001.

Little, Ken to Richard F. Bales, 30 December 2001.

Little, Ken to Richard F. Bales, 4 January 2002.

Little, Ken to Richard F. Bales, 15 January 2002.

Steinkamp, Robert to Richard F. Bales, 17 March 1998.

Vogeler, Ingolf to Richard F. Bales, 1 December 1997.

Vogeler, Ingolf to Richard F. Bales, 23 January 1998.

Other Unpublished Materials

Aurora Committee on Fire and Water Resolution on Tribune Slander of Fire Department, 20 November 1871, Aurora (Illinois) Regional Fire Museum.

Chicago Guarantee Survey Company records.

Chicago Title Insurance Company records. These materials consist primarily of ante-fire plats that reveal the size of the lots in the subdivision that the O'Learys lived in and ante-fire deed records that identify the O'Leary neighbors and disclose the legal descriptions of the land they owned. Other items include Chicago ordinances and miscellaneous plats.

DeHaan, John D. and Richard E. Tontarski. "The Great Chicago Fire of 1871: A Cause-and-Origin Examination of the Great Fire of 1871 (Was It Really the Cow?)." Unpublished manuscript, August 1987.

House Number Ordinance, "New & Old House Numbers, City of Chicago," Bureau of Maps and Plats, Dept. of Public Works, City of Chicago. A cross-reference of new and old Chicago addresses.

Roche, Liliana Gomez. "From Ruins to Relics and Revitalization: The Debris from the Great Chicago Fire." Unpublished manuscript, Loyola University of Chicago, 4 November 1996.

Interviews

Basich, Mary, descendant of Mrs. Catherine O'Leary, interview by Richard F. Bales, 2 February 1999.

Connolly, Nancy Knight, descendant of Mrs. Catherine O'Leary, interview by Richard F. Bales, 25 June 2001.

DeHaan, John D., author of *Kirk's Fire Investigation*, interview by Richard F. Bales, 1 October 2000.

Grenier, Kenneth, retired Survey Officer, Chicago Title Insurance Company; Charles O'Connor, retired Superintendent of Maps Department, City of Chicago; Nicholas Raimondi, co-owner of National Survey Service, Inc., interview by Richard F. Bales, 28 November 1995.

Hannon, Greg, President of Chicago Guarantee Survey Company, interview by Richard F. Bales, 19 July 2001.

Lewis, David, curator of the Aurora (Illinois) Regional Fire Museum, interview by Richard F. Bales, 30 January 2002.

Little, Ken, co-author of *History of Chicago Fire Houses of the 19th Century*, interview by Richard F. Bales, 1 April 2001.

Schell, Herman, Chicago Fire historian, interview by Richard F. Bales, 26 February 1998.

Index